THE BIRTH OF CRIMINOLOGY

Readings from the Eighteenth and Nineteenth Centuries

Edited by
BRUCE DICRISTINA
University of North Dakota

Copyright ©2012 CCH Incorporated.

Published by Wolters Kluwer Law & Business in New York.

Wolters Kluwer Law & Business serves customers worldwide with CCH, Aspen Publishers, and Kluwer Law International products. (www.wolterskluwerlb.com)

No part of this publication may be reproduced or transmitted in any form or by any means, electronic or mechanical, including photocopy, recording, or utilized by any information storage or retrieval system, without written permission from the publisher. For information about permissions or to request permissions online, visit us at www.wolterskluwerlb.com, or a written request may be faxed to our permissions department at 212-771-0803.

To contact Customer Service, e-mail customer.service@wolterskluwer.com, call 1-800-234-1660, fax 1-800-901-9075, or mail correspondence to:

> Wolters Kluwer Law & Business
> Attn: Order Department
> PO Box 990
> Frederick, MD 21705

Printed in the United States of America.

1 2 3 4 5 6 7 8 9 0
ISBN 978-1-4548-0317-1

Library of Congress Cataloging-in-Publication Data

The birth of criminology : readings from the eighteenth and nineteenth centuries / edited by Bruce DiCristina.
    p. cm.
  Includes index.
  ISBN 978-1-4548-0317-1
  1. Criminal law–Philosophy.   2. Punishment–Philosophy.   3. Criminology–Philosophy.
I. DiCristina, Bruce.
  K5103.B57 2011
  364.9'033–dc23

                                                                                                              2011050481

Summary of Contents

Contents	vii
Preface	xi
Acknowledgments	xiii

Introduction
THE BIRTH OF CRIMINOLOGY — 1

PART ONE
THE EMERGENCE OF THE CLASSICAL SCHOOL — 13

Chapter 1
Francis Hutcheson — 22
from A System of Moral Philosophy — 23

Chapter 2
Montesquieu — 31
from The Spirit of Laws — 32

Chapter 3
Cesare Beccaria — 43
from An Essay on Crimes and Punishments — 44

Chapter 4
Jeremy Bentham — 55
from An Introduction to the Principles of Morals and Legislation — 56

PART TWO
PHYSIOGNOMY, PHRENOLOGY, AND THE ITALIAN SCHOOL — 69

Chapter 5
Johann Caspar Lavater — 83
from Essays on Physiognomy — 84

Chapter 6
Franz Joseph Gall — 89
from On the Functions of the Brain and of Each of Its Parts, Volume IV: Organology — 91

Chapter 7
Cesare Lombroso — 100
  Criminal Anthropology: Its Origin and Application (complete) — 101
from The Female Offender (with William Ferrero) — 109

Chapter 8
Enrico Ferri — 114
from The Positive School of Criminology: Three Lectures — 115

Chapter 9
Raffaele Garofalo 125
from Criminology 126

PART THREE
MORAL STATISTICS AND THE NINETEENTH-CENTURY FRENCH SCHOOL 133

Chapter 10
Adolphe Quetelet 145
from A Treatise on Man and the Development of His Faculties 146

Chapter 11
André-Michel Guerry 158
from Essay on the Moral Statistics of France 159

Chapter 12
Gabriel Tarde 170
from Penal Philosophy 171

Chapter 13
Émile Durkheim 186
from The Rules of Sociological Method 187
from Two Laws of Penal Evolution 190

PART FOUR
THE ROOTS OF CRITICAL CRIMINOLOGY 201

Chapter 14
Karl Marx 222
from Capital: A Critique of Political Economy, Volume I 223

Chapter 15
Frederick Engels 232
from The Condition of the Working Class in England in 1844 233

Chapter 16
Peter Kropotkin 244
Law and Authority: An Anarchist Essay (complete) 244

Chapter 17
Harriet Martineau 255
from Society in America, Volume I 256

Chapter 18
W. E. B. Du Bois 264
from The Philadelphia Negro: A Social Study 265

Appendix: Timeline of the Selected Readings 281
Author Index 283
Subject Index 287

Contents

Preface	xi
Acknowledgments	xiii

Introduction
THE BIRTH OF CRIMINOLOGY — 1

Historical Context	1
The Subject Matter of Criminology	5
Historical Trajectories in Criminological Thought	5
Note to the Reader	9
REFERENCES	10

PART ONE
THE EMERGENCE OF THE CLASSICAL SCHOOL — 13

Theoretical Framework	13
Forerunners: Hutcheson and Montesquieu	16
Primary Founders: Beccaria and Bentham	17
Limitations and Contemporary Relevance	20
REFERENCES	20

Chapter 1
Francis Hutcheson — 22

from **A System of Moral Philosophy**	23
The rights arising from injuries and damages done by others: and the abolition of right	23
Of the nature of civil laws and their execution	25

Chapter 2
Montesquieu — 31

from **The Spirit of Laws**	32
Of the severity of punishments in different governments	32
Of the ancient French laws	32
That when people are virtuous few punishments are necessary	32
Of the power of punishments	33
Insufficiency of the laws of Japan	33
Of the spirit of the Roman Senate	35
Of the Roman laws in respect to punishments	35
Of the just proportion between punishments and crimes	36
Of the rack	36
Of pecuniary and corporal punishments	37
Of the law of retaliation	37
Of the punishment of fathers for the crimes of their children	37
That liberty is favored by the nature and proportion of punishments	37
Of certain accusations that require particular moderation and prudence	38
Of the crime against nature	39

Of the crime of high treason — 40
  Of the misapplication of the terms sacrilege and high treason — 40
  Of thoughts — 41
  Of indiscreet speeches — 41
  Of writings — 42
  Breach of modesty in punishing crimes — 42

Chapter 3
Cesare Beccaria — 43
  from An Essay on Crimes and Punishments — 44
  Of the origin of punishments — 44
  Of the right to punish — 44
  Of the proportion between crimes and punishments — 45
  Of estimating the degree of crimes — 46
  Of the intent of punishments — 46
  Of torture — 46
  Of the advantage of immediate punishment — 49
  Of acts of violence — 49
  Of the mildness of punishments — 50
  Of the punishment of death — 51
  Of pardons — 53
  Conclusion — 54

Chapter 4
Jeremy Bentham — 55
  from An Introduction to the Principles of Morals and Legislation — 56
  Of the principle of utility — 56
  Of the four sanctions or sources of pain and pleasure — 58
  Cases unmeet for punishment — 60
  Of the proportion between punishments and offences — 63

PART TWO
PHYSIOGNOMY, PHRENOLOGY, AND THE ITALIAN SCHOOL — 69
  Physiognomy — 71
  Phrenology — 73
  The Italian School — 75
  REFERENCES — 80

Chapter 5
Johann Caspar Lavater — 83
  from Essays on Physiognomy — 84
  Socrates — 84

Chapter 6
Franz Joseph Gall — 89
  from On the Functions of the Brain and of Each of Its Parts, Volume IV: Organology — 91
  Natural history of the carnivorous instinct in man — 91
  What is the fundamental quality of the disposition to murder—of the disposition to kill? — 94

Seat of the carnivorous organ, and its external appearance in the
　　　　human cranium						95

Chapter 7
## Cesare Lombroso						100
　　from Criminal Anthropology: Its Origin and Application		101
　　　History of the discovery—atavism of the criminal			102
　　　Epilepsy of born criminals						104
　　　New studies: Ferri, Garofalo, Marro				105
　　　Practical applications						107
　　from The Female Offender (with William Ferrero)			109
　　　The criminal type in women and its atavistic origin		109

Chapter 8
## Enrico Ferri							114
　　from The Positive School of Criminology: Three Lectures		115
　　　Lecture II								115

Chapter 9
## Raffaele Garofalo						125
　　from Criminology, The Natural Crime				126
　　　The need of a sociologic notion of crime				126
　　　Rationale of the natural crime					126
　　　The delimitation of criminality					129

PART THREE
MORAL STATISTICS AND THE
## NINETEENTH-CENTURY FRENCH SCHOOL				133
　　Moral Statistics							133
　　The French School							137
　　A Concluding Note							142
　　REFERENCES								142

Chapter 10
## Adolphe Quetelet						145
　　from A Treatise on Man and the Development of His Faculties,
　　　Of the Development of the Propensity to Crime			146
　　　Of crimes in general, and of the repression of them		146
　　　On the influence of seasons on the propensity to crime		147
　　　On the influence of sex on the propensity to crime		148
　　　Of the influence of age on the propensity to crime		151
　　　Conclusions							156

Chapter 11
## André-Michel Guerry						158
　　from Essay on the Moral Statistics of France			159
　　　Introduction							159
　　　Geographical distribution [of crimes against persons and property]	160

Chapter 12
## Gabriel Tarde							170
　　from Penal Philosophy						171
　　　Crime: Preponderance of social causes				171

Chapter 13
Émile Durkheim — 186
  from **The Rules of Sociological Method** — 187
    Crime as a normal social fact — 187
  from **Two Laws of Penal Evolution** — 190
    The law of quantitative variations — 190
    Explanation of the first law — 195

PART FOUR
THE ROOTS OF CRITICAL CRIMINOLOGY — 201
  Marxist Criminology — 202
  Anarchist Criminology — 206
  Feminist Criminology — 211
  Critical Race Theory — 214
  A Note on the Idea of Progress — 217
  REFERENCES — 217

Chapter 14
Karl Marx — 222
  from **Capital: A Critique of Political Economy, Volume I** — 223
    Expropriation of the agricultural population from the land — 223
    Bloody legislation against the expropriated, from the end of the 15th century. Forcing down of wages by acts of parliament — 227

Chapter 15
Frederick Engels — 232
  from **The Condition of the Working Class in England in 1844** — 233
    Results [of industrial capitalism] — 233
    The attitude of the bourgeoisie towards the proletariat — 239

Chapter 16
Peter Kropotkin — 244
  Law and Authority: An Anarchist Essay — 244

Chapter 17
Harriet Martineau — 255
  from **Society in America, Volume I** — 256
    Allegiance to law — 256
    Political non-existence of women — 261

Chapter 18
W. E. B. Du Bois — 264
  from **The Philadelphia Negro: A Social Study, The Negro Criminal** — 265
    History of Negro crime in the city — 265
    Negro crime since the war — 267
    A special study in crime — 271
    Some cases of crime — 277

Appendix: Timeline of the Selected Readings — 281
Author Index — 283
Subject Index — 287

PREFACE

Several anthologies covering the principal works of criminology have been published, but most of them devote relatively little attention to the writings of the eighteenth and nineteenth centuries. This reader, *The Birth of Criminology*, has been designed to help fill this gap in the literature and to encourage criminologists to maintain an awareness of the history of their field. It provides researchers, instructors, and students of criminology with a collection of key readings from these formative years. It includes selections from the classical school, physiognomy and phrenology, the Italian school of positive criminology, moral statistics, the nineteenth-century French school, and several works that anticipated the emergence of critical criminology. Many of the perspectives embodied in these readings have endured while others have faded into obscurity, but all of them represent significant viewpoints in the history of criminological thought.

The Birth of Criminology differs from the few existing readers in the field that focus on works written before the twentieth century in at least three notable ways. First, it devotes considerable attention to the classical school of criminology. Not only does it provide lengthy selections from the works of Cesare Beccaria and Jeremy Bentham, but it also presents readings by two prominent forerunners of the classical school, Francis Hutcheson and Montesquieu. Second, it devotes an entire section to critical thought on law, crime, and punishment—that is, to several important precursors of contemporary critical criminology. The works of the early Marxists (including Karl Marx), anarchists, feminists, and critical race theorists (e.g., W. E. B. Du Bois) provide important insights into the overall range of perspectives that addressed issues of criminological interest prior to the twentieth century. Although these perspectives were not mainstream at the time and may not be today, they do occupy a significant place in the history of criminological thought. Finally, the selections presented in this reader generally are longer than those provided by other readers that present works written before the twentieth century. A decision was made to sacrifice some breadth of coverage for a little more depth. Space limitations, unfortunately, require something to give in one area or the other.

Before proceeding, a brief comment on the publication dates of the selected readings may be warranted. There is a slight discrepancy concerning the subtitle of this book, since a few of the selected readings were published in the early twentieth century. However, these early-twentieth-century readings were either later editions of works originally published in the 1800s or, in one case (a 1901 lecture by Enrico Ferri), a concise and very informative presentation of a perspective developed during the 1800s.

ACKNOWLEDGMENTS

I wish to thank the reviewers of the initial book proposal and draft for their helpful advice that undoubtedly improved the overall quality of this publication. A debt is owed to Sherrie M. Fleshman for her excellent translation of "Crime as a Normal Social Fact," a reading from Émile Durkheim's *Les Règles de la méthode sociologique* [*The Rules of Sociological Method*], and to Moussa Nombre for his advice on the translation of several key terms and statements. I also am indebted to my colleagues, Martin Gottschalk and Roni Mayzer, for their suggestions on a variety of matters that arose during the writing and compilation of this book. And of course, my gratitude extends to the staff at Wolters Kluwer, especially David Herzig for the opportunity to create this book and Susan Boulanger for her support and guidance throughout the process.

Finally, I would like to thank the publishers of the following works for permission to include selections from these publications. Complete citations are presented in the chapter introductions.

André-Michel Guerry. Extracts from *Essay on the Moral Statistics of France*; edited and translated by Hugh P. Whitt and Victor W. Reinking; Lewiston, NY: The Edwin Mellen Press. Copyright © 2002. Reprinted by permission of publisher.

Émile Durkheim. Extracts from "Two Laws of Penal Evolution"; translated by William Jeffrey, Jr.; *University of Cincinnati Law Review*, Volume 38. Copyright © 1969. Reprinted by permission of publisher.

THE BIRTH
OF CRIMINOLOGY

Introduction

THE BIRTH OF CRIMINOLOGY

The progress of science is often portrayed as a majestic and inevitable evolution of ideas in a logical sequence of successively closer approximations to the truth. . . . (T)his conception does not apply to criminology wherein myth and fashion and social conditions have often exercised an influence quite unrelated to the soundness of theories or to the implications of accumulated evidence. One of the sources of protection against invasion by fads, and against these extra theoretical influences . . . is sound appreciation of its own past. (Lindesmith and Levin 1937:671)

Criminology was established as a distinct multidisciplinary field of inquiry by the late nineteenth century, but the development of its foundation goes back much further. Indeed, if one views crime as a secular political label that has been attached to historically sinful behavior, theories of crime have existed for thousands of years in that spiritual explanations of sin can be found among some of the early religious texts. Nevertheless, it was during the eighteenth and nineteenth centuries that the foundation was set for the birth of criminology as a distinct field of inquiry in Western nations.[1]

Historical Context

The foundation for criminology in Europe and North America was forged during a period of rapid and dramatic social change. Over the course of the eighteenth and nineteenth centuries, several phenomena interacted to initiate a change in social life that arguably is greater than the changes that had occurred over the previous five millennia. This transformation created conditions under which the development of criminology and other social sciences seemed reasonable and perhaps even necessary. Below I have provided a brief sketch of several elements of this transformation and how they encouraged and shaped the emergence of criminology.

---

1. The scope of this reader is limited to the early history of criminology in Europe and North America. Accordingly, the development of criminological theory and research in Asia and other parts of the world will not be examined.

During the eighteenth and nineteenth centuries, a fundamental shift occurred in intellectual life. This era began with the Enlightenment, and it was marked by a growing emphasis on "reason" and empirical inquiry. Otherworldly theological perspectives were challenged and gradually replaced by this-worldly philosophical and scientific viewpoints. To borrow the language of Auguste Comte ([1830–1842] 1893), the theological mode of thinking gave way to metaphysical thought and, eventually, to positivism. The leading intellectuals became more secular in their reasoning, pushing religious doctrine and arguments emphasizing the influence of supernatural entities further and further into the background. In the legal realm this shift entailed a call for a new and predominantly secular understanding of law, crime, and punishment. The concept of crime was increasingly separated from that of sin, and it became less acceptable to offer spiritual explanations of criminal behavior and to rationalize punishments in terms of such explanations. The criminal was no longer a possessed person, or someone who was unable to resist the promptings of the "Tempter"; she or he was not an individual with an evil or otherwise defective spirit, or someone who simply was not among the "chosen people." Likewise, it became increasingly unreasonable to view punishment as a means to appease a supernatural force, or to destroy or expel an evil spirit, or to purge an individual's soul of the sin that taints it. Rather, secular conceptions of crime, secular explanations of criminal behavior, and secular rationale for penal policy increasingly became representative of the "rational" viewpoint. But, of course, this new understanding of law, crime, and punishment had to be developed by someone or some group; thus an intellectual void was created, one that could be filled by the field of criminology.

This fundamental shift in intellectual life was closely associated with a fundamental change in political structures and ideologies. During the late 1700s, striking transformations began to occur in the governments of Western societies. These changes are perhaps best exemplified by the American Revolution and, more importantly, the French Revolution. More than any other political revolution of this period, the French Revolution symbolized the fall of hereditary monarchies and the rise of modern democracies (republics). The ideals of this revolution—liberty, equality, and fraternity—reflected the aforementioned shift in intellectual life and were central to the broader cultural change that was occurring in the West. Of course, these transformations in governmental structure and political ideology also affected the content of law and formal responses to criminal behavior. Many of the laws and systems of stratification under the monarchy stood in opposition to the new political system and, accordingly, had to be replaced. This added momentum to the existing scholarly efforts to develop rational systems of law, a rational conception of crime and criminals, and rational responses to crime. It represented another implicit call for a field such as criminology.

The political context for the birth of criminology also includes at least two other important phenomena: the emergence of nation-states and the practice of colonialism by Western societies.[2] Around the time of the Enlightenment,

---

2. These were not exclusively political phenomena; for instance, they also were tied to the expansion of particular economic interests.

the traditional state that had characterized the political system of many European societies was in the process of being replaced by the nation-state.[3] Compared to the traditional state, the territory of a modern nation-state has boundaries that are more precisely defined, its central government exercises greater control over the people within its borders, and its citizens generally embrace a distinct national identity (nationalism) (Giddens 1991). Each of these properties has implications for matters of crime and justice, but one seems especially relevant to the emergence of criminology. The expansion of centralized governmental control that is characteristic of nation-states prompted more attention to questions of when and how to exercise that control, questions that have concerned the field of criminology from the beginning.

Regarding Western colonialism, it began in around the sixteenth century and involved the expansion of political domination by Europeans to territories outside of Europe. As an extension of the Age of Exploration, colonialism increased the exposure of Europeans to alternative societies—people who looked different and who had different languages, values, rules, and systems of justice. From a European standpoint, these people usually were regarded as inferior, and by extension their ways of life were viewed as inferior. This general mindset is expressed in some of the descriptions of criminals provided by eighteenth- and nineteenth-century scholars. The physical appearance and psychological dispositions of European criminals, at times, were compared to the actual or presumed characteristics of various non-European populations; the purpose of such comparisons was to make criminals appear inferior to the average European. This way of thinking can be found in many early works of criminology.[4]

The changes in intellectual and political life during the eighteenth and nineteenth centuries were certainly important, but there was another change that was perhaps even more important—the transformation of economic life. This transformation is associated with the development of colonialism, but it is best represented by the Industrial Revolution and the rise of modern capitalism. During this era, agrarian economies gave way to factory-based systems of production. The new system of production, combined with the growth of science, contributed to significant advances in technology. Material goods suddenly were produced with much greater efficiency and in much larger quantities, and the variety of goods manufactured increased at a remarkable rate. This transformation also depended on and contributed to rapid expansion in the division of labor. Many new specializations emerged throughout the economic system, and individuals became more focused in their economic roles. In short, due to this economic transformation, the material conditions of social life and the roles people played within their communities changed dramatically.

---

3. Anthony Giddens (1987:154–155), citing the work of Charles Tilly (1975), notes: "In the sixteenth century, there were some 500 more or less autonomous states and principalities in Europe; by the turn of the twentieth century these had shrunk to twenty-five."

4. Colonialism also allowed for another penal option: the transportation of offenders to the colonies.

However, the emergence of industrial capitalism also contributed to a new set of problems, including a new form of class struggle, rapid population growth and urbanization, and complications associated with managing a highly differentiated society. Class conflicts existed before the emergence of industrial capitalism and they persisted after its establishment. They continued in a new form as tensions arose between wage laborers and the owners of the new industries. The competitive, profit-oriented nature of capitalism created a continual pressure to keep wages low, workdays long, and working conditions barely tolerable. The suffering of workers under the early stages of industrial capitalism, especially when there was a large surplus labor force, was very apparent. To make matters more complicated for the working class, during the eighteenth and nineteenth centuries, there was a population explosion and the number and size of cities increased at an incredible rate. Unfortunately, the infrastructure of these cities did not keep pace with their growth and, consequently, many people lacked food, clothing, shelter, sanitary living conditions, and health care. Finally, given the growing concern with efficiency, the need to manage an ever-increasing population, and the need to effectively organize interactions among a large number of occupational specializations, governments, industries, and other social institutions (e.g., schools) increasingly came to embrace bureaucratic principles and various practices that would promote a more disciplined population.

These socioeconomic problems locked a segment of the population into a state of desperation and raised persistent concerns regarding the development of effective means of social control. On their own, these problems may have been enough to stimulate the emergence of criminology. Many of the scholars who were responsible for the development of criminology were concerned with these issues. Some of them proposed policies to control dangerous subpopulations; others described how the laws unjustly support the interests of some segments of society over the interests of other segments. And while some of these scholars looked for the causes of crime within individuals, others were more inclined to examine the effects of the social environment on criminality.

In simple terms, the changes in social life that were occurring during the eighteenth and nineteenth centuries, and the fear and uncertainty they created, prompted people to take a closer look at the nature of social life in general and the nature of law, crime, and punishment in particular. This was an environment in which various spheres of systematic social inquiry could emerge and prosper. The creation, or at least the further development, of political science, economics, psychology, sociology, anthropology, criminology, and perhaps most other social sciences was easily rationalized in this context. While the official objectives of these disciplines often may differ significantly from their latent functions, their very presence is easy to understand. The changes taking place were so striking that people were encouraged to ask a series of related questions: Why were these changes occurring? Where were they taking us? And how can we alter the course of these changes for the benefit of society, or at least some segment of society? Criminology offered answers to some of these questions, those pertaining to changes in the nature of law, crime, and punishment.

The Subject Matter of Criminology

Criminology has been defined in different ways. Occasionally an author will limit the overall scope of criminology to the study of crime and criminals, especially the causes of crime. Such a conception may be useful for purposes of setting up disciplinary boundaries (e.g., separating criminology from criminal justice), but it tends to overlook or dismiss two very noteworthy descriptions of the field. In 1885, Raffaele Garofalo published the first edition of his *Criminology* (*Criminologia*), one of the first books to apply the label of "criminology" to the field. This book, at least by the time of the French edition of 1905, provided analyses of the "notion of crime," of the characteristics of criminals and the causes of criminality, and of the existing theories of law and criminal procedure. It also presented suggestions for a "rational system of punishment" and an "international penal code." As conceived by Garofalo ([1914] 1968), criminology is concerned with not only the study of crime and criminals but also issues of law and punishment. This broader conception was later embraced in a more sociological form by Edwin Sutherland, who, in the fourth edition of his *Principles of Criminology* (1947), provided perhaps the most influential definition of the field:

> Criminology is the body of knowledge regarding crime as a social phenomenon. It includes within its scope the processes of making laws, of breaking laws, and of reacting toward the breaking of laws. (Sutherland 1947:1)

It is this broader conception of criminology that has guided the selections presented in this book. Thus the readings will cover not only analyses of the causes of crime but also important issues related to legal theory and penology, issues that were a central concern for early criminologists and are still a concern for criminologists today. As Sutherland suggests, there is a kind of unity that exists across the three "principal divisions" of criminology, and this is a position that was embraced to some extent by scholars of very diverse orientations long before Sutherland. It is suggested by the work of not only Garofalo but also Cesare Beccaria, Jeremy Bentham, and Émile Durkheim. It even is implied in the works of several critical theorists of the nineteenth century, including Frederick Engels and Peter Kropotkin. Because of this common tendency to examine laws, criminal behavior, and responses to crime together, I will not attempt to draw a rigid distinction between the fields of criminology and criminal justice.[5]

Historical Trajectories in Criminological Thought

From its early stages of development until today, criminology has been a multidisciplinary field that embodies many different theoretical and research perspectives. Regarding the founding perspectives of the field, they have been classified in different ways (see Horton 2000; Rafter 2009), and currently

---

5. One distinction that appears to exist between criminology and criminal justice is that the latter is more concerned with administrative issues regarding the day-to-day operations of the police, courts, prisons, and other components of the criminal justice system. This difference may help separate the two fields, but criminology still has much to say about the assumptions and knowledge claims that rationalize these operations.

there is little consensus as to which system of classification is the most useful. Nevertheless, I believe the divisions outlined below offer a helpful framework for understanding several key historical developments in criminology. These divisions include the classical school, physical appearance theories (e.g., physiognomy and phrenology), the Italian school of positive criminology, research on moral statistics, the nineteenth-century French school, and the precursors of contemporary critical criminology (e.g., early Marxist theory). Although some of the core concepts and propositions of these divisions have become antiquated, many of their basic insights still can be found in the more recent theories of the field.

The classical school typically is viewed as the first major branch of criminology. It emerged during the eighteenth century and is based largely on an integration of social contract and utilitarian reasoning. The label "classical school" appears to have been coined by members of the Italian school who wished to highlight the more contemporary empirical nature of their own work. Nonetheless, it would be a mistake to conclude that the architects of the classical school opposed science or even discounted its relevance (see Beirne 1993; Newman and Marongiu 2009). They were theorists of the Enlightenment, and while their analyses tended to be more philosophical than empirical, they generally embraced science. Moreover, key elements of the classical school are embodied in contemporary deterrence, economic, and rational choice theories, all of which have been refined, at least in part, through empirical research.[6] To illustrate the birth and development of the classical school, I have included selections from the works of Francis Hutcheson, Montesquieu, Beccaria, and Bentham. The works of Hutcheson and Montesquieu contain several "classical" contentions that anticipated the later writings of Beccaria and Bentham, two scholars who generally are held to be the founders of the classical school.

Despite a favorable reaction from many intellectuals and political leaders, the classical school had its critics. For instance, the Roman Catholic Church opposed its secular nature and placed publications by Montesquieu, Beccaria, and Bentham on its *Index Librorum Prohibitorum* (a list of forbidden books). Immanuel Kant, one of the most prominent philosophers of the Enlightenment, dismissed its utilitarian emphasis on deterrence in favor of retribution. And perhaps most importantly, by the end of the nineteenth century, the scholars of the Italian school, such as Cesare Lombroso and Enrico Ferri, criticized the classical school's presumed position on free will and portrayed it as a fundamentally flawed conceptual framework. Interestingly, at the same time that it was presenting itself as a representative of a more advanced paradigm, the Italian school, especially during its early stages of development, actively embraced the ancient idea that an association exists between physical appearances (how a person looks) and moral character.

Physical appearance theories suggest that deviants often have a visible physical abnormality of one kind or another, and of course "evil" people

---

6. Several criminologists also have associated routine activities theory with the classical school (see Einstadter and Henry 2006; Akers and Sellers 2009; and Bernard, Snipes, and Gerould 2010).

have long been portrayed as having a hideous appearance. This idea was systematized with the development of physiognomy in Greece more than two thousand years ago, and it was later given a more scientific form in nineteenth-century phrenology and the atavist theory of the Italian school. Studies of the relationship between physical appearances and crime continued well into the twentieth century (e.g., Hooton 1939; Sheldon 1949), but they eventually became the target of widespread criticism for their empirical shortcomings, race and class biases, and problematic policy implications. Nonetheless, theories of this type still linger in the margins of criminology and represent a part of its history. To chart the early development of physical appearance theories in criminology, I have included selections from the work of Johann Caspar Lavater, Franz Joseph Gall, and Lombroso. Lavater was the most prominent physiognomist of the eighteenth century, Gall arguably was the most important contributor to the field of phrenology, and Lombroso's atavist theory represents the most controversial physical appearance theory of criminology.

Although Lombroso was both the creator of atavist theory and the founder of the Italian school of positive criminology, it would be a mistake to describe the Italian school exclusively in terms of its speculations and research on the relationship between physical appearances and crime. Perhaps more than anything else, this branch of criminology emphasized the scientific study of criminals; it maintained that criminal behavior is caused by factors beyond the control of offenders and that criminality should be studied through the use of systematic empirical methods (ideally, the methods of the natural sciences). It was not the first branch of criminology to accept this orientation, but it may have done more than any other to promote it. The Italian school was devoted to the scientific spirit and shares responsibility for the dominance of this spirit in criminology today. In its later formulations, it also made a significant contribution to the multidisciplinary currents that flow through the field, for it eventually offered considerable support for efforts to explain criminal behavior in terms of a combination of biological, psychological, social, and "telluric" factors.[7] To illustrate the emergence and growth of the Italian school, I have included readings from its three most prominent members: Lombroso, Ferri, and Garofalo.

Between the genesis of the classical school and the birth of the Italian school, another branch of criminology emerged and contributed to its scientific emphasis. This branch centered on the examination of moral statistics. During the first half of the nineteenth century, several nations began to systematically collect quantitative data on crime and other "moral" phenomena (e.g., suicides and marriages). This seemingly was a natural extension of the rise of modern capitalism, the expansion of bureaucratic organization, and the growth of science. The data collected provided quantitatively oriented researchers with an opportunity to apply their skills in a new area of inquiry. These researchers, the moral statisticians of the nineteenth century, embraced determinism (on some level) and applied empirical methods

---

7. Telluric factors are elements of the physical environment, such as the climate of an area and its natural resources.

prior to the appearance of the Italian school. Thus their work represents another key precursor to the development of contemporary scientific criminology. Moreover, their examinations of age and crime, sex and crime, and the geographical distribution of crime were forerunners to contemporary life-course, gender-ratio, and ecological research. Examples of their work can be found in the readings by Adolphe Quetelet and André-Michel Guerry, two researchers who examined French crime statistics during the early to mid-1800s.

The development of moral statistics was followed by the emergence of a French school of criminology that emphasized the effects of the social environment. During the late 1800s, this school was contrasted with the Italian school, which had a reputation for having an almost exclusively biological/psychological orientation. This reputation was based largely on Lombroso's work, especially his early work; and while it certainly was understandable, it also was exaggerated (see Zimmern 1898). For instance, Ferri's best-known publication was his *Criminal Sociology*, and even Lombroso, as his work continued to develop, gave more attention to possible social causes of crime. Nevertheless, the French school was clearly more sociological than the Italian school. Among the writings of the French school, one can find precursors to contemporary learning, anomie/strain, and control theories as well as contributions to the sociology of law and punishment. Gabriel Tarde and Émile Durkheim are two prominent representatives of the nineteenth-century French school and, accordingly, examples of their work have been included in this book.[8]

In one way or another, many of the founding perspectives of criminology challenged existing religious beliefs and criminal justice practices, but only a few presented a fundamental challenge to broader economic, political, gender, and race relations. The writings of the nineteenth-century Marxists, anarchists, feminists, and critical race theorists provided direct criticism of existing social arrangements and, here and there, anticipated the work of contemporary critical criminologists. Marxists focused their criticism on the economic arrangements of industrial capitalism, anarchists found the political arrangements of the emerging nation-states to be unacceptable, feminists actively opposed the existing patriarchal structures, and the early critical race theorists challenged the institution of slavery and the persistent discrimination that followed formal emancipation. To illustrate several nineteenth-century currents of critical criminological thought, I have included selections from the works of Karl Marx, Frederick Engels, Peter Kropotkin, Harriet Martineau, and W. E. B. Du Bois. They are among the most prominent scholars in the development of Marxism, anarchism, feminism, and critical race theory; there is little doubt that critical criminology, as it exists today, is indebted to them and their followers in other fields.

This list of historical trajectories in criminological thought should not be read as representing a pattern of progressive development in the field; it is not

---

8. It also is possible to envisage an eighteenth-century French school of criminology represented by the writings of Montesquieu and Voltaire, among others. However, such a school, to the best of my knowledge, has not been demarcated by the literature of criminology and, thus, will be left beyond the scope of this book.

being presented as a sequence of steps in the construction of better and better knowledge. The different divisions signify different areas of development, but I do not wish to impose the notion of progress. Such a conclusion would be difficult to defend and, regardless, goes well beyond the scope of this book. In addition, this list is neither mutually exclusive nor exhaustive. On the one hand, there is some noticeable overlap across the different divisions. This was touched on in the discussion of the relationship between the Italian school and the French school, but there are other examples as well. For instance, Ferri, a member of the Italian school, embraced a variation of Marxist theory (see Beck 2005), and Quetelet, a moral statistician, was influenced by the assumptions of phrenology later in his career (see Beirne 1993).

On the other hand, to this list of divisions in criminological thought, one may add the "classical penitentiary school" (e.g., Howard 1777), the psychological tradition (e.g., Rush [1786] 1947), studies of heredity and crime (e.g., Dugdale 1877), and research on the effects of the physical environment, such as weather conditions (e.g., Dexter [1899] 2000). Yet these divisions are at least partially covered by those just mentioned. For example, Bentham's ([1787, 1791] 1995) work on the panopticon prison design creates a link between the classical school of criminology and the classical penitentiary school, while the Italian school includes theory and research on psychological factors, heredity, and the physical environment. Lombroso's inquiries extended to studies of the "insane criminal," and he accepted heredity as an important source of crime (Lombroso 1895–1896; also see Lombroso Ferrero 1911); Garofalo ([1914] 1968) implied that his views may be better described as "criminal psychology" than as criminal anthropology; and Ferri's ([1901] 1913) conception of the Italian school suggests that it subsumes not only scientific studies of biological, psychological, and social factors, but also research on telluric conditions (e.g., the climate and natural resources). Quetelet ([1831] 1984) and Guerry ([1833] 2002) also provided an examination of the relationship between seasons and crime, and almost a century earlier Montesquieu ([1748] 1899) examined the relationship between climate and the law.

Note to the Reader

In summary, the readings in this book center on theories and research from the eighteenth and nineteenth centuries, an era of rapid social change that set the foundation for the birth and development of criminology. They address the three major areas of inquiry (law, crime, and responses to crime) and are organized around the divisions of criminological thought noted in the preceding section.

The authors of the selected readings were prominent scholars with international reputations, and many of them influenced the development of not only criminology but other fields as well. Most of these scholars did not and perhaps would not describe themselves as criminologists, yet their thoughts on law, crime, and punishment occupy an important place in the history of criminological thought. Given the cursory manner in which many of these authors have been covered by the popular textbooks of the field, some readers may be surprised by the actual range of topics they explore in their writings and the sophistication of some of their arguments. Readers also may be surprised by the insensitivity many of these authors express toward people who differ from them. The language of the readings has not been edited to moderate the level of gender, racial, religious, national, or cultural insensitivity, which is extreme in some of these works. While the claims made in several readings are offensive to contemporary sensibilities, their exclusion would only distort the history of the field and the views of its founders.

REFERENCES

Akers, Ronald L., and Christine S. Sellers. 2009. *Criminological Theories: Introduction, Evaluation, and Application*. 5th ed. New York: Oxford University Press.

Beck, Naomi. 2005. "Enrico Ferri's Scientific Socialism: A Marxist Interpretation of Herbert Spencer's Organic Analogy." *Journal of the History of Biology* 38:301–325.

Beirne, Piers. 1993. *Inventing Criminology: Essays on the Rise of 'Homo Criminalis'*. Albany, NY: State University of New York Press.

Bentham, Jeremy. [1787, 1791] 1995. *The Panopticon Writings*. Edited by Miran Božovič. London: Verso.

Bernard, Thomas J., Jeffrey B. Snipes, and Alexander L. Gerould. 2010. *Vold's Theoretical Criminology*. 6th ed. New York: Oxford University Press.

Comte, Auguste. [1830–1842] 1893. *The Positive Philosophy of Auguste Comte*. Freely translated and condensed by Harriet Martineau. London: Kegan Paul, Trench, Trubner & Co.

Dexter, Edwin Grant. [1899] 2000. "Influence of Weather Upon Crime." In *Pioneering Perspectives in Criminology: The Literature of 19th Century Criminological Positivism*, edited by David M. Horton, 393–402. Incline Village, NV: Copperhouse.

Dugdale, Richard L. 1877. *The Jukes: A Study in Crime, Pauperism, Disease, and Heredity*. New York: G. P. Putnam's Sons.

Einstadter, Werner J., and Stuart Henry. 2006. *Criminological Theory: An Analysis of Its Underlying Assumptions*. 2nd ed. Lanham, MD: Rowman & Littlefield.

Ferri, Enrico. [1901] 1913. *The Positive School of Criminology: Three Lectures*. Translated by Ernest Untermann. Chicago: Charles H. Kerr & Company.

Garofalo, Raffaele. [1914] 1968. *Criminology*. Translated primarily from the fifth French edition by Robert Wyness Millar. Montclair, NJ: Patterson Smith.

Giddens, Anthony. 1987. *Sociology: A Brief but Critical Introduction*. 2nd ed. New York: Harcourt Brace Jovanovich.

Giddens, Anthony. 1991. *Introduction to Sociology*. New York: W. W. Norton and Company.

Guerry, André-Michel. [1833] 2002. *Essay on the Moral Statistics of France*. Translated by Hugh P. Whitt and Victor W. Reinking. Lewiston, NY: Edwin Mellen Press.

Hooton, Earnest. 1939. *Crime and the Man*. Cambridge, MA: Harvard University Press.

Horton, David M., ed. 2000. *Pioneering Perspectives in Criminology: The Literature of 19th Century Criminological Positivism*. Incline Village, NV: Copperhouse.

Howard, John. 1777. *The State of the Prisons in England and Wales*. Warrington, Lancashire: William Eyers.

Lindesmith, Alfred, and Yale Levin. 1937. "The Lombrosian Myth in Criminology." *The American Journal of Sociology* 42(5):653–671.

Lombroso, Cesare. 1895–1896. "Criminal Anthropology: Its Origin and Application." *The Forum* 20:33–49.

Lombroso Ferrero, Gina. 1911. *Criminal Man: According to the Classification of Cesare Lombroso*. New York: G. P. Putnam's Sons.

Montesquieu. [1748] 1899. *The Spirit of Laws*. Translated by Thomas Nugent. New York: The Colonial Press.

Newman, Graeme R., and Pietro Marongiu. 2009. "Introduction to the *Treatise*." In Cesare Beccaria's *On Crimes and Punishments*, vii–lv. New Brunswick, NJ: Transaction Publishers.

Quetelet, Adolphe. [1831] 1984. *Research on the Propensity for Crime at Different Ages*. Translated by Sawyer F. Sylvester. Cincinnati, OH: Anderson Publishing.

Rafter, Nicole, ed. 2009. *The Origins of Criminology: A Reader*. New York: Routledge.

Rush, Benjamin. [1786] 1947. "The Influence of Physical Causes Upon the Moral Faculty." In *The Selected Writings of Benjamin Rush*, edited by Dagobert D. Runes, 181–211. New York: Philosophical Library.

Sheldon, William H. 1949. *Varieties of Delinquent Youth: An Introduction to Constitutional Psychiatry*. New York: Harper & Brothers.

Sutherland, Edwin H. 1947. *Principles of Criminology*. 4th ed. Chicago: J. B. Lippincott Company.

Tilly, Charles. 1975. *The Formation of National States in Europe*. Princeton, NJ: Princeton University Press.

Zimmern, Helen. [1898] 2000. "Criminal Anthropology in Italy." In *Pioneering Perspectives in Criminology: The Literature of 19th Century Criminological Positivism*, edited by David M. Horton, 47–64. Incline Village, NV: Copperhouse.

PART ONE

THE EMERGENCE OF THE CLASSICAL SCHOOL

The classical school of criminology emerged during the eighteenth century as a product of the Enlightenment and the work of scholars from several nations. For better or worse, it was compatible with modern capitalism (e.g., both encouraged some form of systematic cost/benefit analysis), the expanding bureaucratic organization of social institutions, and the growing interest in maintaining a disciplined population. But it also was compatible with the cultural shift that stressed greater respect for humanity and that found openly harsh punishments increasingly objectionable. The classical school pursued the creation of more rational and more humane systems of justice. It encouraged a secular understanding of crime and carefully designed punishments guided by the utilitarian principle, social contract reasoning, and ultimately deterrence philosophy.

Theoretical Framework

The classical school, especially as it is represented by the work of Cesare Beccaria, is based on the traditions of utilitarianism and social contract theory. Although elements of utilitarianism are present in the writings of the Greek philosopher Epicurus, who lived from 341 to 270 B.C. (Scarre 1994),[1] it gradually evolved into a distinct branch of philosophy during the seventeenth and eighteenth centuries through the work of Richard Cumberland,[2] David Hume, and Jeremy Bentham, among others; it then was developed further by James Mill, John Stuart Mill, and Henry Sidgwick during the nineteenth century (Beck 1979). Utilitarianism maintains that actions and social arrangements should be evaluated in terms of the extent

---

1. Geoffrey Scarre (1994) notes that the views of Epicurus have been widely misunderstood and that his anticipation of utilitarianism is often overlooked. Scarre also notes that Epicurus has had some harsh critics—for instance, "For his denial of the immortality of the soul, Epicurus was later condemned by Dante to the Sixth Circle of the Inferno, the Circle of heretics" (Scarre 1994:221).

2. According to Ernest Albee (1896:24), Richard Cumberland, in his *De legibus naturae* (1672), was the first English scholar to present the utilitarian principle.

to which they produce happiness (pleasure) and reduce unhappiness (pain); if they produce a net increase in pleasure or a net decrease in pain, they are acceptable. In this connection, the classical school defines a just criminal justice system as one that effectively pursues the utilitarian goal of "the greatest happiness of the greatest number."[3] While this statement has been interpreted in different ways, at a minimum it suggests that the criminal justice system of a society should serve the interests of the general public. In other words, its purpose should not be to maintain only the interests of a ruling minority (e.g., the royal family and religious elite), although it certainly may reinforce their interests to the extent that they are tied to the interests of the general public.

Like utilitarianism, key elements of social contract theory can be traced back to ancient Greek philosophy—in particular, to Socrates's rationale for submitting to the death penalty as reported by Plato in his dialogue entitled "Crito." Nonetheless, its first elaborate formulation was presented in the seventeenth century by Thomas Hobbes in his work *Leviathan* (1651). Following Hobbes, several alternative versions of social contract theory were constructed, most notably by John Locke and Jean-Jacques Rousseau. Although Hobbes, Locke, and Rousseau proposed different conceptions of "the state of nature" and supported different forms of government, each one suggested that it is reasonable for individuals to agree to give up some of their liberties in exchange for the security and other benefits that can be acquired by living together in a society under its government. Without such an agreement (the social contract) and the mechanisms to enforce it, individuals would be subject to uncertainties and coercion from other individuals or groups that would be more oppressive than the terms of the agreement. As conceived by Hobbes (in Ebenstein 1962:368), it would be a situation "where every man is enemy to every man." Hobbes, Locke, and Rousseau provide different descriptions of the exact nature of the problem, but all three embraced the idea of a social contract as a basis for maintaining security in the societies of their era.

The classical school, particularly in the work of Beccaria, justifies punishment using a variety of social contract reasoning. Where a just social contract exists, the government has the right to impose punishments on those who violate it; that is, it has the right to impose punishments on those who break the laws of the society. However, in the classical school, a government's right to punish is constrained by the utilitarian principle. Foremost, the social contract must be a just contract according to utilitarian standards; the exchange of liberties for security must be oriented toward "the greatest happiness of the greatest number." If the social contract does not have this orientation, it is unjust and punishment, overall, is unjust. Beyond this general requirement, from the viewpoint of the classical school, there is a relatively long list of specific requirements that need to be met for a punishment to be acceptable. For Beccaria ([1764] 1819:160), "it should be public, immediate, and necessary, the least possible in the case given, proportioned to the crime, and determined by the laws."

---

3. This wording of the utilitarian principle comes from Beccaria ([1764] 1819:xii).

Underlying the classical school is a partially implicit theory of human nature and crime. Different interpretations of this theory exist in the literature of criminology, but the traditional interpretation, which is perhaps still the most common one, begins with the assumption that humans tend to be hedonistic, rational, and free. It is suggested that our actions are driven by a desire to maximize pleasure and minimize pain. Prior to acting, we weigh the amount of pleasure that may be derived from a particular course of action against the amount of pain that may be suffered. We then choose the course of action that is anticipated to bring the greatest pleasure, even if it is a criminal act. This framework clearly supports deterrence as a penal orientation designed to reduce crime. If people can be given the impression that the commission of a crime will cause them more pain than pleasure, they will not commit the crime. Moreover, if the acts defined as crimes cause more pain than pleasure for the members of a society, then a system that effectively deters such offenses will be in line with the objective of promoting "the greatest happiness of the greatest number."

In this standard description of the classical school, it usually is emphasized that individuals freely choose between different courses of action, but this description has become the subject of some debate and appears to be misleading. While the primary founders of this school often suggest that humans are hedonistic and in some sense rational beings, they arguably embraced a deterministic standpoint that limits, if not excludes, the presumed assumption of free will (see Beirne 1993; Newman and Marongiu 2009). This closes much of the gap between the classical and positive schools of criminology. For more than a century, the two schools have been separated to a substantial degree by the free will/determinism issue—with the classical school presupposing free will and the positive school determinism (see Ferri ([1901] 1913). But this distinction appears to have been exaggerated and may not provide a sound basis for separating the two schools. Nevertheless, even though one of the main customary distinctions may no longer hold, differences still exist. Historically, the classical school has been more inclined to view criminals as rational beings, to stress deterrence as a penal philosophy over correction or incapacitation, to emphasize the examination of criminal laws and penal processes rather than individual criminals or crime rates, and to engage in nonempirical reasoning (logic) rather than the systematic collection and analysis of empirical data.

Many scholars, directly or indirectly, contributed to the emergence of the classical school, including Thomas Hobbes, John Locke, Francis Hutcheson, Montesquieu, Voltaire, Claude Adrien Helvétius, Jean Le Rond d'Alembert, Denis Diderot, David Hume, Étienne Bonnot de Condillac, Cesare Beccaria, Pietro and Alessandro Verri,[4] and Jeremy Bentham (see Paolucci 1963; Blackstone 1965; Monachesi 1973; Newman and Marongiu 1990, 2009; Beirne 1993). The readings in this section trace the development of this school from the work of two scholars who helped set the stage for its emergence (Hutcheson and Montesquieu) to its primary founders (Beccaria and Bentham).

---

4. The Verri brothers assisted Beccaria in the composition of *An Essay on Crimes and Punishments*.

Forerunners: Hutcheson and Montesquieu

Francis Hutcheson (1694–1746) was a Scottish philosopher whose writings represent an important part of the intellectual context that generated the classical school (see Beirne 1993).[5] He typically is not classified as a member of the classical school, but several of his insights are reflected in the works of Beccaria and Bentham. Hutcheson was born in Drumalig, Ireland. He later moved to Scotland and studied theology at the University of Glasgow. After he received his degree and spent a decade directing a private academy in Dublin, he returned to the University of Glasgow and accepted a position as Professor of Moral Philosophy. He eventually became one of the leading figures of the Scottish Enlightenment and in the development of the "science of man," influencing the work of both Adam Smith (his most prominent student) and David Hume.

Although Hutcheson's work represents an important precursor to the classical school (and, more broadly, utilitarianism),[6] it deviates somewhat from the standard classical viewpoint. Contrary to the classical school's focus on egoistic hedonism to explain human behavior, Hutcheson argued that we possess a "moral sense" that leads us to accept conduct that actually opposes our selfish interests. We develop an inclination to care for others, and we derive some degree of pleasure from acts of self-sacrifice. In this connection, Hutcheson proposed that our moral sense encourages conduct that is oriented toward "the greatest Happiness for the greatest Numbers" ([1725] 2004:125), an early statement of the utilitarian principle that would eventually guide the classical school.

The reading presented in Chapter 1 includes several excerpts from Hutcheson's *A System of Moral Philosophy* (1755), where he argues in favor of deterrence and opposes excessive punishment.[7] These commitments—support for the utilitarian principle, deterrence philosophy, and the moderation of punishments—became key elements of the classical school of criminology.

Charles-Louis de Secondat, Baron de Montesquieu (1689–1755), was a French philosopher of the Enlightenment who, much like Hutcheson, helped establish the foundation for the emergence of the classical school (see Beirne 1993).[8] Montesquieu was born into a noble family near Bordeaux, France. He received a law degree from the University of Bordeaux and served as a provincial magistrate for about a decade. In this position, he administered several jails and reportedly was involved in the torture of accused offenders (Shklar 1987). He also sentenced offenders to deportation and execution. This fact, on the surface at least, may strike some readers as ironic, for he later became an advocate for the moderation of punishments.

---

5. The following information on Hutcheson is based on several sources, including Albee (1896), Blackstone (1965), Beirne (1993), and Radcliffe (1995).

6. Ernest Albee (1896) concluded that Hutcheson was almost a utilitarian but not quite.

7. William T. Blackstone (1965) notes that Hutcheson wrote *A System of Moral Philosophy* between 1734 and 1737, but it was not published until 1755, almost a decade after his death. For this reason, the work of Hutcheson is presented in the first chapter, prior to the work of Montesquieu.

8. The following information on Montesquieu is based primarily on Sorel (1888), Ebenstein (1962), Shklar (1987), Beirne (1993), and Turner, Beeghley, and Powers (1998).

Judith N. Shklar (1987:28) has described him as "a nobleman and a magistrate who wrote radical books."

Montesquieu clearly had experience with the justice system of his era, but he also maintained a close connection with the scholarly community. He welcomed science and made a significant contribution to the development of the social sciences. His first major work was *The Persian Letters* (1721), a satire on French institutions that brought him widespread recognition. Almost three decades later, he completed *The Spirit of Laws* (1748), his most important work.[9] Both of these books were condemned by the Catholic Church and added to its *Index Librorum Prohibitorum*. The latter work, though sometimes overlooked, warrants attention from scholars who are interested in the history of criminological thought. In *The Spirit of Laws*, Montesquieu describes three kinds of governments—despotisms sustained by fear, monarchies sustained by honor, and republics sustained by political virtue. He spoke in favor of the separation and balance of governmental powers—executive, legislative, and judicial. He also provided noteworthy insights into the severity and proportionality of punishment that later would be echoed in the works of Beccaria and Bentham. Several of these insights on penal policy are presented in Chapter 2, which contains excerpts from *The Spirit of Laws*.

Primary Founders: Beccaria and Bentham

Although the works of Hutcheson and Montesquieu helped set the stage for the emergence of the classical school, it is Beccaria and Bentham who generally are regarded as the founders of this school.

Cesare Bonesana, Marchese Beccaria (1738–1794), was an Italian scholar who, with some help from his friends, authored an essay that became the cornerstone of the classical school.[10] This work, *An Essay on Crimes and Punishments* (1764), represents the paradigm of the classical school more than any other single publication. Capturing the spirit of the Enlightenment, it was a humanistic philosophical treatise and, as Piers Beirne (1993) points out, an early contribution to the developing "science of man."[11] It calls for a secular criminal justice system, embraces both the utilitarian principle and social contract theory, and provides an outline for a system of punishment based on deterrence. In it, Beccaria argues against torture, the death penalty, excessive punishments, and other perceived problems with eighteenth-century systems of justice. From a contemporary standpoint, *On Crimes and Punishments* may not seem particularly threatening to the political or religious elite, yet it was initially published anonymously and the Roman Catholic Church quickly placed this essay on its list of prohibited books. Nonetheless, soon after it was published it was applauded by

---

9. Jonathan H. Turner, Leonard Beeghley, and Charles H. Powers (1998:9–10) conclude, "*The Spirit of Laws* can be considered one of the first sociological works in both style and tone."

10. The following information on Beccaria is based on Paolucci (1963), Monachesi (1973), Jenkins (1984), Newman and Marongiu (1990, 2009), and Beirne (1993).

11. Beirne (1993) persuasively argues that Beccaria's perspective embodies the Scottish Enlightenment's "science of man" (e.g., the views of Hutcheson) and "the humanism of the French *philosophes*" (e.g., the views of Montesquieu).

many prominent scholars and political leaders, including Voltaire, Helvétius, d'Alembert, Hume, Friedrich II of Prussia, Maria Theresa of Austria, Catherine the Great of Russia, John Adams, and Thomas Jefferson.

Beccaria was born into an aristocratic family in Milan. He attended the University of Pavia, received a law degree in 1758, and then returned to Milan. There he developed a friendship with Pietro and Alessandro Verri and several other young scholars who had an interest in promoting social change, including penal reform. With the encouragement and guidance of the Verri brothers, and the intellectual stimulation of the other members of this group,[12] Beccaria wrote *On Crimes and Punishments*. Whether Beccaria should be regarded as the sole author of this essay or a coauthor is still the subject of some debate (see Paolucci 1963; Newman and Marongiu 1990). Nevertheless, setting this issue aside, we know that the essay was widely read and quoted, helped guide reforms that were occurring or about to occur in Western societies,[13] and became the centerpiece of the classical school. In Chapter 3, several excerpts from *An Essay on Crimes and Punishments* are presented. The selections illustrate Beccaria's utilitarian and social contract reasoning regarding several issues of criminological interest, including the right to punish, torture, the death penalty, and the mildness, promptness, certainty, and proportionality of punishment.

Jeremy Bentham (1748–1832) was an English scholar who praised Beccaria's work and further refined the classical school of criminology.[14] He was born into a middle-class family in London, received a degree from Oxford at the age of 15, and went on to become the "intellectual father" of the University of London (Wallas 1923). His *Fragment on Government* (1776), which was first published anonymously, and *The Defence of Usury* (1787) had earned him some acclaim, but his most important work was *An Introduction to the Principles of Morals and Legislation* (first edition, 1789), which contains an extensive presentation of his utilitarian views on law, crime, and punishment.

In the field of criminology today, Bentham is known primarily for his utilitarian articulation of the classical school and his "panopticon" proposal. Although his views on crime and punishment reflected many of the points made by Beccaria, Bentham generally was more systematic in his arguments and more thoroughly utilitarian. Unlike Beccaria, Bentham did not draw upon social contract theory to support his conclusions. He kept his inquiry centered on the contention that we should evaluate the actions of individuals and governments in terms of their "utility." An act produces utility only if it results in a net increase in pleasure (or a net decrease in pain) for the society in question. Accordingly, a deviant act that produces a net increase in pleasure should not be punished as a crime, and a punishment that produces a net

---

12. The group later came to be known as the "academy of fists."
13. Elio Monachesi (1973:49) concludes, "It is not an exaggeration to regard Beccaria's work as being of primary importance in paving the way for penal reform for approximately the last two centuries."
14. The following information on Bentham is based on multiple sources, including Atkinson (1905), Wallas (1923), and Geis (1973).

increase in pain, a definite possibility given that "all punishment in itself is evil" (Bentham [1823] 1907:170), is unacceptable. In addition, compared to Beccaria, Bentham was more willing to consider variations in the mental states of offenders when contemplating punishments and their potential deterrent effect. For instance, in his discussion of situations in which punishment should not be imposed, he suggested that it is necessary to reflect upon issues of "infancy," "insanity," and "intoxication"—characteristics of offenders that could make punishment "inefficacious" (Bentham [1823] 1907).

Bentham's utilitarian theory is his most salient contribution to the classical school, but he made another noteworthy contribution, one that resides on its margins and has been declared "the great disaster of Bentham's life" (Wallas 1923:52). This disaster was the panopticon—a building plan designed to efficiently observe and control a large number of people. In 1787, Bentham developed this plan with the assistance of his brother, Samuel, and believed that it would be a useful design for prisons, workhouses, poorhouses, "mad-houses," factories, hospitals, and schools (see Bentham [1787, 1791] 1995). He made a proposal to the English government for its use, but after an extended delay, it was rejected. The panopticon design eventually was used in the United States at Western State Penitentiary (Pittsburgh) and Stateville Penitentiary (near Joliet, Illinois), but at these institutions it was only partially implemented and was found to be problematic.

Bentham's work was not just a product of the Enlightenment; it may have embodied the spirit of modern capitalism more than the work of any other major theorist of the classical school. In fact, Karl Marx ([1867] 1987: 570–571), the most prominent critic of capitalism, described Bentham as an "insipid, pedantic, leather-tongued oracle of the ordinary bourgeois intelligence of the 19th century." Yet despite the concerns of Marx and more contemporary social theorists (e.g., Foucault 1979), it appears that Bentham's *intent* was not to reinforce or extend a new form of oppression but rather to provide a rational alternative to a penal system that was openly cruel and largely incompatible with the new cultural sensibilities of the West. Like Beccaria before him, Bentham favored, and seemingly viewed his work as promoting, elevated levels of happiness for most members of society. Moreover, although he has been described as an "arm-chair" criminologist (Geis 1973), his work influenced legal reforms in both England and France. And consistent with his Enlightenment education, he embraced science and stated that his work "on the subject of legislation or any other branch of moral science, is an attempt to extend the experimental method of reasoning from the physical branch to the moral" (in Wallas 1923:47).

To provide a better understanding of Bentham's contribution to the classical school, Chapter 4 presents several selections from *An Introduction to the Principles of Morals and Legislation*. The selections outline the rationale behind Bentham's utilitarian system of punishment. They include his description of "the principle of utility," the four basic sanctions that bind people to a pattern of behavior, situations in which punishment should not be imposed, and the rules that should be used to establish a just and proportionate punishment for an offense.

Limitations and Contemporary Relevance

Through the work of Hutcheson, Montesquieu, Beccaria, and Bentham the classical school emerged as arguably the first form of criminology. Of course, as with almost any paradigm that has existed for longer than two centuries, its list of critics is extensive. The Roman Catholic Church, as suggested, found the classical school to be threatening and criticized its secular orientation. On the other hand, Marxists, as well as other critical theorists, view it as a largely conservative framework oriented toward the preservation of the existing social order rather than its continued development and possible transcendence. In other words, while the classical school once had a critical edge and played a part in the social changes of the eighteenth and early nineteenth centuries, it now stands in opposition to change.[15] Beyond this, Immanuel Kant ([1797] 1965) was critical of its utilitarian framework, especially the suggestion that punishment of an individual should be a means for pursuing the greatest happiness rather than an end in itself.[16] Moreover, the researchers of the Italian school of positive criminology were critical of its lack of empirical inquiry regarding the possible causes of crime.

Despite these and other criticisms, the classical school is an important part of the history of criminology and, in its current form, remains an influential branch of the field. Although it took shape during the eighteenth century and seemingly reached its peak during the early nineteenth century, the imprint of this school can be found in several contemporary perspectives, including modern deterrence theory (e.g., Stafford and Warr 1993), the economic approach to crime (e.g., Becker 1968), rational choice theory (e.g., Cornish and Clarke 1986), and perhaps even routine activities theory (e.g., Cohen and Felson 1979). These perspectives are part of the neoclassical school or, if you prefer, "contemporary classicism."

REFERENCES

Albee, Ernest. 1896. "The Relation of Shaftesbury and Hutcheson to Utilitarianism." *The Philosophical Review* 5(1):24–35.

Atkinson, Charles Milner. 1905. *Jeremy Bentham: His Life and Work*. London: Methuen and Company.

Beccaria, Cesare. [1764] 1819. *An Essay on Crimes and Punishments*. 2nd American ed. Philadelphia: Philip H. Nicklin.

Beck, Robert N. 1979. *Handbook in Social Philosophy*. New York: Macmillan Publishing Company.

Becker, Gary S. 1968. "Crime and Punishment: An Economic Approach." *Journal of Political Economy* 76(2):169–217.

Beirne, Piers. 1993. *Inventing Criminology: Essays on the Rise of 'Homo Criminalis.'* Albany, NY: State University of New York Press.

---

15. It even has been suggested that the classical school always has had a conservative orientation: "Beccaria's work stands as a conservative monument, the first great effort to cure crime without curing the society which produced it" (Jenkins 1984:128).

16. "Judicial punishment can never be used merely as a means to promote some other good for the criminal himself or for civil society, but instead it must in all cases be imposed on him only on the ground that he has committed a crime. . . . The law concerning punishment is a categorical imperative, and woe to him who rummages around in the winding paths of a theory of happiness looking for some advantage to be gained by releasing the criminal from punishment or by reducing the amount of it. . . . " (Kant [1797] 1965:100).

Bentham, Jeremy. [1787, 1791] 1995. *The Panopticon Writings*. Edited by Miran Božovič. London: Verso.

Bentham, Jeremy. [1823] 1907. *An Introduction to the Principles of Morals and Legislation*. Oxford: Clarendon Press.

Blackstone, William T. 1965. *Francis Hutcheson and Contemporary Ethical Theory*. Athens, GA: University of Georgia Press.

Cohen, Lawrence E., and Marcus Felson. 1979. "Social Change and Crime Rate Trends: A Routine Activity Approach." *American Sociological Review* 44:588–608.

Cornish, Derek B., and Ronald V. Clarke, eds. 1986. *The Reasoning Criminal*. New York: Springer-Verlag.

Ebenstein, William. 1962. *Great Political Thinkers: Plato to the Present*. 3rd ed. New York: Holt, Rinehart and Winston.

Ferri, Enrico. [1901] 1913. *The Positive School of Criminology: Three Lectures*. Translated by Ernest Untermann. Chicago: Charles H. Kerr & Company.

Foucault, Michel. 1979. *Discipline and Punish: The Birth of the Prison*. Translated by Alan Sheridan. New York: Vintage Books.

Geis, Gilbert. 1973. "Jeremy Bentham." In *Pioneers in Criminology*, 2nd ed., edited by Hermann Mannheim, 51–68. Montclair, NJ: Patterson Smith.

Hutcheson, Francis. [1725] 2004. *An Inquiry into the Original of Our Ideas of Beauty and Virtue*. Indianapolis: Liberty Fund.

Hutcheson, Francis. [1755] 1968. *A System of Moral Philosophy*. New York: Augustus M. Kelley Publishers.

Jenkins, Philip. 1984. "Varieties of Enlightenment Criminology: Beccaria, Godwin, de Sade." *British Journal of Criminology* 24(2):112–130.

Kant, Immanuel. [1797] 1965. *The Metaphysical Elements of Justice*. Translated by John Ladd. Indianapolis: Bobbs-Merrill.

Marx, Karl. [1867] 1987. *Capital: A Critique of Political Economy*. Volume I. Translated by Samuel Moore and Edward Aveling. New York: International Publishers.

Monachesi, Elio. 1973. "Cesare Beccaria." In *Pioneers in Criminology*, 2nd ed., edited by Hermann Mannheim, 36–50. Montclair, NJ: Patterson Smith.

Montesquieu. [1748] 1899. *The Spirit of Laws*. Translated by Thomas Nugent. New York: The Colonial Press.

Newman, Graeme R., and Pietro Marongiu. 1990. "Penological Reform and the Myth of Beccaria." *Criminology* 28(2):325–346.

Newman, Graeme R., and Pietro Marongiu. 2009. "Introduction to the *Treatise*." In Cesare Beccaria's *On Crimes and Punishments*, vii–lv. New Brunswick, NJ: Transaction Publishers.

Paolucci, Henry. 1963. "Introduction." In Cesare Beccaria's *On Crimes and Punishments*, ix–xxiii. New York: Macmillan.

Radcliffe, Elizabeth S. 1995. "Hutcheson, Francis." In *The Cambridge Dictionary of Philosophy*, edited by Robert Audi, 350–351. Cambridge: Cambridge University Press.

Scarre, Geoffrey. 1994. "Epicurus as a Forerunner of Utilitarianism." *Utilitas* 6(2):219–231.

Shklar, Judith N. 1987. *Montesquieu*. Oxford: Oxford University Press.

Sorel, Albert. 1888. *Montesquieu*. Translated by Melville B. Anderson and Edward P. Anderson. Chicago: A. C. McClurg and Company.

Stafford, Mark C., and Mark Warr. 1993. "A Reconceptualization of General and Specific Deterrence." *Journal of Research in Crime and Delinquency* 30(2):123–135.

Turner, Jonathan H., Leonard Beeghley, and Charles H. Powers. 1998. *The Emergence of Sociological Theory*. 4th ed. Belmont, CA: Wadsworth.

Wallas, Graham. 1923. "Jeremy Bentham." *Political Science Quarterly* 38(1):45–56.

CHAPTER 1

FRANCIS HUTCHESON

This chapter presents a reading from Francis Hutcheson's *A System of Moral Philosophy* (1755), Volume II, pp. 86–87, 92–97, 310–311, 329–340, and 342–347; originally published by R. and A. Foulis, Glasgow; reprinted by Augustus M. Kelley Publishers, New York, 1968. Most of this work, if not all of it, was written between 1734 and 1737, but it was not published until 1755, nearly a decade after Hutcheson's death. Several minor changes have been made to the text. Most notably, marginal notes and footnotes have been excluded, and characters have been updated to contemporary English. The footnotes were brief and contained an occasional illegible word or phrase. However, spelling and punctuation have been left largely the same to ensure that the text retains much of its eighteenth-century style. For readers unfamiliar with this style, an apparent typographical error most likely is nothing more than acceptable eighteenth-century English.

Hutcheson was writing during the first half of the eighteenth century, before the Industrial Revolution and the major political revolutions of the era (e.g., the French Revolution). The Enlightenment had yet to reach its peak, and executions by burning, by "hanging, drawing, and quartering," and by means of other grisly public spectacles were still occurring in Europe. In this context, Hutcheson offered several lines of argument that eventually were embodied in the classical school of criminology. A number of these arguments are presented in the following selections. In these excerpts, Hutcheson supports deterrence as a justification for punishment and is explicitly concerned with "the safety and happiness of the community." He suggests that punishments should be public but that brutal executions, the "horrid spectacles of torture," may create conditions that lead to more cruelty and thus should be "very rare" (if not abolished). Beyond this, Hutcheson argues that the experience of suffering should be "equal for equal crimes." Accordingly, for the same offense, fines "should be in proportion to the wealth of the criminals" and corporal punishments should be less intense for weaker offenders. He also touches on other matters of criminological interest, including "compensation" for victims, "rewards" as another sanction of laws, punishments for "corporations," and the conditions under which people should disobey authority and resist punishment.

In Hutcheson's work, there is a blend of religion and rudimentary scientific thought. This uneasy combination of religion and science was common during the 1700s. It existed not only in the work of Hutcheson, but also in the writings of Johann Caspar Lavater (Chapter 5) and Benjamin Rush, whose work occupies a significant place in the history of the psychology of crime.

---

from A SYSTEM OF MORAL PHILOSOPHY
by Francis Hutcheson

THE RIGHTS ARISING FROM INJURIES AND DAMAGES DONE BY OTHERS: AND THE ABOLITION OF RIGHT

I. The violation of any perfect right of another, is an *injury*, whether by violence to his person, attacks upon his character, restraints upon his right of liberty, depriving him of his goods, spoiling them, stopping the profits he had a right to, or withholding what he had a right to claim; whether any of these things be done with a malicious design, or a selfish one, or by culpable negligence; whether by acting or omitting contrary to our duty. The damage includes, beside the value of the goods taken away, spoiled, or detained, all losses or inconveniences ensuing upon the want of them; and all interception of gain which would have accrued.

The damage one has done he is sacredly obliged to compensate to the utmost of his power. The injury is persisted in till this be done: nor can one otherways sincerely repent, or recover the character of honesty. The person injured has a right to compel the author of it to this compensation: without this right, bad men would trample on all the rights of their fellows. 'Tis generally for the publick interest, as well as that of the sufferer, not to remit this right of compelling even by force to make compensation, and of inflicting further evils as punishments; and that not only for the future security of such who suffered, but for the general safety; that all bad men may be deterred from the like attempts, by fear of the like punishments. . . .

III. In natural liberty men have a right by force to defend themselves and their neighbours, and all their perfect rights; and to compel others by violence to fulfil any perfect claims they have upon them. We are bound no doubt first to try all gentle methods; but when these fail of success, we have a right to use violence, with what assistance we can obtain from any others who are persuaded of the justice of our cause. In civil societies (as we shall see hereafter) the wisdom and force of the state should be employed for these purposes, to prevent the evils to be feared from the passion of interested men under fresh impressions of apprehended injuries. Citizens are generally understood to have committed these rights of violent prosecution and defence to the magistrate, wherever his aid can be obtained; and to have precluded themselves from exercising them in such cases. The rules about violent defence and prosecution must differ in these different states of liberty, or civil polity, and that in these three particulars, 1. the causes, 2. the time of beginning violence, and 3. the term to which it may be continued.

1. The causes, in natural liberty, are any violations of perfect rights great, or small. 'Tis true one is obliged in humanity to use all gentle methods at first, and to use no more violence or severity than may be necessary for his own safety, and that of others. We should always be ready to offer a reference, or to submit any disputed point of right to arbitrators. If the injury be the effect of a sudden passion, of which the author will soon repent, and it be reparable; 'tis the humane part to bear it rather than rush into fatal violence in our defence. But if the injury be designed deliberately, and persisted in after friendly remonstrances, one has a right to defend himself by violence even with the death of the invader. To deny men the right of violent defence to the utmost in maintaining their smaller rights of the perfect kind, would expose all good men, and all their properties, as a perpetual prey to the insolent and injurious. A small injury may be repeated every hour by the same person, or by others equally insolent; life would be intolerable without a remedy for such evils. The publick interest and safety requires that men should be violently deterred from such insolent attempts.

As to the prosecution of smaller rights, 'tis hard to say that inconsiderable injuries can justify our going to the utmost extremity, or that it is necessary to proceed to any fatal violence to compel men to fulfil any trifling contract, or perform some small matter we have a right to claim. We can abstain from all future commerce with such persons: and 'tis better to suffer a small loss than the reflection that for an unnecessary advantage we were intituled to, or for recovery of what was of no great value, we had taken away the life of our fellow, when we could be otherways secured against like injuries for the future.

A subject under civil government should use no violence against such as are amenable to laws, except in defence against injuries irreparable, either in their own nature, or through the insolvency of the invader. In other cases the safer remedy is an action at law. If the invaders are not amenable to laws, such as fugitives, robbers, or pirates; the rights of natural liberty remain against them; as they do also where-ever the hope of detecting and convicting them fails, as in the case of thieves in the night-time. 'Tis by actions at law alone that we are to compel such as are amenable to them, to fulfil our claims upon them.

IV. 2. The time when violence is justly begun in natural liberty, is when one has sufficiently declared an unjust and hostile disposition, and desists not upon such admonition, or remonstrance, as we have time to use. One is not obliged to receive the first attack or assault; this may frequently prove fatal; or occasion an irreparable damage. Defence and prevention of injury in this state, is generally less difficult than forcibly obtaining reparation. In all these matters, when our danger is not immediate, since the keenest passions are apt to arise, 'tis best to be directed in all methods of defence and prosecution, by wise arbitrators not immediately concerned in the injury.

Under civil government, tho' the injury intended be irreparable, yet unless the danger be so imminent that we cannot be defended by the magistrate, we should apply to him for defence; as we should always commit to him the violent prosecution of our rights against our fellow-subjects.

V. 3. The term to which violence should be continued in natural liberty, is until the danger be repelled, full compensation obtained of all damage and expences occasioned by the injury, full performance of all we can justly claim, and security against like injuries for the future. The interest of society, as well as that of the individual, requires that all these things be obtained.

The publick, or mankind as a system, have even a further right of inflicting such further evils as are necessary to deter others from the like attempts. This last right the person who was in danger of immediate wrong should not execute alone, but in conjunction with others who have no private cause of resentment. Some horrid attempts, such as those of murder, assassination, poisoning, robbery, or piracy, shew so desperate a wickedness, that scarce any sufficient security can be obtained to society against the repetition of the like crimes, but the deaths of the criminals. And as men are much allured to injustice by hopes of secrecy, or of impunity by flight, or successful resistance, it must be necessary for society that the punishments of such as are taken and convicted be made so great as shall generally over-balance the invitation to such crimes from the hopes of impunity, and deter others from the like attempts. This is allowed just under civil government, when crimes abound, and many, one half perhaps, of the guilty escape conviction, that the punishment should be doubled at least, on this very account, that the greatness of the evil should outweigh the hopes of impunity. The very same reasons for punishments, and for increasing, or diminishing them, hold in natural liberty, tho' the execution will not generally be so easy or regular. The punishment of crimes in this state of liberty is rather more necessary, and is justified by all the same reasons. That the execution in this state may be attended with more inconveniences, does not prove that there is no right of punishing, or that all the right must arise from civil polity. For by the same way of reasoning we should deny to men in liberty all rights of self-defence, and hold that they too arise from civil polity.

Under civil government private men should proceed no further in violence against such as are amenable to laws than till the present danger be repelled. All the other rights should be left to the magistrate.

We should always remember on this subject that no injury or wickedness should make the author cease to be the object of our good-will: and that all our rights to violence are limited by these ends, viz. the repelling the injury, obtaining our right, with compensation of damages, and getting security for ourselves and the society against like injuries for the future. What is inflicted on wicked men for these beneficent and necessary purposes is just, as far as it is naturally subservient to and requisite for them: what is not requisite for them, is unjust and cruel, even toward the worst of mankind. Such are all private tortures, the sating an angry and revengeful spirit by insults, prostitution to any lusts of ours, or forcing the criminal's conscience, if he has any, in matters of religion. 'Tis very cruel and unjust to create further misery than is requisite for these purposes: when these are answered, and as far as consists with them, all humanity, mercy, and compassion toward bad men is amiable and virtuous. The noblest spring of punishment is extensive goodness, or a regard to the safety and happiness of the community....

OF THE NATURE OF CIVIL LAWS AND THEIR EXECUTION

I. The legislative and executive are powers exerted within the state: Of these in the first place.

As the end of all laws should be the general good and happiness of a people, which chiefly depends on their virtue: it must be the business of legislators to promote, by all just and effectual methods, true principles of virtue, such as shall lead men to piety to God, and all just, peaceable, and kind dispositions towards their fellows; that they may be inclined to every good office, and faithful in every trust committed to them in their several stations. It is poor policy merely to punish crimes when they are committed. The noble art is to contrive such previous education, instruction, and discipline, as shall prevent vice, restrain these passions, and correct these confused notions of great happiness in vicious courses, which enslave men to them. As pious dispositions toward God, a firm persuasion of his goodness, and of his providence governing the world, and administering justice in a future state by rewarding justice, temperance, and all social dispositions, and punishing the contrary, are the sources of the most sublime happiness, so they are the strongest incitements to all social, friendly and heroick offices. The civil power should take care that the people be well instructed in these points, and have all arguments presented to their understandings, and all rational inducements proposed which can raise these persuasions, and confirm these dispositions. Truth with equal advantages will always prevail against error, where errors have not been rooted by such early prejudices as prevent a fair examination. The magistrate should therefore provide proper instruction for all, especially for young minds, about the existence, goodness, and providence of God, and all the social duties of life, and the motives to them....

X. The sanctions of laws are the rewards and punishments. Rewards have place in all civil laws as well as punishments. There is one general reward understood, the continuance of the protection of the state and the enjoyments of the advantages of a civilized life. And in many laws there are other special rewards: such as premiums, and advancements to honour, and to profitable offices, which also give opportunities of honourable actions, which are to good men a sweet reward.

Esteem or honour is either of the *simpler kind*, viz. the mere reputation of integrity and such dispositions as fit a man for a social life; or that of distinguished *eminence*, such as is due only to great abilities and singular services and virtues, or such at least as are above the common rate. To the former, every one who has not forfeited it by some crime of a more atrocious nature than is readily incident to men in the main good, has a natural perfect right; so it can be no matter of civil reward. The taking it away or excluding one from the rights attending it, may indeed be a severe punishment. The magistrate has no more power over it than over the lives and properties of the people. He justly may take any of them away for a crime deserving it, but not without a crime. Nor will the opinions of wise men follow an unjust sentence.

Our inward estimation of the eminent kind will not follow the decree of the state or of the prince, but the opinions we have of the merits of the person. The magistrate indeed is the proper judge of any outward deference, precedence, or other marks of honour; and his decree gives men an external right to claim them. While the magistrate in this matter generally follows the real merit of persons, honours may be very useful in a state. But when honours are conferred without merit, or continued hereditarily to those who are universally known to have degenerated from the virtues which procured them to the family, they become despicable of themselves, tho' the power attending them may be courted by the ambitious. Such conduct in any prince or state, in conferring or continuing honours without merit, has a most pernicious effect. Such a reverence and deference attends high titles in weak minds that those who enjoy them are often screened from the just resentments of a nation: the moral sentiments of a people are weakened, when they see the most scandalous vices adorned and attended by what should naturally be always the retinue of eminent virtue.

Hereditary honours have been conferred upon presumption that the posterity of the eminently virtuous, would either by nature, imitation, or good education, prove eminent the same way: and with a design to make the rewards of eminent services more agreeable, as they conferred a dignity upon the descendants of the virtuous. The expectation of such dignity may raise young minds to nobler views suited to their station. If a censorial power, of degrading such as act unbecomingly to their dignity, be vigorously exercised; hereditary honours cannot be intirely condemned as useless. The natural causes of honour or merit may be abundantly seen by what was said above upon the degrees of virtue. But as they are made political rewards, they must not be employed in exact proportion to the degrees of moral goodness, but as they shall most encourage the virtues most necessary to the state.

XI. The other sort of sanctions are punishments; the peculiar end of which is the deterring all from like vicious practices, and giving publick security against others, as well as the offender. When this right of punishing which belonged to all in natural liberty, is conveyed in a civil state to the magistrate, he obtains the sole right in all ordinary cases, and has the direct power of life and death over criminals.

There is just ground of distinguishing *chastisements* from punishments as they are solely intended for reforming the offender, and are not peculiar to magistrates. They may be inflicted privately; whereas *punishments* should be publick, and the crime intimated to all, that they may be deterred from it. Both these are distinct from the *compensation* of damage, "which respects the repairing any loss sustained by another." And men are often obliged to it who had done nothing viciously or unjustly. The violence used in war has also a different end, at least such as is used before conquest, to wit the defending or prosecuting our rights. What is done after a victory with a view to deter all, would have the nature of punishment.

The true principle of heart which should excite a man in inflicting any evils on his fellow-creatures should always be some kind affection; generally those of a more extensive nature should influence the magistrate in punishments; and those of a less extensive should move men in chastisement, and compelling to compensation. Nothing can make a good man's own heart approve him in these steps but a consciousness that he acted from some kind principle, and that such steps were necessary to some superior good. Nay in justifying the divine punishments we have always recourse to like considerations, which shew that they flow from goodness; such as the supporting the authority and enforcing the influence of his laws calculated for the highest happiness of his rational creatures, which must be desirable to perfect goodness it self; as must also the demonstrating his love to virtue, and his steddy purpose of restraining vice by the most powerful motives: and for these reasons we repute the divine punishments to be just and good.

Since the end of punishment is the general safety; the precise measure of human punishment is the necessity of preventing certain crimes for the publick safety, and not always the moral turpitude of the actions; tho' this often is proportioned to the detriment arising from crimes. But as it is not always so, some of the worst vices must go unpunished, as we said above; and some actions very dangerous to the community, and yet flowing from no great depravity of heart, must be restrained by great severity: such as insurrections against a just prince upon some specious pretence of the preferable title of another. As the evils of civil wars are very great, men must be strongly deterred from entring rashly into them. When crimes arguing none of the greatest depravity are very inviting by hopes of secrecy and impunity, the severity of the punishment upon those who are convicted must by its terror over-ballance these allurements: thus theft must be more severely punished, even when men are induced to it by some straits of their families, than some greater crimes flowing from worse dispositions.

Punishments for the publick crimes in the abuse of power, or usurpation of it contrary to law, should be more severe than for crimes of a more private nature, as the effects of the former are far more pernicious. The ruin of some great states has been owing to too much lenity in punishing such crimes of magistrates.

Severe punishments are necessary too for small guilt whensoever there is danger of such frequent transgressions as might be destructive to a state in certain exigencies. Thus the desertion of soldiers in a time of war, either from cowardice, or impatience for a peaceful life with their families, must be severely punished. In times of peace this is less necessary; and it is cruel without necessity to detain them long in a service grown disagreeable to them.

Nay some actions flowing from the best dispositions must be strictly restrained when the publick interest requires it. Thus an inferior officer of too keen valour may be punished sometimes justly for a brave attempt contrary to the express orders of his general: as the greatest confusion would arise if inferiors disobeyed express orders of their superiors upon any appearances of advantage to be obtained over the enemy. As greater evils must ensue from relaxing military discipline, than can readily upon obedience to the imprudent commands of superiors, which are not plainly treacherous, and ruinous to an army; a good man may see it to be his duty to obey such orders as he certainly knows to be imprudent, and to abstain from wise measures which his superiors prohibit; unless he can prevail upon them by reasoning to alter their orders. One who acts otherways must be punished, as laws must regard the distant effects of actions upon the whole body.

XII. Internal designs not discovered by action, tho' they could be proved, are seldom punished in milder governments. Men may project and talk of designs, who are not wicked enough to execute them. When by expressing such intentions and defending them, they may have corrupted others, they may justly be punished; and the magistrate may always justly demand a security for the good behaviour of such as have entertained them. When the design is come to action, and to such efforts as might have been successful, had they not been defeated by superior force or accident, the criminal deserves the same punishment, whether he succeeds in his attempt or not, as the same depravity is discovered, and the same danger to society from his future attempts. Thus one who gave poison, or who discharged a gun at his neighbour with a design on his life is to be punished as a murderer be the event what it will.

It is proper that in every state there should be a power of dispensing with the sanctions as to ordinary crimes, when singular reasons occur for it, and sufficient security against like crimes can be otherways obtained. But for crimes of magistrates against the publick rights of a people, or for gross abuses of power, or attempts against the plan of polity to encrease their own power or influence there should be no impunity.

The publick interest may sometimes require the giving impunity, nay rewards, to some who have been guilty of the worst of private crimes, to employ them in some necessary services. Thus to break all faith in bands of robbers or pyrates, and destroy all mutual confidence among them, pardons, and even rewards are justly given to such as betray the band, or deliver up any partners: as by such conduct such confederacies against mankind are broken without effusion of innocent blood; tho' the worst of the party may most readily take the advantage of betraying their partners, from these hopes.

XIII. That *respect of persons*, which is unjust in judgment, consists in regarding such circumstances of them as neither affect the guilt of the action, nor its importance toward any publick detriment, nor the quantity of the suffering. As when men are differently punished on account of kindred to the judge, of being zealous for his party or faction civil or religious, or of prior benefits conferred, or services promised or expected; while yet the guilt and detriment to society is equal. But circumstances shewing greater or less guilt, or rather greater or less tendency to the detriment of society, or such as encrease or diminish the sense of the punishment, should be considered as far as human courts can do it, to make the sentences well proportioned and just. In *pecuniary fines* the sums exacted from different persons for the same crimes or equal ones, should be in proportion to the wealth of the criminals.

The sum which is severe upon the poor may be a trifle to the wealthy. In *corporal* punishments, the weakness of the criminals should alleviate the punishments: and infamous punishments should be lessened as the sufferers are in greater dignities. For thus alone the sense of suffering shall be equal for equal crimes.

It may justly be questioned however, whether in increasing of punishments on account of horrid crimes, there be not a certain pitch of suffering beyond which nothing severer should be inflicted. If death is the penalty of any deliberate murder or robbery, one's indignation would move him to inflict something worse upon the more horridly cruel murderers, and to torture such as had tortured others; or to use tortures where the gentler kinds of death inflicted seem scarce sufficient to deter men from the crime. But on the other hand, horrid spectacles of torture, especially if they are frequently presented, may have a very bad effect upon the minds of spectators. They may harden their hearts, and abate the natural sense of compassion by overstraining it, and make it lose its force; as we see in the overstrained fibres of the body. Beside the terrible efforts they may tempt wicked men to in their robberies, to secure themselves against conviction, or to avenge themselves for the sufferings of their fellows. We may find perhaps that nations where they are used have seldom so tender feelings of humanity as those where they are not. And that an easy death, with any subsequent infamy upon the carcase that may affect spectators, without causing any real misery to the criminal, may sufficiently answer the purposes of human justice. If tortures are ever allowed, they must be very rare.

XIV. No man should be punished for the crime of another; nor is any one liable to compensation of damage who did not contribute to it by some action or omission contrary to his duty, nor shared in any gain by it, nor occasioned it by any contrivance or action destined for his own advantage. As children are truly joint proprietors with their parents in the stock of the family; and have a most sacred claim not only for maintenance, but a comfortable subsistence, upon that stock as far as it will afford it, and the parent bound to furnish it out of this stock: it seems plainly unjust that the whole should be forfeited by the crime of a parent; not to mention also the just and strong claim of the wife, even that of a fair purchaser by the fortune she brought, or by her own industry in improving the common stock. It is true the parent may be the natural administrator, or manager for the company, and thus his debts contracted prudently or imprudently always affect it, nay his prodigality may squander it all. But in many civilized nations, this natural joint right of the whole family is recognised by the civil laws; by allowing an inhibition or interdict upon an extravagant or imprudent parent at the suit of the children or any proper person in their name. And this is plainly according to justice and natural equity. It is scarce therefore defencible with any shadow of justice, that civil laws should appoint a punishment on the guilty which equally or more severely affects the innocent.

XV. As to the punishment of corporations, the following maxims seem just.

1. If all the guilty, or as many of them as are sufficient for compensation of damage and a publick example, are found, nothing can be further demanded from the corporation.

2. When this cannot be obtained, no innocent man should be punished in his person or any private fortune of his he holds independently of the corporation, for any crime of its magistrates or other citizens.

3. As merit and demerit are personal and not properly residing in corporations; if all the criminals are dead or banished out of it, no punishments can be justly inflicted on it or its members. Punishments or fines exacted out of the publick stock have not the proper effect intended. Bad men feel and are deterred only by what shall affect themselves. They are not moved by the sufferings of communities.

4. As to compensation of damages; when it cannot be obtained from the criminals, it next falls upon any in power who by grosly culpable negligence shared in the guilt, and it should be levied out of their private fortunes. If these fail, the common stock of the corporation is liable, and where this fails it may be exacted out of the private fortunes of its members . . .

5. As corporations have generally sufficient power to restrain their members from injuries, the governors should be obliged to give sufficient security against future injuries, and should be vested with further powers if the former were not sufficient. Nay they may be divested of any such privileges as are apt to be abused, when no other sufficient security can be obtained against their being abused to the detriment of the publick. But without some great necessity, or when other securities can be obtained, it is very unjust to deprive a large innocent body of men of any privilege of importance to them upon the crime of a few, or even of their magistrates.

6. As to any rights which smaller corporations enjoy as parts of a great body politick and with relation to it, such as a right of representation in the supreme council; no mal-administration of even the magistrates or councils of such corporation should forfeit a right of importance not only to all the innocent members, but to the whole state.

7. Bodies incorporated merely for trade and for the benefit of a few partners, may justly be deprived of their privileges upon their non-compliance with the terms or conditions upon which they were granted. And the corporation may be dissolved. . . .

XVII. To these rights of governors correspond the obligations on subjects to obedience active or passive, as we shall shew more particularly in a few observations.

1. When the command of a governor is truly just and wise, and within the power committed to him by the constitution; a subject is always bound to obey notwithstanding of any private inconveniencies or danger to himself; and that even in conscience, tho' he could artfully evade the penalties of the law. This holds particularly in paying of taxes and in military service.

2. When the matter commanded is within the power committed to the governor, but he is using his power imprudently in commanding it; if modest representations will not move him to change his orders, and they are only burdensome and dangerous to us in particular and not contrary to any perfect right of the innocent, or injurious to others, it is our duty to obey, tho' the governors sinned in commanding. In war the commander may often be very guilty in imprudent orders given, and inferiors may see that they are not only dangerous to themselves who execute them, but even prejudicial in a small degree to the publick cause. But as dissolving all military discipline must be a much greater evil to a nation than the loss that can be readily sustained by executing the imprudent orders; and all discipline must be lost where the inferior assumes to himself to disobey orders he judges imprudent; it is often the duty of inferiors to execute them while they judge them imprudent.

If the orders are judged treacherous, or so pernicious that the execution of them would be more destructive than breaking through in this case the rules of discipline, a good man would disobey, and take his hazard. It is in like manner our duty to pay taxes or tributes, tho' we judge that they are unequally imposed, and to be applied to imprudent purposes, when they are imposed by that person or council to whom that power is committed. There are many commands, civil and military, about the prudence or justice of which inferiors are not proper judges, wanting access to the reasons of them. Upon presumption of the wisdom and justice of their governors, they may act innocently and virtuously, when their superiors are very criminal; and they often owe such obedience to the general interest of their country, when they know that the orders are imprudent.

3. But if a subject is persuaded of the injustice of a war, or of a sentence he is commanded to execute in consequence of an iniquitous law, he should refuse active obedience, and bear patiently for a good conscience the sufferings he may be exposed to.

XVIII. 1. But when a governor exceeds the powers vested in him by the constitution, assuming such as are not granted to him; unless it be in cases of singular necessity, it is always just and honourable to oppose such usurpation of power on its first appearance, whatever specious pretences are made for it of good designs and intentions; as the precedent is dangerous, and will readily be followed in worse cases, to the subversion of the constitution, and all rights established by it.

2. Suppose the governor does not exceed the legal powers vested in him, but is abusing some immoderate powers granted him in an imprudent plan of polity to purposes eversive of the publick safety and liberty; subjects may justly refuse obedience, and by a joint resistance oblige him to consent to such limitations and restrictions as are necessary for the common safety, a private man, when he has no hopes of a sufficient concurrence of others, must fly from oppression or resist it as he can. It would be wrong, without hopes of success, to involve himself and a few friends to no purpose in greater mischiefs, or to obey commands injurious to others.

3. Suppose the plan of polity good, and a prince also in the main faithful to his high trust, but possessed with some groundless prejudice or violent anger against any private subject, and aiming at his destruction without any just cause: no man can innocently obey his unjust orders in destroying an innocent man, and one should suffer rather than execute them. The innocent person thus intended for destruction would have a right to all violent methods of defence, even against the prince in person, were he only to regard the right of the prince against him; but for the sake of his country, not to deprive it of a prince in the main good, or expose it to any great evils which might ensue upon his death; it may be the duty of the subject to fly rather than use violence, or to be a martyr for his country's interest, when he cannot escape by flight.

But to say that in no case men have a right of resistance, or that in no case they can assume to themselves to judge of the commands of their superiors, is monstrous. All ends of government, all safety, all important rights of a people would be precarious, and be lost without redress, as soon as supreme power came into wicked hands. They who cannot judge of the justice of commands given, can surely as little judge of titles to supreme power. This doctrine therefore must for ever establish every usurper who once gets into possession. A wicked prince or usurper, a senate, or a few Democratick deputies once in possession are for ever secure: upon their orders, which none must assume to question or judge about, their soldiers might rob, pillage or massacre any whom they suspected; nor could there be any redress.

4. As to persons condemned to punishment according to just laws, they seem obliged to bear it, and owe to the publick that reparation of the mischief done by their example. Their declining it by artful contrivances to make an escape is scarce justifyable, tho' it is generally excused on account of the greatness of the temptation. As the society has a right to punish, they can have none to resist by violence. Nor is it lawful to tempt any officers of justice by bribes to be unfaithful in their trust, or to use violence against them.

5. One condemned upon an unjust law or false accusation seems to have a right to make his escape by any methods which are not injurious to the innocent. Nay as one may have a right of self-defence, or of defending an innocent man by violence against any aggressor, tho' the aggressor was in an invincible error, and so innocent too: in some cases the like may be just in an innocent man, or in his friends against some inferior officers of justice, when all the detriment arising from such efforts shall be a far less evil than the execution of the unjust sentence upon the innocent, and eminently worthy.

The case is much more obviously favourable where the laws are notoriously unjust and oppressive toward great numbers; or plain usurpations upon the natural and unalienable rights of all rational beings. Such are all those which invade the rights of conscience by persecution for innocent religious opinions. Had one sufficient force by the concurrence of others, he would have a right to compell the legislator by force to rescind such unjust decrees. Much more must he have a right to defend himself against their tyranny in this point by any violence against the execution of such laws when he has probability of success.

Thus the general duties of magistrates and subjects are discoverable from the nature of the trust committed to them, and the end of all civil power. Political prudence to exercise the rights vested in magistrates wisely according to the several exigencies of publick affairs, is a most important part of human knowledge, and must be acquired by much observation, and experience in political affairs, by knowledge of the interests and constitutions of neighbouring states, by civil history, and political writings.

CHAPTER 2

MONTESQUIEU

The reading in this chapter is from Montesquieu's *The Spirit of Laws* ([1748] 1899), Volume I, Books VI and XII, pp. 81–92 and 185–196; translated by Thomas Nugent; New York: The Colonial Press. Section numbers have been removed and footnote symbols have been changed. Although this work was published before Hutcheson's *A System of Moral Philosophy*, it was written at a later date.

The Spirit of Laws stands out among the founding works of the classical school of criminology for its empirical content. It is an example of early comparative historical research and, more generally, early social science. Because of its empirical component, it provides contemporary readers with concrete information on the systems of justice that existed prior to 1750 in Europe and other parts of the world. Even though Montesquieu's study inevitably was influenced by the ethnocentrism embedded in the descriptive information he examined, his conclusions provide an illustration of the way in which an "enlightened" thinker of the mid-eighteenth century viewed crime and punishment in his society and other societies.

In the following selections, Montesquieu presents his views on the forms of crime and punishment found in societies governed by despots, monarchs, and democratic arrangements (republics). The readings offer a brief introduction to the range of acts that have been treated as crimes in different times and places, as well as the kinds of punishments that were imposed on offenders. More importantly, Montesquieu supports the moderation of punishments and proportionality between crimes and punishments, two fundamental proposals of the classical school. He associates moderate and proportionate punishments with more advanced societies, suggesting that the supporters of severe and disproportionate punishments possess a despotic and uncivilized mindset. In addition, Montesquieu questions the use of torture; he argues that punishment should "flow" from the "nature of the crime," whether it is an offense against religion, morals, public tranquility, or the security of individuals; he discusses problems associated with prosecuting individuals for witchcraft, heresy, and "the crime against nature"; and he examines excesses in the conceptualization of "high treason" and in the punishment of thoughts, speeches, and writings.

from THE SPIRIT OF LAWS
by Montesquieu

OF THE SEVERITY OF PUNISHMENTS IN DIFFERENT GOVERNMENTS

The severity of punishments is fitter for despotic governments, whose principle is terror, than for a monarchy or a republic, whose spring is honor and virtue.

In moderate governments, the love of one's country, shame, and the fear of blame are restraining motives, capable of preventing a multitude of crimes. Here the greatest punishment of a bad action is conviction. The civil laws have therefore a softer way of correcting, and do not require so much force and severity.

In those states a good legislator is less bent upon punishing than preventing crimes; he is more attentive to inspire good morals than to inflict penalties.

It is a constant remark of the Chinese authors,[1] that the more the penal laws were increased in their empire, the nearer they drew towards a revolution. This is because punishments were augmented in proportion as the public morals were corrupted.

It would be an easy matter to prove that in all, or almost all, the governments of Europe, penalties have increased or diminished in proportion as those governments favored or discouraged liberty.

In despotic governments, people are so unhappy as to have a greater dread of death than regret for the loss of life; consequently their punishments ought to be more severe. In moderate states they are more afraid of losing their lives than apprehensive of the pain of dying; those punishments, therefore, which deprive them simply of life are sufficient.

Men in excess of happiness or misery are equally inclinable to severity; witness conquerors and monks. It is mediocrity alone, and a mixture of prosperous and adverse fortune, that inspire us with lenity and pity.

What we see practised by individuals is equally observable in regard to nations. In countries inhabited by savages who lead a very hard life, and in despotic governments, where there is only one person on whom fortune lavishes her favors, while the miserable subjects lie exposed to her insults, people are equally cruel. Lenity reigns in moderate governments.

When in reading history we observe the cruelty of the sultans in administration of justice, we shudder at the very thought of the miseries of human nature.

In moderate governments, a good legislator may make use of everything by way of punishment. Is it not very extraordinary that one of the chief penalties at Sparta was to deprive a person of the power of lending out his wife, or of receiving the wife of another man, and to oblige him to have no company at home but virgins? In short, whatever the law calls a punishment is such effectively.

OF THE ANCIENT FRENCH LAWS

In the ancient French laws we find the true spirit of monarchy. In cases relating to pecuniary mulcts, the common people are less severely punished than the nobility.[2] But in criminal[3] cases it is quite the reverse; the nobleman loses his honor and his voice in court, while the peasant, who has no honor to lose, undergoes a corporal punishment.

THAT WHEN PEOPLE ARE VIRTUOUS FEW PUNISHMENTS ARE NECESSARY

The people of Rome had some share of probity. Such was the force of this probity that the legislator had frequently no further occasion than to point out the right road, and they were sure to follow it; one would imagine that instead of precepts it was sufficient to give them counsels.

The punishments of the regal laws, and those of the Twelve Tables, were almost all abolished in the time of the republic, in consequence either of the Valerian[4] or

---

1. I shall show hereafter that China is, in this respect, in the same case as a republic or a monarchy.

2. Suppose, for instance, to prevent the execution of a decree, the common people paid a fine of forty sous, and the nobility of sixty livres.—"Somme Rurale," book II. p. 198, edit. Got. of the year 1512.
3. See the "Council of Peter Defontaines," chap. xiii., especially the 22d art.
4. It was made by Valerius Publicola soon after the expulsion of the kings, and was twice renewed, both times by magistrates of the same family. As Livy observes, lib. X., the question was not to give it a greater force, but to render its injunctions more perfect. "Diligentius sanctum," says Livy, ibid.

of the Porcian law.[5] It was never observed that this step did any manner of prejudice to the civil administration.

This Valerian law, which restrained the magistrates from using violent methods against a citizen that had appealed to the people, inflicted no other punishment on the person who infringed it than that of being reputed a dishonest man.[6]

OF THE POWER OF PUNISHMENTS

Experience shows that in countries remarkable for the lenity of their laws the spirit of the inhabitants is as much affected by slight penalties as in other countries by severer punishments.

If an inconvenience or abuse arises in the state, a violent government endeavors suddenly to redress it; and instead of putting the old laws in execution; it establishes some cruel punishment, which instantly puts a stop to the evil. But the spring of government hereby loses its elasticity; the imagination grows accustomed to the severe as well as the milder punishment; and as the fear of the latter diminishes, they are soon obliged in every case to have recourse to the former. Robberies on the highway became common in some countries; in order to remedy this evil, they invented the punishment of breaking upon the wheel, the terror of which put a stop for a while to this mischievous practice. But soon after robberies on the highways became as common as ever.

Desertion in our days has grown to a very great height; in consequence of which it was judged proper to punish those delinquents with death; and yet their number did not diminish. The reason is very natural: a soldier accustomed to venture his life, despises, or affects to despise, the danger of losing it. He is habituated to the fear of shame; it would have been therefore much better to have continued a punishment[7] which branded him with infamy for life; the penalty was pretended to be increased, while it really diminished.

Mankind must not be governed with too much severity; we ought to make a prudent use of the means which nature has given us to conduct them. If we inquire into the cause of all human corruptions, we shall find that they proceed from the impunity of criminals, and not from the moderation of punishments.

Let us follow nature, who has given shame to man for his scourge; and let the heaviest part of the punishment be the infamy attending it.

But if there be some countries where shame is not a consequence of punishment, this must be owing to tyranny, which has inflicted the same penalties on villains and honest men.

And if there are others where men are deterred only by cruel punishments, we may be sure that this must, in a great measure, arise from the violence of the government which has used such penalties for slight transgressions.

It often happens that a legislator, desirous of remedying an abuse, thinks of nothing else; his eyes are open only to this object, and shut to its inconveniences. When the abuse is redressed, you see only the severity of the legislator; yet there remains an evil in the state that has sprung from this severity; the minds of the people are corrupted, and become habituated to despotism.

Lysander[8] having obtained a victory over the Athenians, the prisoners were ordered to be tried, in consequence of an accusation brought against that nation of having thrown all the captives of two galleys down a precipice, and of having resolved in full assembly to cut off the hands of those whom they should chance to make prisoners. The Athenians were therefore all massacred, except Adymantes, who had opposed this decree. Lysander reproached Phylocles, before he was put to death, with having depraved the people's minds, and given lessons of cruelty to all Greece.

"The Argives," says Plutarch,[9] "having put fifteen hundred of their citizens to death, the Athenians ordered sacrifices of expiation,[10] that it might please the gods to turn the hearts of the Athenians from so cruel a thought."

There are two sorts of corruptions—one when the people do not observe the laws; the other when they are corrupted by the laws: an incurable evil, because it is in the very remedy itself.

INSUFFICIENCY OF THE LAWS OF JAPAN

Excessive punishments may even corrupt a despotic government; of this we have an instance in Japan.

---

5. "Lex Porcia pro tergo civium lata." It was made in the 454th year of the foundation of Rome.
6. "Nihil ultra quam improbe factum adjecet."—Liv.
7. They slit his nose or cut off his ears.
8. Xenoph. "Hist." lib. III.
9. Morals of those who are intrusted with the direction of the state affairs.
10. Montesquieu appears to have followed Amyot, who was mistaken here. Plutarch says that the Athenians carried the victims of expiation around the assembly. It was done as an act of purification.—Crévier.

Here almost all crimes are punished with death,[11] because disobedience to so great an emperor as that of Japan is reckoned an enormous crime. The question is not so much to correct the delinquent as to vindicate the authority of the prince. These notions are derived from servitude, and are owing especially to this, that as the emperor is universal proprietor, almost all crimes are directly against his interests.

They punish with death lies spoken before the magistrate;[12] a proceeding contrary to natural defence.

Even things which have not the appearance of a crime are severely punished; for instance, a man that ventures his money at play is put to death.

True it is that the character of this people, so amazingly obstinate, capricious, and resolute as to defy all dangers and calamities, seems to absolve their legislators from the imputation of cruelty, notwithstanding the severity of their laws. But are men who have a natural contempt for death, and who rip open their bellies for the least fancy—are such men, I say, mended or deterred, or rather are they not hardened, by the continual prospect of punishments?

The relations of travellers inform us, with respect to the education of the Japanese, that children must be treated there with mildness, because they become hardened to punishment; that their slaves must not be too roughly used, because they immediately stand upon their defence. Would not one imagine that they might easily have judged of the spirit which ought to reign in their political and civil government from that which should prevail in their domestic concerns?

A wise legislator would have endeavored to reclaim people by a just temperature of punishments and rewards; by maxims of philosophy, morality, and religion, adapted to those characters; by a proper application of the rules of honor, and by the enjoyment of ease and tranquillity of life. And should he have entertained any apprehension that their minds, being inured to the cruelty of punishments, would no longer be restrained by those of a milder nature, he would have conducted himself[13] in another manner, and gained his point by degrees; in particular cases that admitted of any indulgence, he would have mitigated the punishment, till he should have been able to extend this mitigation to all cases.

But these are springs to which despotic power is a stranger; it may abuse itself, and that is all it can do: in Japan it has made its utmost effort, and has surpassed even itself in cruelty.

As the minds of the people grew wild and intractable, they were obliged to have recourse to the most horrid severity.

This is the origin, this the spirit, of the laws of Japan. They had more fury, however, than force. They succeeded the extirpation of Christianity; but such unaccountable efforts are a proof of their insufficiency. They wanted to establish a good polity, and they have shown greater marks of their weakness.

We have only to read the relation of the interview between the Emperor and the Deyro at Meaco.[14] The number of those who were suffocated or murdered in that city by ruffians is incredible; young maids and boys were carried off by force, and found afterwards exposed in public places, at unseasonable hours, quite naked, and sewn in linen bags, to prevent their knowing which way they had passed: robberies were committed in all parts; the bellies of horses were ripped open, to bring their riders to the ground; and coaches were overturned, in order to strip the ladies. The Dutch, who were told they could not pass the night on the scaffolds without exposing themselves to the danger of being assassinated, came down, etc.

I shall here give one instance more from the same nation. The Emperor having abandoned himself to infamous pleasures, lived unmarried, and was consequently in danger of dying without issue. The Deyro sent him two beautiful damsels; one he married out of respect, but would not meddle with her. His nurse caused the finest women of the empire to be sent for, but all to no purpose. At length, an armorer's daughter having pleased his fancy,[15] he determined to espouse her, and had a son. The ladies belonging to the court, enraged to see a person of such mean extraction preferred to themselves, stifled the child. The crime was concealed from the Emperor; for he would have deluged the land with blood. The excessive severity of the laws hinders, therefore, their execution: when the punishment surpasses all measure, they are frequently obliged to prefer impunity to it.

---

11. See Kempfer.
12. "Collection of Voyages that contributed to the establishment of the East India Company," tom. iii. p. 428.
13. Let this be observed as a maxim in practice, with regard to cases where the minds of people have been depraved by too great a severity of punishments.
14. "Collection of Voyages that contributed to the establishment of the East India Company," tom. v. p. 2.
15. "Collection of Voyages that contributed to the establishment of the East India Company," tom. v. p. 2.

OF THE SPIRIT OF THE ROMAN SENATE

Under the consulate of Acilius Glabrio and Piso, the Asilian law[16] was made to prevent the intriguing for places. Dio says[17] that the Senate engaged the Consuls to propose it, by reason that C. Cornelius, the Tribune, had resolved to cause more severe punishments to be established against this crime; to which the people seemed greatly inclined. The Senate rightly judged that immoderate punishments would strike, indeed, a terror into people's minds, but must have also this effect, that there would be nobody afterwards to accuse or condemn; whereas, by proposing moderate penalties, there would be always judges and accusers.

OF THE ROMAN LAWS IN RESPECT TO PUNISHMENTS

I am strongly confirmed in my sentiments upon finding the Romans on my side; and I think that punishments are connected with the nature of governments when I behold this great people changing in this respect their civil laws, in proportion as they altered their form of government.

The regal laws, made for fugitives, slaves, and vagabonds, were very severe. The spirit of a republic would have required that the Decemvirs should not have inserted those laws in their Twelve Tables; but men who aimed at tyranny were far from conforming to a republican spirit.

Livy says,[18] in relation to the punishment of Metius Suffetius, dictator of Alba, who was condemned by Tullius Hostilius to be fastened to two chariots drawn by horses, and torn asunder, that this was the first and last punishment in which the remembrance of humanity seemed to have been lost. He is mistaken; the Twelve Tables are full of very cruel laws.[19]

The design of the Decemvirs appears more conspicuous in the capital punishment pronounced against libellers and poets. This is not agreeable to the genius of a republic, where the people like to see the great men humbled. But persons who aimed at the subversion of liberty were afraid of writings that might revive its spirit.[20]

After the expulsion of the Decemvirs, almost all the penal laws were abolished. It is true they were not expressly repealed; but as the Porcian law had ordained that no citizen of Rome should be put to death, they were of no further use.

This is exactly the time to which we may refer what Livy says[21] of the Romans, that no people were ever fonder of moderation in punishments.

But if to the lenity of penal laws we add the right which the party accused had of withdrawing before judgment was pronounced, we shall find that the Romans followed the spirit which I have observed to be natural to a republic.

Sylla, who confounded tyranny, anarchy, and liberty, made the Cornelian laws. He seemed to have contrived regulations merely with a view to create new crimes. Thus distinguishing an infinite number of actions by the name of murder, he found murderers in all parts; and by a practice too much followed, he laid snares, sowed thorns, and opened precipices, wheresoever the citizens set their feet.

Almost all Sylla's laws contained only the interdiction of fire and water. To this Cæsar added the confiscation of goods,[22] because the rich, by preserving their estates in exile, became bolder in the perpetration of crimes.

The emperors, having established a military government, soon found that it was as terrible to the prince as to the subject; they endeavored therefore to temper it, and with his view had recourse to dignities, and to the respect with which those dignities were attended.

The government thus drew nearer a little to monarchy, and punishments were divided into three classes:[23] those which related to the principal persons in the state,[24] which were very mild; those which were inflicted on persons of an inferior rank,[25] and were more severe; and, in fine, such as concerned only persons of the lowest condition,[26] which were the most rigorous.

---

16. The guilty were condemned to a fine; they could not be admitted into the rank of senators, nor nominated to any public office.—Dio, book XXXVI.
17. Book XXXVI.
18. Lib. I.
19. We find there the punishment of fire, and generally capital punishments, theft punished with death, etc.
20. Sylla, animated with the same spirit as the Decemvirs, followed their example in augmenting the penal laws against satirical writers.
21. Book I.
22. "Pœnas facinorum auxit, cum locupletes eo facilius scelere se obligarent, quod integris patrimoniis exularent."—Suet. in "Jul. Cæsare."
23. See the 3d law, sec. legis ad leg. Cornel. "de Sicariis," and a vast number of others in the Digest and in the Codex.
24. Sublimiores.
25. Medios.
26. Infimos. Leg. 3, sec. legis ad leg. Cornel. "de Sicariis."

Maximinus, that fierce and stupid prince, increased the rigor of the military government which he ought to have softened. The Senate were informed, says Capitolinus,[27] that some had been crucified, others exposed to wild beasts, or sewn up in the skins of beasts lately killed, without any manner of regard to their dignity. It seemed as if he wanted to exercise the military discipline, on the model of which he pretended to regulate the civil administration.

In "The Consideration on the Rise and Declension of the Roman Grandeur,"[28] we find in what manner Constantine changed the military despotism into a military and civil government, and drew nearer to monarchy. There we may trace the different revolutions of this state, and see how they fell from rigor to indolence, and from indolence to impunity.

OF THE JUST PROPORTION BETWEEN PUNISHMENTS AND CRIMES

It is an essential point, that there should be a certain proportion in punishments, because it is essential that a great crime should be avoided rather than a smaller, and that which is more pernicious to society rather than that which is less.

"An impostor,[29] who called himself Constantine Ducas, raised a great insurrection at Constantinople. He was taken and condemned to be whipped; but upon informing against several persons of distinction, he was sentenced to be burned as a calumniator." It is very extraordinary that they should thus proportion the punishments between the crime of high treason and that of calumny.

This puts me in mind of a saying of Charles II, King of Great Britain. He saw a man one day standing in the pillory; upon which he asked what crime the man had committed. He was answered, "Please your majesty, he has written a libel against your ministers." "The fool!" said the King, "why did he not write against me? They would have done nothing to him."

"Seventy persons having conspired against the Emperor Basil, he ordered them to be whipped, and the hair of their heads and beards to be burned. A stag, one day, having taken hold of him by the girdle with his horn, one of his retinue drew his sword, cut the girdle, and saved him; upon which he ordered that person's head to be cut off, 'for having,' said he, 'drawn his sword against his sovereign.' "[30] Who could imagine that the same prince could ever have passed two such different judgments?

It is a great abuse amongst us to condemn to the same punishment a person that only robs on the highway and another who robs and murders. Surely, for the public security, some difference should be made in the punishment.

In China, those who add murder to robbery are cut in pieces:[31] but not so the others; to this difference it is owing that though they rob in that country they never murder.

In Russia, where the punishment of robbery and murder is the same, they always murder.[32] The dead, say they, tell no tales.

Where there is no difference in the penalty, there should be some in the expectation of pardon. In England they never murder on the highway, because robbers have some hopes of transportation, which is not the case in respect to those that commit murder.

Letters of grace are of excellent use in moderate governments. This power which the prince has of pardoning, exercised with prudence, is capable of producing admirable effects. The principle of despotic government, which neither grants nor receives any pardon, deprives it of these advantages.

OF THE RACK

The wickedness of mankind makes it necessary for the law to suppose them better than they really are. Hence the deposition of two witnesses is sufficient in the punishment of all crimes. The law believes them, as if they spoke by the mouth of truth. Thus we judge that every child conceived in wedlock is legitimate; the law having a confidence in the mother, as if she were chastity itself. But the use of the rack against criminals cannot be defended on a like plea of necessity.

We have before us the example of a nation blessed with an excellent civil government,[33] where without any inconvenience the practice of racking criminals is rejected. It is not, therefore, in its own nature necessary.[34]

---

27. Jul. Cap., Maximini duo.
28. Chap. xvii.
29. "History of Nicephorus, Patriarch of Constantinople."
30. In Nicephorus's history.

31. Du Halde, tom. i. p. 6.
32. "Present State of Russia," by Perry.
33. The English.
34. The citizens of Athens could not be put to the rack (Lysias, "Orat. in Agorat.") unless it was for high treason. The torture was used within thirty days after condemnation. (Curius Fortunatus, "Rhetor. Schol." lib. II.) There was no preparatory torture. In regard to the Romans, the 3d and 4th laws, "ad leg. Juliam Majest.," show that birth, dignity, and the military profession exempted people from the rack, except in cases of high treason. See the prudent restrictions of this practice made by the laws of the Visigoths.

So many men of learning and genius have written against the custom of torturing criminals, that after them I dare not presume to meddle with the subject. I was going to say that it might suit despotic states, where whatever inspires fear is the fittest spring of government. I was going to say that the slaves among the Greeks and Romans—but nature cries out aloud, and asserts her rights.

OF PECUNIARY AND CORPORAL PUNISHMENTS

Our ancestors, the Germans, admitted of none but pecuniary punishments. Those free and warlike people were of opinion that their blood ought not to be spilled but with sword in hand. On the contrary, these punishments are rejected by the Japanese,[35] under pretence that the rich might elude them. But are not the rich afraid of being stripped of their property? And might not pecuniary penalties be proportioned to people's fortunes? And, in fine, might not infamy be added to those punishments?

A good legislator takes a just medium; he ordains neither always pecuniary nor always corporal punishments.

OF THE LAW OF RETALIATION

The use of the law of retaliation[36] is very frequent in despotic countries, where they are fond of simple laws. Moderate governments admit of it sometimes; but with this difference, that the former exercise it in full rigor, whereas among the latter it ever receives some kind of limitation.

The law of the Twelve Tables admitted two: first, it never condemned to retaliation, but when the plaintiff could not be satisfied in any other manner.[37] Secondly, after condemnation they might pay damages and interest,[38] and then the corporal was changed into a pecuniary punishment.[39]

OF THE PUNISHMENT OF FATHERS FOR THE CRIMES OF THEIR CHILDREN

In China, fathers are punished for the crimes of their children. This was likewise the custom of Peru[40]—a custom derived from the notion of despotic power.

Little does it signify to say that in China the father is punished for not having exerted that paternal authority which nature has established, and the laws themselves have improved. This still supposes that there is no honor among the Chinese. Amongst us, parents whose children are condemned by the laws of their country, and children[41] whose parents have undergone the like fate, are as severely punished by shame, as they would be in China by the loss of their lives. . . .

THAT LIBERTY IS FAVORED BY THE NATURE AND PROPORTION OF PUNISHMENTS

Liberty is in perfection when criminal laws derive each punishment from the particular nature of the crime. There are then no arbitrary decisions; the punishment does not flow from the capriciousness of the legislator, but from the very nature of the thing; and man uses no violence to man.

There are four sorts of crimes. Those of the first species are prejudicial to religion, the second to morals, the third to the public tranquillity, and the fourth to the security of the subject. The punishments inflicted for these crimes ought to proceed from the nature of each of these species.

In the class of crimes that concern religion, I rank only those which attack it directly, such as all simple sacrileges. For as to crimes that disturb the exercise of it, they are of the nature of those which prejudice the tranquillity or security of the subject, and ought to be referred to those classes.

In order to derive the punishment of simple sacrileges from the nature of the thing,[42] it should consist in depriving people of the advantages conferred by religion in expelling them out of the temples, in a temporary or perpetual exclusion from the society

---

35. See Kempfer.
36. It is established in the Koran. See the chapter of the Cow.
37. "Si membrum rupit, ni cum eo pacit, talio esto."—Aulus Gellius, lib. XX. cap. i.
38. Ibid.
39. See also the law of the Visigoths, book VI. tit. iv. secs. 3 and 5.

40. See Garcilaso, "History of the Civil Wars of the Spaniards."
41. "Instead of punishing them," says Plato, "they ought to be commended for not having followed their fathers' example."—Book IX. of Laws.
42. St. Louis made such severe laws against those who swore, that the Pope thought himself obliged to admonish him for it. This prince moderated his zeal, and softened his laws.—See his "Ordinances."

of the faithful, in shunning their presence, in execrations, comminations, and conjurations.

In things that prejudice the tranquillity or security of the state, secret actions are subject to human jurisdiction. But in those which offend the Deity, where there is no public act, there can be no criminal matter, the whole passes between man and God, who knows the measure and time of His vengeance. Now if magistrates confounding things should inquire also into hidden sacrileges, this inquisition would be directed to a kind of action that does not at all require it: the liberty of the subject would be subverted by arming the zeal of timorous as well as of presumptuous consciences against him.

The mischief arises from a notion which some people have entertained of revenging the cause of the Deity. But we must honor the Deity and leave him to avenge his own cause. And, indeed, were we to be directed by such a notion, where would be the end of punishments? If human laws are to avenge the cause of an infinite Being, they will be directed by his infinity, and not by the weakness, ignorance, and caprice of man.

An historian[43] of Provençe relates a fact which furnishes us with an excellent description of the consequences that may arise in weak capacities from the notion of avenging the Deity's cause. A Jew was accused of having blasphemed against the Virgin Mary; and upon conviction was condemned to be flayed alive. A strange spectacle was then exhibited: gentlemen masked, with knives in their hands, mounted the scaffold, and drove away the executioner, in order to be the avengers themselves of the honor of the blessed Virgin. I do not here choose to anticipate the reflections of the reader.

The second class consists of those crimes which are prejudicial to morals. Such is the violation of public or private continence, that is, of the police directing the manner in which the pleasure annexed to the conjunction of the sexes is to be enjoyed. The punishment of those crimes ought to be also derived from the nature of the thing; the privation of such advantages as society has attached to the purity of morals, fines, shame, necessity of concealment, public infamy, expulsion from home and society, and, in fine, all such punishments as belong to a corrective jurisdiction, are sufficient to repress the temerity of the two sexes. In effect these things are less founded on malice than on carelessness and self-neglect.

We speak here of none but crimes which relate merely to morals, for as to those that are also prejudicial to the public security, such as rapes, they belong to the fourth species.

The crimes of the third class are those which disturb the public tranquillity. The punishments ought therefore to be derived from the nature of the thing, and to be in relation to this tranquillity; such as imprisonment, exile, and other like chastisements, proper for reclaiming turbulent spirits, and obliging them to conform to the established order.

I confine those crimes that injure the public tranquillity to things which imply a bare offence against the police; for as to those which by disturbing the public peace attack at the same time the security of the subject, they ought to be ranked in the fourth class.

The punishments inflicted upon the latter crimes are such as are properly distinguished by that name. They are a kind of retaliation, by which the society refuses security to a member, who has actually or intentionally deprived another of his security. These punishments are derived from the nature of the thing, founded on reason, and drawn from the very source of good and evil. A man deserves death when he has violated the security of the subject so far as to deprive, or attempt to deprive, another man of his life. This punishment of death is the remedy, as it were, of a sick society. When there is a breach of security with regard to property, there may be some reasons for inflicting a capital punishment: but it would be much better, and perhaps more natural, that crimes committed against the security of property should be punished with the loss of property; and this ought, indeed, to be the case if men's fortunes were common or equal. But as those who have no property of their own are generally the readiest to attack that of others, it has been found necessary, instead of a pecuniary, to substitute a corporal, punishment.

All that I have here advanced is founded in nature, and extremely favorable to the liberty of the subject.

OF CERTAIN ACCUSATIONS THAT REQUIRE PARTICULAR MODERATION AND PRUDENCE

It is an important maxim, that we ought to be very circumspect in the prosecution of witchcraft and heresy. The accusation of these two crimes may be vastly injurious to liberty, and productive of infinite oppression, if the legislator knows not how to set bounds to it. For as it does not directly point at a

---
43. Father Bougerel.

person's actions, but at his character, it grows dangerous in proportion to the ignorance of the people; and then a man is sure to be always in danger, because the most exceptional conduct, the purest morals, and the constant practice of every duty in life are not a sufficient security against the suspicion of his being guilty of the like crimes.

Under Manuel Comnenus, the Protestator[44] was accused of having conspired against the emperor, and of having employed for that purpose some secrets that render men invisible. It is mentioned in the life of this emperor[45] that Aaron was detected, as he was poring over a book of Solomon's, the reading of which was sufficient to conjure up whole legions of devils. Now by supposing a power in witchcraft to rouse the infernal spirits to arms, people look upon a man whom they call a sorcerer as the person in the world most likely to disturb and subvert society; and, of course, they are disposed to punish him with the utmost severity.

But their indignation increases when witchcraft is supposed to have the power of subverting religion. The history of Constantinople[46] informs us that in consequence of a revelation made to a bishop of a miracle having ceased because of the magic practices of a certain person, both that person and his son were put to death. On how many surprising things did not this single crime depend? That revelations should not be uncommon, that the bishop should be favored with one, that it was real, that there had been a miracle in the case, that this miracle had ceased, that there was an art magic, that magic could subvert religion, that this particular person was a magician, and, in fine, that he had committed that magic act.

The Emperor Theodorus Lascarus attributed his illness to witchcraft. Those who were accused of this crime had no other resource left than to handle a red-hot iron without being hurt. Thus among the Greeks a person ought to have been a sorcerer to be able to clear himself of the imputation of witchcraft. Such was the excess of their stupidity that to the most dubious crime in the world they joined the most dubious proofs of innocence.

Under the reign of Philip the Long, the Jews were expelled from France, being accused of having poisoned the springs with their lepers. So absurd an accusation ought to make us doubt all those that are founded on public hatred.

I have not here asserted that heresy ought not to be punished; I said only that we ought to be extremely circumspect in punishing it.

OF THE CRIME AGAINST NATURE

God forbid that I should have the least inclination to diminish the public horror against a crime which religion, morality, and civil government equally condemn. It ought to be proscribed, were it only for its communicating to one sex the weaknesses of the other, and for leading people by a scandalous prostitution of their youth to an ignominious old age. What I shall say concerning it will in no way diminish its infamy, being levelled only against the tyranny that may abuse the very horror we ought to have against the vice.

As a natural circumstance of this crime is secrecy, there are frequent instances of its having been punished by legislators upon the deposition of a child. This was opening a very wide door to calumny. "Justinian," says Procopius,[47] "published a law against this crime; he ordered an inquiry to be made not only against those who were guilty of it, after the enacting of that law, but even before. The deposition of a single witness, sometimes of a child, sometimes of a slave, was sufficient, especially against such as were rich, and against those of the green faction."

It is very odd that these three crimes, witchcraft, heresy, and that against nature, of which the first might easily be proved not to exist; the second to be susceptible of an infinite number of distinctions, interpretations, and limitations; the third to be often obscure and uncertain—it is very odd, I say, that these three crimes should amongst us be punished with fire.

I may venture to affirm that the crime against nature will never make any great progress in society unless people are prompted to it by some particular custom, as among the Greeks, where the youths of that country performed all their exercises naked; as amongst us, where domestic education is disused; as amongst the Asiatics, where particular persons have a great number of women whom they despise, while others can have none at all. Let there be no customs preparatory to this crime; let it, like every other violation of morals, be severely proscribed by the civil magistrate; and nature will soon defend or resume her rights. Nature, that fond, that indulgent parent, has strewed her pleasures with a bounteous hand,

---

44. Nicetas, "Life of Manuel Comnenus," book IV.
45. Ibid.
46. "History of the Emperor Maurice," by Theophylactus, chap. II.

47. "Secret History."

and while she fills us with delights she prepares us, by means of our issue, in whom we see ourselves, as it were, reproduced—she prepares us, I say, for future satisfactions of a more exquisite kind than those very delights.

OF THE CRIME OF HIGH TREASON

It is determined by the laws of China that whosoever shows any disrespect to the emperor is to be punished with death. As they do not mention in what this disrespect consists, everything may furnish a pretext to take away a man's life, and to exterminate any family whatsoever.

Two persons of that country who were employed to write the Court gazette, having inserted some circumstances relating to a certain fact that was not true, it was pretended that to tell a lie in the Court gazette was a disrespect shown to the Court, in consequence of which they were put to death.[48] A prince of the blood having inadvertently made some mark on a memorial signed with the red pencil by the emperor, it was determined that he had behaved disrespectfully to the sovereign; which occasioned one of the most terrible persecutions against that family that ever was recorded in history.[49]

If the crime of high treason be indeterminate, this alone is sufficient to make the government degenerate into arbitrary power. I shall descant more largely on this subject when I come to treat[50] of the composition of laws.

OF THE MISAPPLICATION OF THE TERMS SACRILEGE AND HIGH TREASON

It is likewise a shocking abuse to give the appellation of high treason to an action that does not deserve it. By an imperial law[51] it was decreed that those who called in question the prince's judgment, or doubted the merit of such as he had chosen for a public office, should be prosecuted as guilty of sacrilege.[52] Surely it was the cabinet council and the prince's favorites who invented that crime.

By another law, it was determined that whosoever made any attempt to injure the ministers and officers belonging to the sovereign should be deemed guilty of high treason, as if he had attempted to injure the sovereign himself.[53] This law is owing to two princes[54] remarkable for their weakness—princes who were led by their ministers as flocks by shepherds; princes who were slaves in the palace, children in the council, strangers to the army; princes, in fine, who preserved their authority only by giving it away every day. Some of those favorites conspired against their sovereigns. Nay, they did more, they conspired against the empire—they called in barbarous nations; and when the emperors wanted to stop their progress the state was so enfeebled as to be under a necessity of infringing the law, and of exposing itself to the crime of high treason in order to punish those favorites.

And yet this is the very law which the judge of Monsieur de Cinq-Mars built upon[55] when endeavoring to prove that the latter was guilty of the crime of high treason for attempting to remove Cardinal Richelieu from the ministry. He says: "Crimes that aim at the persons of ministers are deemed by the imperial constitutions of equal consequence with those which are levelled against the emperor's own person. A minister discharges his duty to his prince and to his country: to attempt, therefore, to remove him, is endeavoring to deprive the former one of his arms,[56] and the latter of part of its power." It is impossible for the meanest tools of power to express themselves in more servile language.

By another law of Valentinian, Theodosius, and Arcadius,[57] false coiners are declared guilty of high treason. But is not this confounding the ideas of things? Is not the very horror of high treason diminished by giving that name to another crime?

THE SAME SUBJECT CONTINUED

Paulinus having written to the Emperor Alexander, that "he was preparing to prosecute for high treason a judge who had decided contrary to his edict," the emperor answered, "that under his reign there was no such thing as indirect high treason."[58]

---

48. Father Du Halde, tom. i. p. 43.
49. Father Parennin in the "Edifying Letters."
50. Book XXIX.
51. Gratian, Valentinian, and Theodosius. This is the second in the Code "de Crimin. Sacril."
52. "Sacrilegii instar est dubitare an is dignus sit quem elegerit imperator."—Code "de Crimin. Sacril." This law has served as a model to that of Roger in the "Constitution of Naples," tit. 4.
53. The 5th law, "ad leg. Jul. Maj."
54. Arcadius and Honorius.
55. "Memoirs of Montresor," tom. i.
56. "Nam ipsi pars corporis nostri sunt."—The same law of the Code "ad leg. Jul. Maj."
57. It is the 9th of the Code Theod. "de falsa moneta."
58. "Etiam ex aliis causis majestatis crimina cessant meo sæculo."—Leg. I "eod ad leg. Jul. Maj."

Faustinian wrote to the same emperor, that as he had sworn by the prince's life never to pardon his slave, he found himself thereby obliged to perpetuate his wrath, lest he should incur the guilt of *læsa majestas*. Upon which the emperor made answer, "Your fears are groundless,[59] and you are a stranger to my principles."

It was determined by a *senatus-consultum*[60] that whosoever melted down any of the emperor's statues which happened to be rejected should not be deemed guilty of high treason. The Emperors Severus and Antoninus wrote to Pontius,[61] that those who sold unconsecrated statues of the emperor should not be charged with high treason. The same princes wrote to Julius Cassianus, that if a person in flinging a stone should by chance strike one of the emperor's statues he should not be liable to a prosecution for high treason.[62] The Julian law requires this sort of limitations; for in virtue of this law the crime of high treason was charged not only upon those who melted down the emperor's statues, but likewise on those who committed any such like action,[63] which made it an arbitrary crime. When a number of crimes of *læsa majestas* had been established, they were obliged to distinguish the several sorts. Hence Ulpian, the civilian, after saying that the accusation of *læsa majestas* did not die with the criminal, adds that this does not relate to all the treasonable acts established by the Julian law,[64] but only to that which implies an attempt against the empire, or against the emperor's life.

THE SAME SUBJECT CONTINUED

There was a law passed in England under Henry VIII, by which whoever predicted the king's death was declared guilty of high treason. This law was extremely vague; the terror of despotic power is so great that it recoils upon those who exercise it. In the king's last illness, the physicians would not venture to say he was in danger; and surely they acted very right.[65]

OF THOUGHTS

Marsyas dreamed that he had cut Dionysius's throat.[66] Dionysius put him to death, pretending that he would never have dreamed of such a thing by night if he had not thought of it by day. This was a most tyrannical action: for though it had been the subject of his thoughts, yet he had made no attempt[67] towards it. The laws do not take upon them to punish any other than overt acts.

OF INDISCREET SPEECHES

Nothing renders the crime of high treason more arbitrary than declaring people guilty of it for indiscreet speeches. Speech is so subject to interpretation; there is so great a difference between indiscretion and malice; and frequently so little is there of the latter in the freedom of expression, that the law can hardly subject people to a capital punishment for words unless it expressly declares what words they are.[68]

Words do not constitute an overt act; they remain only in idea. When considered by themselves, they have generally no determinate signification; for this depends on the tone in which they are uttered. It often happens that in repeating the same words they have not the same meaning; this depends on their connection with other things, and sometimes more is signified by silence than by any expression whatever. Since there can be nothing so equivocal and ambiguous as all this, how is it possible to convert it into a crime of high treason? Wherever this law is established, there is an end not only of liberty, but even of its very shadow.

In the manifesto of the late Czarina against the family of the D'Olgoruckys,[69] one of those princes is condemned to death for having uttered some indecent words concerning her person: another, for having maliciously interpreted her imperial laws, and for having offended her sacred person by disrespectful expressions.

Not that I pretend to diminish the just indignation of the public against those who presume to stain the glory of their sovereign; what I mean is, that if despotic princes are willing to moderate their power, a milder chastisement would be more proper on

---

59. "Alienam sectæ meæ solicitudinem concepisti."—Leg. 2 "eod. ad leg. Jul. Maj."
60. See the 4th law in ff. "ad leg. Jul. Maj."
61. See the 5th law ibid.
62. Ibid.
63. "Aliudve quid simile admiserint."—Leg. 6 ff. "ad leg. Jul. Maj."
64. In the last law in ff. "ad leg. Jul. de Adulteris."
65. See Burnet's "History of the Reformation."

66. Plutarch's "Life of Dionysius."
67. The thought must be joined with some sort of action.
68. "Si non tale sit delictum in quod vel scriptura legis descendit vel ad exemplum legis vindicandum est," says Modestinus in the seventh law, in ff. "ad leg. Jul. Maj."
69. In 1740.

those occasions than the charge of high treason—a thing always terrible even to innocence itself.[70]

Overt acts do not happen every day; they are exposed to the eye of the public; and a false charge with regard to matters of fact may be easily detected. Words carried into action assume the nature of that action. Thus a man who goes into a public market-place to incite the subject to revolt incurs the guilt of high treason, because the words are joined to the action, and partake of its nature. It is not the words that are punished, but an action in which words are employed. They do not become criminal, but when they are annexed to a criminal action: everything is confounded if words are construed into a capital crime, instead of considering them only as a mark of that crime.

The Emperors Theodosius, Arcadius, and Honorius wrote thus to Rufinus, who was *præfectus prætorio*: "Though a man should happen to speak amiss of our person or government, we do not intend to punish him:[71] if he has spoken through levity, we must despise him; if through folly, we must pity him; and if he wrongs us, we must forgive him. Therefore, leaving things as they are, you are to inform us accordingly, that we may be able to judge of words by persons, and that we may duly consider whether we ought to punish or overlook them."

OF WRITINGS

In writings there is something more permanent than in words, but when they are in no way preparative to high treason they cannot amount to that charge.

And yet Augustus and Tiberius subjected satirical writers to the same punishment as for having violated the law of majesty. Augustus,[72] because of some libels that had been written against persons of the first quality; Tiberius, because of those which he suspected to have been written against himself. Nothing was more fatal to Roman liberty. Cremutius Cordus was accused of having called Cassius in his annals the last of the Romans.[73]

Satirical writings are hardly known in despotic governments, where dejection of mind on the one hand, and ignorance on the other, afford neither abilities nor will to write. In democracies they are not hindered, for the very same reason which causes them to be prohibited in monarchies; being generally levelled against men of power and authority, they flatter the malignancy of the people, who are the governing party. In monarchies they are forbidden, but rather as a subject of civil animadversion than as a capital crime. They may amuse the general malevolence, please the malcontents, diminish the envy against public employments, give the people patience to suffer, and make them laugh at their sufferings.

But no government is so averse to satirical writings as the aristocratic. There the magistrates are petty sovereigns, but not great enough to despise affronts. If in a monarchy a satirical stroke is designed against the prince, he is placed on such an eminence that it does not reach him; but an aristocratic lord is pierced to the very heart. Hence the decemvirs, who formed an aristocracy, punished satirical writings with deaths.[74]

BREACH OF MODESTY IN PUNISHING CRIMES

There are rules of modesty observed by almost every nation in the world; now it would be very absurd to infringe these rules in the punishment of crimes, the principal view of which ought always to be the establishment of order.

Was it the intent of those Oriental nations who exposed women to elephants trained up for an abominable kind of punishment—was it, I say, their intent to establish one law by the breach of another?

By an ancient custom of the Romans it was not permitted to put girls to death till they were ripe for marriage. Tiberius found an expedient of having them debauched by the executioner before they were brought to the place of punishment:[75] that bloody and subtle tyrant destroyed the morals of the people to preserve their customs.

When the magistrates of Japan caused women to be exposed naked in the market-places, and obliged them to go upon all fours like beasts, modesty was shocked:[76] but when they wanted to compel a mother—when they wanted to force a son—I cannot proceed; even Nature herself is struck with horror.

---

70. "Nec lubricum linguæ ad pœnam facile trahendum est."—Modestin. in the seventh law in ff. "ad leg. Jul. Maj."
71. "Si id ex levitate processerit, contemnendum est; si ex insania, miseratione dignissimum; si ab injuria, remittendum."—Leg. unica Cod. "Si quis Imperat. maled."
72. Tacit. "Annal." book I. This continued under the following reigns. See the first law in the Code "de famosis libellis."
73. Tacit. "Annal." book IV.
74. The law of the Twelve Tables.
75. Suetonius, in "Tiberio."
76. "Collection of Voyages that Contributed to the Establishment of the East India Company," tom. v. part II.

CHAPTER 3

CESARE BECCARIA

This chapter presents a reading from Beccaria's *An Essay on Crimes and Punishments* (1819), pp. 15–19, 28–35, 47, 59–68, 74–79, 93–108, and 158–160; second American edition; Philadelphia: Philip H. Nicklin. The first edition of this essay was published in Italian in 1764. Since then, many different editions have been published in numerous languages. The second American edition, which includes "A Commentary" by Voltaire, is an anonymous translation of one of the Italian editions, perhaps the fifth (although it is not specified in the text). Like the fifth Italian edition, it has 47 chapters, and the chapters are presented in the same order. However, unlike the fifth Italian edition, the second American edition does not include Beccaria's prefatory note "To the Reader."* In the selections presented below, the original chapter headings have been retained, but the chapter numbers have been removed. The full text of the second American edition is available through the HathiTrust Digital Library (hathitrust.org).

On Crimes and Punishments was widely read and applauded in Europe during the latter half of the eighteenth century. At that time, a significant shift in European culture was well under way. In the decades leading up to its publication, Hutcheson, Montesquieu, and other scholars of the Enlightenment shaped an intellectual climate that could readily embrace many of its arguments. Its publication was well timed, for there was an audience aptly prepared to appreciate its contents. In fact, the intellectual environment, as suggested by the readings in Chapters 1 and 2, already included some of these contents; Beccaria's arguments were not entirely new. Of course, *On Crimes and Punishments* was strongly opposed by some people, but this did not stop its translation into French, English, and several other languages, nor did it prevent favorable reviews from many highly respected scholars and political leaders.

More than any other work, *On Crimes and Punishments* defines the classical school of criminology. It proposed criminal justice reforms based on a largely secular paradigm that combines utilitarianism and social contract theory. Within this framework, Beccaria maintained that punishment should be designed for the purpose of deterrence. The following selections illustrate

---

* In 2009, Graeme R. Newman and Pietro Marongiu provided a new translation of the fifth Italian edition (specifically, the "Harlem" edition of 1766), which was published by Transaction Publishers. In their "A Note on the Text," Newman and Marongiu also provide a helpful overview of the different versions of this book and the challenge of identifying the definitive edition.

this general orientation. They present Beccaria's views on "the origin of punishments," "the right to punish," and "the intent of punishments." They also present his opposition to torture and capital punishment, and his insights regarding the proportionality, swiftness, visibility, mildness, and certainty of punishment.

from AN ESSAY ON CRIMES AND PUNISHMENTS
by Cesare Beccaria

OF THE ORIGIN OF PUNISHMENTS

LAWS are the conditions under which men, naturally independent, united themselves in society. Weary of living in a continual state of war, and of enjoying a liberty, which became of little value, from the uncertainty of its duration, they sacrificed one part of it, to enjoy the rest in peace and security. The sum of all these portions of the liberty of each individual constituted the sovereignty of a nation and was deposited in the hands of the sovereign, as the lawful administrator. But it was not sufficient only to establish this deposit; it was also necessary to defend it from the usurpation of each individual, who will always endeavour to take away from the mass, not only his own portion, but to encroach on that of others. Some motives therefore, that strike the senses were necessary to prevent the despotism of each individual from plunging society into its former chaos. Such motives are the punishments established against the infractors of the laws. I say that motives of this kind are necessary; because experience shows, that the multitude adopt no established principle of conduct; and because society is prevented from approaching to that dissolution, (to which, as well as all other parts of the physical and moral world, it naturally tends,) only by motives that are the immediate objects of sense, and which being continually presented to the mind, are sufficient to counterbalance the effects of the passions of the individual which oppose the general good. Neither the power of eloquence nor the sublimest truths are sufficient to restrain, for any length of time, those passions which are excited by the lively impressions of present objects.

OF THE RIGHT TO PUNISH

EVERY punishment which does not arise from absolute necessity, says the great Montesquieu, is tyrannical. A proposition which may be made more general thus: every act of authority of one man over another, for which there is not an absolute necessity, is tyrannical. It is upon this then that the sovereign's right to punish crimes is founded; that is, upon the necessity of defending the public liberty, entrusted to his care, from the usurpation of individuals; and punishments are just in proportion, as the liberty, preserved by the sovereign, is sacred and valuable.

Let us consult the human heart, and there we shall find the foundation of the sovereign's right to punish, for no advantage in moral policy can be lasting which is not founded on the indelible sentiments of the heart of man. Whatever law deviates from this principle will always meet with a resistance which will destroy it in the end; for the smallest force continually applied will overcome the most violent motion communicated to bodies.

No man ever gave up his liberty merely for the good of the public. Such a chimera exists only in romances. Every individual wishes, if possible, to be exempt from the compacts that bind the rest of mankind.

The multiplication of mankind, though slow, being too great, for the means which the earth, in its natural state, offered to satisfy necessities which every day became more numerous, obliged men to separate again, and form new societies. These naturally opposed the first, and a state of war was transferred from individuals to nations.

Thus it was necessity that forced men to give up a part of their liberty. It is certain, then, that every individual would choose to put into the public stock the smallest portion possible, as much only as was sufficient to engage others to defend it. The aggregate of these, the smallest portions possible, forms the right of punishing; all that extends beyond this, is abuse, not justice.

Observe that by *justice* I understand nothing more than that bond which is necessary to keep the interest of individuals united, without which men would return to their original state of barbarity. All punishments which exceed the necessity of preserving this bond are in their nature unjust. We should be cautious how we associate with the word *justice* an idea of any thing real, such as a physical power, or a being that actually exists. I do not, by any means, speak of the justice of God, which is of another kind, and refers immediately to rewards and punishments in a life to come. . . .

OF THE PROPORTION BETWEEN CRIMES AND PUNISHMENTS

IT is not only the common interest of mankind that crimes should not be committed, but that crimes of every kind should be less frequent, in proportion to the evil they produce to society. Therefore the means made use of by the legislature to prevent crimes should be more powerful, in proportion as they are destructive of the public safety and happiness, and as the inducements to commit them are stronger. Therefore there ought to be a fixed proportion between crimes and punishments.

It is impossible to prevent entirely all the disorders which the passions of mankind cause in society. These disorders increase in proportion to the number of people and the opposition of private interests. If we consult history, we shall find them increasing, in every state, with the extent of dominion. In political arithmetic, it is necessary to substitute a calculation of probabilities to mathematical exactness. That force which continually impels us to our own private interest, like gravity, acts incessantly, unless it meets with an obstacle to oppose it. The effects of this force are the confused series of human actions. Punishments, which I would call political obstacles, prevent the fatal effects of private interest, without destroying the impelling cause, which is that sensibility inseparable from man. The legislator acts, in this case, like a skilful architect, who endeavours to counteract the force of gravity by combining the circumstances which may contribute to the strength of his edifice.

The necessity of uniting in society being granted, together with the conventions which the opposite interests of individuals must necessarily require, a scale of crimes may be formed, of which the first degree should consist of those which immediately tend to the dissolution of society, and the last of the smallest possible injustice done to a private member of that society. Between these extremes will be comprehended all actions contrary to the public good which are called criminal, and which descend by insensible degrees, decreasing from the highest to the lowest. If mathematical calculation could be applied to the obscure and infinite combinations of human actions, there might be a corresponding scale of punishments, descending from the greatest to the least; but it will be sufficient that the wise legislator mark the principal divisions, without disturbing the order, lest to crimes of the *first* degree be assigned punishments of the *last*. If there were an exact and universal scale of crimes and punishments, we should there have a common measure of the degree of liberty and slavery, humanity and cruelty of different nations.

Any action which is not comprehended in the above mentioned scale will not be called a crime, or punished as such, except by those who have an interest in the denomination. The uncertainty of the extreme points of this scale hath produced a system of morality which contradicts the laws, a multitude of laws that contradict each other, and many which expose the best men to the severest punishments, rendering the ideas of *vice* and *virtue* vague and fluctuating, and even their existence doubtful. Hence that fatal lethargy of political bodies, which terminates in their destruction.

Whoever reads, with a philosophic eye, the history of nations, and their laws, will generally find, that the ideas of virtue and vice, of a good or bad citizen, change with the revolution of ages, not in proportion to the alteration of circumstances, and consequently conformable to the common good, but in proportion to the passions and errors by which the different lawgivers were successively influenced. He will frequently observe that the passions and vices of one age are the foundation of the morality of the following; that violent passion, the offspring of fanaticism and enthusiasm, being weakened by time, which reduces all the phenomena of the natural and moral world to an equality, become, by degrees, the prudence of the age, and an useful instrument in the hands of the powerful or artful politician. Hence the uncertainty of our notions of honour and virtue; an uncertainty which will ever remain, because they change with the revolutions of time, and names survive the things they originally signified; they change with the boundaries of states, which are often the same both in physical and moral geography.

Pleasure and pain are the only springs of actions in beings endowed with sensibility. Even amongst the motives which incite men to acts of religion, the invisible legislator has ordained rewards and punishments. From a partial distribution of these will arise that contradiction, so little observed, because so common, I mean that of punishing by the laws the crimes which the laws have occasioned. If an equal punishment be ordained for two crimes that injure society in different degrees, there is nothing to deter men from committing the greater as often as it is attended with greater advantage.

OF ESTIMATING THE DEGREE OF CRIMES

THE foregoing reflections authorise me to assert that crimes are only to be measured by the injury done to society.

They err, therefore, who imagine that a crime is greater or less according to the intention of the person by whom it is committed; for this will depend on the actual impression of objects on the senses, and on the previous disposition of the mind; both which will vary in different persons, and even in the same person at different times, according to the succession of ideas, passions, and circumstances. Upon that system it would be necessary to form, not only a particular code for every individual, but a new penal law for every crime. Men, often with the best intention, do the greatest injury to society, and, with the worst, do it the most essential services.

Others have estimated crimes rather by the dignity of the person offended than by their consequences to society. If this were the true standard, the smallest irreverence to the Divine Being ought to be punished with infinitely more severity than the assassination of a monarch.

In short, others have imagined, that the greatness of the sin should aggravate the crime. But the fallacy of this opinion will appear on the slightest consideration of the relations between man and man, and between God and man. The relations between man and man are relations of equality. Necessity alone hath produced, from the opposition of private passions and interests, the idea of public utility, which is the foundation of human justice. The other are relations of dependence, between an imperfect creature and his Creator, the most perfect of beings, who has reserved to himself the sole right of being both lawgiver and judge; for he alone can, without injustice, be, at the same time, both one and the other. If he hath decreed eternal punishments for those who disobey his will, shall an insect dare to put himself in the place of divine justice, or pretend to punish for the Almighty, who is himself all sufficient, who cannot receive impressions of pleasure or pain, and who alone, of all other beings, acts without being acted upon? The degree of sin depends on the malignity of the heart, which is impenetrable to finite beings. How then can the degree of sin serve as a standard to determine the degree of crimes? If that were admitted, men may punish when God pardons, and pardon when God condemns; and thus act in opposition to the Supreme Being. . . .

OF THE INTENT OF PUNISHMENTS

FROM the foregoing considerations it is evident that the intent of punishments is not to torment a sensible being, nor to undo a crime already committed. Is it possible that torments and useless cruelty, the instrument of furious fanaticism or the impotency of tyrants, can be authorised by a political body, which, so far from being influenced by passion, should be the cool moderator of the passions of individuals? Can the groans of a tortured wretch recall the time past, or reverse the crime he has committed?

The end of punishment, therefore, is no other than to prevent the criminal from doing further injury to society, and to prevent others from committing the like offence. Such punishments, therefore, and such a mode of inflicting them, ought to be chosen, as will make the strongest and most lasting impressions on the minds of others, with the least torment to the body of the criminal. . . .

OF TORTURE

THE torture of a criminal during the course of his trial is a cruelty consecrated by custom in most nations. It is used with an intent either to make him confess his crime, or to explain some contradictions into which he had been led during his examination, or discover his accomplices, or for some kind of metaphysical and incomprehensible purgation of infamy, or, finally, in order to discover other crimes of which he is not accused, but of which he may be guilty.

No man can be judged a criminal until he be found guilty; nor can society take from him the public protection until it have been proved that he has violated the conditions on which it was granted. What right, then, but that of power, can authorise the punishment of a citizen so long as there remains any doubt of his guilt? This dilemma is frequent. Either he is guilty, or not guilty. If guilty, he should only suffer the punishment ordained by the laws, and torture becomes useless, as his confession is unnecessary. If he be not guilty, you torture the innocent; for, in the eye of the law, every man is innocent whose crime has not been proved. Besides, it is confounding all relations to expect that a man should be both the accuser and accused; and that pain should be the test of truth, as if truth resided in the muscles and fibres of a wretch in torture. By this method the robust will escape, and the feeble be condemned. These are the inconveniencies of this pretended test of truth, worthy only of a cannibal, and which the Romans, in many respects barbarous, and whose savage virtue has been too much admired, reserved for the slaves alone.

What is the political intention of punishments? To terrify and be an example to others. Is this intention answered by thus privately torturing the guilty and the innocent? It is doubtless of importance that no crime should remain unpunished; but it is useless to make a public example of the author of a crime hid in darkness. A crime already committed, and for which there can be no remedy, can only be punished by a political society with an intention that no hopes of impunity should induce others to commit the same. If it be true, that the number of those who from fear or virtue respect the laws is greater than of those by whom they are violated, the risk of torturing an innocent person is greater, as there is a greater probability that, *cæteris paribus,* an individual hath observed, than that he hath infringed the laws.

There is another ridiculous motive for torture, namely, *to purge a man from infamy.* Ought such an abuse to be tolerated in the eighteenth century? Can pain, which is a sensation, have any connection with a moral sentiment, a matter of opinion? Perhaps the rack may be considered as the refiner's furnace.

It is not difficult to trace this senseless law to its origin; for an absurdity, adopted by a whole nation, must have some affinity with other ideas established and respected by the same nation. This custom seems to be the offspring of religion, by which mankind, in all nations and in all ages, are so generally influenced. We are taught by our infallible church, that those stains of sin contracted through human frailty, and which have not deserved the eternal anger of the Almighty, are to be purged away in another life by an incomprehensible fire. Now infamy is a stain, and if the punishments and fire of purgatory can take away all spiritual stains, why should not the pain of torture take away those of a civil nature? I imagine, that the confession of a criminal, which in some tribunals is required as being essential to his condemnation, has a similar origin, and has been taken from the mysterious tribunal of penitence, where the confession of sins is a necessary part of the sacrament. Thus have men abused the unerring light of revelation; and, in the times of tractable ignorance, having no other, they naturally had recourse to it on every occasion, making the most remote and absurd applications. Moreover, infamy is a sentiment regulated neither by the laws nor by reason, but entirely by opinion; but torture renders the victim infamous, and therefore cannot take infamy away.

Another intention of torture is to oblige the supposed criminal to reconcile the contradictions into which he may have fallen during his examination; as if the dread of punishment, the uncertainty of his fate, the solemnity of the court, the majesty of the judge, and the ignorance of the accused, were not abundantly sufficient to account for contradictions, which are so common to men even in a state of tranquillity, and which must necessarily be multiplied by the perturbation of the mind of a man entirely engaged in the thoughts of saving himself from imminent danger.

This infamous test of truth is a remaining monument of that ancient and savage legislation, in which trials by fire, by boiling water, or the uncertainty of combats, were called *judgments of God;* as if the links of that eternal chain, whose beginning is in the breast of the first cause of all things, could ever be disunited by the institutions of men. The only difference between torture and trials by fire and boiling water is, that the event of the first depends on the will of the accused, and of the second on a fact entirely physical and external: but this difference is apparent only, not real. A man on the rack, in the convulsions of torture, has it as little in his power to declare the truth, as, in former times, to prevent without fraud the effects of fire or boiling water.

Every act of the will is invariably in proportion to the force of the impression on our senses. The impression of pain, then, may increase to such a degree, that, occupying the mind entirely, it will compel the sufferer to use the shortest method of freeing himself from torment. His answer, therefore, will be an effect as necessary as that of fire or boiling water, and he will accuse himself of crimes of which he is innocent: so that the very means employed to distinguish the innocent from the guilty will most effectually destroy all difference between them.

It would be superfluous to confirm these reflections by examples of innocent persons who, from the agony of torture, have confessed themselves guilty: innumerable instances may be found in all nations, and in every age. How amazing that mankind have always neglected to draw the natural conclusion! Lives there a man who, if he has carried his thoughts ever so little beyond the necessities of life, when he reflects on such cruelty, is not tempted to fly from society, and return to his natural state of independence?

The result of torture, then, is a matter of calculation, and depends on the constitution, which differs in every individual, and it is in proportion to his strength and sensibility; so that to discover truth by this method, is a problem which may be better solved by a mathematician than by a judge, and may be thus stated: *The force of the muscles and the sensibility of the nerves of an innocent person being given, it is required to find the degree of pain necessary to make him confess himself guilty of a given crime.*

The examination of the accused is intended to find out the truth; but if this be discovered with so much difficulty in the air, gesture, and countenance of a man at ease, how can it appear in a countenance distorted by the convulsions of torture? Every violent action destroys those small alterations in the features which sometimes disclose the sentiments of the heart.

These truths were known to the Roman legislators, amongst whom, as I have already observed, slaves only, who were not considered as citizens, were tortured. They are known to the English, a nation in which the progress of science, superiority in commerce, riches, and power, its natural consequences, together with the numerous examples of virtue and courage, leave no doubt of the excellence of its laws. They have been acknowledged in Sweden, where torture has been abolished. They are known to one of the wisest monarchs in Europe, who, having seated philosophy on the throne by his beneficent legislation, has made his subjects free, though dependent on the laws; the only freedom that reasonable men can desire in the present state of things. In short, torture has not been thought necessary in the laws of armies, composed chiefly of the dregs of mankind, where its use should seem most necessary. Strange phenomenon! that a set of men, hardened by slaughter, and familiar with blood, should teach humanity to the sons of peace.

It appears also that these truths were known, though imperfectly, even to those by whom torture has been most frequently practised; for a confession made during torture, is null, if it be not afterwards confirmed by an oath, which if the criminal refuses, he is tortured again. Some civilians and some nations permit this infamous *petitio principii* to be only three times repeated, and others leave it to the discretion of the judge; therefore, of two men equally innocent, or equally guilty, the most robust and resolute will be acquitted, and the weakest and most pusillanimous will be condemned, in consequence of the following excellent mode of reasoning. *I, the judge, must find some one guilty. Thou, who art a strong fellow, hast been able to resist the force of torment; therefore I acquit thee. Thou, being weaker, hast yielded to it; I therefore condemn thee. I am sensible, that the confession which was extorted from thee has no weight; but if thou dost not confirm by oath what thou hast already confessed, I will have thee tormented again.*

A very strange but necessary consequence of the use of torture is, that the case of the innocent is worse than that of the guilty. With regard to the first, either he confesses the crime which he has not committed, and is condemned, or he is acquitted, and has suffered a punishment he did not deserve. On the contrary, the person who is really guilty has the most favourable side of the question; for, if he supports the torture with firmness and resolution, he is acquitted, and has gained, having exchanged a greater punishment for a less.

The law by which torture is authorised, says, *Men, be insensible to pain. Nature has indeed given you an irresistible self-love, and an unalienable right of self-preservation; but I create in you a contrary sentiment, an heroical hatred of yourselves. I command you to accuse yourselves, and to declare the truth, amidst the tearing of your flesh and the dislocation of your bones.*

Torture is used to discover whether the criminal be guilty of other crimes besides those of which he is accused, which is equivalent to the following reasoning. *Thou art guilty of one crime, therefore it is possible that thou mayest have committed a thousand others; but the affair being doubtful I must try it by my criterion of truth. The laws order thee to be tormented because thou art guilty, because thou mayest be guilty, and because I choose thou shouldst be guilty.*

Torture is used to make the criminal discover his accomplices; but if it has been demonstrated that it is not at a proper means of discovering truth, how can it serve to discover the accomplices, which is one of the truths required? Will not the man who accuses himself yet more readily accuse others? Besides, is it just to torment one man for the crime of another? May not the accomplices be found out by the examination of the witnesses, or of the criminal; from the evidence, or from the nature of the crime itself; in short, by all the means that have been used to prove the guilt of the prisoner? The accomplices commonly fly when their comrade is taken. The uncertainty of their fate condemns them to perpetual exile, and frees society from the danger of further injury; whilst the punishment of the criminal, by deterring others, answers the purpose for which it was ordained. . . .

OF THE ADVANTAGE OF IMMEDIATE PUNISHMENT

THE more immediately after the commission of a crime a punishment is inflicted, the more just and useful it will be. It will be more just, because it spares the criminal the cruel and superfluous torment of uncertainty, which increases in proportion to the strength of his imagination and the sense of his weakness; and because the privation of liberty, being a punishment, ought to be inflicted before condemnation but for as short a time as possible. Imprisonment, I say, being only the means of securing the person of the accused until he be tried, condemned, or acquitted, ought not only to be of as short duration, but attended with as little severity as possible. The time should be determined by the necessary preparation for the trial, and the right of priority in the oldest prisoners. The confinement ought not to be closer than is requisite to prevent his flight, or his concealing the proofs of the crime; and the trial should be conducted with all possible expedition. Can there be a more cruel contrast than that between the indolence of a judge and the painful anxiety of the accused; the comforts and pleasures of an insensible magistrate, and the filth and misery of the prisoner? In general, as I have before observed, *The degree of the punishment, and the consequences of a crime, ought to be so contrived as to have the greatest possible effect on others, with the least possible pain to the delinquent.* If there be any society in which this is not a fundamental principle, it is an unlawful society; for mankind, by their union, originally intended to subject themselves to the least evils possible.

An immediate punishment is more useful; because the smaller the interval of time between the punishment and the crime, the stronger and more lasting will be the association of the two ideas of *crime* and *punishment*; so that they may be considered, one as the cause, and the other as the unavoidable and necessary effect. It is demonstrated, that the association of ideas is the cement which unites the fabric of the human intellect, without which pleasure and pain would be simple and ineffectual sensations. The vulgar, that is, all men who have no general ideas or universal principles, act in consequence of the most immediate and familiar associations; but the more remote and complex only present themselves to the minds of those who are passionately attached to a single object, or to those of greater understanding, who have acquired an habit of rapidly comparing together a number of objects, and of forming a conclusion; and the result, that is, the action in consequence, by these means becomes less dangerous and uncertain.

It is, then, of the greatest importance that the punishment should succeed the crime as immediately as possible, if we intend that, in the rude minds of the multitude, the seducing picture of the advantage arising from the crime should instantly awake the attendant idea of punishment. Delaying the punishment serves only to separate these two ideas, and thus affects the minds of the spectators rather as being a terrible sight than the necessary consequence of a crime, the horror of which should contribute to heighten the idea of the punishment.

There is another excellent method of strengthening this important connection between the ideas of crime and punishment; that is, to make the punishment as analogous as possible to the nature of the crime, in order that the punishment may lead the mind to consider the crime in a different point of view from that in which it was placed by the flattering idea of promised advantages.

Crimes of less importance are commonly punished either in the obscurity of a prison, or the criminal is *transported,* to give by his slavery an example to societies which he never offended; an example absolutely useless, because distant from the place where the crime was committed. Men do not, in general, commit great crimes deliberately, but rather in a sudden gust of passion; and they commonly look on the punishment due to a great crime as remote and improbable. The public punishment, therefore, of small crimes will make a greater impression, and, by deterring men from the smaller, will effectually prevent the greater.

OF ACTS OF VIOLENCE

SOME crimes relate to *person,* others to *property.* The first ought to be punished corporally. The great and rich should by no means have it in their power to set a price on the security of the weak and indigent; for then riches, which, under the protection of the laws, are the reward of industry, would become the aliment of tyranny. Liberty is at an end whenever the laws permit that, in certain cases, a man may cease to be *a person,* and become *a thing.* Then will the powerful employ their address to select from the various combinations of civil society all that is in their own favour. This is that magic art which transforms subjects into beasts of burden, and which, in the hands of the strong, is the chain that binds the weak and incautious. Thus it is that in some governments, where there is all the appearance of Liberty, tyranny lies concealed, and insinuates itself into some neglected corner of the constitution, where it gathers strength insensibly. Mankind generally oppose, with resolution, the assaults of barefaced and open tyranny, but disregard the little insect that gnaws through the dike, and opens a sure though secret passage to inundation. . . .

OF THE MILDNESS OF PUNISHMENTS

THE course of my ideas has carried me away from my subject, to the elucidation of which I now return. Crimes are more effectually prevented by the *certainty* than the *severity* of punishment. Hence in a magistrate the necessity of vigilance, and in a judge of implacability, which, that it may become an useful virtue, should be joined to a mild legislation. The certainty of a small punishment will make a stronger impression than the fear of one more severe, if attended with the hopes of escaping; for it is the nature of mankind to be terrified at the approach of the smallest inevitable evil, whilst hope, the best gift of Heaven, hath the power of dispelling the apprehension of a greater, especially if supported by examples of impunity, which weakness or avarice too frequently afford.

If punishments be very severe, men are naturally led to the perpetration of other crimes, to avoid the punishment due to the first. The countries and times most notorious for severity of punishments were always those in which the most bloody and inhuman actions and the most atrocious crimes were committed; for the hand of the legislator and the assassin were directed by the same spirit of ferocity, which on the throne dictated laws of iron to slaves and savages, and in private instigated the subject to sacrifice one tyrant to make room for another.

In proportion as punishments become more cruel, the minds of men, as a fluid rises to the same height with that which surrounds it, grow hardened and insensible; and the force of the passions still continuing, in the space of an hundred years the *wheel* terrifies no more than formerly the *prison.* That a punishment may produce the effect required; it is sufficient that the *evil* it occasions should exceed the *good* expected from the crime, including in the calculation the certainty of the punishment, and the privation of the expected advantage. All severity beyond this is superfluous, and therefore tyrannical.

Men regulate their conduct by the repeated impression of evils they know, and not by those with which they are unacquainted. Let us, for example, suppose two nations, in one of which the greatest punishment is *perpetual slavery,* and in the other *the wheel*: I say, that both will inspire the same degree of terror, and that their can be no reasons for increasing the punishments of the first, which are not equally valid for augmenting those of the second to more lasting and more ingenious modes of tormenting, and so on to the most exquisite refinements of a science too well known to tyrants.

There are yet two other consequences of cruel punishments, which counteract the purpose of their institution, which was, to prevent crimes. The *first* arises from the impossibility of establishing an exact proportion between the crime and punishment; for though ingenious cruelty hath greatly multiplyed the variety of torments, yet the human frame can suffer only to a certain degree, beyond which it is impossible to proceed, be the enormity of the crime ever so great. The *second* consequence is impunity. Human nature is limited no less in evil than in good. Excessive barbarity can never be more than temporary, it being impossible that it should be supported by a permanent system of legislation; for if the laws be too cruel, they must be altered, or anarchy and impunity will succeed.

Is it possible without shuddering with horror, to read in history of the barbarous and useless torments that were cooly invented and executed by men who were called sages? Who does not tremble at the thoughts of thousands of wretches, whom their misery, either caused or tolerated by the laws, which favoured the few and outraged the many, had forced in despair to return to a state of nature, or accused of impossible crimes, the fabric of ignorance and superstition, or guilty only of having been faithful to their own principles; who, I say, can, without horror, think of their being torn to pieces, with slow and studied barbarity, by men endowed with the same passions and the same feelings? A delightful spectacle to a fanatic multitude!

OF THE PUNISHMENT OF DEATH

THE useless profusion of punishments, which has never made men better, induces me to inquire, whether the punishment of *death* be really just or useful in a well governed state? What *right,* I ask, have men to cut the throats of their fellow-creatures? Certainly not that on which the sovereignty and laws are founded. The laws, as I have said before, are only the sum of the smallest portions of the private liberty of each individual, and represent the general will, which is the aggregate of that of each individual. Did any one ever give to others the right of taking away his life? Is it possible that, in the smallest portions of the liberty of each, sacrificed to the good of the public, can be contained the greatest of all good, life? If it were so, how shall it be reconciled to the maxim which tells us, that a man has no right to kill himself, which he certainly must have, if he could give it away to another?

But the punishment of death is not authorised by any right; for I have demonstrated that no such right exists. It is therefore a war of a whole nation against a citizen, whose destruction they consider as necessary or useful to the general good. But if I can further demonstrate that it is neither necessary nor useful, I shall have gained the cause of humanity.

The death of a citizen cannot be necessary but in one case: when, though deprived of his liberty, he has such power and connections as may endanger the security of the nation; when his existence may produce a dangerous revolution in the established form of government. But, even in this case, it can only be necessary when a nation is on the verge of recovering or losing its liberty, or in times of absolute anarchy, when the disorders themselves hold the place of laws: but in a reign of tranquillity, in a form of government approved by the united wishes of the nation, in a state well fortified from enemies without and supported by strength within, and opinion, perhaps more efficacious, where all power is lodged in the hands of a true sovereign, where riches can purchase pleasures and not authority, there can be no necessity for taking away the life of a subject.

If the experience of all ages be not sufficient to prove, that the punishment of death has never prevented determined men from injuring society; if the example of the Romans; if twenty years' reign of Elizabeth, empress of Russia, in which she gave the fathers of their country an example more illustrious than many conquests bought with blood; if, I say, all this be not sufficient to persuade mankind, who always suspect the voice of reason, and who choose rather to be led by authority, let us consult human nature in proof of my assertion.

It is not the intenseness of the pain that has the greatest effect on the mind, but its continuance; for our sensibility is more easily and more powerfully affected by weak but repeated impressions, than by a violent but momentary impulse. The power of habit is universal over every sensible being. As it is by that we learn to speak, to walk, and to satisfy our necessities, so the ideas of morality are stamped on our minds by repeated impressions. The death of a criminal is a terrible but momentary spectacle, and therefore a less efficacious method of deterring others than the continued example of a man deprived of his liberty, condemned, as a beast of burden, to repair, by his labour, the injury he has done to society, *If I commit such a crime,* says the spectator to himself, *I shall be reduced to that miserable condition for the rest of my life.* A much more powerful preventive than the fear of death which men always behold in distant obscurity.

The terrors of death make so slight an impression, that it has not force enough to withstand the forgetfulness natural to mankind, even in the most essential things, especially when assisted by the passions. Violent impressions surprise us, but their effect is momentary; they are fit to produce those revolutions which instantly transform a common man into a Lacedæmonian or a Persian; but in a free and quiet government they ought to be rather frequent than strong.

The execution of a criminal is to the multitude a spectacle which in some excites compassion mixed with indignation. These sentiments occupy the mind much more than that salutary terror which the laws endeavour to inspire; but, in the contemplation of continued suffering, terror is the only, or at least predominant sensation. The severity of a punishment should be just sufficient to excite compassion in the spectators, as it is intended more for them than for the criminal.

A punishment, to be just, should have only that degree of severity which is sufficient to deter others. Now there is no man who, upon the least reflection, would put in competition the total and perpetual loss of his liberty, with the greatest advantages he could possibly obtain in consequence of a crime. Perpetual slavery, then, has in it all that is necessary to deter the most hardened and determined, as much as the punishment of death. I say it has more. There are many who can look upon death with intrepidity and firmness, some through fanaticism, and others through vanity, which attends us even to the grave;

others from a desperate resolution, either to get rid of their misery, or cease to live: but fanaticism and vanity forsake the criminal in slavery, in chains and fetters, in an iron cage, and despair seems rather the beginning than the end of their misery. The mind, by collecting itself and uniting all its force, can, for a moment, repel assailing grief; but its most vigorous efforts are insufficient to resist perpetual wretchedness.

In all nations, where death is used as a punishment, every example supposes a new crime committed; whereas, in perpetual slavery, every criminal affords a frequent and lasting example; and if it be necessary that men should often be witnesses of the power of the laws, criminals should often be put to death: but this supposes a frequency of crimes; and from hence this punishment will cease to have its effect, so that it must be useful and useless at the same time.

I shall be told that perpetual slavery is as painful a punishment as death, and therefore as cruel. I answer, that if all the miserable moments in the life of a slave were collected into one point, it would be a more cruel punishment than any other; but these are scattered through his whole life, whilst the pain of death exerts all its force in a moment. There is also another advantage in the punishment of slavery, which is, that it is more terrible to the spectator than to the sufferer himself; for the spectator considers the sum of all his wretched moments whilst the sufferer, by the misery of the present, is prevented from thinking of the future. All evils are increased by the imagination, and the sufferer finds resources and consolations of which the spectators are ignorant, who judge by their own sensibility of what passes in a mind by habit grown callous to misfortune.

Let us, for a moment, attend to the reasoning of a robber or assassin, who is deterred from violating the laws by the gibbet or the wheel. I am sensible, that to develop the sentiments of one's own heart is an art which education only can teach; but although a villain may not be able to give a clear account of his principles, they nevertheless influence his conduct. He reasons thus: "What are these laws that I am bound to respect, which make so great a difference between me and the rich man? He refuses me the farthing I ask of him, and excuses himself by bidding me have recourse to labour, with which he is unacquainted."

"Who made these laws? The rich and the great, who never deigned to visit the miserable hut of the poor, who have never seen him dividing a piece of mouldy bread, amidst the cries of his famished children and the tears of his wife. Let us break those ties, fatal to the greatest part of mankind, and only useful to a few indolent tyrants. Let us attack injustice at its source. I will return to my natural state of independence, I shall live free and happy on the fruits of my courage and industry. A day of pain and repentance may come, but it will be short; and for an hour of grief I shall enjoy years of pleasure and liberty. King of a small number as determined as myself, I will correct the mistakes of fortune, and I shall see those tyrants grow pale and tremble at the sight of him, whom, with insulting pride, they would not suffer to rank with their dogs and horses."

Religion then presents itself to the mind of this lawless villain, and, promising him almost a certainty of eternal happiness upon the easy terms of repentance, contributes much to lessen the horror of the last scene of the tragedy.

But he who foresees that he must pass a great number of years, even his whole life, in pain and slavery, a slave to those laws by which he was protected, in sight of his fellow-citizens, with whom he lives in freedom and society, makes an useful comparison between those evils, the uncertainty of his success, and the shortness of the time in which he shall enjoy the fruits of his transgression. The example of those wretches, continually before his eyes, makes a much greater impression on him than a punishment, which instead of correcting, makes him more obdurate.

The punishment of death is pernicious to society, from the example of barbarity it affords. If the passions, or the necessity of war, have taught men to shed the blood of their fellow creatures, the laws, which are intended to moderate the ferocity of mankind, should not increase it by examples of barbarity, the more horrible as this punishment is usually attended with formal pageantry. Is it not absurd, that the laws, which detest and punish homicide, should, in order to prevent murder, publicly commit murder themselves? What are the true and most useful laws? Those compacts and conditions which all would propose and observe in those moments when private interest is silent, or combined with that of the public. What are the natural sentiments of every person concerning the punishment of death? We may read them in the contempt and indignation with which every one looks on the executioner, who is nevertheless an innocent executor of the public will, a good citizen, who contributes to the advantage of society, the instrument of the general security within, as good soldiers are without. What then is the origin of this contradiction? Why is this sentiment of mankind indelible to the scandal of reason? It is, that, in a secret corner of the mind, in which the original impressions of nature are still preserved, men discover a sentiment which tells them, that their lives are not lawfully in the power of any one, but of that necessity only which with its iron sceptre rules the universe.

What must men think, when they see wise magistrates and grave ministers of justice, with indifference and tranquillity, dragging a criminal to death, and whilst a wretch trembles with agony, expecting the fatal stroke, the judge, who has condemned him, with the coldest insensibility, and perhaps with no small gratification from the exertion of his authority, quits his tribunal, to enjoy the comforts and pleasures of life? They will say, "Ah! those cruel formalities of justice are a cloak to tyranny, they are a secret language, a solemn veil, intended to conceal the sword by which we are sacrificed to the insatiable idol of despotism. Murder, which they would represent to us an horrible crime, we see practised by them without repugnance or remorse. Let us follow their example. A violent death appeared terrible in their descriptions, but we see that it is the affair of a moment. It will be still less terrible to him who, not expecting it, escapes almost all the pain." Such is the fatal though absurd reasonings of men who are disposed to commit crimes, on whom the abuse of religion has more influence than religion itself.

If it be objected, that almost all nations in all ages have punished certain crimes with death, I answer, that the force of these examples vanishes when opposed to truth, against which prescription is urged in vain. The history of mankind is an immense sea of errors, in which a few obscure truths may here and there be found.

But human sacrifices have also been common in almost all nations. That some societies only either few in number, or for a very short time, abstained from the punishment of death, is rather favourable to my argument; for such is the fate of great truths, that their duration is only as a flash of lightning in the long and dark night of error. The happy time is not yet arrived, when truth, as falsehood has been hitherto, shall be the portion of the greatest number.

I am sensible that the voice of one philosopher is too weak to be heard amidst the clamours of a multitude, blindly influenced by custom; but there is a small number of sages scattered on the face of the earth, who will echo to me from the bottom of their hearts; and if these truths should happily force their way to the thrones of princes be it known to them, that they come attended with the secret wishes of all mankind; and tell the sovereign who deigns them a gracious reception, that his fame shall outshine the glory of conquerors, and that equitable posterity will exalt his peaceful trophies above those of a Titus, an Antoninus, or a Trajan.

How happy were mankind if laws were now to be first formed! now that we see on the thrones of Europe benevolent monarchs, friends to the virtues of peace, to the arts and sciences, fathers of their people, though crowned, yet citizens; the increase of whose authority augments the happiness of their subjects, by destroying that intermediate despotism which intercepts the prayers of the people to the throne. If these humane princes have suffered the old laws to subsist, it is doubtless because they are deterred by the numberless obstacles which oppose the subversion of errors established by the sanction of many ages; and therefore every wise citizen will wish for the increase of their authority. . . .

OF PARDONS

AS punishments become more mild, clemency and pardon are less necessary. Happy the nation in which they will be considered as dangerous! Clemency, which has often been deemed a sufficient substitute for every other virtue in sovereigns, should be excluded in a perfect legislation, where punishments are mild, and the proceedings in criminal cases regular and expeditious. This truth will seem cruel to those who live in countries where, from the absurdity of the laws and the severity of punishments, pardons and the clemency of the prince are necessary. It is indeed one of the noblest prerogatives of the throne, but, at the same time, a tacit disapprobation of the laws. Clemency is a virtue which belongs to the legislator, and not to the executor of the laws; a virtue which ought to shine in the code, and not in private judgment. To shew mankind that crimes are sometimes pardoned, and that punishment is not the necessary consequence, is to nourish the flattering hope of impunity, and is the cause of their considering every punishment inflicted as an act of injustice and oppression. The prince in pardoning gives up the public security in favour of an individual, and, by his ill-judged benevolence, proclaims a public act of impunity. Let, then, the executors of the laws be inexorable, but let the legislator be tender, indulgent, and humane. He is a wise architect who erects his edifice on the foundation of self-love, and contrives that the interest of the public shall be the interest of each individual, who is not obliged, by particular laws and irregular proceedings, to separate the public good from that of individuals, and erect the image of public felicity on the basis of fear and distrust; but, like a wise philosopher, he will permit his brethren to enjoy in quiet that small portion of happiness, which the immense system, established by the first cause, permits them to taste on this earth, which is but a point in the universe.

A small crime is sometimes pardoned if the person offended chooses to forgive the offender. This may be an act of good nature and humanity, but it is contrary to the good of the public: for although a private citizen may dispense with satisfaction for the injury he has received, he cannot remove the necessity of example. The right of punishing belongs not to any individual in particular, but to society in general, or the sovereign. He may renounce his own portion of this right, but cannot give up that of others.

CONCLUSION

I CONCLUDE with this reflection, that the severity of punishments ought to be in proportion to the state of the nation. Among a people hardly yet emerged from barbarity, they should be most severe, as strong impressions are required; but, in proportion as the minds of men become softened by their intercourse in society, the severity of punishments should be diminished, if it be intended that the necessary relation between the object and the sensation should be maintained.

From what I have written results the following general theorem, of considerable utility, though not conformable to custom, the common legislator of nations:

That a punishment may not be an act of violence, of one, or of many, against a private member of society, it should be public, immediate, and necessary, the least possible in the case given, proportioned to the crime, and determined by the laws.

CHAPTER 4

JEREMY BENTHAM

The reading in this chapter is from Jeremy Bentham's *An Introduction to the Principles of Morals and Legislation* ([1823] 1907), pp. 1–5, 24–28, and 170–188; Oxford: Clarendon Press. The first edition of this book was printed in 1780, but it was not published until 1789. The reading comes from the "New Edition," which was published in 1823 and includes Bentham's final revisions. Several minor changes have been made to the text. Most notably, marginal notes and chapter numbers have been excluded, and footnotes have been renumbered and reformatted. On several occasions, Bentham inserts a footnote into a footnote, creating two levels of notes. Where this occurs, the text of the second-level note has been marked by an asterisk (*) and placed immediately after the first-level note.

The Principles of Morals and Legislation is arguably the second most significant work of the classical school of criminology. It was written near the end of the Enlightenment and was published in the same year the French Revolution began. In this work, Bentham increases the precision of the classical school and moves it in the direction of a thoroughly utilitarian framework. The selections presented below include nearly four complete chapters from this book. The first selection presents Bentham's "principle of utility," the basis of his proposed legal reforms. In the second selection, Bentham discusses the distinctions among "physical," "political," "moral," and "religious" sanctions—four "sources of pain and pleasure" that shape our behavior. The third selection provides Bentham's overview of the four general ways in which punishment can violate the principle of utility. He concluded that punishment should not be administered where it is "groundless," "inefficacious," "unprofitable," or "needless." In the final selection, Bentham proposes 13 rules that should guide efforts to determine a just and proportionate punishment for an offense. These rules reiterate and extend several proposals that were supported by Beccaria, but they also deviate from Beccaria's views at a few points.

As noted earlier, it is commonly suggested that the members of the classical school assumed that humans are hedonistic, rational, and free. Regarding the assumption of hedonism, Bentham maintained that humans are "governed by pain and pleasure." Concerning human rationality, he suggested that although some individuals calculate with greater precision than others, "all men calculate," even "madmen." Regarding free will, Bentham's position becomes more complex. Indeed, there is reason to question this assumption as a component of Bentham's work and, more generally, as a defining characteristic of the classical school. For instance, if we are governed by pain and pleasure, if they "determine what we shall do," can we have free will? Bentham suggested that our expectations of pain and pleasure determine our behavior and that these expectations are shaped by many factors. Is this viewpoint ultimately a subtle form of determinism?

from AN INTRODUCTION TO THE PRINCIPLES OF MORALS AND LEGISLATION

by **Jeremy Bentham**

OF THE PRINCIPLE OF UTILITY.

I. NATURE has placed mankind under the governance of two sovereign masters, *pain* and *pleasure*. It is for them alone to point out what we ought to do, as well as to determine what we shall do. On the one hand the standard of right and wrong, on the other the chain of causes and effects, are fastened to their throne. They govern us in all we do, in all we say, in all we think: every effort we can make to throw off our subjection, will serve but to demonstrate and confirm it. In words a man may pretend to abjure their empire: but in reality he will remain subject to it all the while. The *principle of utility*[1] recognises this subjection, and assumes it for the foundation of that system, the object of which is to rear the fabric of felicity by the hands of reason and of law. Systems which attempt to question it, deal in sounds instead of sense, in caprice instead of reason, in darkness instead of light.

But enough of metaphor and declamation: it is not by such means that moral science is to be improved.

II. The principle of utility is the foundation of the present work: it will be proper therefore at the outset to given an explicit and determinate account of what is meant by it. By the principle[2] of utility is meant that principle which approves or disapproves of every action whatsoever, according to the tendency which it appears to have to augment or diminish the happiness of the party whose interest is in question: or, what is the same thing in other words, to promote or to oppose that happiness. I say of every action whatsoever; and therefore not only of every action of a private individual, but of every measure of government.

III. By utility is meant that property in any object, whereby it tends to produce benefit, advantage, pleasure, good, or happiness, (all this in the present case comes to the same thing) or (what comes again to the same thing) to prevent the happening of mischief, pain, evil, or unhappiness to the party whose interest is considered: if that party be

---

1. Note by the Author, July 1822.
To this denomination has of late been added, or substituted, the *greatest happiness* or *greatest felicity* principle: this for shortness, instead of saying at length *that principle* which states the greatest happiness of all those whose interest is in question, as being the right and proper, and only right and proper and universally desirable, end of human action: of human action in every situation, and in particular in that of a functionary or set of functionaries exercising the powers of Government. The word *utility* does not so clearly point to the ideas of *pleasure* and *pain* as the words *happiness* and *felicity* do: nor does it lead us to the consideration of the *number*, of the interests affected; by the *number*, as being the circumstance, which contributes, in the largest proportion, to the formation of the standard here in question; the *standard of right and wrong*, by which alone the propriety of human conduct, in every situation, can with propriety be tried. This want of a sufficiently manifest connexion between the ideas of *happiness* and *pleasure* on the one hand, and the idea of *utility* on the other, I have every now and then found operating, and with but too much efficiency, as a bar to the acceptance, that might otherwise have been given, to this principle.

2. The word principle is derived from the Latin *principium*: which seems to be compounded of the two words *primus*, first, or chief, and *cipium*, a termination which seems to be derived from *capio*, to take, as in *mancipium, municipium*; to which are analogous, *auceps, forceps*, and others. It is a term of very vague and very extensive signification: it is applied to any thing which is conceived to serve as a foundation or beginning to any series of operations: in some cases, of physical operations; but of mental operations in the present case.

The principle here in question may be taken for an act of the mind; a sentiment; a sentiment of approbation; a sentiment which, when applied to an action, approves of its utility, as that quality of it by which the measure of approbation or disapprobation bestowed upon it ought to be governed.

the community in general, then the happiness of the community: if a particular individual, then the happiness of that individual.

IV. The interest of the community is one of the most general expressions that can occur in the phraseology of morals: no wonder that the meaning of it is often lost. When it has a meaning, it is this. The community is a *fictitious body,* composed of the individual persons who are considered as constituting as it were its *members.* The interest of the community then is, what?—the sum of the interests of the several members who compose it.

V. It is in vain to talk of the interest of the community, without understanding what is the interest of the individual.[3] A thing is said to promote the interest, or to be *for* the interest, of an individual, when it tends to add to the sum total of his pleasure: or, what comes to the same thing, to diminish the sum total of his pains.

VI. An action then may be said to be conformable to the principle of utility, or, for shortness sake, to utility, (meaning with respect to the community at large) when the tendency it has to augment the happiness of the community is greater than any it has to diminish it.

VII. A measure of government (which is but a particular kind of action, performed by a particular person or persons) may be said to be conformable to or dictated by the principle of utility, when in like manner the tendency which it has to augment the happiness of the community is greater than any which it has to diminish it.

VIII. When an action, or in particular a measure of government, is supposed by a man to be conformable to the principle of utility, it may be convenient, for the purposes of discourse, to imagine a kind of law or dictate, called a law or dictate of utility: and to speak of the action in question, as being conformable to such law or dictate.

IX. A man may be said to be a partizan of the principle utility, when the approbation or disapprobation he annexes to any action, or to any measure, is determined by and proportioned to the tendency which he conceives it to have to augment or to diminish the happiness of the community: or in other words, to its conformity or unconformity to the laws or dictates of utility.

X. Of an action that is conformable to the principle of utility one may always say either that it is one that ought to be done, or at least that it is not one that ought not to be done. One may say also, that it is right it should be done; at least that it is not wrong it should be done: that it is a right action; at least that it is not a wrong action. When thus interpreted, the words *ought,* and *right* and *wrong,* and others of that stamp, have a meaning: when otherwise, they have none.

XI. Has the rectitude of this principle been ever formally contested? It should seem that it had, by those who have not known what they have been meaning. Is it susceptible of any direct proof? it should seem not: for that which is used to prove every thing else, cannot itself be proved: a chain of proofs must have their commencement somewhere. To give such proof is as impossible as it is needless.

XII. Not that there is or ever has been that human creature breathing, however stupid or perverse, who has not on many, perhaps on most occasions of his life, deferred to it. By the natural constitution of the human frame, on most occasions of their lives men in general embrace this principle, without thinking of it: if not for the ordering of their own actions, yet for the trying of their own actions, as well as of those of other men. There have been, at the same time, not many, perhaps, even of the most intelligent, who have been disposed to embrace it purely and without reserve. There are even few who have not taken some occasion or other to quarrel with it, either on account of their not understanding always how to apply it, or on account of some prejudice or other which they were afraid to examine into, or could not bear to part with. For such is the stuff that man is made of: in principle and in practice, in a right track and in a wrong one, the rarest of all human qualities is consistency.

XIII. When a man attempts to combat the principle of utility, it is with reasons drawn, without his being aware of it, from that very principle itself.[4] His arguments, if they prove any thing, prove not

---

3. Interest is one of those words, which not having any superior *genus,* cannot in the ordinary way be defined.

4. 'The principle of utility, (I have heard it said) is a dangerous principle: it is dangerous on certain occasions to consult it.' This is as much as to say, what? that it is not consonant to utility, to consult utility: in short, that it is *not* consulting it, to consult it.
Addition by the Author, July 1822.
Not long after the publication of the Fragment on Government, anno 1776, in which, in the character of an all-comprehensive and all-commanding principle, the principle of *utility* was brought to view, one person by whom observation to the above effect was made was *Alexander Wedderburn,* at that time Attorney or Solicitor General, afterwards successively Chief Justice of the Common Pleas, and Chancellor of England, under the successive titles of Lord Loughborough and Earl of Rosslyn. It was made—not indeed in my hearing, but in the hearing of a person by whom it was almost immediately communicated to me. So far from being self-contradictory, it was a shrewd and perfectly true one. By that distinguished functionary, the state of the

that the principle is *wrong,* but that, according to the applications he supposes to be made of it, it is *misapplied.* Is it possible for a man to move the earth? Yes; but he must first find out another earth to stand upon. . . .

OF THE FOUR SANCTIONS OR SOURCES OF PAIN AND PLEASURE.

I. IT has been shown that the happiness of the individuals, of whom a community is composed, that is their pleasures and their security, is the end and the sole end which the legislator ought to have in view: the sole standard, in conformity to which each individual ought, as far as depends upon the legislator, to be *made* to fashion his behaviour. But whether it be this or any thing else that is to be *done,* there is nothing by which a man can ultimately be *made* to do it, but either pain or pleasure. Having taken a general view of these two grand objects (*viz.* pleasure, and what comes to the same thing, immunity from pain) in the character of *final* causes; it will be necessary to take a view of pleasure and pain itself, in the character of *efficient* causes or means.

II. There are four distinguishable sources from which pleasure and pain are in use to flow: considered separately, they may be termed the *physical,* the *political,* the *moral,* and the *religious:* and inasmuch as the pleasure and pains belonging to each of them are capable of giving a binding force to any law or rule of conduct, they may all of them be termed sanctions.[5]

III. If it be in the present life, and from the ordinary course of nature, not purposely modified by the interposition of the will of any human being, nor by any extraordinary interposition of any superior invisible being, that the pleasure or the pain takes place or is expected, it may be said to issue from or to belong to the *physical sanction.*

IV. If at the hands of a *particular* person or set of persons in the community, who under names correspondent to that of *judge,* are chosen for the particular purpose of dispensing it, according to the will of the sovereign or supreme ruling power in the state, it may be said to issue from the *political sanction.*

V. If at the hands of such *chance* persons in the community, as the party in question may happen in the course of his life to have concerns with, according to each man's spontaneous disposition, and not according to any settled or concerted rule, it may be said to issue from the *moral* or *popular* sanction.[6]

VI. If from the immediate hand of a superior invisible being, either in the present life, or in a

---

Government was thoroughly understood: by the obscure individual, at that time not so much as supposed to be so: his disquisitions had not been as yet applied, with any thing like a comprehensive view, to the field of Constitutional Law, nor therefore to those features of the English Government, by which the greatest happiness of the ruling *one* with or without that of a favoured few, are now so plainly seen to be the only ends to which the course of it has at any time been directed. The *principle of utility* was an appellative, at that time employed—employed by me, as it had been by others, to designate that which, in a more perspicuous and instructive manner, may, as above, be designated by the name of the *greatest happiness principle.* 'This principle (said Wedderburn) is a dangerous one.' Saying so, he said that which, to a certain extent, is strictly true: a principle, which lays down, as the only *right* and justifiable end of Government, the greatest happiness of the greatest number—how can it be denied to be a dangerous one? dangerous it unquestionably is, to every government which has for its *actual* end or object, the greatest happiness of a certain *one,* with or without the addition of some comparatively small number of others, whom it is matter of pleasure or accommodation to him to admit, each of them, to a share in the concern, on the footing of so many junior partners. *Dangerous* it therefore really was, to the interest—the sinister interest—of all those functionaries, himself included, whose interest it was, to maximize delay, vexation, and expense, in judicial and other modes of procedure, for the sake of the profit, extractible out of the expense. In a Government which had for its end in view the greatest happiness of the greatest number, Alexander Wedderburn might have been Attorney General and then Chancellor: but he would not have been Attorney General with £15,000 a year, nor Chancellor, with a peerage with a veto upon all justice, with £25,000 a year, and with 500 sinecures at his disposal, under the name of Ecclesiastical Benefices, besides *et cæteras.*

5. Sanctio, in Latin, was used to signify the *act of binding,* and, by a common grammatical transition, *any thing which serves to bind a man:* to wit, to the observance of such or such a mode of conduct. According to a Latin grammarian,* the import of the word is derived by rather a far-fetched process (such as those commonly are, and in a great measure indeed must be, by which intellectual ideas are derived from sensible ones) from the word *sanguis,* blood: because, among the Romans, with a view to inculcate into the people a persuasion that such or such a mode of conduct would be rendered obligatory upon a man by the force of what I call the religious sanction (that is, that he would be made to suffer by the extraordinary interposition of some superior being, if he failed to observe the mode of conduct in question) certain ceremonies were contrived by the priests: in the course of which ceremonies the blood of victims was made use of.

A Sanction then is a source of obligatory powers or *motives:* that is, of *pains* and *pleasures;* which, according as they are connected with such or such modes of conduct, operate, and are indeed the only things which can operate, as *motives.* See Chap. x. [Motives].

*Servius. See Ainsworth's Dict. ad verbum *Sanctio.*

6. Better termed *popular,* as more directly indicative of its constituent cause; as likewise of its relation to the more common phrase *public opinion,* in French *opinion publique,* the name there given to that tutelary power, of which of late so much is said, and by which so much is done. The latter appellation is

future, it may be said to issue from the *religious sanction*.

VII. Pleasures or pains which may be expected to issue from the *physical, political,* or *moral* sanctions, must all of them be expected to be experienced, if ever, in the *present* life: those which may be expected to issue from the *religious* sanction, may be expected to be experienced either in the *present* life or in a *future*.

VIII. Those which can be experienced in the present life, can of course be no others than such as human nature in the course of the present life is susceptible of: and from each of these sources may flow all the pleasures or pains of which, in the course of the present life, human nature is susceptible. With regard to these then (with which alone we have in this place any concern) those of them which belong to any one of those sanctions, differ not ultimately in kind from those which belong to any one of the other three: the only difference there is among them lies in the circumstances that accompany their production. A suffering which befalls a man in the natural and spontaneous course of things, shall be styled, for instance, a *calamity;* in which case, if it be supposed to befall him through any imprudence of his, it may be styled a punishment issuing from the physical sanction. Now this same suffering, if inflicted by the law, will be what is commonly called a *punishment;* if incurred for want of any friendly assistance, which the misconduct, or supposed misconduct, of the sufferer has occasioned to be withholden, a punishment issuing from the *moral* sanction; if through the immediate interposition of a particular providence, a punishment issuing from the religious sanction.

IX. A man's goods, or his person, are consumed by fire. If this happened to him by what is called an accident, it was a calamity: if by reason of his own imprudence (for instance, from his neglecting to put his candle out) it may be styled a punishment of the physical sanction: if it happened to him by the sentence of the political magistrate, a punishment belonging to the political sanction; that is, what is commonly called a punishment: if for want of any assistance which his *neighbour* withheld from him out of some dislike to his *moral* character, a punishment of the *moral* sanction: if by an immediate act of *God's* displeasure, manifested on account of some *sin* committed by him, or through any distraction of mind, occasioned by the dread of such displeasure, a punishment of the *religious* sanction.[7]

X. As to such of the pleasures and pains belonging to the religious sanction, as regard a future life, of what kind these may be we cannot know. These lie not open to our observation. During the present life they are matter only of expectation: and, whether that expectation be derived from natural or revealed religion, the particular kind of pleasure or pain, if it be different from all those which lie open to our observation, is what we can have no idea of. The best ideas we can obtain of such pains and pleasures are altogether unliquidated in point of quality. In what other respects our ideas of them *may* be liquidated will be considered in another place.[8]

XI. Of these four sanctions the physical is altogether, we may observe, the ground-work of the political and the moral: so is it also of the religious, in as far as the latter bears relation to the present life. It is included in each of those other three. This may operate in any case, (that is, any of the pains or pleasures belonging to it may operate) independently of *them:* none of *them* can operate but by means of this. In a word, the powers of nature may operate of themselves; but neither the magistrate, nor men at large, *can* operate, nor is God in the case in question *supposed* to operate, but through the powers of nature.

XII. For these four objects, which in their nature have so much in common, it seemed of use to find a common name. It seemed of use, in the first place, for the convenience of giving a name to certain pleasures and pains, for which a name equally characteristic could hardly otherwise have been found: in the second place, for the sake of holding up the efficacy of certain moral forces, the influence of which is apt not to be sufficiently attended to. Does the political sanction exert an influence over the conduct of mankind? The moral, the religious sanctions do so too. In every inch of his career are the operations of the political magistrate liable to be aided or impeded by these two foreign powers: who, one or other of them, or both, are sure to be either his rivals or his allies. Does it happen to him to leave them out in his calculations? he will be sure almost to find himself mistaken in the result. Of all this we shall find abundant proofs in the sequel of this work.

---

however unhappy and inexpressive; since if *opinion* is material, it is only in virtue of the influence it exercises over action, through the medium of the affections and the will.

7. A suffering conceived to befall a man by the immediate act of God, as above, is often, for shortness' sake, called a *judgment*: instead of saying, a suffering inflicted on him in consequence of a special judgment formed, and resolution thereupon taken, by the Deity.

8. See ch. xiii. [Cases unmeet] par. 2, note.

It behoves him, therefore, to have them continually before his eyes; and that under such a name as exhibits the relation they bear to his own purposes and designs. . . .

CASES UNMEET FOR PUNISHMENT.

§1. General view of cases unmeet for punishment.

I. THE general object which all laws have, or ought to have, in common, is to augment the total happiness of the community; and therefore, in the first place, to exclude, as far as may be, every thing that tends to subtract from that happiness: in other words, to exclude mischief.

II. But all punishment is mischief: all punishment in itself is evil. Upon the principle of utility, if it ought at all to be admitted, it ought only to be admitted in as far as it promises to exclude some greater evil.[9]

III. It is plain, therefore, that in the following cases punishment ought not to be inflicted.

1. Where it is *groundless*: where there is no mischief for it to prevent; the act not being mischievous upon the whole.

2. Where it must be *inefficacious*: where it cannot act so as to prevent the mischief.

3. Where it is *unprofitable*, or too *expensive*: where the mischief it would produce would be greater than what it prevented.

4. Where it is *needless*: where the mischief may be prevented, or cease of itself, without it: that is, at a cheaper rate.

§2. Cases in which punishment is groundless.

These are,

IV. 1. Where there has never been any mischief: where no mischief has been produced to any body by the act in question. Of this number are those in which the act was such as might, on some occasions, be mischievous or disagreeable, but the person whose interest it concerns gave his *consent* to the performance of it.[10] This consent, provided it be free, and fairly obtained, is the best proof that can be produced, that, to the person who gives it, no mischief, at least no immediate mischief, upon the whole, is done. For no man can be so good a judge as the man himself, what it is gives him pleasure or displeasure.

V. 2. Where the mischief was *outweighed*: although a mischief was produced by that act, yet the same act was necessary to the production of a benefit which was of greater value[11] than the mischief. This may be the case with any thing that is done in the way of precaution against instant calamity, as also with any thing that is done in the exercise of the several sorts of powers necessary to be established in every community, to wit, domestic, judicial, military, and supreme.[12]

VI. 3. Where there is a certainty of an adequate compensation: and that in all cases where the offence can be committed. This supposes two things: 1. That the offence is such as admits of an adequate compensation: 2. That such a compensation is sure

---

9. What follows, relative to the subject of punishment, ought regularly to be preceded by a distinct chapter on the ends of punishment. But having little to say on that particular branch of the subject, which has not been said before, it seemed better, in a work, which will at any rate be but too voluminous, to omit this title, reserving it for another, hereafter to be published, intituled *The Theory of Punishment.** To the same work I must refer the analysis of the several possible modes of punishment, a particular and minute examination of the nature of each, and of its advantages and disadvantages, and various other disquisitions, which did not seem absolutely necessary to be inserted here. A very few words, however, concerning the *ends* of punishment, can scarcely be dispensed with.

The immediate principal end of punishment is to control action. This action is either that of the offender, or of others: that of the offender it controls by its influence, either on his will, in which case it is said to operate in the way of *reformation;* or on his physical power, in which case it is said to operate by *disablement:* that of others it can influence no otherwise than by its influence over their wills; in which case it is said to operate in the way of *example*. A kind of collateral end, which it has a natural tendency to answer, is that of affording a pleasure or satisfaction to the party injured, where there is one, and, in general, to parties whose ill-will, whether on a self-regarding account, or on the account of sympathy or antipathy, has been excited by the offence. This purpose, as far as it can be answered *gratis*, is a beneficial one. But no punishment ought to be allotted merely to this purpose, because (setting aside its effects in the way of control) no such pleasure is ever produced by punishment as can be equivalent to the pain. The punishment, however, which is allotted to the other purpose, ought, as far as it can be done without expense, to be accommodated to this. Satisfaction thus administered to a party injured, in the shape of a dissocial pleasure,** may be styled a vindictive satisfaction or compensation: as a compensation, administered in the shape of a self-regarding profit, or stock of pleasure, may be styled a lucrative one. See B. I. tit. vi. [Compensation]. Example is the most important end of all, in proportion as the *number* of the persons under temptation to offend is to *one*.

*This is the work which, from the Author's papers, has since been published by Mr. Dumont in French, in company with The *Theory of Reward* added to it, for the purpose of mutual illustration. It is in contemplation to publish them both in English, from the Author's manuscripts, with the benefit of any amendments that have been made by Mr. Dumont. [Note to Edition of 1823.]

**See ch. x. [Motives].

10. See B. I. tit. [Justifications].

11. See supra, ch. iv. [Value].

12. See Book I. tit. [Justifications].

to be forthcoming. Of these suppositions, the latter will be found to be a merely ideal one: a supposition that cannot, in the universality here given to it, be verified by fact. It cannot, therefore, in practice, be numbered amongst the grounds of absolute impunity. It may, however, be admitted as a ground for an abatement of that punishment, which other considerations, standing by themselves, would seem to dictate.[13]

§3. Cases in which punishment must be inefficacious.

These are,

VII. 1. Where the penal provision is *not established* until after the act is done. Such are the cases, 1. Of an *ex-post-facto* law; where the legislator himself appoints not a punishment till after the act is done. 2. Of a sentence beyond the law; where the judge, of his own authority, appoints a punishment which the legislator had not appointed.

VIII. 2. Where the penal provision, though established, is *not conveyed* to the notice of the person on whom it seems intended that it should operate. Such is the case where the law has omitted to employ any of the expedients which are necessary, to make sure that every person whatsoever, who is within the reach of the law, be apprized of all the cases whatsoever, in which (being in the station of life he is in) he can be subjected to the penalties of the law.[14]

IX. 3. Where the penal provision, though it were conveyed to a man's notice, *could produce no effect* on him, with respect to the preventing him from engaging in any act of the *sort* in question. Such is the case, 1. In extreme *infancy*; where a man has not yet attained that state or disposition of mind in which the prospect of evils so distant as those which are held forth by the law, has the effect of influencing his conduct. 2. In *insanity*; where the person, if he has attained to that disposition, has since been deprived of it through the influence of some permanent though unseen cause. 3. In *intoxication*; where he has been deprived of it by the transient influence of a visible cause: such as the use of wine, or opium, or other drugs, that act in this manner on the nervous system: which condition is indeed neither more nor less than a temporary insanity produced by an assignable cause.[15]

X. 4. Where the penal provision (although, being conveyed to the party's notice, it might very well prevent his engaging in acts of the sort in question, provided he knew that it related to those acts) could not have this effect, with regard to the *individual* act he is about to engage in: to wit, because he knows not that it is of the number of those to which the penal provision relates. This may happen, 1. In the case of *unintentionality*; where he intends not to engage, and thereby knows not that he is about to engage, in the *act* in which eventually he is about to engage.[16] 2. In the case of *unconsciousness*; where, although he may know that he is about to engage, in the *act* itself, yet, from not knowing all the material *circumstances* attending it, he knows not of the *tendency* it has to produce that mischief, in contemplation of which it has been made penal in most instances. 3. In the case of *missupposal*; where, although he may know of the tendency the act has to produce that degree of mischief, he supposes it, though mistakenly, to be attended with some circumstance, or set of circumstances, which, if it had been attended with, it would either not have been productive of that mischief, or have been productive of such a greater degree of good, as has determined the legislator in such a case not to make it penal.[17]

---

13. This, for example, seems to have been one ground, at least, of the favour shown by perhaps all systems of laws, to such offenders as stand upon a footing of responsibility: shown, not directly indeed to the persons themselves; but to such offences as none but responsible persons are likely to have the opportunity of engaging in. In particular, this seems to be the reason why embezzlement, in certain cases, has not commonly been punished upon the footing of theft: nor mercantile frauds upon that of common sharping.*

*See tit. [Simple merc. Defraudment].

14. See B. II. Appendix, tit. iii. [Promulgation].

15. Notwithstanding what is here said, the cases of infancy and intoxication (as we shall see hereafter) cannot be looked upon in practice as affording sufficient grounds for absolute impunity. But this exception in point of practice is no objection to the propriety of the rule in point of theory. The ground of the exception is neither more nor less than the difficulty there is of ascertaining the matter of fact: viz. whether at the requisite point of time the party was actually in the state in question; that is, whether a given case comes really under the rule. Suppose the matter of fact capable of being perfectly ascertained, without danger or mistake, the impropriety of punishment would be as indubitable in these cases as in any other.*

The reason that is commonly assigned for the establishing an exemption from punishment in favour of infants, insane persons, and persons under intoxication, is either false in fact, or confusedly expressed. The phrase is, that the will of these persons concurs not with the act; that they have no vicious will; or, that they have not the free use of their will. But suppose all this to be true? What is it to the purpose? Nothing: except in as far as it implies the reason given in the text.

*See B. I. tit. iv. [Exemptions], and tit. vii. [Extenuations].

16. See ch. viii. [Intentionality].

17. See ch. ix. [Consciousness].

XI. 5. Where, though the penal clause might exercise a full and prevailing influence, were it to act alone, yet by the *predominant* influence of some opposite cause upon the will, it must necessarily be ineffectual; because the evil which he sets himself about to undergo, in the case of his *not* engaging in the act, is so great, that the evil denounced by the penal clause, in case of his engaging in it, cannot appear greater. This may happen, 1. In the case of *physical danger;* where the evil is such as appears likely to be brought about by the unassisted powers of *nature.* 2. In the case of a *threatened mischief;* where it is such as appears likely to be brought about through the intentional and conscious agency of man.[18]

XII. 6. Where (though the penal clause may exert a full and prevailing influence over the *will* of the party) yet his *physical faculties* (owing to the predominant influence of some physical cause) are not in a condition to follow the determination of the will: insomuch that the act is absolutely *involuntary.* Such is the case of physical *compulsion* or *restraint*, by whatever means brought about; where the man's hand, for instance, is pushed against some object which his will disposes him *not* to touch; or tied down from touching some object which his will disposes him to touch.

§4. Cases where punishment is unprofitable.

These are,

XIII. 1. Where, on the one hand, the nature of the offence, on the other hand, that of the punishment, are *in the ordinary state of things,* such, that when compared together, the evil of the latter will turn out to be greater than that of the former.

XIV. Now the evil of the punishment divides itself into four branches, by which so many different sets of persons are affected. 1. The evil of *coercion* or *restraint:* or the pain which it gives a man not to be able to do the act, whatever it be, which by the apprehension of the punishment he is deterred from doing. This is felt by those by whom the law is *observed.* 2. The evil of *apprehension:* or the pain which a man, who has exposed himself to punishment, feels at the thoughts of undergoing it. This is felt by those by whom the law has been *broken,* and who feel themselves in *danger* of its being executed upon them. 3. The evil of *sufferance:*[19] or the pain which a man feels, in virtue of the punishment itself, from the time when he begins to undergo it. This is felt by those by whom the law is broken, and upon whom it comes actually to be executed. 4. The pain of sympathy, and the other *derivative* evils resulting to the persons who are in *connection* with the several classes of original sufferers just mentioned.[20] Now of these four lots of evil, the first will be greater or less, according to the nature of the act from which the party is restrained: the second and third according to the nature of the punishment which stands annexed to that offence.

XV. On the other hand, as to the evil of the offence, this will also, of course, be greater or less, according to the nature of each offence. The proportion between the one evil and the other will therefore be different in the case of each particular offence. The cases, therefore, where punishment is unprofitable on this ground, can by no other means be discovered, than by an examination of each particular offence; which is what will be the business of the body of the work.

XVI. 2. Where, although in the *ordinary state* of things, the evil resulting from the punishment is not greater than the benefit which is likely to result from the force with which it operates, during the same space of time, towards the excluding the evil of the offences, yet it may have been rendered so by the influence of some *occasional circumstances.* In the number of these circumstances may be, 1. The multitude of delinquents at a particular juncture; being such as would increase, beyond the ordinary measure, the *quantum* of the second and third lots, and thereby also of a part of the fourth lot, in the evil of the punishment. 2. The extraordinary value of the services of some one delinquent; in the case where the effect of the punishment would be to deprive the community of the benefit of those services. 3. The displeasure of the *people;* that is, of an indefinite number of the members of the *same* community, in cases where (owing to the influence

---

18. The influences of the *moral* and *religious* sanctions, or, in other words, of the motives of *love of reputation* and *religion,* are other causes, the force of which may, upon particular occasions, come to be greater than that of any punishment which the legislator is *able,* or at least which he will *think proper,* to apply. These, therefore, it will be proper for him to have his eye upon. But the force of these influences is variable and different in different times and places: the force of the foregoing influences is constant and the same, at all times and every where. These, therefore, it can never be proper to look upon as safe grounds for establishing absolute impunity: owing (as in the above-mentioned cases of infancy and intoxication) to the impracticability of ascertaining the matter of fact.

19. See ch. v. [Pleasures and Pains].
20. See ch. xii. [Consequences] iv.

of some occasional incident) they happen to conceive, that the offence or the offender ought not to be punished at all, or at least ought not to be punished in the way in question. 4. The displeasure of *foreign powers;* that is, of the governing body, or a considerable number of the members of some *foreign* community or communities, with which the community in question is connected.

§5. Cases where punishment is needless.

These are,

XVII. 1. Where the purpose of putting an end to the practice may be attained as effectually at a cheaper rate: by instruction, for instance, as well as by terror: by informing the understanding, as well as by exercising an immediate influence on the will. This seems to be the case with respect to all those offences which consist in the disseminating pernicious principles in matters of *duty;* of whatever kind the duty be; whether political, or moral, or religious. And this, whether such principles be disseminated *under,* or even *without,* a sincere persuasion of their being beneficial. I say, even *without;* for though in such a case it is not instruction that can prevent the writer from endeavouring to inculcate his principles, yet it may the readers from adopting them: without which, his endeavouring to inculcate them will do no harm. In such a case, the sovereign will commonly have little need to take an active part: if it be the interest of *one* individual to inculcate principles that are pernicious, it will as surely be the interest of *other* individuals to expose them. But if the sovereign must needs take a part in the controversy, the pen is the proper weapon to combat error with, not the sword.

OF THE PROPORTION BETWEEN PUNISHMENTS AND OFFENCES.

I. WE have seen that the general object of all laws is to prevent mischief; that is to say, when it is worth while; but that, where there are no other means of doing this than punishment, there are four cases in which it is *not* worth while.

II. When it *is* worth while, there are four subordinate designs or objects, which, in the course of his endeavours to compass, as far as may be, that one general object, a legislator, whose views are governed by the principle of utility, comes naturally to propose to himself.

III. 1. His first, most extensive, and most eligible object, is to prevent, in as far as it is possible, and worth while, all sorts of offences whatsoever:[21] in other words, so to manage, that no offence whatsoever may be committed.

IV. 2. But if a man must needs commit an offence of some kind or other, the next object is to induce him to commit an offence *less* mischievous, *rather* than one *more* mischievous: in other words, to choose always the *least* mischievous, of two offences that will either of them suit his purpose.

V. 3. When a man has resolved upon a particular offence, the next object is to dispose him to do *no more* mischief than is *necessary* to his purpose: in other words, to do as little mischief as in consistent with the benefit he has in view.

VI. 4. The last object is, whatever the mischief be, which it is proposed to prevent, to prevent it at as *cheap* a rate as possible.

VII. Subservient to these four objects, or purposes, must be the rules or canons by which the proportion of punishments[22] to offences is to be governed.

VIII. Rule 1. The first object, it has been seen, is to prevent, in as far as it is worth while, all sorts of offences; therefore,

The value of the punishment must not be less in any case than what is sufficient to outweigh that of the profit[23] *of the offence.*[24]

---

21. By *offences* I mean, at present, acts which appear to him to have a tendency to produce mischief.

22. The same rules (it is to be observed) may be applied, with little variation, to rewards as well as punishment: in short, to motives in general, which, according as they are of the pleasurable or painful kind, are of the nature of *reward* or *punishment*: and, according as the act they are applied to produce is of the positive or negative kind, are styled impelling or restraining. See ch. x. [Motives] xliii.

23. By the profit of an offence, is to be understood, not merely the pecuniary profit, but the pleasure or advantage, of whatever kind it be, which a man reaps, or expects to reap, from the gratification of the desire which prompted him to engage in the offence.*

It is the profit (that is, the expectation of the profit) of the offence that constitutes the *impelling* motive, or, where there are several, the sum of the impelling motives, by which a man is prompted to engage in the offence. It is the punishment, that is, the expectation of the punishment, that constitutes the *restraining* motive, which, either by itself, or in conjunction with others, is to act upon him in a *contrary* direction, so as to induce him to abstain from engaging in the offence. Accidental circumstances apart, the strength of the temptation is as the force of the seducing, that is, of the impelling motive or motives. To say then, as authors of great merit and great name have said, that the punishment ought not to increase with the strength of the temptation, is as much as to say in mechanics, that the moving force or *momentum* of the *power* need not increase in proportion to the momentum of the *burthen*.

*See ch. x. [Motives] §1.

24. Beccaria, dei diletti, §6. id. trad. par. Morellet, §23.

If it be, the offence (unless some other considerations, independent of the punishment, should intervene and operate efficaciously in the character of tutelary motives[25]) will be sure to be committed notwithstanding:[26] the whole lot of punishment will be thrown away: it will be altogether *inefficacious*.[27]

IX. The above rule has been often objected to, on account of its seeming harshness: but this can only have happened for want of its being properly understood. The strength of the temptation, *cæteris paribus*, is as the profit of the offence: the quantum of the punishment must rise with the profit of the offence: *cæteris paribus*, it must therefore rise with the strength of the temptation. This there is no disputing. True it is, that the stronger the temptation, the less conclusive is the indication which the act of delinquency affords of the depravity of the offender's disposition.[28] So far then as the absence of any aggravation, arising from extraordinary depravity of disposition, may operate, or at the utmost, so far as the presence of a ground of extenuation, resulting from the innocence or beneficence of the offender's disposition, can operate, the strength of the temptation may operate in abatement of the demand for punishment. But it can never operate so far as to indicate the propriety of making the punishment ineffectual, which it is sure to be when brought below the level of the apparent profit of the offence.

The partial benevolence which should prevail for the reduction of it below this level, would counteract as well those purposes which such a motive would actually have in view, as those more extensive purposes which benevolence ought to have in view: it would be cruelty not only to the public, but to the very persons in whose behalf it pleads: in its effects, I mean, however opposite in its intention. Cruelty to the public, that is cruelty to the innocent, by suffering them, for want of an adequate protection, to lie exposed to the mischief of the offence: cruelty even to the offender himself, by punishing him to no purpose, and without the chance of compassing that beneficial end, by which alone the introduction of the evil of punishment is to be justified.

X. Rule 2. But whether a given offence shall be prevented in a given degree by a given quantity of punishment, is never any thing better than a chance; for the purchasing of which, whatever punishment is employed, is so much expended in advance. However, for the sake of giving it the better chance of outweighing the profit of the offence,

The greater the mischief of the offence, the greater is the expense, which it may be worth while to be at, in the way of punishment.[29]

XI. Rule 3. The next object is, to induce a man to choose always the least mischievous of two offences; therefore

Where two offences come in competition, the punishment for the greater offence must be sufficient to induce a man to prefer the less.[30]

XII. Rule 4. When a man has resolved upon a particular offence, the next object is, to induce him to do no more mischief that what is necessary for his purpose: therefore

The punishment should be adjusted in such manner to each particular offence, that for every part of the mischief there may be a motive to restrain the offender from giving birth to it.[31]

---

25. See ch. xi. [Dispositions] xxix.

26. It is a well-known adage, though it is to be hoped not a true one, that every man has his price. It is commonly meant of a man's virtue. This saying, though in a very different sense, was strictly verified by some of the Anglo-Saxon laws: by which a fixed price was set, not upon a man's virtue indeed, but upon his life: that of the sovereign himself among the rest. For 200 shillings you might have killed a peasant: for six times as much, a nobleman: for six-and-thirty times as much you might have killed the king.* A king in those days was worth exactly 7,200 shillings. If then the heir to the throne, for example, grew weary of waiting for it, he had a secure and legal way of gratifying his impatience: he had but to kill the king with one hand, and pay himself with the other, and all was right. An earl Godwin, or a duke Streon, could have bought the lives of a whole dynasty. It is plain, that if ever a king in those days died in his bed, he must have had something else, besides this law, to thank for it. This being the production of a remote and barbarous age, the absurdity of it is presently recognized: but, upon examination, it would be found, that the freshest laws of the most civilized nations are continually falling into the same error.** This, in short, is the case wheresoever the punishment is fixed while the profit of delinquency is indefinite: or, to speak more precisely, where the punishment is limited to such a mark, that the profit of delinquency may reach beyond it.

*Wilkins' Leg. Anglo-Sax. p. 71, 72. See Hume, Vol. I. App. I. p. 219.

**See in particular the *English Statute laws* throughout, *Bonaparte's* Penal Code, and the recently enacted or not enacted *Spanish* Penal Code.—Note by the Author, July 1822.

27. See ch. xiii. [Cases unmeet], §I.

28. See ch. xi. [Dispositions], xlii.

29. For example, if it can ever be worth while to be at the expense of so horrible a punishment as that of burning alive, it will be more so in the view of preventing such a crime as that of murder or incendiarism, than in the view of preventing the uttering of a piece of bad money. See B. I. tit. [Defraudment touching the Coin] and [Incendiarism].

30. Espr. des Loix, L. vi. c. 16.

31. If any one have any doubt of this, let him conceive the offence to be divided into as many separate offences as there are distinguishable parcels of mischief that result from it. Let it consist, for example, in a man's giving you ten blows, or stealing from you ten shillings. If then, for giving you ten blows, he is

XIII. Rule 5. The last object is, whatever mischief is guarded against, to guard against it at as cheap a rate as possible: therefore

The punishment ought in no case to be more than what is necessary to bring it into conformity with the rules here given.

XIV. Rule 6. It is further to be observed, that owing to the different manners and degrees in which persons under different circumstances are affected by the same exciting cause, a punishment which is the same in name will not always either really produce, or even so much as appear to others to produce, in two different persons the same degree of pain: therefore

That the quantity actually inflicted on each individual offender may correspond to the quantity intended for similar offenders in general, the several circumstances influencing sensibility ought always to be taken into account.[32]

XV. Of the above rules of proportion, the four first, we may perceive, serve to mark out the limits on the side of diminution; the limits *below* which a punishment ought not to be *diminished*: the fifth, the limits on the side of increase; the limits *above* which it ought not to be *increased*. The five first are calculated to serve as guides to the legislator: the sixth is calculated, in some measure, indeed, for the same purpose; but principally for guiding the judge in his endeavours to conform, on both sides, to the intentions of the legislator.

XVI. Let us look back a little. The first rule, in order to render it more conveniently applicable to practice, may need perhaps to be a little more particularly unfolded. It is to be observed, then, that for the sake of accuracy, it was necessary, instead of the word *quantity* to make use of the less perspicuous term *value*. For the word *quantity* will not properly include the circumstances either of certainty or proximity: circumstances which, in estimating the value of a lot of pain or pleasure, must always be taken into the account.[33] Now, on the one hand, a lot of punishment is a lot of pain; on the other hand, the profit of an offence is a lot of pleasure, or what is equivalent to it. But the profit of the offence *is* commonly more *certain* than the punishment, or, what comes to the same thing, *appears* so at least to the offender. It is at any rate commonly more *immediate*. It follows, therefore, that, in order to maintain its superiority over the profit of the offence, the punishment must have its value made up in some other way, in proportion to that whereby it falls short in the two points of *certainty* and *proximity*. Now there is no other way in which it can receive any addition to its *value*, but by receiving an addition in point of *magnitude*. Wherever then the value of the punishment falls short, either in point of *certainty*, or of *proximity*, of that of the profit of the offence, it must receive a proportionable addition in point of *magnitude*.[34]

XVII. Yet farther. To make sure of giving the value of the punishment the superiority over that of the offence, it may be necessary, in some cases, to take into the account the profit not only of the *individual* offence to which the punishment is to be annexed, but also of such *other* offences of the *same sort* as the offender is likely to have already committed without detection. This random mode of calculation, severe as it is, it will be impossible to avoid having recourse to, in certain cases: in such, to wit, in which the profit is pecuniary, the chance of detection very small, and the obnoxious act of such a nature as indicates a habit: for example, in the case of frauds against the coin. If it be *not* recurred to, the practice of committing the offence will be sure to be, upon the balance of the account, a gainful practice. That being the case, the legislator will be absolutely sure of *not* being able to suppress it, and the whole punishment that is bestowed upon it will be thrown away. In a word (to keep to the same expressions we set out with) that whole quantity of punishment will be *inefficacious*.

XVIII. Rule 7. These things being considered, the three following rules may be laid down by way of supplement and explanation to Rule 1.

To enable the value of the punishment to outweigh that of the profit of the offence, it must be increased, in point of magnitude, in proportion as it falls short in point of certainty.

---

punished no more than for giving you five, the giving you five of these ten blows is an offence for which there is no punishment at all: which being understood, as often as a man gives you five blows, he will be sure to give you five more, since he may have the pleasure of giving you these five for nothing. In like manner, if for stealing from you ten shillings, he is punished no more than for stealing five, the stealing of the remaining five of those ten shillings is an offence for which there is no punishment at all. This rule is violated in almost every page of every body of laws I have ever seen.

The profit, it is to be observed, though frequently, is not constantly, proportioned to the mischief: for example, where a thief, along with the things he covets, steals others which are of no use to him. This may happen through wantonness, indolence, precipitation, &c. &c.

32. See ch. vi. [Sensibility].

33. See ch. iv. [Value].
34. It is for this reason, for example, that simple compensation is never looked upon as sufficient punishment for theft or robbery.

XIX. Rule 8. *Punishment must be further increased in point of magnitude, in proportion as it falls short in point of proximity.*

XX. Rule 9. *Where the act is conclusively indicative of a habit, such an increase must be given to the punishment as may enable it to outweigh the profit not only of the individual offence, but of such other like offences as are likely to have been committed with impunity by the same offender.*

XXI. There may be a few other circumstances or considerations which may influence, in some small degree, the demand for punishment: but as the propriety of these is either not so demonstrable, or not so constant, or the application of them not so determinate, as that of the foregoing, it may be doubted whether they be worth putting on a level with the others.

XXII. Rule 10. *When a punishment, which in point of quality is particularly well calculated to answer its intention, cannot exist in less than a certain quantity, it may sometimes be of use, for the sake of employing it, to stretch a little beyond that quantity which, on other accounts, would be strictly necessary.*

XXIII. Rule 11. *In particular, this may sometimes be the case, where the punishment proposed is of such a nature as to be particularly well calculated to answer the purpose of a moral lesson.*[35]

XXIV. Rule 12. The tendency of the above considerations is to dictate an augmentation in the punishment: the following rule operates in the way of diminution. There are certain cases (it has been seen[36]) in which, by the influence of accidental circumstances, punishment may be rendered unprofitable in the whole: in the same cases it may chance to be rendered unprofitable as to a part only. Accordingly,

In adjusting the quantum of punishment, the circumstances, by which all punishment may be rendered unprofitable, ought to be attended to.

XXV. Rule 13. It is to be observed, that the more various and minute any set of provisions are, the greater the chance is that any given article in them will not be borne in mind: without which, no benefit can ensue from it. Distinctions, which are more complex than what the conceptions of those whose conduct it is designed to influence can take in, will even be worse than useless. The whole system will present a confused appearance: and thus the effect, not only of the proportions established by the articles in question, but of whatever is connected with them, will be destroyed.[37] To draw a precise line of direction in such case seems impossible. However, by way of memento, it may be of some use to subjoin the following rule.

Among provisions designed to perfect the proportion between punishments and offences, if any occur, which, by their own particular good effects, would not make up for the harm they would do by adding to the intricacy of the Code, they should be omitted.[38]

XXVI. It may be remembered, that the political sanction, being that to which the sort of punishment belongs, which in this chapter is all along in view, is but one of four sanctions, which may all of them contribute their share towards producing the same effects. It may be expected, therefore, that in adjusting the quantity of political punishment, allowance should be made for the assistance it may meet with from those other controlling powers. True it is, that from each of these several sources a very powerful assistance may sometimes be derived. But the case is, that (setting aside the moral sanction, in the case where the force of it is expressly adopted into and modified by the political[39]) the force of those other powers is never determinate enough to be depended upon. It can never be reduced, like political punishment, into exact lots, nor meted out in number, quantity, and value. The legislator is therefore obliged to provide the full complement of punishment, as if he were sure of not receiving any assistance whatever from any of those quarters. If he does, so much the better: but lest he should

---

35. A punishment may be said to be calculated to answer the purpose of a moral lesson, when, by reason of the ignominy it stamps upon the offence, it is calculated to inspire the public with sentiments of aversion towards those pernicious habits and dispositions with which the offence appears to be connected; and thereby to inculcate the opposite beneficial habits and dispositions.

It is this, for example, if any thing, that must justify the application of so severe a punishment as the infamy of a public exhibition, hereinafter proposed, for him who lifts up his hand against a woman, or against his father. See B. I. tit. [Simp. corporal injuries].

It is partly on this principle, I suppose, that military legislators have justified to themselves the inflicting death on the soldier who lifts up his hand against his superior officer.

36. See ch. xiii. [Cases unmeet], §4.

---

37. See B. II. tit. [Purposes], Append. tit. [Composition].

38. Notwithstanding this rule, my fear is, that in the ensuing model, I may be thought to have carried my endeavours at proportionality too far. Hitherto scarce any attention has been paid to it. Montesquieu seems to have been almost the first who has had the least idea of any such thing. In such a matter, therefore, excess seemed more eligible than defect. The difficulty is to invent; that done, if any thing seems superfluous, it is easy to retrench.

39. See B. I. tit. [Punishments].

not, it is necessary he should, at all events, make that provision which depends upon himself.

XXVII. It may be of use, in this place, to recapitulate the several circumstances, which, in establishing the proportion betwixt punishments and offences, are to be attended to. These seem to be as follows:

I. *On the part of the offence:*

1. The profit of the offence;
2. The mischief of the offence;
3. The profit and mischief of other greater or lesser offences, of different sorts, which the offender may have to choose out of;
4. The profit and mischief of other offences, of the same sort, which the same offender may probably have been guilty of already.

II. *On the part of the punishment:*

5. The magnitude of the punishment: composed of its intensity and duration;
6. The deficiency of the punishment in point of certainty;
7. The deficiency of the punishment in point of proximity;
8. The quality of the punishment;
9. The accidental advantage in point of quality of a punishment, not strictly needed in point of quantity;
10. The use of a punishment of a particular quality, in the character of a moral lesson.

III. *On the part of the offender:*

11. The responsibility of the class of persons in a way to offend;
12. The sensibility of each particular offender;
13. The particular merits or useful qualities of any particular offender, in case of a punishment which might deprive the community of the benefit of them;
14. The multitude of offenders on any particular occasion.

IV. *On the part of the public,* at any particular conjuncture:

15. The inclinations of the people, for or against any quantity or mode of punishment;
16. The inclinations of foreign powers.

V. *On the part of the law:* that is, of the public for a continuance:

17. The necessity of making small sacrifices, in point of proportionality, for the sake of simplicity.

XXVIII. There are some, perhaps, who, at first sight, may look upon the nicety employed in the adjustment of such rules, as so much labour lost: for gross ignorance, they will say, never troubles itself about laws, and passion does not calculate. But the evil of ignorance admits of cure:[40] and as to the proposition that passion does not calculate, this, like most of these very general and oracular propositions, is not true. When matters of such importance as pain and pleasure are at stake, and these in the highest degree (the only matters, in short, that can be of importance) who is there that does not calculate? Men calculate, some with less exactness, indeed, some with more: but all men calculate. I would not say, that even a madman does not calculate.[41] Passion calculates, more or less, in every man: in different men, according to the warmth or coolness of their dispositions: according to the firmness or irritability of their minds: according to the nature of the motives by which they are acted upon. Happily, of all passions, that is the most given to calculation, from the excesses of which, by reason of its strength, constancy, and universality, society has most to apprehend:[42] I mean that which corresponds to the motive of pecuniary interest: so that these niceties, if such they are to be called, have the best chance of being efficacious, where efficacy is of the most importance.

---

40. See Append. tit. [Promulgation].
41. There are few madmen but what are observed to be afraid of the strait waistcoat.
42. See ch. xii. [Consequences], xxxiii.

PART TWO

PHYSIOGNOMY, PHRENOLOGY, AND THE ITALIAN SCHOOL

During the mid- to late nineteenth century, the Italian school of positive criminology emerged in opposition to the classical school. Ironically, Beccaria, an Italian whose work defines much of the classical school, became a target for later Italian scholars who envisioned a more thoroughly scientific criminology. For the founders of the Italian school, the classical school overestimated the extent to which criminals have free will and failed to make systematic observations regarding possible biological, psychological, social, and environmental (telluric) causes of crime. In contrast, the Italian school explicitly embraced determinism, conducted many empirical studies, and presented its arguments using a more developed scientific vocabulary. Although the members of the classical school embraced determinism more than is generally acknowledged (see Beirne 1993), it is true that they provided few systematic empirical studies of crime. The Italian school, thus, identified a void in its predecessor's paradigm, and given the growing acceptance of the natural sciences and the common concern regarding social disorder (including crime), it also had an audience that was primed to listen to its proposals.

The Italian school represents just one branch of positive criminology,[1] and positive criminology, as a whole, can be viewed as just one of many frameworks that exist within a much broader tradition of positivism. This tradition extends across several fields, takes many different forms, and thus lacks a single, precise meaning. Focusing primarily on the field of sociology, Peter Halfpenny (1982) identified 12 different meanings of positivism, and there is little doubt that his list could be extended considerably with the examination of other fields. Multiple meanings of positivism have existed from the time Auguste Comte described this framework in his writings on "positive philosophy" and "positive polity" (see Comte [1830–1842] 1893, [1851–1854] 1966). Halfpenny argued that within Comte's work, the term *positivism* is used in at least four distinct ways, and of course, it became even more

---

1. Other forms of positive criminology can be found in the writings of the moral statisticians and the scholars of the nineteenth-century French school (described in Part Three).

ambiguous as it was adopted and used by other theorists. To simplify matters, it may be argued that positivism is just science, but this does not get us very far, for *science* itself is an elusive term. Historically the label "science" has been attached to many different kinds of information and numerous methods. Johann Caspar Lavater (1840:37), for instance, extends this label to "mathematics," "experimental philosophy," "physic(s)," "theology," and "belles lettres."

Fortunately, for purposes of this inquiry, there is no need to identify and evaluate all the different forms of positivism. The focus here is on the birth of criminology. In this context it is enough to note that while the term is used in different ways, most of its uses in this field appear to have four things in common. First, most forms of positivism in criminology assume that our behavior, individual or collective, is shaped by natural causes of one kind or another (e.g., biological, psychological, or social factors); free will is denied or significantly limited, and supernatural causes, such as spirits, are excluded from consideration. Second, they hold that these causal factors have a consistent effect on behavior; in other words, law-like relationships exist between phenomena. Third, they emphasize that these causes can be identified through systematic observation, especially through the application of the methods of the natural sciences, or at least the presumed methods of the natural sciences. Put differently, methods of interpretive understanding have little or no place within this paradigm. Finally, most conceptions of positivism in criminology suggest that upon identifying the causes of crime, we often have the capacity to alter them and, thus, change the course of individual or collective behavior. Hence control of behavior is perhaps their most common practical objective.[2] These qualities, to varying degrees, were embraced not only by members of the Italian school but also by the early moral statisticians and members of the nineteenth-century French school. Nonetheless, it is the development of the Italian school that is our present concern.

One of the more interesting historical facts about the Italian school is that it preserved in a new "scientific" form the ancient tradition of

---

2. It may be argued that most branches of positivism in criminology apply an orientation that is primarily logical and empirical, and thus an additional quality should be added to this list—namely, an emphasis on following the rules of logic. This quality may be prominent in the work of some positivists. However, in practice, many positivists in criminology and other social sciences have a tendency to dismiss logic in favor of poor empirical data. Consider, for instance, the importance that is often bestowed upon self-report data when theories of deviance are tested; it defies logic in many instances (see DiCristina 2006). To have a logically consistent empirical test of a theory, the assumptions of the data-collection technique must be more plausible than the theory. With self-report data, it frequently is assumed that people will provide largely accurate information about their own deviant behavior to strangers (i.e., to the researchers conducting the self-report survey). This is a very questionable assumption, and where this assumption is less plausible than the theory being tested, logic is sacrificed in favor of inadequate data. Indeed, in such cases, it makes more sense to view the theory as the hard fact against which a speculative data set is being tested. Given this and other issues regarding the quality of crime data, I have excluded logic as a defining characteristic of positivism in criminology. As suggested earlier, this represents a point at which the classical school may be distinguished from the positive school, since, arguably, the classical school as a whole occupied itself more with logic (reason) than with the systematic collection and analysis of empirical data.

associating deviant inclinations with the physical appearance of individuals. Theories that include this contention—that is, physical appearance theories—propose that dishonest and dangerous people commonly have one or more distinctive physical characteristics. Accordingly, from an examination of the facial features, skull configuration, or various other dimensions of a person's body (e.g., arm length), it would be possible to determine whether or not the individual posed a threat to other people. This assumption has a long history and is central to physiognomy, phrenology, and the atavist theory of the Italian school. The readings that follow this introduction illustrate the changing content of physical appearance theories over the course of the eighteenth and nineteenth centuries and the place of this kind of theory within the Italian school. But, just as important, the readings also highlight that the work of this school goes well beyond physical appearance research and even includes a noteworthy interdisciplinary orientation.

Physiognomy

Physiognomy proposes that important elements of an individual's character, including vicious and virtuous inclinations, are reflected in his/her facial features. Other parts of the body may reflect various traits as well, but the focus of physiognomy generally is on facial features. For example, a close examination of a person's eyes or nose may reveal a tendency to be deceitful or an inclination for theft; likewise, the shape of a person's chin may suggest a cowardly disposition. The actual proposals, of course, differ somewhat from one physiognomist to another, and the development of this discipline entailed many reinterpretations of the various facial features. This is a very old discipline; it has been around at least since the time of the ancient Greeks. Socrates was examined by a physiognomist (and received an unfavorable evaluation) more than two thousand years ago, and discussions of physiognomy can be found in the works of Pythagoras and Aristotle (see Evans 1941; Tsouna 1998). The interest in physiognomy continued through the Middle Ages and was maintained during the Renaissance in part through the contributions of Giambattista della Porta. It then persisted into the Enlightenment, where it perhaps was best represented in the work of Johann Caspar Lavater.

Lavater (1741–1801) was born in Zürich, Switzerland, and received an education in theology.[3] He was a pastor who wrote extensively on physiognomy and attempted to affirm its relevance and scientific standing. Over the course of his career, he became the most prominent physiognomist of the eighteenth century. Lavater and his work were well known throughout Europe. His *Essays on Physiognomy*, first published in German during the 1770s, received a level of attention that was comparable to Beccaria's *On Crimes and Punishments*. As John Graham (1961:562) notes, it "was reprinted, abridged, summarized, pirated, parodied, imitated, and reviewed so often that it is difficult to imagine how a literate person of the time could have failed to have some general knowledge of the man and his

---

3. The following information on Lavater is based primarily on Graham (1961), Staum (1995), and Percival (2003).

theories."[4] In fact, it has been reported that Charles Darwin was almost denied passage on the *H.M.S. Beagle* because the captain accepted Lavater's views and questioned whether someone with a nose like Darwin's could complete the trip (Graham 1961).

It is relatively easy to understand the popularity of Lavater's work in eighteenth-century Europe. This was a time when Christianity was struggling to maintain its influence and natural science was emerging as a competing worldview. Lavater's physiognomy, being an expression of his theological training and his interest in science, could accommodate both causes to some degree; it "seemed to reconcile any conflict between science and religion, placing the former at the service of the latter" (Graham 1961:563). His physiognomy was not a materialist theory; for Lavater, the face is the "magic mirror of the soul" (in Staum 1995:446). In addition, physiognomy, like other physical appearance paradigms (e.g., phrenology and atavist theory), could be used for political purposes to categorize certain segments of the population as either good citizens or inferiors who threaten the "proper" social order.[5] Finally, another, more aesthetic, reason for the popularity of Lavater's *Essays* has been suggested (Graham 1961; Percival 2003): The early editions of this work were "richly illustrated" and "appealed to the tastes of a wealthy audience" (Percival 2003:78). They were, in a sense, works of art.

Chapter 5 presents an excerpt from the third edition of Lavater's *Essays on Physiognomy* (1840). In this selection, Lavater attempts to defend physiognomy as a science by reexamining an illustration of the countenance of Socrates. Long before the work of Lavater, the physiognomist Zopyrus examined Socrates and concluded that he had many deviant character traits; specifically, he was found to be "stupid, brutal, sensual, and addicted to drunkenness" (Lavater 1840:113). This conclusion had been used by critics of physiognomy to discredit the discipline. In response to these critics, Lavater provides a reinterpretation of Socrates's facial features in an attempt to highlight Zopyrus's mistakes and reaffirm the relevance of physiognomy as a means for judging the character of an individual.

Throughout much of its history, the development of physiognomy occurred together with the science of the era. From the beginning it incorporated an impression of science, a hint of determinism, and some rudimentary component of empirical inquiry. Accordingly, to the extent that it offered an explanation of criminal behavior, it represented a precursor to positive criminology.[6] Nonetheless, during the Enlightenment, physiognomists'

---

4. John Graham (1961:562) continues: "By 1810, there had been published sixteen German, fifteen French, two American, one Dutch, one Italian, and no less than twenty English versions—a total of fifty-five editions in less than forty years."

5. Martin Staum (1995) points out that physiognomy, and later phrenology, had some appeal for both conservatives and liberals. The conservative potential of these disciplines for designating certain groups as inferior and rationalizing social hierarchies is obvious, but they also appeared to attract favorable attention from many liberals. The liberal appeal of physiognomy and phrenology stemmed from their scientific appearance. Nevertheless, from a contemporary standpoint, they typically are classified as conservative paradigms and pseudosciences.

6. According to Staum (1995:446), ". . . Lavater thought maximum knowledge of indelible, excessive passions would come from studying inmates of prisons or asylums." Whether or not Lavater ever attempted such a study is unclear.

claims of being scientific frequently were rejected and the discipline ultimately was classified as a pseudoscience. This, however, was not the end of physiognomy—not entirely at least. At the beginning of the nineteenth century, it was reconfigured into a more scientific form: phrenology. Although it has been noted that Hippocrates, the "father of medicine," had an influence on the early development of physiognomy (Evans 1941; Tsouna 1998), phrenology was more "distinctly medical" in its origin and was based more extensively on empirical research (Riegel 1933). This, combined with the fact that it also was more materialistic and deterministic, and embraced a more elaborate theory of brain functioning, helped to elevate its status as a "science" above that of physiognomy.

Phrenology

Phrenology—also known as craniology, cranioscopy, and organology—proposes that an individual's intellectual and moral tendencies are reflected in his/her skull configuration.[7] Specifically, it assumes that the human mind consists of different faculties (intellectual and moral) that are located in different parts ("organs") of the brain. The brain is held to be the material basis of the mind. Each part of the brain is said to vary in size according to the strength of the faculty it represents. For instance, when a given faculty is strong, its part of the brain will be larger; when it is weak, its part will be smaller. In turn, the shape of the brain is said to determine the shape of the skull. Where a given part of the brain is relatively large, the area of the skull that covers it will protrude; where a given part is relatively small, the corresponding area of the skull will recede. Therefore, by examining the shape of someone's skull, one should be able to assess the relative strength of the person's intellectual and moral faculties. For example, it would be possible to estimate the strength of a person's instinct to kill or to possess things, and thus one could infer a given propensity for violent or property crime.

This "science" was first established by Franz Joseph Gall (1758–1828) at the end of the eighteenth century and was further developed by other researchers—most notably, Johann Gaspar Spurzheim (Gall's assistant and collaborator) and George Combe.[8] Gall was born in Tiefenbronn, Germany, into a relatively wealthy and well-respected family.[9] In 1781, he moved to Vienna, Austria, where he lived until the first years of the 1800s. There he earned a doctorate in medicine, established a private medical practice, and gradually constructed most of his phrenological perspective.[10] However, the materialism of his viewpoint brought criticism from the Catholic Church and

---

7. The following information on phrenology is based on Riegel (1933), Critchley (1965), Young (1968), Staum (1995), van Wyhe (2002), Rafter (2005), and Simpson (2005).

8. In phrenology, Spurzheim, perhaps more than any other phrenologist, is responsible for the idea that the faculties of the mind can be altered over the course of an individual's life (see Staum 1995; Rafter 2005). Accordingly, to the extent that these malleable faculties are a source of criminality, criminals can be rehabilitated.

9. The following information on Gall comes from several sources, including Critchley (1965); Young (1968); Savitz, Turner, and Dickman (1977); Staum (1995); van Wyhe (2002); and Simpson (2005).

10. Gall was more inclined to describe his work as organology, the physiology of the brain, or the doctrine of the skull, rather than phrenology (see van Wyhe 2002:22).

the Holy Roman Emperor, Francis II, who placed a ban on his lectures and publications.[11] In response, Gall left Vienna in 1805, went on an extended lecture tour through several countries in Europe, and ultimately made Paris his home in 1807.

Gall was one of the first researchers to conduct systematic empirical inquiries into the localization of mental faculties in different parts of the brain. By the end of his career, he held that there were at least 27 brain organs, each of which represents a specific mental faculty. The number of these organs was later increased by other phrenologists—most notably, Spurzheim. Nonetheless, in Gall's conceptual scheme there are various organs that increase the propensity for crime. As suggested earlier, there is an organ that represents a disposition to kill and another associated with theft, and the strength of these dispositions in an individual, according to Gall, can be estimated through an examination of the person's skull. Overall, Gall's phrenological research and theory warrant recognition. His work offered psychology a distinctive biological orientation, it anticipated nineteenth-century evolutionary theory, and it contributed to the development of cerebral localization theory in the neurosciences (see Critchley 1965; Young 1968; Simpson 2005). Moreover, it arguably established Gall as one of the first "scientific criminologists" (Critchley 1965:780; also see Savitz, Turner, and Dickman 1977).

The reading in Chapter 6 comes from Gall's *On the Functions of the Brain and of Each of Its Parts* (1835). This is a six-volume work that was completed in 1825, but it was not published in English until seven years after Gall's death. The selected reading is from Volume IV, which is entitled *Organology*. In this reading, Gall offers his thoughts on the "carnivorous instinct" and provides an example of phrenological reasoning that correlates a disposition to kill with a particular skull configuration.

Phrenology, much like physiognomy, had many critics and lacked credibility. The empirical support for many of its conclusions was weak, and the phrenologists after Gall gradually drifted away from the discipline's empirical roots; they came to resemble fortune tellers more than scientists (see Riegel 1933; Critchley 1965; Young 1968; Rafter 2005). In addition, as a physical appearance paradigm, phrenology was laden with political implications and could be used to help rationalize class, gender, and racial hierarchies. As Martin Staum (1995:455) notes, "Gall was far from egalitarian and apparently ready to freeze the social hierarchy." It also appears that Gall did not embrace democracy (see Critchley 1965:780). Nonetheless, in its initial form (especially as it was developed by Gall), phrenology had an influence on theories of anatomy, the neurosciences, and psychology. Moreover, given its proposal of biopsychological causes of crime and its emphasis on empirical inquiry, it made a contribution to the development of positive criminology. In fact, Nicole Rafter (2005:65–66) concludes that the nineteenth-century phrenologists provided "the first comprehensive explanation of criminal behavior," helped alter popular conceptions of "criminal responsibility," and supported crime prevention through means of rehabilitation and incapacitation.

---

11. In his research on this matter, van Wyhe (2002:25) concluded, "there is no evidence that the Viennese clergy opposed Gall's system."

The framework of phrenology represented a noteworthy alternative to the deterrence philosophy of the classical school as well as the retributive views held by Kant and others.

The Italian School

Within the emerging field of criminology, the theories of phrenology eventually gave way to a more elaborate physical appearance theory—atavist theory, the first prominent theory of the Italian school of positive criminology. Cesare Lombroso, the primary founder of the Italian school, developed atavist theory early in his career. An atavist is a throwback to an earlier stage of evolution, someone "who reproduces in his person the ferocious instincts of primitive humanity and the inferior animals" (Lombroso 1911:xv). Lombroso maintained that such a person is more likely to engage in crime than a "normal" person.[12] He also proposed that atavists have a set of physical characteristics that are less evolved; such characteristics may include a retreating forehead, large ears, excessive dimensions of the jaw and cheekbone, and unusually long arms. Thus, from an examination of the facial features, skull configuration, and general dimensions of a person body, it would be possible to determine whether or not the person is an atavist and, hence, a "born criminal." Once an atavist is identified, he or she may then be incapacitated and thus denied the opportunity to harm other members of society. The deterministic nature of this theory is clear, and Lombroso and his disciples conducted many empirical studies in an effort to identify the defining characteristics of these born criminals. However, it would be a mistake to define Lombroso's career in terms of this theory alone, and it would be even more of a mistake to present it as the only theory of the Italian school. The Italian school was shaped by the work of not only Lombroso but also Enrico Ferri, Raffaele Garofalo, and other Italian scholars (e.g., William Ferrero). But let us return to Lombroso.

Cesare Lombroso (1835–1909) was born in Verona, Italy.[13] He studied at several universities, received degrees in both medicine and surgery, and went on to become a professor of psychiatry and of criminal anthropology at the University of Turin. He may have been the most visible criminologist of his era. "In the history of criminology," writes Marvin E. Wolfgang (1972:232), "probably no name has been eulogized or attacked so much as that of Cesare Lombroso." Lombroso was a critic of the classical school and the most prominent advocate of criminal anthropology, the best-known branch of the Italian school.[14] Criminal anthropology, especially as it initially was established,

---

12. Marvin Wolfgang (1972:247) as well as George Vold and Thomas Bernard (1986:37) note that Charles Darwin, in *The Descent of Man* (1871), presented a comparable idea. At about the same time as Lombroso, Darwin stated that some people may be "reversions to a savage state." However, Lombroso (1895–1896:35) later wrote that the core contention of his atavist theory came to him in 1864 during an autopsy that he was performing on a well-known criminal: "I instantly perceived that the criminal must be a survival of the primitive man and the carnivorous animals."

13. One of the better overviews of Lombroso's career is provided by Wolfgang (1972). Also see Vold and Bernard (1986).

14. Criminal anthropology often is treated as synonymous with this school, although such a treatment tends to discount the contributions of Ferri and Garofalo.

emphasized biological and psychological factors as causes of crime, and it maintained that these factors could be identified through careful scientific research.

Lombroso's viewpoint reflects a combination of German materialism, the positivism of Comte, and the evolutionary theory of Darwin (see Wolfgang 1972). He conducted most of his research during the mid- to late 1800s, and he published the first edition of his most important work, *Criminal Man*, in 1876. The fifth and final edition of this work appeared in three volumes over the years 1896 and 1897. While Lombroso is probably best known for his atavist theory, his research went well beyond the study of atavism and crime. In his later work, he acknowledged several different kinds of criminals; he proposed additional biological and psychological causes of crime; and he gave more attention to the possible influence of various social and environmental factors, although the biological and psychological causes seemingly retained more importance within his perspective. Regarding his policy views, Lombroso generally agreed with the classical school's emphasis on designing punishments to protect society, but he rejected its deterrence philosophy. Specifically, he advocated individualized penal responses based primarily on the type of offender rather than the crime. He held that atavists, upon committing a crime (even a minor crime), should be "confined for life," whereas "occasional criminals" often can be, and should be, reformed (see Lombroso 1895–1896:46).

The readings in Chapter 7 are from the work of Lombroso. In the first selection, "Criminal Anthropology: Its Origin and Application" (1895–1896), Lombroso presents a concise history of the development of his perspective and its use in various nations. The second selection is a chapter from *The Female Offender* ([1893] 1903), a book that Lombroso coauthored with his son-in-law, William Ferrero. The chapter is entitled "The Criminal Type in Women and Its Atavistic Origin" and provides some of Lombroso's controversial conclusions regarding female criminality.

Arguably the second most important contributor to the Italian school of positive criminology was Enrico Ferri (1856–1929).[15] Compared to Lombroso, Ferri gave more weight to social factors as causes of crime and, therefore, applied the label "criminal sociology" to his branch of the Italian school. Indeed, when Lombroso broadened his viewpoint, it was due in part to the influence of Ferri (see Lombroso 1911).[16] Ferri was born into a family of modest means in San Benedetto Po, Italy. He received a law degree from the University of Bologna in 1877, and he later studied with Lombroso at the University of Turin. Ferri had a very active career as a lawyer, professor, and politician. In his most famous case as a lawyer, he successfully defended a group of poor farmers who had revolted against the inhumane conditions they experienced and who subsequently were accused of initiating a civil war.

---

15. The following information on Ferri is based on several sources, including Sellin (1972), Vold and Bernard (1986), and Beck (2005).

16. It is likely that Lombroso's expanding viewpoint also was due to a growing awareness of the history of criminology (e.g., early-nineteenth-century ideas on the relationship between social factors and crime) and harsh criticisms of his atavist theory (see Lindesmith and Levin 1937).

As a professor, Ferri taught penal law at universities in Bologna, Siena, Pisa, and Rome. He also became a member of the Italian Socialist Party and served in the Italian Parliament for many years.

For much of his life, Ferri supported a Marxist version of scientific socialism, a viewpoint that centers on an integration of Marxism and the evolutionary theories of Charles Darwin and Herbert Spencer (see Beck 2005). However, late in his career Ferri's political orientation began to shift and he eventually left the Socialist Party. He reportedly attempted to get socialists to collaborate with Benito Mussolini's fascist movement and altered his evolutionary theory in a way that made fascism a stage of social evolution following socialism (see Beck 2005:320–322). Referring to the founders of the classical school, Ferri once stated, "... the revolutionary of yesterday is very often the conservative of to-day" (Ferri 1898:xvii). Interestingly, his work combined revolutionary and conservative ideas into a single framework; he thus could be viewed as serving both ends of the political spectrum simultaneously.

Ferri's contribution to the Italian school was significant, though perhaps not as interesting as his broader political views. His most important work was *Criminal Sociology*, which was first published in 1881 under a different title. Overall five editions were published, the last of which appeared in two volumes during the years 1929 and 1930. In his work, Ferri explicitly embraced an interdisciplinary approach to the study of crime. He argued that crime was caused by the interaction of three factors: "anthropological" (biological and psychological factors), "telluric" or "physical" (e.g., natural resources and climate), and "social" (e.g., economic, political, and cultural conditions). He retained the anthropological categories of "born" and "insane" criminals but also emphasized the existence of "habitual," "occasional," and "passionate" criminals. Accordingly, on policy matters, he maintained that efforts to reduce crime should not focus exclusively on the biological and psychological characteristics of offenders because the social environment often is the key source of criminality and may need to be changed.

Ferri provides a useful summary of his viewpoint in a 1901 lecture on the causes of criminal behavior, a lecture that was later published in *The Positive School of Criminology* ([1901] 1913). This lecture is presented in Chapter 8.

Of the other researchers who made contributions to the development of the Italian school, Baron Raffaele Garofalo (1852–1934) is the most noteworthy.[17] Garofalo was born into a noble family in Naples, Italy, and eventually was given the title of Baron. Like Ferri, he received a formal education in law and had a successful legal and political career. Professionally, he served as a prosecutor and magistrate, was a member of the Senate of Italy, and taught criminal law and procedure at the University of Naples. In his writings, he promoted a more consistently conservative branch of the Italian school, and his views were commonly at odds with those of Ferri.[18] Garofalo's best-known work, *Criminology*, was first published in 1885 and was revised and

---

17. The following information on Garofalo is largely based on Allen (1972) and Vold and Bernard (1986).
18. Garofalo's opposition to Ferri's viewpoint is perhaps best represented in his book *The Socialist Superstition* (*La Superstition socialiste*, 1895).

updated on several occasions. In his preface to the English edition, Garofalo ([1914] 1968:xxix), using a language that is still common in the political realm, declared, "The time has come to proclaim warfare on crime in the name of civilization. . . ." He then proceeded to propose: "The task of the twentieth century is to eradicate those traces of primitive barbarity which we know as criminality" (p. xxx).

Like Lombroso and Ferri, Garofalo applauded experimental science and was interested in reforming the existing systems of justice. However, his viewpoint arguably represented another distinct branch of the Italian school, and not simply because he may have been more conservative than the other major contributors. Whereas Lombroso described his views as criminal anthropology and Ferri emphasized the importance of criminal sociology, Garofalo, at least by the early 1900s, suggested that his views centered primarily on "criminal psychology." In this way, he separated his viewpoint somewhat from theories that give more weight to physical appearances or social factors (see Garofalo [1914] 1968:xxx–xxxi).[19] Nevertheless, perhaps his most important contribution to not only the Italian school but also to criminology in general was his "sociologic notion of crime"—specifically, his theory of "the natural crime." Garofalo had noted that criminologists were attempting to scientifically describe criminals without having a clear scientific conception of crime. This, of course, is a serious problem, since we cannot reasonably identify a criminal before we have a clear image of crime. In part through an application of Spencer's theory of social evolution, which was well known in Italy during the late 1800s, Garofalo ([1914] 1968:43–44) attempted to specify "the true crimes of contemporary society." He held that such crimes are "natural crimes," and a true science of criminology will focus on such crimes and the people who commit them.[20] From Garofalo's viewpoint, people who commit natural crimes because they have deficient moral sentiments are true criminals, and such people often need to be removed from society (e.g., by means of the death penalty or some other form of incapacitation). The reading in Chapter 9 is from Garofalo's discussion of "The Natural Crime," the first chapter of his *Criminology*.

Today discussions of the Italian school of positive criminology can prompt mixed reactions from scholars. On the one hand, it was scarred by its atavist theory, its claims regarding the inferiority of some races (and other populations),[21] and its support for physical appearance research, which continued

---

19. Garofalo ([1914] 1968:xxxii–xxxiii) suggested that some environmental conditions contribute to crime, but he discounted efforts to change them as a means to reduce crime: "(T)he contention that, in lieu of punishing, we should aim to modify the environment and thus suppress the causes of crime, is not one entitled to serious regard. The law-maker cannot accomplish that which is the work of time alone."

20. Émile Durkheim, a representative of the nineteenth-century French school of criminology, was critical of Garofalo's theory of the natural crime, but there is little doubt that it had an influence on Durkheim's own sociological conception of crime (see Durkheim [1893] 1984). The work of Durkheim is examined in Part Three.

21. Nicole Rafter (2008:302) notes: "To criminal anthropologists, the crime problems of southern Italy—the Mafia, the Camorra, and brigandage—proved that Sicilians, Sardinians and other inhabitants of the lower third of the country were racially inferior to the law-abiding citizens of the North."

for several decades after the death of Lombroso. Large-scale efforts to identify a relationship between physical appearances and crime were undertaken until the mid-twentieth century. The studies of Ernst Kretschmer (1921, 1951), Earnest Hooton (1939), and William Sheldon (1949) are among the most noteworthy. However, the physical appearance theories that emerged from this research, like their forerunners, were constructed on a weak empirical foundation. These theories were especially problematic when combined with the hereditary assumptions that supported the eugenics movement. Thus, when confronted by the atrocities of World War II and a growing concern for human rights during the mid-1900s,[22] they were pushed to the margins of criminology. In addition, while individuals on the political left generally find physical appearance theories to be offensive, those on the right often oppose the Italian school's secular orientation and the inclination of some of its members to support socialism. Lombroso, reportedly, favored socialist reforms (see Wolfgang 1972:238), and Ferri, as noted, advocated a Marxist form of scientific socialism.

On the other hand, the Italian school, in its later formulations (especially in the work of Ferri), supported an interdisciplinary orientation, a framework that appears to be reemerging with greater clarity within criminology today. Moreover, it placed a heavy emphasis on systematic observation and, thereby, added momentum to the development of scientific methods in the field. It was not the first branch of criminology to embrace the spirit of the natural sciences and, in practice, its methods often lacked rigor and sophistication, but it certainly promoted a scientific orientation and is partially responsible for its current prominence in the field. Of course, while this is a progressive quality for contemporary criminologists who embrace positivism, it is yet another problem for researchers who favor interpretive methods and other forms of inquiry that deviate considerably from the rules of positivism.

Before proceeding, one additional point must be noted. The perspectives of phrenology and the Italian school are connected to the development of both psychological theories and hereditary theories. Gall, as noted earlier, has been credited with giving psychology a biological framework; Lombroso was a professor of psychiatry who wrote extensively on insanity and crime;[23] and Garofalo's viewpoint placed an emphasis on "criminal psychology." In addition, Lombroso concluded that heredity is an important "organic cause of criminal tendencies" (see Lombroso-Ferrero 1911:137–139), and Garofalo ([1914] 1968) suggested that biological evolution plays a major role in the historical development of criminal law. Nevertheless, for the reader who wishes to develop a better understanding of the early development of criminal psychology (especially moral insanity), it is useful to explore the works of Benjamin Rush ([1786] 1947, 1806), Philippe Pinel ([1806] 1962), James Cowles Prichard (1835), and Isaac Ray ([1838] 1962). Nicole Rafter (2004) provides a helpful analysis of the importance of these theorists to the development of criminology. For readers interested in the early theories and

---

22. In 1948, the General Assembly of the United Nations adopted the Universal Declaration of Human Rights.

23. In fact, in 2004, the *American Journal of Psychiatry* acknowledged and briefly summarized Lombroso's place in the history of psychiatry (Carrà and Barale 2004).

research on the relationship between heredity and crime, the works of Richard L. Dugdale (1877), Francis Galton (1883), and, moving into the early twentieth century, Charles Goring ([1913] 1972) are useful starting points.

REFERENCES
Allen, Francis A. 1972. "Raffaele Garofalo: 1852–1934." In *Pioneers in Criminology*, 2nd ed., edited by Herman Mannheim, 318–340. Montclair, NJ: Patterson Smith.
Beck, Naomi. 2005. "Enrico Ferri's Scientific Socialism: A Marxist Interpretation of Herbert Spencer's Organic Analogy." *Journal of the History of Biology* 38:301–325.
Beirne, Piers. 1993. *Inventing Criminology: Essays on the Rise of 'Homo Criminalis'*. Albany, NY: State University of New York Press.
Carrà, Giuseppe, and Francesco Barale. 2004. "Cesare Lombroso, M.D., 1835–1909." *American Journal of Psychiatry* 161(4):624.
Comte, Auguste. [1830–1842] 1893. *The Positive Philosophy of Auguste Comte*. Freely translated and condensed by Harriet Martineau. London: Kegan Paul, Trench, Trubner & Co.
Comte, Auguste. [1851–1854] 1966. *System of Positive Polity*. 4 vols. Translated by Richard Congreve. New York: Burt Franklin.
Critchley, MacDonald. 1965. "Neurology's Debt to F. J. Gall (1758–1828)." *British Medical Journal* 2:775–781.
Darwin, Charles. 1871. *The Descent of Man*. London: John Murray.
DiCristina, Bruce. 2006. "The Epistemology of Theory Testing in Criminology." In *Philosophy, Crime, and Criminology,* edited by Bruce A. Arrigo and Christopher R. Williams, 134–164. Chicago: University of Illinois Press.
Dugdale, Richard L. 1877. *The Jukes: A Study in Crime, Pauperism, Disease, and Heredity*. New York: G. P. Putnam's Sons.
Durkheim, Emile. [1893] 1984. *The Division of Labor in Society*. Translated by W. D. Halls. New York: The Free Press.
Evans, Elizabeth C. 1941. "The Study of Physiognomy in the Second Century A.D." *Transactions and Proceedings of the American Philological Association* 72:96–108.
Ferri, Enrico. 1898. *Criminal Sociology*. 3rd ed. (abridged). Edited by W. D. Morrison. New York: D. Appleton and Company.
Ferri, Enrico. [1901] 1913. *The Positive School of Criminology: Three Lectures*. Translated by Ernest Untermann. Chicago: Charles H. Kerr and Company.
Gall, Francois (Franz) Joseph. [1825] 1835. *On the Functions of the Brain and of Each of Its Parts*. Vols. I–VI. Translated by Winslow Lewis. Boston: Marsh, Capen, and Lyon.
Galton, Francis. 1883. *Inquiries into Human Faculty and Its Development*. London: Macmillan.
Garofalo, Raffaele. 1895. *La Superstition socialiste*. Paris: Félix Alcan.
Garofalo, Raffaele. [1914] 1968. *Criminology*. Translated primarily from the fifth French edition by Robert Wyness Millar. Montclair, NJ: Patterson Smith.
Goring, Charles. [1913] 1972. *The English Convict: A Statistical Study*. Montclair, NJ: Patterson Smith.
Graham, John. 1961. "Lavater's Physiognomy in England." *Journal of the History of Ideas* 22(4):561–572.
Halfpenny, Peter. 1982. *Positivism and Sociology: Explaining Social Life*. London: George Allen and Unwin.
Hooton, Earnest. 1939. *Crime and the Man*. Cambridge, MA: Harvard University Press.

Kretschmer, Ernst. 1921. *Körperbau und Charakter*. Berlin: Springer-Verlag.
Kretschmer, Ernst. 1951. *Physique and Character: An Investigation of the Nature of Constitution and of the Theory of Temperament*. 2nd ed. revised. New York: Humanities Press.
Lavater, John (Johann) Caspar. 1840. *Essays on Physiognomy: Designed to Promote the Knowledge and the Love of Mankind*. 3rd ed. Translated by Thomas Holcroft. London: B. Blake.
Lindesmith, Alfred, and Yale Levin. 1937. "The Lombrosian Myth in Criminology." *The American Journal of Sociology* 42(5):653–671.
Lombroso, Cesare. 1895–1896. "Criminal Anthropology: Its Origin and Application." *The Forum* 20:33–49.
Lombroso, Cesare. 1911. "Introduction." In Gina Lombroso-Ferrero's *Criminal Man: According to the Classification of Cesare Lombroso*, pp. xi–xx. New York: G.P. Putnam's Sons.
Lombroso, Cesare, and William Ferrero. [1893] 1903. *The Female Offender*. New York: D. Appleton and Company.
Lombroso-Ferrero, Gina. 1911. *Criminal Man: According to the Classification of Cesare Lombroso*. New York: G.P. Putnam's Sons.
Percival, Melissa. 2003. "Johann Caspar Lavater: Physiognomy and Connoisseurship." *British Journal for Eighteenth-Century Studies* 26:77–90.
Pinel, Philippe. [1806] 1962. *A Treatise on Insanity*. Translated by D. D. Davis. New York: Hafner Publishing.
Prichard, James Cowles. 1835. *A Treatise on Insanity*. London: Sherwood, Gilbert and Piper.
Rafter, Nicole. 2004. "The Unrepentant Horse-Slasher: Moral Insanity and the Origins of Criminological Thought." *Criminology* 42(4):979–1008.
Rafter, Nicole. 2005. "The Murderous Dutch Fiddler: Criminology, History and the Problem of Phrenology." *Theoretical Criminology* 9(1):65–96.
Rafter, Nicole. 2008. "Criminology's Darkest Hour: Biocriminology in Nazi Germany." *The Australian and New Zealand Journal of Criminology* 41(2):287–306.
Ray, Isaac. [1838] 1962. *A Treatise on the Medical Jurisprudence of Insanity*. Cambridge, MA: Harvard University Press.
Riegel, Robert E. 1933. "The Introduction of Phrenology to the United States." *The American Historical Review* 39(1):73–78.
Rush, Benjamin. [1786] 1947. "The Influence of Physical Causes Upon the Moral Faculty." In *The Selected Writings of Benjamin Rush*, edited by Dagobert D. Runes, 181–211. New York: Philosophical Library.
Rush, Benjamin. 1806. *Essays, Literary, Moral and Philosophical*. 2nd ed. Philadelphia: Thomas and William Bradford.
Savitz, Leonard, Stanley H. Turner, and Toby Dickman. 1977. "The Origin of Scientific Criminology: Franz Joseph Gall as the First Criminologist." In *Theory in Criminology: Contemporary Views*, edited by Robert F. Meier, 41–56. Beverly Hills, CA: Sage Publications.
Sellin, Thorsten. 1972. "Enrico Ferri: 1856–1929." In *Pioneers in Criminology*, 2nd ed., edited by Herman Mannheim, 361–384. Montclair, NJ: Patterson Smith.
Sheldon, William H. 1949. *Varieties of Delinquent Youth: An Introduction to Constitutional Psychiatry*. New York: Harper & Brothers.
Simpson, Donald. 2005. "Phrenology and the Neurosciences: Contributions of F. J. Gall and J. G. Spurzheim." *ANZ Journal of Surgery* 75:475–482.
Staum, Martin. 1995. "Physiognomy and Phrenology at the Paris Athénée." *Journal of the History of Ideas* 56(3):443–462.

Tsouna, Voula. 1998. "Doubts about Other Minds and the Science of Physiognomics." *The Classical Quarterly* 48(1):175–186.

van Wyhe, John. 2002. "The Authority of Human Nature: The *Schädellehre* of Franz Joseph Gall." *The British Journal for the History of Science* 35(1):17–42.

Vold, George B., and Thomas J. Bernard. 1986. *Theoretical Criminology*. 3rd ed. New York: Oxford University Press.

Wolfgang, Marvin E. 1972. "Cesare Lombroso: 1835–1909." In *Pioneers in Criminology*, 2nd ed., edited by Herman Mannheim, 232–291. Montclair, NJ: Patterson Smith.

Young, Robert M. 1968. "The Functions of the Brain: Gall to Ferrier (1808–1886)." *Isis* 59(3):250–268.

CHAPTER 5

JOHANN CASPAR LAVATER

The reading in this chapter is entitled "Socrates," and it is from John (Johann) Caspar Lavater's *Essays on Physiognomy* (1840), third edition, pp. 113–122 and plate XV (an illustration); translated by Thomas Holcroft; London: B. Blake. The first edition of this work was published in German in four volumes during the years 1775–1778 under the title *Physiognomische Fragmente, zur Beförderung der Menschenkenntniss und Menschenliebe* (*Physiognomonical Fragments, for the Promotion of the Knowledge and Love of Mankind*). The full text of the third edition is available through the HathiTrust Digital Library (hathitrust.org).

The first edition of Lavater's *Essays on Physiognomy* appeared only a decade after the publication of Beccaria's *On Crimes and Punishments*, but it was a very different work. Lavater, who was both a pastor and the foremost physiognomist of his era, approached the explanation of deviance from an angle that differs markedly from that of the classical school. In brief, he argued that elements of a person's soul, a person's dispositions, can be identified through a careful examination of the person's facial features. Yet, although Lavater's paradigm is readily distinguishable from that of the classical school, the spirit of the Enlightenment did leave an imprint upon it. This perhaps is most evident in his efforts to defend the standing of physiognomy as a science, an effort that is apparent in his essay on Socrates.

In this essay Lavater, in an attempt to reaffirm the relevance of physiognomy, examines the facial features of Socrates as portrayed in an engraving. The essay is intriguing in several ways. First, it documents the fact that physiognomy has a long history and, at least in the distant past, was taken seriously by some prominent intellectuals, including Socrates. More than two thousand years ago, Socrates was examined by a physiognomist who concluded that he had several negative character traits. Socrates did not dismiss his negative evaluation; instead, he maintained that he was able to overcome his problematic dispositions "by the continual practice of virtue." Second, as suggested above, this essay demonstrates that Lavater viewed physiognomy as a science, despite its errors. To support his position, he maintained that physiognomists, like physicians in the field of medicine, make mistakes, but that is not an adequate basis for the rejection of all their work.

Finally, Lavater's essay on Socrates portrays physiognomy as a discipline of some complexity, an image that is often overlooked in the secondary literature. For example, he emphasized that an adequate examination of a person's countenance should include the analysis of both "solid" ("permanent") and "flexible" features, the former representing "original dispositions" and the latter representing the "development" of these dispositions over a person's lifetime. In other words, from this viewpoint, a person's character is not fixed at birth; there is opportunity for change and, for the deviant, some possibility of reform. In Lavater's words: "A man of the best native inclinations may degenerate, and another with the worst may become good" (p. 115).

---

from ESSAYS ON PHYSIOGNOMY
by Johann Caspar Lavater

SOCRATES

The well-known judgment of the physiognomist Zopyrus, concerning Socrates—

"That he was stupid, brutal, sensual, and addicted to drunkenness—"

Has been repeatedly cited in modern times against physiognomy; but this science has been as repeatedly supported by the answer of Socrates, to his disciples, who ridiculed the judgment of the physiognomist.

"By nature I am addicted to all these vices, and they were only restrained, and vanquished, by the continual practice of virtue."

Permit me to add something on this subject.

However insignificant, in itself, this anecdote may be, or though, like anecdotes in general, it should be but half true, yet is it pregnant with physiognomonical discussion.

Let us suppose it to be literal truth; what will be the consequence?

It will not militate against physiognomy, whatever it may do against the knowledge of Zopyrus.

Suppose that Zopyrus was mistaken, that he overlooked all traits of excellence, and dwelt upon the rude, the massy. How will this injure the science of physiognomy?

That physiognomist who, from his zeal for the science, should affirm, "I never err," would be like the physician who, from the ardour of his zeal for the honour of his art, should affirm, "My patients never die."

Whoever, because of one, or one hundred, errors of the physiognomist, should reject the science of physiognomy, would be like the man who, because there are ignorant physicians, or because that the patients of the greatest physicians die, should reject all physical aid.

But to come nearer to the point.

All antiquity, certainly, attests that Socrates had a very ordinary countenance.

All the busts of Socrates, however different from each other, still have a similarity of ugliness. To this we may add what was said by Alcibiades, who, certainly, was well acquainted with Socrates, as he also was with what was beautiful, and what deformed; "That he resembled the figure of Silenus."[1] I understand the remark of Alcibiades to refer to the general form of the countenance. We perceive there can be no doubt of the ugliness of Socrates.

Yet was Socrates, from all that we know concerning him, the wisest, best, most incomparable of men. Be this all granted; we shall ever carefully avoid denying what is highly probable in order to establish our own propositions.

"Consequently, the wisest and best of men had the countenance of the most stupid and debauched; or, rather, had a gross, rude, forbidding, ugly, countenance." How may this objection be answered?

I. The deformity of Socrates was, in the opinion of most who maintain the circumstance, a thing so remarkable, so extraordinary, that it was universally considered as a contradiction, an anomaly of nature.—Accurately examined, is this for or against physiognomy?—A direct contrary relation, between the external and internal, was expected. This want of conformity, this dissonance, produced general astonishment.—Let any one determine what was the origin of their general expectation and astonishment.

II. Were this dissonance as great as it has been asserted to be, it will only form an exception to a general rule, which will be as little conclusive against

---

1. It is difficult, says Winckelmann, for human nature to be more debased than in the figure of Silenus.

physiognomy, as a child born with twelve fingers would against the truth, that men have five fingers on each hand. We must allow there are unusual exceptions, mistakes of nature, errors of the press, if I may so speak, which as little destroy the legibility, and the explicability of the human countenance, as ten or twenty errors, in a large volume, would render the whole unintelligible.

III. This, however, is capable of a very different answer; and the best reply that I can make is, that—"Characters, pregnant with strong and contending powers, generally contain in the great mass, the prominent features of the face, somewhat of severe, violent, and perplexed; consequently are very different from what the Grecian artists, and men of taste, name beauty. While the signification, the expression, of such prominent features are not studied and understood, such countenances will offend the eye that searches only for beauty." The countenance of Socrates is manifestly of this kind.

IV. In the study of physiognomy, it cannot be too much inculcated, nor too often repeated, by a writer on the science, that dispositions, and their development, talents, powers, their application and use, the solid and flexible parts, the prominent and fugitive traits must be most accurately distinguished, if we would form an accurate judgment on the human countenance. This appears to have been neglected in the judgment formed on the countenance of Socrates. Zopyrus, Alcibiades, Aristotle, most of the physiognomists with whom I am acquainted, all its opponents, nay, its very defenders, have, in this, been deficient.

To the unphysiognomonical eye, the form of the countenance of Socrates might appear distorted, although the mutable features might have displayed celestial beauty.

A man of the best native inclinations may degenerate, and another with the worst may become good. The noblest talents may rust in indolence, and the most moderate, by industry, be astonishingly improved. If the first dispositions were excellent, it will require an acute observer to read their neglect in the countenance, especially if unimpassioned. In like manner, if they were unfavourable, it will require the most experienced eye to read their improvement. Original dispositions are most discoverable in the form of the solid and prominent parts; and their development, and application, in the flexible features.—Whoever is accustomed to attend only to the flexible traits, and their motion, and has not, as often happens, devoted himself to the study of the solid parts, and permanent traits, he, like Zopyrus, in the countenance of Socrates, will neither discover what is excellent, and characteristic of the disposition, nor the improvement of what may have been apparently bad; consequently his judgment must be erroneous. It is incumbent upon me to make this evident. Be it supposed that the great propensities of Socrates were prominent in his countenance, though it were rude and unpleasing, and that these permanent features were not studied, but that the gross, rude, massy traits met the acute eye of the Greek, who was in search of beauty alone. Be it further supposed, as each observer will remark, that the improvement of all, which may be denominated bad in the disposition, is only visible when the features are in action. Nothing will then be more probable than physiognomonical error, or more plausible than false conclusions against the science.

V. I have repeatedly spoken of good and bad dispositions: the elucidation of my subject requires that I should here explain myself with greater accuracy.

A man born with the happiest propensities or dispositions may become bad; or with the most unfortunate, may, after his own manner, become good.

To speak with precision, no man has good or bad dispositions; no man is born either vicious or virtuous; we must be children before we are men, and children are neither born with vice or virtue: they are innocent. Time will improve some few to a high degree of virtue, and sink some few others to as low a degree of vice. The multitude will find a medium: they appear to want the power of being either virtuous or vicious in any extraordinary degree. All, however, whom for a moment we have considered innocent, all sin, as all die; none may escape sin and death. By sin I mean a propensity to sensual gratifications, which are attended with a troubled conscience, and the degradation of the native powers. I shall just observe that original sin, that subject of ridicule in this our philosophic age, is, in this sense, most demonstrable to a true philosopher, a dispassionate observer of nature.

It is no less true, to speak philosophically, that is, according to experience, that there is, originally, only physical irritability in men, however great their progress may afterwards be in vice or virtue; an impulse to act, to exist, to extend the faculties; which impulse, considered as the spring of action, is good; but which has in itself neither morality nor immorality. If this irritability, this power, be so formed that it is generally addicted, being surrounded by certain objects, or placed under such and such, almost unavoidable, circumstances, to bad thoughts and bad actions, which disturb the peace and happiness of mankind; if they are so formed that, in the present state of the world and its inhabitants, they have scarcely the power of being employed to good, they are then called immoral propensities; and moral, when they are, generally speaking, the reverse.

Experience indubitably teaches us that where the power and irritability are great, there, also, will numerous passions take birth which will generally induce immoral thoughts and actions.

"Helvetius says, the abuse of power (and the same may be said of all the faculties of man) is as inseparable from power as the effect from the cause."

Qui peut tout ce qu'il veut, veut plus que ce qu'il doit.[2]

Hence the sense of the affirmation that man has evil propensities is clear. It might as well be affirmed he has the best propensities; since nothing more is meant than that with respect to certain objects, he is or is not irritable. It is possible he may apply his proportion of power to good, though it is often applied to evil; that circumstances may happen which shall produce irritability where it is wanting, or that he shall remain unmoved under the strongest incitements; consequently, that either virtue itself is there, or an appearance of virtue, which will be called virtue and strength of mind.

VI. Let us apply what has been said to an engraving of Socrates, with which we here present our readers in Plate XV.

According to this head, after Reubens, which we shall first consider, Socrates had certainly great propensities to become eminent. If he resembled this copy, and I have no doubt but that his appearance was better, for this may be the twentieth copy, each of which is less accurate, the declaration of Zopyrus, that he was stupid, was incontrovertibly erroneous; nor was Socrates less mistaken when he was so ready to allow that he was, by nature, weak. It may have been, and perhaps was, an inevitable effect of the weight of these features, that the perspicuity of his understanding was, sometimes, as if enveloped by a cloud. But had Zopyrus, or any true physiognomist, been accustomed accurately to remark the permanent parts of the human face, he never could have said Socrates was naturally stupid.

Whoever considers this forehead as the abode of stupidity has never been accustomed to observe the forehead. If Zopyrus, or any other ancient, has held

PLATE XV: SOCRATES
(The name of the artist who created this engraving was illegible. The image was provided by Washington and Lee University Library.)

this arching, this prominence, or these cavities, as tokens of stupidity, I can only answer they have never been accustomed to consider or compare foreheads. How great soever the effects of a good or bad education, of fortunate or disastrous circumstances, and whatever other influence, of better or worse, may become, a forehead like this will ever remain the same, with respect to its great outlines of character, and never can escape the accurate physiognomist. In these high and roomy arches, undoubtedly, the spirit dwells which will penetrate clouds of difficulties, and vanquish hosts of impediments.

The sharpness also of the eyebones, the eyebrows, the knitting of the muscles between the brows, the breadth of the nose, the depth of the eyes, the projection of the pupil under the eyelid, how does each separately, and all combined, testify the great natural propensities of the understanding, or rather the powers of the understanding called forth!—And how inferior must this twentieth or thirtieth copy be, compared to the original! What painter, however good, is accurate in his foreheads? Nay, where is the shade that defines them justly? How much less an engraving from the last of a succession of copies!

"This countenance, however, has nothing of that noble simplicity, that cool, tranquil, artless, unassuming candour, so much admired in the original.

---

2. He who can do all he will, will do more than he ought.

Something of deceit and sensuality are clearly perceptible in the eye."

In the countenance before us, yes; but a countenance of this pregnancy and power may exert an astonishing degree of force in the command of its passions, and by such exertion may become what others are from a kind of imbecility; and further, I affirm the living countenance may have traits too evident to be mistaken, which yet no art of the painter, no stroke of the engraver, can express. This subject was slightly mentioned in a former fragment: I here repeat, with a greater degree of precision,—

The most disgusting vices are often concealed under the fairest faces; some minute trait, inexpressible by the graver, to be seen only occasionally, when the features are in motion, will denote the most enormous vice. Similar deceptions are found in a distorted, or rather in a strong and pregnant countenance; such as is that of Socrates. The most beauteous, noble, and active characteristics of wisdom and virtue, may discover themselves only by certain indefinable traits, visible to a spectator when the features are in action.

The greatest likenesses of such faces, which are strikingly like because of the strength and sharpness of the prominent features, are, for that very reason, generally, libels on the originals. The present portrait of Socrates, although it might have been called the strongest of likenesses, by the multitude, might yet have been the greatest of libels upon the man. To exaggerate the prominent, and to omit the minute, is a libellous rule alike for the reasoner or the painter. Of this, all sophistical reasoners, all vile painters, avail themselves. In this light I consider most of the portraits of Socrates. I think it probable, nay certain, with respect to myself, that the countenance would, on the first view, have produced similar effects. The sharp, compressed, and heavy parts shocked, or bedimmed, the eye of the Greek, accustomed to consider beauteous forms, so that the spirit of the countenance escaped his penetration. The mind is invisible to those who understand not the body of physiognomy, that is to say, the outlines and form of the solid parts.

VII. The engraving we have in view, the rational physiognomist will say, is, at least, as remarkable, as extraordinary, as was the character of Socrates. —This may well lead us to suspect that there is still a possibility left of reconciling it to the science of physiognomy.

Much we have seen; more we have to see.—We boldly affirm there are traits in this countenance expressive of extraordinary greatness, fortitude unshaken; however degrading single features may be, the whole bears the stamp of manly perseverance. —To what we have already said in its favour, we shall further add—in the upper part of the chin is powerful understanding; and, in the lower, strength and courage, which denote an almost total absence of fear. The thick, short neck, below, is, by the general judgment of all nations, the feature of resolution—*Stiff-necked*.

If we remember that, in painting such countenances, the large traits are always rendered somewhat more large, that the more minute lines of the countenance in action are wanting, and that, though the likeness is preserved, still the soul is fled from the face, we shall not be surprised to find, in this countenance, so much of the great, and of the little; of the inviting, and the forbidding.

Of this we should certainly be convinced could we contemplate living nature. How differently would these immoveable eyes speak, could we behold them animated, inspecting the soul of the listener, while the noble Greek was teaching honour towards God, hope of immortality, simplicity, and purity of heart!—Can any man of observation doubt of this?

This, now so fatal, mouth, which may be proved not to have been accurately drawn, as it also may that much which all living mouths have is here wanting, do you not feel, oh! philanthropists! oh! men of observation! that it must assume a form infinitely different in a moment so picturesque?

Let me be permitted a short digression; suffer me to bewail the artist and the painter.

Designers, statuaries, and painters, usually caricature nature in those parts where she has somewhat caricatured herself. They generally are ready to seize those unfortunate moments, those moments of relaxed indolence, into which the persons who sit or stand to them sink, with such facility, and into which it is almost impossible to prevent sinking. These they perpetuate, because imitation is then most easy, and incite exclamation, or perhaps laughter, in the spectator. A likeness is given by a portrait painter as it is by a satirist; we know who the picture is meant for, though it is *un*like. Satires and bad portraits ever find superficial admirers, but for such the artist should not labour; his great endeavour should be to portray the beauty of truth, and thus secure the admiration of those who are worthy to admire.

The lucky moment of the countenance of man, the moment of actual existence, when the soul, with all her faculties, rushes into the face, like the rising sun, when the features are tinged with heavenly serenity, who seeks, who patiently awaits this moment? By whom are such, by whom can such, moments be depicted?

IX. We return to Socrates.

He confessed that industry, that the exercise of his faculties, had amended his character. This, according to our principles, ought to be expressed in the countenance. But where and how? It was not visible in the solid parts, but it was in the flexible features, and, particularly, in their action and illumination, which no painting, much less engraving, can express. A strong degree of debasement must, also, still exist in Socrates, consequently, might still be perceptible in his countenance. Have not the wisest their moments, their hours, of folly? the best their intervals of passion, and vice, if hot in act, at least, in thought?—Must Socrates, alone, stand an exception?

On summing up all these considerations concerning the countenance of Socrates, and this physiognomonical anecdote, will they oppose, or support, the science of physiognomy?

X. I am willing to grant that heavenly wisdom, sometimes, condescends to reside in wretched earthly vessels, despicable in the eyes of men, in vindication of its own honour, which must not be attributed to mortal man; and that its true beauty may remain concealed, nay, be reviled by the multitude, that these vessels may not ascribe to themselves that worth and those qualities which are the gift of God.

XI. But never will I allow that actual reformation, preeminent wisdom, proved fortitude, and heroic virtue, can exist, and not be impressed upon the countenance, unless it voluntarily distorts itself, or is distorted by accident.

But what is the dead Socrates to us? How much more might we have learnt from him in the moment of living existence! Let us rather take an animated being, and thence determine who most has reason, the antagonist, or the defender of physiognomy.

Let the opponent bring the wisest and best man he knows, with the most stupid or vicious countenance. The search will be tedious ere such a one be found; and, when found, we will discuss what may seem contradictory, according to our principles, and will own ourselves confuted, if it be not confessed that the man proves either not so good and wise as he was supposed, or that there are manifest traits of excellent wisdom and goodness which had passed unobserved.

CHAPTER 6

FRANZ JOSEPH GALL

This chapter presents a reading from François (Franz) Joseph Gall's *On the Functions of the Brain and of Each of Its Parts,* Volume IV, *Organology* (1835), pp. 60–68 and 105–119; translated by Winslow Lewis, Jr.; Boston: Marsh, Capen, and Lyon. This is an English translation of the French edition, which was published in 1825 under the title *Sur les fonctions du cerveau et sur celles de chacune de ses parties.* Footnote symbols have been changed and one note has been removed. The deleted footnote apparently was added by the editor of the English edition; it is not in the original French edition. Unfortunately, I have been unable to find the illustrations referred to in the text in either the 1825 French edition or the 1835 English edition.

Gall established the foundation for phrenology during the last decade of the eighteenth century and the first years of the nineteenth century. Unlike the physiognomy of Lavater, Gall's phrenology was more scientific in its methods and conclusions. Given his medical background, his understanding of human anatomy, his empirical research, and his interest in issues of crime and punishment, it is easy to grasp why Gall has been referred to as one of the first "scientific criminologists." As noted earlier, Gall's work also helped provide psychology with a distinctive biological orientation, and it was a precursor to the evolutionary theories that would develop later in the nineteenth century. Both of these points are evident in his description of the "carnivorous instinct."

In the selected reading, Gall argues that we possess a carnivorous instinct that explains our disposition to kill. He maintains that the strength of this instinct, which varies across individuals, can be estimated by examining a particular region of the skull. Through such an examination, we thus should be able to get a rough idea of how dangerous someone is to the physical well-being of others. However, Gall adds that before we draw a conclusion regarding the extent to which someone poses a threat, it is necessary to estimate the strength of the person's other dispositions (e.g., goodness), because they may offset a strong disposition to kill. Beyond this, Gall holds that the energy of the carnivorous instinct often can be controlled or redirected through education and the development of moral habits.

On the next page, there is a list of 26 brain organs proposed by Gall and two illustrations indicating the areas of the skull that need to be examined to estimate their strength. This information comes from an 1807 publication. As his research moved forward, the number and descriptions of these organs were adjusted to accommodate new data and propositions. By the end of his career, Gall held that there were at least 27 brain organs, each one representing a specific mental disposition/faculty. The selected reading focuses on the carnivorous instinct, which corresponds to his earlier description of "the organ of slaughter."

Name and Location of Organs

1. Sexual Love
2. Parental and Filial Love
3. Friendship or Fidelity
4. Fighting
5. Slaughter
6. Address
7. Cupidity
8. Good-nature
9. Mimicry or Imitation
10. Vain-glory or Vanity
11. Constancy or Firmness
12. Aptness to Learn Things
13. Aptness to Learn Places
14. Aptness to Recollect Persons
15. Sense of Color
16. Aptness to Learn Music
17. Aptness to Learn Numbers
18. Aptness to Learn Words
19. Aptness to Learn Languages
20. Mechanic Art
21. Prudence or Circumspection
22. Loftiness
23. Rhetorical Acuteness
24. Metaphysical Subtlety
25. Wit
26. Theosophy

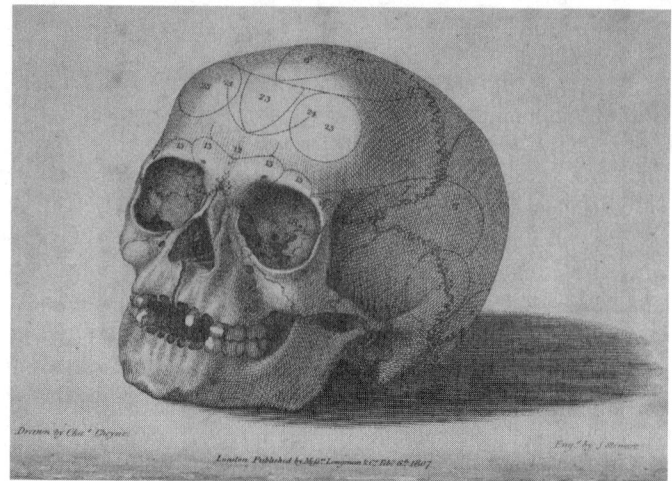

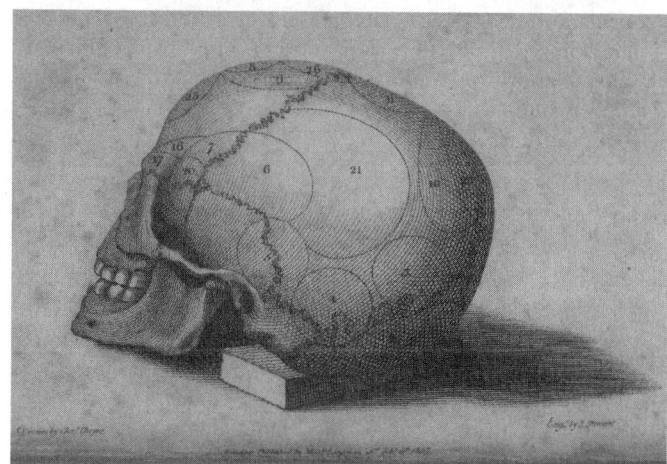

Adapted from C. H. E. Bischoff and C. W. Hufeland, *Some Account of Dr. Gall's New Theory of Physiognomy, Founded Upon the Anatomy and Physiology of the Brain, and the Form of the Skull* (London: Longman, Hurst, Rees, and Orme, 1807). Drawn by C. Cheyne and engraved by J. Stewart. Copies provided by the Rare Book and Manuscript Library, University of Pennsylvania.

from ON THE FUNCTIONS OF THE BRAIN AND OF EACH OF ITS PARTS, VOLUME IV, ORGANOLOGY

by **Franz Joseph Gall**

NATURAL HISTORY OF THE CARNIVOROUS INSTINCT IN MAN

The first question presented to our notice is, whether man is naturally carnivorous, or is destined by nature to be exclusively frugivorous, using animal food, only in consequence of degenerating from his primitive destination.

Man is omnivorous. Flesh nourishes him full as well as vegetables. In the structure of his teeth, jaws, stomach, and intestines, he holds a medium between the frugivora and carnivora; relishing all animals, from the oyster to the pheasant, and all vegetables from the potato to the pine-apple. If the Creator had designed him to be nourished by vegetables only, nothing certainly could have turned him from his destiny. If, in certain climates, he is more exclusively carnivorous or frugivorous, it depends on the influence exerted upon him by surrounding objects and circumstances,—one kind of climate favoring the development of one organ, and repressing that of another, and vice versâ. Since then man was designed to feed on flesh, it is necessary, that, like the other carnivora, he should be induced, by an internal impulse, to kill other animals, and the history of all times shows that he is really endowed with this quality. It only remains for me, therefore, to show how differently this instinct is manifested in different individuals, and the part it sometimes bears in insanity and idiocy, in order to prove, that, in man, and other animals, it is an independent and peculiar function, and must consequently result from a particular organ.

In the fifth section of the first volume, I have described the different degrees of the manifestation of this disposition. To save the reader the trouble of recurring to that volume, and to present the whole subject at once, I will repeat the passages relative to the carnivorous instinct, or disposition, to murder.

There is in man, an inclination, which varies in degree, from simple indifference at seeing animals suffer, and from simple pleasure at witnessing the destruction of life, to the most imperious desire of killing. Our sensibility revolts at this doctrine, but it is, nevertheless, only too true. Whoever would judge justly of the phenomena of nature, must have the courage to acknowledge things as they are, and, in general, not to make man better than he is.[1]

We observe that, among children as among adults, among coarse people as well as those who have received education, some are sensitive, and others indifferent to the sufferings of their fellows. Some even find pleasure in tormenting animals, in seeing them tortured, and in killing them, without our being able to charge it either to habit, or to a defect of education. I could cite several instances, in which this inclination, when very energetic, has decided individuals in their choice of employment. A student used to shock his companions by the particular pleasure he took in tormenting insects, birds, and other animals. It was to satisfy this propensity, as he himself said, that he made himself a surgeon. An apothecary's boy experienced such a violent propensity to kill, that he took up the trade of a hangman. The son of a shopkeeper, whose mind took the same turn, embraced that of a butcher. A rich Dutchman used to pay the butchers, who made large contracts for supplying vessels with beef, to let him kill the cattle.

We may also judge of the existence of this propensity and of its diversity, by the impression produced on spectators by the punishment to which criminals are subjected. Some cannot support the spectacle; others seek it as an amusement. The Chevalier Selwyn made particular exertions to be placed near the criminal who was undergoing punishment. They relate an anecdote of La Condamine, that, one day, making efforts to penetrate the crowd assembled at the place of execution, and being repulsed by the soldiers, the executioner exclaimed, "Let the gentleman pass, he is an amateur." M. Bruggmans, professor at Leyden, mentioned to us a Dutch clergyman, who had so decided a desire for killing, and for witnessing death, that he took the place of almoner of a regiment, solely to have an opportunity of seeing a great number of men

---
1. Vol. 1. p. 259.

destroyed. This same individual raised at his house, the females of various domestic animals, and when they brought forth young, his favorite occupation was to cut their throats. He used to take charge of killing all the animals that were to be cooked. He corresponded with the executioners throughout the country, and would travel several miles on foot, to be present at executions; so that the executioners always secured to him the distinction of a place near them. On the field of battle we find striking examples of the different degree in which this disposition exists. One soldier, at the view of the blood which he causes to flow, feels the intoxication of carnage; another, moved by pity, inflicts feeble blows, or at least spares the conquered; turns away at the sight of a child, of a woman, and of an old man, and checks himself after a victory.

The man enslaved by the cruel propensity of which I here speak, still preserves the faculty of vanquishing it, or of giving it a direction which is not injurious. But the power of subduing a vicious propensity, is weakened in such an individual, in proportion as he has received less education, or the organs of the qualities of a superior order are less developed. If it happens that this propensity is carried to the highest degree, the man experiences but little opposition between his pernicious propensities and his external duties; and though even in this case he is not deprived of moral liberty, or the faculty of being determined by motives, he still finds pleasure in homicide. I shall include in this case all the robbers, who, not content with plunder, have shown the sanguinary inclination to torment and kill without necessity. John Rosbeck was not satisfied, like his companions, with ill-treating his victims to make them confess the place where their treasures were concealed; he invented and exercised the most atrocious cruelties, for the sole pleasure of seeing the sufferings and the blood of children, women, and old men. His first imprisonment continued nineteen months; he was shut up in a subterranean dungeon, so narrow that he could hardly breathe. His feet were loaded with chains; he was up to the ankles in dirty water; and when he was taken from this sink, it was to undergo cruel torture. Still he would confess nothing; he was set at liberty, and the first use he made of his freedom, was to commit a robbery in open day. He soon committed new murders, and was finally put to death. At the beginning of the last century, several murders were committed in Holland, on the frontiers of the country of Cleves. The author of these crimes was a long time unknown. Finally, an old minstrel, who used to go to play the violin at all the weddings in the neighborhood, was suspected from some conversation among his children. Carried before the magistrate, he confessed thirty-four distinct murders, and asserted that he had committed them without malice, and without any intention to rob, solely because he found in them extraordinary pleasure. This fact was communicated to us by M. Serrurier, magistrate at Amsterdam.

The well-known Sabatino, condemned at Palermo, for various crimes, at the moment he ascended the scaffold, confessed that he had killed a man with a musket shot two years before. When asked what could have induced him to commit such an outrage, he coolly replied, that he had fired his musket on the man, to satisfy himself that the powder was good! Journal des Maires, Saturday, Sep. 19, 1818.

Louis XV., says M. Lacratelle,[2] had a well-founded aversion to the brother of the duke de Bourbon Condé, the Count de Charolais, a prince who would have revived all the crimes of Nero, if, to the misfortune of mankind, he had been permitted to occupy a throne. Even in the sports of his childhood, he manifested an instinct of cruelty which might make one shudder. He amused himself in torturing animals: his violence to his servants was absolutely ferocious. They pretend that he tried to mingle cruelty even with his debaucheries, and that he practised divers barbarities on the very courtezans who were brought to him. The popular tradition, confirmed by several records, accuses him of several homicides. He committed murder, as is said, without interest, resentment, or anger. He used to fire at bricklayers, in order to enjoy the barbarous pleasure of seeing them fall from the top of the houses, on which they worked.

These last facts, fortunately very rare, show us that this detestable propensity is sometimes altogether independent of education, of examples of seduction or habit, and that it has its source solely in a bad organization. In fact, there are sometimes committed crimes so barbarous, with circumstances so revolting and disgusting, that it would be difficult to explain them in any other manner. Prochaska[3] relates that a woman of Milan used to lure children to her house by flatteries, kill them, salt their flesh, and devour them daily. He also cites the example of a man, who, in the indulgence of this atrocious propensity, killed a traveller and a young girl, to devour them. I have already mentioned the daughter of a cannibal,

---

2. Historie de France, tom. ii. p. 59.
3. Opera Minora. tom. II. p. 98.

who, though educated at a distance from him, partook, from an early age, of this savage passion.

We cannot deny, then, that certain individuals have propensities to crimes, and even to those of the most atrocious character. Helvetius himself, the great antagonist of the innateness of the qualities of the mind and soul, is obliged to allow "that there are men so unfortunately constituted, as never to be happy, but in doing deeds which will send them to the gallows." Cardinal Polignac,[4] also speaks of men "born vicious, for whom crime has actual charms, and who are borne along by a furious passion, which obstacles only irritate."[5]

Professor Bruggmans, of Leyden, showed the skull of a leader of Dutch robbers, who had precipitated several persons into canals, for the sole gratification of seeing them struggle with death. "What can they do with me," he said on his trial; "am I not an honest man?" Schinderhannes and his accomplice took the greatest pleasure in telling the story of their crimes, and their eyes would sparkle during the recital. Every circumstance calculated to heighten the effect, was dwelt upon with the most intense delight. There have been some, who, at the very moment of their execution, when calling up to their recollection the pleasures in which they had reveled during life, have boasted that none have equaled those produced by the exercise of cruelty.

If any of my readers deem this portrait of man too deeply shaded, let them retrace the whole history of ancient and modern nations. Is there a single spot on the globe, that has not been reddened with human blood? Let them read the history of God's chosen people; the history of the Romans; the discovery of America;—let them follow the Spaniards to Cuba, to Mexico and Peru;—let them open the history of Inquisitions, and of the religious wars;—let them call to mind the Sicilian Vespers, St. Bartholomew's day, and the French revolution. Every where we tread on battle-fields; every where we encounter funeral piles, wheels, and a thousand instruments of torture invented to abridge man's life. What an immense diversity of machines of destruction and death fill our arsenals! In fine, is not military glory ever placed above all others?

If you would see, in all his nakedness, the man whose bosom harbors the most atrocious passions, observe him when the very multitude of his crimes renders every sort of disguise superfluous. Look at him who hires the midnight assassin, or at the assassin himself, who barters his stabs for gold, and makes a business of destroying his neighbor's life; at the poisoner, and at those robber chiefs, surrounded by the most ferocious wretches, whom they lead to rapine and murder. Especially observe those miscreants, born with the thirst of blood, when seated on the throne, where no law can reach them, and no considerations whatever check their unbridled fury. Behold Caligula, cutting out the tongues of innocent people, throwing them to wild beasts to be devoured, forcing parents to assist in the execution of their children, giving the unfortunate wretches their choice of the wheel or the rack, and amusing himself with their agony, summing up his rage in one wish, that the Romans had but one neck, that he might decapitate them at a single stroke, feeding wild-beasts, kept for the shows, on living men, and whose strongest wishes were for famine, pestilence, conflagration, earthquake, and the loss of an army. Look at Nero, poisoning Brittanicus, murdering his mother, and the husband of the woman he wished to violate; passing the night in the streets, with a rabble of unbridled youths, fighting, robbing and killing; sacrificing to his fury his own wife Octavia, Burrhus, Seneca, Lucan, Petronius, and his mistress Poppæa; setting fire to the four corners of Rome, and then ascending an elevated tower, to enjoy the terrible sight at his ease, with the wish that he could see the whole world on fire; covering the Christians with wax and other combustibles, and burning them by night, that they might serve for lamps; laying a plan to murder all the governors of provinces, all the generals of the army, all the exiles and all the Gauls in Rome; to poison the whole senate at their meal, to burn Rome a second time, and, at the same moment, turn the wild beasts reserved for the shows, into the streets, to prevent the people from extinguishing the fire. Behold a Louis XI., the ungrateful, unnatural and rebellious son, whose father died from very fear of being killed by his own son; who, formed by nature for a cruel and implacable tyrant, wished to reign only by terror; and looked on France as a meadow, that he might mow every year, and as close as he pleased. Few tyrants have slain more citizens by the hands of the executioner, and the most refined methods of destruction. The chronicles of the time reckon four thousand subjects, executed publicly or privately, in his reign. Dungeons, iron cages, and chains, that loaded the victims of his barbarity, are the monuments he left behind him. While criminals were put to the torture, he stationed himself behind a lattice, &c. &c. Nothing but gibbets

---

4. De l' Esprit, p. 578.
5. Anti Lucrece, trad. par. M. de Bougainville, Louis, 1754, p. 184.

were to be seen around his palace, and he personally assisted in the execution of his vengeance. When the Duke of Nemours was executed for high treason, he caused the children of this unfortunate prince to be placed upon the scaffold, that they might be sprinkled with the blood of their father. They descended covered with his blood, and in this state were conducted to Rochelle, and put into scuttle-shaped dungeons, where the cramped condition of their bodies operated as a perpetual torture. Forever covered with relics and images, and wearing a leaden figure of Our Lady in his bonnet, he asked pardon for his murders, and then, proceeded to commit new ones. Look at Sylla, Tiberius, Domitian, Marcus Caius, Aurelian, Caracalla, Septimius Severus, Henry VIII., Catherine de Medicis.

It would take years to enumerate the scenes of horror, which the earth has exhibited; and those, who would know the hearts of ordinary men, must transport themselves into times when there existed no restraint on the passions. Who is ignorant of the horrible scenes that have stigmatized the French revolution? Who has not heard the names of Rossignol, of Pethion, of Marat, of Chalier, of Robespierre, of Danton, of Carrier, of Henriot, of Collot d' Herbois, of Fouquier, Tinville, &c.? Think of the murders, that are every day committed with all the refinements of cruelty, in spite of education, morality, religion, and the laws. When, too, will the barbarous and infamous custom of duelling cease to be authorized? Who, now, will dare to maintain, that there is not in man an innate propensity, which leads him to the destruction of his own species? Where is the creature, that evinces more ferocity towards all other animals, not excepting his fellows, than man?[6] . . .

WHAT IS THE FUNDAMENTAL QUALITY OF THE DISPOSITION TO MURDER—OF THE DISPOSITION TO KILL?

To answer this question at all satisfactorily, we must first go back to the circumstance that led to the discovery of this propensity, viz. the difference between the skulls of the carnivorous, and those of the frugivorous animals; the former having a prominence above the ear, produced by a large cerebral mass, which the latter have not. My position in regard to the discovery of this quality, was the same, as for all the other fundamental qualities or faculties and their organs. It would have been impossible for me to discover such a quality or faculty, unless it had been manifested in the highest, or, at least, a very marked degree of activity; and I was under the necessity of giving it a name, derived from this high degree of activity. Another reason for this cause was, that the carnivora must not only be forcibly impelled by this inward propensity to kill creatures necessary for their support, but it must also teach them the kind of death to be inflicted on their prey. Hence the denomination, *instinct of murder*. As man is the most formidable of all the carnivora,—as he confines his ravages to no single one, nor a few species, like the greater part of the other carnivora, that kill only for nourishment, and indulges his ravenous propensity upon every living thing, not even excepting his own species, he may be called carnivorous, (*carnassier,*) with a better title to the name, than any other creature. But never, as some of my opponents, with equal assurance and folly, have sedulously endeavored to make people believe, never, in speaking of the *instinct of murder*, did I mean thereby, a propensity to *homicide*. My principle is, and I shall always adhere to it, that to designate a fundamental quality or faculty, common to man and the lower animals, we must choose a name that will be applicable to it in the brutes, as well as in our own species. But, certainly, a propensity to murder impelling to homicide, would be totally inapplicable to the natural destination of the carnivorous animals.

The propensity to destroy, or *destructiveness,* as Dr. Spurzheim calls it, gives a too general and extensive signification to the carnivorous instinct. Spurzheim derives from the same propensity, the acts of quarreling, pinching, breaking, tearing, burning, biting, devastating, demolishing, overturning, &c. The architect who demolishes in order to build,—the gardener who roots up one tree, for the purpose of planting another, cannot be charged with destroying; otherwise, there is no animal, frugivorous, or carnivorous, destitute of the propensity. And, finally, this appellation does not at all convey to the mind of the reader, the idea of the quality, whose natural history we have been considering. Perhaps I, or my successors, may succeed in determining its fundamental power with more precision. For the present, it is enough for the reader to know exactly what I understand by the quality in question, and how the gradual development of its organ may, subsequently, become the material cause of the propensity to homicide.

---

6. In vol. 1. sect. iv. I have shown, that the existence of a propensity does not necessarily suppose its action, nor exclude moral liberty.

If man had sufficient force of mind to recognize the true place assigned him by nature, he would discover here, too, a wise institution. When man came from the hands of his Creator, the Supreme Being surely foresaw that he would live with his fellows in a state of eternal war. Would it have been just for nature to withhold from him the means of ridding himself of his enemies? Have not they done their duty, who have condemned criminals to death; or they who, with fire and sword, have destroyed the enemies of their country? And if the human species should remain at peace, for a few ages only, it would, for that reason, inundate the whole surface of the globe; every animal would be displaced, the whole equilibrium of nature disturbed, and its order completely inverted. This is the why—the final cause—that war has such singular charms, to civilized as well as savage nations; that they seem to be born and to live for it; and that, of all other passions, it is the one of which they make the greatest show. It is well proved, that the first ideas of religion were warlike ideas; that one of the first attributes given to God by men, was that of *God of battles, God of armies.*

I ever recognize and revere the supreme foresight, and submit to its laws. Let those who seek for glory, in leading nations to the work of butchering one another, and who slaughter their fellow-men by thousands, know that they act not altogether of their own will; that nature has placed in their hearts the rage for destroying their own species; that, little as they suspect it, they are merely one of the instruments it employs for thinning the human population. Thus they figure by the side of devastating pestilences, and of all the disasters by which man is assailed, from within and from without.

The expression, *instinct of murder,* therefore, may be excused, even where man kills his fellow-man; for they will never be said to commit homicide, who destroy those of whom the country must be rid. I would, therefore, wish to keep my first name; but, as the multitude will always be tempted to confound murder with homicide, I prefer, for the present, that of *carnivorous instinct.*

SEAT OF THE CARNIVOROUS ORGAN, AND ITS EXTERNAL APPEARANCE IN THE HUMAN CRANIUM

We ought not to expect to find a large development of the carnivorous organ in all murderers. There are unfortunate circumstances, in which an organ, even but moderately developed, may be so excited, as to acquire a high degree of activity. People who make rhymes in the delirium of fever, are not always poets. We frequently see persons, whose conduct has always been irreproachable, from a concurrence of unfortunate circumstances, committing actions which they have sincerely abhorred, and which they detested even after they had committed them. No crime is naturally more repugnant to my feelings than homicide; still, looking to the very bottom of my heart, I would not venture to affirm, that I am beyond the reach of temptation under all possible events. A father, after educating a beloved daughter in the sentiments of honor and virtue, and believing he has secured her happiness by a settled match, sees this child, the object of his tenderest affection, dishonored by a vile seducer. At the moment of the consummation of the crime, this unfortunate father, hurried on by feelings as proper as they are heart-rending, becomes the murderer of the wretch who dishonors him. Would it not be a deplorable error, in legislation as well as the physiology of the brain, to confound such a father with the consummate cut-throat?

Besides, the physiologist well knows that depravement of moral character, or a propensity to murder, is sometimes the effect of a chronic and masked disease of the brain. We have very often found the skulls of homicides, like those of maniacs who have been such for many years. In treating of lesions of the brain, I have related several cases, where the whole moral character was found to be changed after one of these lesions. Who is not aware of the consequences of diseases or mutilations of the generative organs? None of my readers can be ignorant, how blindly the propensity to suicide acts, as well as that other mental affection, still more dreadful, in which the patient not only destroys himself, but, believing that he is inspired from on high, sacrifices others, and ordinarily those whom he most loves, his wife, and children. Such affections strongly show the necessity of caution in forming our opinion in cases of homicide, and that a righteous judge must have a profounder knowledge of man than is generally possessed by those, who, in applying the law to criminals, consider only so much of the action as falls within the cognizance of their senses, and are capable of nothing but a literal interpretation of the law.

It must also be borne in mind, that the same degree of activity of an organ, may produce entirely different actions in different individuals. If we except idiotism and insanity, and cases of an entirely circumscribed excitation, actions are never determined by the activity of a single organ. The manifestation of a certain power will differ according to the strength and modifications of the action of the other organs. The propensity to murder, combined with courage, acts very differently from what it does when combined with deliberate malice; and still more so, when combined with philanthropy, &c. The possessor of superior intellectual powers, will know how to give his propensity a more favorable direction, than the man of feeble intellect. Education, habit, example, religion, morality, laws, &c., act on a man endowed with moral liberty, as so many motives for conforming to the social order, even in spite of his propensities. These are sufficient reasons, why a large development of the carnivorous instinct is not to be sought for in every individual who has been hurried to the commission of homicide, without being particularly disposed to it by his primitive organization. They will explain, too, why I am very far from considering a person as disposed to commit homicide, for the sole reason that he has the organ of this instinct largely developed. All we can confidently maintain is, that, *cæteris paribus,* a person who has this organ large, will be more easily induced to commit homicide, than one not naturally disposed to it by his organization. Amid the tumult of violent passions, the transports of jealousy, vengeance, and anger, the idea of revenging himself by fire and sword will be suggested to the former, while the thoughts of the other will take a quite different direction.

Having thus prepared the mind of the reader by these remarks, I now proceed to speak of the organ itself. Facts relating to this subject are so numerous, I must be contented with recording a few, which particularly suggest some interesting reflections.

Comparing many skulls or heads together, we shall find some, in which the temporal and inferior-parietal region, that is to say, immediately over the ears, is flattened; while in others, this region is prominent and rounded out. This convexity exists precisely in the place where the temporal bones are so thin as to be transparent, and where, consequently, the cerebral parts beneath show their real dimension. When the development of this cerebral part is excessive, the whole portion of the cranium, from the inferior edge of the parietal bone, even to the ear, swells out; when less developed, the prominence is limited to the temporal bones. This region is marked vi. both on the brains and skulls.

In two of the Schinderhannes band, who had been guilty of more than twenty homicides, the organ of murder is very apparent. This region was extremely prominent, forming a segment of a sphere, in a soldier at Berlin, who was subject to an irresistible propensity to commit homicide, and who, on the approach of his paroxysms, which he was always aware of beforehand, caused himself to be confined, that he might be prevented from shedding blood. We found the same conformation in the girl that helped her mother kill her father, and who spoke of the parricidal deed with a smile, regarding it as nothing extraordinary. In a half-idiotical young man, who had killed a child from no other cause than obedience to a blind impulse; in a fellow called Hommedieu, whose skull M. Brüggmann showed us at Leyden, and who pushed people from the dykes into the ditches below, solely for the pleasure of seeing them struggle with death; in a homicide belonging to Brunswick, who, with no other motive than the pleasure of killing, committed his second murder on a child; in twenty-five women guilty of infanticide, whom we had an opportunity of seeing in different houses of correction; in an assassin at Frankfort, who was executed after his second homicide; in another criminal, to whom murder had become a habit; in Bouhours, who killed her victims with a hammer, in order to rob them of their money; in all the skulls of homicides in the collections of M. M. Habert, Sax, and Weigel;—in the skulls of all these people, I say, the same region was very prominent, and, consequently, the same cerebral part was very much developed.

In Bouhours, three organs had acquired a high degree of development. The excessive activity of one produced a propensity to steal; of the second, to murder; and of the third, to fight;—an unhappy concourse, which can only explain the atrocious conduct of this monster.

Lepelley des Longs-Champs had the organ of murder largely developed, while that of courage was small. He planned a murder, which he made Heluin, more courageous than himself, execute. The latter was strongly disposed to steal, which explains why he was always ready to commit homicide, for money. I have subjected the skulls of Valet and Mercier to the same test; Valet committed a quadruple homicide on his mother and three aunts. Mercier assisted in the massacre, but without giving a single blow himself, only he prevented the women from escaping. He had been promised a sum of money by Valet. In Valet's skull, the organ of murder is well developed. In Mercier's, it is not. The organs of self-defence, (courage,) of circumspection, and of benevolence, are all small. The organ of sentiment of property, on the contrary, is very prominent; hence, we have baseness, malice, want of foresight, or stupidity, and, to finish the unfortunate combination, an inveterate propensity to steal. I have plaster casts of these crania, which are in the Royal Garden.

The skull of Voirin, hatter, guillotined at Paris nearly ten years ago, for having committed two murders, is very remarkable. If, when I first saw this head, I had never before known the organ, possessing the degree of development, which produces the propensity to murder, I should have discovered it in this subject. The region above indicated is extraordinarily developed, and very prominent, which explains the impulse that hurried him on to the commission of homicide. The following passage is taken from the record of the accusation of this murderer.

Perrin was descending the stair-case, holding a light, and preceding Voirin. Suddenly he felt a violent blow on his head. His hat fell off and extinguished the light. Frightened for his life, he struggled with his assassin, who redoubled his blows, sprung upon his victim, threw him on the ground, and, placing his knee upon his chest, continued to strike him. Perrin, however, did not entirely give up; he had strength enough left to seize his murderer by the hair; he also bit his hand severely, and wrested from him a piece of iron with which he was armed. Voirin got back the iron, and struck Perrin again, who still evinced compassionate and generous feelings for his assassin. "Wretched man," said he, "I have known you from infancy, and you are bent on murdering me! But I knew your father. I would not harm you; save yourself." He was about to open the door to let him out, when Voirin sprang upon him, and began striking him again. In the mean time, Perrin succeeded in opening the door, and called for aid. Hearing his cries, Voirin now determined to commit the crime. "I am a lost man," he exclaimed, "I am a monster, a cut-throat." These expressions would seem to refer to some previous crime. He even said, "that he was urged on by a frightful impulse, which prompted him to kill." Arrested at the very moment of finishing the murder, he exclaimed, "I feel the bitterest remorse; I am impelled by an irresistible power to shed the blood of my fellows; two months ago, I bought pistols for the purpose of blowing out my brains; I am sorry I did not do it."

When M. Danloux, after the murder of Geyer, observed the accounts of Voirin's expenses, and censured him for them, and even suspected his honesty, Voirin said that there was a woman who supplied his extravagance. In his defence he accounted for his money, by saying that he won it at play, a short time after the murder of Geyer.

Voirin, indeed, was not an idiot, and, consequently, not absolutely incapable of reflecting, or of being guided by motives of an elevated order. For this reason, he wished to destroy himself, that he might prevent the crime to which he felt himself impelled; but his very low forehead shows, that his intellectual faculties were extremely small. The upper part of the frontal bone is flattened, indicating a want of benevolence. The head of the fratricide Dautun, is cast almost in the same mould. When, to such an unfortunate organization, there is joined a want of education and of moral and religious instruction, it is easy to foresee how such a character would terminate, how little soever circumstances might impel him to the crime. It is for this reason, that I insist so strenuously on the instruction of the lower classes, who have far stronger excitements to vice and crime, than others.[7] How often have we had occasion to observe, that those persons are the really guilty, who suffer the mind of the people to stagnate and corrupt in ignorance and superstition. The following account presents many points of resemblance between Voirin and the author of a crime, committed at Albi, in 1808.

"The court of criminal justice of Tarn," says M. Coutele,[8] "condemned to death, Jan. 21, 1809, a man who was convicted of having killed his brother-in-law. The jury and the spectators were struck with the unwavering ferocity, manifested by this person during the trial. He had the most sinister aspect, and such was the expression of his sombre and savage look, and haggard eyes, that none could see him without a shudder. The judges were convinced they had never seen the figure of a mantiger drawn in such strong relief.

"The court had followed the traces of his crime, but no evidence had fixed it upon him as the author, because no witness had seen it. He confessed it himself voluntarily, and of his own accord, and with the utmost sang-froid, detailed every circumstance that attended it. The dreadful story made the large audience that listened to it, shudder with very horror. After confessing all with calmness, and with an air of familiarity with the subject, he declared *that he had been urged on by an impulse to this murder*, adding, *that he could not resist the temptation of killing*

---

7. V. Sect.
8. Observations on the medical constitution of the year 1808, at Albi, part II. by M. Coutele, M. D. at Albi, 1809, p. 163 and 165.

and shedding blood. He seemed to be aware, that, if left to himself, his existence would be a calamity to his species.

"In the special examinations, he had already made known a series of crimes, previously committed on his nearest relations. Among others, he made several attempts to poison his mother and stepfather.

"The announcement of his sentence did not intimidate him. He heard it without fear or remorse; he declined to appeal, and requested them to hasten his death. He refused all spiritual aid, appeared to be unmoved by the thought of his near destruction, and mounted the scaffold without emotion.

"The great importance," continues Dr. Coutele, from whom I have taken this account, "of ascertaining whether the conformation of the skull in this subject corresponded with his well-known character and the expression of his countenance, induced me not to neglect examining it.

"Decending into the pit, shortly after the execution, I hesitated for a moment to take up the head, which had been separated from the trunk. The eyes glared, and the features retained, to the full, their fierce and threatening expression. I soon found, by the touch, a prominence in the temporal region, just over the ear; having exposed the squamous portion of the bone, I found, on its posterior third, a round bump, from three to four millimetres (0.11811 to .15748 of an inch) high in the centre, and a dozen centimetres (4.7244 of an inch) in circumference at the base. It bore some resemblance to those little balls of ivory or stone, that children play with. The two prominences were perfectly symmetrical."

The whole region over the ears is more remarkable than in any other cranium. In that of Madeline Albert, of Moulines, it is so developed, that, without exaggeration, it might be thought to have been blown up. (Pl. lxviii. fig. 1.) This monster killed her mother, brothers and sisters with a hatchet. During the preparation for her trial, she spoke continually and with pleasure, of her atrocious deed. For the convenience of the artist in drawing her figure, she willingly placed herself in the attitude she took, when meditating the crime, (Pl. lxix. fig. 1.) Excepting the organ of murder, (vi.) the whole head is but moderately developed. The forehead is low and narrow. From all appearances, this girl had none of the resources furnished by education, for combating the pernicious impulses, to which her internal organization made her a prey.

Since the publication of my large work, I have obtained six skulls and casts of murderers, all of which show the organ much developed, viz.; the cast of Merlin, who murdered his father for refusing him money; that of Boutiller, who murdered his mother for the purpose of robbing her; that of Foulard, who murdered his mistress, in a fit of intoxication, to get possession of her jewels; and that of Guichat, an assassin and robber. These four murderers had, besides the organ of the propensity to murder, so large a development of the organ of the sentiment of property, that there was also a propensity to steal. The next, the skull of a hussar, and pump-maker by trade, who killed his mistress for her infidelities, presents the organ of the propensity to murder only, largely developed.

A society of physicians[9] charged M. Trolliet, physician of the Hotel-Dieu, to send me a cast of a remarkable criminal, executed at Lyons. His name was Lelievre, and he styled himself Chevalier. He was accused of robbing the bank of France, where he held some office, of sixty thousand francs, (about twelve thousand dollars.) He had poisoned his mistress, and his first three wives, killed two of his children, and robbed another. He was for seven or eight years, employed in the prefecture of Rhone, in quality of chief of the bureau. The cast shows an unfortunate combination of several organs largely developed, viz. those of the propensity to murder, to cunning, and to theft. The organs of calculation, wit, mimickry, &c. are large, with a small development of the organ of circumspection; consequently, we have heedlessness, perverse inclinations, and a temper of mind to be extremely pleased with their indulgence!!

Dr. Spurzheim saw, in the Hunterian Museum, two Carib skulls, which swelled out greatly over the ears. See, also, Pl. lxxiv. fig. 2. vi. the skull of an adult Carib.

I have constantly observed, that bloody spectacles have a peculiar charm to those women in whom this organ is large. They are fond of the chase; they would like to be men, to follow the profession of arms; they bestow their affections on military men exclusively; battles are never murderous enough for their taste; and, in reading the newspapers, their curiosity is excited only by the accounts of murders and executions. Like Aurelian and Louis XI., they are fond of attending executions, and, if decency permitted, they would adopt the example of Catherine de Medicis, and be pleased to make their children spectators of such revolting spectacles.

---

9. I beg these gentlemen to receive my warmest thanks. If such zeal were every where manifested, what progress would not the science make in a few years!

In the engraving of the Marquis of Toirus, who excelled in the chase, and whose principal passion was that of arms, I observe this organization expressed in a very high degree.

I have elsewhere said, that painters, draftsmen, engravers, and sculptors, sacrifice truth to erroneous notions of beauty, and endeavor to render less striking those uncommon forms, which they sometimes meet with in their models. Still, there occur, from time to time, forms so striking, that the likeness absolutely depends on it, and then the artist is obliged, in spite of himself, to remain true to nature. In this way we obtain some faithful portraits of remarkable persons. The busts and portraits of Caligula, Nero, Sylla, Septimius Severus, the most cruel and warlike of the Roman emperors; Charles IX., Richard Coeur-de-Lion, Philip II. of Spain, the sanguinary and cruel Mary of England, Catherine de Medicis, Ravaillac, the famous corsair Storzenbecker, the fierce and sanguinary Knipperdolling, (pl. lxix. fig. 2.) and bishop Bonner, who, in the space of four years, sent more than two hundred victims to the flames, all bear the outward mark of a cruel and bloody character.

The action of this organ, when very active, must be necessarily modified by the co-existence of one or many other faculties, equally very active. Combined with love of fighting, it constitutes the warrior, brave to temerity, as well as the invincible brigand. Combined with a high degree of lasciviousness, it constitutes those debauchees, who, like Nero, the author of Justine, and Count Charrolois, stained their debaucheries with blood, and sacrificed the same victims, both to their lust and their blood-thirsty temper.

In treating of the dispositions to theft, pride, devotion, &c, I shall show how they modify the propensity to murder, when they accompany it.

From what has been said, my readers will comprehend, why even Montaigne, who had probably reflected on such facts, could not help expressing the following sentiments:—"I could not be convinced, before seeing it, that there are spirits so brutal as to murder for the single pleasure of the thing; who would hack and hew the limbs of a fellow-being, rack their ingenuity to invent new means of torture, and enjoy the charming sight of the writhings, the dreadful cries and groans of a man dying in agony,—the utmost refinement of cruelty. *Ut homo, hominem, non iratus, non timens, tantum spectaturus occidat.* Seneca, epist. 90.—2.

"I seldom take a wild animal alive, which I do not restore to liberty. Pythagoras bought them of the fishermen and fowlers for the same purpose. The barbarous treatment of brutes, indicates a natural propensity to cruelty. When the Romans had become accustomed to the shows of the murders of wild beasts, they were not long in getting to those of men and gladiators. Nature, I fear, has implanted in man some instinct of inhumanity."[10]

It is proved, therefore, by the natural history of man and brutes—of man, in disease as well as health—that the murderous, or sanguinary instinct, is an innate primitive power, and, consequently, a fundamental quality, resulting from a particular cerebral part, placed just above the ears, in the majority of the carnivorous and omnivorous animals.

---

10. Montagine, Essais liv. 2. chap. 2.

CHAPTER 7

CESARE LOMBROSO

This chapter includes two readings from the works of Cesare Lombroso. The first selection is his article "Criminal Anthropology: Its Origin and Application" (1895–1896), which was published in *The Forum*, volume 20, pp. 33–49. The second selection, written by Lombroso and William Ferrero, is entitled "The Criminal Type in Women and Its Atavistic Origin." It is a chapter from *The Female Offender* ([1893] 1903), pp. 103–114 and illustrations; New York: D. Appleton and Company. In the text, reference is made to an illustration (Plate III, No. 10), which either was not included in the book or was not numbered.

During the 1870s, Lombroso founded the Italian school of positive criminology and established its most prominent branch (criminal anthropology) and its most controversial theory (atavist theory). On the one hand, Lombroso's work opposed many of the propositions and policies of the classical school, which by this time had existed for a full century; on the other, it shared several qualities with early-nineteenth-century phrenology. His work placed a heavy emphasis on biological causes of human behavior and unique physical traits as indicators of atavism, although this emphasis diminished somewhat in the later stages of his career.

In the first reading, Lombroso provides a history of criminal anthropology. He begins with a brief critique of several court practices and suggests his opposition to the orientation of the classical school. He then describes his discovery of atavism as a cause of criminality, his research on epilepsy and crime, and his classification of different kinds of criminals, which changed over the course of his career. In addition, in this reading Lombroso comments on studies by Ferri, Garofalo, and other members of the Italian school; he offers a few criminal justice policy proposals; and he describes some of the ways in which his views have been applied outside of Italy. Interestingly, he commented that while the work of criminal anthropologists had been neglected in Italy, it was being applied in the United States and other nations. Regarding the United States, he noted that it guided the "system of education" at the Elmira Reformatory.

In the second selection, Lombroso and Ferrero present a number of their conclusions regarding atavism in women and its relationship to female criminality. They find that the "criminal type" is less common among female offenders than male offenders. They explain this in terms of an evolutionary process of "sexual selection" and the proposition that women "congenitally ... are less inclined to crime than men." They suggest that women are innately more "conservative" and conclude that female atavists tend to have male characteristics (e.g., "masculine strength"). Nonetheless, they also acknowledge that "opportunities for evil-doing" affect the extent to which women are involved in crime. Overall, this reading offers an illustration of atavist theory, a late-nineteenth-century viewpoint on the differences between male and female offenders, and the kind of science engaged in by Lombroso and other criminal anthropologists of the Italian school.

CRIMINAL ANTHROPOLOGY: ITS ORIGIN AND APPLICATION
by Cesare Lombroso

One thing strikes you when you enter one of our courts,—the sight of judges, state employees like others, who think that they cannot fulfil their functions unless they are masked in a costume of the Middle Ages. The same spirit pervades their judgments. These are often evoked from remote ages. Antiquity is more honored than the truth. The lawyer who can cite in behalf of his client a law of the twelve tables has a better chance to gain his case. Worse yet, the courts are often led astray by formulas that had some sense at the time of their origin, but have none now and simply turn justice from the true path. In Italy, for example, sentences are often annulled because the clerk had forgotten to preface them with the formula, "In the name of His Majesty, by the grace of God and the will of the people, King of Italy." The law prescribes times for the accomplishment of certain formalities. Now justice is often denied to poor wretches who are quite in the right, because they come a half an hour too late, or because they have made a mistake of a few moments in the execution of these formalities.

What is the reason of all this? It is because of the tendency of the human mind to reduce to a minimum the number of mental associations required in a given task. The literal interpretation prevails in practice over all considerations of justice. Legal provisions can be only the rude and imperfect indication of the legislative will, useful only as a guide to the magistrate in attaining justice by a personal mental effort. But they have taken the place of justice and right, and the magistrate has to apply them literally. To judge rightly he ought, in each case, to have resort to his own consciousness, to give free course to those associations of ideas and emotions of which the complexity is so great. He ought to compare the answer of his own consciousness with the customary interpretation of the law. If they do not agree he should examine the differences, analyze the provisions of the law, and, comparing the idea of the more frequent cases for which the law was made with the idea involved in the specific case, modify the application as justice requires.

But this is a long, complex, difficult task. If the comparison be not obvious enough, the judge becomes lost in doubt, and every new case requires a renewed effort. How much simpler it is to apply general provisions of law, drawing from them their logical inferences, not bothering with all the concomitant associations of ideas and emotions, but merely following a longer or shorter chain of reasoning. Once this habit of idio-emotional, or let us call it professional, judgment is formed the mind continues to consider only the logical relations of the general principle to the specific case. It excludes all collateral associations of ideas and feelings, numerous and varied as they are, which lead to a just solution of the actual question. The lofty and complex sentiment of justice is reduced to a sentiment of satisfaction in the logical application of the general principle. All notion of the wrong done to the victim, and the causes of that wrong, is excluded. In brief, the idio-emotional judgment results in the substitution of pure logic for observation and investigation of facts, a characteristic of the primitive periods of science and of periods of scientific degeneracy and decadence.

The consequences of this heedlessness are enormous. The judges pronounce judgment as if the crime formed the simplest incident in the life of the criminal. The criminal, on the other hand, does all that he can to prove the contrary by the rarity of his repentance and his continual relapses, which often reach 80 per cent, with enormous peril and expense to society, and discredit to justice,—which is often only a futile fencing with the criminal for the sole benefit of some rhetorician. The trouble is still greater when the same penalty is administered to a man who kills and steals from cupidity, and to one who has been impelled to crime by a great and noble passion,—patriotism, for instance, or love. It is a long time—thirty years—since I began to think that to avoid these pitfalls the criminal and not the crime must be studied. How did I reach this conclusion? How did I succeed in establishing it?

I. HISTORY OF THE DISCOVERY.—ATAVISM OF THE CRIMINAL

I arrived in Paris in 1861, a very young clinical professor of mental disease, a boy, with my head full of philology and comparative physiology. I soon saw that the most serious lack in this science was that of anatomical and anthropological knowledge. They were studying insanity in general without studying individual lunatics. I set to work. I insisted that we should study lunatics as we would a special variety of the human race, noting the skin, the form, the skull, and particularly the functions, sensibility, etc. My colleagues laughed at me and called me the "Doctor of the steelyard." Little by little the idea prevailed, and now they seem almost to have forgotten who it was that introduced the new somatic school. I had a strong desire to study the morally insane who have since been shown to be the born criminals. It was a principle of mine to deny everything which I did not see, and as there were none of these in our clinic I was inclined to deny their existence. Nevertheless, to make sure of the facts, I commenced to occupy myself with criminals, to frequent prisons, and carefully to gather skulls and brains of prisoners. One evening there died in one of the prisons of the city a celebrated brigand, robber, and incendiary who had often escaped by means of his great agility. Upon the death of this man, who was a true type of the born criminal and morally insane, I examined his skull. It presented an enormous median occipital fossa in place of the occipital median spine which occurs in the interior of the skull. This is a characteristic wanting in the superior apes and existing in all other vertebrates. I made the autopsy in the yard of the prison in the early hours of the morning. The day was very foggy, in the winter of 1864. The weather and the place did not permit me to make a thorough autopsy, but I recollect how, at that moment, the whole idea of my future work rose before me like a picture.

I instantly perceived that the criminal must be a survival of the primitive man and the carnivorous animals. The idea, though yet embryonic, was perfected a few days later, when I was called as an expert by the tribunal of Bergamo in the case of a sort of Jack the Ripper,—one Verzenti. This young peasant, with cross eyes and enormous jaws, was possessed with a desire to disembowel, chew, and eat morsels of women, young and old, who happened to cross his path. He afterward confided to me in secret the great erotic pleasure which he experienced in this.

Then I went furiously to work in the examination of facts, in museums, in prisons, especially at Pesaro (when I was director of an insane asylum), near a great cellular prison where, with a corps of aides, I could go whenever I wished. Some of these took weights, others measured the figures or sketched the faces of the criminals. As for myself, I noted the more important characteristics, questioned the prisoners, treating them to cigars and wine, and applied to them all the modern methods. While the criminal had his hand in the plethysmograph, which gave me in graphic lines all the psychic impressions and the reactions of the brain, I showed him things likely to interest him strongly,—a woman, a purse, a glass of wine, cigars, and noted the effect of these impressions and especially the effect of electric currents. The result indicated a curious insensibility. To complete my studies I finally shut myself up for three years in the great cellular prison of Turin as a physician, until my health was undermined.

It was there that I perceived that my earlier ideas fell short of the truth. I saw that the criminal was worse than the savage, worse sometimes than the true carnivora, especially as regards analgesia. On one occasion I saw one of these criminals, who was working upon a roof several yards in height, fall to the ground and immediately return to his work as if nothing had happened. On another occasion a woman refused, for many days, to allow herself to be cared for, until the odor warned us of the presence of gangrene. It had, in effect, eaten away four fingers from one hand, where she had been cut by her lover. The total of these facts thus gathered was enormous, so that the image of the criminal arose from them in perfect clearness. The anatomy of criminals showed a great number of completely atavistic changes: surcillary arch and frontal sinus enormous; median occipital fossa; suture of the atlas; virile aspect of the skull in women; double articular face of the occipital condyle; flattening of the palate; large oblique orbits varying from 2 per cent to 58 per cent. These traits are often grouped in the same individuals, producing a *type*, in the proportion of 43 per cent. The convolutions of the brain present frequent atavistic anomalies, such as the separation of the calcareous fissure from the occipital, the formation of an operculum of the occipital lobe, and absolutely atypical variations, such as the transverse furrows of the frontal lobe.

The study of 25,000 living beings confirmed, though less constantly, the frequency of the anomalies revealed by the anatomical table. It showed analogies between savages and delinquents in the proportion of 35 to 36 per cent. Among these anomalies were prognathism; the hair black and crisp; the beard thin; oxicephaly; oblique eyes; small skull; the jaw and the zygomes developed; the forehead retreating obliquely from the eyes; the ears large; analogy between the two sexes; a greater extension of all new characteristics added to the necroscopic characteristics which assimilate the European criminal to the Mongolian and Australian type.

A photographic study of 5,000 criminals furnished a means of verifying and fixing the frequency of the criminal physiognomic type in the proportion of 25 per cent, with the maximum of 56 per cent for assassins, and a minimum of 6 to 8 per cent for bankrupts, swindlers, and bigamists. Photography showed how often the ethnic type is effaced among criminals, while they have with each other a veritable resemblance. It shows the frequency of feminine aspect among certain thieves and pederasts, and virility among many female criminals, especially murderesses. A study of 800 free men showed that there may often be found among these the characteristics of degenerate physiognomy, but very rarely, almost never, combined in the same person, and frequently justified by latent criminality. It often happens that greater shrewdness, wealth, or political influence avert the action of the law and hide the criminal in men of great power,—Crispi, for example, or, in New York, the leaders of the Tammany ring.

The anomalies appeared still stranger on studying the psychology and the biology of these unfortunates. Here the analogy with savages was more striking, especially as to tattooing, which in certain criminals prevails to the extent of 25 per cent, among thieves 16 per cent, among minor criminals 34 per cent, and which often serves, as among the savages, to indicate a sect or to boast of a crime. Tattooing is sometimes composed of true pictographic characters, as in the writing of the Indians reported in the publications of the Smithsonian Institution. Thus one man was tattooed with the figure of a woman, winged and crowned. "I caused her to take flight," he said, "for she fled with me, and by me she lost her virgin's crown." She had in her hands two bleeding hearts, denoting the parents who mourned her. Like savages, criminals display great insensibility to pain, which explains their longevity, their ability to bear wounds, their frequent suicide. As with savages also, their passions are swift but violent, vengeance is considered as a duty, and they have a strong love for gambling, alcohol, and complete idleness. Thus the New Caledonians were accustomed to repeat, without knowing it, the remark of the murderer Lemair, "Better die than work." In connection with this, I remember reading one day in a scientific review that among the Australian savages there were found more left-handed persons than among Europeans. I immediately made observations upon 600 criminals in Turin, and found the proportion of left-handed ones double that in the same number of journeyman printers. Again, having read that savages have greater visual acuteness, I set to work with the oculists and found indeed that the acuteness of their vision was far greater than the normal, contrasting with their dulness of touch, hearing, and sense of color. At another time I read concerning a tribe of American Indians that their plays were almost like combats. Then I studied the games and amusements of young criminals in the reformatories, and I found that almost always these amusements involved wounds, even more often than among the savages. Thus, in one game, the object of a player was to save the head and hands from the wounds of two knives used by the others.

However, these observations were not so original as I at first thought they were. The knowledge of a criminal physiognomic type, which at first appeared most novel, and was most generally denied by the savants, is often instinctive among the common people. There are often persons, especially among women, who are far from suspecting even the existence of criminal anthropology, and who yet, at the sight of those who bear criminal characteristics, instantly experience a lively repulsion and know that they are in the presence of a malefactor. I was acquainted with one lady whose life was quite withdrawn from society, who on two occasions discovered the criminal character of certain young people, not before suspected, but afterward detected by the police. How often we read in the reports of trials, of perfectly honest people, unfamiliar with the slightest anthropological observations, who escape certain death from being warned in time by the sinister glance of the assassin, in which they read his criminal intention. It was in this way that the first letter-carrier who was to have been the victim of the murderer Francesconi had time to flee, haunted by that glance. At my request schoolmasters have shown to forty young girls twenty portraits of thieves and twenty of great men. Four-fifths of these children recognized the first as wretched creatures or as scoundrels, and the second as honest men. The universal although involuntary consciousness of the existence of a physiognomy peculiar to criminals has given birth to the epithets "a thief's face," "the look of an assassin," etc. The only way to explain the opposition to the fact is the reluctance of men to draw a general conclusion from individual observations. But how is this universal consciousness itself to be explained? In young girls there is certainly no knowledge acquired by experience. Then what is there? An intuitive sense, is it said? That is a vulgar explanation with which the public is contented because it has no meaning.

I suspect that the phenomenon is hereditary. The impression left us by our fathers and transmitted to our children has become unconscious knowledge, like that of the little birds born and reared in our houses, who strike their wings and beaks in fright against their cages when they see pass above them birds of prey known only to their ancestors. Every day teaches us the importance of the unconscious part in human actions, and what a rôle is played by atavism and heredity. Who of us can realize, when he bends the knees and joins the hands in prayer, that he is making an hereditary movement transmitted from those epochs of barbarism when war was the normal state?

II.—EPILEPSY OF BORN CRIMINALS

My work was only at its beginning. In the earlier years, possessed by the idea of the skull with its occipital fossa, I believed that the criminal was solely and simply an atavistic phenomenon. I was soon compelled to admit that there are in born criminals, not in others, still stranger anomalies than are presented by savages, and with which atavism has nothing to do. These are: precocious wrinkles, irregular teeth, strabismus, synostosis, osteoma, hernia; meningitic, hepatic, and cardiac lesions. These show the criminal to be abnormal before birth, through the disease of various organs, especially the nervous centres. This again is confirmed by histologic observations, dilation of the cerebral lymphatic vessels, pigmentation of the nerve and connective cells, obtuseness of the senses.

I must confess that in my studies I have never reached the solution of my problems suddenly. Thus, in the study of the nature of the *pellagra,* or Italian leprosy, I reached a solution only by successive stages and by accidents occurring in the path of my studies. This time, also, I was aided by an accident after much time lost in investigation. A soldier at Naples, one Misdea, assassinated without any plausible motive three or four of his companions. It was not noticed in any way, on this occasion, that he had an attack of epilepsy. He showed great coolness in his murder and remembered it sufficiently well, though not quite correctly. The entire life of this man, who was descended from a line of degenerates, murderers, and epileptics, was a mass of crimes and diseases. One day he set out to kill his *fiancée,* fell fainting in a church, and lay there all night, foaming at the mouth. He remembered nothing of it. He was a barber by trade. In his regiment he had been relieved of this duty on account of his disease. He was straightway seized with a boundless rage, tore his razors into bits with his teeth, and spit them out before his superior officers. In studying this curious criminal I divined instantly that the disease, which was confused with and obscured by the atavism of the crime, was epilepsy.

In effect, in epilepsy there is found the same absence of moral sense, the same dulness of the physical senses, the same impulsiveness as among criminals. This discovery, strange enough in appearance, is very simple in reality. We often hear the spontaneous remark that certain attacks of criminal rage are marked by "epileptic fury." The discovery was rejected with great unanimity, even by those who, like Tamburini and Morselli, had seen cases of psychic epilepsy without convulsion and without amnesia as is often seen in the case of criminals. As for me, I am used to this reception from savants and demi-savants. Indeed, I see in it the sign that I have struck a new and fruitful vein. For thirty years my colleagues ridiculed me for maintaining that *pellagra* is a poisoning by spoiled maize; and during all those years I was known in Italy as the "pella-groseine crank." But there is one thing more trustworthy than academicians,—Time. After some years the proofs in this direction became very numerous. Left-handedness was found to be very frequent among epileptics, as well as insensibility to wounds. Dr. Ottolenghi discovered a characteristic peculiar to epileptics and born criminals alone, the interruption and contraction with scotoma of the periphery of the visual field. Rossi demonstrated that the proportion of epileptics among criminals was 40 per cent. Even the official statistics of the criminals showed the proportion to be six times more than normal. Krafft-Ebing, and Panata of Verona, found epilepsy in the case of many sexual psychopaths, which explains almost all the more curious crimes due to luxury. Literature, both the ancient and the most modern, agrees with these views. Shakespeare surmised epilepsy in the mind of Macbeth, who suffered from hallucinations. Goncourt saw epilepsy in the murderer of the girl Eliza. Dostoiewski described all his criminals as epileptic in his "Crime et Châtiment." Zola, without knowing it, gave us a complete type of psychic epilepsy in the murderer of "La Bête Humaine." I was able to found the first editions of my "Delinquent Man" on living documents, taking as a basis atavism and epilepsy.

III.—NEW STUDIES: FERRI, GAROFALO, MARRO

By a strange coincidence, which may be called the maturing of an idea, a young man of Bologna, Ferri, about this time wrote a book in which he demonstrated that if there is no free will all the laws should be changed, for punishment has no influence upon the criminal. He continued in this direction, entered completely into my ideas, and showed that I had not taken sufficient account of the occasional criminal and the habitual criminal. Finally he applied himself to the study of "Fifty Years of Criminality in France," supplying for me another of my defects—that of statistics, which has never been my forte. Later he gave in his "Criminal Sociology" all the sociological bases of our school. At the same time a young magistrate of Naples, Garofalo, who acknowledged no standard of punishment but the defence of society, summed up his studies in the sentence, "The more a man is to be feared, the more he should be confined." Shortly after, Marro, a laborious and learned alienist of minute exactness, contributed powerful support to my theories by studying with the patience of a Benedictine all the moral, physical, and psychical characteristics of five hundred criminals, divided, according to the crime, into thieves, swindlers, etc., and compared them with two hundred normal persons of the same country and age. As a climax of exactness he prepared in twelve personal tables all the observations that he had made and provided for the verification of his conclusions. It will be seen that the little edifice, which was quite rudimental when I began to work alone, was beginning to be completed. Thanks to these critics I was able to add to the criminal born the insane criminal (who is quite as formidable, and resembles him closely), the mattoid (also known as the "crank"), and the criminaloid (a semi-criminal born, who requires a great occasion to violate the laws), and the occasional criminal (who violates them when forced by circumstances). But the gap was not yet entirely filled. One last and almost tragic accident revealed to me the criminal through passion. I was one day in a printing-office, correcting the proofs of my "Delinquent Man" with the chief reader. I came to a page which spoke of a young man in the diplomatic service who, impelled by jealousy only too well justified (his *fiancée* had almost shown him the price of her prostitution), had stabbed her with a knife and afterward stabbed himself. Sentenced to a light punishment, he had disappeared. The proof-reader was this man. Suddenly he threw himself at my feet, declaring that he would commit suicide if I published this story with his name. His face, before very gentle, was completely altered and almost terrifying, and I was really afraid that he would kill himself or me upon the spot. I tore up the proofs, and for several editions omitted his story; but I had discovered the criminal through passion.[1] There is a class of men, young, honest, of gentle appearance, whose beauty of soul corresponds to their beauty of body, in no wise apathetic like born criminals, but of an exaggerated affectionateness. One of these young men, being in love and unable to talk with his lady-love, put his ear to a wall, transported with delight to hear her step. My proof-reader declared that he wished to burn his ears with red-hot iron when he heard his *fiancée* uttering unclean things. All these men are capable of remorse and of repentance, and are impelled to crime by a strong and often just cause. They commit the crime in broad daylight, with whatever weapon is at hand, and never seek to prove an alibi. It is my opinion that many political criminals belong in this category,—Orsini, for example, Sand and Charlotte Corday.

After this the work arose, it may be said, if not complete, certainly vital and fecund. A large number of monographs appeared upon special crimes, which would not have been published before. Balestrini made a wonderful study of infanticide and abortion, and demonstrated that these crimes might almost be stricken from the code,—on the one hand because

---

1. I may add that a few years later this man, who had married an extremely plain woman, and who had told me that at the slightest suspicion of his wife he would kill either her or himself, committed suicide without any known cause. I made a study of his skull and brain and found them of admirable beauty.

criminals through passion are incapable of relapse, and on the other hand because, in the case of abortion especially, what is killed is not a man, but a being inferior in the zoological world. Margri at Pisa undertook a study of theft. Florian took up another on defamation, showing that what resembles defamation and is severely punished by the Italian law—which always goes contrary to right—is a necessity of moral and political liberty; that the liberty of criticism, even when it is offensive, should not be restricted, but favored in every possible way. Sighele studied collective crime. He showed, more amply than I had been able to do, that aggregations of human beings have a character quite opposed to that of the units of which they are made up. Though the majority of the crowd may be good, the crowd itself may be converted into a cruel beast. The passions of each, when shared by a great number of individuals at once, become doubly intense, because the emotion of each is communicated from one to another, and the latent criminality of every individual breaks out through the certainty of impunity or through the influence of some one not so honest. This is the basis of his "Foule Criminelle." In another work, "Le Crime à Deux," he demonstrated that persons associated for evil are more to be feared than any single criminal. Occasional criminals, or criminals through passion, never have accomplices. I, myself, with Laschi, constructed a complete penal system for political crimes, starting from misoneism. In nature the law of inertia prevails, and still more in the human race, which has a horror of the new. Every precipitate change which is not extorted by necessity is painful to it, and in politics is punished, for it goes against the opinions and sentiments of the majority. If organic and moral progress does not take place slowly, through powerful attrition, provoked by exterior and interior circumstances, and if man and society are distinctly conservative, it must be concluded that those efforts in favor of progress which adopt means too abrupt and too violent are not physiological. They may sometimes be a necessity for an oppressed minority, but in the eyes of the law they are anti-social and therefore a crime. Often it is a useless crime, for it awakens reaction in the misoneistic direction, which, since it is solidly based on human nature, has great force. All progress, to be accepted, must be slow, otherwise it is futile and mischievous. Those who wish to impose a political innovation upon society, without tradition, without necessity, offend misoneism and arouse that reaction in the public mind which comes from a dread of the new, and invite the application of the penal laws. Here appears the distinction between revolutions and revolts or seditions. The former are slow, long-prepared, necessary, or at most hastened a little by some neurotic or passional spirit. The latter may be an artificial and precipitate incubation, at an exaggerated temperature, of embryos doomed to certain death. These latter are for the most part the work of mattoids (semi-lunatics), lunatics, and born criminals who have a strong tendency to innovation. The former prevail more among the Germanic and Anglo-Saxon races in cold or temperate climates (Luther, Cromwell); the latter are more often found in Latin, Catholic, and warm countries.

Mr. Henry Ferri made a brilliant beginning with the biological, psychical, psycho-pathological study of homicide in his "Criminels, avec Atlas." Under natural conditions of primitive humanity homicide bore, in many respects, a great part, and Mr. Ferri notes with great perspicacity a double process of evolution, toward diminishing ferocity and moral sentiment, and toward judicial institutions. Homicide, therefore, in the form of sanguinary vengeance, is the embryo of all social rights of repression. He infers that murder is not the product of an abstract voluntary fiat, but that it has its roots deep in the animal organism; that it is the natural effect of physio-pathological, physical, and social causes. He gives us the evidence in insensibility, which is the key of innate criminality; in the indifference, and sometimes the pleasure, taken in the sufferings of others; the cool ferocity of crime; the apathetic impassibility as to the crime itself and its penalties,—evident proof that this psychic analgesia is founded upon physical anæsthesia. He shows the futility of motive, the disdain of human life which is a characteristic of savages, and finally the behavior of born homicides, cynical and vain during their trial, and very different afterward. Ferri reports numerous original observations which show that, contrary to the general belief, many homicides confess their crimes, and do so much more frequently than thieves or pickpockets. Quite novel, and capable of a still greater development, is his study upon moral daltonism, by which, in certain criminals, there exists a strong aversion for certain crimes and for the causes and reasons for committing them. Moreover, despite these abnormal conditions of their general senses, criminals also possess sentiments common to other men, but differently developed, lacking the guide and check of the moral sense. For instance, the religious sentiment, which is very frequent among homicides, has nothing to do with the genesis of the crime, because it represents rather a moral sanction than a true and proper moral sense. The most extraordinary part of this work is the atlas. The figures of arid criminal anthropometry are handled with striking certainty. Accounts are given of 695 investigations of great variety and interest. It is the geography not only of homicide, but of all crimes in all the countries of Europe.

Madame Tarnowski, in her studies of the *filles de joie,* thieves, and village women, demonstrated that the cranial capacity of prostitutes is inferior to that of the female thieves and the villagers, and still more to that of women of good society. *Vice versa* the zygomatic process and the mandibles were more developed among the former, who also showed a greater number of anomalies,—87 per cent; while the thieves had 79 per cent, and the villagers only 12 per cent. According to the author, what distinguishes the thieves from the prostitutes is their utter repugnance to giving any information as to their sexual relations, and the silence that falls upon them when the question is raised as to the causes of their confinement. They deny their offence and will not yield even to proof. The hereditary defects of thieves are less marked than those of prostitutes. The latter have, for example, among their ancestry, 82 per cent of inebriate relatives and 44 per cent of consumptives, while the thieves have only 49 per cent and 19 per cent respectively. Thus the thieves possess fewer signs of physical degeneration. Moreover the number of births among them exceeds that of the other class as 256 to 64, a circumstance approaching the normal.

Kurella and Fraenkel in Germany, Havelock Ellis and Morrison in England, extended the horizons of these studies by their own works and by translations from the Italian. A large number of reviews, entirely special, appeared on every side. "L'Archivio di Antropologia Criminale" is already in its eighteenth year. Kowalewski and Mucewski have two in Russia, Lacassagne one in France, Kurella one in Germany. There sprang also into existence a publishing house devoted exclusively to books on criminal anthropology in Italy, which has already issued more than sixty works in three series. A similar one was established in Germany under the direction of Kurella, and another by Morrison in England, which unfortunately commenced with the poorest of my works, making it still poorer by the cruelest mutilations.

IV.—PRACTICAL APPLICATIONS

It is easy enough to see the practical application of these theories. The criminal code has been conceived through the study of crime as an abstraction. It must be modified by knowledge of the criminal. There should be in it no dream of theological expiations, which man has no right to impose, but it should aim solely at the defence of society. The greatest criminal anomaly—even insanity—should not be considered as an extenuating circumstance. Even lunatics should be arrested in order to protect society, especially the morally insane, who are a great peril, and the masked epileptics. In the punishment of crime the tendency of its authors should be considered. If the author is born criminal, he must be confined for life, though the crime itself is not great. On the other hand, a crime committed by an honest man impelled by some strong motive should be punished with much indulgence, especially political and religious crimes, which often only anticipate by some centuries the thought of the people. In our time, when hours are years and years are centuries, a political idea which appears to be dangerous and even criminal through its excessive novelty, after some time may appear practical and just. Such, for instance, were the ideas of Christ and of Luther, and at the present time the ideas of the equality of all classes and of the participation of workmen in profits. There was a time when it would have been a crime to maintain these ideas. Now they pertain to a possible reform. Then it must be understood that for these crimes there should be no irrevocable penalty, like death. The penalty should be revocable when the novelty has passed away and the idea is no longer criminal.

Vice versa, the hand of the law must fall heavily upon the recidivists, putting aside all sentimentality, especially if they have accomplices. And the complicity must not be judged arithmetically, for whether there are four or ten they are equally dangerous. It is merely preferring formulas to facts to exempt an association with less than six members, as is done in Italy, and to ignore the perils of any criminal association. A man who is not contented to steal himself, but enlists others, is more dangerous, and must be treated without pity. Justice cannot be an emanation from the Eternal Father repressing sin and disregarding interests. It especially should undertake to compensate the victims of crime at the expense of the criminal, making him work in order to pay the indemnity if he is not rich. It is a blunder also, when society has lost through the crime, to compel it to lose still more for the support of the criminal.

All efforts at reform should be concentrated upon occasional criminals. They are the only ones for whom much can be done. They should be removed from all opportunity by procuring them employment and protecting them from the mischievous influence of alcohol, not only by prohibitory laws and fines, which are generally a dead letter, but by giving them mental amusement, which will satisfy that cerebral excitement that is gratified by alcohol. Above all, the tendency to crime which appears in infancy must not be allowed to continue in youth and become habitual. All this has received no application in Italy. I was fairly startled when THE FORUM requested from me an account of the applications made in Italy of my ideas. What can one expect from a race of advocates and rhetoricians? When there is a great evil to correct we are contented to make laws, and speeches which have quite as much force. The speeches vanish, and the laws with them, producing no effect. But people get along contentedly because their apathetic quiet is not disturbed. In their hatred of the new they prefer suffering to change. It is true that a new criminal code has been made in our country since my school sprang up, but it is wholly opposed to my ideas. The penalties in the case of relapses have been almost suppressed with great applause in the Senate and the Chamber of Deputies. These great legislators take no account of the foes of free will or of classic law. Nevertheless the *manicome* (guardian of the insane) is necessary for criminals despite the law, and three establishments have been founded in Italy. The penalty of death, which is a sovereign remedy for us, has been abolished, though murderers continue and even multiply their offences.

No provision for judicial anthropometry has been established. An Italian, one of my dearest disciples, Anfasso, has invented an instrument, the tachianthropometer, which rapidly and automatically takes all the measures of the body (I call it, half in jest, the "anthropometric guillotine"), but after much negotiation the government did not accept it. The only countries where anything has really been done in the direction of my school are North America, England, and Switzerland. We must admit that there is a tendency to crime at a very early age. Children are liars, thieves, etc. This tendency in well-born children disappears with a good education, when they are removed from bad examples and evil incitements, but in the criminal born it is continued in spite of everything. Every effort that we can suggest to combat crime should be concentrated, not upon the criminal born, but upon the occasional criminal, to prevent him from wandering from the right path. This class forms about 75 per cent according to our calculations. Now, almost unconsciously, by that intuition which comes from practical vice joined to religious fanaticism unspoiled by formulas and by the bonds of Catholicism, London and Geneva have found the means to prevent the child not criminal born from being driven to evil through the abandonment of his parents or the want of work or of nourishment, so that he does not become an occasional criminal and afterward an habitual one. In this work the ragged schools, etc., Dr. Barnardo's missions, and the enterprises of the Salvation Army are engaged. While in England millions of rescued children are reported, in Italy there are only 12,000; and these are not really rescued, for the houses of correction and reformatories are in reality universities of crime. In the United States, especially in Boston and New York, great efforts have been made in this direction. In all these countries—in America, England, Norway, and Switzerland—an effort has been made to restrict alcoholic poison, which may transform the honest adult into the criminal. Unfortunately, in some countries, continual immigration composed always of adventurous men, together with the mixture of blood, black and yellow, having no common moral sense, and the evil influence of professional politicians, prevent results as important as at London and Geneva. But the United States alone can boast of having conscientiously applied scientific knowledge of criminal anthropology to criminal therapeutics, for at Washington there has been founded the first bureau for degenerates and abnormal people. The worthy founder of the Elmira Reformatory, with the frankness which is no longer found among our old races, has declared that his whole system of education is based upon the knowledge given by our school as to the criminal, and especially as to his psychology. To give new strength to good tendencies; to make of mischievous tendencies—vanity for instance—the stimulus toward the right way; to engraft the taste for work; to avail one's self of the natural desire of the prisoner to shorten his penalty; to remove from all adult occasional criminals the opportunity for relapse,—that is, according to our school, the greatest possible effort for the cure of crime: and I believe that these efforts would be crowned with still greater success if masses of individuals had not been brought together in the same place, and if the adults had not been employed to care for the young; if, following the example of Barnardo, instead of making the prisoners servants or workmen, they had been made good farmers.

Nevertheless, when I compare these establishments with those which I see in Italy and in France, where there is only the appearance of work, with a varnish of bigotry, I am happy and proud. If the new ideas sprung from our old European soil must perish there for want of people who understand them, they will find in the new world fervent supporters, able to perpetuate and apply them. As the inspiring fruit of the vine, which was the first joy and the first sin of the ancient world, is now commencing to be returned to us from the new world modified and improved, so the true political liberty, a Utopian dream in our ancient continent, has already taken deep and sure root in North America, whence the great thinkers of Europe may draw new force for work, and whither they may direct their last glance, finding consolation for a life misunderstood and disdained.

---

from THE FEMALE OFFENDER
by Cesare Lombroso and William Ferrero

THE CRIMINAL TYPE IN WOMEN AND ITS ATAVISTIC ORIGIN

1. *Quota of the type.*—More instructive than a mere analytical enumeration of the characteristics of degeneration is a synthesis of the different features peculiar to the female criminal type.

We call a *complete type* one wherein exist four or more of the characteristics of degeneration; a half-type that which contains at least three of these; and no type a countenance possessing only one or two anomalies or none.

Out of the female delinquents examined 52 were Piedmontese in the prison of Turin, and 234 in the Female House of Correction were natives of different Italian provinces, especially from the South. In these, consequently, we set aside all special characteristics belonging to the ethnological type of the different regions, such as the brachycephali of the Piedmontese, the dolichocephali of the Sardinians, the oxycephali.

We studied also from the point of view of type the 150 prostitutes whom we had previously examined for their several features; as well as another 100 from Moscow whose photographs Madame Tarnowsky sent us.

And we classified under the same heads the various data furnished by Marro, by Grimaldi, and by Madame Tarnowsky, so as to compare the results obtained by all three.

One glance at Table VII. suffices to show the reader how little these various returns differ. The subjects we examined in the House of Correction resemble those we saw in prison; nor do our results differ much from the averages of the other observers, allowance being made for the personal equation or individual divergences in the mode of regarding the same peculiarity.

The results of the examination may be thus summarised:—

1. The rarity of a criminal type in the female as compared with the male delinquent. In our homogeneous group (286) the proportion is 14 per cent., rising, when all other observations are taken into account, to 18 per cent., a figure lower almost by one-half than the average in the male born criminal, namely, 31 per cent.

In normal women this same type is only present in 2 per cent.

All observers agree as to the rarity of the criminal type. Marro records the absence of the type in 58.7 per cent., Madame Tarnowsky in 55 per cent., we found it wanting in 55.9 per cent. of the cases in the House of Correction, and in 55.8 of those in prison; so that altogether the criminal type results as wanting in 57.5 per cent. of delinquents.

The demi-type is present in almost constant proportions, Marro finding it in 22 per cent., Madame Tarnowsky in 21 per cent., we in 29 per cent. in the House of Correction, and in 28.9 in the prison. Average: 25.20 per cent.

2. Prostitutes differ notably from female criminals in that they offer so much more frequently a special and peculiar type. Grimaldi's figures are 31 per cent. (of anomalies), Madame Tarnowsky's 43 per cent., our own 38 per cent.; making a mean of 37.1 per cent. These results harmonise with the conclusions to which we had already arrived in our study of particular features, and our survey of the various types of born prostitutes as distinguished from ordinary female offenders.

TABLE VII
Type of Degeneration in the Female Criminal and Prostitute

	No.	o type	o characteristic	1 characteristic	2 characteristics	½ type, 3 characteristics	Complete type	4 characteristics	5 characteristics	6 characteristics	7 characteristics	8 characteristics
Soldiers	71	89	37.2	—	51.8	—	11.8	11.8	—	—	—	—
Normal males	200	84	32	—	52	—	16	16	—	—	—	—
Normal females	600	—	—	—	—	—	1.89	—	—	—	—	—
Criminal males	353	64.8	8.2	—	56.6	—	35.2	32.6	—	2.3	0.3	—
Great criminals (men)	346	59.1	11.9	—	47.2	—	40.9	33.9	—	6.7	0.3	—
Male criminals (photographs)	228	61	16	17	28	16	24	14	7.5	1.3	1.3	—
Female criminals (German photos.)	83	15	—	—	—	—	28	—	—	—	—	—
Female criminals (Italian)	122	16	—	—	—	—	26	—	—	—	—	—
F. crims. observed by Marro	41	58.7	4.8	32	21	22	19	7.3	9.7	—	2.4	—
F. crims. observed by Tarnowsky	150	55	3	18	34	21	24	10	10	4	—	—
Females in penal establishments (?)	234	55.9	—	—	—	29	14.9	—	—	—	—	—
Murderesses	106	55.7	—	—	—	31.1	13.2	—	—	—	—	—
Thieves	38	55.2	—	—	—	28.9	16	—	—	—	—	—
Infanticides	45	64.4	—	—	—	26.6	8.7	—	—	—	—	—
Swindlers	18	61.1	—	—	—	27.8	11.1	—	—	—	—	—
Corrupt	16	50	—	—	—	31	18.7	—	—	—	—	—
Poisoners	12	33	—	—	—	25	41.6	—	—	—	—	—
Females in prison (thieves)	52	55.8	—	—	—	28.9	15.3	—	—	—	—	—
Average 286 (Lombroso, Ottolenghi)	—	57	—	—	—	29.3	14	—	—	—	—	—
Female criminals photographed	56	62.4	19.6	26.8	16	19.6	17.8	7.1	10.7	—	—	—
Prostitutes (Grimaldi)	26	38	—	23	15	27	31	26	7.6	7.6	—	—
Prostitutes (Tarnowsky)	100	32.9	—	10	22.66	23.33	43	20	9.33	4	2.66	—
Prostitutes (Lombroso, Ottolenghi)	100	30	—	—	—	32	38	—	—	—	—	—
Average of female criminals	533	57.5	—	—	—	25.7	18.7	—	—	—	—	—
Average of prostitutes	226	33.6	—	—	—	27.5	37.1	—	—	—	—	0.66
Female lunatics (Roncoroni)	40	59	2.5	12.5	45	17.5	22.5	15	7.5	—	—	—

3. In the differentiation of female criminals, according to their offences, our last observations on the 286 criminals (made first without knowing the nature of their crimes and classified afterwards) give the prevalence of the criminal type among thieves as 15.3 and 16 per cent.; among assassins as 13.2 per cent., and as rising to 18.7 per cent. in those accused of corruption, among whom were included old prostitutes.

The least frequency was among swindlers, 11 per cent., and infanticides, 8.7 per cent., such women being indeed among the more representative of occasional criminals.

In a yet more complete table Madame Tarnowsky shows how the percentages among homicides prevail over those among thieves, and how the averages among prostitutes are higher than any others, besides giving us the various proportions of the anomalies.[1]

	Normals 150.	Homicides 100.	Thieves 100.	Prostitutes 100.[2]
0 Anomalies	32 per cent.	10 per cent.	40 per cent.	– per cent.
1 ,,	35 ,,	–	6 ,,	4 ,,
2 ,,	26 ,,	14 ,,	18 ,,	12 ,,
3 ,,	4 ,,	38 ,,	22 ,,	22 ,,
4 ,,	2 ,,	16 ,,	14 ,,	30 ,,
5 ,,	–	16 ,,	20 ,,	16 ,,
6 ,,	–	4 ,,	10 ,,	12 ,,
7 ,,	–	2 ,,	6 ,,	22 ,,

Here we see the crescendo of the peculiarities as we rise from moral women, who are most free from anomalies, to prostitutes, who are free from none, and we note how homicides present the highest number of multiple anomalies.

All the same, it is incontestable that female offenders seem almost normal when compared to the male criminal, with his wealth of anomalous features.

2. *Social and atavistic reasons for the rarity of the type.*—The remarkable rarity of anomalies (already revealed by their crania) is not a new phenomenon in the female, nor is it in contradiction to the undoubted fact that atavistically she is nearer to her origin than the male, and ought consequently to abound more in anomalies.

We saw, indeed, that the crania of male criminals exhibited 78 per cent. of anomalies, as against 27 per cent. in female delinquents and 51 per cent. in prostitutes; but we also saw that the monstrosities in which women abound are forms of disease, consequent on disorder of the ovule. But when a departure from the norm is to be found only in the physiognomy, that is to say, in that portion of the frame where the degenerative stamp, the type declares itself, then even in cases of idiotcy, of madness, and, what is more important for our purpose, of epilepsy, the characteristic face is far less marked and less frequent in the woman. In her, anomalies are extraordinarily rare when compared with man; and this phenomenon, with a few exceptions among lower animals, holds good throughout the whole zoological scale.

For this reason, as Viazzi well observes (Anomalo, 1893), the *common* characters of a genus are more evident in the forms of the female. Most naturalists are agreed[3] that for the type of a species also one must look to the female rather than to the male; and this remark may be applied with equal justice to the moral sphere.

Helen Zimmern, in her "Philosophy of Fashion," observed that women show their individuality better than men in the details of their dress, but that the principal lines of every fashion of attire in every age are due to the active, creative element in man. And in truth, beginning with the primitive Greek chiton, sleeveless and flowing, confined by a belt, from which all feminine and masculine habiliments have successively sprung throughout the course of European civilisation, how many have been the varieties of male attire from age to age, among different nations, while the female dress in its general lines is substantially always the same (Viazzi).

Compilers of public statutes have also noted the conservative tendency of women in all questions of social order; a conservatism of which the primary cause is to be sought in the immobility of the ovule compared with the zoosperm.

To this add that the female, on whom falls the larger share of the duty of bringing up the family, necessarily leads a more sedentary life, and is less exposed than the male to the varying conditions of time and space in her environment. More especially is this the case among the greater number of vertebrates, and still more of savages, where the struggle for life, both for parents and progeny, devolves primarily upon the male, and is the incessant cause of variations and peculiar adaptations in functions and organs (Viazzi).

---

1. "Arch. di psich.," xiv. i., 1893.
2. [Editor's note: There appear to be at least two typographical errors in this table. The sum of the percentages for the "Thieves" column substantially exceeds 100 percent, as does the sum of the percentages for the "Prostitutes" column.]

3. Morelli, "Lezioni di Antropologia" (in course of publication), p. 220.

Now, once we admit that the primitive type of a species is more clearly represented in the female, we must proceed to argue thence that the typical forms of our race, being better organised and fixed in the woman through the action of time and long heredity, joined to fewer ancestral variations, are less subject to transformation and deformation by the influences which determine special and retrogressive variations in the male.

Another very potent factor has been sexual selection. Man not only refused to *marry* a deformed female, but ate her, while, on the other hand, preserving for his enjoyment the handsome woman who gratified his peculiar instincts. In those days he was the stronger, and choice rested with him.

It is almost superfluous to record once again the instance of the aboriginal Australian, who, in reply to an inquiry as to the absence of old women in his country, said, "We eat them all!" and on being remonstrated with for such treatment of his wives, answered, "For one whom we lose, a thousand remain."

It is quite certain that the ladies whom they lost were neither the loveliest nor the most attractive. The only anomalies which prevail are such as form no obstacle to sexual selection, either because the male finds them convenient for other reasons, or has no objection to them, or attaches no importance to them. Such is the cushion of the Hottentot women, which is useful for the transport of children; and when this and other anomalies prevail among the women of any tribe, they assume a stable and perpetual character in virtue of the tenacity peculiar to the feminine organism.

Yet another reason for the comparative rarity of the criminal type in women is that congenitally they are less inclined to crime than men. Atavism must be held to account for this fact, savage females, and still more, civilised females, being by nature less ferocious than males. It is the *occasional* offender whom we meet with most frequently among women; and as occasional criminals have no special physiognomy, they can offer no examples of the type. And woman's inability in this respect is all the greater that even when a *born* offender she is, in the majority of cases, an adulteress, a calumniator, a swindler, or a mere accomplice—offences, every one of them, which require an attractive appearance, and prohibit the development of repulsive facial characteristics.

The primitive woman was rarely a murderess; but she was always a prostitute, and such she remained until semi-civilised epochs. Atavism, again, then explains why prostitutes should show a greater number of retrogressive characteristics than are to be observed in the female criminal.

Various as are these solutions of a singular problem, we may, I think, seek yet another. In female animals, in aboriginal women, and in the women of our time, the cerebral cortex, particularly in the psychical centres, is less active than in the male. The irritation consequent on a degenerative process is therefore neither so constant nor so lasting, and leads more easily to motor and hysterical epilepsy, or to sexual anomalies, than to crime. For a similar reason genius is more common in men than in women; and the lower animals remain insensible to narcotics, which intoxicate the human species, and are not subject to delirium or mania when attacked by fever.

We have now got to the reason why criminality increases among women with the march of civilisation. The female criminal is a kind of occasional delinquent, presenting few characteristics of degeneration, little dulness, &c., but tending to multiply in proportion to her opportunities for evil-doing; while the prostitute has a greater atavistic resemblance to her primitive ancestress, the woman of pleasure, and, as we shall see, has consequently a greater dulness of touch and taste, a greater propensity for tattooing, and so on.

In short, the female criminal is of less typical aspect than the male because she is less essentially criminal; because in all forms of degeneration she deviates to a less degree; because, being organically conservative, she keeps the characteristics of her type even in her aberrations from it; and finally because beauty, being for her a supreme necessity, her grace of form resists even the assaults of degeneracy.

But it cannot be denied that when depravity in woman is profound, then the law by which the type bears the brand of criminality asserts itself in spite of all restraint at any rate as far as civilised races are concerned . . . ; and this is particularly true of the prostitute, whose type approximates so much more to that of her primitive ancestress.

3. *Atavism.*—Atavism helps to explain the rarity of the criminal type in woman. The very precocity of prostitutes—the precocity which increases their apparent beauty—is primarily attributable to atavism. Due also to it is the virility underlying the female criminal type; for what we look for most in the female is femininity, and when we find the opposite in her we conclude as a rule that there must be some anomaly. And in order to understand the significance and the atavistic origin of this anomaly, we have only to remember that virility was one of the special features of the savage women. In proof I have but to refer the reader to the Plates opposite, taken from Ploss's work ("Das Weib," 3rd ed.,

1890), where we have the portraits of Red Indian and Negro beauties, whom it is difficult to recognise for women, so huge are their jaws and cheek-bones, so hard and coarse their features. And the same is often the case in their crania and brains.

The criminal being only a reversion to the primitive type of his species, the female criminal necessarily offers the two most salient characteristics of primordial woman, namely, precocity and a minor degree of differentiation from the male—this lesser differentiation manifesting itself in the stature, cranium, brain, and in the muscular strength which she possesses to a degree so far in advance of the modern female. Examples of this masculine strength may still be found among women in country districts of Italy, and especially in the islands; and the reader should now be able to understand why I detect the criminal type in that Z. . . . (Plate III., No. 10), whose likeness would strike many as being very beautiful.

NEGRO WOMAN

RED INDIAN WOMAN

The excessive obesity of prostitutes, to which we have already drawn attention, is perhaps of atavistic origin.

"The fatness of many prostitutes," observes Parent Duchatelet, "strikes those who look at them *en masse* when many are together in one place. Persons living among these women and observing them every day have certified that this obesity only begins at about the age of 25 to 30 years. It is rarely noticeable in young girls or beginners. To what," he continues, "are we to attribute this peculiarity? The most simple explanation seems to lie in the great number of hot baths which such women are accustomed to take throughout the year, and, above all, to their inactive lives and abundant nourishment."

But the lower orders of prostitutes, who are the fattest, do not take baths; and if their lives in the daytime are inactive, they are not so at night, when their wakeful hours are frequent and diversified by dances and orgies. And if we must admit that, as a rule, they grow fat only after the age of 20 years, yet we have but to look at the likenesses furnished by Magnan to observe that the tendency shows itself sometimes in the very young.

Many attribute this obesity to the mercurial preparations of which these women make so large a use. But it is well known that workers in quicksilver mines and makers of looking-glasses, so far from being fat, are noted for their thinness. Moreover, prostitutes who do not use mercury incline to be fat, and mercurial treatment does not produce fleshiness in those who undergo it.

Hottentot, African, and Abyssinian women when rich and idle grow enormously fat, and the reason of the phenomenon is atavistic.

Maternal and sexual functions produce the cushion of the Hottentot woman, who by increasing in adipose and connective tissue reverts to a peculiarity of primitive women—or is, in other words, an example of atavism. Indeed, in Oceania and in Africa the standard of beauty consists in weight, to increase which, various artifices are resorted to, such as imbibing enormous draughts of milk and beer in a progressive ratio, until at last the venal women of those societies are simple monsters of obesity.

In conclusion, I would remark that in prisons and asylums for the insane, the female lunatics are far more often exaggeratedly fat than the men. In Imola there is a girl of 12 years with hypertrophy of the breasts and buttocks (the former weighing two kilogrammes), so that she is fatter than a Hottentot woman, and has to wear special stays.

CHAPTER 8

ENRICO FERRI

The reading in this chapter contains the content of a lecture given by Enrico Ferri at the University of Naples in April 1901. The text comes from Ferri's second lecture in *The Positive School of Criminology: Three Lectures* ([1901] 1913), pp. 49–94; translated by Ernest Untermann; Chicago: Charles H. Kerr and Company. The three lectures were first published in English in 1906 and then reprinted in 1913. The full text of this publication is available through the HathiTrust Digital Library (hathitrust.org).

Given that this lecture was presented in 1901, it perhaps should not be an entry in an anthology subtitled "Readings from the Eighteenth and Nineteenth Centuries." Yet, Ferri's views, as expressed in this lecture, were developed several years earlier. In fact, the first edition of his best-known work, *Criminal Sociology*, was published in 1881 (under a different title). Thus, although this lecture may not be a nineteenth-century reading in a literal sense, it is in its content, and its content is especially useful for understanding the orientation of the Italian school of positive criminology at the very end of the 1800s.

Ferri influenced the course of the Italian school by drawing more attention to the possible effects of social factors on crime. He established "criminal sociology" as a branch of the Italian school. However, as noted earlier, his orientation was not exclusively sociological. He advocated an interdisciplinary approach to the study of crime that explores the "interaction" of "anthropological" causes (biological and psychological factors), "telluric" causes (e.g., natural resources and climate), and "social" causes (e.g., economic, political, and cultural conditions). Ferri's perspective also included a classification of criminals that was comparable to the classification constructed by Lombroso. He acknowledged "born," "insane," "habitual," "occasional," and "passionate" criminals. Moreover, he drew a distinction between egoistic and altruistic criminals, a distinction that reflects his broader political standpoint and allows some criminals to be viewed as progressive. Remaining true to the sociological component of his orientation, he also maintained that a substantial amount of crime can be eliminated by altering social conditions.

In the following lecture, Ferri differentiates the "classic school" from the "positive school." In doing so, he critiques the juridical emphasis and freewill assumption of the former, and he describes the scientific and interdisciplinary orientation of the latter. He also outlines his classification of criminals.

from THE POSITIVE SCHOOL OF CRIMINOLOGY: THREE LECTURES
by Enrico Ferri

LECTURE II

... When a crime is committed in some place, attracting public attention either through the atrocity of the case or the strangeness of the criminal deed—for instance, one that is not connected with bloodshed, but with intellectual fraud—there are at once two tendencies that make themselves felt in the public conscience. One of them, pervading the overwhelming majority of individual consciences, asks: How is this? What for? Why did that man commit such a crime? This question is asked by everybody and occupies mostly the attention of those who do not look upon the case from the point of view of criminology. On the other hand, those who occupy themselves with criminal law represent the other tendency, which manifests itself when acquainted with the news of this crime. This is a limited portion of the public conscience, which tries to study the problem from the standpoint of the technical jurist. The lawyers, the judges, the officials of the police, ask themselves: What is the name of the crime committed by that man under such circumstances? Must it be classed as murder or patricide, attempted or incompleted manslaughter, and, if directed against property, is it theft, or illegal appropriation, or fraud? And the entire apparatus of practical criminal justice forgets at once the first problem, which occupies the majority of the public conscience, the question of the causes that led to this crime, in order to devote itself exclusively to the technical side of the problem which constitutes the juridical anatomy of the inhuman and antisocial deed perpetrated by the criminal.

In these two tendencies you have a photographic reproduction of the two schools of criminology. The classic school, which looks upon the crime as a juridical problem, occupies itself with its name, its definition, its juridical analysis, leaves the personality of the criminal in the background and remembers it only so far as exceptional circumstances explicitly stated in the law books refer to it: whether he is a minor, a deaf-mute, whether it is a case of insanity, whether he was drunk at the time the crime was committed. Only in these strictly defined cases does the classic school occupy itself theoretically with the personality of the criminal. But ninety times in one hundred these exceptional circumstances do not exist or cannot be shown to exist, and penal justice limits itself to the technical definition of the fact. But when the case comes up in the criminal court, or before the jurors, practice demonstrates that there is seldom a discussion between the lawyers of the defense and the judges for the purpose of ascertaining the most exact definition of the fact, of determining whether it is a case of attempted or merely projected crime, of finding out whether there are any of the juridical elements defined in this or that article of the code. The judge is rather face to face with the problem of ascertaining why, under what conditions, for what reasons, the man has committed the crime. This is the supreme and simple human problem. But hitherto it has been left to a more or less perspicacious, more or less gifted, empiricism, and there have been no scientific standards, no methodical collection of facts, no observations and conclusions, save those of the positive school of criminology. This school alone makes an attempt to solve in every case of crime the problem of its natural origin, of the reasons and conditions that induced a man to commit such and such a crime.

For instance, about 3,000 cases of manslaughter are registered every year in Italy. Now, open any work inspired by the classic school of criminology, and ask the author why 3,000 men are the victims of manslaughter every year in Italy, and how it is that there are not sometimes only as many as, say, 300 cases, the number committed in England, which has nearly the same number of inhabitants as Italy; and how it is that there are not sometimes 300,000 such cases in Italy instead of 3,000?

It is useless to open any work of classical criminology for this purpose, for you will not find an answer to these questions in them. No one, from Beccaria to Carrara, has ever thought of this problem, and they could not have asked it, considering their point of departure and their method. In fact, the classic criminologists accept the phenomenon of criminality as an accomplished fact. They analyze it from the point of view of the technical jurist, without asking how this criminal fact may have been produced, and why it repeats itself in greater or smaller numbers from year to year, in every country. The theory of a free will, which is their foundation, excludes the possibility of this scientific question, for according to it the crime is the product of the fiat of the human will. And if that is admitted as a fact, there is nothing left to account for. The manslaughter was committed, because the criminal wanted to commit it; and that is all there is to it. Once the theory of a free will is accepted as a fact, the deed depends on the fiat, the voluntary determination, of the criminal, and all is said.

But if, on the other hand, the positive school of criminology denies, on the ground of researches in scientific physiological psychology, that the human will is free and does not admit that one is a criminal because he wants to be, but declares that a man commits this or that crime only when he lives in definitely determined conditions of personality and environment which induce him necessarily to act in a certain way, then alone does the problem of the origin of criminality begin to be submitted to a preliminary analysis, and then alone does criminal law step out of the narrow and arid limits of technical jurisprudence and become a true social and human science in the highest and noblest meaning of the word. It is vain to insist with such stubbornness as that of the classic school of criminology on juristic formulae by which the distinction between illegal appropriation and theft, between fraud and other forms of crime against property, and so forth, is determined, when this method does not give to society one single word which would throw light upon the reasons that make a man a criminal and upon the efficacious remedy by which society could protect itself against criminality.

It is true that the classic school of criminology has likewise its remedy against crime—namely, punishment. But this is the only remedy of that school, and in all the legislation inspired by the theories of that school in all the countries of the civilized world there is no other remedy against crime but repression.

But Bentham has said: Every time that punishment is inflicted it proves its inefficacy, for it did not prevent the committal of that crime. Therefore, this remedy is worthless. And a deeper study of the cause of crime demonstrates that if a man does not commit a certain crime, this is due to entirely different reasons, than a fear of the penalty, very strong and fundamental reasons which are not to be found in the threats of legislators. These threats, if nevertheless carried out by police and prison keepers, run counter to those conditions. A man who intends to commit a crime, or who is carried away by a violent passion, by a psychological hurricane which drowns his moral sense, is not checked by threats of punishment, because the volcanic eruption of passion prevents him from reflecting. Or he may decide to commit a crime after due premeditation and preparation, and in that case the penalty is powerless to check him, because he hopes to escape with impunity. All criminals will tell you unanimously that the only thing which impelled them when they were deliberating a crime was the expectation that they would go scot free. If they had had the least suspicion that they might be detected and punished they would not have committed the crime. The only exception is the case in which a crime is the result of a mental explosion caused by a violent outburst of passion. And if you wish to have a very convincing illustration of the psychological inefficacy of legal threats, you have but to think of that curious crime which has now assumed a frequency never known to former centuries, namely the making of counterfeit money. For since paper money—from want or for reasons of expediency—has become a substitute of metal coin in the civilized countries, the making of counterfeit paper money has become very frequent in the nineteenth century. Now a counterfeiter, in committing his crime, must compel his mind to imitate closely the inscription of the bill, letter for letter, including that threatening passage, which says: *"The law punishes counterfeiting . . ."* etc. Can you see before your mind's eye a counterfeiter, in the act of engraving on the stone or the plate these words: *"The law punishes counterfeiting . . . ?"* Others may ignore the penalty that awaits them, but he cannot. This illustration is convincing, for in cases of other crimes one may always assume that the criminal acted without thinking of the future, even when he was not in a transport of passion. But in the case of the counterfeiter the very act of committing the crime reminds him of the threat of the law, and yet he is imperturbable while perpetrating it.

Crime has its natural causes, which lie outside of that mathematical point called the free will of the criminal. Aside from being a juridical phenomenon, which it would be well to examine by itself, every crime is above all a natural and social phenomenon, and should be studied primarily as such. We need not go through so hard a course of study merely for the purpose of walking over the razor edge of juristic definitions and to find out, for instance, that from the time Romagnosi made a distinction between incompleted and attempted crime rivers of ink have been spilled in the attempt to find the distinguishing elements of these two degrees of crime. And finally, when the German legislator concluded to make no distinction between incompleted and attempted crime and to recognize only the completed crime in his code of 1871, we witnessed the spectacle of Carrara praising that legislator for leaving that subtle distinction out of his code. A strange conclusion on the part of a science, which cudgels its brains for a century to find the marks of distinction between attempted and incompleted crime, and then praises the legislator for ignoring it. And another classic jurist, Buccellati, proposed to do away with the theory of attempted crime by simply defining it as a crime by itself, or as—a violation of police laws! A science which comes to such conclusions is a science which moves in metaphysical abstractions, and we shall see that all these finespun questions which abound in classical science lose all practical value before the necessity of saving society from the plague of crime.

The method which we, on the other hand, have inaugurated is the following: Before we study crime from the point of view of a juristic phenomenon, we must study the causes to which the annual recurrence of crimes in all countries is due. These are natural causes, which I have classified under the three heads of anthropological, telluric and social. Every crime, from the smallest to the most atrocious, is the result of the interaction of these three causes, the anthropological condition of the criminal, the telluric environment in which he is living, and the social environment in which he is born, living and operating. It is a vain beginning to separate the meshes of this net of criminality. There are still those who would maintain the one-sided standpoint that the origin of crime may be traced to only one of these elements, for instance, to the social element alone. So far as I am concerned, I have combatted this opinion from the very inauguration of the positive school of criminology, and I combat it today. It is certainly easy enough to think that the entire origin of all crime is due to the unfavorable social conditions in which the criminal lives. But an objective, methodical, observation demonstrates that social conditions alone do not suffice to explain the origin of criminality, although it is true that the prevalence of the influence of social conditions is an incontestable fact in the case of the greater number of crimes, especially of the lesser ones. But there are crimes which cannot be explained by the influence of social conditions alone. If you regard the general condition of misery as the sole source of criminality, then you cannot get around the difficulty that out of one thousand individuals living in misery from the day of their birth to that of their death only one hundred or two hundred become criminals, while the other nine hundred or eight hundred either sink into biological weakness, or become harmless maniacs, or commit suicide without perpetrating any crime. If poverty were the sole determining cause, one thousand out of one thousand poor ought to become criminals. If only two hundred become criminals, while one hundred commit suicide, one hundred end as maniacs, and the other six hundred remain honest in their social condition, then poverty alone is not sufficient to explain criminality. We must add the anthropological and telluric factor. Only by means of these three elements of natural influence can criminality be explained. Of course, the influence of either the anthropological or telluric or social element varies from case to case. If you have a case of simple theft, you may have a far greater influence of the social factor than of the anthropological factor. On the other hand, if you have a case of murder, the anthropological element will have a far greater influence than the social. And so on in every case of crime, and every individual that you will have to judge on the bench of the criminal.

The anthropological factor. It is precisely here that the genius of Cesare Lombroso established a new science, because in his search after the causes of crime he studied the anthropological condition of the criminal. This condition concerns not only the organic and anatomical constitution, but also the psychological, it represents the organic and psychological personality of the criminal. Every one of us inherits at birth, and personifies in life, a certain organic and psychological combination. This constitutes the individual factor of human activity, which either remains normal through life, or becomes criminal or insane. The anthropological factor, then, must not be restricted, as some laymen would restrict it, to the study of the form of the skull or the bones of the criminal. Lombroso had to begin his studies with the anatomical conditions of the criminal, because the skulls may be studied most easily in the museums. But he continued by also studying the brain and the other physiological conditions of the individual, the state of sensibility, and the circulation of matter. And this entire series of studies is but a necessary scientific introduction to the study of the psychology of the criminal, which is precisely the one problem that is of direct and immediate importance. It is this problem which the lawyer and the public prosecutor should solve before discussing the juridical aspect of any crime, for this reveals the causes which induced the criminal to commit a crime. At present there is no methodical standard for a psychological investigation, although such an investigation was introduced into the scope of classic penal law. But for this reason the results of the positive school penetrate into the lecture rooms of the universities of jurisprudence, whenever a law is required for the judicial arraignment of the criminal as a living and feeling human being. And even though the positive school is not mentioned, all profess to be studying the material furnished by it, for instance, its analyses of the sentiments of the criminal, his moral sense, his behavior before, during and after the criminal act, the presence of remorse which people, judging the criminal after their own feelings, always suppose the criminal to feel, while, in fact, it is seldom present. This is the anthropological factor, which may assume a pathological form, in which case articles 46 and 47 of the penal code remember that there is such a thing as the personality of the criminal. However, aside from insanity, there are thousands of other organic and psychological conditions of the personality of criminals, which a judge might perhaps lump together under the name of extenuating circumstances, but which science desires to have thoroughly investigated. This is not done today, and for this reason the idea of extenuating circumstances constitutes a denial of justice.

This same anthropological factor also includes that which each one of us has: the race character. Nowadays the influence of race on the destinies of peoples and persons is much discussed in sociology, and there are one-sided schools that pretend to solve the problems of history and society by means of that racial influence alone, to which they attribute an absolute importance. But while there are some who maintain that the history of peoples is nothing but the exclusive product of racial character, there are others who insist that the social conditions of peoples and individuals are alone determining. The one is as much a one-sided and incomplete theory as the other. The study of collective society or of the single individual has resulted in the understanding that the life of society and of the individual is always the product of the inextricable net of the anthropological, telluric and social elements. Hence the influence of the race cannot be ignored in the study of nations and personalities, although it is not the exclusive factor which would suffice to explain the criminality of a nation or an individual. Study, for instance, manslaughter in Italy, and, although you will find it difficult to isolate one of the factors of criminality from the network of the other circumstances and conditions that produce it, yet there are such eloquent instances of the influence of racial character, that it would be like denying the existence of daylight if one tried to ignore the influence of the ethnical factor on criminality.

In Italy there are two currents of criminality, two tendencies which are almost diametrically opposed to one another. The crimes due to hot blood and muscle grow in intensity from northern to southern Italy, while the crimes against property increase from south to north. In northern Italy, where movable property is more developed, the crime of theft assumes a greater intensity, while crimes due to conditions of the blood are decreasing on account of the lesser poverty and the resulting lesser degeneration of the people. In the south, on the other hand, crimes against property are less frequent and crimes of blood more frequent. Still there also are in southern Italy certain cases where criminality of the blood is less frequent, and you cannot explain this in any other way than by the influence of racial character. If you take a geographical map of manslaughter in Italy, you will see that from the minimum, from Lombardy, Piedmont, and Venice, the intensity increases until it reaches its maximum in the insular and peninsular extreme of the south. But even there you will find certain cases in which manslaughter shows a lesser intensity.

For instance, the province of Benevent is surrounded by other provinces which show a maximum of crimes due to conditions of blood, while it registers a smaller number. Naples, again, shows a considerably smaller number of such cases than the provinces surrounding it, but it has a greater number of unpremeditated cases of manslaughter. Messina, Catania and Syracuse have a remarkably smaller number of blood crimes than Trapani, Girgenti and Palermo. It has been attempted to claim that this difference in criminality is due to social conditions, because the agricultural conditions in eastern Sicily are less degrading than those of Girgenti and Trapani, where the sulphur mines compel the miners to live miserably. But we should like to ask the following question in opposition to this idea: Why and in what respect are the agricultural conditions in some provinces better than in others? This condition is merely itself a result, not a cause of the first degree.

Since the theory of historical materialism, which I prefer to call economic determinism, has demonstrated that political, moral and intellectual phenomena are reactions on the economic conditions of any time and place, the attempt has been made to interpret this theory very narrowly and to pretend that the economic condition of a nation is a primary cause and not determined by any other. For my part, ever since I have demonstrated the perfect accord between the Marxian and the Darwinian theories, I have said: Very well, the economic conditions of a nation explain its political, moral, intellectual conditions, but the economic condition is in its turn the result of other factors. For instance, how can the industrialism of England in the nineteenth century be explained? Take away the coal mines (the telluric environment), and you could not have the economic conditions of England as they are. For the economic conditions are a result of favorable or unfavorable telluric conditions which are acted upon by the intelligence and energy of a certain race. Catania, Messina, Syracuse, are in a better economic condition, because they have better geographical conditions and a different race (of Grecian blood) than the other Sicilian provinces. So it is in Apulia and Naples, which have likewise a considerable mixture of Grecian blood. The northern tourists are still attracted by our art and visit the ruins of Taormina or Pesto, which are the relics of the Grecian race. And it is the Grecian blood which explains the lesser frequency of bloody crimes in those provinces. This is therefore evidently the influence of the race. And I maintain that the same fact is due in the province of Benevent to the admixture of Langobardian blood. For the Duchy of Benevent has had an influx of Langobardian elements since the seventh century. And as we know that the German and Anglo-Saxon race has the smallest tendency towards bloody crimes, the beneficial influence of this racial character in Benevent explains itself. On the other hand, there is much Saracen blood in the western and southern provinces of Sicily, and this explains the greater number of bloody crimes there. It is evident that the organic character of the inhabitants of that island, where you may still see the brutal and barbarian features of the Saracen by the side of those of the blond, cool and quiet Norman, contains a transfusion of the blood of diverse races. But it is also true that wherever a certain race has been predominant, there its influence is left behind in the individual and collective life.

Let this be enough so far as the anthropological factor of criminality is concerned. There are, furthermore, the telluric factors, that is to say, the physical environment in which we live and to which we pay no attention. It requires much philosophy, said Rousseau, to note the things with which we are in daily contact, because the habitual influence of a thing makes it more difficult to be aware of it.

This applies also to the immediate influence of the physical conditions on human morality, notwithstanding the spiritualist prejudices which still weigh upon our daily lives. For instance, if it is claimed in the name of supernaturalism and psychism that a man is unhappy because he is vicious, it is equivalent to making a one-sided statement. For it is just as true to say that a man becomes vicious because he is unhappy. Want is the strongest poison for the human body and soul. It is the fountain head of all inhuman and antisocial feeling. Where want spreads out its wings, there the sentiments of love, of affection, of brotherhood, are impossible. Take a look at the figures of the peasant in the far-off arid Campagna, the little government employe, the laborer, the little shopkeeper. When work is assured, when living is certain, though poor, then want, cruel want, is in the distance, and every good sentiment can germinate and develop in the human heart. The family then lives in a favorable environment, the parents agree, the children are affectionate. And when the laborer, a bronzed statue of humanity, returns from his smoky shop and meets his white-haired mother, the embodiment of half a century of immaculate virtue and heroic sacrifices, then he can, tired, but assured of his daily bread, give room to feelings of affection, and he will cordially invite his mother to share his frugal meal. But let the same man, in the same environment, be haunted by the spectre of want and lack of employment, and you will see the moral atmosphere in his family changing as from day into night. There is no work, and the laborer comes home without any wages. The wife, who does not know how to feed the children, reproaches her husband with the suffering of his family. The man, having been turned away from the doors of ten offices, feels his dignity as an honest laborer assailed in the very bosom of his own family, because he has vainly asked society for honest employment. And the bonds of affection and union are loosened in that family. Its members no longer agree. There are too many children, and when the poor old mother approaches her son, she reads in his dark and agitated mien the lack of tenderness and feels in her mother heart that her boy, poisoned by the spectre of want, is perhaps casting evil looks at her and harboring the unfilial thought: "Better an open grave in the cemetery than one mouth more to feed at home!"

It is true, that want alone is not sufficient to prepare the soil in the environment of that suffering family for the roots of real crime and to develop it. Want will weaken the love and mutual respect among the members of that family, but it will not be strong enough alone to arm the hands of the man for a matricidal deed, unless he should get into a pathological mental condition, which is very exceptional and rare. But the conclusions of the positive school are confirmed in this case as in any other. In order that crime may develop, it is necessary that anthropological, social and telluric factors should act together.

We generally forget the conditions of the physical environment in which we live, because supernatural prejudice tells us that the body is a beast which we must forget in order to elevate ourselves into a spiritual life. Manzoni could designate the Middle Ages by the term "dirty," because they neglected the demands of elementary hygiene, and thus of human morality. For where the requirements of our physical body are neglected or offended, there no flower can bloom. The telluric environment has a great influence on our physical activity, by way of our nervous system. We feel differently disposed, according to whether a south or a north wind blows. When Garibaldi was on the Pampas, he observed that his companions were irascible and prone to violent quarrels, when the Pampero blew, and that their behavior changed, when this wind ceased. The great founders of criminal statistics, Quetelet and Guerry, observed that the change of seasons carried with it a change in criminality. Sexual crimes are less frequent in winter than in spring and summer. And with reference to this point I have maintained, and still maintain, that it is due to the combined effects of temperature and social conditions, if crimes against property increase in winter. For lack of employment, the want of food and shelter, intensify the misery and lead to attacks on property. On the other hand, the cold by itself reduces sexual crimes and personal assaults. And those who claim that the longer intercourse between people in summer time has also a social influence, are also partly in the right.

The most eloquent fact in this respect was mentioned by Murro, when he pointed out that this change in the frequency of bloody crimes, greater in the warm months than in winter, applied also to prisoners. Statistics show that breach of discipline is most frequent in hot seasons. The social factor does not enter there, because the social life is there the same in winter and in summer. This is, therefore, a practical proof of the influence of climate, and it is re-enforced by the fact that delirium and epilepsy in insane asylums are also more frequent in hot than in cold months. The influence of the telluric factors, then, cannot be denied, and the influence of the social factor intensifies it, as I have already shown by its most drastic and characteristic example, that of want. One can, therefore, understand that a man, whose morality has been shaken by the pressure of increasing want, may be led to commit a crime against property or persons.

It is certainly quite evident that economic misery has an undeniable influence on criminality. And if you consider, that about 300,000 criminals are sentenced in Italy every year, 180,000 of them for minor crimes, and 120,000 for crimes which belong to the gravest class, you can easily see that the greater part of them are due mainly to social conditions, for which it should not be so very difficult to find a remedy. The work of the legislator may be slow, difficult, and inadequate, so far as the telluric and anthropological factors are concerned. But it could surely be rapid, efficacious and prompt, so far as the social factors influencing criminality are concerned.

We have now demonstrated that crime has its natural source in the combined interaction of three classes of causes, the anthropological (organic and psychological) factor, the telluric factor, and the social factor. And by this last factor we must not only mean want, but any other condition of administrative instability in political, moral, and intellectual life. Every social condition which makes the life of man in society insincere and imperfect is a social factor contributing towards criminality. The economic factor is in evidence in our civilization wherever the law of free competition, which is but a form of disguised cannibalism, establishes the rule: *Your death is my life.* The competition of laborers for a limited number of places is equivalent to saying that those who secure a living do so at the expense of those who do not. And this is a disguised form of cannibalism. While it does not devour the competitor as primitive mankind did, it paralyzes him by calumnies, recommendations, protection, money, which secure the place for the best bargainer and leave the most honest, talented, and self-respecting to the pangs of starvation.

Moreover, the economic factor exerts its crime-breeding influence also under the form of a superabundance of wealth. Indeed, in our present society, which is in the downward stage of transition from glorious bourgeois civilization, which constituted a golden page of human history in the 19th century, wealth itself is a source of crime. For the rich, who do not enjoy the advantage of manual or intellectual work, suffer from the corruption of leisure and vice. Gambling throws them into an unhealthy fever; the struggle and race for money poison their daily lives.

And although the rich may keep out of reach of the penal code, still they have condemned themselves to a life devoted to hypocritical ceremonies, which are devoid of moral sentiment. And this life leads them to a sportive form of criminality. To cheat at gambling is the inevitable fate of these parasites. In order to kill time they give themselves up to games of chance, and those who do not care for that devote themselves to the sport of adultery, which in that class is a pastime even among the best friends, on account of sheer mental poverty. And all because man's mind unoccupied is the devil's own forge, as the English poet says.

We have now surveyed briefly the natural genesis of crime, as a natural social phenomenon, brought about by the interaction of anthropological, telluric, and social influences, which in any determined moment act upon a personality standing on the cross road of vice and virtue, crime and honesty. This scientific deduction gives rise to a series of investigations which satisfy the mind and supply it with a real understanding of things, far better than the theory that a man is a criminal because he wants to be. No, a man commits crime because he finds himself in certain physical and social conditions, from which the evil plant of crime takes life and strength. Thus we obtain the origin of that sad human figure which is the product of the interaction of those factors, an abnormal man, a man not adapted to the conditions of the social environment in which he is born, so that emigration becomes an ever more permanent phenomenon for the greater portion of men, for whom the accident of birth will less and less determine the course of their future life. And the abnormal man who is below the minimum of adaptability to social life and bears the marks of organic degeneration, develops either a passive or an aggressive form of abnormality and becomes a criminal.

Among these abnormal human beings, two groups must be particularly distinguished. Limiting our observations to those who are true aggressively antisocial abnormals, that is to say, who are not adapted to a certain social order and attack it by crimes, we must distinguish those who for egoistic or ferocious reasons attack society by atavistic forms of the struggle for existence by committing socalled common crimes in the shape of fraud or violence, thereby opposing or abolishing conditions in which their fellow beings may live. This is the atavistic type of criminals which represents an involuntary, or retrogressive, form of abnormality, due to an arrested development or an atavistic reversion to a savage and primitive type. These constitute the majority in the world of criminals and must be distinguished from the minority, who are evolutionary, or progressive, abnormals, that may also commit crime in a violent form, but must not be confounded with the others, because they do not act from egoistic motives, but rebel from altruistic motives against the injustice of the present order. These altruistic criminals feel the sufferings and horrors due to the injustice surrounding them and may go so far as to commit murder, which must always be condemned, but which must not be confounded with atavistic or egoistic murder. Recourse to personal violence is always objectionable from the point of view of higher manhood, which desires that human life should always be held in respect. But the reasons for such a crime are different, being egoistic in the one, and altruistic in the other case. The evolutionary abnormal is often an instrument of human progress, not in the form of criminality, but in that of intellectual and moral rebellion against conditions which are sanctioned by laws that frequently punish such an evolutionary rebellion harder than atavistic crime, as they do in Russia, where capital punishment has been abolished for common crimes, but retained for political violations of the law! We are living in an epoch of transition from the old to the new, and contemporaneous humanity has an uneasy moral conscience in this critical time. The ruling classes are losing their clearness of vision, so that they promise monuments to those political murderers who promoted their own historical victories, but would condemn like any common criminal him who now devotes his soul to a revolutionary ideal, would throw into prison the pioneer of new human ideals, just as Russia is excommunicating the rebel Tolstoi. I mention Leo Tolstoi advisedly for the purpose of giving a precise illustration of my heterodox thought in reference to this question. We are opposed to any form of personal violence (with the sole exception of self-defense), we cannot approve of any form of personal assault, no matter what may be its motive. Therefore we cannot have words of praise or excuse for political murder, though it may be inspired by altruistic motives. We can demand that the legislator should distinguish between the psychological sources of these two forms of murder, the egoistic and the altruistic form. But we condemn them both, because they are inhuman forms of violence. Ideas do not make victorious headway by force of arms. Ideas must be combatted by ideas, and it is only by the propaganda of the idea that we can prepare humanity for its future. Violence is always a means of preventing the sincere and fruitful diffusion of an idea. We do not say this merely for the abnormals of the lower classes. We refer with scientific serenity also to the upper classes, who would suppress by violence every manifestation of revolt against the social iniquities, every affirmation of faith in a better future.

This is the conception of our science, which thus succeeds in distinguishing traits of character even among the unlucky and forlorn people of the criminal world, while the classic school of criminology regards a criminal as a sort of abstract and normal man, with the exception of cases of minors, deafmutes, inebriates, and maniacs.

In fact, the classic school of criminology regards all thieves as THE thief, all murderers as THE murderer, and the human shape disappears in the mind of the legislator, while it re-appears before the judge. Before the essayist and legislator, the criminal is a sort of moving dummy, on whose back the judge may paste an article of the penal code. If you leave out of consideration the established cases of exceptional and rare human psychology mentioned in the penal code, all other cases serve the judge merely as an excuse to select from the criminal code the number of that article which will fit the criminal dummy, and if he should paste 404 instead of 407 on its back, the court of appeals would resist any change of numbers. And if this dummy came to life and said: "The question of my number may be very important for you, but if you would study all the conditions that compelled me to take other people's things, you would realize that this importance is very diagrammatic," the judge would answer: "That's all right for the justice of the future, but it isn't now. You are number 404 of the criminal code, and after leaving this court room with this number pasted legally on your back, you will receive another number, for you will enter prison as number 404 and will exchange it for entry number 1525, or some other, because your personality as a man disappears entirely before the enactment of social justice!" And then it is pretended that this man, whose personality is thus absurdly ignored, should leave prison cured of all degeneration, and if he falls back into the path of thorns of his misery and commits another crime, the judge simply pastes another article over the other, by adding number 80 or 81, which refer to cases of relapse, to number 404!

In this way the classic school of criminology came to its unit of punishment, which it heralded as its great progress. In the Middle Ages, the diversity of punishment was greater. But in the 19th century the classic school of criminology combatted dishonoring punishment, corporeal punishment, confiscation, professional punishment, capital punishment, with its ideal of one sole penalty, the only panacea for crime and criminals, *prison.*

We have, indeed, prohibitory measures and fines even today. But in substance the whole punitive armory is reduced to imprisonment, since fines are likewise convertible into so many days or months of imprisonment. Solitary confinement is the ideal of the classic school of criminology. But experience proves that this penalty has as much effect on the disease of criminality, as the remedy of a physician would have, who would sit in the door of a hospital and tell every patient seeking relief: "Whatever may be your disease, I have only one medicine and that is a decoction of rhubarb. You have heart trouble? Well, then, the problem for me is simply—how big a dose of rhubarb decoction shall I give you?"

And measuring doses of penalty is the foundation of the criminal code. That is so true that this code is in its last analysis but a table of criminal logarithms for figuring out penalties. Woe to the judge who makes a mistakes in sentencing a 19 year old offender who was drunk when he sinned, but had premeditated his deed. Woe to the judge, if he misses his calculation in adding or subtracting the third, or sixth, or one half, corresponding to the prescribed extenuating or aggravating circumstances! If he makes a miscalculation, the court of appeals is invoked by the defendant, and the inexorable court of appeals tells the judge: "Figure this over again. You have been unjust." The only question for the judge is this: Add your sums and subtract your deductions, and the prisoner is sentenced to one year, seven months, and thirteen days. Not one day more or less! But the human spectator asks: "If the criminal should happen to be reformed before the expiration of his term, should he be retained in prison?" The judge replies: "I don't care, he stays in one year, seven months, and thirteen days!"

Then the human spectator says: "But suppose the criminal should not yet be fit for human society at the expiration of his term?" The judge replies: "At the expiration of his term he leaves prison, for when he has absolved his last day, he has paid his debt!"

This is the same case as that of the imaginary physician who says: "You have heart trouble? Then take a quart of rhubarb decoction and stay twelve days in the hospital." Another patient says: "I have broken my leg." And the doctor: "All right, take a pint of rhubarb decoction and 17 days in the hospital." A third has inflammation of the lungs, and the doctor prescribes three quarts of rhubarb decoction and three months in the hospital. "But if my inflammation is cured before that time?" "No matter," says the doctor, "you stay in three months." "But if I am not cured of my lung trouble after three months?" "No matter," says the doctor, "you leave after three months."

To such results have wise men been led by a system of penal justice, which is a denial of all elementary common sense. They have forgotten the personality of the criminal and occupied themselves exclusively with crime as an abstract juristic phenomenon. In the same manner, the old style medicine occupied itself with disease as such, as an abstract pathological phenomenon, without taking into account the personality of the patient. The ancient physicians did not consider whether a patient was well or ill nourished, young or old, strong or weak, nervous or fullblooded. They cured fever as fever, pleurisy as pleurisy. Modern medicine, on the other hand, declares that disease must be studied in the living person of the patient. And the same disease may require different treatment, if the condition of the patient is different.

Criminal justice has taken the same historical course of development as medicine. The classic school of criminology is still in the same stage, in which medicine was before the middle of the 19th century. It deals with theft, murder, fraud, as such. But that which claims so much of the attention of society has been forgotten by the classic school. For that school has forgotten to study the murderer, the thief, the forger, and without that study their crimes cannot be understood.

Crime is one of the conditions required for the study of the criminal. But the same crime may require the application of different remedies to the personalities of different criminals, according to the different anthropological and social conditions of the various criminals. There is a fundamental distinction between the anthropological and social types of criminals, whom I have divided into five categories, which are today unanimously accepted by criminalist anthropologists, since the Geneva congress offered an opportunity to explain the misapprehension which led some foreign scientists to believe that the Italian school regarded one of these types (the born criminal) merely as an organic anomaly.

Just a word concerning each one of these five types.

The *born criminal* is a victim of that which I will call (seeing that science has not yet solved this problem) criminal neurosis, which is very analogous to epileptic neurosis, but which is not in itself sufficient to make one a criminal. Our adversaries had the idea that the mere possession of a crooked nose or a slanting skull stamped a man as predisposed by birth to murder or theft. But a man may be a born criminal, that is to say, he may have some congenital degeneration which predisposes him toward crime, and yet he may die at the age of 80 without having committed any crime, because he was fortunate enough to live in an environment which did not offer him any temptation to commit crime. Again, are not many predisposed toward insanity without ever becoming insane? If the same individual were to live under unfavorable conditions, without any education, if he were to find himself in unhealthy telluric surroundings, in a mine, a rice field, or a miasmatic swamp, he would become insane. But if instead of living in conditions that condemn him to lunacy he were to be under no necessity to struggle for his daily bread, if he could live in affluence, he might exhibit some eccentricity of character, but would not cross the threshold of an insane asylum. The same happens in the case of criminality. One may have a congenital predisposition toward crime, but if he lives in favorable surroundings, he will live to the end of his natural life without violating any criminal or moral law. At any rate we must drop the prejudice that only those are criminals on whose backs the judge has pasted a number. For there are many scoundrels at large who commit crime with impunity, or who brush the edge of the criminal law in the most repulsive immorality without violating it.

This misunderstanding was explained at the congress of Geneva by the statement that the interaction of the social and telluric environment is required also in the case of the born criminal. And now we may take it for granted that my classification of five types is everywhere accepted. These are the following: The *born criminal* who has a congenital predisposition for crime; the *insane criminal* suffering from some clinical form of mental alienation, and whom even our existing penal code had to recognize; the *habitual criminal,* that is to say one who has acquired the habit of crime mainly through the ineffective measures employed by society for the prevention and repression of crime. A common figure in our large industrial centers is that of the abandoned child which has to go begging from its earliest youth in order to collect an income for the enterprising boss or for its poor family, without an opportunity to educate its moral sense in the filth of the streets. It is punished for the first time by the law and sent to prison or to a reformatory, where it is inevitably corrupted. Then, when such an individual comes out of prison, he is stigmatized as a thief or forger, watched by the police, and if he secures work in some shop, the owner is indirectly induced to discharge him, so that he must inevitably fall back upon crime.

Thus one acquires crime as a habit, a product of social rottenness, due to the ineffective measures for the prevention and repression of crime. There is furthermore the *occasional criminal,* who commits very insignificant criminal acts, more because he is led astray by his conditions of life than because the aggressive energy of a degenerate personality impels him. If he is not made worse by a prison life, he may find an opportunity to return to a normal life in society. Finally there is the *passionate criminal,* who, like the insane criminal, has received attention from the positive school of criminology; which, however, did not come to any definite conclusions regarding him, such as may be gathered by means of the experimental method through study in prisons, insane asylums, or in freedom. The relations between passion and crime have so far been studied on a field in which no solution was possible. For the classic school considers such a crime according to the greater or smaller intensity and violence of passion and comes to the conclusion that the degree of responsibility decreases to the extent that the intensity of a passion increases, and vice versa. The problem cannot be solved in this way. There are passions which may rise to the highest degree of intensity without reducing the responsibility. For instance, is one who murders from motives of revenge a passionate criminal who must be excused?

The classic school of criminology says "No," and for my part I agree with them. Francesco Carrara says: "There are blind passions, and others which are reasonable. Blind passions deprive one of free will, reasonable ones do not. Blind and excusable passions are fear, honor, love, reasonable and inexcusable ones are hatred and revenge." But how so? I have studied murderers who killed for revenge and who told me that the desire for revenge took hold of them like a fever, so that they "forgot even to eat." Hate and revenge can take possession of a man to such an extent that he becomes blind with passion. The truth is that passion must be considered not so far as its violence or quantity are concerned, but rather as to its quality. We must distinguish between social and antisocial passion, the one favoring the conditions of life for the species and collectivity, the other antagonistic to the development of the collectivity. In the first case, we have love, injured honor, etc., which are passions normally useful to society, and aberrations of which may be excused more or less according to individual cases. On the other hand, we have inexcusable passions, because their psychological tendency is to antagonize the development of society. They are antisocial, and cannot be excused, and hate and revenge are among them.

The positive school therefore admits that a passion is excusable, when the moral sense of a man is normal, when his past record is clear, and when his crime is due to a social passion, which makes it excusable. . . .

We have thus exhausted in a short and general review the subject of the natural origin of criminality.—To sum up, crime is a social phenomenon, due to the interaction of anthropological, telluric, and social factors. This law brings about what I have called criminal saturation, which means that every society has the criminality which it deserves, and which produces by means of its geographical and social conditions such quantities and qualities of crime as correspond to the development of each collective human group.

Thus the old saying of Imetelet[1] is confirmed: "There is an annual balance of crime, which must be paid and settled with greater regularity than the accounts of the national revenue." However, we positivists give to this statement a less fatalistic interpretation, since we have demonstrated that crime is not our immutable destiny, even though it is a vain beginning to attempt to attenuate or eliminate crime by mere schemes. The truth is that the balance of crime is determined by the physical and social environment. But by changing the condition of the social environment, which is most easily modified, the legislator may alter the influence of the telluric environment and the organic and psychic conditions of the population, control the greater portion of crimes, and reduce them considerably. It is our firm conviction that a truly civilized legislator can attenuate the plague of criminality, not so much by means of the criminal code, as by means of remedies which are latent in the remainder of the social life and of legislation. And the experience of the most advanced countries confirms this by the beneficent and preventive influence of criminal legislation resting on efficacious social reforms.

We arrive, then, at this scientific conclusion: In the society of the future, the necessity for penal justice will be reduced to the extent that social justice grows intensively and extensively.

---

1. Editor's note: The quote appears to be from Quetelet.

CHAPTER 9

RAFFAELE GAROFALO

The reading in this chapter is from Raffaele Garofalo's *Criminology* (1914), pp. 3–5 and 33–45; translated by Robert Wyness Millar; Boston: Little, Brown and Company. The first edition of *Criminology* was published in 1885. The excerpt in this chapter is an English translation of the 1905 French edition, with a few changes based on the second Italian edition (1891). In his preface, the translator comments, "... the interests of the English version have at times seemed to require that the Italian edition be laid under direct contribution" (p. xiii). The translator's footnotes have been deleted, and the author's footnotes have been renumbered. The full text of *Criminology* is available through the HathiTrust Digital Library (hathitrust.org).

Garofalo was another prominent member of the Italian school who produced his most important work during the late nineteenth century. In the following selection, he provides his conception of "the natural crime," a "sociologic definition of crime" that was intended to be scientific and to fill a significant gap in the research program of the Italian school. Garofalo noted that although this school was dedicated to the scientific study of criminals, it lacked a clear conception of crime with which criminals could be distinguished from other offenders. He emphasized that criminologists should focus their attention on the study of offenders who commit natural crimes, suggesting that such offenders are true criminals, at least in modern societies.

Because space limitations do not allow for a complete presentation of Garofalo's discussion of the natural crime, some additional information on this reading may be helpful. Garofalo acknowledged that conceptions of crime vary markedly across different societies and concluded that no particular act appears to be regarded as criminal "at all times and in all places." Drawing on the work of Herbert Spencer, he then argued that human evolution is accompanied by the progressive development of "the moral sense." More specifically, it entails growth in the altruistic sentiments of "pity" and "probity," the former referring to "repugnance to cruelty" (p. 21) and the latter to "respect for all that which belongs to others" (p. 31). Garofalo maintained that pity is more a product of "natural heredity" than probity, but he also held that both sentiments have become instinctive to some degree. He suggested that these sentiments existed in an "embryonic" form among our distant ancestors and increased in scope with the growth of civilization. They are salient sentiments of modern people. More importantly, for Garofalo, a natural crime is an act that violates one or both of these sentiments at a fundamental level. Given this definition, some acts that violate the criminal law of a nation—for instance, some offenses against "modesty" (e.g., public nudity) and the state (e.g., flag desecration)—are not "true crimes." The people who commit these offenses, therefore, do not fit Garofalo's conception of a true criminal, the kind of criminal that should be of primary interest to criminologists.

---

from CRIMINOLOGY
by Raffaele Garofalo

THE NATURAL CRIME

§1. The Need of a Sociologic Notion of Crime

The Lack of a Sociologic Definition of Crime. —Toward the close of the 1800s the study of the criminal from the point of view of the natural sciences began to engage marked attention. As a result, his anthropologic and psychologic descriptions have been noted; he has been presented as a type, as a variety of the "genus homo." But when we come to consider how this theory may be applied to legislation, serious difficulties are encountered. By no means every person who is an offender according to legal standards answers the description of the naturalists' criminal man—a circumstance which has thrown doubt upon the practical value of such studies. Nor could the case be otherwise, from the very fact that although the naturalists speak of the *criminal,* they have omitted to tell us what they understand by the word *crime*. This task of definition they have left to the jurists, without attempting to say whether or not criminality from the legal standpoint is coterminous with criminality from the sociologic point of view. It is this lack of definition which has hitherto rendered the naturalists' study of crime a thing apart and caused it to be regarded as a matter of purely scientific interest with which legislation has nothing to do.

Crime not Properly a Juridical Notion. —To my mind, then, the initial step in our investigation should be the attainment of the sociologic notion of crime. It will not do to say that we are dealing with a legal notion and that consequently its definition belongs to the jurists alone. We are here concerned not with a technical term, but with a word which expresses an idea accessible to every one, irrespective of his knowledge of the law. The law-maker has not created this term, but has borrowed it from the popular language. He has not even defined it. All that he has done is to group a certain number of acts and call them crimes. This is why, at the same period of time and often within the confines of a single nation, we find a given act in one locality treated as a crime and in another not punished at all. It follows that the legal classification can in no way foreclose sociologic investigation. For the solution of his doubts regarding the boundaries of criminality, the sociologist cannot turn to the man of law, as he would to the chemist to learn the nature of salts or acid, or to the physicist to be informed of the notion of light or electricity. This notion of crime he must seek for himself. Only when he will have taken the pains to tell us what he understands by crime, shall we know what criminals he is talking about. In a word, we must arrive at the notion of the *natural crime*. In this expression, be it noted, the word "natural" is given the meaning of that which is not conventional, of that which exists in a human society independently of the circumstances and exigencies of a given epoch or the particular views of the law-maker. I employ the phrase "natural crime," because I believe it to be the clearest and least inexact—I do not say the most exact—form of words to designate those acts which no civilized society can refuse to recognize as criminal and repress by means of punishment. . . .

§5. Rationale of the Natural Crime

Injury to Pity or Probity the Essential Element. —From what has been said in §4, we may conclude that the element of immorality requisite before a harmful act can be regarded as criminal by public opinion, is the injury to so much of the moral sense as is represented by one or the other of the elementary altruistic sentiments of *pity* and *probity*.

Moreover, the injury must wound these sentiments not in their superior and finer degrees, but in the average measure in which they are possessed by a community—a measure which is indispensable for the adaptation of the individual to society. Given such a violation of either of these sentiments, and we have what may properly be called *natural crime*. The foregoing, I concede, is not a complete definition, but it furnishes a determinant which I believe to be of the highest importance. I have sought to show the futility of saying in the usual fashion that crime is an act at once immoral and harmful. It is something more: it is a determinate species of immorality. Hundreds of deeds might be mentioned which are both harmful and immoral and still not considered as crimes. And this is so, because the element of immorality which they contain is neither cruelty nor improbity. If, for example, immorality *in general* be spoken of, we are obliged to recognize that this element in some degree exists in every voluntary disobedience to law. But it is nevertheless true that there is a host of acts which are misdemeanors and even crimes in the eye of the law and yet do not tend to lower their authors in the estimation of their friends.

Beyond question, every disobedience to law should be attended with a penal sanction, whether such disobedience does or does not wound the altruistic sentiments. What then is the practical object of your distinction?—some one may inquire. This we shall presently explain, but first, to complete our analysis, we must show why certain violations of a different order of sentiments have been excluded from our category of criminality.

Distinctions: Acts wounding Modesty and Chastity. —The result of our discussion of the subject of modesty sufficiently justifies the exclusion of all acts which wound this sentiment alone. Offenses against chastity are rendered criminal by the interference with individual liberty—the violation of the sentiment of benevolence or pity,—and this even if the offense is accomplished by seduction unattended with force, because of the moral suffering, shame, and other harmful consequences suffered by the victim. But when the woman has submitted of her own free will and no element of seduction is involved, the unchaste act of itself is a matter of indifference. The same reason equally prevents us from classing as crimes certain acts of sexual perversion, although the laws of some countries still endeavor to repress such offenses by means of physical punishments ("peines afflictives"). Civilized society does insist on the observance of public decorum: it will not tolerate complete nudity or the commerce of the sexes in public;—spectacles of this sort would excite mirth or disgust, or, especially among parents, the keenest sense of indignation. But even the last would hardly demand the death of the offenders; they would protest, not against crime, but against indecency. Manifestly, in these cases the only thing that needs to be changed is a modality, namely, the place, and there is nothing to complain of. For this reason, such facts have been, according to the period, visited with the lash, minor restrictions of liberty, or fines, just as the case of drunkenness, but no more than in the last-mentioned case, has it ever been thought proper to invoke the punishments which are set apart for crimes. The public conscience is unable to discover crime in that which becomes a breach of decorum ("inconvenance") only by the single external circumstance of publicity. The seriousness of the breach of decorum, it may be added, depends upon how public the place in question is. This explains why public opinion in these instances can see only police offenses ("contraventions de police"), however they may be classed by the positive law.

Acts wounding Sentiments of Family. —Let us turn now to another class of sentiments which at one time possessed great importance, viz., the sentiments of family. We know that the family was the nucleus of the tribe and hence of the nation, and that the moral sense first appeared under the form of love for one's children,—this being a sentiment not yet altruistic, but purely ego-altruistic. The progress of altruism has greatly diminished the importance of the family group, morality having first passed beyond the limits of the family, to transcend in later stages those of the tribe, the caste, and the people, and, ultimately, to recognize no other boundaries than those of mankind.

But in spite of this constant progression, the family has continued to exist, with its natural rules of obedience, fidelity, and mutual assistance on the part of its members. What then of the violation of such sentiments? Does it always constitute a natural crime? By no means, unless there exists at the same time a violation of one or both of the elementary altruistic sentiments discussed above. Suppose that a son maltreats his parents, a mother abandons her offspring, what sentiment is really wounded here? Is it the sentiment of family—of the family regarded as an aggregation, an organism—or is it not rather the sentiment of pity,—which, it may be noted, is generally more vivid when its objects are related to us by blood?

It is this same universality of pity within the family which renders criminal certain acts in relation to our parents and children, which if committed against outsiders would not be given a criminal character. On the other hand, the idea of the family community—a traditional idea which persists in spite of the laws—denies a criminal character to certain attacks upon property within the family circle, as, for example, larceny between father and son, husband and wife, or brother and sister. And this is not because the sentiment of probity is overborne by the sentiment of family, but simply because the idea of a common ownership diminishes the degree of improbity or renders its existence doubtful.

Disobedience to the paternal authority has long since ceased to be classed as a crime, but adultery continues to be so regarded. That adultery is harmful to the family order, and from this point of view is immoral, cannot admit of the slightest doubt. Nevertheless, save in some exceptional cases, it does not directly wound the elementary altruistic sentiments. It is merely the breach of a duty, the violation of a contract, and, as in the case of other contractual relations, its legal consequences should be limited to the giving rise to a right to rescind on the part of the aggrieved party. We have not yet come to this, but history shows us a progressive diminution in the punishment of adultery. The Israelitish stoning, the Teutonic fustigation, the pillory and other forms of corporal punishment which obtained in the Middle Ages, have all given way to the few months of correctional imprisonment by which the offense is punished at the present day. In brief, that which is nothing more than the violation of a right, and wounds neither the sentiment of pity nor that of probity cannot be deemed a crime by public opinion. On the other hand, the criminal character of bigamy, for example, where the second spouse is unaware of the prior marriage ("bigamie frauduleuse"), is easily recognized. The same is true of the false pretenses ("fausses qualités") under which an adventurer insinuates himself into a respectable family and effects a marriage with one of its members. Although this last-mentioned fact has yet no place in the code, it cannot be gainsaid that a marriage procured by fraud excites public indignation to a much greater degree than the fault of adultery.

In some measure adultery is the political crime of the family. To it may be applied many of the considerations now to be mentioned in relation to political crimes in general.

Political Crimes. —The subject of political crimes presents difficulties of a most serious character. How are we to contend that conspiracy or rebellion against a lawful government is not a true crime? Can there be anything more dangerous to the particular society? Does it not attack the public peace in the directest manner possible? And yet, how else can we explain the sympathy that political offenders often inspire in their bitterest enemies, as opposed to the repugnance which every honest man feels for thieves, swindlers, forgers, and men of that stripe? There is here a clear-cut distinction. One may, to be sure, speak of *political crime,* but the word "crime," standing alone, has nothing to do with the present class of acts. This difference is one which the public conscience never fails to recognize. As an example may be cited its expression by that most philosophic of novelists, Balzac, in "The Magic Skin." The speakers are young men of the literary Bohemia:

"'Oh, well,' resumes the first, 'there is still left to us . . .'

"'What?' inquires another.

"'Crime . . .'

"'There's a word which has all the height of the gallows and all the depth of the Seine,' replies Raphael.

"'Oh! You don't understand me. I mean political crime.'"

In reality, egoism is often alien to political crimes. They are explained, not by the default of moral sense, but rather by a revolutionary ingenuousness which feels capable of making over the world.

Still, there are certain crimes commonly called political which, nevertheless, properly come under our definition. Such, for example, are attacks upon the life of the head of the State or other public officers, the use of bombs and dynamite to further revolutionary propaganda, and similar acts of violence. In these cases it is of little moment what the political object may be, if the sentiment of humanity is wounded. Has there been killing or an attempt to kill, not in the course of war or in the exercise of lawful self-defense? If so, the author, by that fact alone, is a criminal. His degree of criminality may be greater or less, according to the intent and the surrounding circumstances—a matter to which we shall later refer. But if crime arises from the single fact of a serious violation of pity, there must be at least an attempt to commit it. This is so, because we cannot admit that any crime exists before some step has been taken in its accomplishment, even if the design has been fully formed in the author's mind. It may be that public policy, in cases of this character, will treat as a punishable attempt that which is not an attempt in the ordinary sense; here we have a true political crime. The cases to which we have reference, however, are those in which there has been murder, incendiarism, or dynamiting, actual or attempted. In such cases the crime exists independently of the passion which has provoked it. It exists because of the wilful intent to destroy human lives. Only when the act of the fanatic or revolutionary exhibits no such cruelty or carelessness of human life can we distinguish the true political crime, and say that it inherently differs from the natural crime. But the act which is normally a political crime may become a natural crime when a society suddenly returns to a condition in which the collective existence is threatened. War, a state resembling that of the predatory life, relegates the sentiments developed by pacific activity to a subordinate station. Let independence once become the principal concern of a people, and the attempt of a citizen to betray his country to the enemy assumes the worst aspects of immorality. Under such circumstances every citizen must be considered as a soldier; martial law reigns supreme; the laws of peace have disappeared. Treason, desertion, espionage are then true crimes, because tending to national destruction. But at the present day the state of war is a crisis of short duration. As pacific activity succeeds to the predatory activity, the morality of the state of peace succeeds to that of war, and the offense which was esteemed a crime only in relation to that state of war, becomes a political crime or no crime at all; at all events, it ceases to be numbered among the natural crimes. Thus desertion becomes no more than voluntary expatriation; conspiracy and revolt no longer threaten the national life, but only the form of government. As for espionage, it is no more than the revealing of State secrets, which, like many other acts of a similar character, may still be culpable if it involves the selling for money or other object a secret which one is in honor bound to keep. In this case the element of improbity is present, the moral sense is in consequence wounded, and the act continues to be a natural crime.

Non-Political Local Offenses Menacing Public Peace. —There are other offenses which are not political, but which from a local point of view are a menace to public peace. Such, for example, are attempts to subvert a particular governmental institution, disobedience to the constituted authorities, and the refusal of a citizen to perform a public duty legally incumbent upon him. So far as these are concerned, we need only repeat that for public opinion there can be neither crime nor criminal in the absence of injury to the universal moral sense.

§6. The Delimitation of Criminality

And now as to our delimitation of criminality. For us, all crime falls into two extensive categories, according as offense is principally occasioned to the one or the other of the two primordial altruistic sentiments. So far as this distribution is concerned, it is of no consequence what rights may be attacked or how the offense may be classified in the codes.

(1) Offense to the Sentiment of Pity. —The first category—offense to the sentiment of pity or humanity—therefore includes: (*a*) attacks upon human life and all manner of acts tending to produce physical harm to human beings, such as the deliberate infliction of physical torture ("sévices"), mayhem ("mutilations"), the maltreatment of the weak and infirm, the voluntary causing of illness, the imposition upon children of excessive labor or such work as tends to injure their health or stunt their physical development;[1] (*b*) physical acts which produce suffering at once physical and moral, such as the violation of personal liberty in an egoistic end, whether for carnal pleasure or pecuniary gain:—abduction of a female or kidnapping for ransom may be cited as types; and (*c*) acts which directly produce moral suffering. Defamation ("diffamation"), false accusation ("calomnie"), and seduction under promise of marriage are of this last character.

(2) Offense to the Sentiment of Probity. — In the second category—offense to the elementary sentiment of probity—are comprised: (*a*) attacks upon property involving violence, viz.: robbery, extortion by threats, malicious mischief ("dévastation"), arson, and the like; (*b*) attacks unaccompanied by violence, but involving breach of trust: obtaining money by false pretenses; embezzlement; the conveyance of property in fraud of creditors ("insolvabilité volontaire"), bankruptcy occurring through negligence or fraud ("banqueroute"), the revelation of professional secrets, the misappropriation of literary property ("plagiat"), and all the various forms of counterfeiting tending to injure the rights of inventors and manufacturers; and (*c*) all indirect injuries to a person's property or civil rights occasioned by false statements or entries made in some formal or solemn manner, among which may be mentioned perjury, the forgery or spoliation of official documents and records ("faux dans les actes authentiques"), the substitution of children, and the suppression of civil status ("suppression d'état civil").

---

1. These last are not yet recognized by the codes, or at most are classed as police offenses ("contraventions").

Offenses Excluded. —It will be noted that we thus exclude from the field of criminality: (*a*) acts which menace the State as a governmental organization. Of this type are such deeds as may involve one nation in hostilities with another, unauthorized military enlistments, political rioting, meetings to conspire against the government, the utterance of seditious outcries, seditious offenses of the press, affiliation with revolutionary sects or anti-constitutional parties, inciting to civil war, etc. (*b*) Acts which attack the social power but without a political object. Among these would be: resistance to officers of the law (except when involving murder or the infliction of bodily injury), the usurpation of titles, dignities, or public functions, without purpose of unlawful pecuniary gain, the refusal to perform a service owed to the State, smuggling, etc.; (*c*) acts resulting in injury to the public peace, the political rights of citizens, or the respect due to religion, or causing offense to public decency. In this division would fall the unlawful invasion of private dwellings ("violation de domicile"), the exercise of a right by force instead of by legal means, the spreading of false news tending to alarm the public, the act of aiding or abetting the escape of prisoners, election intrigues, offenses against religion or worship, illegal arrests, acts of sexual perversion of which no innocent person has been made the victim; and (*d*) acts which contravene the local or special legislation of a given country, *e.g.*, gambling, the unlawful carrying of arms, clandestine prostitution, and infringements of laws relating to railroads, telegraphs, sanitation, the customs, hunting, fishing, forests, and water-courses, and the civil status of citizens, as well as violations of many kinds of municipal regulations, etc.

Certain Objections Considered. —With respect to the foregoing classification, De Aramburu,[2] followed by Lozano,[3] contends that it would be easily demonstrable that the crimes of one category might with equal propriety be assigned to the other, since, they say, that which is unjust is cruel, and that which is cruel is unjust. On the contrary, I am firmly convinced that the two sentiments are entirely distinct, and that one may be wounded without the other being affected, although it may frequently happen that both are wounded by a single act. Is there, for example, any cruelty in robbing a rich man's house which has been shut up for the summer, or in embezzling a few thousand francs from a metropolitan bank? Clearly, improbity alone is involved. On the other hand, what element of improbity exists in a murder for revenge, occurring solely as the exaggerated reaction against a wrong done to the murderer or his kindred? True, it may be said that it is always wicked to harm any one in any way whatsoever. But wickedness and injustice are not synonymous terms, and in any event, the element of wickedness inherent in the last example is not a violation of the sentiment of justice heretofore designated as "probity."

The further objection has been raised that the altruistic sentiments possess little uniformity and that the boundaries of the field of crime are constantly expanding.[4] We, of course, fully admit that the altruistic sentiments, at a former period and in a different state of society, had by no means attained their present degree of development. This, in fact, was our point of departure in speaking of the progression of these sentiments abreast of civilization. Moreover, it is to be borne in mind that the present-day morality is based on altruism, whereas the morality of other peoples and other ages was based on sentiments of a different nature—patriotism, religion, loyalty to the sovereign, the respect due to caste, the point of honor, and the like. The purpose of our investigation, then, is to discover what are the true crimes of contemporary society,—to ascertain what constitutes a crime in our eyes in the eyes of Europeans of the present century. There is nothing in this to contradict the possibility of a still further development of altruism, or that acts which today are not considered as crimes may one day acquire that character. Progress, assuredly, will tend more and more to the enrichment of the moral sense. "If the moral sense becomes augmented," says Fouillée, "the displeasing things of today will become the odious things of the future. . . . Our sympathy embraces a continually increasing number of objects; it extends not only to humanity, but to the whole of nature; and, for this reason, it is nowadays much more easily wounded than formerly, especially in its moral force."[5]

Thus, it will very probably ensue that many facts today regarded as indifferent will come to be viewed as immoral, and that others simply immoral will be vested with a criminal character. Of the latter class might be instanced the abandonment of illegitimate children, the failure on the part of parents properly

---

2. *De Aramburu, op. cit.*, p. 102. ["La nueva ciencia penal" (Madrid, 1887)—Ed.]

3. *Lozano*, "La escuela antropologica y sociologica criminal," p. 98 (La Plata, 1889).

4. *Colajanni*, "La sociologia criminale," pp. 54, 55; *De Aramburu, op. cit.*, pp. 102–104.

5. *Alfred Fouillée* in Revue des Deux Mondes, 15 March, 1888.

to care for their children, or to give them an adequate education, or again, vivisection, artificial fattening, and other forms of cruelty to animals, which in recent years have aroused the just indignation of zoöphilist societies. The advance will equally affect the sentiment of probity. All those non-punishable acts of chicane which occur in the conduct of civil cases will come to take their place—unless the practical difficulties are insurmountable—beside the other species of frauds which are today punishable, so that the two will become indistinguishable. So, too, a criminal character will come to be given to the abandonment of such persons as already have, or may be awarded by future laws, the right to assistance and support—parents, children, and aged or infirm domestics or workmen, without means of existence.

It is easily understood, however, that the sentiments wounded by the crimes of the future will be the same sentiments with which we have dealt, but these sentiments in their higher and more refined development—a state which the efflux of time will have rendered much more common than at the present day. It is wholly impossible to suppose crimes of a different character, or to suppose that offenses to other sentiments can ever become crimes. As we have already noticed, the tendency is quite the opposite. Offenses not involving injury to the sentiments in question, are treated less and less as crimes in proportion as civilization increases.

So much for the future. Does not this glance at it furnish new proof of the validity of our concept of crime?

The offenses which have no place in our scheme, do not come within the scope of the sociologic study of crime. They are relative to the special conditions of particular countries. They do not reveal in their authors, anomaly—the default of that part of the moral sense which evolution has rendered almost universal. The law-maker, no doubt, ought to adopt measures looking to their chastisement, but from our point of view it is the true crime alone which, in demanding investigation of its natural causes and social remedies, is capable of interesting true science. The excluded offenses often consist merely of violations of prejudice or contraventions of custom, or in any event simply run counter to the laws of a determinate society—laws varying with different countries and unnecessary to the social coexistence. In these cases investigation of biologic causes is unnecessary, and as for remedy, none other is needed than chastisement depending in severity upon the degree of intimidation required.

PART THREE

MORAL STATISTICS AND THE NINETEENTH-CENTURY FRENCH SCHOOL

The development of scientific thought in criminology is associated with several different and sometimes competing research programs. During the eighteenth century, the founders of the classical school, Beccaria and Bentham, embraced science and constructed a secular and subtly deterministic framework upon which they advocated fundamental changes in the administration of criminal justice. At the same time, Lavater presented his system of physiognomy as a theologically compatible science. The taste of science one finds in Lavater's work was soon developed more fully in Gall's phrenology and, later, in Lombroso's studies of atavism. Eventually Lombroso's efforts, together with the research of Ferri and Garofalo, provided the groundwork for the multidisciplinary Italian school of positive criminology. These are just a few of the traditions that directly or indirectly contributed to the growth of science in criminology. Additional influences can be found in the early studies of moral statistics and the nineteenth-century French school of criminology.

Moral Statistics

During the 1800s, several nations began to systematically collect quantitative data on crime, education, "illegitimate births," suicides, and other "moral" phenomena—that is, they began to generate "moral statistics."[1] This provided researchers with an opportunity to examine various social facts using the statistical techniques that were available at the time. The best-known and most influential analyses of moral statistics during the first half of the nineteenth century were conducted by Adolphe Quetelet and André-Michel Guerry. Enrico Ferri ([1901] 1913:72) referred to Quetelet and Guerry as the "great founders of criminal statistics." It even has been suggested that "criminology as a modern social science" was established by

---

1. Piers Beirne (1993:104) notes that Johann Peter Süssmilch has been credited with founding moral statistics in the mid-1700s, while André-Michel Guerry was perhaps the first of the "Franco-Belgian statisticians" to apply the label to quantitative data on crime.

their efforts during the 1830s (Lindesmith and Levin 1937a:655).[2] The quantitative research of Quetelet and Guerry, like that of other scholars of this era (e.g., Rawson W. Rawson 1839; Joseph Fletcher 1849; and Mary Carpenter 1857), involved relatively simple statistical analyses. Nonetheless, their work is significant on both methodological and theoretical grounds. It represented an early form of scientific criminology (early positivism); it examined the relationship between crime and several variables that have retained a high level of interest within the field (e.g., sex, age, and economic conditions); it provided a theory of age and crime that is a noteworthy forerunner to contemporary life-course criminology; and it was a harbinger of modern methods of ecological research and crime mapping.[3]

Lambert Adolphe Jacques Quetelet (1796–1874) was born and educated in Ghent, Belgium, and went on to become one of the nation's most prominent intellectuals.[4] At the University of Ghent, he studied mathematics and astronomy, and at age 23 he received a doctor of science degree. Over his career, he taught courses at both the Athenaeum and the École Militaire in Brussels. He also was the secretary of the Royal Academy of Belgium, the founder of the Royal Observatory of Brussels, and reportedly "an honoured member of nearly every scientific body in the world, which has any pretensions to authority in the conduct of scientific research" (Anon. 1874:114). Today Quetelet is still remembered for his contributions to astronomy, meteorology, and statistics, but he also is recognized for his influence on the growth of the social sciences, especially the development of positivism in sociology and criminology. Regarding the latter, it has been suggested that a combination of at least two factors prompted Quetelet to conduct his studies of crime: the failure of early-nineteenth-century penal practices to control the "dangerous classes" and the development of statistical methods (see Beirne 1993:67–75). Quetelet believed that through a careful statistical examination of crime, its general causes could be identified and such knowledge could then be used to reduce it.

Quetelet referred to his research on social life as "social physics"[5] and, sometimes, "social mechanics." He believed that the social world, including the world of crime, was governed by laws comparable to the laws of physics and that these social laws could be discovered through careful observation and statistical analyses involving a large number of cases. In this connection, his research indicated that crime rates tend to be relatively stable from year to year and that criminal behavior is correlated with several variables—such as the seasons, sex, age, and various economic conditions. However,

---

2. Beyond this, it has been asserted that ". . . moral statistics laid the groundwork for and later evolved into sociology as we understand the discipline today" (Whitt 2002:x).

3. Guerry, and to some extent Quetelet, conducted a form of ecological research more than a century before the publication of Clifford R. Shaw and Henry D. McKay's *Juvenile Delinquency and Urban Areas* (1942).

4. The following information on Quetelet is largely based on Anon. (1874), Hankins (1908), Lurguin (1924), Sylvester (1984), and Beirne (1993).

5. Prior to Quetelet, Comte had used the label "social physics," describing it as "the science which has for its subject the study of social phenomena" (in Coser 1977:28). However, upon seeing Quetelet's use of the term, Comte dropped his reference to "social physics" and replaced it with the label "sociology" as part of an effort to maintain the distinctiveness of his views (see Coser 1977:28–29).

Quetelet also held that we possess a "moral power" that allows us to manipulate the social laws that affect us (Quetelet [1842] 1968:96), and thus with adequate knowledge we have some capacity to shape our social world and reduce crime. This is evident in his conclusion:

> ... since the crimes which are annually committed seem to be a necessary result of our social organization, and since the number of them cannot diminish without the causes which induce them undergoing previous modification, it is the province of legislators to ascertain these causes, and to remove them as far as possible ... *society prepares crime, and the guilty are only the instruments by which it is executed.* (Quetelet [1842] 1968:108—emphasis in original)

Overall, Quetelet made several contributions to the field of criminology. Not only did he draw attention to the potential uses of statistical methods in the study of crime, but he also conducted a form of empirical research in which geographic areas (e.g., départements of France) were the units of analysis. In this research he examined, among other things, the relationship between crime and economic conditions, and he suggested that economic inequality appears to have an effect on crime rates. This form of research, which was more fully developed by Guerry, represents a precursor to modern ecological research. In addition, Quetelet maintained that while everyone has some propensity for crime, this propensity generally varies from one individual to another and across time for any specific individual. What is more, many different factors can influence these variations. In his research, not only did he study the potential influence of economic conditions on crime, but he also examined the possible effects of sex, age, education, profession, alcohol consumption, and the seasons. His examination of sex and crime represents an early inquiry into the gender-ratio problem, and from his research on age and crime, he proposed a theory that is compatible with contemporary life-course criminology. In this theory, Quetelet ([1842] 1968) suggested that an individual's propensity for crime will vary across his/her lifetime due to the changes that occur in physical "strength," "passion," and "reason" ("judgment").

Quetelet conducted his most important research on moral statistics during the 1830s. Thus, if we locate his primary contribution to criminology on a timeline, it falls between the founding of the classical school (as well as the work of Lavater and Gall) and the emergence of the Italian school. In 1831, he published *Research on the Propensity for Crime at Different Ages*. This was his first major study of crime and one of the first works of positive criminology. Four years later he published *A Treatise on Man and the Development of His Faculties* (1835), a work that includes much of the text from his earlier book. A selection from his *Treatise*, which was translated into English in 1842, is presented in Chapter 10. In this selection, Quetelet provides a statistical examination of the relationships among the seasons, sex, age, and crime.[6]

---

6. Quetelet continued to publish into the 1870s, although his most significant contributions to criminology appear to have been made in his first analyses of moral statistics. By the 1840s, he began to give more attention to phrenological and hereditary assumptions and his work incorporated a more pronounced biological component (see Beirne 1993). This perhaps is most evident in his book *Anthropométrie* (1871).

At the same time Quetelet was conducting his research, André-Michel Guerry (1802–1866) was engaged in a similar line of inquiry.[7] Guerry was born in Tours, France, and studied law at the University of Poitiers. Despite his legal training, he soon developed an interest in statistics and eventually earned international recognition for his statistical work. Professionally, he became Director of Criminal Statistics in the Ministry of Justice and also was accepted as a member of the French Academy of Sciences. In the literature of the social sciences, André-Michel Guerry and Jacques Guerry de Champneuf (1788–1852) occasionally are confused due to their similar names and their work on French crime data (see Elmer 1933, 1937; Lindesmith and Levin 1937b; Whitt 2002). In 1821, Champneuf was appointed Director of Criminal Affairs and Pardons, a position he held until 1830. In this position, he initiated the annual publication of the *Compte général de l'administration de la justice criminelle* (*General Report on the Administration of Criminal Justice*), a collection of official data regarding criminal justice in France that eventually was analyzed by Guerry as well as Quetelet. In other words, while Champneuf played an important role in the development of French crime data, Guerry's research stands out in criminology, since he provided an examination of these data; his work went beyond the construction of a data set.

Guerry ([1833] 2002:2, 14), like Quetelet, was both a positivist and an innovative statistician. He held that the "moral sciences" should attempt to adopt the methods of the "natural sciences" and that "the facts of the moral order, like those of the physical order, obey invariable laws." His research also was motivated in large part by a desire to provide factual information that could be used to guide public policies (see Whitt 2002). However, while Guerry, like Quetelet, conducted a form of ecological research, Guerry placed more emphasis on the use of shaded maps to illustrate the geographic distribution of crime and other social phenomena. In 1829, Guerry, together with the Italian geographer Adriano Balbi, introduced the "cartographic method" to the field of criminology in a one-page document entitled "Comparative Statistics of the Educational Situation and the Number of Crimes in the Various Royal Court Districts and Educational Districts of France."[8] Four years later, he published what probably is his best-known study, *Essay on the Moral Statistics of France* (1833). In this work, Guerry presented "criminal statistics" as a science and further developed cartography as a research method for criminology. He continued to conduct research into the 1860s, with his last major publication being *The Moral Statistics of England in Comparison to the Moral Statistics of France* (1864). This was his most elaborate work and, according to Michael Friendly (2007:396), it "contemplated ideas of multivariate explanation well beyond theory and methods available at the time."[9]

---

7. The following information on Guerry is primarily based on Lindesmith and Levin (1937a), Beirne (1993), Whitt (2002), and Friendly (2007).

8. This document is reproduced in an article by Michael Friendly (2007:372).

9. Much like Quetelet, it appears that Guerry also had at least a marginal interest in phrenology; in fact, he contributed to a study of the cranial dimensions of inmates (see Beirne 1993; Whitt 2002).

The reading in Chapter 11 comes from Guerry's *Essay*. In this selection, he calls for scientific inquiry into moral phenomena and provides an early statistical study of crimes against persons and crimes against property. Among other things, the selection explores the relationship between economic conditions and crime and illustrates Guerry's cartographic method.

Guerry conducted his research at the same time as Quetelet, examined similar data sets, and came to many of the same conclusions. They both embraced the methods of positive social science and examined the statistical relationships among crime and sex, age, season, education, and economic conditions. They both found that crime rates tend to be uniform across time. They both questioned popular notions regarding the relationship between education and crime as well as poverty and crime; their data indicated that some of the most educated and most prosperous regions of France had among the highest crime rates. Although the list of similarities between them could be extended further, the main point is that Quetelet and Guerry made several historically significant contributions to the field of criminology. From a contemporary standpoint, their research on moral statistics represented a noteworthy advance over the inquiries of Gall and Spurzheim. But, of course, disciplines rarely, if ever, follow a steady, cumulative path of development. The work of Lombroso, which occurred after the major contributions of Quetelet and Guerry, was arguably a step backward in that it reenergized inquiries into the relationship between physical appearances and crime and, at least temporarily, drew attention away from social conditions that affect crime (see Lindesmith and Levin 1937a). This resurgence in physical appearance theorizing was soon opposed by a group of French scholars who stressed the importance of the social environment; they were the members of the French school of criminology.

The French School

French scholars have made many noteworthy contributions to the birth and development of criminology. Montesquieu's influence on the emergence of the classical school, as noted earlier, was significant, but he was not the only French writer of the eighteenth century to make a contribution to the field. For instance, Voltaire and the Marquis de Sade also provided insights of criminological interest during this era (see Jenkins 1984; Newman and Marongiu 2009). As we move into the early nineteenth century, we find the psychiatric work of Philippe Pinel ([1806] 1962) and, as just noted, the statistical work of Guerry. By the end of the century, the writings of Gabriel Tarde and Émile Durkheim rose to prominence. And during the twentieth century, the research of Michel Foucault had a significant impact on criminology, especially its more critical branches. But this is not all, for the influence of French intellectual life extended to foreign scholars who had prolonged contact with the scholarly communities of France. Many noteworthy scholars from other nations had a close connection with one or more of these communities; some of these scholars moved to France (e.g., Gall) and others had one or more extended visits (e.g., Quetelet and Ferri). In short, French scholarship has a long and remarkable history in the field of criminology. While a complete overview of this scholarship is beyond the scope of this book, more attention is warranted. Specifically, this attention will be directed toward the nineteenth-century "French school."

The existence of a French school of criminology has been noted by several authors (e.g., Zimmern [1898] 2000; Bonger 1916; and Shichor 2010), but its boundaries are not well defined. Typically, where reference is made to it, it does not entail all French scholarship of relevance to criminology. Rather it centers on the work of late-nineteenth-century French theorists who opposed the biological emphasis of Lombroso's criminal anthropology and stressed the examination of social factors that may affect crime.[10] Although there is some variation across the literature, Alexandre Lacassagne, Gabriel Tarde, and Émile Durkheim appear to be the French school's most significant representatives.[11] Lacassagne is perhaps best known for making the following analogy: "the social milieu is a bouillon, a culture for criminality. The microbe is the criminal, an element of no importance until the day he finds the bouillon which he makes ferment" (in Rafter 2009:196). Although Lacassagne was a key figure in the French school, Tarde and Durkheim hold a more prominent place in the history of criminology and, thus, will be the focus here.

Gabriel Tarde (1843–1904) was born into "an old family of minor aristocrats" in Sarlat, France, and studied law at Toulouse and Paris.[12] He had an active professional career—first serving as a provincial magistrate in his hometown, then as the director of the Bureau of Statistics in the Ministry of Justice, and, toward the very end of his career, as Professor of Modern Philosophy at the Collège de France. During the late 1800s, Tarde made scholarly contributions to several fields, including criminology, sociology, and philosophy. Regarding criminology, he opposed the biological positivists of the Italian school, but he also was somewhat critical of the moral statisticians and the work of Durkheim. Tarde rejected Lombroso's atavist theory, arguing that the available empirical evidence simply did not support the idea of an atavistic criminal type. Although Tarde contributed to the compilation of crime statistics in France, he held that the moral statisticians were excessively influenced by the natural sciences and that this hindered their efforts to explain crime (see Beirne 1993:155–159). Finally, although he and Durkheim both emphasized the effect of the social environment on human

---

10. Willem Bonger (1916) referred to the French school as "the school of the environment." However, David Shichor (2010) maintains that while the French school emphasized the effect of social factors more than the criminal anthropologists of the Italian school, it nonetheless was influenced by neo-Lamarckian evolutionary theory.

11. Although other names may be added to this list (e.g., Léonce Manouvrier), a narrow conception of the French school has been applied that excludes several researchers who otherwise may be classified among its members—researchers such as Guerry and the "quasi-Frenchman," Quetelet. [Tarde ([1903] 1912:47) referred to Quetelet as a "quasi-Frenchman."] This classification is not unique. In the early twentieth century, Bonger (1916) classified Guerry and Quetelet with "the statisticians" and not under the French school, but he also commented: "Like every classification this is more or less arbitrary. Several authors might have been placed under two different headings" (p. xxxi). Bonger's classification of authors who addressed "criminality and economic conditions" includes "the precursors" (e.g., Beccaria, Godwin, and Engels), "the statisticians" (e.g., Guerry and Quetelet), "the Italian school" (e.g., Lombroso, Ferri, and Garofalo), "the French school" (e.g., Lacassange, Tarde, and Manouvrier), "the bio-socialists" (e.g., Morrison and Ellis), "the spiritualists" (e.g., Joly and Proal), and "the third school and the socialists" (e.g., Turati and Colajanni).

12. The following information on Tarde is based on several sources including Tosti (1897), Giddings (1903), Lindsey (1912), Vine (1972), and Beirne (1993). The quote in this statement comes from Beirne (1993:143).

behavior, Tarde found Durkheim's theory of the normality of crime to be untenable (see Tarde [1895] 1983).

Tarde's perspective entailed a free will/determinism compromise,[13] embraced a social psychological framework, and centered on the concept of "imitation" (see Vine 1972; Beirne 1993). He proposed at least three "laws of imitation" in his explanation of crime and thus offered a viewpoint that can be classified among the early learning theories of criminology. For Tarde ([1903] 1912:322), "All the important acts of social life are carried out under the domination of example." Accordingly, he believed that criminal behavior, as well as other behavior, is learned through a process of imitating others. One of his laws of imitation suggests that the elite members of society are the source of many crimes in that their misbehavior tends to be imitated by people who occupy a lower social status. In his words, "The superior is imitated by the inferior to a greater extent than the inferior by the superior" (Tarde [1903] 1912:326). However, the radical potential of this suggestion did not carry over to the remainder of his work. In the political realm, he opposed Marxism, anarchism, and the revolutionary movements in France (see Beirne 1993:163, 172–173).

Tarde's two major works in criminology were *La Criminalité comparée* (1886) and *Penal Philosophy* (1890). His other noteworthy publications include *The Laws of Imitation* (1890) and *Social Laws: An Outline of Sociology* (1899). The reading in Chapter 12 is a selection from the fourth edition of *Penal Philosophy* ([1903] 1912), in which he attempts to explain crime in terms of his laws of imitation. It presents a simple learning theory and exemplifies a social psychological branch of the French school.

Although the contributions of Tarde were significant, Émile Durkheim (1858–1917) may have been the most important researcher associated with the French school, at least if we consider both the direct and indirect influences of his work on the field of criminology.[14] Durkheim was born in Epinal, in eastern France, and eventually studied at the École Normale Supérieure in Paris, "the traditional training ground for the intellectual elite of France" (Coser 1977:143). Unlike Tarde, Durkheim did most of his work in a university environment. He was a professor of sociology at the University of Bordeaux and later at the Sorbonne in Paris. He is best known for his contribution to the development of sociology; indeed, he generally is regarded as one of the three most significant classical sociological theorists, together with Karl Marx and Max Weber. Durkheim embraced positive social science,[15] applied a

---

13. It has been suggested that Tarde's writings on crime and punishment have a neoclassical orientation in that he attempted to find a compromise between the assumptions of free will and determinism (see Beirne 1993:170–174).

14. Concise summaries of Durkheim's work can be found in most textbooks on classical sociological theory. Extensive examinations of his writings have been provided by several sociologists, including Talcott Parsons (1949), Steven Lukes (1972), Anthony Giddens (1979), and Dominick LaCapra (1985). See Garland (1990) and Cotterrell (1999) for extensive analyses of Durkheim's theory of punishment and his theory of law, respectively.

15. Peter Halfpenny (1982:32) contends that Durkheim presented another distinct form of sociological positivism by combining "Comte's sociology and descriptive social statistics." Despite his neglect of the work of Guerry and his criticisms of Quetelet, Durkheim appears to have been influenced by the tradition of moral statistics; in fact, his book *Suicide* ([1897] 1951) arguably falls within this tradition (see Whitt 2002).

macro-level sociological orientation, and emphasized a reciprocal relationship between culture (the "common consciousness") and social structure (e.g., the division of labor) when explaining social phenomena. Although his explanations often applied a functionalist viewpoint and he frequently is described as a conservative theorist, a critical spirit nonetheless can be found here and there within his work. This spirit perhaps is most evident in his frequent expressions of concern over the institution of inherited wealth, which he regarded as obsolete and divisive in modern societies.

Although Durkheim's primary influence was in the field of sociology, his work also had an effect on other fields, such as anthropology and criminology. In anthropology (on the subject of religion), Durkheim's *The Elementary Forms of Religious Life* ([1912] 1995) has been described as "A great classic, and quite indispensable reading" (Montagu 1974:615). In criminology, his influence goes a few steps further. His theory of "anomic suicide" provided the backdrop for the emergence of the anomie tradition, most notably Robert Merton's (1938) theory of social structure and anomie. His theories of "egoistic suicide" and "moral education" provided some of the context for the development of control theories—in particular, Travis Hirschi's (1969) social bond theory. Durkheim also proposed an interesting conception of crime, one that challenges Garofalo's description of "the natural crime." In brief, Durkheim suggested that crime is culturally relative. Long before Howard Becker (1963), Durkheim argued that an extrinsic factor rather than an intrinsic property makes a given act a crime. He concluded that the "essence" of crime is to be found outside of the criminal act itself—in the "common consciousness" of a society and the institutions that represent and protect it.[16] Beyond this, Durkheim presented a noteworthy (though often criticized) theory of law and a relatively elaborate theory of punishment. Regarding the latter, David Garland (1990:23) commented, "Durkheim did more than anyone else to develop a sociological account of punishment. . . ."

Durkheim constructed his theories during the late 1800s and early 1900s. Three of his four major books—*The Division of Labor in Society* ([1893] 1984), *The Rules of Sociological Method* ([1895] 1982), and *Suicide* ([1897] 1951)—contain important discussions of crime, but not one of them has law, crime, or punishment as its primary subject matter. Durkheim's analyses of these phenomena, on most occasions, were part of an effort to develop a better understanding of some other dimension of social life, such as the content and strength of the common consciousness or the principal form of social solidarity in a society. Other significant analyses of law, crime, and punishment can be found in his lectures (e.g., Durkheim [1900] 1958; [1902–1903] 1973) and a few articles and reviews (e.g., Durkheim [1900] 1969).

Chapter 13 provides two readings from Durkheim's work. The first selection, an excerpt from *The Rules*, is his argument that crime should be viewed as a normal social fact because, among other things, it is closely connected to

---

16. As noted in Part Four, before Durkheim the theorists who established much of the foundation for contemporary critical criminology also suggested that an extrinsic factor makes a given act a "crime." For critical theorists, this factor, in simple terms, centers on the wishes and interests of the dominant subpopulation of a society.

healthy social conditions. Although Tarde and other social theorists have questioned this argument, it certainly is thought provoking. The other selection is an excerpt from his article "Two Laws of Penal Evolution" ([1900] 1969), in which he describes his "law of quantitative variations." Here he contends that punishments tend to be less severe in societies that are more developed and more democratic; that is, they are less intense where the division of labor is more advanced and government is less "absolute." He explains part of this relationship in terms of a historical shift in conceptions of crime and the content of criminal law—a shift from "religious criminality" to "human criminality" that is said to accompany societal development.

Because Durkheim's theories of crime and punishment are based on his general theory of social evolution, it is useful to have some understanding of the latter to better understand the former. With this in mind, a few notes on his theory of social evolution may be helpful to readers who do not have a background in classical sociological theory. Durkheim ([1893] 1984) described social evolution in terms of changes in a society's dynamic density, division of labor, common consciousness ("conscience collective"), and predominant form of social solidarity. To understand Durkheim's criminological perspective, it is especially important to understand his views regarding the general way in which the common consciousness changes with societal development. In simple terms, the common consciousness refers to the beliefs and sentiments that are shared by most members of a society. For Durkheim, most crimes are acts that violate strong and precise collective sentiments, deep feelings of respect that make up the core of the common consciousness. He maintains that most penal laws are oriented toward the preservation of these sentiments. Because they are shaped by many different factors, these sentiments vary from one society to another and, consequently, different societies have different conceptions of crime and different penal laws. Nonetheless, Durkheim concluded that the content of the common consciousness tends to change in a particular way through the process of social development.

According to Durkheim, as a society develops from a simple premodern form to a complex modern form, the core of the common consciousness shifts from a set of strong sentiments related to "collective things" to sentiments related to "the individual" (see Durkheim [1893] 1984, [1900] 1969). In other words, the culture of a society moves from an intense feeling of respect for the family, church, and nation to an intense feeling of respect for the lives, property, and freedom of individuals. We evolve from the worship of collective entities to the worship of humanity in general. Durkheim uses this conception of cultural development to explain historical variations in criminal law (the transition from "religious criminality" to "human criminality"), punishment (the transition from intense physical punishments to the deprivation of liberty), and crime (e.g., the perceived decline in homicide rates).[17] He also

---

17. In a lecture published in *Professional Ethics and Civic Morals* ([1900] 1958), Durkheim presented a theory in which he attempts to explain a perceived historical decline in homicide rates. There he provides his most extensive examination of homicide, explaining the historical decline primarily in terms of a general decline in respect for "collective things" (e.g., family, church, and state). For an overview of Durkheim's perspective on homicide, see DiCristina (2004, 2006).

suggested that during periods of rapid social development, the common consciousness of a society may temporarily break down, creating a state of excessive anomie, a condition of insufficient regulation that can affect the level of deviant behavior.

Durkheim's conclusions have been criticized on several grounds (see Garland 1990). One significant problem with his work is that he frequently neglects the existence and effects of group conflict. He often overlooks the extent to which power is unevenly distributed across different groups in society, and how the more powerful groups may be able to shape the law and systems of punishment to serve their own interests at the expense of others. In addition, it can be argued that Durkheim was too sociological in his orientation, causing him to neglect theories of biology and psychology that may have prompted him to alter his perspective. In any case, a complete overview and critique of Durkheim's theory of social evolution and his overall criminological perspective go well beyond this introduction.

A Concluding Note

If one combined the work of the moral statisticians with that of the French school, which seems reasonable given the amount of overlap between the two, the combination arguably shares more with contemporary criminology than any of the other major divisions of criminological thought that existed prior to the twentieth century. Their ideas, however, are embodied primarily in mainstream criminology; the imprint of the moral statisticians and the French school, at least as they have been defined here, is considerably less visible in the work of critical criminologists. While critical theorists generally prefer sociological frameworks to those of biology and psychology, they oppose sociological theories that appear to rationalize inequitable distributions of wealth, power, and prestige. Their common goal is to help emancipate one or more segments of society that they perceive as oppressed (e.g., the working class, women, or a minority racial group), something that generally cannot be accomplished without a fundamental change in the culture and structure of a society. Few moral statisticians or intellectuals of the late-nineteenth-century French school of criminology appear to have centered their work on this goal.

REFERENCES

Anon. 1874. "Monsieur Quetelet." *Journal of the Statistical Society of London* 37(1):114–115.

Becker, Howard S. 1963. *Outsiders: Studies in the Sociology of Deviance.* New York: The Free Press.

Beirne, Piers. 1993. *Inventing Criminology: Essays on the Rise of 'Homo Criminalis'.* Albany, NY: State University of New York Press.

Bonger, William (Willem) A. 1916. *Criminality and Economic Conditions.* Translated by Henry P. Horton. Boston: Little, Brown and Company.

Carpenter, Mary. 1857. "On the Importance of Statistics to the Reformatory Movement, with Returns from Female Reformatories, and Remarks on Them." *Journal of the Statistical Society of London* 20(1):33–40.

Coser, Lewis A. 1977. *Masters of Sociological Thought: Ideas in Historical and Social Context.* 2nd ed. New York: Harcourt Brace Jovanovich.

Cotterrell, Roger. 1999. *Émile Durkheim: Law in a Moral Domain*. Stanford, CA: Stanford University Press.

DiCristina, Bruce. 2004. "Durkheim's Theory of Homicide and the Confusion of the Empirical Literature." *Theoretical Criminology* 8(1):57–91.

DiCristina, Bruce. 2006. "Durkheim's Latent Theory of Gender and Homicide." *British Journal of Criminology* 46(2):212–233.

Durkheim, Emile. [1893] 1984. *The Division of Labor in Society*. Translated by W. D. Halls. New York: The Free Press.

Durkheim, Emile. [1895] 1982. *The Rules of Sociological Method*. Translated by W. D. Halls. New York: The Free Press.

Durkheim, Emile. [1897] 1951. *Suicide: A Study in Sociology*. Translated by John A. Spaulding and George Simpson. New York: The Free Press.

Durkheim, Emile. [1900] 1958. *Professional Ethics and Civic Morals*. Translated by Cornelia Brookfield. Glencoe, IL: The Free Press.

Durkheim, Emile. [1900] 1969. "Two Laws of Penal Evolution." Translated by William Jeffrey, Jr. *University of Cincinnati Law Review* 38(1):32–60.

Durkheim, Emile. [1902–1903] 1973. *Moral Education: A Study in the Theory and Application of the Sociology of Education*. Translated by Everett K. Wilson and Herman Schnurer. New York: The Free Press.

Durkheim, Emile. [1912] 1995. *The Elementary Forms of Religious Life*. Translated by Karen E. Fields. New York: The Free Press.

Elmer, M. C. 1933. "Century-Old Ecological Studies in France." *The American Journal of Sociology* 39(1):63–70.

Elmer, M. C. 1937. Comment on "The Lombrosian Myth in Criminology." *The American Journal of Sociology* 42(6):899–900.

Ferri, Enrico. [1901] 1913. *The Positive School of Criminology: Three Lectures*. Translated by Ernest Untermann. Chicago: Charles H. Kerr and Company.

Fletcher, Joseph. 1849. "Moral and Educational Statistics of England and Wales." *Journal of the Statistical Society of London* 12(2):151–176.

Friendly, Michael. 2007. "A.-M. Guerry's *Moral Statistics of France*: Challenges for Multivariable Spatial Analysis." *Statistical Science* 22(3):368–390.

Garland, David. 1990. *Punishment and Modern Society: A Study in Social Theory*. Chicago: The University of Chicago Press.

Giddens, Anthony. 1979. *Émile Durkheim*. New York: The Viking Press.

Giddings, Franklin H. 1903. "Introduction." In Gabriel Tarde's *The Laws of Imitation*, iii–vii. New York: Henry Holt and Company.

Guerry, André-Michel. [1833] 2002. *Essay on the Moral Statistics of France*. Translated by Hugh P. Whitt and Victor W. Reinking. Lewiston, NY: Edwin Mellen Press.

Halfpenny, Peter. 1982. *Positivism and Sociology: Explaining Social Life*. London: George Allen and Unwin.

Hankins, Frank H. 1908. *Adolphe Quetelet as Statistician*. Doctoral dissertation. Columbia University.

Hirschi, Travis. 1969. *Causes of Delinquency*. Berkeley: University of California Press.

Jenkins, Philip. 1984. "Varieties of Enlightenment Criminology: Beccaria, Godwin, de Sade." *British Journal of Criminology* 24(2):112–130.

LaCapra, Dominick. 1985. *Emile Durkheim: Sociologist and Philosopher*. Chicago: The University of Chicago Press.

Lindesmith, Alfred, and Yale Levin. 1937a. "The Lombrosian Myth in Criminology." *The American Journal of Sociology* 42(5):653–671.

Lindesmith, Alfred, and Yale Levin. 1937b. "Rejoinder." *The American Journal of Sociology* 42(5):901.

Lindsey, Edward. 1912. "Editorial Preface." In Gabriel Tarde's *Penal Philosophy*, xxi–xxv. Boston: Little, Brown and Company.

Lukes, Steven. 1972. *Émile Durkheim: His Life and Work*. New York: Harper & Row.

Lurguin, Constant. 1924. "The Fiftieth Anniversary of Quetelet's Death." *Journal of the American Statistical Association* 19:520–522.

Merton, Robert K. 1938. "Social Structure and Anomie." *American Sociological Review* 3(5):672–682.

Montagu, Ashley, ed. 1974. *Frontiers of Anthropology*. New York: G. P. Putnam's Sons.

Newman, Graeme R., and Pietro Marongiu. 2009. "Introduction to the *Treatise*." In Cesare Beccaria's *On Crimes and Punishments*, vii–lv. New Brunswick, NJ: Transaction Publishers.

Parsons, Talcott. 1949. *The Structure of Social Action*. New York: The Free Press.

Pinel, Philippe. [1806] 1962. *A Treatise on Insanity*. Translated by D. D. Davis. New York: Hafner Publishing.

Quetelet, Adolphe. [1831] 1984. *Research on the Propensity for Crime at Different Ages*. Translated by Sawyer F. Sylvester. Cincinnati, OH: Anderson Publishing.

Quetelet, Adolphe. [1842] 1968. *A Treatise on Man and the Development of His Faculties*. Translated by R. Knox. New York: Burt Franklin.

Quetelet, Adolphe. 1871. *Anthropométrie*. Bruxelles: C. Muquardt.

Rafter, Nicole, ed. 2009. *The Origins of Criminology: A Reader*. New York: Routledge.

Rawson, Rawson W. 1839. "An Inquiry into the Statistics of Crime in England and Wales." *Journal of the Statistical Society of London* 2(5):316–344.

Shaw, Clifford R., and Henry D. McKay. 1942. *Juvenile Delinquency and Urban Areas*. Chicago: University of Chicago Press.

Shichor, David. 2010. "The French-Italian Controversy: A Neglected Historical Topic in Criminological Literacy." *Journal of Criminal Justice Education* 21(3):211–228.

Sylvester, Sawyer F. 1984. "Introduction." In Adolphe Quetelet's *Research on the Propensity for Crime at Different Ages*, vii–xviii. Cincinnati, OH: Anderson Publishing.

Tarde, Gabriel. [1895] 1983. "Criminality and Social Health." In *Durkheim and the Law*, edited by Steven Lukes and Andrew Scull, 76–92. Oxford: Martin Robertson.

Tarde, Gabriel. [1903] 1912. *Penal Philosophy*. Translated by Rapelje Howell. Boston: Little, Brown and Company.

Tosti, Gustavo. 1897. "The Sociological Theories of Gabriel Tarde." *Political Science Quarterly* 12(3):490–511.

Vine, Margaret S. Wilson. 1972. "Gabriel Tarde (1843–1904)." In *Pioneers in Criminology*, 2nd ed., edited by Herman Mannheim, 292–304. Montclair, NJ: Patterson Smith.

Whitt, Hugh P. 2002. "Inventing Sociology: André-Michel Guerry and the *Essai sur la statistique morale de la France*." In André-Michel Guerry's *Essay on the Moral Statistics of France*, ix–xxxvii. Lewiston, NY: Edwin Mellen Press.

Zimmern, Helen. [1898] 2000. "Criminal Anthropology in Italy." In *Pioneering Perspectives in Criminology: The Literature of 19th Century Criminological Positivism*, edited by David M. Horton, 47–64. Incline Village, NV: Copperhouse.

CHAPTER 10

ADOLPHE QUETELET

The reading in this chapter is a selection from Adolphe Quetelet's *A Treatise on Man and the Development of His Faculties* ([1842] 1968), pp. 82–83, 90–96, and Plate 4; translated by R. Knox; New York: Burt Franklin. In 1835, the first edition of the *Treatise* was published in French under the title *Sur l'homme et le développement de ses facultés, ou Essai de physique sociale*. The selection in this chapter comes from a reprint of the 1842 English translation. While section numbers have been retained, footnote symbols have been changed to a numerical series. Quetelet's *Treatise* draws heavily on his earlier work, *Research on the Propensity for Crime at Different Ages*, which was first published in 1831. In fact, much of the reading below first appeared in this earlier work. For this reason I am presenting a selection from Quetelet's *Treatise* before the reading from Guerry's *Essay on the Moral Statistics of France*, a study that was first published in 1833.

Quetelet began his research on crime well after the establishment of the classical school and well before the emergence of the Italian school. The French Revolution had occurred more than three decades earlier and the Industrial Revolution was transforming Western societies. At this time, there was a growing concern for the establishment of predictable, if not calculable, interactions among individuals and different units of society, a concern that was associated with the breakdown of traditional ways of life and the expansion of capitalism, bureaucratic arrangements, and the social sciences. This, in other words, was a context that was conducive to the quantification and statistical analysis of empirical information on crime and criminals, the kind of research that was carried out by Quetelet and other moral statisticians of this era.

Quetelet's analyses of French crime statistics were important in several ways. He provided a demonstration of how statistical methods may be used in the study of crime and, more generally, a model for a form of positivism in the social sciences. Moreover, he examined the relationships among criminal behavior and several variables that remain of interest to contemporary criminologists (e.g., sex, age, education, and economic conditions). The following selection presents Quetelet's examination of the relationships among criminal behavior and the seasons, sex, and age. Although the study of crime rates across different seasons currently receives little attention from criminologists, it nonetheless represents a noteworthy part of the history of criminology and still may be of some marginal interest. More importantly, Quetelet's analysis of the relationship between sex and crime is a significant precursor to contemporary studies of the gender-ratio problem, while his examination of the relationship between age and crime anticipates contemporary life-course criminology.

from A TREATISE ON MAN AND THE DEVELOPMENT OF HIS FACULTIES

by Adolphe Quetelet

OF THE DEVELOPMENT OF THE PROPENSITY TO CRIME

1. Of Crimes in General, and of the Repression of them

Supposing men to be placed in similar circumstances, I call the greater or less probability of committing crime, the *propensity to crime*. My object is more especially to investigate the influence of season, climate, sex, and age, on this propensity.

I have said that the circumstances in which men are placed ought to be similar, that is to say, equally favourable, both in the existence of objects likely to excite the propensity and in the facility of committing the crime. It is not enough that a man may merely have the intention to do evil, he must also have the opportunity and the means. Thus the propensity to crime may be the same in France as in England, without, on that account, the *morality* of the nations being the same. I think this distinction of importance.[1]

There is still another important distinction to be made; namely that two individuals may have the same propensity to crime, without being equally *criminal*, if one, for example, were inclined to theft, and the other to assassination.[2]

Lastly, this is also the place to examine a difficulty which has not escaped M. Alphonse de Candolle in the work above mentioned: it is this, that our observations can only refer to *a certain number of known and tried offences, out of the unknown sum total of crimes committed*. Since this sum total of crimes committed will probably ever continue unknown, all the reasoning of which it is the basis will be more or less defective. I do not hesitate to say, that all the knowledge which we possess on the statistics of crimes and offences will be of no utility whatever, unless we admit without question that *there is a ratio, nearly invariably the same, between known and tried offences and the unknown sum total of crimes committed*. This ratio is necessary, and if it did not really exist, every thing which, until the present time, has been said on the statistical documents of crime, would be false and absurd. We are aware, then, how important it is to legitimate such a ratio, and we may be astonished that this has not been done before now. The ratio of which we speak necessarily varies according to the nature and seriousness of the crimes: in a well-organised society, where the police is active and justice is rightly administered, this ratio, for murders and assassinations, will be nearly equal to unity; that is to say, no individual will disappear from the society by murder or assassination, without its being known: this will not be precisely the case with poisonings. When we look to thefts and offences of smaller importance, the ratio will become very small, and a great number of offences will remain unknown, either because those against whom they are committed do not perceive them, or do not wish to prosecute the perpetrators, or because justice itself has not sufficient evidence to act upon. Thus, the greatness of this ratio, which will generally be different for

---

1. This has been very clearly established by M. Alphonse de Candolle, in an article entitled *Considerations sur la Statistique des Delits*, inserted in the *Bibliothèque Universelle de Genève*, Feb. 1830. The author regards the propensity of individuals to crime as depending on their morality, the temptation to which they are exposed, and the greater or less facility they may find to commit offences. Of these three causes, the first belongs more especially to the man; the other two are, properly speaking, external to him. As it is with man that I am occupied, I have endeavoured, in the course of my researches, that the causes external to him might be constantly nearly equal, so that they might be left out of the computation. I have necessarily been obliged to take into account natural influencing causes, such as climate, seasons, sex, and age.

2. In an article on *Hygiène Morale*, M. Villermé has fully shown how fatal the *regime* of prisons may become to the unfortunate person who is often confined for slight offences, and cast into the midst of a collection of wicked wretches, who corrupt him. "I have been told," says he, "by a person who accompanied Napoleon to the Isle of Elba, that, in the particular and at that time philosophical conversations of the ex-emperor,

---

he has several times been heard to say, that under whatever relation we may view man, *he is as much the result of his physical and moral atmosphere as of his own organisation*. And the idea, now advanced by many others, which is contained in this phrase, is the most general as well as the most just that can be formed on the subject before us.—*Annales d'Hygiène Publique*, Oct. 1830.

different crimes and offences, will chiefly depend on the activity of justice in reaching the guilty, on the care with which the latter conceal themselves, on the repugnance which the individuals injured may have to complain, or perhaps on their not knowing that any injury has been committed against them. Now, if all the causes which influence the magnitude of the ratio remain the same, we may also assert that the effects will remain invariable. This result is confirmed in a curious manner by induction, and observing the surprising constancy with which the numbers of the statistics of crime are reproduced annually—a constancy which, no doubt, will be also reproduced in the numbers at which we cannot arrive: thus, although we do not know the criminals who escaped justice, we very well know that every year between 7000 and 7300 persons are brought before the criminal courts, and that 61 are regularly condemned out of every 100; that 170,000 nearly are brought before courts of correction, and that 85 out of 100 are condemned; and that, if we pass to details, we find a no less alarming regularity; thus we find that between 100 and 150 individuals are annually condemned to death,[3] 280 condemned to perpetual hard labour, 1050 to hard labour for a time, 1220 to solitary confinement (*à la réclusion*), &c.; so that this budget of the scaffold and the prisons is discharged by the French nation, with much greater regularity, no doubt, than the financial budget; and we might say, that what annually escapes the minister of justice is a more regular sum than the deficiency of revenue to the treasury. . . .

3. On the Influence of Seasons on the Propensity to Crime

The seasons have a well-marked influence in augmenting and diminishing the number of crimes. We may form some idea from the following table, which contains the number of crimes committed in France against persons and property, during each month, for three years, as well as the ratio of these numbers. We can also compare the numbers of this table with those which I have given to show the influence of seasons on the development of mental alienation, and we shall find the most remarkable coincidences, especially for crimes against persons, which would appear to be most usually dependent on failures of the reasoning powers:[4]—

Months.	Crimes against		Ratio: 1827-28.	Crimes against		Ratio: 1830-31.
	Persons.	Property.		Persons.	Property.	
January,	282	1,095	3.89	189	666	3.52
February,	272	910	3.35	194	563	2.90
March,	335	968	2.89	205	602	2.94
April,	314	841	2.68	197	548	2.78
May,	381	844	2.22	213	569	2.67
June,	414	850	2.05	208	602	2.90
July,	379	828	2.18	188	501	2.66
August,	382	934	2.44	247	596	2.41
September,	355	896	2.52	176	584	3.32
October,	285	926	3.25	207	586	2.83
November,	301	961	3.20	223	651	2.95
December,	347	1,152	3.33	181	691	3.82
Total,	3847	11,205	2.77	2428	7159	2.94

First, the epoch of maximum (June) in respect to the number of crimes against persons, coincides pretty nearly with the epoch of minimum in respect to crimes against property, and this takes place in summer; whilst, on the contrary, the minimum of the number of crimes against persons, and the maximum of the number of crimes against property, takes place in winter. Comparing these two kinds of crimes, we find that in the month of January nearly four crimes take place against property to one against persons, and in the month of June only two to three. These differences are readily explained by considering that during winter misery and want are more especially felt, and cause an increase of the number of crimes against property, whilst the violence of the passions predominating in summer, excites to more frequent personal collisions.

The periods of maxima and minima also coincide with those of the maxima and minima of births and deaths, as we have already shown.

The *Comptes Généraux* of France also contain data on the hours at which crimes have been committed, but only for thefts in Paris and the neighbourhood. These data are hitherto too few to draw any satisfactory conclusions from them.

---

3. The number of persons condemned to death has, however, diminished from year to year; is this owing to the increasing repugnance which tribunals feel to apply this punishment, for the abolition of which we have so many petitioners at the present day?

4. The observations which we possess are neither so numerous nor so carefully compiled as to enable us to affirm that any direct ratio exists between the propensity to crimes against persons and the tendency to mental alienation; yet the existence of this ratio becomes more probable if we consider that we find again the same coincidence regarding the influence of age.

4. On the Influence of Sex on the Propensity to Crime

... At the commencement, we may observe that, out of 28,686 accused, who have appeared before the courts in France, during the four years before 1830, there were found 5416 women, and 23,270 men, that is to say, 23 women to 100 men. Thus, the propensity to crime in general gives the ratio of 23 to 100 for the sexes. This estimate supposes that justice exercises its duties as actively with regard to women as to men; and this is rendered probable by the fact, that the severity of repression is nearly the same in the case of both sexes; in other words, that women are treated with much the same severity as men.

We have just seen that, in general, the propensity to crime in men is about four times as great as in women, in France; but it will be important to examine further, if men are four times as criminal, which will be supposing that the crimes committed by the sexes are equally serious. We shall commence by making a distinction between crimes against property and crimes against persons. At the same time, we shall take the numbers obtained for each year, that we may see the limits in which they are comprised:—

Years.	Crimes against Persons.			Crimes against Property.		
	Men.	Women.	Ratio.	Men.	Women.	Ratio.
1826,	1639	268	0.16	4073	1008	0.25
1827,	1637	274	0.17	4020	998	0.25
1828,	1576	270	0.17	4396	1156	0.26
1829,	1552	239	0.15	4379	1203	0.27
Averages,	1601	263	0.16	4217	1091	0.26
1830,	1412	254	0.18	4196	1100	0.26
1831,	1813	233	0.13	4567	993	0.22
Averages,	1612	243	0.15	4381	1046	0.24

Although the number of crimes against persons may have diminished slightly, whilst crimes against property have become rather more numerous, yet we see that the variations are not very great; they have but little modified the ratios between the numbers of the accused of the two sexes. We have 26 women to 100 men in the accusations for crimes against property, and for crimes against persons the ratio has been only 16 to 100.[5] In general, crimes against persons are of a more serious nature than those against property, so that our distinction is favourable to the women, and we may affirm that men, in France,

---

5. These conclusions only refer to the results of the four years before 1830. The numbers of the following years, which have been since added to the table, give almost the same ratios.

---

are four times as criminal as women. It must be observed, that the ratio 16 to 26 is nearly the same as that of the strength of the two sexes. However, it is proper to examine things more narrowly, and especially to take notice of individual crimes, at least of those which are committed in so great a number, that the inferences drawn from them may possess some degree of probability. For this purpose, in the following table I have collected the numbers relating to the four years before 1830, and calculated the different ratios; the crimes are classed according to the degree of magnitude of this ratio. I have also grouped crimes nearly of the same nature together, such as issuing false money, counterfeits, falsehoods in statements or in commercial transactions, &c.

Nature of Crimes.	Men.	Women.	Women to 100 Men.
Infanticide,	30	426	1320
Miscarriage,	15	39	260
Poisoning,	77	73	91
House robbery (vol domestique),	2648	1602	60
Parricide,	44	22	50
Incendiarism of buildings and other things,	279	94	34
Robbery of churches,	176	47	27
Wounding of parents (blessures envers ascendans),	292	63	22
Theft,	10,677	2249	21
False evidence and suborning,	307	51	17
Fraudulent bankruptcy,	353	57	16
Assassination,	947	111	12
False coining (fausse monnaie), counterfeit making, false affirmations in deeds, &c.	1669	177	11
Rebellion,	612	60	10
Highway robbery,	648	54	8
Wounds and blows,	1447	78	5
Murder,	1112	44	4
Violation and seduction,	685	7	1
Violation on persons under 15 years of age,	585	5	1

As we have already observed, to the commission of crime the three following conditions are essential—the will, which depends on the person's morality, the opportunity, and the facility of effecting it. Now, the reason why females have less propensity to crime than males, is accounted for by their being more under the influence of sentiments of shame and modesty, as far as morals are concerned; their dependent state, and retired habits, as far as occasion or opportunity is concerned; and their physical weakness, so far as the facility of acting is concerned. I think we may attribute the differences observed in the degree of criminality to these three principal causes. Sometimes the whole three concur at the same time: we ought, on such occasions, to expect to find their influence very marked, as in rapes and seductions; thus, we have only 1 woman to 100 men in crimes of this nature. In poisoning, on the contrary, the number of accusations for either sex is nearly equal. When force becomes necessary for the destruction of a person, the number of women who are accused becomes much fewer; and their numbers diminish in proportion, according to the necessity of the greater publicity before the crime can be perpetrated: the following crimes also take place in the order in which they are stated—infanticide, miscarriage, parricide, wounding of parents, assassinations, wounds and blows, murder.

With respect of infanticide, woman has not only many more opportunities of committing it than man, but she is in some measure impelled to it, frequently by misery, and almost always from the desire of concealing a fault, and avoiding the shame or scorn of society, which, in such cases, thinks less unfavourably of man. Such is not the case with other crimes involving the destruction of an individual: it is not the degree of the crime which keeps a woman back, since, in the series which we have given, parricides and wounding of parents are more numerous than assassinations, which again are more frequent than murder, and wounds and blows generally; it is not simply weakness, for then the ratio for parricide and wounding of parents should be the same as for murder and wounding of strangers. These differences are more especially owing to the habits and sedentary life of females; they can only conceive and execute guilty projects on individuals with whom they are in the greatest intimacy: thus, compared with man, her assassinations are more often in her family than out of it; and in society she commits assassination rather than murder, which often takes place after excess of drink, and the quarrels to which women are less exposed.

If we now consider the different kinds of theft, we shall find that the ratios of the propensity to crime are arranged in a similar series: thus, we have successively house robbery, robbery in churches, robberies in general, and, lastly, highway robbery, for which strength and audacity are necessary. The less conspicuous propensity to cheating in general, and to fraudulent bankruptcy, again depend on the more secluded life of females, their separation from trade, and that, in some cases, they are less capable than men—for example, in coining false money and issuing counterfeits.

If we attempt to analyse facts, it seems to me that the difference of morality in man and woman is not so great as is generally supposed, excepting only as regards modesty; I do not speak of the timidity arising from this last sentiment, in like manner as it does from the physical weakness and seclusion of females. As to these habits themselves, I think we may form a tolerable estimate of their influence by the ratios which exist between the sexes in crimes of different kinds, where neither strength has to be taken into consideration, nor modesty—as in theft, false witnessing, fraudulent bankruptcy, &c.; these ratios are about 100 to 21 or 17, that is to say, about 5 or 6 to 1. As to other modes of cheating, the difference is a little greater, from the reasons already stated. If we try to give a numerical expression of the intensity of the causes by which women are influenced, as, for example, the influence of strength, we may estimate it as being in proportion to the degree of strength itself, or as 1 to 2 nearly; and this is the ratio of the number of parricides for each sex. For crimes where both physical weakness and the retired life of females must be taken into account, as in assassinations and highway robberies, following the same plan in our calculations, it will be necessary to multiply the ratio of power or strength ½ by the degree of dependence 1-5, which gives 1-10, a quantity which really falls between the values 12-100 and 8-100, the ratios given in the table. With respect to murder, and blows and wounds, these crimes depend not merely on strength and a more or less sedentary life, but still more on being in the habit of using strong drinks and quarrelling. The influence of this latter cause might almost be considered as 1 to 3 for the sexes. It may be thought that the estimates which I have here pointed out, cannot be of an exact nature, from the impossibility of assigning the share of influence which the greater modesty of woman, her physical weakness, her dependence, or rather her more retired life, and her feebler passions, which are also less frequently excited by liquors, may have respectively on any crime in particular. Yet, if such were the characters in which the sexes more particularly differ from each other, we might, by analyses like those now given, assign their respective influence with some probability of truth, especially if the observations were very numerous. I do not speak of modes of justice, of legislation in general, of the state of knowledge, of means of providing for physical wants, &c., which may powerfully contribute to increase or diminish the number of crimes, but whose influence is generally not very evident as regards the ratio of the accused of each sex.

Perhaps it may be said, that if it be true that the morality of woman is not greater than that of man, house robbery should be as frequent for the one as for the other. This observation would be just, if it were proved that the class of individuals by whom house robberies are committed, were equally composed of men and women; but there are no data on this subject. All that can be laid down is, that men and women who live in a domestic state, rather commit crimes against property than against persons, which very materially confirms the observations made above, on the influence of retired life and sedentary habits. The *Compte Général de l'Administration de la Justice* in 1829, for the first time, gives the professions of the accused; and in the article *Domestiques*, we find 318 men and 147 women employed as farm-servants; and 149 men and 175 women as personal domestics: the total number of men is greater than that of women. Now, of these numbers, there were 99 accused of crimes against persons, and 590 of crimes against property: the ratio of these numbers is 1 to 6 nearly, and it has preserved exactly the same value in the years 1830 and 1831. But we have had occasion to see that this ratio for the mass of society is 1 to 3, when particular circumstances are not taken into consideration; and it would be only as 263 to 1091, or 1 to 4 nearly, if society were composed of women alone: thus, in all the cases, I think it has been sufficiently shown that men and women, when in the state of servants, commit crimes against property in preference to others.

As to capital crimes, we may arrange them in the following manner:—

Adultery, domestic quarrels, and jealousy, cause almost an equal number of poisonings in both sexes; but the number of assassinations, and especially of murders, of women by their husbands, is greater than that of husbands by their wives. The circumstances bearing on this subject have been stated already.

Of 903 murders which have taken place from hatred, revenge, and other motives, 446 have been committed in consequence of quarrels and contentions at taverns; thus, more than one-third of the total number of murders have taken place under circumstances in which women are not usually involved.

The four last volumes of the *Comptes Généraux*, contain some interesting details on the intellectual state of the accused of both sexes: they may be stated as follows:—

Intellectual State.	Men.	Women.	Ratio: 1828-29.	Men.	Women.	Ratio: 1830-31.
Unable to read or write,	6,537	2152	3.0	6,877	2042	3.3
Able to read and write imperfectly,	3,308	497	6.6	3,422	451	7.6
Could read and write well,	1,399	110	12.7	1,373	82	16.7
Had received an excellent education to the 1st degree,	283	5	56.6	314	5	62.8
Intellectual state not mentioned,	374	104	3.6	2	..	..
	11,901	2868	4.2	11,988	2580	4.6

These numbers give us no information on the population, since we do not know what is the degree of knowledge diffused in France; but we see, at least, that there is a great difference in the sexes. I think we might explain these results by saying, that in the lower orders, where there is scarcely any education, the habits of the women approach those of the men; and the more we ascend in the classes of society, and consequently in the degrees of education, the life of woman becomes more and more private, and she has less opportunity of committing crime, all other things being equal. These ratios differ so much from each other, that we cannot but feel how

Apparent Motives: 1826-1829 inclusive.	Accused for				Total.
	Poisoning.	Murder.	Assassination.	Incendiarism.	
Cupidity, theft,	20	39	237	66	362
Adultery,	48	9	76	..	133
Domestic dissensions,	48	120	131	34	333
Debauchery, jealousy,	10	58	115	37	220
Hatred, revenge, & divers motives,	23	903	460	229	1615
Total,	149	1129	1019	366	2663

much influence our habits and social position have on crime.

It is to be regretted that the documents of justice for the Low Countries do not contain any thing on the distinction of the sexes; we only see (according to the returns of the prisons and the houses of correction and detention, in the *Recueil Official*), that on the 1st of January 1827, the number of men was 5162, that of women 1193, which gives 100 women to 433 men. Making use of the documents which have been disclosed to me by M. le Baron de Keverberg, I found that in 1825 this ratio was 100 to 314.

According to the report of M. Ducpétiaux, on the state of prisons in Belgium, we enumerated 2231 men and 550 women, as prisoners on the 1st of January 1833, which gives a ratio of 405 to 100: among these prisoners were found 1364 men and 326 women who could not read or write; so that the intellectual state of the prisoners of both sexes was nearly the same; the ratio of the whole population to those who could neither read nor write, was as 100 to 61 among the men, and 100 to 60 among the women. To the number of prisoners just mentioned, may be added 419 individuals confined in the central military prison, of whom 282 could neither read nor write; this gives a ratio of 67 in 100.[6]

If we examine the accounts of the correctional (or minor) tribunals of France, we find the ratio between the accused of both sexes to be 529,848 to 149,565, or 28 females to 100 males. Thus, with respect to less serious offences, which are judged by the correctional tribunals, the women have there been rather more numerous compared with the men than in the case of weightier crimes.

5. Of the Influence of Age on the Propensity to Crime

Of all the causes which influence the development of the propensity to crime, or which diminish that propensity, age is unquestionably the most energetic. Indeed, it is through age that the physical powers and passions of man are developed, and their energy afterwards decreases with age. Reason is developed with age, and continues to acquire power even when strength and passion have passed their greatest vigour. Considering only these three elements, strength, passion, and judgement[7] (or reason), we may almost say, *à priori*, what will be the degree of the propensity to crime at different ages. Indeed, the propensity must be almost nothing at the two extremes of life; since, on the one hand, strength and passion, two powerful instruments of crime, have scarcely begun to exist, and, on the other hand, their energy, nearly extinguished, is still further deadened by the influence of reason. On the contrary, the propensity to crime should be at its maximum at the age when strength and passion have attained their maximum, and when reason has not acquired sufficient power to govern their combined influence. Therefore, considering only physical causes, the propensity to crime at different ages will be a property and sequence of the three quantities we have just named, and might be determined by them, if they were sufficiently known.[8] But since these elements are not yet determined, we must confine ourselves to seeking for the degrees of the propensity to crime in an experimental manner; we shall find the means of so doing in the *Comptes Généraux de la Justice*. The following table will show the number of crimes against persons and against property, which have been committed in France by each sex during the years 1826, 27, 28, and 29, as well as the ratio of these numbers; the fourth column points out how a population of 10,000 souls is divided in France, according to age; and the last column gives the ratio of the total number of crimes to the corresponding number of the preceding column; thus there is no longer an inequality of number of the individuals of different ages.

---

6. According to the statistical tables of France, of young persons inscribed for military service in 1827, we enumerate (Bulletin de M. Férussac, Nov. 1829, p. 271)—

	Absolute No.	Relative No.
Young persons able to read,	13,794	5
Young persons able to read and write,	100,787	37
Young persons not able to read or write,	157,510	58
	272,091	100

This ratio of 58 in 100 is a little less unfavourable than that of prisons, which is 60 in 100.

7. I am not speaking of the intellectual state, of religious sentiments, of fear, shame, punishment, &c., because these qualities depend more or less directly on reason.

8. Here we are more especially considering crimes against persons; for crimes against property, it will be necessary to take notice of the wants and privations of man.

Individuals' Age.	Crimes against		Crimes against Property in 100.	Population according to Age.	Degrees of the Propensity to Crime.
	Persons.	Property.			
Less than 16 years,	80	440	85	3304	161
16 to 21 years,	904	3723	80	887	5217
21 to 25 years,	1278	3329	72	673	6846
25 to 30 years,	1575	3702	70	791	6671
30 to 35 years,	1153	2883	71	732	5514
35 to 40 years,	650	2076	76	672	4057
40 to 45 years,	575	1724	75	612	3757
45 to 50 years,	445	1275	74	549	3133
50 to 55 years,	288	811	74	482	2280
55 to 60 years,	168	500	75	410	1629
60 to 65 years,	157	385	71	330	1642
65 to 70 years,	91	184	70	247	1113
70 to 80 years,	64	137	68	255	788
80 and upwards,	5	14	74	55	345

This table gives us results conformable to those which I have given in my *Recherches Statistique* for the years 1826 and 1827. Since the value obtained for 80 years of age and upwards is based on very small numbers, it is not entitled to much confidence. Moreover, we see that man begins to exercise his propensity to crimes against property at a period antecedent to his pursuit of other crimes. Between his 25th and 30th year, when his powers are developed, he inclines more to crimes against persons. It is near the age of 25 years that the propensity to crime reaches its maximum; but before passing to other considerations, let us examine what difference there is between the sexes. The latter columns of the following table show the degrees of propensity to crime,[9] reference being had to population, and the greatest number of each column being taken as unity:—

---

9. To give a new proof of the almost identity of results of each year, I have thought proper to present here the numbers collected between 1830 and 1831; we may compare them with those of the preceding tables, which are nearly exactly double, because they refer to four years:—

Individuals' Age.	Crimes against		Crimes against Property in 100 Crimes.	Accused.		Women to 100 Men.
	Persons.	Property.		Men.	Women.	
Under 16 years,	27	214	88	211	30	14
16 to 21 years,	394	1,888	83	1,911	371	19
21 to 25 years,	643	1,708	72	1,913	438	23
25 to 30 years,	758	1,872	70	2,185	445	20

Individuals' Age.	Accused.		Women to 1000 Men.	Degrees of the Propensity to Crime.			
	Men.	Women.		In General.	Men.	Women.	Calculated.
Under 16 years,	438	82	187	0.02	0.02	0.02	0.02
16 to 21 years,	3,901	726	186	0.76	0.79	0.64	0.66
21 to 25 years,	3,762	845	225	1.00	1.00	0.98	1.00
25 to 30 years,	4,260	1017	239	0.97	0.96	1.00	0.92
30 to 35 years,	3,254	782	240	0.81	0.80	0.83	0.81
35 to 40 years,	2,105	621	295	0.59	0.56	0.75	0.71
40 to 45 years,	1,831	468	256	0.55	0.54	0.60	0.60
45 to 50 years,	1,357	363	267	0.46	0.44	0.51	0.51
50 to 55 years,	896	203	227	0.33	0.33	0.33	0.42
55 to 60 years,	555	113	204	0.24	0.24	0.22	0.34
60 to 65 years,	445	97	218	0.24	0.24	0.23	0.27
65 to 70 years,	230	45	196	0.16	0.17	0.14	0.21
70 to 80 years,	163	38	233	0.12	0.12	0.12	0.12
80 & upwards,	18	1	56	0.05	0.06	0.01	0.04
All ages,	23,270	5416	233	0.41	..	..	..

Individuals' Age.	Crimes against		Crimes against Property in 100 Crimes.	Accused.		Women to 100 Men.
	Persons.	Property.		Men.	Women.	
30 to 35 years,	662	1,741	72	2,004	399	20
35 to 40 years,	376	1,088	74	1,167	297	26
40 to 45 years,	279	725	72	800	204	25
45 to 50 years,	200	643	76	692	151	21
50 to 55 years,	161	426	73	487	100	21
55 to 60 years,	91	245	73	270	66	24
60 to 65 years,	55	147	73	162	40	25
65 to 70 years,	31	100	77	113	18	16
70 to 80 years,	29	58	66	67	20	30
80 and upwards,	6	1	14	6	1	16
All ages,	3712	10,856	74	11,988	2580	22

Women, compared to men, are rather later in entering on the career of crime, and also sooner come to the close of it. The maximum for men takes place about the 25th year, and about the 30th for women; the numbers on which our conclusions are founded are still very few; yet we see that the two lines which represent the relative value for each sex are almost parallel. The latter column contains results calculated by the following very simple formula:—

$$y = (1 - \sin. x)\frac{1}{1 + m}, \text{ supposing } m = \frac{1}{2x - 18}.$$

In this manner the degree of the propensity to crime is expressed according to age (*en fonction de l'âge*) x. We must take, as we see, for the axis of the abscissæ, one-fourth of the corrected circumference (*circonférence rectifiée*), and divided into decimal parts. The results of this formula generally agree better with the results obtained for women. I have endeavoured to render them sensible by the construction of a curve, the greater or less divergences of which from the axis AB (see *plate* 4) indicates the degree of the propensity to crime. The equation becomes a sinusoide—

$$y = 1 - \sin. x,$$

for ages above 30 years, because m evidently is equal to unity. It is not to be expected that we should find mathematical precision, for several reasons, of which the principal are—

1. The numbers obtained for four years are not so great that we may adopt their results with perfect confidence.

2. To calculate the propensity to crime, we must combine these numbers with those which the tables of population have furnished; and it is pretty generally agreed that the table of the *Annuaire* does not give the state of the population of France with sufficient accuracy.

3. The propensity to crime can only be calculated from the whole of the individuals who compose the population; and as those who occupy the prisons are generally persons of more than 25 years of age, and who, from their state of captivity, cannot enter into the ratio for persons above 25 years of age, there must necessarily be a void (*lacune*). If, instead of taking crimes collectively, we examine each in particular in proportion to age, we shall have a new proof that the maximum of crimes of different kinds takes place between the 20th and 30th years,

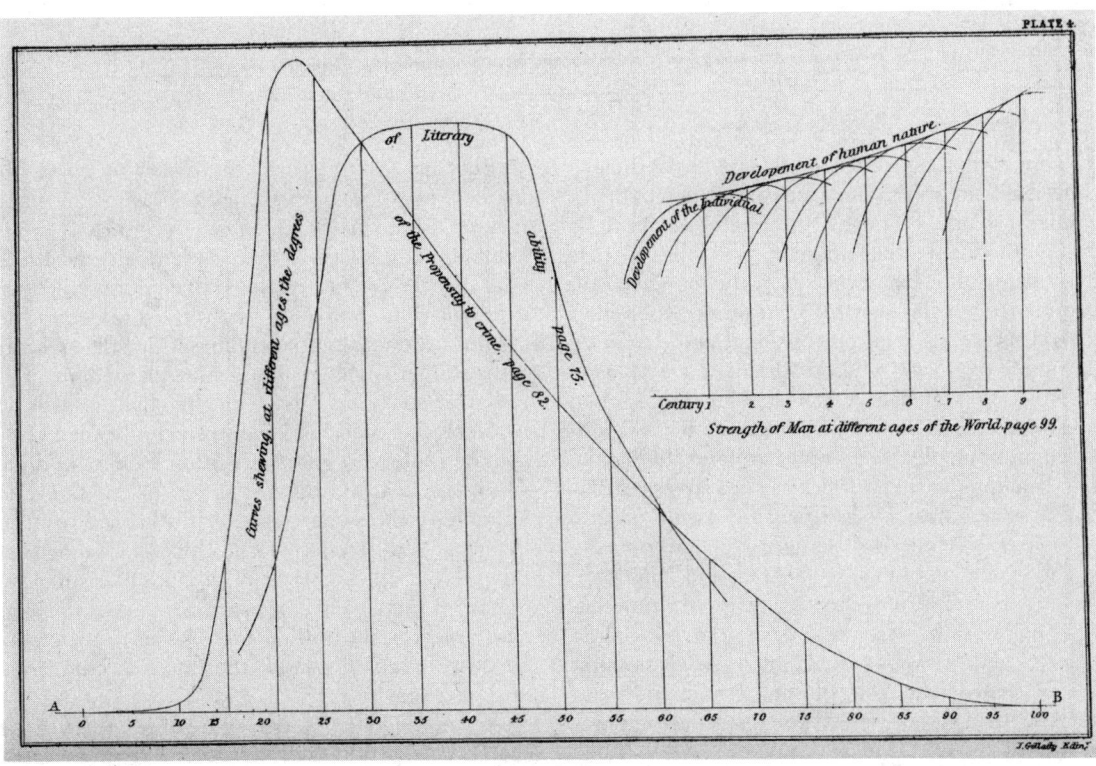

PLATE 4

and that it is really about that period that the most vicious disposition is manifested. Only the period of maximum will be hastened or retarded some years for some crimes, according to the quicker or slower development of certain qualities of man which are proportioned to those crimes. These results are too curious to be omitted here; I have presented them in the following table, according to the documents of France, from 1826 to 1829 inclusively, classing them according to the periods of maxima, and taking into account the population of different ages. I have omitted the crimes which are committed in smallest number, because the results from that alone would have been very doubtful.

Nature of the Crimes.	Under 16 Years.	16 to 21.	21 to 25.	25 to 30.	30 to 35.	35 to 40.	40 to 45.	45 to 50.	50 to 55.	55 to 60.	60 to 65.	65 to 70.	70 to 80.	80 and upwards.
Violations on children under 15 years,	4	120	71	96	73	39	34	45	22	18	26	17	21	2
House robbery,	54	965	845	766	528	351	249	207	112	56	61	34	14	..
Other thefts,	332	2479	2050	2292	1716	1249	1016	707	433	263	190	98	65	10
Violation and seduction,	9	155	156	148	99	38	40	27	9	5	3	1	2	..
Parricide,	6	13	12	13	6	3	2	1	4	2	..	..	..	..
Wounds and blows,	6	180	300	359	219	129	101	95	55	35	23	10	7	1
Murder,	15	139	198	275	172	103	84	49	48	30	25	17	9	..
Infanticide,	1	40	99	134	76	44	30	8	7	1	8	4	2	..
Rebellion,	5	67	129	156	115	51	51	35	29	16	16	5	5	..
Highway robbery,	21	80	111	149	107	60	62	46	22	21	8	6	4	..
Assassination,	10	90	144	203	183	100	104	89	53	32	24	13	15	1
Wounding parents,	2	47	64	73	72	40	30	16	8	2	1	..	..	..
Poisoning,	5	6	17	30	27	15	20	12	6	2	5	4	1	..
False witnessing and suborning,	2	23	46	48	44	42	42	35	23	15	15	11	7	..
Various misdemeanours,	8	86	202	276	312	244	207	185	129	78	75	28	28	2

Thus the propensity to theft, one of the first to show itself, prevails in some measure throughout our whole existence; we might be led to believe it to be inherent to the weakness of man, who falls into it as if by instinct. It is first exercised by the indulgence of confidence which exists in the interior of families, then it manifests itself out of them, and finally on the public highway, where it terminates by having recourse to violence, when the man has then made the sad essay of the fullness of his strength by committing all the different kinds of homicide. This fatal propensity, however, is not so precocious as that which, near adolescence, arises with the fire of the passions and the disorders which accompany it, and which drives man to violation and seduction, seeking its first victims among beings whose weakness opposes the least resistance. To these first excesses of the passions, of cupidity, and of strength, is soon joined reflection, plotting crime; and man, become more self-possessed and hardened, chooses to destroy his victim by assassination or poisoning. Finally, his last stages in the career of crime are marked by address in deception, which in some measure supplies the place of strength. It is in his decline that the vicious man presents the most hideous spectacle; his cupidity, which nothing can extinguish, is rekindled with fresh ardour, and assumes the mask of swindling; if he still uses the little strength which nature has left to him, it is rather to strike his enemy in the shade; finally, if his depraved passions have not been deadened by age, he prefers to gratify them on feeble children. Thus, his first and his last stages in the career of crime have the same character in this last respect: but what a difference! That which was somewhat excusable in the young man, because of his inexperience, of the violence of his passions, and the similarity of ages, in the old man is the result of the deepest immorality and the most accumulated load of depravity.

From the data of the preceding tables, it is scarcely possible not to perceive the great influence which age exercises over the propensity to crime, since each of the individual results tend to prove it. I shall not hesitate to consider the scale of the different degrees of the propensity to crime, at different ages, deserving of as much confidence as those which I have given for the stature, weight, and strength of man, or, finally, those for mortality.

Account has also been taken of the ages of accused persons, who have appeared before the minor or correctional courts of France, but only preserving the three following heads, which refer but to the four years preceding 1830:—

Ages.	Criminal Courts.		Correctional Courts.	
	Men.	Women.	Men.	Women.
Under 16 years,	2	2	5	6
From 16 to 21,	17	13	14	16
More than 21,	81	85	81	78
	100	100	100	100

Thus, the correctional cases are, in early age, all things being equal, more frequent than criminal cases; they are the first steps of crime, and consequently those most easily ascended. In Belgium, only four heads of ages have been made, and the results of correctional and criminal courts have been united, which renders our comparisons more difficult, since, as we have just seen, the numbers in each are not the same; it is also to be regretted that care has not been taken to distinguish the sexes. Be this as it may, by taking the total number of the accused and suspected (*prévenus*) as unity, we obtain the following results:—

Ages.	Suspected (or Committed) and Accused.				
	1826.	1827.	1828.	1829.	Average Number.
Under 16 years,	4	5	5	5	5
From 16 to 21,	13	11	12	11	12
From 21 to 70,	81	82	81	82	81
Above 70 years,	2	2	2	2	2
	100	100	100	100	100

These results are very similar to those of the correctional courts of France, and the latter elements ought certainly to predominate, when we make no distinction between the accused and those merely committed, since the latter are always more numerous than the accused. Yet it would seem that with us there are fewer offences between the ages of 16 and 21 than in France.

We do not find that the number of children brought annually before the courts of Belgium has diminished, either in an absolute sense, or compared with the numbers of other accused and committed persons. The same is nearly the case with France, as we see by the following table, in which I have preferred giving the absolute numbers:—

Years.	Under 16 Years.	16 to 21.	More than 21.	Total.
Accused.				
1826,	124	1,101	5,763	6,988
1827,	136	1,022	5,771	6,939
1828,	143	1,278	5,975	7,396
1829,	117	1,226	6,030	7,373
1830,	114	1,161	5,687	6,962
1831,	127	1,121	6,358	7,606
Committed.				
1826,	5,042	12,799	86,196	104,037
1827,	5,233	13,291	73,588	92,112
1828,	5,228	14,902	71,622	91,752
1829,	5,306	14,431	79,438	99,175
1830,*	2,852	6,452	47,812	57,116
1831,	5,651	17,659	84,433	107,743

*Those committed for different kinds of offences are not included in these numbers.

We must not, however, conclude from these results that education, which for some time has been diffused with such activity, has been of no effect in diminishing the number of crimes committed by young persons; several years more are necessary before its influence can become apparent, and before it can carry its effects into the bosom of families.

It is a matter of regret, that as yet we possess so few accounts of the ages of criminals, calculated to render appreciable the influence of places and the customs of different nations. In general, we remark, that the number of children in prisons in England is much greater than with us; this would appear to be owing, especially in the metropolis, to children being trained in a manner to theft, while the really guilty act through their intermediation. In the penitentiary of Millbank, in the year 1827, 1250 individuals were registered as under 21 years of age out of a total number of 3020, which gives a ratio of 41 to 100, being more than double that of France and the Low Countries.[10]

---

10. Bulletin de M. de Férussac, Mai 1828.

The condemned persons in the jail of Philadelphia in 1822, 1823, and 1824, were proportioned as follows:[11]—

Ages.	1822.	1823.	1824.	Totals.
Under 21 years,	52	72	58	182
From 21 to 30 years,	151	143	122	416
From 30 to 40 years,	72	67	79	218
Above 40 years,	55	49	28	132

The total for the three years was 948. Taking the ratio of this sum to 1000, we find the following values, opposite to which I have placed those of France:—

	Philadelphia.	France.
Under 21 years,	19	19
From 21 to 30,	44	35
From 30 to 40,	23	23
Above 40 years,	14	23
	100	100

Thus the prisons of Philadelphia present exactly the same number of criminals as those of France for individuals under 19 and for those between 30 and 40 years of age; they have fewer old men, but more men between 21 and 30, which may be owing to the nature of the population of the two countries.

France, Belgium, and Philadelphia, agree then pretty nearly as to the number of criminals in proportion to the ages; but England differs very sensibly from the average values presented by these countries, and that is owing, no doubt, as I observed before, not so much to the character of the English people as to the modes of eluding the rigour of the laws which the malefactors make use of, acting through the inter-medium of children whom they have trained up as instruments of crime.

Conclusions

In making a summary of the principal observations contained in this chapter, we are led to the following conclusions:—

1st, Age (or the term of life) is undoubtedly the cause which operates with most energy in developing or subduing the propensity to crime.

2d, This fatal propensity appears to be developed in proportion to the intensity of the physical power and passions of man: it attains its maximum about the age of 25 years, the period at which the physical development has almost ceased. The intellectual and moral development, which operates more slowly, subsequently weakens the propensity to crime, which, still later, diminishes from the feeble state of the physical powers and passions.

3d, Although it is near the age of 25 that the maximum in number of crimes of different kinds takes place, yet this maximum advances or recedes some years for certain crimes, according to the quicker or slower development of certain qualities which have a bearing on those crimes. Thus, man, driven by the violence of his passions, at first commits violation and seduction; almost at the same time he enters on the career of theft, which he seems to follow as if by instinct till the end of life; the development of his strength subsequently leads him to commit every act of violence—homicide, rebellion, highway robbery still later, reflection converts murder into assassination and poisoning. Lastly, man, advancing in the career of crime, substitutes a greater degree of cunning for violence, and becomes more of a forger than at any other period of life.

4th, The *difference of sexes* has also a great influence on the propensity to crime: in general, there is only 1 woman before the courts to 4 men.

5th, The propensity to crime increases and decreases nearly in the same degrees in each sex; yet the period of maximum takes place rather later in women, and is near the 30th year.

6th, Woman, undoubtedly from her feeling of weakness, rather commits crimes against property than persons; and when she seeks to destroy her kind, she prefers poison. Moreover, when she commits homicide, she does not appear to be proportionally arrested by the enormity of crimes which, in point of frequency, take place in the following order:—infanticide, miscarriage, parricide, wounding of parents, assassination, wounds and blows, murder: so that we may affirm that the number of the guilty diminishes in proportion as they have to seek their victim more openly. These differences are no doubt owing to the habits and sedentary life of woman; she can only conceive and execute guilty projects on individuals with whom she is in constant relation.

7th, The *seasons*, in their course, exercise a very marked influence on crime: thus, during summer, the greatest number of crimes against persons are committed, and the fewest against property; the contrary takes place during winter.

8th, It must be observed that age and the seasons have almost the same influence in increasing or

---
11. American Review, 1827, No. 12.

diminishing the number of mental disorders and crimes against persons. . . .

14th, The higher we go in the ranks of society, and consequently in the degrees of education, we find a smaller and smaller proportion of guilty women to men; descending to the lowest orders, the habits of both sexes resemble each other more and more. . . .

I cannot conclude this chapter without again expressing my astonishment at the constancy observed in the results which the documents connected with the administration of justice present each year.

"Thus, as I have already had occasion to repeat several times, we pass from one year to another, with the sad perspective of seeing the same crimes reproduced in the same order, and bringing with them the same punishments in the same proportions." All observations tend likewise to confirm the truth of this proposition, which I long ago announced, that *every thing which pertains to the human species considered as a whole, belongs to the order of physical facts:* the greater the number of individuals, the more does the influence of individual will disappear, leaving predominance to a series of general facts, dependent on causes by which society exists and is preserved. These causes we now want to ascertain, and as soon as we are acquainted with them, we shall determine their influence on society, just in the same way as we determine effects by their causes in physical sciences.[12] It must be confessed, that, distressing as the truth at first appears, if we submit to a well followed out series of observations the physical world and the social system, it would be difficult to decide in respect to which of the two the acting causes produce their effects with most regularity. I am, however, far from concluding that man can do nothing for man's amelioration. I think, as I said at the commencement of this work, that he possesses a moral power capable of modifying the laws which affect him; but this power only acts in the slowest manner, so that the causes influencing the social system cannot undergo any sudden alternation; as they have acted for a series of years, so will they continue to act in time to come, until they can be modified. Also, I cannot repeat too often, to all men who sincerely desire the well-being and honour of their kind, and who would blush to consider a few francs more or less paid to the treasury as equivalent to a few heads more or less submitted to the axe of the executioner, that there is a budget which we pay with a frightful regularity—it is that of prisons, chains, and the scaffold: it is that which, above all, we ought to endeavour to abate.

---

12. M. Guerry comes to the same conclusions from his researches on crimes, *Essai sur la Statistique Morale*, p. 69:—"One of the most general conclusions we can make is, that they all concur to prove that the greater number of facts of a moral nature, considered in the mass, and not individually, are determined by regular causes, the variations of which take place within narrow limits, and which may be submitted, like those of a material nature, to direct and numerical observation." As this idea has continually presented itself to me in all my researches on man, and as I have exactly expressed it in the same terms as those of the text, in my conclusions on the *Recherches sur le Penchant au Crime*, a work which appeared a year before that of M. Guerry, I have thought it necessary to mention the point here, to prevent misunderstanding.

CHAPTER 11

ANDRÉ-MICHEL GUERRY

The reading in this chapter is from André-Michel Guerry's *Essay on the Moral Statistics of France* ([1833] 2002), pp. 1–3, 71–86, and 139–142; edited and translated by Hugh P. Whitt and Victor W. Reinking; Lewiston, NY: The Edwin Mellen Press. Copyright © 2002 by The Edwin Mellen Press. Reprinted with permission. In addition to the footnotes provided by Guerry, two footnotes added by the translators have been included in this selection. The footnotes also have been renumbered.

    Guerry examined French crime statistics at the same time as Quetelet, during the first half of the nineteenth century. The variables and data examined by the two researchers, their analyses, and their findings were very similar. However, in his research, Guerry placed more emphasis on the use of the "cartographic method," constructing several shaded maps to illustrate the geographic distribution of crime and other social phenomena. An example of this method is presented in the following selection from Guerry's *Essay*. This reading begins with his "Introduction," where he expresses his support for science and, specifically, his opinion that the "moral sciences" should utilize the methods of the "natural sciences" as much as possible. This is followed by his analysis of the geographic distribution of violent crimes and property crimes in France, where he explores, among other things, the relationship between economic conditions and crime.

    Overall, the reading in this chapter provides another example of an early-nineteenth-century statistical analysis of crime and demonstrates that cartography, a method of ecological research, has been a part of criminology for nearly two centuries. Guerry's work stands as an important methodological forerunner to Durkheim's study of suicide during the late nineteenth century and the early/mid-twentieth century ecological studies by Clifford R. Shaw, Henry D. McKay, and other members of the Chicago School.

from ESSAY ON THE MORAL STATISTICS OF FRANCE
by André-Michel Guerry

INTRODUCTION

The observation and study of facts are the bases of our knowledge. This principle has contributed to the rapid development of the natural sciences, but not always to that of the moral and political sciences. While it is true that the moral sciences recommend this approach in theory, they nonetheless neglect it in practice. There is discussion rather than observation, and scant regard for the facts either with respect to issues or to the solutions proposed, so that what one writer regards as certain another dismisses as erroneous. The result is a plethora of opinions that are not grounded on a solid observational foundation.

The employment of the method of observation in the study of moral and political questions not only contributes to the progress of science, but also to concerns that are perhaps more important and more immediate. The theoretical systems of our day do not long remain mere abstractions; they move from their written form to the public sphere and soon penetrate our institutions, where they exert an influence for good or for ill on society. It is therefore important that the moral sciences adopt, to the greatest extent possible, the rigorous methods of the natural sciences, paying attention to facts, collecting them, observing them, and then diffusing knowledge. In so doing, the moral sciences will be able to invalidate false systems while at the same time verifying useful truths. By shedding light on the weighty questions of criminal legislation, statistics has already demonstrated the usefulness of its application and the success which one would hope for in research of this type. Until recently, statistical analysis was limited almost exclusively to the tabulation of facts relative to the vital statistics of nations and the knowledge of their commercial and agricultural riches; no one had yet dreamed of the necessity of collecting, in a special work, statistics that would evaluate the moral condition of a nation's population. Because we are persuaded of the importance and utility of such a work, we have felt compelled to undertake it.

It is upon France that our attention is focused. We offer, in a series of tables for the kingdom as a whole and for each of its departments, a collection of empirically based documents, methodically presented and coordinated with one another, which, taken together, represent the moral condition of society.

In indicating in a brief text our understanding of the principal results and a few of the relationships which they demonstrate, we have duly avoided any speculative consideration of causes and causal chains so as not to stray from the object of statistics, which, by limiting itself to facts in their most concise form, does not directly show how they are linked. The study of causes is slow, difficult, and fraught with error. In order to be fruitful in such delicate and complex matters, it is necessary that the work which we publish today be replicated after a period of years. In this way, the facts could be embraced in one single look, not only in cross-section, but also over time; their causes and reciprocal action would become more apparent, and erroneous theoretical induction from the data would be rectified.

We have made use of various graphical techniques to render our results more striking. Without excluding the enumerations in the tables which the reader may reflect upon at his pleasure, our graphical presentations provide advantages which are also real, but of another type. The gradations of shading of our maps make geographical relationships which would be obscured in a long series of figures instantly stand out, while quantitative relationships are expressed with precision through graphs for which a single look leaves a durable impression in memory. If it is necessary to justify the employment of these methods by appealing to the authority of an illustrious name, we cite Mr. Al[exander] von Humboldt, who has often made the most ingenious use of them, and who does not think that science should be scornful of borrowing anything helpful. "All that relates to extent and to quantification," he says, "is properly presented by geometrical constructions. Statistical projections which speak to the eye without fatiguing the mind have the advantage of fixing attention on a great number of important points."[1]

No systematic spirit has guided us; we have sought support from no theory. To have done so would have been to demonstrate philosophical short-sightedness and to poorly understand the interests of one's country by attaching oneself to facts favorable to a doctrine to the neglect of those which seem contrary to it. We have, in addition, carefully made known the sources we have drawn upon, thus supplying the means by which one may be assured of our exactitude and of our sincerity. . . .

GEOGRAPHICAL DISTRIBUTION

Crimes Against Persons

The five regions of the kingdom, ranked according to the number of crimes committed there in proportion to their population appear in the order [shown in table 15] for the six-year period 1825–1830.

Based on Table 15, the departments of the southern region are, over those six years, those where the greatest number of crimes against persons are found. Crimes there were twice as numerous as in the western and central regions, whose crime rates were roughly the same. The differences for individual departments taken separately are even greater.

On the average, each year, one person in every 2,199 inhabitants of the department of Corsica is accused of crimes against persons; in the department of Lot, this figure is one in 5,885; it is one in 6,173 in Ariège, and one in 17,085 for France as a whole. At the other end of the scale, the rate is no more than one in 32,000 inhabitants in the Côte-d'Or and Indre, one in 33,000 in the departments of Somme and Sarthe, one in 35,000 in the Ardennes, and, finally, one in 37,000 in La Creuse, whose rate is approximately fifteen times less than Corsica's. In this latter department the number of accusations has grown smaller each year, falling by more than half since 1825.

Of all crimes against persons, those directed against parents imply the greatest moral perversion. It is important therefore to know if crimes of this type are equally concentrated in the south. But since it is probable that local causes in that region which increase crimes against persons also increase attacks on parents, we compare the data on crimes against parents with the total number of crimes against persons rather than with population.

It is in the southern and central regions, in Berry, Limousin, Auvergne, and Provence, and in parts of Languedoc and Guyenne that attacks against parents are least numerous in comparison with the total number of crimes against persons. It is in the north, the east, and the west that they are more frequent. Corsica, Lot, Ariège, Pyrénées-Orientales, Haut-Rhin and Lozère, the six departments ranked first on crimes against persons, rank only 81st, 54th, 67th, 74th, 40th, and 72nd on assaults on parents. Undoubtedly, for these latter crimes the rank order of departments cannot be determined with great precision, but they are nevertheless close enough to permit approximation.

The areas of the kingdom where there is the greatest respect for parents are generally those where young soldiers most quickly leave military service to return to their families. It is in these areas that one also finds fewer illegitimate births and suicides. . . .

Because population concentration softens morals while at the same time reducing the chance of escaping the pursuit of justice, some would say it reduces the frequency of crimes against persons. By consulting Table A1 . . . , it can be seen that the effect of population concentration is at most very limited, if it exists at all, since a large number of crimes of this type are committed in the departments of Bouches-du-Rhône, Hérault, Var, Haut-Rhin and Moselle, where there are very populous cities. Replacing population density with the ratio of rural to urban population would not make this influence stand out any better, since although the departments of Corsica, Lot, Ariège, Aveyron, and Lozère have sparse populations, the southeastern region is nonetheless the one with the largest urban population. The western and central regions, with the smallest urban populations, are those which show the smallest number of crimes against persons. This is the opposite of what we should have seen had the position we spoke of above been generally true.

---

1. Al[exander] von Humboldt, *Political Essay on the Kingdom of New Spain*, Volume 1, Introduction.

We might also cite W. Playfair. The reflections abstracted from his *Commercial and Political Atlas* apply perfectly to our work:

"The giving form and shape to what otherwise would only have been an abstract idea has often rendered easy and accurate a conception that was in itself imperfect and acquired with difficulty.—Men of great rank or active business, can only pay attention to general outlines; nor is the attention to particulars of use any farther than as they give a general information. And it is hoped, that with the assistance of these charts, such information will be got without the fatigue and trouble of studying the particulars of which it is composed." (*The Commercial and Political Atlas*, Vol. 1, p. 4, London 1786)

TABLE 15
Ratio of the Number Accused of Crimes Against Persons to Population
(One Accused per ... Inhabitants)

Region	1825		1826		1827		1828		1829		1830		Average
South	9,072	S	9,972	S	11,830	S	11,743	S	11,277	S	13,080	S	11,003
East	17,972	E	15,535	E	16,980	E	16,361	E	16,661	C	18,512	E	17,349
North	17,983	N	19,995	W	17,880	N	18,476	N	20,414	E	19,151	N	19,964
West	20,140	C	22,485	C	19,475	C	21,471	C	22,388	N	22,807	C	20,984
Central	22,293	W	24,168	N	20,852	W	22,756	W	23,759	W	26,548	W	22,168

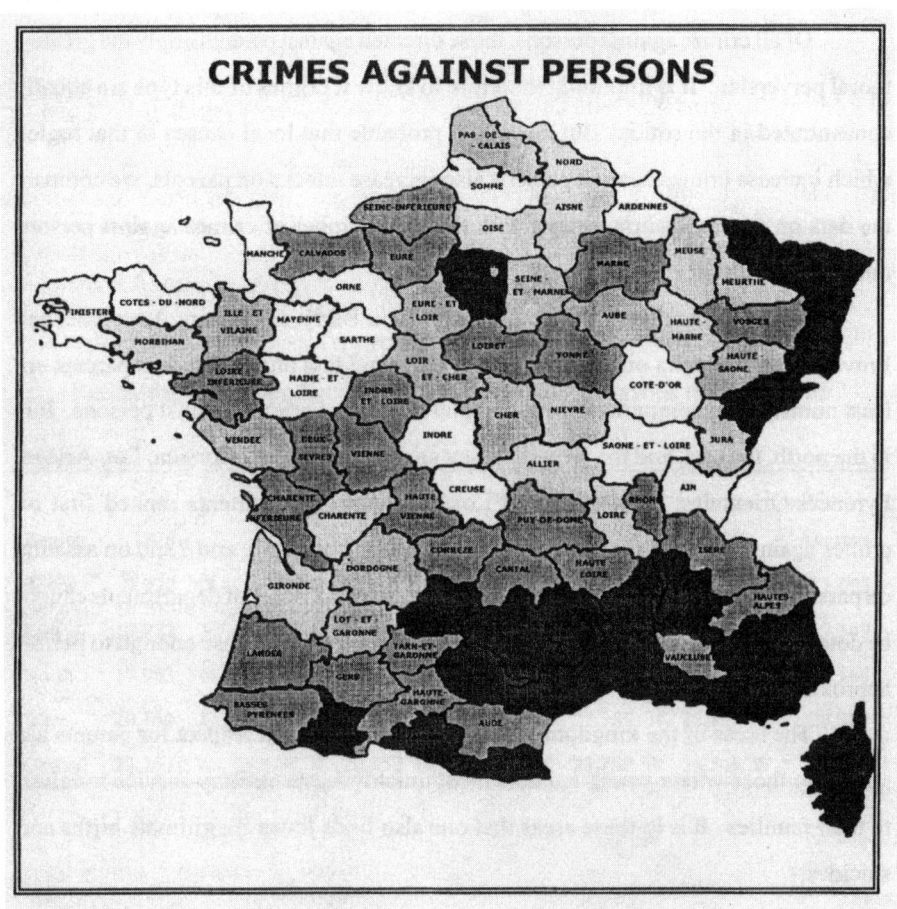

MAP 1: CRIMES AGAINST PERSONS

The lottery has been represented in Parliament as the principal cause of all domestic theft, assault and battery against parents, and poisonings, if not of all types of crime. It is difficult to conceive how the lottery—an institution which we are in any case far from approving—could by itself produce all these crimes. Poisonings are much too uncommon for their distribution by department to be anything but very uncertain. It is more or less the same with assault and battery against parents. It would be mistaken to draw conclusions from data for a single year, which could represent exceptional figures. We now know that a fairly large proportion of these crimes are committed in departments where the lottery is seldom played and in others where it is not played at all because there are no lottery bureaus. In any case, even if we assume that domestic theft, assaults against parents, and poisonings are in reality more common in the departments where more is bet on the lottery than in the others, it might very well be a simple coincidence or the spurious correlation of two effects, independent of one another but both produced by a common cause.

In each period in history, there are general causes that are claimed to explain everything and whose effects are seen everywhere. Thus it is that in France, for example, the differences which have been observed between the moral character of different peoples, in their customs and prejudices, have been successively attributed, always according to the dominant ideas of the time and in an exclusive manner, to climate, to temperature, to diet, and finally, in recent times, to elementary education, to the industrial system, to the actions of the clergy, and to the enjoyment of political rights. Especially today, when people's spirits are thrown into lively discussions of public affairs, one is inclined to view the moral character of different peoples as the variable result of institutions. Natural influences, which seem to go almost unnoticed, nonetheless operate with no less force and are worthy of as much attention.

TABLE 16
CRIMES AGAINST PARENTS

Rank Order	Department	Number of Crimes Against Parents per 1,000 Crimes Against Persons
1	Landes	133
2	Charente	129
3	Charente-Inférieure	125
4	Aisne	116
5	Meurthe	110
6	Côtes-du-Nord	107
7	Somme	106
8	Marne	104
9	Morbihan	100
10	Seine-et-Oise	94
....	....	....
77	Aube	13
78	Loire	12
79	Cantal	11
80	Aude	10
81	Corsica	2
82	Indre	–
83	Nièvre	–
84	Jura	–
85	Hautes-Pyrénées	–
86	Corrèze	–

Among the causes of the unequal geographical distribution of crimes against persons, there is one which until now has not received enough attention. This factor is regional differences in acquired or early organization which, despite the regularity of our new administrative divisions, makes it necessary to recognize the kingdom as made up of several distinct nations, each with its own language, manners, customs, and traditional prejudices. In similar circumstances, a Basque or an inhabitant of Languedoc will behave very differently than a person from Normandy; similarly, someone from Lower Brittany will not behave like a resident of Auvergne or Berry. Moreover, these variations in character-types in many of our old provinces are so striking that they have long been consecrated in popular proverbs. Unfortunately, the natural history of man, in which we should take a vigorous interest, is too little advanced to be of any use here. Distinctions of type or race have been scarcely glimpsed for only part of Europe, and then only on the basis of historical documents and in an entirely incomplete and superficial matter. The study of physiological characteristics would seem likely to lead to more empirically-based and satisfactory results,[2] but it will undoubtedly be a long time yet before we have sufficiently numerous observations to rigorously determine a geographical distribution of races in this country.

In addition to the facts which we have collected, and whose linkage with the distribution of crime can be studied, there are other extremely important data which we regret not being able to offer to our readers. Even if the end result of examining them should prove negative, it would not be fruitless, since, in research of this type, in which *a priori* explanations are almost always erroneous, it is usually only by the path of exclusion that one can hope to arrive at the truth.

In order to appraise ease of transport, we have drawn up the fold-out map of royal highways per square league;[3] we hope that a similar study would be published of departmental highways, communal roads, and navigable rivers. It would also be useful to know whether these roads traverse forests or uncultivated land for any long stretch, and to know, for each department, the property divisions, the physical aspect of the countryside, the principal industry, the type of cultivation, and, consequently, the customs and usual occupations of

---

2. W. F. Edwards.—*Physiological Characteristics of the Human Races, Considered in Their Relationship to History* (Paris, 1829).
3. This map is not available to us.—trans.

its inhabitants. It is true that these pieces of information are for the most part in our possession, but since until now they have been indicated in a vague and imprecise manner, they ought to be sufficiently based on observation and sufficiently precise as to be expressed numerically and to permit the classification of departments in rank order, all of which is in a large number of cases impossible today. Finally, our desire would be that, for capital crimes only, the *Compte général de la justice criminelle*, so perfect in other respects, would distinguish in the future between crimes committed by city-dwellers and those committed by inhabitants of the countryside, and, in addition, that it would present the major findings by administrative districts,[4] as is done for correctional matters. This would be one of the best ways of demonstrating the local causes of crimes and delivering the most active police surveillance to those places where it is most necessary.

Some will perhaps wonder at our seemingly endless requests for new information and more extensive details. It is quite generally thought that, once a statistical framework is set in place, nothing remains but to periodically fill it in without searching for more information. This is gravely mistaken. Statistics, thus considered, would be of highly restricted utility. Of course, as a first priority, facts that have been previously presented should always continue to be collected in the same form so as to show development over time. On the other hand, supplemental or secondary data that might be tied to these primary facts should not be neglected. It is seldom that a single table gives the complete answer to a question. The simpler a question appears, the more often it is discovered to be complex. By continuing to extend the scope of research as the issue is broken up into parts, one arrives at an understanding of all its elements, illuminating it on all sides. If, on the other hand, one stops with the first partial results, it is necessary to use untested hypotheses to compensate for the knowledge of the facts that remain unknown, and one thus becomes involved in an interminable series of errors.

Crimes Against Property

The five regions of the kingdom, arranged on the basis of the relationship between their populations and the number of crimes against property committed, appear in the order [shown in Table 17].

The maximum is consistently found in the northern region, which only ranks third for crimes against persons; and except for the year 1830, for which the results may have been affected by causes we have indicated above, the minimum always falls in the central region, where crimes against property are generally twice as uncommon as in the northern region. Following the department of the Seine, where there is one accused for every 1,368 inhabitants, or twelve times more than in the departments of Haute-Loire and La Creuse, the greatest number of crimes is in part of Normandy, and, after that, in the departments of Seine-et-Oise, Eure-et-Loire, and Pas-de-Calais.

By way of happy compensation, the parts of the kingdom which have the most crimes against persons show very few against property. However, Alsace and the departments of Corsica, Seine-et-Oise, Moselle, and Lozère are exceptions which are once again highly ranked, just as they were in the preceding map.

Proportionally to population, crimes against property are usually more common in populous cities than in those whose inhabitants are less numerous. Some believe it is possible to conclude from this that high population density is the principal cause of crimes against property. This would be carrying the generalization too far, since fewer crimes of this type are committed in some departments where one finds major cities—Nantes, Bordeaux, Nîmes, Toulouse, Montpellier, and Marseille—than in the northern departments where the largest towns are Troyes, Châlons, Arras, Evreux and Chartres. Some have undoubtedly attributed to population concentration the influence actually due to various other factors which frequently coincide with high population density without necessarily being causally linked with it as a result. Since these factors vary together, it is difficult because of their similar distributions to distinguish how great an effect is due to each factor.

Wealth, as indicated by the amounts of taxes on both income and property (Column A, Table A1 . . .) and by regional revenues, is more closely related than population density to crimes against property, so that it thus appears to be an indirect cause of such crimes. It should be noted that it is true that the maximum level of wealth as measured by the combination of these two elements falls in the northern departments, where one also finds the most crimes against property, and that the minimum falls in the

---

4. Here, Guerry is asking for the equivalent of modern county and census tract data. He calls for breakdowns by *arrondisements*, which were in most departments roughly the equivalent of counties in the United States. For Paris, an *arrondisement* was one of the city's twenty wards.—trans.

TABLE 17
RATIO OF THE NUMBER ACCUSED OF CRIMES AGAINST PROPERTY TO POPULATION
(ONE ACCUSED PER ... INHABITANTS)

Region	1825	1826	1827	1828	1829	1830	Average
North	4,226	N 4,181	N 4,238	N 3,681	N 3,561	N 3,773	N 3,924
East	6,194	E 7,089	E 6,896	E 6,637	W 7,362	C 7,463	E 6,924
South	7,912	W 7,472	W 7,324	S 7,313	S 7,369	E 7,686	W 7,534
West	7,992	S 8,423	S 7,354	W 7,353	E 7,403	W 7,745	S 7,945
Central	8,382	C 8,703	C 9,792	C 8,148	C 7,626	S 8,279	C 8,285

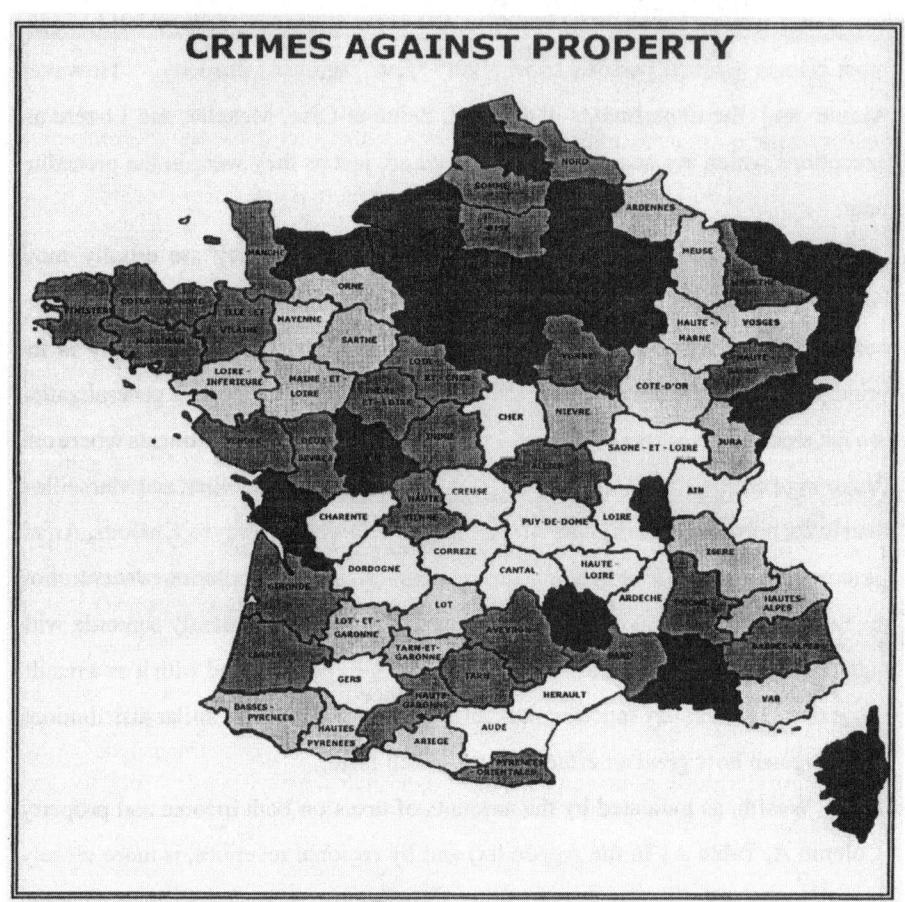

MAP 2: CRIMES AGAINST PROPERTY

central region, where these crimes are the most uncommon. But then, on the other hand, average wealth is almost as high in the south as in the north, following the direction of a curve that, beginning in the department of Charente, crosses parts of Guyenne, Languedoc, and Provence. If wealth indirectly produces crimes against property in the north, why is the same not true in the south?

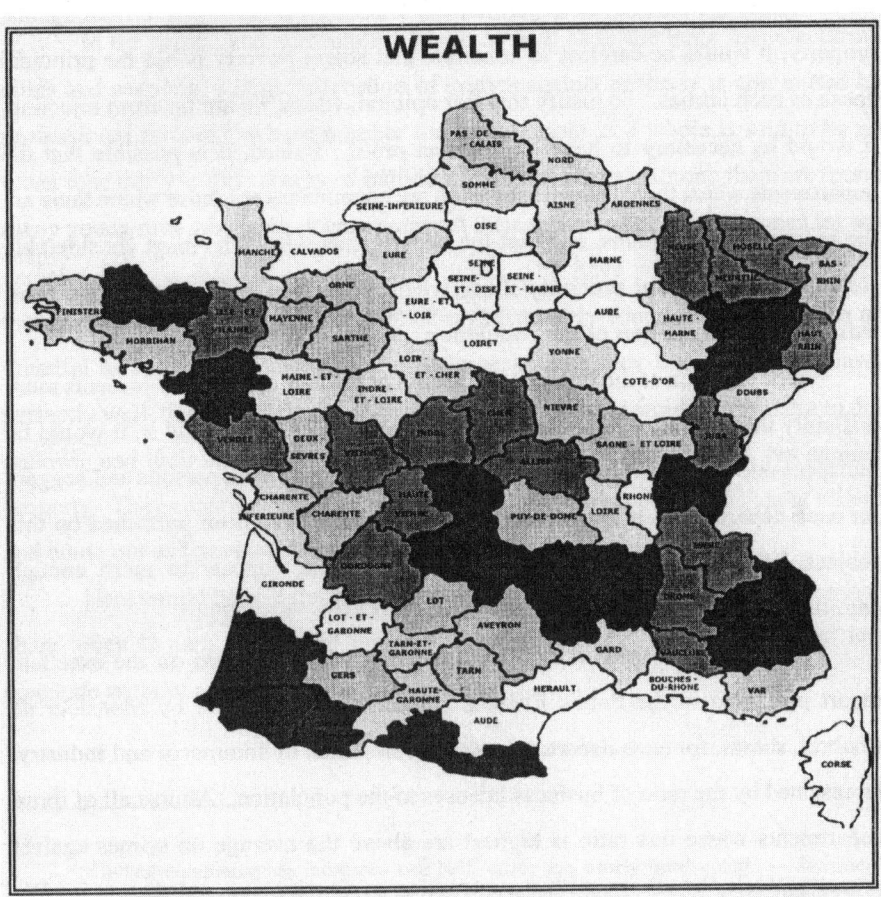

Map 3: Wealth

Although the poorest departments are those with the fewest crimes against property, it would be careless to conclude that abject poverty is not the principal cause of such crimes. To justify this last opinion, which we are far from rejecting, it would be necessary to have more direct proof. Indeed, it is possible that the departments where there is the least wealth are nonetheless not those where there are the most indigent persons, and that the departments where the most considerable fortunes are found are precisely those where poverty is at the same time most extreme for a certain part of the population.

The question of the influence of wealth or poverty on morality presents more difficulty than might be supposed at first glance. In order to study it, it would be indispensable to establish the proportional numbers of indigent persons and beggars for each department. It is true that some documents have been published on this subject, but they are of a dubious nature and do not appear to merit enough confidence to be included in the present analysis.

Column B of Table A1 . . . , which is based on the excellent report presented to the Public Finance Administration in 1830 by Monsieur de Chabrol, shows, for each department, the development of commerce and industry, represented by the ratio of business licenses to the population. Almost all of those departments where this ratio is highest are above the average on crimes against property; while the others, with the exception of Corsica, are well below it. We could point out that there are, as always, exceptions: for part of Brittany, for example, where there is the least industry but where theft is very common, or for the departments of Ardennes, the Meuse, and the Côte-d'Or, where, in contrast, one finds few crimes against property coupled with very active industry. But we must emphasize the general findings.

This apparent connection between crimes against property and the development of commerce and industry merits careful study, since France is not the only country where it has been noticed.[5]

In the capital and surrounding areas, as well as in the large manufacturing cities and seaports, a large proportion of crimes against property is committed by professional thieves,[6] whose number for the kingdom as a whole is said to be no fewer than thirty to forty thousand individuals of both sexes. Among them are found many young men who have openly prepared themselves in our reformatories for the exercise of their infamous craft. Ex-convicts who have served their sentences, though they are objects of terror for society, are rarely found guilty of crimes as dreadful as is imagined in the world at large. Since they know the penal laws perfectly well, they carefully avoid committing actions that would carry them to the gallows, and their crimes are thus no longer directed against persons, but against property. They enter the *bagnes* as premeditated murderers or other kinds of killers and come out as thieves and forgers.

Here would be an appropriate place to examine an opinion which we cannot share, even though it is found in worthy and esteemed writings. We shall not conclude without a few words on the subject.

Attacks against persons are, it is said, *the most serious* of all crimes. Assuredly, they are the most serious for those who are the victims, but is this equally true for those who are found guilty? Do such crimes presuppose greater corruption and perversity than crimes against property? We do not think so. Assault and battery, simple homicide, even manslaughter, when they are not with the object of facilitating a theft, are most often due to being caught up in a violent passion which can leave behind remorse—a fit of jealousy, an uncontrollable rage, a desire to rebuff a provocation or avenge an injustice. In particular circumstances, such crimes may even have a sense of honor as their source; while it is true that we know them to be wrong, we are inclined to excuse them.

In contrast, crimes against property, which are planned out for a long time and endlessly repeated, are evidence of a distressing perseverance in wrongdoing, and presuppose depravity no less than cowardice. Never do they excite any sympathy. The swindler, the forger, the fraudulent bankrupt of our northern departments who, with his polished etiquette and wide-ranging education, coldly accomplishes the ruin of twenty families whose trust he has abused, is, in our eyes, more vile, more immoral than the illiterate inhabitant of our southern departments, who strikes down his adversary in a brawl and kills him. . . .

---

5. Whilst commerce has increased one half, crime has nearly quadrupled.—*Statistical Illustrations of the British Empire* (London, 1827, Preface); Girard, *Report to the Academy of Sciences on a Memoire by Monsieur de Morogues Entitled* "On the Usefulness of Machines and Their Inconveniences, etc.," page 17 (Paris, 1832).

6. This observation applies with even greater force to the city of London, where thieves, more numerous and more skilled than here in France, have formed a kind of corporation or trade guild—a regularly organized society—*Minutes of Evidence before the Select Committee on Secondary Punishments* (London, September 1831, page 103).—*Report from the Select Committee on Criminal Commitments and Convictions* (London, July 1828, page 5). (*Minutes of Evidence Taken before Select Committee on Secondary Punishments* [London, June 1832, page 64]).

TABLE A1
RANK ORDER OF VARIOUS MORAL STATISTICS: DATA BY DEPARTMENT

Departments (a)	Region	Size of Principal City*	A. Wealth	B. Commerce and Industry	C. Distribution of Clergy	D. Crimes Against Parents	E. Infanticides	F. Donations to The Clergy	G. Lottery	H. Military Desertion
Ain	East	Medium	73	58	11	71	60	69	41	55
Aisne	North	Medium	22	10	82	4	82	36	38	82
Allier	Central	Medium	61	66	68	46	42	76	66	16
Basses-Alpes	East	Small	76	49	5	70	12	37	80	32
Hautes-Alpes	East	Small	83	65	10	22	23	64	79	35
Ardèche	South	Small	84	1	28	76	47	67	70	19
Ardennes	North	Medium	33	4	50	53	85	49	31	62
Ariège	South	Small	72	60	39	74	28	63	75	22
Aube	East	Medium	14	3	42	77	54	9	28	86
Aude	South	Medium	17	35	15	80	35	27	50	63
Aveyron	South	Medium	50	70	3	51	5	23	81	10
Bouches-du-Rhône	South	Large	2	26	30	45	74	55	3	23
Calvados	North	Medium	10	48	7	57	56	11	13	12
Cantal	Central	Medium	59	7	6	79	83	66	82	1
Charente	West	Medium	87	47	79	2	7	81	60	61
Charente-Inférieure	West	Medium	18	5	86	3	38	72	35	74
Cher	Central	Medium	63	56	83	69	11	86	44	51
Corrèze	Central	Medium	74	80	46	86	16	82	84	2
Corsica	—	Medium	?	83	1	81	2	84	83	9
Côte-d'Or	East	Medium	16	12	37	49	27	18	33	78
Côtes-du-Nord	West	Medium	70	86	30	6	69	15	72	47
Creuse	Central	Small	78	82	75	75	24	75	85	4
Dordogne	West	Medium	60	72	77	64	18	79	77	44
Doubs	East	Medium	31	57	24	38	25	6	18	73
Drôme	East	Medium	66	41	22	21	13	62	54	46
Eure	North	Medium	20	17	27	39	45	45	47	27
Eure-et-Loir	Central	Medium	11	21	16	18	62	14	48	72
Finistère	West	Medium	36	84	66	24	78	25	36	77
Gard	South	Medium	26	31	81	15	39	59	20	40
Haute-Garonne	South	Large	23	40	23	62	59	13	25	15
Gers	South	Medium	40	30	12	43	13	32	74	30
Gironde	West	Large	8	20	69	27	80	48	4	13
Hérault	South	Medium	12	34	67	47	51	28	19	43
Ille-et-Vilaine	West	Medium	55	77	19	12	31	22	37	50
Indre	Central	Medium	54	55	84	82	19	83	69	29
Indre-et-Loire	Central	Medium	27	25	58	48	3	41	15	49
Isère	East	Medium	65	46	53	52	27	73	23	26
Jura	East	Medium	62	54	32	84	66	43	39	71
Landes	West	Small	81	68	63	1	43	56	73	28
Loir-et-Cher	Central	Medium	19	23	57	65	37	70	46	54
Loire	Central	Medium	24	79	34	78	77	34	42	6
Haute-Loire	Central	Medium	75	85	8	73	17	65	62	3

TABLE A1
(continued)

Departments (a)	Region	Size of Principal City*	A. Wealth	B. Commerce and Industry	C. Distribution of Clergy	D. Crimes Against Parents	E. Infanticides	F. Donations to The Clergy	G. Lottery	H. Military Desertion
Loire-Inférieure	West	Large	80	76	73	56	52	29	12	45
Loiret	Central	Medium	9	24	54	44	22	16	17	60
Lot	South	Medium	42	67	20	54	15	68	78	24
Lot-et-Garonne	West	Medium	7	53	49	26	32	46	52	34
Lozère	South	Small	77	69	2	72	45	42	86	5
Maine-et-Loire	West	Medium	34	52	43	19	36	20	24	76
Manche	North	Medium	32	73	9	33	70	3	59	21
Marne	North	Medium	13	6	47	8	58	39	22	81
Haute-Marne	East	Small	25	7	18	63	55	4	56	65
Mayenne	West	Medium	38	75	40	59	40	8	61	58
Meurthe	East	Medium	57	11	26	5	71	1	21	70
Meuse	North	Medium	52	2	33	17	65	12	58	59
Morbihan	West	Medium	48	81	31	9	29	7	32	69
Moselle	North	Large	53	19	13	35	9	2	16	68
Nièvre	Central	Medium	44	33	80	83	20	80	63	37
Nord	North	Large	28	38	74	14	81	38	7	64
Oise	North	Medium	15	14	60	31	86	50	43	57
Orne	North	Medium	35	62	21	29	50	31	57	25
Pas-de-Calais	North	Medium	45	39	44	36	79	10	27	48
Puy-de-Dôme	Central	Medium	51	78	52	42	63	61	53	8
Basses-Pyrénées	West	Medium	79	71	38	34	72	60	34	7
Hautes-Pyrénées	South	Medium	85	51	17	85	75	71	76	20
Pyrénées-Orientales	South	Medium	71	37	4	67	84	77	11	18
Bas-Rhin	East	Large	46	16	64	23	48	51	5	53
Haut-Rhin	East	Medium	58	29	65	40	53	17	10	56
Rhône	East	Large	6	18	35	37	33	21	2	14
Haute-Saône	East	Small	69	27	25	25	68	57	65	83
Saône-et-Loire	East	Medium	49	61	59	11	10	58	45	31
Sarthe	Central	Medium	41	45	41	41	57	19	49	75
Seine	North	Large	1	9	85	60	67	53	1	33
Seine-Inférieure	North	Large	3	22	62	28	61	74	9	36
Seine-et-Marne	North	Medium	4	13	56	16	73	26	29	67
Seine-et-Oise	North	Medium	5	8	45	10	30	24	6	42
Deux-Sèvres	West	Medium	39	59	72	30	4	85	71	84
Somme	North	Medium	21	36	48	7	64	33	30	80
Tarn	South	Medium	47	44	14	13	9	47	67	17
Tarn-et-Garonne	South	Medium	29	50	29	66	41	52	64	39
Var	South	Medium	43	39	61	55	49	40	26	52
Vaucluse	South	Medium	64	28	78	61	76	54	8	41
Vendée	West	Small	56	64	70	50	44	30	68	79
Vienne	West	Medium	68	43	71	20	1	44	40	38

TABLE A1
(continued)

Departments (a)	Region	Size of Principal City*	A. Wealth	B. Commerce and Industry	C. Distribution of Clergy	D. Crimes Against Parents	E. Infanticides	F. Donations to The Clergy	G. Lottery	H. Military Desertion
Haute-Vienne	Central	Medium	67	63	76	68	6	78	55	11
Vosges	East	Medium	82	42	51	58	34	5	14	85
Yonne	Central	Medium	30	15	55	32	22	35	51	66

(a) The figures in the eight lettered columns of the table indicate the rank of each department in the series of 86 departments classified by wealth, industry, etc. The maximum is always indicated by "1" and the minimum by "86." Departments whose figures are identical are classified in alphabetical order.

* "Large" indicates the ten departments where the ten largest cities are found, and "Small" the ten departments whose principal cities have the smallest populations.

A. Wealth—Share of taxes on personal and movable property per inhabitant (*Proposition de lois pour la fixation des dép. et des recettes de 1821. État C and E*, No. 2. Calculated by Monsieur Villot—*Bull. univ.* Section VI, January, 1826). *Maximum*—North and Southwest.—*Minimum*—Central, Lorraine and Dauphiné (?).

B. Commerce and Industry—Ratio of the number of patents to the population, 1830—(*Rapport au roi sur l'administration des fiances*, by Monsieur de Chabrol. Tables and statistical documents, *État X*). (*Maximum*—Northeast—*Minimum*—Central, Brittany, Southeast—Coincides with the distribution of instruction.

C. Distribution of Clergy—Ratio of the number of Catholic priests in active service to the population. (*Almanach officiel du clergé, 1829*).—*Maximum*—Corsica, Southeast and Normandy. *Minimum*—Flanders, Picardy, central and west (?). Coincides with crimes against persons and with donations to the poor.

D. Crimes against Parents—Ratio of the number of crimes against parents to all crimes against persons—Average of the six years 1825–1830—(*Compte général de l'administration de la justice criminelle*).—*Maximum*—Northeast and west (?)—*Minimum*—Central, south and Corsica.

E. Infanticide—Ratio of infanticides to population—Average of the six years 1825–1830—(*Compte général de l'administration de la justice criminelle*).—*Maximum*—Corsica and central. *Minimum*—North, east and Auvergne (?)

F. Donations to Clergy—Ratios of the number of bequests and donations *inter vivos* to population—Average of the ten years 1815–1824. (*Bull, des lois, ordonn. d'autorisation.*)—*Maximum*—Northeast, Anjou, Brittany and Normandy—*Minimum*—Central and southeast.

G. Lottery—Ratio of the proceeds bet on the royal lottery to the population—Average of the seven years 1822–1826. (*Comptes rendus par le ministre des finances—Développemens par départemens et par produits, sur les contributions et les revenus publics*)—*Maximum*—Northeast and departments with large cities (?)—*Minimum*—Central.

H. Military Desertion—Ratio of the number of young soldiers accused of desertion to the force of the military contingent, minus the deficit produced by the insufficiency of available billets—Average of the three years 1825–1827—(*Compte du ministre du guerre, 1829, état V*)—*Maximum*—Central and southwest—*Minimum*—Northeast—The maximum coincides with the minimum of crimes against persons and crimes against property, and the minimum corresponds with the maximum of instruction.

CHAPTER 12

GABRIEL TARDE

The selection presented in this chapter comes from Gabriel Tarde's *Penal Philosophy* (1912), pp. 322–342 and 362–371; translated by Rapelje Howell; Boston: Little, Brown and Company. The first edition of *Penal Philosophy* was published in 1890, and by 1903 four editions had been printed. The reading presented below is an excerpt from the 1912 English translation of the fourth edition. Subsection numbers have been removed and footnotes have been renumbered. The full text of this translation is available through the Hathi-Trust Digital Library (hathitrust.org).

Tarde's work represents an example of the late-nineteenth-century French school of criminology. He opposed the atavist theory of the Italian school and, instead, favored a sociological framework. The following selection from *Penal Philosophy* highlights this framework and Tarde's efforts to explain patterns of criminal behavior. In this reading, Tarde argues that imitation accounts for a wide variety of behavior patterns, and he proposes three "laws of imitation" to help explain variations in criminal behavior across different places and during different time periods. The first law maintains that imitation increases with increments in the amount of contact between people; the second contends that "inferior" people have a tendency to imitate "superior" people; and the third law asserts that through a process of imitation "customs" give way to "fashions," and "fashions" often lead to new "customs." Tarde maintained that these laws can be used to explain patterns of homicide, rape, arson, theft, counterfeiting, and other crimes, and he offered several examples in an attempt to support his claim.

While it would be a mistake to refer to Tarde as the field's first learning theorist (e.g., proposals regarding a relationship between moral instruction and crime existed prior to Tarde's work), his theory of imitation nevertheless represents an important precursor to the twentieth-century learning theories of Edwin Sutherland, Daniel Glaser, Ronald Akers, and other criminologists. In fact, both Sutherland and Akers explicitly refer to imitation in their theories, although both also add that the learning of criminal behavior goes well beyond just imitation.

from PENAL PHILOSOPHY
by Gabriel Tarde

CRIME: PREPONDERANCE OF SOCIAL CAUSES

(I) **The tendency towards imitation, its force and its forms, its study by means of the phenomenon of crowds. How a suspicion soon becomes a conviction among a crowd. Genesis of popularity and unpopularity. The spirit of sect and the spirit of the group. The group, as well as the family, a primitive social factor; double origin of societies.**

Before anything else, we ought summarily to define and analyze the powerful, generally unconscious, always partly mysterious, action by means of which we account for all the phenomena of society, namely imitation. In order to judge of its inherent power, we must first of all observe its manifestations among idiots. In them the imitative inclination is no stronger than in ourselves,[1] but it acts without encountering the obstacle which is met with in our ideas, our moral habits, and our wishes. Now, a case is cited of an idiot[2] who "after having taken part in the slaughtering of a pig took a knife and attacked a man." Others carry out the imitative tendency in setting fire to buildings.

All the important acts of social life are carried out under the domination of example. One procreates or one does not procreate, because of imitation; the statistics of the birth rate have shown us this. One kills or one does not kill, because of imitation; would we today conceive of the idea of fighting a duel or of declaring war, if we did not know that these things had always been done in the country which we inhabit? One kills oneself or one does not kill oneself, because of imitation; it is a recognized fact that suicide is an imitative phenomenon to the very highest degree; at any rate it is impossible to refuse to give this character to those "suicides in large numbers of conquered peoples escaping by means of death the shame of defeat and the yoke of the stranger, like that of the Sidonians who were defeated by Artaxerxes Orchus, of the Tyrians defeated by Alexander, of the Sagontines defeated by Scipio, of the Achaeans defeated by Metellus, etc."[3]

After this how can we doubt but that one steals or does not steal, one assassinates or does not assassinate, because of imitation? But it is especially in the great tumultuous assemblages of our cities that this characteristic force of the social world ought to be studied. The great scenes of our revolutions cause it to break out, just as great storms are a manifestation of the presence of the electricity in the atmosphere, while it remains unperceived though none the less a reality in the intervals between them. A *mob* is a strange phenomenon. It is a gathering of heterogeneous elements, unknown to one another;[4] but as soon as a spark of passion, having flashed out from one of these elements, electrifies this confused mass, there takes place a sort of sudden organization, a spontaneous generation. This incoherence becomes cohesion, this noise becomes a voice, and these thousands of men crowded together soon form but a single animal, a wild beast without a name, which marches to its goal with an irresistible finality. The majority of these men had assembled out of pure curiosity, but the fever of some of them soon reached the minds of all, and in all of them there arose a delirium. The very man who had come running to oppose the murder of an innocent person is one of the first to be seized with the homicidal contagion, and moreover, it does not occur to him to be astonished at this.

There is no need for me to recall certain never to be forgotten pages of Taine's dealing with the fourteenth of July and its consequences in the provinces.[5] How can these things be so? In the most

---

1. As a general thing, as we know, it is not impulses which are strong in the case of the insane, even in the case of those who are called "impulsives"; but it is the brakes within which are weak.
2. "La folie héréditaire," by *Saury*.
3. "Le suicide dans l'armée," by *Mesnier*.
4. Of course, it necessarily follows that these men assembled together should resemble one another on some essential points such as nationality, religion, social class.
5. Read again what is said about the massacres of September ("Révolution," vol. IV, pp. 295 *et seq.*). Among the Septemberists "some having come with good intentions are seized with vertigo at the contact of the bloody whirlwind, and, by a sudden stroke of revolutionary feeling, are converted to the religion of murder. A certain Grapin, delegated by his section to save two prisoners, sits down beside Maillard, and passes sentences with him during sixty hours."—There must without doubt also have been many such men as Grapin during the night of St. Bartholomew.

simple manner imaginable. The manner in which the mob acts shows us the force under the domination of which it became organized. Let us imagine ourselves carried back to the time of the Commune; a man wearing a white blouse, crossing a square, passes close to an over-excited crowd; he looks like a suspicious person to someone. In a moment, with the rapidity of a conflagration, this suspicion spreads, and instantly, what happens? *"A suspicion is enough,* all protest is useless, every proof is a delusion; *the conviction is profound."*[6] Supposing that each one of these people had been alone in his own house, never could a mere suspicion in the mind of each one of them, without proofs to support it, have been changed into a conviction. But they are together, and the suspicion of each of them, by virtue of imitative force, keener, and acting more promptly in times of emotion, is reinforced by the suspicions of all the others; the result of which ought to be that, from being very weak, a belief in the guilt of the unfortunate fellow suddenly becomes very strong, without the shadow of an argument being necessary. Reciprocal imitation, when it is exercised over *similar* beliefs, and, generally speaking, over *similar* psychological states, is a true multiplication of the intensity proper to these beliefs, to these various states, in each one of those who feel them simultaneously.

When, on the contrary, in imitating one another, several persons exchange *different* states, which is what ordinarily takes place in social life, when, for example, one communicates to the other a taste for Wagnerian music and in return the other communicates to him a love for realistic fiction; these persons no doubt establish between themselves a bond of mutual assimilation, just as when they express to each other two similar ideas or needs which take root in this manner. But in the first case, the assimilation is, for each of them, a *complication* of their internal state—this is essentially an effect of civilization—and in the second case the assimilation is, for each of them, a mere *reinforcement* of their inner life. Between these two cases there is the musical interval between unison and a chord. A mob has the simple and deep power of a large unison. This explains why it is so dangerous to associate too much with minds which reflect one's own thoughts and one's own feelings; in doing this one soon arrives at the *sect spirit,* which is entirely analogous to the *mob spirit.*

The war madness, that intermittent attack which peoples suffer, can be accounted for by means of the preceding statements. In a country in which civilization has multiplied its relations, that is to say developed imitative force, thirty or forty millions of men are exchanging their fancies and their conceptions, their passions and their desires. The inner state of each one of them in this way becomes complicated, as a consequence of the dissimilarity between classes, interests, habits, and minds which have a tendency to become fused together. From this there result the ardor of cupidity, the fever of luxury. But at the same time, upon one point, their inner state ought merely to be reinforced by their being brought into contact with one another; namely in that which touches the feeling which a hostile nation, or one reputed to be such, inspires in them. This hatred, as compared with all the other desires put together, would be extremely weak in each one of them if they were by themselves; but it is common to all; they express it to one another; the imitative reinforcement must thus be exercised over it in particular and give rise, from time to time, to sublime or extravagant outbursts of patriotism which, in the very midst of a world of reason, to the great surprise of the wise, break out with a force in proportion to the progress of civilization. Why be astonished at this? It is inevitable.[7]

Let us return to the phenomenon of mobs; it is interesting from the point of view of social embryology, because it shows us by what means a new society has been able, and often has been compelled, to spring into existence outside of the family; I do not say maintain itself, once it has come into existence, without the aid of the family. There are, we say, two distinct germs of societies, the family and the mob; and, according as it shall have had one or the other as its principal source, as it shall have increased in its course by affluents derived from one or the other of

---

6. Maxime du Camp.

7. The elective genesis of the most inexplicable popularity and unpopularity is another excellent example of the part played by imitation in social life. When several successive elections take place with regard to one man or one idea, the vote of one Department manifestly carries that of another, and the enthusiasm for or against is as irresistible as a rising tide. After having been favorably regarded many times, the most ordinary man appears to be a great man and everywhere encounters the sincere enthusiasm of people who did not know him, but who heard him greeted with acclamation around them, also sincerely by a crowd to whom he is just as much an unknown; or else it is just the other way, he is suspected, then spurned, and then treated like the very worst scoundrel and the indignation which he inspires in honest property holders for no apparent reason would go as far as murder, should he be so unfortunate as to show himself before them. The history of "Boulangisme" is very instructive in this respect.

them, a nation will clothe itself with absolutely different characteristics. No doubt the two origins resemble each other in many ways. In both cases, the society is the product of a suggestion, and not of a contract. A contract is the meeting of several wills born independently of one another, and which have happened to agree; a pure hypothesis. A suggestion is the product of wills which are born agreeing with the superior will from which they proceed; such is the primitive social fact. Every mob, like every family, has a head and obeys him scrupulously.[8] But the superstitious and constitutional respect of the son for his father in the ancient household is one thing, and the infatuation of a day aroused by a leader of riots is quite another thing. When the family spirit, whether agricultural or rural, dominates in the social life, imitation-custom reigns there exclusively, with that majestic particularism and serenity which were characteristic of the Egyptian and the Chinese world; when the mob spirit takes its place, imitation-fashion effects its levelings and its changes, its assimilations of vast extent and its transformations in short periods of time. In the country the family-society predominates, the population is only kept up or increased by means of the domestic peopling; in towns the mob-society predominates, from all sides come people detached from their home and confusedly brought together. This is partly why I thought it best to attach so much importance, in the preceding chapter, to the distinction between urban brigandage and rural brigandage. It is not immaterial to know whether the inclination to crime is the fruit of a bad family education or of a dangerous companionship. It is always either a family, or a sect, or a café full of comrades, which drives to crime the individual who is wavering; and, in this last case, the enthusiasm which carries him away recalls, to almost the very highest degree, the popular current which drives a rioter to commit murder.

(II) The laws of imitation. Men imitate one another in proportion as they are in close contact. The superior is imitated by the inferior to a greater extent than the inferior by the superior. Propagation from the higher to the lower in every sort of fact: language, dogma, furniture, ideas, needs. The great fields of imitation; formerly aristocracies, today capitals. Similarity of the former and the latter.

After these few words as to the force and the forms of imitation, we must set forth its general laws, which must be applied to crime as well as to every other aspect of societies. But the limits of this work will only allow us a brief indication of the subject. We already know that the example of any man, almost like the attraction of a body, radiates around himself, but with an intensity which becomes weaker as the distance of the men touched by his ray increases. "Distance" should not here be understood merely in the geometrical sense, but especially in the psychological sense of the word; the increase in the relations established by correspondence or by printing, of the intellectual communications of all kinds between fellow-citizens scattered over a vast territory, has the effect of diminishing in this sense the distance between them. Thus it may happen, let us repeat, that the honest example of an entire surrounding but distant society may be neutralized in the heart of a young vagabond by the influence of a few companions. From the economic, philological, religious, and political point of view, it is the same. In the vicinity of the largest cities there are still to be found villages, having but slight relations with them, where the old needs and the old ideas are preserved, where they order their cloth from the weaver, where they like to eat brown bread, where they speak nothing but dialect, where they believe in sorcerers and witchcraft.... This consideration must never be lost sight of.

Now instead of taking each example by itself, let us examine the connection between several examples and let us seek to find the result of the exchange. First of all, however mean and however despised an individual may be, repeated contact with him does not fail to stamp the highest and the proudest persons with a certain vague tendency to copy him. We have the proof of this in the contagion of *accents*; the proudest master, if he lives alone in the country with his servants, eventually borrows some of their intonations and even of their phrases. It is thus that the coldest body sends heat to the hottest body. But, just as in reality the heating of the hot body by the cold body is approximately nothing if it be compared with the great heat imparted to the cold body by the hot body, similarly one can often ignore, the more often even, in our societies, the impressive action exercised by the example of slaves upon their masters, of children upon adults, of the laity upon the

---

8. One can see in these remarks in "Etudes sur les mœurs religieuses et sociales de l'extrême Orient," by *Alfred Lyall* (Thorin, 1885) how, even in India, where the tie of blood seems at first sight to be the only social bond, the prestige of a celebrated individual, of an ascetic famed for his austerity, of a dreaded brigand, suffices to rally around him a clientèle of companions and to form a new caste.

clergy (in the prosperous days of the theocracy), of the ignorant upon the literate, the ingenuous upon the clever, the poor upon the rich, the plebeians upon the patricians (in the prosperous period of the aristocracy), of the inhabitants of the country upon the inhabitants of cities, of the provincials upon the Parisians, in a word, of the inferior upon the superior, and only take into account the opposite action, which is the true explanation of history. There is during every period a recognized superiority, sometimes wrongly recognized as such. It is the privilege of the man who, richer in needs and ideas, has more examples to give than he has to receive. The unequal exchange of examples, such as it is governed by this law, has the effect of causing the social world to progress towards a leveling state which may be compared to that universal uniformity of temperature which the law of the radiation of the heat of bodies has a tendency to establish.

It sometimes happens, too often in fact, that the political and military power is found in the hands of the nation or the class having the fewest civilizing examples to show. In such a case as this, the class or the nation which is in subjection, believing itself to be superior to the one which rules it, limits itself to a submission but refuses to be assimilated. This is one of the frequent causes of acts of oppression and of bloody revolts. For the conqueror, before everything, either wittingly or unknown to himself, wishes to be copied, and does not believe his victory to be a real one as long as this is not done; so greatly does he feel that imitative contagion is the very best social action. Also he strives in every manner, by brutal violence or by oppression disguised in some way, to force upon the vanquished, not only his yoke, but his own type.

Philip II, for example, made use of the former against the Moors of Andalusia. They were the most industrious, the richest, the most civilized, and not the least faithful of his subjects. But they jealously guarded their national usages, their manner of dressing, of eating, of living, without allowing the Spanish customs to penetrate among them. Everything which was said against them at that time, all the hatred which they inspired in the people and the clergy of the conquering race, arose from this fact. "A victorious people," Fourneron says correctly on this subject, "will always have grievances against those who profit by the laws without becoming absorbed into their unity."[9] That is to say, against those who obey but do not imitate themselves.

The decrees which Philip II, in 1566, enacted against the Moors to the applause of all Christians, had as their real object a compulsory imitation by the Moors of the Christians in everything and for everything. "After the first of January following," says the author cited, "the Moors could possess neither weapons, nor slaves, nor costumes after their own fashion . . . they had immediately to provide themselves with doublets and breeches, to cease to hide under the 'habarah' and the 'feredjeh' the faces and shoulders of their women, who were compelled thenceforward to wear caps and farthingales . . . forget their own language and learn Spanish within a period of six months . . . etc." Here we see demented despotism, and we know the sea of blood it caused to flow. But, during the periods and among the nations who boast the most of their democratic tolerance, do we not find a reigning sect, Puritan or Jacobin, pursuing the same object, at bottom, by taking possession of the national education and molding the children in the same form as its own, or simply, without decrees and without battles, by excluding from every branch of their employ, by excommunicating in a thousand ways, anybody who persists in having *a style* which is not its own?

It is none the less true that imitation imposed upon people in this manner scarcely ever spreads, and never sinks in very deep; in other words, it is the *social superior,* the person with most ideas of a civilizing kind, even when he is distinct from the political superior and opposed to the latter, who eventually prevails, excepting in cases of a radical extermination such as was that of the Moors in the sixteenth century.

History abounds in illustrations of this truth. Go into the home of a peasant and look at his household effects. From his fork and his glass to his shirt, from his andirons to his lamp, from his axe to his gun, there is not one piece of his furniture, of his clothing, or one of his implements, which, before having come down to his cottage, was not originally an object of luxury for the use of kings or warrior chiefs, or ecclesiastical chiefs, then of the lords, afterwards of the citizens of towns, and lastly of the neighboring landowners. Draw this peasant into conversation. You will find he has not a single idea on law, agriculture, politics, or arithmetic, a single sentiment of family or patriotism, a single wish, a single desire, which was not originally a peculiar discovery or initiative, propagated from the social heights, gradually down to his low level. His language, the French which he is beginning to speak correctly, is an echo of the neighboring town, itself an echo of Paris just as the dialect which he still speaks (let us assume that we are dealing with the south of France) had

---

9. This author adds: "The same repugnance is observable even today against the Jews among the Christians of the Danube and against the Chinese among the Americans of the West."

been communicated to him from the neighboring castles, themselves modeled after the Provençal courts, or as he had started to speak Latin after the time of Julius Caesar because the nobility of Gaul had been eager to copy the language of the conquerors. His very hatred of the Old Régime was whispered to him by the leaders of the Old Régime; his need of equality comes to him from the Jacobin clubs which in turn had received it from the salons of the philosophers where the innovations of Rousseau were discussed by fine ladies and clever men. His jealous love of the land comes to him from the great feudal landowners whose soul it was and whom his ancestors, for centuries, had as neighbors and as masters,—a twofold reason for imitating them.

It is especially in fostering the spread of example that a social hierarchy is useful; an aristocracy is a fountain reservoir necessary for the fall of imitation in successive cascades, successively enlarged. If industry on a large scale has become a possibility in our day, if the diffusion of needs, of tastes, of identical ideas in the hearts of immense masses of people has opened up the vast outlets which it needs, is it not to the old inequalities that we are indebted for this existing equality?

But let us beware of thinking that this movement is going to cease; in democratic times the work of the nobility is carried on, and on a larger scale, by capitals.[10] The latter in many ways resemble the former. The nobility, in their days of splendor, shine by reason of wit, luxury, generosity, courage, gallantry, and a spirit of enterprise; they purchase these brilliant gifts by furnishing a larger contingent to madness, crime, suicide, the duel, illegitimate births, to vices and maladies of every sort. Capitals are no less luxurious, no less ruinous, no less gay and full of innovation. They show the same egoism and the same insolence; they have a profound contempt for the provinces in return for the profound admiration which they themselves inspire in the former, and treat them in precisely the same manner as the gentlemen of former days used to treat the common people, who were only too happy to pay their debts and for their extravagances; they also show a lower birth rate and a higher death rate; and, owing to the cankers which gnaw them, to tuberculosis, syphilis, alcoholism, pauperism, and prostitution, they would inevitably perish if, like every living aristocracy, they were not renewed very quickly by the influx of new elements.[11] They maintain themselves by means of immigration as did the Roman patriarchate by means of adoption. Thus the moralist of today, in order that he may predict what the morality of tomorrow will be, should keep his eye on the examples furnished by great cities, just as the moralist of yesterday was right in being concerned with what took place in the midst of courts, salons, and castles.

(III) Application to criminality. Vices and crimes were formerly propagated from the nobles to the people. Examples: drunkenness, poisoning, murder by command. Deliberations of the Council of Ten. Counterfeit money. Pillage and theft.

Let us see how all this applies to our subject. Strange as it may seem, there are serious reasons for maintaining that the vices and the crimes of today, which are to be found in the lowest orders of the people, descended to them from above. In every nascent or renascent society when the producing of wine becomes difficult or limited, drunkenness is a royal luxury and a privilege of the aristocracy. It is quite certain that the kings of Homer's time got drunk far more often than did their subjects, the Merovingian chiefs than their vassals, and the lords of the Middle Ages than their serfs. Even as late as the sixteenth century, in Germany "the celebrated autobiography of the knight of Schweinichen furnishes a proof that the coarsest

---

10. Conversely, we find the work of capitals carried on by the nobility which they have created and which survives them. Everything is relative in fact, and by capitals we must understand, whether in the midst of the forests of ancient Germany or among the primitive Latins, a borough greater in size than the neighboring villages. Here is born and is always formed a body of patricians. With his usual penetration, Niebuhr has reduced the fundamental contrast of Roman history, that between the Patricians and the Plebeians, to the distinction which serves as its source, between "Rome-city" and "Rome-country." This contest, to tell the truth, is the foundation of every history. Each day under our eyes grows the conflict in which we see it assuming its latest form; the electoral duel between the workman and the peasant. It has its source finally in the human organism where muscle, which rural life nourishes too much, separates and is united to sinews, which the urban life has developed to excess.

11. Just as the nobilities of the Old Régime, democratic capitals today are still the conservators of the duel. In my study on this subject I thought I had shown that the duel had become an essentially urban phenomenon and that except for a few large cities this prejudice would rapidly have disappeared. From 1880 to 1889, out of 598 duels among civilians registered in the Ferréus Annual, 491 originated in Paris, according to my reckoning. Of the others, 107 originated in Marseilles, Nîmes, Lyons, Limoges, etc. No country duel exists, so to speak, just as though honor in the country were of too inferior a kind to be deserving of a recourse to arms against the party who offends it. The kind of urban duel which predominates is the literary duel, a rather inoffensive kind, after all.

drunkenness did not dishonor a person of rank."[12] He tells us as a matter of course that, the first three nights after his marriage, he went to bed in an absolute state of intoxication, as did all the guests composing the wedding party.

The smoking habit, at present so widespread in every sort of surroundings, perhaps already more widespread among the people than among the socially elect, where they have begun to combat this passion, was propagated in the same manner. James I of England, Roscher tells us, put a very heavy tax upon tobacco in 1604, "because," says the law, "the lower classes, incited by the example of the upper classes, impair their health, taint the air, and corrupt the soil."[13] The irreligiousness of the masses, which today here and there contrasts with the relative religiousness of the last survivors of the old aristocracy, is just as much due to this same cause. Vagabondage, under its thousand and one existing forms, is an essentially plebeian offense; but by going back into the past, it would not be very difficult to connect our vagabonds, our street singers, with the noble pilgrims and the noble minstrels of the Middle Ages.

Poaching, another hotbed of crime, which in the past, together with smuggling, has played a part which may be compared with that played by vagabondage at the present time, is still more directly connected with the life of the lords. One ought to read, in Taine's "Ancien régime," of the importance of poachers in the eighteenth century in all the countries where there were forests. For the very reason that hunting was a feudal privilege, the wretch who indulged in it by main force, with an audacity and a passion hard to realize, was driven to it less by reason of his poverty than because of the vague delusion that he would to some extent ennoble himself. At this time there were poaching parties in imitation of the great hunting parties of the king; poachers to the number of from twenty-five to fifty often exchanged murderous shots with the gamekeepers, and in this manner served their apprenticeship as brigands.

Poisoning is now a crime of the illiterate;[14] as late as the seventeenth century it was the crime of the upper classes, as is proven by the epidemic of poisonings which flourished at the court of Louis XIV, from 1670 to 1680, following the importation of certain poisons by the Italian Exili. The Marquise de Brinvilliers is the direct ancestress of the common Locustes of our villages. At the table of every king at first, and afterwards of all the principal lords, during the Middle Ages and as late as the sixteenth century, it was always customary that no dish should be offered the master without previously having been tasted, "tried," out of fear that it might be poisoned. This characteristic shows the former frequency of this crime in courts and castles, especially in Italy. Italy in the Middle Ages was the nation after which the others were modeled.

Must not murder by bravos, by "bravi," so much used in Germany and Italy in the Middle Ages, have been the transition phase which homicide passed through in descending from the highest stratum of society to the lowest? The fact remains that the power to kill, from which was derived the right to kill, has been, in every primitive society, the distinguishing indication of the upper classes. The "Grands jours d'Auvergne," however pleasant they may have been made out in the valuable account given by Flechier, are sufficient to show us what were in this respect, even until the seventeenth century, the tendencies of the nobility in backward countries.[15] The evolution

---

12. "Recherches sur divers sujets d'économie politique," by *Roscher*.

13. Pipes were smoked at the court of Louis XIII. (See *Quicherat*, "Histoire du Costume," p. 478.)

14. There are still exceptions to the rule, for example that dramatic Ain-Fezza case which has just come to an end while I am correcting the proofs of this page.

15. It was not only in Auvergne, it was in many other provinces also that those terrible extra-judicial tribunals met; and against whom were their forces always directed? Against the bandits of the nobility. In our day when an exceptional form of justice is brought into play, for example in 1810, it has only to punish brigands who have been recruited from the lowest ranks of the people. In the sixteenth century, during the religious wars, kings, queens, princes, great vassals, gentlemen, all brave men, moreover, thought they had a right, not only to kill in a duel their enemy who had been overcome, but to assassinate him, either from motives of vengeance, or for ambition's sake and sometimes through greed. (See especially "Ducs de Guise," by *Formeron*.) In those days one became famous through the number of bold assassinations one had committed, for example Baron de Vittaud, whom the gentle Marguerite de Valois herself went to see at the Augustine Convent in order to confide to him the mission of killing Du Guast, the king's favorite, who had outraged her. Philip II decorated and ennobled his bravos. The massacre of St. Bartholomew is only the best known of the bloody orgies of this time. The further back we go into the past, the more do the customs of the scum of the nobility, I do not say of its élite in normal times, everywhere resemble those of the Sicilian or Corsican bandits of our day. Let us add it is true that the extraordinary number of fatal duels or of homicides, properly so-called (for at that time it is hard to distinguish between duels and assassinations in many cases) committed during the sixteenth century and again under the Fronde by the nobility, is due to a great extent to that monopoly of the right of wearing a sword which was so fatal to them. There were gentlemen of the Old Régime, like the Corsicans of today, who were turning to murder owing to the habit of carrying weapons, so much so that by forbidding them to do so their criminality was suddenly diminished by three fourths under the Second Empire. To the habit of wearing a sword was related that of going on horseback in the streets, which, given up toward the end of the sixteenth century, had also (see Voltaire) a great homicidal influence.

of the political assassination is instructive. There was a time when kings, the heads of republics, themselves assassinated; for example Clovis. What is more, it was their near relatives whom they killed by preference; parricide, fratricide, uxoricide, cold blooded infanticide, after the manner of a Tropmann, were the Merovingian specialty, as can be seen from each page of the writings of Gregory of Tours.

Later on, the princes commit assassinations which are paid for; this is especially proved by the archives of Venice. Lamansay, who has consulted them,[16] has found in them, from 1415 to 1768, more than one hundred deliberations of the Council of Ten relating to commissions of this sort. Here is a sample taken at random. "1448, September 5. The Council of Ten charge Lawrence Minio to inform the person who is unknown that he accepts the latter's offer which consists in putting to death Count Francis [Sforza], and that, after the execution, he can promise him from ten to twenty thousand ducats."[17]

Finally there comes a time,—and fortunately as a general rule far sooner than in Venice,—when men of the State would blush to make this sort of bargain; and this is the time when regicides and tyrannicides spontaneously spring up from the hot-headed populace. It is noticeable that the great recrudescences of private homicide, as far as we are able to judge with respect to a past lacking in statistics, have immediately followed the outbreak of external wars or civil wars, that is to say the great debauches of official homicide called "reasons of State." Is there not reason to believe, finally, that the cruelty of the old justices, who were so bloodthirsty, was a terrible example solemnly given by the upper classes of society, to ferocious minds, and that the excesses of public vengeance may have aroused or stimulated those of private revenge?

Arson, the crime of the lower classes today, was one of the prerogatives of the feudal lords. "Did we not hear the Margrave of Brandenburg boasting one day of having, during his lifetime, burned one hundred and seventy villages?"[18] Counterfeiting today takes refuge in a few caverns in the mountains, in a few underground places in towns; we know that for a long time it was a royal monopoly. Now governments limit themselves to sometimes putting false rumors in circulation. Finally theft, so degrading in our day, has had a brilliant past. Montaigne tells us, without being very indignant about it, that many young gentlemen of his acquaintance, to whom their fathers did not give enough money, got funds by stealing. Why should they have had any scruples on the matter when, at this same time, the king, Henry III, plundered and ransomed as he saw fit the merchants of Paris; when it was customary in the best disciplined armies to plunder captured towns and to extort enormous ransoms from prisoners of war, even of a private war, captured as a result of ambushes and betrayals? The sequestration of persons,[19] so much used quite recently among the Sicilian brigands, strangely resembles this proceeding of extortion, just as their "abigeato" recalls the military "razzias."

In one of the popular German songs of the sixteenth century, republished by Janssen, we read that the brigandage of the nobility is intolerable, that gentlemen seem to consider stealing as "an honorable action" and they go so far as to teach it "just as children are taught to read." Werner Roleswinck has supplied us with ample details as to the manner in which young gentlemen were brought up to steal in Westphalia (1487). When they went on a campaign, they sang, in the dialect of their country: "Let us steal, let us plunder without shame! The best people in the country do it!" The same customs, in less violent but more crafty form, as was fitting, were imputed to the legists; here the difference between rural theft and urban theft is felt.

In every plan of reform in Germany during the fifteenth century, the "brigandage of the nobility" is mentioned. A chronicler of the same period says that "the brigand knights make the roads very unsafe." Goetz of Berlichingen and Frank of Sickingen are, in the sixteenth century, brilliant personifications of this seigniorial criminality. In Italy the spectacle was at this time similar; the owners of castles plundered and held to ransom, throughout their fiefs, travelers, merchants, and boatmen. In France we are comparatively privileged in this respect; our nobility and especially our royalty, with some exceptions becoming more numerous during the sixteenth century, owing to the Italian contagion, were of a

---

16. "Revue historique," September and October, 1882, article on "Assassinat politique à Venise."

17. Jean-Marie Visconti had bravos of another sort; he let loose his dogs upon the citizens of Milan.

18. "L'Allemagne à la fin du moyen âge," by *Jean Janssen* (French translation, 1887).

19. In the course of a criminal trial which was brought to my notice by a distinguished archaeologist, the Vicomte de Gérard, and which was carried on in 1653–54 before the inferior court of Sarlat, I note that one of the victims was incarcerated for eight days in a dungeon in the castle of M—, on bread and water and only obtained his liberty upon the payment of a large sum of money.

mildness and a probity which were remarkable among all the others. None the less is it true that our kings had hardly any scruples about indulging in arbitrary confiscation, and that our gentlemen, even during the seventeenth century, if we are to judge by a thousand deductions drawn from the literature of the times, had very broad notions on the subject of delicacy. In the "Bourgeois gentilhomme," Dorante, who represents the type of the elegant cavalier, of the fashionable lover, commits a veritable abuse of confidence to the prejudice of Jourdain; he undertakes for the latter to carry a very valuable diamond to Dorimène (a peculiar commission moreover), and he gives it to her as coming from himself, Dorante. Here we have a little trick which it did not seem improper at that time to attribute to a courtier. However, we know whether Molière was a good courtier or not. In the memoirs of Rochefort, we read of a characteristic which proves that the great lords of the time of the Fronde made sport, not merely of killing, but of stealing. One day, he tells us, when he was in happy company "it was suggested that they go and rob on the Pont-Neuf; this was a form of amusement which the Duke of Orléans had made fashionable at that time." Rochefort says, however, that he had some hesitancy about this; at the same time he looked on, perched up on the bronze horse. "The others began to waylay the passers-by and took four or five cloaks. But, someone who had been robbed having gone and complained, the archers came and our fellows took to their heels."

And yet we say that the last descendants of these pickpockets of feudal times are now the most unblemished representatives of French honor and honesty! If heredity were the principal "factor" as far as morality is concerned, could this be as it is? Furthermore, everywhere in Europe, until the sixteenth century, there existed the right to the estate of a deceased alien, a right which was in truth one of stealing, for the benefit of the lords, and affecting all those who were shipwrecked upon their coasts. This propagation from those above to those below applies to urban crime and rural crime equally well. When, in a country such as Sicily, we see country brigandage flourish by reason of a continual recruiting among the lower agricultural classes, we may be sure that at an earlier period the upper rural classes, which at the present time limit themselves to protecting this bold plundering, themselves used formerly to practice it. Similarly, when a band of obscure insurgents terrorizes a capital and holds a government in check, let us recall the fact that there was a time when statesmen were not ashamed to carry out the massacres and annoyances which they suppress in our day.[20]

Finally, there is no need for me to recall the fact that during all the periods of their prosperity, monarchic or aristocratic courts, just as capitals at the present time, were a school of adultery, of license and moral corruption for the rest of the nation. Every offense against morals has as its cause the examples which have come from above. Rape, even more than plunder and burning, was the great diversion of the old warriors, of the military and dominant class, at a time when a castle or a town was captured and at once sacked. Brantôme cheerfully relates these ferocious orgies. Of how many criminal assaults has the habit of rape and plunder in wartime, considered for centuries as a right of war, been the cause even in times of peace and in the very midst of industrious and agricultural people!

What has just been said does not imply that there was a time, even during the most barbarous period, when murder, theft, rape, and arson were a monopoly belonging exclusively to the higher ranks of the nation; but it does mean that when a man of the lower ranks was found to be a murderer, a thief, a "struprator," an incendiary, he stood out by reason of the terror which he inspired, ennobled himself to a certain extent, and broke into government circles. In barbarous times—that is to say, times of *social illogicalness,* of isolation and of chronic hostility—every active, enterprising, and adventurous man hopes to become the leader of a band, just as, in a century of peace and of great agglomerations, he hopes to become the *head of a household.* Then, provided his criminal industry prospers, he succeeds in having himself proclaimed king, as was done by that Marcone, a brigand of Calabria who, in 1560, had himself styled "king Marcone." This thing, which has often happened in Italy, may serve as a partial

---

20. With regard to the history of Spanish literature, Brunetière ("Revue des Deux Mondes," March, 1891), observes that the chivalrous romance was the forerunner of the knavish romance, which dealt with the exploits of brigands and swindlers. In literature there was but a step between such men as Amadis aux Cartouche and Amadis aux Mandrin. Are not these latter in their own way "a sort of knight errant"? Or else should we say that in proportion as a society is formed, becomes organized and regulated, it is the knights of former times who become the beggars of today? . . . Could there not be a peculiar way of interpreting the point of honor which would be to do no work with one's two hands and, not having a farthing, in wishing to live as a gentleman? In our day this point of honor would very quickly lead people to the convict prison or the gallows. In the time of Charles V history tells us that it just as easily led them to the conquest of Mexico or Peru.

explanation of the origin of feudalism, not only of Christian feudalism, but of every sort of feudalism, for example Greek and Hindu feudalism.[21] "The little [Italian] governments which originated [in the fifteenth century] through some exploit of brigandage, are very numerous and of a savage character" says Gebhart. Does not this essentially criminal character of the ruling classes, in Italy during the fifteenth and sixteenth centuries, to a certain extent account for the very distressing spread of sanguinary criminality among the Italian lower classes of our day? And do not we Frenchmen to a certain extent owe our lesser propensity to homicide, to the relatively mild character of our former rulers?

(IV) At the present time they are propagated from the great cities to the country. Women cut to pieces. The lovers' vitriol.

While crime formerly spread, like every industrial product, like every good or bad idea, from the nobility to the people, and while the nobility, in those remote times, drew to itself the audacious and criminal elements of the people, today we can see crime spreading from the great cities to the country, from the capitals to the provinces, and these capitals and great cities having an irresistible attraction for the outcasts and scoundrels of the country, or the provinces, who hasten to them to become civilized after their own manner, a new kind of ennobling.[22]

For the time being this latter fact is a fortunate one for the provinces, which are being purified by means of this emigration and passing through an era of comparative security. Never, perhaps, in rural regions has there been less fear of assassination and even of robbery with violence than at the present time. But unfortunately the attraction of the great cities for criminals is closely connected with the influence exercised by them over the remainder of the nation, with the fascinating power their example has in all matters. As a consequence it is to be feared that the benefits derived from this betterment of conditions in the provinces is but temporary. The capitals send to the provinces not only their political and literary likes and dislikes, their style of wit or folly, the cut of their clothes, the shape of their hats and their accent, but they also send their crimes and their misdemeanors.

Indecent assault upon children is an essentially urban crime, as is demonstrated by its chart; in its spread it is seen to form a dark spot around the great cities. Each variety of murder or theft invented by evil genius is born or takes root in Paris, Marseilles, Lyons, etc., before becoming widespread throughout France. The series of corpses cut to pieces began in 1876 with the Billoir case and was for a long time confined to Paris, Toulouse, and Marseilles; but it was carried on in the Departments of Nièvre, Loir-et-Cher, and Eure-et-Loir.[23] The feminine idea of throwing vitriol in the face of a lover is entirely

---

21. Moreover, let us not forget that this criminal contagion of the aristocracy has at all times been compensated for, and more often than not, advantageously, especially in the eighteenth century by their beneficial contagion. The peculiar character with which the virtues as well as the vices of a people clothe themselves, is derived by these people from their former chiefs. Although the sentiment of chivalrous honor became vulgarized in France, where it was expressed by means of too frequent duels; and although lofty pride and independence today characterize the Spaniard, energy and a love of freedom the Englishman, this is not a mere question of race. In this we may see the consequences of a time-honored influence exercised by the nobles of these different nations. Obviously it is by imitating the classes which used to be the upper ones, that every Spaniard aspires to be a hidalgo and that the most plebeian of Frenchmen will fight a duel today. In former times single combat was a privilege of the aristocracy, as was the honor of knighthood.

22. Let us observe, while on the subject, that the substitution of capitals for aristocracies as the social summit destined to spread the various currents of imitation according to the law of their progress from above to below is itself perhaps a consequence of this law. Is not emigration from the country to the city, which has for more than a century caused the great centres to preponderate, perchance connected with the emigration, under the Old Régime, of the country nobility to the court? Under Henry IV, as is seen in the case of Olivier de Serres, the French nobility still lived upon their landed properties. After the time of Louis XIII we find a movement of concentration by the great lords to the court of the king. This tendency has been criticized and with good reason; but

while criticizing it, its critics have unconsciously and universally imitated it. The lesser nobility which could not go to court compensated themselves for this lack of power by concentrating in the larger or smaller towns of their neighborhood, where they observed the manners and the amusements of the court; or else assembled together in some castle, richer and more hospitable than the others, an imitation in miniature of Versailles. At the same time the rich townsmen, financiers and magistrates, came together around the court in Paris, or around the provincial aristocracies in each one of the little "Faubourgs Saint-Germain" which was included in nearly every town in France. (On this subject see "La ville sous l'ancien régime," by *Babeau*.) Finally, the workmen, the very peasants, began to look upon the towns as the country gentlemen of former times looked upon the court. For the latter the court was the Eden they dreamed of, the country which most abounded in game as far as good sinecures were concerned, of pleasant and refined pleasures to be sampled; and it is because this conviction has for a long time prevailed that the town has become little by little for our farmers a terrestrial paradise, the place where all profit is made without work and where every pleasure is to be found.

23. See "Contagion du meutre," by *Aubry*, pp. 137 *et seq.* In England and even in France, Billoir had had precursors, but this was a fact of which he probably was unaware. The English Billoir was called Greenaer, and he himself had been preceded by Theodore Gardelle and Catherine Hayes. (See "Causes célèbres de l'Angleterre," by *Lewis*, 1884.) Consult also "Dépeçage criminel," by *Raroux*, with notes and commentaries by *A. Lacassagne*. (Lyons, Storck.)

Parisian; it was the widow Gras who, in 1875, had the honor of inventing this, or rather of re-inventing it. But I know of villages where this seed has borne fruit, and the peasant women themselves now try their hand at the handling of vitriol.[24] In 1881, a young actress, Clotilde J—, threw vitriol over her lover, at Nice. "When she was asked at what time she first thought of avenging herself, 'since the day,' she replied, 'when I read *in a Paris newspaper* an article dealing with the revenge of women.'"[25] Another instrument of feminine hatred is the revolver; its use in a much talked of case in Paris was very soon followed by a similar shot at Auxerre.[26] In 1825, in Paris, Henriette Cornier cruelly put to death a child of which she had the care; not long afterwards, other children's nurses yielded, for no other reason than this, to an irresistible desire to cut the throats of their employers' children.

With regard to thefts the same thing applies. There is not a single means of swindling employed at village fairs which did not first see the light of day upon a sidewalk of Paris. "There were," says Corre (in "Crime et suicide"), "following the Pranzini and Prado cases, a few attempts at imitating them on a small scale carried out upon prostitutes. But what more striking example of suggesto-imitative assault could there be than the series of mutilations of women, begun in the month of September 1888 *in London,* in the Whitechapel district! Never perhaps has the pernicious influence of *general news* been more apparent. The newspapers were filled with the exploits of Jack the Ripper, and, in less than a year, as many as eight absolutely identical crimes were committed in various crowded streets of the great city. This is not all; there followed a repetition of these same deeds outside of the capital and very soon there was even a spreading of them abroad. At Southampton attempt to mutilate a child; at Bradford horrible mutilation of another child; at Hamburg murder accompanied by disemboweling of a little girl; in the United States disemboweling of four negroes [Birmingham], disemboweling and mutilation of a colored woman [Milville]; in Honduras disemboweling ... etc. The Gouffe case had its almost immediate counterpart in Copenhagen.... Infectious epidemics spread with the air or the wind; epidemics of crime follow the line of the telegraph."

It may be objected, it is true, in looking at the chart of French criminality, that many rural centres, far away from the great centres, are nevertheless making progress in the matter of crime.

But let us study this chart closely, let us go into detail, and, after having seemed to depart from the preceding reflections, we shall be compelled to come back to them. We shall see that the influence exercised by the example of the great cities over criminality is not only direct, as we have just pointed out, but at the same time and more especially indirect, like that of the old nobility, through the spread and the attraction of their pleasures, their luxuries, and their vices, a forerunner of and a preparation for the contagion of their offenses. They attract the country people because the latter began by imitating them in everything. Thus the progress of this imitation may be measured by the progress of rural emigration, which is almost entirely directed towards Paris or the other great centres. An exodus within and without which is ever increasing, because the proportion of the rural population as compared with the total population is constantly decreasing, and, in less than twenty-five years, has been lowered from three-quarters to two-thirds.

Now when we say change of place we almost always mean change of class as well; and when one is out of one's sphere, socially, it is not long before one is beyond the pale of the law. In 1876, it was calculated that, out of every 100,000 Frenchmen who had stayed at home, there were eight accused of some crime; that, out of the same number of Frenchmen who had emigrated to the interior of the country, there were twenty-nine; that out of the same number of foreigners residing in France, there were forty-one. The more detached from his native soil and his family a man is, the more is he led astray. When he once more acquires a fatherland and a family, he at once becomes better. For example: "The Department of Nord[27] has two or three times as many naturalized foreigners as the Department of Doubs, and the criminality of its immigrants is one-fourth as great."

This is not all; the example of the great centres not only affects persons who are young, active, enterprising, and who hasten to them; it also affects, it deeply and invisibly stamps the individuals who have stayed at home; and, if one of the latter, through the cultivation of vines, through industry or through speculation, becomes rich and raises himself above the others, the first use he will

---

24. It often happens that because of their clumsiness they disfigure themselves through the spurting of the liquid over their own face.
25. Paul Aubry, *op. cit.*
26. The Clovis Hugues case followed by the Francey case.

27. See "La France criminelle," by *Henry Joly,* p. 61.

make of his fortune will be to copy some Parisian, in so far as will be consistent with his natural rusticity, and to awaken to this ungainly and tormenting imitation all his neighbors. They are rural townsmen who are an outcome and a counterpart of the citizen gentlemen of the Old Régime. It is as though a caricature of Paris itself had appeared in the midst of the village. This applies to all those farmers who have become rich too quickly in the Department of Hérault, through wine growing, and in Normandy through even the breeding of cattle, as well as to the commercial upstarts who have spread everywhere. . . .

(VII) By means of another of the laws of imitation; the law of insertion, the alternate passing from fashion to custom, an irregular rhythm. Examples drawn from the history of languages, of religions, of industries. The same law applies to feelings of morality or immorality.

The manner in which we state the question already shows that in our opinion crime is a peculiar social fact, but after all a social fact like any other.[28] It is an off-shoot of the national tree, but a branch nourished by the common sap and subject to the laws which are common to all. We have seen that, taken by itself, it grows in conformity with the rule of imitation from *above* to *below,* just as do all the other fruitful and useful branches of the same trunk. We might have added that, again like them, it becomes changed or develops through the intermittent insertion of new buds or new grafts of *imitation-fashions* which come to replenish and nourish, sometimes to drive back, a stock of *imitation-customs,* but they themselves have a tendency to take root, to swell the legacy of custom and tradition. Every industry feeds itself in this manner by means of an afflux of improvements, innovations today, traditions tomorrow. Every science, every art, every language, every religion, obeys this law of the passing from custom to fashion and the return from fashion to custom, but custom which has expanded. For with each step in advance taken by it the territorial domain of imitation becomes larger, the field of social assimilation and of human fraternity expands, and it is not, as we know, the least salutary effect of imitative cause from the point of view of morality.

Here a few explanations will be necessary. At the beginning, or rather at each beginning of history, what do we find? As many dialects, as many forms of worship, as many embryonic systems of law, as many industrial or artistic processes, as many standards of morality, let us add as many kinds of vices and crimes, as there are families or groups of families. And in the end, when the same whirlwind of civilization has for a long time commingled all these tribes, what do we find? A common language, a common religion, or a science in common, a common body of law, a common form of government, an industry in common, a common art, a common standard of morality, and finally, a standard of immorality and a criminality which are uniform, spread over the entire continent where the distinct elements used to exist in the beginning.[29]

How has this change taken place? If we observe its phases we shall see; for it is not enough to say that warfare and victory have in the long run resulted in this unity; they only aroused it. Conquest can account for the subjection but not for the assimilation of the vanquished; but by breaking down the barriers between the tribes which it amalgamates into towns, and later on those between the towns which it binds together into federations, and still later those between the federations which it organizes into States, and into States which become larger and larger, it opens the door, from century to century, to the prestige of the foreigner, which becomes superimposed upon the prestige of the ancestor.

Furthermore, the door never stays open very long to the invasion from outside, the infatuation for words, for gods, for laws, for trades, for maxims, for tastes, for vices, and for crimes which are external. One will always find a dialect, a religion, a body of law, a standard of morality, a form of aestheticism, a form of depravity or brigandage, after having extended its rule owing to this widening of its field, with jealousy shutting itself up behind ramparts which have become more extensive but once more insurmountable, and there becoming perpetuated through the sanction of custom alone. From this there arises that peculiar resistance offered by

---

28. *Aristotle,* in his "Politics," expresses himself as follows: "The raising of flocks and herds, agriculture, *brigandage,* fishing and hunting, these are the means of *natural* industry available to man for the procuring of his subsistence." If we concede to the economists that all wealth which is not acquired as the fruit of labor is the result of plunder, whether brutal or disguised in some manner, we can form an accurate idea of the enormously important part played by crime in the social functions.

29. On the other hand, although in the beginning it was found that everything differed according to locality, yet everything remained practically unchanged from one century to another, there were many differences but little differentiation; and in the end everything became uniform everywhere, but everything went through a rapid change: it seems as though the difference in time and the difference in space are the counterpart of each other.

a local, provincial, or national dialect or worship, in the interval between salutary epidemics of fashion, to the importation of phrases or beliefs taken from its nearest neighbors. For example, in primitive Germania, before the invasion, each little people had its dialect, its vocabulary, its law, etc. The result of the invasion was to let loose upon these tribes themselves a current of *fashion* which compelled them to imitate the prestige of the vanquished. All their institutions then became partly Romanized or Christianized, as did their languages, under the influence of the universal impulse. Nevertheless it is true that their new religion, their new languages, their new civil and criminal law, etc., very soon became just as exclusively dear to them as the customs of their ancestors had been.

But I will pass over those Merovingian and Carolingian times which were so obscure, at the same time pointing out that the reign of Charlemagne is remarkable, like the period of the invasions, for a great overthrow of the inclosing walls of the law, politics, industry, and other matters, under the blows of a powerful agent of renovation. Afterwards the frontiers became once more established, and each nationality was again shut up within itself. But if by nationality is to be understood less a political division than a social reality, we shall see that, since the Merovingian age, nationalities, groups of individuals which have become sufficiently like one another, have already diminished in number and increased in extent.

The heroic period of the Crusades, before the time of Saint Louis, marks another great tornado of external imitation of every kind. This was the time when several new and broad streams of imitation, having their source in a number of inventions and discoveries of the greatest importance, for example of the rediscovery of the Roman law, of Aristotle partly exhumed, of the idea of the Gothic style of architecture or the heroic song, overflow and cover with their silt all local customs, all social philosophies or religions, all local styles of architecture and literature, drowning some and reviving others. Then follows a period of comparative rest under Saint Louis, when the kingdoms which have grown become separately organized, and when the great schools of jurisprudence, philosophy, architecture, and poetry become concentrated and limited, are transmitted and perpetuated in the same manner as a hereditary legacy, a national or regional tradition. The Renaissance, the discovery of America, and the Reformation put an end to this work of formation, and under their torrential deposit of countless novelties quickly transformed languages, beliefs, sciences, letters, arts, and commerce. Instead of a transformation there would have been an absolute overthrow, had not the seventeenth century come to bind up the sheaf of this harvest, and, as a tradiational consolidation of its progress, sanction it. Then comes the eighteenth century, and, with the same enthusiasm but on a still larger scale, it takes up once more the work of the sixteenth. But already, in our own day, do we not feel that the flood of cosmopolitism raised by our French philosophers is subsiding, and that the end of our century is working to separate the nations, grown very large it is true, just as much as the age which preceded it had contributed towards uniting them?

To each branch or to each subdivision of social activity we ought separately to apply in detail the law of this irregular, but continuous, rhythm, were it not for the fact that this subject would lead us too far afield.[30] There would be many corollaries to be deduced from it; I will do no more than point out one of the most simple, but not the least worthy of notice from the point of view of the future of morality. A traveler who traverses a still savage or barbarian archipelago or continent everywhere meets with small groups of people, so greatly attached to their ancestral institutions that at first sight everything about them appears to be aboriginal. Each one of these groups is convinced that they have their own particular language exclusively their own, that they "drink in their very own glass" every religious, political, and artistic idea which they may have acquired.

However, in covering an extensive region, this traveler notices that, in spite of the difference in race, the languages of these various peoples, today hermetically sealed, betray a common stock of roots, their religions a common stock of legends and mysteries, their arts a common stock of implements, methods, and subjects, etc. Should he desire, in the face of this remarkable similarity, to cling to the hypothesis of aboriginality from which he started, he will find great difficulty, as they did before the advent of Darwin,[31] in reconciling the resemblance between the species of a common

---

30. It would be a very poor interpretation of the facts to see in this rhythm an example of Spencer's rhythmic movement, that is to say, an action followed by a reaction. Let us be careful not to confuse *action* and *reaction,* the latter destroying the former, with *sowing* and *taking root,* the latter of these carrying on and forming the completion of the former.

31. Let us observe in passing that the law of Malthus and Darwin, the tendency of each species to spread itself and also to vary indefinitely, without doubt requires a completion by means of a tendency, not contrary, but consecutive to and alternating with the former, a tendency to become fixed.

genus, of a common family, or of a common order, with the hypothesis of their having been created independently. He will temporarily escape the difficulty by explaining all these correspondences of parts and analogies shown by the comparative anatomy of societies, by means of the presumed identity of human nature and the assumed invariableness of its necessary development in all times and at all places. But taken in detail this conception results in an absurdity, and it is contradicted by an observation of our civilized and half civilized nations, among whom we can establish similar correspondences of parts and analogies the cause of which is to us sufficiently clear.

It is with the energy befitting an ancestral custom that Catholicism, for centuries, has continued to exist in Ireland and Brittany; nevertheless we know the names of the missionaries who imported and spread it in those countries by the help of a great impulse of opinion hospitable to the foreigner, hostile to men's ancestors, similar to our revolutionary crises. Everywhere, in the whole world, the steam engine has been installed in workshops and factories of every kind which have become, in less than a century, local, hereditary, and ineradicable industries, in the very spot where the tourist sees them today. But we know that the steam engine came to us from Watt, that it spread little by little, starting with a little corner of England, and that, wherever workmen venerate it as an ancestor, it was at first received as an intruder. There has not been a single weaving machine, spinning machine, or sewing machine, which has not shared this same fate. National though it be in Germany, music was brought there from Italy; however Grecian Greek sculpture may be, Greece received the germ of it from the Orient or from Egypt; however original Etruscan art may have been, it was imported from Phoenicia. Many an expression, many a construction in our language, originally introduced from love of neologism, is only kept later on from love of archaism. There is not one literary innovation which, having become general, does not take on a classic appearance, otherwise called a traditional one.

It is useless to insist any further. We can draw the conclusion that every social matter, that is to say, all individual initiative, every special method of thought, feeling, or action, put in circulation by a man, has a tendency to be spread through fashion, among primitive peoples as well as among those who are civilized, and after having become widespread, to take root in the form of a custom, among civilized peoples as well as among primitive ones.

The thing which concerns us is to observe that it is not merely language, dogma, industrial and artistic instruments and talents, but moral or immoral feelings, moral or immoral habits as well, which have a tendency to become general and to become fixed in this manner.

How many African tribes, among whom drunkenness has already been raised to an institution, received from us, less than a hundred years ago, their first drink of spirits, and only took it with a grimace! How many millions of Europeans there are who resemble these savages in this! The bad habit of smoking, with which the whole of Europe and all the old world became innoculated from a few American colonies, has everywhere become acclimated to such an extent that the cigarette has become in Spain what the pipe of peace was among the Red-Skins, a national emblem. The bottle, which used formerly in all countries to be devoted to drunkenness, also becomes a sort of fetish, just as the gun, in Sicily and Corsica, is the object of a holy veneration[32] due to the traditional homicides of which it is the instrument, or as the flint knife of the Aztec sacrificer, used to open human victims in accordance with the rites, was an object of religious veneration. The "phallus," worn round their necks by Roman children under the Empire, symbolized the cult of that religion of pleasure which, coming from Syria, had taken possession of Rome and all romanity and had there so soon taken such firm root.

An epidemic of vice as well as one of virtue never fails soon to become *predisposed*. There is not a virtue, barbarian or civilized, hospitality or probity, bravery or industry, chastity or benevolence, which, today firmly rooted in the morals of a people, was not brought there yesterday or the day before. There is no atrocity, no oddity, no corruption, no superstition,—anthropophagy, religious murder of old men and the sick, tattooing, sorcery, divination by means of dreams or auguries, massacre of a political adversary or confiscation of his possessions, interrogatories by torture, the duel, the jury, the inquisition, etc.,—which, wherever it is found to be established as a constitutional evil, did not begin by being an exotic germ brought by a social current of air. What an absurd thing the duel is! And with what ancestral authority it is imposed upon civilized people, upon whole continents![33] At

---

32. "A man lends neither his gun nor his wife," says a Sicilian proverb. The gun comes before the wife.

33. It is even impressed upon the minds of the learned men who concern themselves with it. In his pamphlet "Du duel au point de vue médico-légal" (Lyons, Storck, 1890), *Teissier* is of

the same time is it possible to have any doubt but that originally it was, like every form of ordeal, like the "Wergeld," the invention of an individual, very unworthy of its great success? Assuredly, the notion of a judgment from on high being obtained by means of a combat between the two parties litigant, when the only reason for going before a court is to avoid fighting, could not have come into existence spontaneously in so many places at once.

It would therefore be a mistake to suppose that every people among whom is found endemic the habit of devouring their captives, of sacrificing the old men, of selling or killing the newly born, of treating slaves with inhumanity and, in the first place of having slaves at all, or else of becoming passionately attached to the bloody games of the circus, to burning at the stake, or to bull fights, are born cruel. Or that people given to pederasty, such as the Arabs or the Greeks, are born infamous; or that people, classes, devoted by national custom to stealing domestic animals, to smuggling, to usury, to financial speculation, are born thieves. The truth is, rather, that they have become so through unfortunately allowing the microbe of some disastrous foreign example to penetrate among them.

It would be a mistake of the same kind to imagine that the native kindness, honesty, and modesty of the civilized population of our Europe is a sufficient protection against the invasion and the acclimation of certain forms of cruelty, of corruption, of abominations, at the very mention of which they become scandalized. The more civilized a people are and the more they are subject to the domination of fashion, the more suddenly and rapidly does the avalanche of example sweep down from the heights of the cities to the lowest rural depths. The various people of the Roman Empire, peacefully settled about their blue sea, were the mildest, the most humane, even the most enervated, that the world ever saw until the eighteenth century in France, and yet they could not do without seeing thousands of gladiators slaughtered at every great festival, because it was the custom in the city of Rome, which had received this custom from Taranto, I believe.

Thus it is that our eighteenth century wound up in the butchery of the French Revolution, each murder in Paris being at once repeated in Paris itself and reverberating soon in massacres or robberies throughout the whole of France. This was nothing more than a *fashion,* but it had a perceptible tendency to become strengthened into a tradition through the authority of its "great ancestors." The unfortunate part of it is that, whenever any crime or vice can be authorized by means of the example of one's ancestors, it appears to be excusable, even respectable and patriarchal, which obtains for it the sympathy of everybody and the indulgence of the jury. Such are knife blows ("coltellate") in Italy, assassinations through revenge in Corsica, the "sfregio" in Naples, or, in certain localities which have become too commercial, forgery of commercial documents, or elsewhere voluntary setting fire to houses by the owner himself to the injury of the insurance companies. There are cantons and districts in which this last crime is perpetrated so frequently that the companies refuse to renew fire insurance policies.

The "sfregio" is used by Neapolitan lovers just as the "vitriol" is used by French mistresses; it allows the former to force people to marry them by threatening a scar on the face, just as the latter do by means of the threat of a burn which will be still more disfiguring. Both of these disfigurations had in the beginning the character of an epidemic, then, at least the first of them, an endemic character. The razor cut on women's faces has become such a national institution around Naples that, according to Garofalo,[34] "there are villages where not one young girl, unless she be protected by her ugliness, has a chance of escaping it if she does not make up her mind to marry the first man who proposes to her." Even the jury looked upon this old usage with such favor that it had to be compelled to do its duty. Imperial Rome looked upon the games of its Circus and its Amphitheatre as being so innocent that it was honestly and sincerely scandalized at the human victims sacrificed by the Druids, in about the same way as we take umbrage at the polygamy of the Arabs without stopping to think of the prostitution in our great cities. England carried on a campaign against the slave-trade without the slightest hesitancy about allowing thousands of children and women to be buried alive in its coal mines. In order to perceive

---

the opinion that dueling is *necessary* in the army. Just as though the Roman armies, to whom the duel was never known, had been lacking in discipline and courage.—This writing includes, moreover, several interesting statements, for example the following: that since 1878 there have taken place in France 647 duels which were not military, and that there has been, on an average, one death in seventy-seven duels, and that the greatest number of duels take place in the spring, and the smallest number in autumn. Can anybody be found who will account for this regular maximum and minimum by means of the action of physical factors? If not, I wonder why the same explanation would not better apply to suicide and homicide.

34. "La Criminologie," French translation, 1888, p. 280.

the odious character of a custom, it must be contemplated from without and from a distance. We reproach the savages who poison their arrows, and we exhaust our brains to devise strange engines of destruction, grape-shot, torpedoes, which in the twinkling of an eye can sink the most formidable vessel of war and mow down two hundred thousand men in an hour on a single battlefield.

There is nothing to equal the progress of our political and military inhumanity, unless it be the depth of its unconsciousness; our newspaper polemics breathe nothing but deadly hatred; instigation to murder, the glorification of assassination, no longer astonish anybody in them. But it is especially in the direction of fraud that condoned crime has developed. The inroads made by immorality upon morality, by dishonesty upon honesty, are as continuous as they are imperceptible. The tendency, in drawing-rooms, seems by preference to be, as we are aware, to go to the extreme limit of respectability, and to strive to extend that limit; so much so that after a certain length of time, in a very lively society, a person can only continue to be respectable by saying the most indecent things possible. The part played by this tendency in gatherings for pleasure is the same as that played by ability in serious matters. It is carried to the extreme limit of honesty and causes this vague dividing line to recede so far that, in certain highly civilized and very busy communities, one can with perfect honesty indulge in the very greatest dishonesty, with the consent of general opinion. If it were not for the courts, do you not suppose that the tendency of wine merchants to color their goods with aniline, in other words to poison their customers, would very soon become an ineffaceable tradition, a customary practice in storage sheds, like "stock clauses" in the deeds of conveyancers?

CHAPTER 13

ÉMILE DURKHEIM

This chapter includes two readings from the works of Émile Durkheim. The first selection, entitled "Crime as a Normal Social Fact," is from the fourth edition of *Les Règles de la méthode sociologique* [*The Rules of Sociological Method*] (1907), pp. 81–90; Paris: Félix Alcan. This reading was translated by Sherrie M. Fleshman. The first edition of *The Rules* was published in 1895. The title of this reading has been added by the editor; it was not provided by Durkheim. The second selection is from Durkheim's "Two Laws of Penal Evolution," *University of Cincinnati Law Review*, Volume 38 (1969), pp. 32–43 and 50–59; translated by William Jeffrey, Jr. Copyright © 1969 by the *University of Cincinnati Law Review*. Reprinted with permission. "Two Laws of Penal Evolution" was first published in French in 1900.

Durkheim was another important contributor to the French school of criminology. Compared to the moral statisticians, and even compared to Tarde, Durkheim was more thoroughly sociological in his work. He embraced a form of sociological positivism and valued quantitative analyses of social phenomena, but he also had an interest in history and appreciated ethnographic research. More often than not, Durkheim examined law, crime, and punishment as a means for understanding other social phenomena— such as variation in the predominant form of social solidarity, the content of the common consciousness, and the strength of collective sentiments. In spite of this (or perhaps because of it), he was able to provide several intriguing analyses that made a significant contribution to criminology. Two of these analyses are presented in the following readings.

In the first reading, Durkheim argues that crime is a normal social phenomenon, something that is not only inevitable in all societies but also intimately tied to healthy social conditions. His argument includes the suggestion that a modern society with a very low crime rate would be repressive and, thus, unhealthy. The second reading presents one of Durkheim's two laws of penal evolution, "the law of quantitative variations." Here he argues that the severity of punishment in a society varies with its level of development and the concentration of governmental power. In this reading he also describes his ideas of "religious criminality" and "human criminality," a distinction that is said to reflect a critical historical shift in the content of the common consciousness.

In view of the current literature describing Durkheim's contributions to criminology, these two readings are noteworthy in that they present pivotal arguments in his overall criminological perspective but contain no reference to anomie, the concept for which he is perhaps best known. In fact, in his discussions of anomie, Durkheim did not provide an extensive examination of crime or punishment—unless, of course, one views suicide as a crime. While Durkheim certainly made a contribution to the development of anomie theory, his criminological perspective, as the present readings demonstrate, goes well beyond this theory.

---

from THE RULES OF SOCIOLOGICAL METHOD
by Émile Durkheim

CRIME AS A NORMAL SOCIAL FACT[1]

If there is one fact whose pathological character seems to be incontestable, it is crime. All criminologists agree on this point. If they explain this pathology in different ways, they are unanimous in acknowledging it. The problem, however, requires less hasty treatment.

. . . Crime is not seen solely in most societies of any particular species, but in all societies of all types. There is not one society in which there does not exist criminality. Criminality changes form, acts that qualify as criminal are not the same everywhere; but, everywhere and always, there have been men who conduct themselves in such a way as to attract penal repression to themselves. If, at least, in the measure that societies pass from inferior types to those that are more elevated, the rate of criminality, that is to say the relationship between the annual number of crimes and that of the population, tended to decrease, we can believe that, all the while remaining a normal phenomenon, crime, however, tends to lose its character of normality. But we have no reason that leads us to believe in the reality of this regression. Many facts would seem moreover to prove the existence of a movement in the opposite direction. Since the beginning of the century, statistics furnish us with the means to follow the progression of crime; it has increased everywhere. In France, the increase is near 300%. There is not therefore a single phenomenon that presents in a more unimpeachable way all the symptoms of normality, as it seems to be tightly linked to the conditions of all collective life. Making crime a social disease, would be to admit that disease is not something accidental, but, on the contrary, derives, in certain cases, from the fundamental condition of the living being; this would be to erase every distinction between the physiological and the pathological. Without a doubt, it could be that crime itself has abnormal forms; that which comes when, for example, it reaches an exorbitant rate. It is unquestionable, in effect that this excess is by nature morbid. That which is normal, is simply that there is criminality, provided that this criminality reaches and does not surpass for each social type, a certain level that perhaps is not impossible to establish. . . . [2]

We find ourselves in the presence of an outwardly rather paradoxical conclusion. We should not be mistaken. Classifying crime among the phenomena of normal sociology, is not merely to say that it is an inevitable phenomenon however regrettable, due to the incorrigible wickedness of men; it is to avow that it is a factor of public health, an integral part of all healthy societies. This result is, at first glance, surprising enough that it caused us to be disconcerted for a long time. However, once one overcomes this first impression of surprise, it is not difficult to find reasons that explain this normality and, at the same time, confirm it.

In the first place, crime is normal because a society that is exempt from it is completely impossible.

Crime, as we have shown elsewhere, consists of an act that offends certain collective sentiments, possessed of singular energy and distinction. In order that, in a given society, the reputed criminal

---

1. Translator's note: Where possible, the translator has retained the formality of the subjunctive tense.

2. In that crime is a phenomenon of normal sociology, it does not follow that the criminal is an individual normally constituted from the biological and psychological perspectives. The two questions are independent of each other. We can better understand this independence, when we have shown further on the difference that there is between psychological facts and sociological facts.

acts can cease being committed, it is necessary, therefore, that the sentiments that these acts hurt be found in all individual consciousnesses without exception, and with the degree of force necessary to contain contradictory sentiments. But, supposing that this condition could be effectively reached, crime would not disappear, it would only change form; because the very same cause that would thus dry up the sources of criminality, would immediately open new sources.

In effect, in order that the collective sentiments protected by the penal laws of a people, at a given moment in its history, succeed in penetrating the consciousnesses that had previously been closed to them, or succeed in gaining a stronger hold where they had not been sufficiently rooted, it is necessary that they acquire a superior intensity to that which they had had before. It is necessary that the community in its entirety feel them with more vivacity; because they cannot mine from another source the greater force that will permit them to assert themselves upon the individuals who, not long ago, were the most refractory. In order that murderers disappear, it is necessary that the horror of spilled blood become greater in those social strata that recruit murderers; but, for that, it is necessary that the horror become greater in all reaches of society. Moreover, the very absence of crime would contribute directly to producing this result; because a sentiment seems much more respectable when it is always and uniformly respected. But we overlook the fact that these strong states of collective consciousness cannot be reinforced without the weaker states, the violation of which previously gave birth to nothing but purely moral faults, being reinforced at the same time; because the weaker states are only the prolongation of the stronger states. Thus, theft and simple unscrupulous action offend one and the same altruistic sentiment, the respect of property of others. However, this same sentiment is offended less by one of these acts than the other; and, on the other hand, as there is not within the average consciousness sufficient intensity to vividly feel the lesser of these two offenses, it is the object of a greater tolerance. That is why we simply reprimand the unscrupulous whereas the thief is punished. But if this same sentiment becomes stronger, to the point of silencing in all consciousnesses the penchant which disposes men towards theft, it becomes more sensitive to the damage that, until now, was only felt mildly; thus it will react more acutely against them; they will be the object of a more energetic reprobation that will pass on certain of them, from the simple moral faults that they are, to the state of crimes. For example, the unscrupulous contracts or those that are improperly executed, that only lead to public reprimand or civil reparation, will become misdemeanors. Imagine a society of saints, an exemplary and perfect cloister. In such a society, that which we call crimes would be unknown; but the sins that seem venial to the common man would be raised to the same level of scandal as is the ordinary misdemeanor in the opinion of ordinary consciousness. If then this society found itself armed with the power of judging and punishing, it would call these acts criminal and treat them as such. It is for the same reason that the honest cultivated man judges the least moral shortcoming with a severity that the masses reserve for true misdemeanors. In former times, violence against people was more frequent than it is today because respect for individual dignity was weaker. As this respect grew, these crimes became more rare; but also, many of the acts that are harmful to this sentiment have entered into the penal law that did not previously include them.[3]

We could perhaps ask ourselves, in order to exhaust all of the possible logical hypotheses, why this unanimity could not extend to all collective sentiments without exception; why even the weakest would not have enough energy to forestall all dissent. Society's moral consciousness would be found completely in all individuals and with a vitality sufficient to impede all acts that are offensive, purely moral faults as well as crimes. But a uniformity equally universal and equally absolute is essentially impossible; because the immediate physical milieu in which each one of us is placed, our hereditary antecedents, the social influences on which we rely vary from one individual to another and, as a consequence, diversify consciousnesses. It is not possible that everyone can be the same to such an extent, if only because each of us has his own constitution and that these constitutions occupy different portions of space. That is why, even with inferior peoples, where individual originality is underdeveloped, it exists nonetheless. So therefore, because there cannot be societies where individuals do not diverge more or less from the collective type, it is inevitable as well, among these differences, that there are those that present a criminal character. What bestows upon them this character, is not their intrinsic

---

3. Slander, insults, defamation, fraudulent misrepresentation, etc.

importance, but the importance given to them by the common consciousness. If therefore this is stronger, if it has enough authority to render these differences weaker in absolute value, it will be more sensitive, more exacting, and reactive against the least deviation with the energy that it displays elsewhere against the greatest dissents. It attributes to them the same gravity, that is to say, it marks them as criminal.

Crime is therefore necessary; it is tied to the fundamental conditions of all social life, but, in that same way, it is useful; because the conditions to which it is dependent are themselves indispensable to the normal evolution of morality and of the law.

In effect, it is no longer possible today to dispute that not only the law and morality vary from one social type to another, but that they change within the same type if the conditions of collective existence are modified. But, in order that these transformations be possible, it is necessary that the collective sentiments at the basis of morality are not obstinate to change, and consequently, that they only have moderate energy. If they were too strong, they would no longer be pliable. Every arrangement, in effect, is an obstacle to rearrangement, and even more so if the original arrangement is stronger. The more a structure is strongly integrated the more it resists all modification and this is true of functional arrangements as well as anatomical arrangements. But if there were no crime, this condition would not be fulfilled; because such a hypothesis implies that the collective sentiments would reach a degree of intensity unparalleled in history. Nothing is good indefinitely and without limit. It is necessary that the authority which moral consciousness enjoys not be excessive; otherwise, none would dare to raise a hand against it, and it would set itself too easily in an immutable form. In order that individual originality evolve, it is necessary that it see the light of day; but, in order that the originality of the idealist who dreams of surpassing his century be able to manifest itself, it is necessary that the originality of the criminal, who is below his time, be possible. One cannot be without the other.

That is not all. Beyond this indirect utility, it happens that crime itself plays a useful role in this evolution. Not only does it imply that the way remains open to necessary changes, in certain cases, it directly prepares these changes. Where crime exists, collective sentiments are not only in the necessary state of malleability to take on a new form, but sometimes crime contributes to predetermining the form that they will take. Many times, in effect, it is only an anticipation of the morality to come, a progression towards that which will be. According to Athenian law, Socrates was a criminal and his condemnation was completely just. However, his crime, the independence of his thoughts, was useful, not only for humanity, but for his country. It served to prepare a morality and a new faith of which the Athenians had need because the traditions by which they had lived until then were no longer in harmony with their conditions of existence. But the case of Socrates is not isolated; it is reproduced periodically in history. The liberty of thought that we currently enjoy would never have been proclaimed, if the rules that prohibited it had not been violated before being solemnly repealed. However, at that moment, that violation was a crime, because it was an offense to sentiments that were still very alive in the average consciousness. And yet this crime was useful because it was a prelude to the transformation that, from day to day, became more necessary. Liberal philosophy had as its precursors, heretics of all sorts that were justly struck down by the secular arm during the course of the Middle Ages and up to the eve of the contemporary age.

From this point of view, the fundamental facts of criminology are presented to us in an entirely new aspect. Contrary to current ideas, the criminal no longer appears as a completely unsociable being, as a sort of parasitic element, a foreign and inassimilable body, introduced to the bosom of society;[4] he is a normal part of social life. Crime, for its part, should not be conceived as an evil that cannot be too strictly contained; but, far from being the moment of self-congratulations when crime descends too far beneath the ordinary level, we can be certain that this apparent progress is at one and the same time associated with some social disturbance. It is thus that the number of assaults and batteries never falls as low as in times of poverty.[5] At the same

---
4. We have, ourselves, committed the error of speaking thusly of the criminal, due to the error of failing to apply our rule (*Division du travail social*, p. 395, 396).

5. However, in that crime is a normal sociological fact, it does not follow that we should not hate it. Pain, also, has nothing desirable; individuals hate it as society hates crime, and yet it rises from normal physiology. Not only does it by necessity derive its very make-up from every living being, but it plays a useful role in life and for this reason it cannot be replaced. It would therefore be a singular distortion of our thought to present it as an apology for crime. We would not even dream of protesting against such an interpretation, if we did not know to what strange accusations and to what misunderstandings we are liable, when we attempt to study moral facts objectively and to speak of them in a language that is not that of the common man.

time and as a consequence, the theory of punishment is revised or, better yet, needs to be revised. If, in effect, crime is an illness, punishment is its remedy and cannot be conceived otherwise; all discussions that it raises bear on the point of knowing what the punishment must be in order to fulfill its role as remedy. But if crime is not pathological, the purpose of punishment cannot be to cure it and its true function must be sought elsewhere. . . .

---

from TWO LAWS OF PENAL EVOLUTION
by Émile Durkheim

I. THE LAW OF QUANTITATIVE VARIATIONS[*]

This law may be formulated as follows: *The severity of punishment is greater where societies are of a less advanced type and where the central power is more absolute in character.*

Let us begin by explaining the meaning of these expressions.

The first factor has no great need of definition. It is relatively easy to know whether one society is more or less advanced than another. We need only see in what degree they are established, and if on this point they are equals, then, which of them is the more highly organized. Moreover, this hierarchy of societies does not imply that the spectrum of societies forms any single linear sequence. On the contrary, it is certain that the series should rather be depicted as a tree with many more or less different branches.[1] On this "tree," however, societies are located higher or lower, as they are found at varying distances from their common source. Only on the condition that we consider them from this point of view is it possible to speak of a general evolution of societies.

The second factor we have distinguished, however, requires a lengthier discussion. We say that governmental power is absolute when it encounters among other social institutions nothing which is of a nature to balance it, or to set effective limits to it. A complete absence of all limitations, of course, is found nowhere; it could even be said that such a situation is inconceivable. Tradition and religious beliefs serve as checks upon even the strongest governments. Furthermore, there are always some secondary social organs which are liable on occasion to assert themselves and resist. The subordinate powers to which a supreme regulative power is applied are never deprived of all individual energy. It happens, however, that this factual limitation has about it nothing which is legally obligatory on the government that sustains it. Even though the government observe a certain measure of restraint in the exercise of its prerogatives, it is not held to this by statute or customary law. In this situation it has at its disposal a power which may be called absolute. No doubt, if the government allows itself to go to excess, the social forces which it wrongs may coalesce to react and to curb it. With some foresight of this potential reaction, and for its avoidance, government may limit itself with self-restraint. This restraint, however, whether it be the government's own doing, or be positively imposed upon it, is essentially contingent. It does not result from the normal functioning of institutions. When it is due to the government's own initiative, this restraint is presented as a gracious concession, a voluntary abandonment of legitimate rights. Whenever it is the result of collective resistances, restraint is frankly revolutionary in character.

Absolute government may be characterized in another way. The legal order gravitates around two poles, the relations composing it being either (1) unilateral or (2) bilateral and reciprocal. At least, these are the two ideal types around which relations oscillate. The first type is exclusively constituted by rights attributed to one party as against the other, without the latter enjoying any rights correlative to his obligations. In the second type, the legal link results from a perfect reciprocity between the rights conferred upon each of the two parties. Real rights, especially the right of property, represent the most developed form of the first kind of relations: a proprietor has rights over his property, which it does not have over him. Contract, particularly the just

---

1. *Cf.* E. DURKHEIM, LES REGLES DE LA METHODE SOCIOLOGIQUE 20 (1893). [Translated as THE RULES OF SOCIOLOGICAL METHOD, by S. Solovay and J. Mueller 19 (Chicago, 1938).]

contract, *i.e.,* one in which there is a perfect equivalence in the societal value of the "things" (*prestations*) which are exchanged, is the typical case of reciprocal relations. Now, the more that the relations of the supreme power to the rest of society have a unilateral character—in other words, the more they resemble those which link a person with the property he owns—the more absolute is the government. Conversely, government is less absolute when its relations with other societal functions are more nearly bilateral in character. The most perfect example of absolute sovereignty is the *patria potestas* of the Romans, as defined in the ancient civil law, where a son was assimilated to a chattel.

Thus, what makes a central power more or less absolute is the absence, in more or less radical degree, of any counterbalances regularly organized for the purpose of moderating it. We may foresee that what gives birth to this kind of power is the more or less complete union, in one and the same hand, of all the directive functions of a society. Because of their vital importance, these functions cannot in fact be concentrated in only one person, without conferring on him an exceptional preponderance over all the rest of society. This preponderance constitutes absolutism. The holder of such an authority finds himself invested with a force that frees him from all collective restraint, and results, at least to a certain degree, in a situation where he thinks only of himself and his own interests and convenience, and can impose his every wish. This hyper-centralization releases a social force *sui generis* of such an intensity as to dominate all others and subject them to itself. And this preponderance does not make itself felt solely in fact, but in law as well, because he who has a privilege of this kind is invested with such prestige that he seems to have a more-than-human nature, making it inconceivable that he could be subject to regular obligations, as ordinary human beings are.

Brief and imperfect though this analysis may be, at least it will suffice to forewarn us against certain errors that are still very prevalent. We can see in fact—and contrary to the confusion propagated by Spencer—that governmental absolutism does not vary with the number and the importance of governmental functions. However numerous these may be, government is not absolute, whenever these functions are not concentrated in the hands of only one man. This is what is happening today in the major European societies, particularly in France. The field of governmental action is extended in other ways than it was under Louis XIV, but the rights which the State has over society are not without reciprocal duties; in no way do they resemble proprietary rights. In fact, the situation is that not only are the supreme regulatory functions divided up among distinct and relatively autonomous but interdependent organs, but they are not exercised without a certain participation by other societal functions. Thus, from the fact that the State can make its action felt at a great many points, it does not follow that the State becomes more absolute. True, it *may* become so, but this requires many other circumstances in addition to the increased complexity of the powers which have been vested in it. Conversely, a mediocre range of functions does not constitute an obstacle to the State's taking on this character. When governmental functions are in fact few in number or lacking in activity, this is because the society's own life is generally poor and languishing. The varying degree of development of the central regulatory organ merely reflects the general development of the collective life, just as the dimensions of an individual's nervous system vary according to the importance of organic changes. The directive functions in a society are rudimentary only when other societal functions also have the same nature; the relation between the two remains constant. Consequently, governmental functions retain their supremacy, and their absorption by one and the same individual suffices to put him above the level of others, to raise him infinitely above the society. Nothing is simpler than the governments of some petty barbarian kings, yet no governments are more absolute in character.

This remark leads to another, which more directly concerns our subject: the more or less absolute character of a government is not integral to any specific type of society. Since, in fact, absolute government may be found where the collective life is extremely simple, as well as where the collective life is very complex, it does not belong more exclusively to primitive societies than to any others. One may, it is true, believe that the concentration of governmental powers always accompanies the concentration of the societal mass, either as its result or as a factor contributing to determine it. Nothing of the kind. The Roman city-state, particularly after the expulsion of the kings, was free from all absolutism, down to the last century of the Republic, because the various segments or partial societies (*gentes*) of which it was formed had achieved, under the Republic, a very high degree of concentration and fusion. Indeed, forms of government deserving to be called "absolute" may be observed in the most varied types of society: in seventeenth-century France, or at the end of the Roman state, or in a multitude of barbarian monarchies. Conversely, a single people can, under different circumstances, pass from an absolute government to a completely different one. Nevertheless, a single society can no more change its type in the course of its evolution than an animal can change its species during its individual existence. France of the seventeenth century and France of the nineteenth century belong to the same type, and yet the supreme regulatory organ was transformed. It is impossible to admit that, from Napoleon I to Louis Philippe, French society passed from one societal type to another, yet underwent a reverse change, in passing from Louis Philippe to Napoleon III. Changes like these contradict the very notion of species.[2]

The particular form of political organization, therefore, does not depend on any "congenital" constitution of the society, but depends, instead, on individual, transitory and contingent conditions. For this reason, the two factors in the evolution of penal systems—the nature of the societal type and the nature of the governmental organ—are to be carefully distinguished. Being independent, they act independently of each other, sometimes even in opposition to one another. For example, it happens that in a transition from a primitive to some other, more advanced, type of society, punishment is not observed to decrease as might have been expected. This is because at the same time the governmental organization neutralizes the effects of the social organization. The process is extremely complex.

With our formulation of the law explained, we now need to show that it conforms to the facts. Since a review of all peoples or nations is out of the question, we shall select for comparison those whose penal institutions have achieved a certain degree of development and are known with sufficient certainty. Moreover, as we have attempted elsewhere to show, the essential element in a sociological demonstration is not the amassing of factual data, but the establishment of series of regular variations "the terms of which are connected with each other in a gradation of the greatest possible continuity and adequate extent."[3]

In a great many ancient societies, death pure and simple did not constitute the supreme punishment. For those crimes considered the most atrocious, death was worsened by additional corporal punishments whose effect was to make death more frightful. Among the Egyptians, we encounter, in addition to hanging and beheading, the stake, torture with ashes, and crucifixion. In burnings at the stake, the executioner began by making several incisions in the hands of the condemned individual by means of pointed cane stalks; only then was the criminal placed on a fiery bed of thorns and burned alive. The punishment with ashes consisted in suffocating the condemned person under a heap of ashes. "It is even probable," says Thonissen, "that the judges were accustomed to inflict upon the guilty all the additional suffering that they believed to be required by the nature of the crime or the demands of public opinion."[4] The peoples of Asia appear to have pushed cruelty even further. "Among the Assyrians, the guilty were thrown to the wild beasts or into a fiery furnace; or they were burned in a bronze vat over a slow fire; or their eyes were put out. Strangulation and decapitation were rejected as being insufficient measures! Among the various tribes of Syria, criminals were stoned to death, shot full of arrows, hanged, or crucified; their bones and entrails were burned with torches; they were cut in quarters; they were thrown from rocky crags . . . they were crushed beneath the feet of animals, etc."[5] The Laws of Manu distinguished between simple death (by beheading), and aggravated or qualified death. This latter was of seven kinds: empalement on a stake, fire, crushing beneath an elephant's feet, drowning, boiling oil poured in the ears and the mouth, torn to pieces by dogs in a public square, and cut to pieces with razor-sharp knives.

Among these same peoples, simple death was used unsparingly, even to prodigality. An enumeration of all the cases requiring it is impossible. One

---

2. It seems to us hardly scientific to classify societies according to their level of civilization, as Spencer and Steinmetz do, because then we are obliged to attribute *one and the same society* to a plurality of species, according to the political forms in which it has been successively clothed, or according to the degrees of civilization through which it has successively passed. What would we say of a zoologist who thus fragmented an animal among several species? A society has, nevertheless, even more than an organism, a definite personality, self-identical in certain respects throughout its existence; in consequence, a classification that fails to recognize this fundamental unity seriously distorts reality. We may indeed so classify social conditions, but not societies; and these social conditions remain confused and "in the air," when detached from the permanent substratum linking the two. Only the analysis of this substratum, then, and not the changing life supported by it, can provide the bases of a rational classification. Cf. E. Durkheim, *supra* note 1, ch. 4, esp. at 88 [translation, 88].

3. E. Durkheim, *supra* note 1, at 134 [translation, 135].
4. 1 J. Thonissen, Etudes sur l'histoire du droit criminel des peuples anciens 142 (1869).
5. *Id.* at 69.

fact will show how numerous they were: according to a story in Diodorus, an Egyptian king, consigning the condemned to death in the desert, succeeded in founding a new city there. By employing the condemned on public works, another king accomplished the construction of numerous dikes and the excavation of canals.[6]

In the next rank below the death punishment are found the "expressive" mutilations. In Egypt, for example, counterfeiters and those who altered public inscriptions had both hands cut off; the perpetrator of rape on a free woman was punished by the removal of his genitals; a spy had his tongue cut out, etc.[7] Similarly, according to the Laws of Manu, the tongue was cut out of a man of the lowest class who had gravely insulted the Dwidjas; the hip of a Soudra who had been so audacious as to sit beside a Brahman was marked, etc.[8] In addition to these characteristic mutilations, all sorts of corporal punishments were used among both peoples. Punishments of this kind were most often arbitrarily fixed by the judge.

The Hebrew people certainly did not belong to a type superior to those last-mentioned; in fact, a concentration of the societal mass did not occur until a relatively late era, under the kings. Until that time there was no Israelite state, but merely a juxtaposition of more or less autonomous tribes or clans, which only coalesced momentarily to meet a common danger.[9] Nevertheless, the Mosaic law was much less severe than that of Manu or the sacred books of Egypt. Capital punishment was not accompanied by similar refinements in cruelty. Indeed, it appears that, during a long period, stoning was the only customary punishment; burning, beheading, and strangulation appear only in the Rabbinical texts.[10] Mutilation, so widely practiced by other peoples of the Orient, appears only once in the Pentateuch.[11] When the crime was a "wounding," the *talion*, it is true, could entail mutilations, but the culprit could always escape them by means of a pecuniary composition. Such a composition was prohibited only for murder.[12] As for other corporal punishments, which dwindled to flogging, they were certainly applied in a great number of delicts,[13] but the maximum was fixed at 40 stripes, and, in practice, the number stayed at 39.[14] What is the source of this comparative mildness? The answer is that, among the Hebrew people, absolute government was never able to establish itself in any enduring fashion. We have noted that for a long time the Hebrew people lacked all political organization. Although it is true that a monarchy was later established, the power of the kings continued to be very limited. "The sentiment in Israel was always strong that the king was for his people, not the people for its king; he had to help Israel, not make use of it for his own self-interest."[15] Even though it sometimes happened that an exceptional authority was obtained by certain individuals, by reason of their personal prestige, the spirit of the people remained fundamentally democratic.

It may be noted that penal law continued to be very rigorous. When we pass from the earlier societies to the social type of the city-state, which is incontestably superior, we ascertain a sharply marked regression in the penal law. At Athens, although capital punishment was augmented in certain cases, this was nonetheless the great exception.[16] As a rule, it consisted of death by the hemlock, by the sword, or by strangulation. "Expressive" mutilations disappeared. This seems also to be true of corporal punishments, except for slaves and, perhaps, for persons of low social status.[17] Even considered at her apogee, however, Athens represents a relatively archaic form of the city-state. In fact, her organization on the basis of clans (*genē*, phratries) was never so completely effaced as at Rome, where the *curiae* and the *gentes* early became mere historic memories, whose meaning the Romans themselves did not know with any certainty. Accordingly, the system of punishments was much more severe at Athens than at Rome. First, the Athenian law, as we said, did not entirely ignore "aggravated" death. Demosthenes alludes to the guilty ones nailed to the gallows.[18] Lysias cites the names of assassins, brigands, and spies who had been clubbed to death.[19] Antiphon speaks of a female poisoner being broken on the wheel of torture.[20] Sometimes

---

6. Diodorus Siculus, I, 60 and 65.
7. J. Thonissen, *supra* note 4, at 160.
8. Laws of Manu, VIII, §281.
9. I. Benzinger, Hebraische Archaologie 202-03, 71, & §41 (1894).
10. Cf. *id.* at 333; 2 Thonissen, *supra* note 4, at 28.
11. Deuteronomy 25:11–12.
12. Numbers 35:31.
13. This is explained in a passage of Deuteronomy 25:1–2.
14. Josephus, Jewish Antiquities, IV, 238, 248.
15. I. Benzinger, *supra* note 9, at 312.
16. Cf. 2 K. Hermann, Lehrbuch der griechische Antiquitaten, Rechtsalter-thumer 124–125 (1884).
17. *Id.* at 126–127.
18. Demosthenes, Contra Midias 105; cf. Plato, Republic, II, 362.
19. Lysias, Contra Agoratos 56, 67, 68; Demosthenes, On the False Legation, 137.
20. Antiphon, Prosecution for Poisoning 20.

death was preceded by torture.[21] In addition, the death penalty was pronounced in a considerable number of cases: "treason, injury to the Athenian people, attack against the political institutions, alteration of the national law, falsehoods offered to the tribunal of the popular assembly, abuse of diplomatic offices . . . extortion, impiety, sacrilege, etc., etc., incessantly required the intervention of the dreadful ministry of the Eleven."[22] At Rome, on the other hand, capital crimes were far less numerous. The *Leges Porciae* limited the use of capital punishment throughout the duration of the Republic.[23] And, apart from very exceptional circumstances, death was not combined with any accessory torture or other aggravation. Crucifixion was restricted to slaves only. Moreover, the Romans prided themselves on the relative mildness of their repressive system, for example, Livy, who said, "Let no nation claim to have established milder punishments,"[24] and Cicero's reference to the ancestors "who wanted your liberty guarded by the mildness of laws, and not besieged by the harshness of punishments."[25]

But when governmental power tended to become absolute in the Empire, the penal law worsened. First, capital crimes became more numerous. Adultery, incest, all sorts of outrages against the *mores*, and especially the ever-increasing multitude of crimes of high treason, were punished with death. At the same time, severer punishments were instituted. The stake, which had been reserved for exceptional political crimes, was employed against incendiarists, perpetrators of sacrilege, magicians, parricides, and perpetrators of crimes of high treason; the condemnation *ad opus publicum* was established; mutilations were applied to certain criminals (*e.g.*, castration in certain cases of offenses against the *mores*; cutting off a hand, for counterfeiters, etc.). Finally, torture made its appearance; it was from the Imperial period that the Middle Ages borrowed it much later.

If we turn now from the city-state to the Christian societies, we see penal law evolve according to the same law.

It would be a mistake to judge the penal law under the feudal regime on the basis of the Middle Ages' reputation for atrocity. When the facts are examined, it will be verified that the penal law was then much milder than in the preceding societal types, at least if these types are considered in the corresponding phase of their evolution, that is, in their formative period and, so to say, their first youth. Only on this condition can the comparison have demonstrative value. Capital crimes were not very numerous. According to Beaumanoir, the only truly inexpiable acts were murder, treason, homicide, and rape.[26] To these the *Establishments of Saint Louis* added abduction and arson.[27] These were the principal cases of "high justice." Although brigandage was not so characterized, it too was a capital crime. So, also, were two delicts regarded as particularly prejudicial to the rights of a seigneur: offenses committed in markets, and the delicts involved in damaging roadways (the violent overthrowing of toll-houses).[28] The only religious crimes then repressed by capital punishment were heresy and infidel belief. The perpetrators of sacrileges owed only a fine or other compensatory penalty, as did also the blasphemers. The decision by Saint Louis, in the initial religious fervor of his youth, that these latter were to be marked on their foreheads and have their tongues pierced, drew down on him the censure of Pope Clement IV. The Church did not unleash an implacable severity against her enemies until a later period. As for the punishments themselves, there was nothing unusual about them. The only aggravations of capital punishment consisted in dragging the condemned on a hurdle to the execution, and in burning the condemned alive. Mutilations were rare. In other respects we know that the Church's repressive system was humane. The punishments she preferred to employ were penances and mortifications. She rejected public mortification—the iron collar and the pillory—although such punishments, apparently, would not have exceeded her jurisdiction. It is true that, when the Church decided that sanguinary repression was necessary, she delivered the culprit over to secular justice. Nonetheless, it was a fact of the greatest importance that the highest moral

---

21. LYSIAS, *supra* note 19, 54; PLUTARCH, PHOCION, xxxiv.
22. J. THONISSEN, *supra* note 4, at 100.
23. F. WALTER, HISTOIRE DU DROIT CRIMINEL CHEZ LES ROMAINS §821 (tr. J. Piquet-Damesme, 1863); W. Rein, DAS KRIMINALRECHT DER ROMER, VON ROMULUS BIS AUF JUSTINIAN 55 (1844).
24. LIVY, I, 28: "Nulli gentium mitiores placuisse poenas."
25. CICERO, PRO RABIRIO PERDUELLIONIS REO, 3: "vestram libertatem, non acerbitate suppliciorum infestam, sed lenitate legum munitam esse voluerunt."

26. COUTUME DU BEAUVOISIS, ch. xxx, no. 2.
27. 1 ETABLISSEMENTS DE SAINT LOUIS, chs. 4 and 40.
28. *Cf.* 2 A. DU BOYS, HISTOIRE DU DROIT CRIMINEL DES PEUPLES MODERNES CONSIDERE DANS SES RAPPORTS AVEC LE PROGRES DE LA CIVILISATION 231 (1854–60).

power of the period thus bore witness to her horror of these kinds of punishments.[29]

In general, this was the situation down to the fourteenth century. From that time on, the royal power was established more and more solidly. To the extent that it was consolidated, we see the penal law strengthened. First, the crimes of lese majesty, unknown to the feudal system, made their appearance, and their list is a lengthy one. Even religious crimes were thus characterized, one result being that sacrilege became a capital crime. The same was true of simple dealings with infidels, and of any attempt "to cause belief in, or to argue about anything which is or could be contrary to the sacred faith of Our Saviour." At the same time, an increased rigor in the application of punishments became manifest. Those guilty of capital crimes could be broken upon the wheel (it was in this era that torture on the wheel appeared), buried alive, quartered, flayed alive, or boiled. In certain cases, the children of a condemned person shared his punishment.[30]

The apogee of absolute monarchy marked the apogee of repression. The capital punishments still in use in the seventeenth century were those enumerated above. In addition, a new punishment, the galleys, was instituted, a punishment so terrible that condemned wretches sometimes cut off an arm or a hand to escape it. This very practice became so frequent that it was made subject to the death penalty by a proclamation in 1677. As for the corporal punishments, they were innumerable: tearing out or piercing of the tongue, cutting off the lips, cropping or tearing off the ears, branding with a hot iron, whipping with a cudgel or lash, the iron collar, etc. Finally, it should not be forgotten that torture was often employed, not only as an element of judicial procedure, but as the penalty itself. In the same period, capital crimes multiplied, because the crimes of lese majesty had become more numerous.[31]

Such was the penal law until the middle of the eighteenth century. There then occurred throughout Europe the protest that has become linked with the name of Beccaria. The Italian criminologist was, of course, not the initial cause of the reaction which developed without interruption. The movement had commenced before his time; numerous works, forgotten today, had already appeared, calling for reforms in penal systems. It is, nevertheless, beyond dispute that his *Dei delitti e delle pene* (1764) struck the mortal blow at the old and detestable routines of the criminal law.

An ordinance of 1788 had earlier introduced some reforms, not without importance, but the new aspirations were chiefly satisfied by the penal code of 1810. When this code appeared, it was received with unreserved admiration, not only in France, but in the principal countries of Europe. The code in fact achieved significant progress in mitigation or alleviation, but in reality it still clung far too much to the past. New ameliorations were not slow in being called for. One complaint was that the death penalty, even though it was no longer aggravated as it had been under the *ancien régime,* was still too prodigally employed. The retention of branding, the iron collar, and mutilation of the hand for parricides, were regarded as inhumane. The response to these criticisms was the revision in 1832. This introduced into our penal system a much greater mildness by discarding all mutilations, reducing the number of capital crimes and, finally, granting to the judges the means of mitigating all punishments on the ground of extenuating circumstances. There is no need to show that since that time the movement has continued in the same direction, until today the complaint begins to be heard that the regime has become too "comfortable" for criminals. . . .

IV. EXPLANATION OF THE FIRST LAW

To facilitate this exposition, we shall consider separately the two factors we have distinguished, and because the second factor plays the less important role, we shall begin by temporarily setting it aside. We seek, then, to know how it happens that punishments become milder as we pass from primitive societies to more advanced societies,

---

29. This relative mildness of punishment was even more accentuated in the democratically governed parts of society, namely, the free communes. "In the free towns, as in the communes properly so called, one finds a tendency to alter punishments to fines, and to employ infamy rather than corporal punishment or coercive penalties as a means of repression. Thus, at Mont Chabrier, whoever stole two sous was obliged to wear them suspended around his neck, and to go about like this all day and all night, and then a fine of five sous was inflicted upon him." 2 Du Boys, *supra* note 28, at 370. Kohler has remarked a similar phenomenon in the Italian cities. Kohler, Das Strafrecht der Italienischen Statuten vom 12–16. Jahrhundert [1885–97].

30. *Cf.* 5 Du Boys, *supra* note 28, at 234, 237 ff.

---

31. 6 *id.* at 62–81.

without concerning ourselves, for the moment, with any distortions that may result from the more or less absolute character of governmental power.

We might be tempted to explain this alleviation as being due to a parallel refinement in the *mores*. Increasingly, we have a horror of violence; violent, *i.e.,* cruel, punishments inspire in us an increasing repugnance. Unfortunately, this explanation is self-contradictory, for if, on the one hand, our greater humanity causes us to shun cruel punishments, it should, on the other hand, make the inhuman acts repressed by punishment appear all the more odious to us. If our more developed altruism clashes with the idea of making another suffer, then, for the same reason, crimes that contravene these sentiments seem to us more abominable and, as a result, we inevitably tend to repress them with greater severity. This tendency, however, is only partially and weakly neutralized by the opposing tendency (although this has the same altruistic origin) that leads us to inflict on the culprit the least possible punishment. Obviously, our sympathy for the culprit should be less than our sympathy for his victim. Consequently, refinement of the *mores* should sooner express itself in aggravated punishment, at least for all those crimes which injure another. In fact, when this moral refinement began to appear in history in a marked manner, it was indeed manifested in this fashion. In primitive societies, murders and mere thefts are only feebly repressed because the relevant *mores* are so very coarse. At Rome, for a long time, violence was not regarded as vitiating contracts, indeed, as not having any punishable quality at all. From the time when the sympathetic feelings of man for man have been affirmed and developed, these crimes have been more severely punished. This movement would have continued, had some other cause not intervened.

Because punishment results from crime and expresses the manner in which the public conscience is affected, we must seek the determining cause of the evolution of punishment in the evolution of crime.

With no need to present and discuss all the detailed evidence which justifies the distinction, we think it will be agreed without difficulty that all acts deemed criminal by all the different societies known to us can be divided into two fundamental categories: (1) crimes directed against collective "things" (ideal or material, it makes no difference), the principal ones being the public authority and its representatives, the *mores,* traditions, and religion, and (2) crimes which injure only individuals (murders, thefts, violence, and fraudulent dealings of all kinds). These two forms of criminality are sufficiently different to warrant designating them by different terms. The first category can be termed *religious criminality,* because outrages against religion are its most essential part, and because crimes against traditions or the chiefs of the State always have a more or less religious character. For the second category we can reserve the term *human criminality*. With this classification established, we know that crimes of the first category, to the virtual exclusion of all the others, constitute the criminal law in primitive societies. We know also that these crimes decline in parallel with the advance in evolution, since outrages against human beings increasingly take over this area. For primitive peoples, crime consists almost entirely in failing to perform cult duties, in violating ritual prohibitions, in deviating from the ancestral customs, and in disobeying the interdictions of authority, where this latter is established in sufficient strength. On the other hand, for Europeans of the present day, crime consists essentially in injury to some *human* interest.

It follows, therefore, that these two categories of criminality differ profoundly, because the collective sentiments offended by them are not of the same nature. A further result is that repression cannot be the same for both categories.

The collective sentiments contravened or encroached upon by the particular criminality of primitive societies are "collective" for two reasons. Not only do they have the collectivity for their subject and are, therefore, to be encountered in the generality of individual consciences, but, in addition, *they have collective "things" as their object.* By definition, these "things" are beyond the circle of our private interests. The ends to which we are thus linked infinitely exceed the small horizon of each of us. They do not concern us personally; they concern the collective entity. It follows that the acts required of us for their attainment are not slanted to the inclination of our individual natures, but do violence to them, for these acts consist of sacrifices and privations of all sorts which men are required to impose upon themselves, either to please their gods, or to satisfy the demands of custom, or to obey authority. We do not have any innate penchant for fasting, self-mortification, forbidding ourselves particular kinds of meats, sacrificing our best animals on an altar, inconveniencing ourselves out of respect for some custom, etc. Consequently, just as sensations come to us from the external world, certain sentiments are within us without our efforts—even, to some extent, in spite of ourselves—and they so appear to us as a consequence of the restraint they exercise on us. We need, therefore, to set them apart from ourselves, relating them to some external force as their cause, just as we do for our sensations. Furthermore, we are obliged to conceive of this force as a power not only foreign but also superior to us, inasmuch as it orders and we obey. This voice that speaks in us with such an imperative tone, enjoining us to do violence to our natures, can emanate only from some being different from us, a being which dominates us as well. Under whatever specific form men may imagine this force (gods, ancestors, august personalities of whatever kind), it always has, from this relation to them, something of the transcendant, the superhuman. This is the reason why that part of morality is wholly impregnated with religiosity. The duties prescribed to us by morality link us with a personality infinitely surpassing our own—the collective personality that we represent to ourselves in its abstract purity or, as most often happens, with the assistance of genuinely religious symbols.

In this situation, the crimes that violate these sentiments and consist in omissions of these special duties, can only appear to us as being directed against those transcendant beings, since in reality they affect them. As a result, these crimes seem to us particularly odious, because the higher the nature or the dignity of the offended is above that of the offender, the more revolting is the offense. The more some person is bound to show respect, the more abominable is his lack of it. The same act which is simply blameworthy when it involves one's equal, becomes impious when it involves someone who is one's superior. The horror it arouses can be allayed only by violent repression. For the sole purpose of placating his gods by maintaining regular relations with them, a worshipper must normally submit to a thousand privations. To what privations, then, should he not be subjected when he has outraged the gods? Even if the pity inspired by the culprit were lively enough, it could not serve as an effective counterpoise to the indignation aroused by the sacrilegious act, nor could it, in consequence, appreciably moderate the punishment. The two sentiments are much too unequal. The sympathy felt by men for one of their kind, especially one degraded for some fault, cannot restrain the effects of the reverential fear that is felt for divinity. Compared with that power, which so very greatly exceeds his own, the individual appears so small that his sufferings lose their relative value and become a negligible quantity. What is an individual's sorrow, when it is a matter of appeasing a *god*?

The situation is otherwise with those collective sentiments whose object is the individual, because in this instance each of us is an object. Whatever concerns Man himself concerns everyone, for we are all humans. The feelings that protect human dignity, affect us deep in our hearts. I am not at all suggesting that we respect the lives and properties of our fellow-men from some merely utilitarian calculation, in order to obtain from them a precisely, reciprocal respect. If we disapprove of acts which lack this respect, we do so because they offend the feelings of sympathy we have for mankind in general. These sentiments are disinterested precisely because they have a general object. Therein lies the great difference that separates the moral individualism of Kant from that of the Utilitarians. In a sense, both make the development of the individual the object of moral conduct. For the Utilitarians, however, the individual in question is the sensible, empirical individual as he is to be found in each particular conscience. For Kant, on the other hand, it is the human personality, humanity in general, an abstraction from the diverse and concrete forms in which it presents itself to observation. Nevertheless, however universal it may be, such an objective is intimately related to the one toward which our egoistic propensities incline us. The difference between Man in general and the men that we are is not the same as the difference between a man and a god. The nature of this ideal being differs from ours only in degree; it is merely a model, of which we are varied exemplars. The sentiments attaching us to it are in part, then, the extension of those attaching us to ourselves. This is merely what the current maxim says: Do not do to another what you would not have him do to you.

As a consequence, it is not equally necessary, for our explanation of these sentiments and the actions to which they stimulate us, to search for some transcendental origin. To explain the respect we feel for humanity, there is no need to suppose that it is imposed upon us by some external power superior to humanity. It already seems intelligible to us, from the mere fact that we know and perceive ourselves to be humans. We are aware, indeed, that this respect conforms to the natural inclination of our sensibilities. Thus the attacks that deny it do not seem to us to be so much directed against some superhuman entity as were those mentioned above. We do not perceive in them any acts of lese divinity, but simply acts of lese humanity. No doubt, it is remote from this ideal that it should lack all transcendency. It is the nature of the ideal to surpass the real, and to dominate it, but its transcendency is much less marked. Although this abstract Man does not blend itself with any of us, each of us realizes it in part. However lofty the design may be, since it is essentially human, so also, in some measure, is it immanent in us.

Thus the conditions of repression are no longer the same as those in the first case. There is no longer the same distance between the offender and the offended; they are more on a par. This is even more so since in each particular case the human person injured by the crime presents himself in the nature of a particular individuality, identical in all points with that of the criminal. Hence the moral scandal embodied in the criminal act is something less revolting and therefore does not require so violent a repression. The attack of one man against another man does not arouse the same indignation as does the attack of a man against a god. At the same time, the sentiments of compassion inspired in us by one who suffers punishment can no longer be so easily or so completely stifled by the sentiments he has wounded, which react against him, for they both have the same nature. The first are only a variety of the second. What tempers the collective anger, the spirit of punishment, is the sympathy we feel for everyone who suffers, the horror aroused in us by all destructive violence. On the other hand, it is precisely this sympathy and this horror which kindle that anger. In these circumstances, the very cause that sets in motion the repressive machinery tends to impede its operation. One and the same mental state urges us to punish but also to moderate the punishment. A mitigating influence cannot fail to make itself felt. It can seem perfectly natural to sacrifice unreservedly the human dignity of a criminal to the outraged majesty of a divinity. Still, there is a real and ineluctable contradiction in avenging an offended human dignity, in the person of the victim, by violating the integrity of the person of the criminal. The only means, not of removing the antinomy (since it is not rigorously solvable) but of mitigating it, is to lighten the punishment as much as possible.

Since—to the extent that there has been any advance—crime is increasingly reduced only to attacks against persons, while the forms of religious criminality are declining, the average punishment inevitably continues to grow weaker. This weakening does not derive from any softening of the *mores*, but rather from the fact that religiosity, whose influence was primitively so strongly marked in both the criminal law and its underlying collective sentiments, continues to diminish. No doubt, the sentiments of human sympathy become at the same time more intense, but this greater vitality does not suffice to explain the progressive moderation of punishments. Instead, it would, by itself alone, tend to make us more severe about all the crimes of which mankind is the victim and to heighten their repression. The true reason is that the compassion whose object is the condemned man, is no longer overwhelmed by contrary sentiments which do not permit it to make its action felt.

Still, it will be asked: If this is so, how is it that the punishments attached to attacks against persons share in the general regression? Because, while these have lost less than the others, it is also certain that they are generally less prominent than they were two or three centuries ago. If, nevertheless, the nature of this kind of crime is such as to call forth less severe punishments, this effect should have manifested itself in the beginning, as soon as the criminal character of these acts was formally recognized. The punishments they involve should thus have achieved, at once and at a single stroke, the degree of mildness they called for, rather than to have become progressively milder. However, the fact that has determined this progressive softening is that, at the time these attacks (having long stood at the threshold of the criminal law) penetrated it and were definitely classified within it, religious criminality occupied nearly the whole of the area. As a consequence of this preponderant position, religious criminality began to draw into its orbit any newly recognized delicts and to stamp them with its imprint. So long as crime is, in a general manner, thought of as being essentially an offense directed against divinity, crimes committed by man against man will also be thought of along the same lines. We believe that these crimes also revolt us because they are forbidden by the gods and, for this reason, are insulting to them. Habits of mind are such that it seems hardly possible for a moral precept to have a sufficiently well founded authority unless the precept borrows authority from what is regarded as the unique source of all morality. This is the origin of the theories, so widespread even today, according to which morality lacks any and all basis whatever, if it is not supported by religion or, at least, by rational theology, *i.e.*, if the categorical imperative does not emanate from some transcendental Being. To the extent that human criminality develops and religious criminality retreats, however, the former more and more distinctly discloses its own individual aspect and its distinctive traits as we have described them. It frees itself of the influences it has undergone which have hindered it from being itself. If today there are still many minds to whom the criminal law and, more generally, all morality, are inseparable from the idea of God, nonetheless their number is diminishing, and those who still cling to this archaic conception do not link the two ideas so closely as Christians did in the earlier ages. Human morality increasingly throws off its primitively confessional character. In the course of this development there has occurred the regressive evolution of punishments that make the most serious breaches in the prescriptions of this morality.

In the course of an interaction which requires notice here, human criminality, as it gains ground, reacts upon religious criminality and, so to speak, assimilates it to itself. Although attacks against persons constitute the principal crimes today, attacks against collective "things" (crimes against the family, against the *mores,* against the State) can still occur. On the other hand, these collective "things" themselves tend increasingly to lose the religiosity formerly so characteristic of them. From being divine, as they once were, they become human realities. We no longer hypostatize the family or society in the form of transcendental and mystical entities. We now see in them little more than groups of people who concert their efforts to realize human goals. As a result of this, crimes directed against these collectivities share the character of those that directly injure individuals, and the punishments that affect the former are themselves becoming milder.

Such is the cause that has determined the progressive abatement of punishments. The result has been produced mechanically. The manner in which collective sentiments react against crime has changed because the sentiments have changed. New forces have come into play; the effect cannot remain the same. This great transformation has not occurred for the purpose of some preconceived end, nor has it occurred under the influence of any utilitarian considerations. Once completed, however, the transformation is found to be quite naturally adapted to useful ends. Simply because it has necessarily resulted from the new conditions in which societies find themselves, the transformation could not fail to be in a harmonious relation with these conditions. In fact, the severity of punishments serves only to make the energy of social constraint felt by individual consciences. Furthermore, it is of no use unless it varies with the severity of that constraint. It is appropriate, then, that the severity of punishments grows milder to the same extent that collective coercion is lightened, becomes more flexible, and less exclusive of free thought. This is the great change that has occurred in the course of moral evolution. Although societal discipline—of which morality properly so called is merely the highest expression—increasingly extends its field of action, it loses more and more of its authoritarian rigor. Because it takes on something more human, societal discipline allows more room for individual spontaneities; in fact, it encourages them. It has less need, therefore, to be imposed by violence. For this result, however, it is also necessary that the sanctions ensuring this respect become less restrictive of all initiative and reflection.

We can now return to the second factor in penal evolution, which we have thus far put to one side: the nature of the governmental organ. The foregoing considerations enable us to explain more easily the manner in which this factor operates.

The establishment of an absolute power necessarily has the effect of elevating its holder above the rest of humanity, making him something more than human, particularly when the power with which he is armed is virtually unlimited. Indeed, whenever government takes this form, he who exercises the power seems to men like a divinity. Although he may not be made into a special god, at the very least an emanation of divine power is perceived in the power with which he is invested. Consequently, this religiosity cannot fail to have its ordinary effects on punishment. For one thing, assaults directed against a being so obviously superior to all of his offenders will not be regarded as ordinary crimes, but rather as sacrileges, and therefore to be suppressed with violence. Among all peoples subject to an absolute government, this is the source of that exceptional standing assigned by the criminal law to crimes of lese majesty. For another, since nearly all the laws in these same societies are deemed to emanate from the sovereign and to express his wishes, the principal violations of law appear to be directed against him. The reprobation excited by these acts is thus much more severe than it is when the authority of which they have run afoul is more dispersed and, therefore, more moderate. The fact that authority is concentrated to such a high degree, while rendering it more intense, also renders it more sensitive to everything that offends it and more violent in its reactions. Thus it is that the gravity of most crimes finds itself increased by several degrees; in consequence, the average severity of punishments is very greatly augmented....

PART FOUR

THE ROOTS OF CRITICAL CRIMINOLOGY

Almost all of the historical divisions of criminology covered to this point have embraced one or more positions that were threatening to the religious or political elite of the societies in which they emerged. Works by Montesquieu, Beccaria, and Bentham offended the teachings of the Roman Catholic Church and were placed on its *Index Librorum Prohibitorum*; Gall's writings and lectures on phrenology were found to be too materialistic and were banned by the Holy Roman Emperor, Francis II; Ferri, one of the most important members of the Italian school, embraced a variation of Marxism, a specter that haunted capitalist societies from the mid-nineteenth century to nearly the end of the twentieth century; and Durkheim, a prominent member of the French school, opposed the forced division of labor in modern societies, especially the institution of inherited wealth. Despite these and other critical standpoints, the classical school, physiognomy and phrenology, the Italian school, moral statistics, and the French school (narrowly defined) generally did not pose a significant direct challenge to the capitalist, patriarchal, and ethnocentric/racist social arrangements that existed during the eighteenth and nineteenth centuries.[1] Indeed, with a few exceptions (e.g., Ferri), they tended to ignore or reinforce these arrangements.[2]

Yet these were not the only divisions of criminology evolving during this era. There were several scholars who did not fit neatly into these divisions, who directly challenged one or more of the aforementioned social arrangements, and who also offered analyses of law, crime, or punishment that were very critical. These scholars constructed much of the foundation for the

---

1. The claim that the French school of criminology posed little threat to these social arrangements requires a narrow and, admittedly, debatable conception of this school. If the French school is defined to include the writings of the nineteenth-century French socialists (e.g., Charles Fourier) and French anarchists (e.g., Pierre-Joseph Proudhon), it too may be viewed as a noteworthy contributor to the emergence of critical criminological thought.

2. Michael J. Lynch (2000:147) has argued that "... during the rise of capitalism, criminology emerged as part of the apparatus of the 'science of oppression' established by Enlightenment philosophy." Its target was the "dangerous classes." Also see Foucault (1979).

eventual emergence of critical criminology and include the early Marxists (e.g., Karl Marx and Frederick Engels), anarchists (e.g., Peter Kropotkin), feminists (e.g., Harriet Martineau), and critical race scholars (e.g., W. E. B. Du Bois). Much of their work centered on critiquing and changing fundamental components of the dominant culture and social structure of society. The Marxists supported an economic transition from capitalism to communism, anarchists pursued the removal of coercive government, feminists sought the abolition of patriarchal institutions, and critical race scholars pursued the elimination of racism and racist social arrangements.

Marxist Criminology

Marxist theories of law, crime, and punishment hold an important place in the history of critical criminology. To understand these theories, it first is necessary to have a general understanding of Marxism. The arrival of Marxism stemmed from a concern over the socioeconomic transformations that were occurring in Europe during the eighteenth and nineteenth centuries—primarily, the rise of industrial capitalism and the problems that accompanied it. Although different types of Marxism currently exist, the emphasis here will be on traditional Marxism, the general worldview of Karl Marx and his associate Frederick Engels. Below is a brief sketch of a few traditional Marxist themes that might be helpful to readers who are not familiar with their work, but first a few biographical notes are warranted.

Karl Marx (1818–1883) was born into a middle-class family in Trier, Prussia (Germany).[3] He attended the University of Berlin and later the University of Jena, where he received a doctorate in philosophy in 1841. He was very active politically. During his lifetime, he was associated with the Communist League and contributed to the founding of the International Working Men's Association in London. Early on, the adverse response to his political activities prompted Marx to move about between Germany, France, and Belgium. He finally settled in England, where at times he lived in poverty but nonetheless completed some of his most significant work.

Marx was the primary architect of one of the most influential social theories of the nineteenth and twentieth centuries. His work has guided many social movements and has had an effect on several disciplines—from sociology (where he is regarded as one of the most important classical theorists) to political science, philosophy, economics, history, and even criminology. Like most of the theorists examined in this book, Marx embraced science. Engels ([1883] 1999:164–165), a friend and coauthor on several works, described him as a "man of science" and commented: "Just as Darwin discovered the law of development of organic nature, so Marx discovered the law of development of human history. . . ." Marx's most important book, and also the most significant work of Marxism, is *Capital, Volume I* (1867).[4] Other notable works by

---

3. Because of his prominent status in the history of sociology, summaries of Marx's work can be found in most textbooks on classical sociological theory. See Greenberg (1981) and Lynch and Groves (1989) for extensive overviews of Marxist criminology; see Garland (1990) for a helpful examination of the Marxist theory of punishment.

4. There are three volumes of *Capital*. Volumes II and III were prepared by Engels and published after Marx's death in 1885 and 1894, respectively.

Marx include his "Economic and Philosophical Manuscripts" (1844), *The German Ideology* (1845–1846, with Engels), and *The Communist Manifesto* (1848, also with Engels).

Yet, as just suggested, Marx is not the sole architect of Marxism. Frederick Engels (1820–1895) also made a contribution. Engels was born into a relatively wealthy manufacturing family in Barmen, Germany. Like Marx, he eventually moved to England and lived there for many years. In addition to the works he coauthored with Marx, Engels produced several other noteworthy publications. These include *The Condition of the Working Class in England in 1844* (1845), *Socialism: Utopian and Scientific* (1880), *Dialectics of Nature* (1873–1883), and *The Origin of the Family, Private Property, and the State* (1884). While Marx generally is regarded as the superior scholar, Engels may have had a deeper devotion to science. For instance, Kai Nielsen (1995:227) noted: "Engels, and not Marx, presented a Marxist account of natural science and integrated Darwinian elements in Marxian theory."

Marxism begins with the assumption that within a given society, the mode of production is the primary determinant of social life (although not the only determinant). In simple terms, the mode of production refers to the economic system of a society, the general way in which goods are produced and distributed. For Marx and Engels, it has a very significant influence on the structure of other institutions, including government, religion, education, and families. Thus, within a traditional Marxist framework, if you want to develop an adequate understanding of a society, you would begin by identifying its mode of production. Different modes of production—such as feudalism, capitalism, and communism—result in fundamentally different types of societies. The work of Marx and Engels was primarily a critique of capitalism, and of course they advocated a transition to communism.

Capitalism, the dominant mode of production in the world today, allows for private ownership of the means of production—things such as the tools, machines, raw materials, and land used in the production process. It is driven by a highly competitive pursuit of profits in a theoretically free market and allows for private control of those profits. Because private ownership of productive property is encouraged and protected, capitalism results in a society with different economic classes—namely (as labeled by Marx and Engels), the bourgeoisie, petty bourgeoisie, proletariat, and lumpenproletariat (lower proletariat). The two most significant classes in this framework are the bourgeoisie and the proletariat. The bourgeoisie (capitalists) are the owners and controllers of the means of production; they represent a small percentage of the overall population but nevertheless control most of the wealth and constitute the ruling class. The proletariat, on the other hand, are laborers who sell their skills and physical effort to the bourgeoisie for a wage; they represent a much larger segment of the population, control relatively little wealth, and constitute the working class. Marx and Engels argued that in such an economy the proletariat become increasingly alienated,[5]

---

5. In his "Economic and Philosophical Manuscripts," Marx ([1844] 1964) describes four types of alienation suffered by workers—estrangement from the products of their labor, from their productive activity, from their "species-life," and from each other (i.e., "man is alienated from other men").

exploited, and demoralized, and are propelled into a conflict with the bourgeoisie.

From the traditional Marxist viewpoint, capitalist societies, like other societies in which the means of production are privately owned (e.g., feudal societies), generate class struggle. The bourgeoisie and the proletariat have conflicting interests. For instance, the bourgeoisie want to maximize profits, an objective that is furthered by reducing wages, increasing the length of the workday, and improving the efficiency of the production process through the development of new technologies. Conversely, the proletarians have an interest in humane conditions that allow them to reach their human potential. This is promoted by the provision of a steady and fair income, safe working conditions, and opportunities to develop their physical and mental abilities. According to Marx and Engels, as a capitalist system evolves, class struggle generally intensifies and will eventually lead to a revolution in which the proletarians overthrow the bourgeoisie. "What the bourgeoisie, therefore, produces, above all, is its own grave-diggers. Its fall and the victory of the proletariat are equally inevitable" (Marx and Engels [1848] 1999:77). Where this victory occurs, the proletariat, in theory, will initiate a transition to a new mode of production—communism.

Communism is an economic system based on collective ownership and control of the means of production. "The distinguishing feature of Communism is not the abolition of property generally, but the abolition of bourgeois property" (Marx and Engels [1848] 1999:78). Moreover, it is guided by the following principle, which was originally proposed by Jean J. C. Louis Blanc and later adopted by Marx: "from each according to his ability, to each according to his needs." Communist societies, from a Marxist viewpoint, do not have different economic classes. They are classless in that there is no distinction between the owners of the means of production and the workers; everyone would relate to the means of production in essentially the same way. Consequently, there would be no great difference in wealth across the people of a communist society; economic inequality would be very low. Likewise, there would be no class struggle since there would be no classes. What is more, because the economy is not driven by the pursuit of profit, and because the means of production and goods produced would be shared, a communist society, in theory, would be far less competitive and far more cooperative than a capitalist society. "In place of the old bourgeois society, with its classes and class antagonisms, we shall have an association, in which the free development of each is the condition for the free development of all" (Marx and Engels [1848] 1999:85).[6]

Thus Marxist criminologists pay special attention to the socioeconomic system of a society when explaining crime and proposing responses to crime. They view capitalist societies as highly criminogenic with unjust legal systems. The alienation, exploitation, suffering, and self-interest generated by capitalism are said to drive a substantial portion of the population into a

---

6. Elsewhere Engels ([1847] 1999:99) describes "the aim of the Communists" in the following terms: "To organise society in such a way that every member of it can develop and use all his capabilities and powers in complete freedom and without thereby infringing the basic conditions of this society."

criminal lifestyle; at the same time, the criminal justice system protects the interests of the bourgeoisie at the expense of the proletariat. On the other hand, Marxist criminologists view "full communism" as offering an environment in which crime can be reduced to its lowest level and justice elevated to its highest level. From their viewpoint, alienation, exploitation, suffering, and self-interest would be greatly reduced, and the criminal justice system would be cut to a fraction of its former size and would protect the interests of the masses. In short, Marxist criminologists are very critical of capitalism and support a transition to communism.

For those who value economic equality (not just equal opportunity) and cooperative social interactions, the appeal of Marxism during the late 1800s and much of the 1900s is easy to understand. Nonetheless, the theories of Marx and Engels have faced more than a century of criticism and are problematic in several ways. To begin, it is commonly suggested that Marxism embraces a utopian ideal that is based on a flawed conception of human nature. Regarding this issue, Sigmund Freud ([1930] 1961:71) concluded that the "psychological premises" of communism are "an untenable illusion," and thus the "abolition of private property" is unlikely to deliver us from our evil ways. Marxism, in other words, is inclined to accept the idea of "social instincts" (innate altruism) but discounts the idea of innate hedonism or egoism, of a "carnivorous" or "death" instinct, or of some other selfish/aggressive tendency that may be present at birth in every normal human.[7] Traditional Marxism also has been criticized on other grounds. For instance, class conflicts have not evolved as predicted, and proletarian revolutions simply have not occurred in advanced capitalist societies. Likewise, the socialist societies that emerged during the twentieth century, such as the Soviet Union and Cuba, did not and have not evolved into the type of communist society anticipated by Marx—a "full communist" society in which the state "withers away." Beyond this, it has been argued that Marxist theorists give too much weight to the mode of production in their efforts to explain social life; that is, Marxism suffers from the problem of economic reductionism.

Despite its shortcomings, the critical orientation of Marxism is clear, as is its influence on the development of critical criminology. "One thing that we can be sure about," writes Martin D. Schwartz and Suzanne E. Hatty (2003:ix), "is that modern critical criminology has its roots in the long tradition of Marxist criminology. . . ." In Chapters 14 and 15, one can find a glimpse of that tradition as it was first intimated in the works of Marx and Engels. Chapter 14 presents a reading from Marx's *Capital, Volume I* (1915, based primarily on the third German edition). In this selection, he argues that the emergence of capitalism in England depended in part on the theft of lands occupied by peasants. The displaced peasants, nascent

---

7. For a Marxist account of human nature and the effects of capitalism by one of the first Marxist criminologists, see Willem Bonger's *Criminality and Economic Conditions* (1916), Book II, Chapter I.

proletarians, were then controlled by "a bloody legislation against vagabondage."

Although Marx, as one would guess, made the most important contribution to the development of Marxism, Engels arguably made a more direct substantive contribution to criminology. In *The Condition of the Working Class in England in 1844* ([1845] 1887), Engels provides a classic critical analysis of crime and law. Here he suggests that many crimes by individual proletarians were acts of rebellion, but he also maintains that such crimes represented the "earliest, crudest and least fruitful" type of rebellion, and that ". . . theft was the most primitive form of protest . . ." (p. 143). Moreover, he contends that ". . . the law is sacred to the bourgeois, for it is his own composition, enacted with his consent, and for his benefit and protection" (p. 152). These are common Marxist themes, but Engels says much more than this. Several excerpts from *The Condition of the Working Class* are presented in Chapter 15. In these readings, Engels presents his conception of "social murder," provides his views on the demoralizing effects of early industrial capitalism, illustrates the class bias that existed in the laws of nineteenth-century England, and describes the workhouses that were used to control the surplus population.

The writings of Marx and Engels, directly or indirectly, have influenced several generations of criminologists and legal scholars—from the work of Enrico Ferri (1898), Willem (William) Adrian Bonger (1916), Evgeny B. Pashukanis ([1924] 1978), and Georg Rusche and Otto Kirchheimer ([1939] 2003) to the more contemporary works of David M. Gordon (1973), Richard Quinney (1980), David F. Greenberg (1981), Mark Colvin and John Pauly (1983), and Michael J. Lynch and W. Byron Groves (1989), to name a few. While it is true that the Marxist influence on critical criminology has faded somewhat over the last two decades, its significance, as Schwartz and Hatty (2003) suggest, should not be dismissed. After all, it is unlikely that there is another branch of criminology, critical or otherwise, that has stimulated as much theory and research on the relationships between capitalism and crime, class and crime, and class biases in the content and administration of the law.

Anarchist Criminology

Like Marxism, the emergence of modern anarchism stemmed from a concern over the social transformations that were occurring during the eighteenth and nineteenth centuries. In fact, there is considerable overlap across the two viewpoints, and Marxists and anarchists often worked together during the nineteenth century. For instance, in the International Working Men's Association, they jointly opposed capitalism and its defenders. Yet there also were conflicts between the two groups, conflicts based on a significant philosophical difference. Whereas the Marxist concern centered on the socioeconomic system (the development of industrial capitalism), anarchists, as a whole, focused their critique on coercive governmental authority. Thus anarchists were deeply disappointed when the leaders of the Marxist movement in Russia instituted their "dictatorship of the proletariat" following the Russian Revolution of 1917. Even if it was intended to be a temporary political arrangement, one that would facilitate a transition to full communism and then wither away, it made little difference to the anarchists. It was a political system that stood in opposition to anarchism, and hence it was rejected by the anarchists (e.g., see Berkman 1925; Goldman 1925). But let's return to the eighteenth and nineteenth centuries.

Together with the rise of industrial capitalism, a fundamental political shift was occurring as republics began to replace monarchies and nation-states evolved. This political change extended public participation in government, but it also was accompanied by the expansion of formal governmental control. Surveillance of the public, for instance, became more systematic with the development of formal metropolitan police forces during the early 1800s. Over the course of this era, industrial capitalism produced more wealth to protect, the expansion of the division of labor generated more specializations to coordinate, rapid population growth resulted in more interpersonal conflicts to manage, and science created significant advancements in communication and transportation. These and other conditions (e.g., rapid urbanization) encouraged or facilitated the expansion of governmental control. But at the same time, concern over this expansion prompted a countermovement, the development of modern anarchism. This countermovement also was promoted by concerns that emerged where older oppressive political systems were maintained—as in Russia under its nineteenth-century tsars.

Anarchist philosophy has a long history, takes different forms, and is associated with the work of a variety of writers.[8] Although it has been traced back as far as the ancient Greeks, to the views of Aristippus and Zeno (see Kropotkin [1905] 1975), modern anarchism began to emerge during the late eighteenth century primarily through the writings of the British author and philosopher William Godwin. Moving into the nineteenth century, anarchist theory began to flourish and diversify. During this era, in France, Pierre-Joseph Proudhon developed a form of anarchism centered on "mutualism" and associated with "anarcho-syndicalism." In Russia, Mikhail Bakunin advocated a "collectivist" and revolutionary form of anarchism; Leo Tolstoy supported a version of anarchism that embraced nonviolent Christian beliefs and pacifism; and Peter Kropotkin developed perhaps the most scholarly form of "anarchist communism." In the United States, Henry David Thoreau and, by the early twentieth century, Emma Goldman were among the most prominent anarchists.[9]

Although anarchism takes several forms, a common theme runs through them: We should do as much as we can to eliminate coercive governmental authority. Beyond this, true anarchists, those who apply the concept of anarchism in its purest form, oppose all types of domination. They maintain that

---

8. Brief overviews of the various forms of anarchism can be found in many textbooks on political theory and political ideology (e.g., Baradat 1997). For a review of anarchist theory in criminology, see Ferrell (1997, 1999).

9. Goldman has been referred to as "the most influential anarchist in United States history" (Baradat 1997:157), although she credits Thoreau with being "the greatest American Anarchist" (see Goldman [1917] 1969:56).

we should not dominate others and we should resist domination by others.[10] The more scholarly anarchists were not advocates of disorder (at least not for its own sake); rather, they were people who embraced an optimistic conception of human nature and found the domination of individuals or groups to be unacceptable. While there is considerable variation from one version of anarchism to another, most versions identify and oppose multiple forms of institutionalized domination—such as the domination of thoughts by established religion,[11] the domination of basic material needs by the institution of private property, and the domination of actions by the state (see Kropotkin [1905] 1975; Goldman [1917] 1969). Anarchists wish to create conditions under which human freedom can be maximized, conditions that allow us "to obtain the full development of all (our) faculties" (Kropotkin [1905] 1975:108–109).

Much like traditional Marxism, the scholarly forms of anarchism generally have a very hopeful outlook and tend to view humans as naturally altruistic. Because of this, they also confront a similar criticism: They often appear utopian. For theorists who embrace a more pessimistic outlook on human nature (e.g., who presuppose innate egoism), the claims of anarchists, like the claims of Marxists, may appear unreasonable. In response it may be argued that the various pessimistic conceptions of human nature are merely ideological beliefs that help rationalize systems of domination. Yet, if anarchists are wrong about the altruistic inclinations of humans, the pursuit of an anarchist agenda, rather than providing more opportunities for the development of our faculties, might elevate oppression and suffering, for it could result in less control over our selfish and destructive impulses. Nevertheless, the point to be emphasized here is that prior to the twentieth century, anarchist scholarship made a distinctive contribution to the existing theories of law, crime, and punishment.

Among the anarchists of the eighteenth and nineteenth centuries, Godwin and Kropotkin may have made the most noteworthy contributions to early criminological thought. I will begin with a few words about Godwin and then proceed to the life and work of Kropotkin.

William Godwin (1756–1836) was born in Cambridgeshire, England, into a middle-class family.[12] After he completed his education at Hoxton College, he became a minister, the occupation of his father. However, he eventually left the ministry and pursued a career in literature and philosophy. In the 1790s he married Mary Wollstonecraft, one of the most important

---

10. Some forms of anarchism deviate from this ideal, such as Max Stirner's "individualist anarchism." Advocates of individualist anarchism often have a right-wing orientation and embrace anarchist philosophy only in a limited or contradictory manner. As Kropotkin ([1905] 1975:114–115) suggested in a brief critique, individualist anarchism opposes the domination of individuals by government and other social institutions, but it allows "certain better endowed individuals" to develop more fully and, ultimately, dominate those who are less endowed. Because it begins with opposition to domination and ends with the reestablishment of domination (though perhaps of a different kind), it results in the negation of its own starting point.

11. Some anarchists were religious (e.g., Tolstoy), but even they tended to oppose organized, authoritative religious institutions.

12. For a brief discussion of Godwin's contribution to criminology, see Jenkins (1984). For more extensive examinations of his life and anarchist philosophy, see Paul (1876) and Kramnick (1972).

representatives of eighteenth-century feminism.[13] It also was during this decade that Godwin wrote his most significant book, *Enquiry Concerning Political Justice and Its Influence on Modern Morals and Happiness*; the first edition was published in 1793 and the final (third) edition was published in 1798. In this work, he seemingly followed the shifting currents of eighteenth-century liberalism as far as they would take him, and then he took an additional step, proposing a form of "philosophical anarchism" (see Watkins 1948; Kramnick 1972). He criticized government and other institutions (e.g., school systems and churches) for subverting individual autonomy. Government, for Godwin, was an institution that was destined to fade away. Although key elements of anarchist thought can be found among the works of ancient Greek philosophers, Godwin may have been "the first to formulate the political and economic conceptions of anarchism" (Kropotkin [1905] 1975:112). Moreover, while he was critical of governmental authority, laws, and punishment, and while he supported fundamental change, he generally embraced nonviolent intellectual means in the pursuit of his anarchist agenda. As one reviewer of *Political Justice* noted, "he is no Quaker, but his dislike of violence is so pronounced as almost to align him with Tolstoi" (Hall 1948:346).[14]

Writing during the Enlightenment, Godwin arguably presented one of the first critical theories of criminology (see Jenkins 1984). *Political Justice*, which has been referred to as "the bible of anarchism" (Kramnick 1972:123), contains a fairly extensive analysis of law, crime, and punishment. Anticipating the work of later generations of critical theorists, Godwin ([1798] 1985) argued that a class bias existed in the laws and that economic inequality was a major cause of crime. He held that anarchism, as he conceived it, would reduce this inequality and, ultimately, eliminate most crime. In this connection, Godwin was critical of punishment in general, rejecting its most common justifications. He provided a classic anarchist critique of punishment as a means of retribution, incapacitation ("restraint"), reformation, and deterrence ("example")—a critique that reinforced his broader rejection of governmental authority, for if state-administered punishment is not necessary to maintain peace, the state lacks a major reason for its existence.

While Godwin's style of argument was literary and philosophical, at least one of the early anarchists adopted a more scientific orientation, Peter Alexeivich Kropotkin (1842–1921).[15] Kropotkin, who has been described as "the

---

13. Their marriage is of some interest in that Godwin ([1798] 1985) initially opposed the institution of marriage.

14. The general nature of Godwin's nonviolent orientation, from a critical standpoint, is somewhat problematic. Kramnick (1972) points out that Godwin's opposition to aggressive political action served conservative interests on at least one occasion. Kramnick also highlights an element of intellectual elitism in Godwin's vision of social change. In that vision, the gradual transition to an anarchist form of social life would be guided by reason (knowledge), but it is the intellectual elite who will be the source of this reason.

15. The following information on Kropotkin is based on several sources, including J. S. K. (1921), Baldwin ([1927a] 2002, [1927b] 2002), and Shub (1953).

greatest of all the anarchists" (Shub 1953:227), was born into an aristocratic family in Moscow, Russia. In fact, he was born a prince, but he apparently rejected the title during his youth (Baldwin [1927b] 2002). He entered military school when he was 13 and later became an officer in the army. In 1867, he resigned from the service and enrolled at the university in St. Petersburg, where he studied mathematics and geography. Kropotkin eventually became well respected for his geographic studies of various regions of Europe and Asia (see J. S. K. 1921). But he was not just a scientist; he also was an activist and a social theorist. He held memberships in the International Working Men's Association, the Jura Federation, and the "Circle of Tchaykovsky," organizations that to varying degrees embodied revolutionary currents of communism and anarchism (see Baldwin [1927b] 2002). In 1874 Kropotkin's association with the revolutionary movement in Russia against the tsar resulted in his imprisonment.[16] After more than a year of confinement, he escaped and fled to England. Over the next four decades Kropotkin resided in Switzerland and France (where he was once again imprisoned), but he spent most of these years in England. In 1917, after more than forty years of living in exile, he returned to Russia, and it is there that he died in 1921.

Kropotkin's intellectual orientation involved a combination of scientific, anarchist, and communist thought. He held that anarchism "must be treated by the same methods as the natural sciences . . . on the solid basis of induction applied to human institutions" (in Baldwin [1927b] 2002:21; also see Kropotkin [1905] 1975:118). He also had an interest in social evolution, but he rejected social Darwinism. Rather than framing human evolution in competitive terms, he viewed cooperation as more important for purposes of human adaptation and survival. On this basis, Kropotkin proposed a form of anarchist communism, a theory that opposes both the existence of coercive governments and class hierarchies based on private property. For Kropotkin ([1905] 1975:118), ". . . anarchist communism is the only form of communism that has any chance of being accepted in civilized societies. . . ." Predictably, he "opposed Lenin from the start . . ." (Shub 1953:227). He was critical of Marx and very critical of the government instituted by Lenin and the Bolsheviks following the Russian Revolution. In addition, like most anarchists, he was critical of organized religion; in fact, he suggested that priests support unjust laws that often further their selfish interests (see Kropotkin 1886:10).

Kropotkin's most important works include *The Conquest of Bread* (1892), *Memoirs of a Revolutionist* (1899), *Fields, Factories, and Workshops* (1899), and *Mutual Aid* (1902). He also produced several publications that directly address the subject matter of criminology: *Law and Authority: An Anarchist Essay* (1886), *In Russian and French Prisons* (1887), and "Prisons and Their

---

16. Kropotkin was more willing than Godwin and Tolstoy to support some violence in the pursuit of his anarchist ideal. He regarded revolutions as a natural phenomenon in the evolution of human societies, although he did encourage efforts to keep their damage to a minimum (see Baldwin [1927a] 2002, [1927b] 2002).

Moral Influence on Prisoners" (1887).[17] The first of these, *Law and Authority*, was one of Kropotkin's "revolutionary pamphlets" and is presented in Chapter 16. It provides a critique of law and punishment, institutions that are said to protect the interests of the "dominant minority" and cause crime. This selection offers a useful introduction to anarchist criminology.

Anarchist thought on law, crime, and punishment was quite visible during the nineteenth century and into the early twentieth century. However, by the 1930s, it lost much of its appeal and visibility. But this was not the end of anarchism; it did not disappear entirely and began to reemerge during the 1960s. In criminology, it appeared explicitly during the 1970s largely through the work of Harold Pepinsky (1978), Larry Tifft (1979), and Dennis Sullivan (Tifft and Sullivan 1980); it then received additional support from the writings of Jeff Ferrell (1993).[18] Although anarchist theory sometimes is overlooked by the textbooks of criminology, it nevertheless occupies a noteworthy place in the history of critical criminology. Its critiques of punishment are congruent with many of the views expressed in the writings of contemporary penal abolitionism, peacemaking criminology, and restorative justice.

Feminist Criminology

While the early Marxist and anarchist theorists drew attention to class biases in the law, the early feminists drew attention to gender biases.[19] Over the course of the nineteenth century, several prominent researchers acknowledged and attempted to explain the common observation that women commit fewer crimes than men (the "gender-ratio problem"). As noted previously, the relationship between sex and crime was addressed by the moral statisticians in the 1830s (e.g., Quetelet [1835] 1968) and, at the end of the nineteenth century, by the Italian school (e.g., Lombroso and Ferrero [1893] 1903). However, it was among the early feminist scholars

---

17. Roger N. Baldwin (2002:219) states that the essay "Prisons and Their Moral Influence on Prisoners" is based on a speech delivered by Kropotkin in 1877. However, he also notes that it was prompted by Kropotkin's prison experience in France during the years 1883–1886. With this in mind, and given that this essay also refers to the work of Enrico Ferri (who did not graduate from the University of Bologna until 1877 and did not publish his *Criminal Sociology* until the 1880s), it seems likely that the speech Baldwin referred to actually occurred in 1887 or later. Accordingly, 1887 has been used as the date of this essay.

18. Drawing on the work of Paul Feyerabend (1975), I have presented an argument supporting a form of anarchism in criminological research, an orientation that opposes the privileging of particular methods of inquiry (see DiCristina 1995). Of course, Kropotkin probably would question my lack of enthusiasm for the application of the methods of the natural sciences in criminological research.

19. Some of the early feminists also were outspoken critics of slavery and questioned class-based inequities. This concern for multiple forms of oppression has continued and has even been extended. As Jody Miller (2003:15) notes, "contemporary feminist scholars strive to be attentive to the interlocking nature of race, class, and gender oppression. . . ." (Also see Jurik 1999.) In this connection, feminists sometimes sound a lot like anarchists. "Feminism," writes Jeanne Flavin and Amy Desautels (2006:23), "gives great weight to identifying strategies for social change and ending domination in all its forms." Indeed, feminism and anarchism have been associated in some ways for more than two centuries—for instance, through the relationship between Mary Wollstonecraft and William Godwin and in the works of Emma Goldman.

that patriarchal arrangements, and the injustices they create and maintain, became a central concern.

Over the past two centuries, several overlapping branches of feminism have emerged. Today a distinction frequently is drawn among liberal, radical, Marxist, socialist, and postmodern feminism. To this list, we also may add multicultural and materialist feminism. Each variation of feminism, in turn, implies an alternative form of feminist criminology, and most of these forms represent separate yet overlapping branches of critical criminology.[20] The critical forms of feminist criminology share several qualities.[21] First, to borrow the words of Meda Chesney-Lind and Barbara Bloom (1997:45), they oppose "the overall masculinist nature of criminology by pointing to the repeated omission and misrepresentation of women in criminological theory." Criminology is a field dominated by men, and this is reflected in its theories and research. While the works of mainstream nineteenth-century criminology did not overlook women's crime entirely, the nature of women's crime and women's victimization (e.g., wife battery) generally were treated as subjects of secondary significance.

Second, the critical forms of feminist criminology emphasize gender as not only an important sociological concept but also an important criminological concept. They maintain that the examination of gender is necessary to resolve the "gender-ratio problem"; it seems indispensable when attempting to provide an adequate explanation of the overrepresentation of men in both official and unofficial crime statistics. In fact, gender may be the most stable predictor of criminal behavior cross-nationally and historically. Age often is presented as a strong predictor of criminal behavior, with young people portrayed as having a higher propensity for crime. But this relationship tends to be reversed when "suite crimes" are examined. Such crimes are primarily the work of adults in their 30s and older because, at a minimum, very few young people occupy an economic or political position that gives them the opportunity to commit such crimes. In contrast, gender appears to relate to "suite crime" in roughly the same way that it relates to "street crime"; men are overrepresented in both cases. What is more, through the analysis of gender, feminists also draw attention to the "generalizability problem": the shortcomings associated with attempts to extend popular theories of men's crime to women's crime. Such theories typically do not include gender as a variable.

Third, the critical forms of feminist criminology embrace rich descriptive (qualitative) studies—especially research that centers on the lives and experiences of women who have been victims, have engaged in crime, have been punished, and have worked within the criminal justice system. Feminists do not universally reject quantitative research and the possibility of objective knowledge, but many will question both. Feminists commonly maintain that some variables are not readily quantifiable, and that in these cases quantification results in superficial and often misleading information. Moreover,

---

20. Liberal feminism may be the only branch of feminist criminology that resides outside of critical criminology.

21. The following list of shared qualities is derived primarily from Chesney-Lind and Bloom (1997), Jurik (1999), Wonders (1999), Miller (2003), and Flavin and Desautels (2006).

they commonly emphasize the socially constructed and gendered nature of knowledge. This clearly is the case among postmodern feminists, where multiple images of reality are acknowledged and the idea of absolute truth is discredited.[22] They maintain that "identity—difference based on race, class, gender, or other categories—is not a fact but is instead socially constructed by the larger society," especially by the subpopulations that have the greatest power (Wonders 1999:117). Postmodern feminists add that the construction of such differences contributes to oppression.

Finally, the critical forms of feminist criminology advocate fundamental changes in the culture and social structure of society to eliminate the exploitation and oppression of women and, frequently, other groups. They challenge patriarchal beliefs that rationalize the subjugation of women and that discourage women from actively trying to improve their social position. Likewise, they challenge patriarchal institutional arrangements—including oppressive family structures, economic structures, and political arrangements.

The eighteenth- and nineteenth-century feminist scholars, theorists such as Harriet Martineau, have received little attention from both mainstream and critical criminologists. This, in part, is due to the fact that among their writings there appear to be relatively few direct and extensive discussions of criminal law, crime, or punishment.[23] Yet studies of criminological interest do exist in this literature. Martineau's *Society in America* (1837), for instance, includes analyses that anticipate not only noteworthy views of twentieth-century feminist scholarship but also views of contemporary critical criminology.

Harriet Martineau (1802–1876) was born into a middle-class family in Norwich, England.[24] Despite the obstacles of being a woman in a very patriarchal society and losing her hearing during adolescence, Martineau went on to become an accomplished author and sociologist. She made a significant contribution to the founding of sociology, and it may even be argued that she was the discipline's "founding mother" as well as the "founder of feminist sociology" (see Lengermann and Niebrugge-Brantley 2000). Her *Illustrations of Political Economy*, a series of stories that demonstrate various principles of

---

22. Feminist epistemologies include "feminist empiricism," standpoint feminism, and postmodern feminism (see Flavin and Desautels 2006).

23. During the nineteenth century several women made significant contributions to criminology. For instance, Mary Carpenter, an English social reformer, wrote extensively on juvenile delinquency and corrections (e.g., Carpenter 1851, 1853, [1864] 1969). Important contributions also were made by Pauline Tarnowsky (1889) and Ida B. Wells-Barnett ([1894] 1969). Tarnowsky conducted research within the tradition of the Italian school (specifically, criminal anthropology), while Wells-Barnett's research on lynching represents a precursor to the development of critical race theory. In fact, Wells-Barnett has been described as a "lifelong activist on behalf of African-American and women's rights" (Lengermann and Niebrugge-Brantley 2000:313).

24. The life and work of Martineau have been examined in a number of books. She wrote an autobiography in 1855, which was later edited by Maria Weston Chapman and published in 1877. Since that time, several studies of Martineau's work have been written; see Wheatley (1957), Webb (1960), and Hill and Hoecker-Drysdale (2002). Brief discussions of Martineau's contribution to sociology can be found in Lipset (1962) and Lengermann and Niebrugge-Brantley (2000).

sociology, was published from 1832 to 1834. From 1836 to 1837, her best-known work, *Society in America*, was published in three volumes. A year later she published *How to Observe Morals and Manners*, which Seymour Martin Lipset (1962:7) described as possibly "the first book on the methodology of social research." Martineau also provided an influential translation of Auguste Comte's *Positive Philosophy*, which included substantial editing. Overall, while she favored reform over revolutionary change and apparently opposed the socialist standpoint on several economic issues,[25] her work contained a clear critical current in that she was a strong supporter of women's rights and the abolition of slavery. Like many contemporary feminists, Martineau examined social problems related to gender, race, and class;[26] she also embraced qualitative research.

Martineau's *Society in America* certainly had a critical edge, especially at the time it was written. Chapter 17 presents two selections from this work. In the first reading ("Allegiance to Law"), she describes a tendency in American society to overlook some very harmful acts by well-respected citizens—that is, a tendency to redefine or ignore certain crimes committed by middle- and upper-class white males ("gentlemen"). In the second reading ("Political Non-Existence of Women"), she addresses the question: How can a democracy apply a law in a just manner to a group when that group had no input regarding its content? In self-described democracies where women, not to mention racial minorities and the poor, have little or no opportunity to participate in the political process, is it just to apply the laws to any of these subpopulations? The tendency to overlook harmful acts of the elite (i.e., the failure to treat such acts as crimes) and the political exclusion of various segments of society are central concerns of critical criminology and, as Martineau's work confirms, they are not new concerns.

Critical Race Theory

Just as class and gender oppression have been subjects of concern for a long time, so has oppression based on race and ethnicity. This, of course, was a concern of Martineau and other critics of slavery. But more generally, it was a concern of the researchers who constructed much of the foundation for the emergence of critical race theory. Racism and ethnocentrism, just like class bias and sexism, were often explicit in the works of eighteenth- and nineteenth-century researchers. From the classical school, to the Italian school, and on to the French school, racist and ethnocentric assumptions were rarely hidden as they tend to be today. Indeed, as several selections in this anthology

---

25. In a review of R. K. Webb's *Harriet Martineau: A Radical Victorian*, John Saville (1960:293) provided a brief comment on Martineau's rather uncritical position regarding several important economic issues: "She was a superb popularizer of *laissez faire* dogmas; a firm supporter of the New Poor Law; an opponent of the ten hour Bill; . . . an opponent of trade unions in anything but their friendly society rôle which she thought in any case incompatible with their trade function; a bitter critic of the Builders' strike of 1859–60; . . ." On the other hand, Martineau also commented: "Wealth is power; and large amounts of power ought not to rest in the hands of individuals" (in Lipset 1962:41).

26. Patricia Madoo Lengermann and Jill Niebrugge-Brantley (2000:296) note that in her studies of "the wage labor of working-class women," Martineau "brings together the double oppressions of class and gender."

demonstrate, these assumptions often were presented as if they were well-known facts. Nonetheless, here and there researchers came forward who questioned these "facts."

Critical race theory (CRT), as it is commonly described, is a relatively new area of scholarship and activism.[27] It emerged during the 1970s as a form of legal scholarship, firmly established itself as a distinct movement by the end of the 1980s, and has found a niche within not only law but also education, philosophy, political science, sociology, and criminology. Some of the key contributors to CRT are Derrick Bell, Kimberlé W. Crenshaw, Richard Delgado, Alan Freeman, Charles R. Lawrence III, Mari J. Matsuda, and Patricia J. Williams. The core perspectives of CRT have been influenced by traditional civil rights scholarship, critical legal studies, and feminist thought. CRT represents an effort to go beyond traditional civil rights scholarship and examine issues of "race, racism, and power" at a more fundamental level (Delgado and Stefancic 2001:2–3). It acknowledges and embraces the experiences of racial minorities and "challenges the experience of whites as the normative standard" (Taylor 1998:122). It maintains that racism is common and, while sometimes subtle, is embedded in the basic social institutions of society, including the criminal justice system. Racism, from this viewpoint, helps to maintain a distribution of wealth, power, and prestige that favors the white population, especially the white elites. CRT scholars also challenge the contention that there is some intrinsic property, some essence, that distinguishes one race from another. Instead, they hold that race is a social construct. As Richard Delgado and Jean Stefancic (2001:7) note, ". . . races are categories that society invents, manipulates, or retires when convenient."

Katherine K. Russell (1999) has identified a few basic themes of critical race theory and its approach to criminology. She suggests that criminologists who embrace CRT maintain that we must understand racism if we wish to develop an adequate understanding of the criminal justice system. An examination of racism is necessary to understand how the system is "used to maintain White supremacy and the subordination of people of color" (p. 180). But the pursuit of understanding is not enough. CRT also calls for efforts to make fundamental changes in the criminal justice system and other social institutions, changes that will acknowledge and address "historical and contemporary injustices" (p. 180). Consequently, much like other critical criminologists, CRT scholars commonly make their values explicit in their writings; they rarely engage in the struggle to appear value-neutral.

Although critical race theory generally is described as emerging during the 1970s, the spirit of this perspective appears to have been around for more than a century. Indeed, much of its foundation was constructed during the 1800s and early 1900s through the work of several researchers and activists, including Frederick Douglas, Ida B. Wells-Barnett, and W. E. B. Du Bois. Of these scholars, Du Bois arguably made the most influential contribution to

---

27. The following description of critical race theory is based primarily on Taylor (1998), Gordon (1999), Russell (1999), and Delgado and Stefancic (2001).

the emergence of CRT (see Gordon 1999), and he also provided an extensive analysis of race and crime.

William Edward Burghardt Du Bois (1868–1963) was an African American scholar who was born soon after the Civil War in Barrington, Massachusetts.[28] He received a Ph.D. in history from Harvard in 1895 and held academic positions at Wilberforce University, the University of Pennsylvania, and Atlanta University. Although his Ph.D. was in history, most of his research was sociological. In fact, he was the chair of the Sociology Department at Atlanta University from 1934 until 1944. Du Bois also was an influential activist who supported civil rights and workers' rights. He was one of the founders of the National Association for the Advancement of Colored People (NAACP), he was a key contributor to the Pan-African Congresses, and he was a critic of capitalism and an advocate of socialism. While his work was largely overlooked by sociologists throughout much of the twentieth century, he made an important contribution to the field. In fact, Du Bois has been referred to as "arguably one of the most brilliant social theorists this country has ever produced, and without question ... one of the most imaginative, perceptive, and prolific founders of the sociological discipline—American or otherwise" (Zuckerman 2004:3). Du Bois conducted groundbreaking studies in urban sociology, rural sociology, the sociology of religion, and the sociology of race; and he examined issues concerning economics, international relations, the family, and other social phenomena (see Zuckerman 2004). Moreover, he was one of the first American criminologists and "a pioneer in sociological criminology" (Gabbidon 1996, 2001:590).

Du Bois was a prolific writer who addressed issues of race, crime, and criminal justice in several publications, including "The Negro and Crime" (1899a), *The Philadelphia Negro: A Social Study* (1899b), "The Spawn of Slavery: The Convict Lease System in the South" (1901), *The Black North in 1901* ([1901] 1969), *Some Notes on Negro Crime, Particularly in Georgia* (1904), and *Morals and Manners Among Negro Americans* (1914). As the dates of these publications indicate, his research began during the late nineteenth century and continued well into the twentieth century. His work has been overlooked by many criminologists, but it was pioneering, rich in empirical data and theory. Du Bois embraced social science and engaged in both quantitative and qualitative research. He rejected the biological reasoning of his era and explained African American crime rates primarily in terms of social phenomena such as migration and the resulting "lack of harmony" with the social environment, the transition from slavery to freedom, discrimination, and a lack of opportunities. His critical orientation toward criminal justice and his concern with both class and race are captured in this quotation: "... in convictions by human courts the rich always are favored somewhat at the expense of the poor, the upper classes at the expense of the unfortunate classes, and whites at the expense of Negroes" (Du Bois 1899b:249).

---

28. The following biographical information is based on several sources, including Gabbidon (1996, 2001), Wilson et al. (1996), and Zuckerman (2004).

The final chapter of this book contains an excerpt from the *The Philadelphia Negro* in which Du Bois explores "The Negro Criminal."[29] This selection, written by Du Bois relatively early in his career, represents an important sociological examination of the nature of crime by African Americans during the late nineteenth century. It also represents early opposition to the biological explanations of race and crime that were popular at the time and remained popular well into the twentieth century.[30]

A Note on the Idea of Progress

The theories of the early Marxists, anarchists, feminists, and critical race scholars were a significant addition to the list of criminological viewpoints that had been constructed by the end of the nineteenth century. By this time, criminology had a multidisciplinary orientation that included a wide variety of theories from across the political spectrum, a characteristic that it still possesses today.

However, I do not wish to imply that criminology *progressed* through a series of stages represented by the various divisions covered in this book. The discussions of the classical school, the Italian school, the French school, and the early critical theories—in that order—should not be read as suggesting a sequence of stages through which criminological knowledge moved closer and closer to the truth. These divisions represent different paradigms (or sets of paradigms) and, thus, offer different understandings of law, criminals, and punishment. The development of criminology can be described in terms of the proliferation of theories and data, which may be categorized in various ways, but I do not wish to imply the notion of progress. That said, each of the divisions covered in this book has left a lasting imprint on the history of criminology. The classical school, the Italian school, and the French school, at one time or another, occupied a central (if not dominant) position in the field; the various critical theories, on the other hand, resided primarily on the margins of criminology—opposing the mainstream and, in some ways, the discipline itself.

REFERENCES

Baldwin, Roger N., ed. 2002. *Anarchism: A Collection of Revolutionary Writings by Peter Kropotkin*. Mineola, NY: Dover Publications.

Baldwin, Roger N. [1927a] 2002. "The Significance of Kropotkin's Life and Teaching." In *Anarchism: A Collection of Revolutionary Writings by Peter Kropotkin*, edited by Roger N. Baldwin, 1–12. Mineola, NY: Dover Publications.

Baldwin, Roger N. [1927b] 2002. "The Story of Kropotkin's Life." In *Anarchism: A Collection of Revolutionary Writings by Peter Kropotkin*, edited by Roger N. Baldwin, 13–30. Mineola, NY: Dover Publications.

---

29. *The Philadelphia Negro* has been described as "the first definitive study of blacks in American society," "a superb sociology treatise," and "an enduring classic in American scholarship" (Wilson et al. 1996:78–79, 82).

30. Shaun L. Gabbidon, Helen Taylor Greene, and Vernetta D. Young (2002) provide a helpful collection of late-nineteenth- and early-twentieth-century writings in criminology and criminal justice by several African American scholars, including Ida B. Wells-Barnett, W. E. B. Du Bois, Monroe N. Work, E. Franklin Frazier, and Earl R. Moses.

Baradat, Leon P. 1997. *Political Ideologies: Their Origins and Impact.* 6th ed. Upper Saddle River, NJ: Prentice Hall.

Berkman, Alexander. 1925. *The Bolshevik Myth (Diary 1920–1922).* London: Boni and Liveright.

Bonger, William (Willem) A. 1916. *Criminality and Economic Conditions.* Translated by Henry P. Horton. Boston: Little, Brown and Company.

Carpenter, Mary. 1851. *Reformatory Schools: For the Children of the Perishing and Dangerous Classes and for Juvenile Offenders.* London: C. Gilpin.

Carpenter, Mary. 1853. *Juvenile Delinquents, Their Condition and Treatment.* London: W. & F. G. Cash.

Carpenter, Mary. [1864] 1969. *Our Convicts.* Montclair, NJ: Patterson Smith.

Chesney-Lind, Meda, and Barbara Bloom. 1997. "Feminist Criminology: Thinking About Women and Crime." In *Thinking Critically About Crime,* edited by Brian D. MacLean and Dragan Milovanovic, 45–55. Vancouver: Collective Press.

Colvin, Mark, and John Pauly. 1983. "A Critique of Criminology: Toward an Integrated Structural-Marxist Theory of Delinquency Production." *American Journal of Sociology* 89(3):513–551.

Delgado, Richard, and Jean Stefancic. 2001. *Critical Race Theory: An Introduction.* New York: New York University Press.

DiCristina, Bruce. 1995. *Method in Criminology: A Philosophical Primer.* Albany, NY: Harrow and Heston.

Du Bois, W. E. B. 1899a. "The Negro and Crime." *The Independent* 51(May):1355–1357.

Du Bois, W. E. B. 1899b. *The Philadelphia Negro: A Social Study.* Philadelphia: University of Pennsylvania Press.

Du Bois, W. E. B. 1901. "The Spawn of Slavery: The Convict Lease System in the South." *Missionary Review of the World* 14(October):737–745.

Du Bois, W. E. B. [1901] 1969. *The Black North in 1901.* New York: Arno Press.

Du Bois, W. E. B., ed. 1904. *Some Notes on Negro Crime, Particularly in Georgia.* Atlanta, GA: Atlanta University Press.

Du Bois, W. E. B., ed. 1914. *Morals and Manners among Negro Americans.* Atlanta, GA: Atlanta University Press.

Engels, Frederick. [1845] 1887. *The Condition of the Working Class in England in 1844.* Translated by Florence Kelley Wischnewetzky. New York: John W. Lovell Company.

Engels, Frederick. [1847] 1999. "Draft of a Communist Confession of Faith." In *The Communist Manifesto with Related Writings,* edited by John E. Toews, 99–104. Boston: Bedford/St. Martin's.

Engels, Frederick. [1883] 1999. "Speech at Karl Marx's Funeral." In *The Communist Manifesto with Related Writings,* edited by John E. Toews, 164–165. Boston: Bedford/St. Martin's.

Ferrell, Jeff. 1993. *Crimes of Style: Urban Graffiti and the Politics of Criminality.* New York: Garland Publishing.

Ferrell, Jeff. 1997. "Against the Law: Anarchist Criminology." In *Thinking Critically About Crime,* edited by Brian D. MacLean and Dragan Milovanovic, 146–154. Vancouver: Collective Press.

Ferrell, Jeff. 1999. "Anarchist Criminology and Social Justice." In *Social Justice/Criminal Justice: The Maturation of Critical Theory in Law, Crime, and Deviance,* edited by Bruce A. Arrigo, 93–108. Belmont, CA: Wadsworth Publishing Company.

Ferri, Enrico. 1898. *Criminal Sociology,* edited by W. D. Morrison. 3rd ed. (abridged). New York: D. Appleton and Company.

Feyerabend, Paul. 1975. *Against Method: Outline of an Anarchistic Theory of Knowledge*. London: Verso.
Flavin, Jeanne, and Amy Desautels. 2006. "Feminism and Crime." In *Rethinking Gender, Crime, and Justice: Feminist Readings*, edited by Claire M. Renzetti, Lynne Goodstein, and Susan L. Miller, 11–28. Los Angeles: Roxbury Publishing Company.
Foucault, Michel. 1979. *Discipline and Punish: The Birth of the Prison*. Translated by Alan Sheridan. New York: Vintage Books.
Freud, Sigmund. [1930] 1961. *Civilization and Its Discontents*. Translated by James Strachey. New York: W. W. Norton & Company.
Gabbidon, Shaun L. 1996. "An Argument for Including W.E.B. Du Bois in the Criminology and Criminal Justice Literature." *Journal of Criminal Justice Education* 7(1):99–112.
Gabbidon, Shaun L. 2001. "W.E.B. Du Bois: Pioneering American Criminologist." *Journal of Black Studies* 31(5):581–599.
Gabbidon, Shaun L., Helen Taylor Greene, and Vernetta D. Young, eds. 2002. *African American Classics in Criminology and Criminal Justice*. Thousand Oaks, CA: Sage Publications.
Garland, David. 1990. *Punishment and Modern Society: A Study in Social Theory*. Chicago: The University of Chicago Press.
Godwin, William. [1798] 1985. *Enquiry Concerning Political Justice and Its Influence on Modern Morals and Happiness*. 3rd ed. London: Penguin Books.
Goldman, Emma. [1917] 1969. *Anarchism and Other Essays*. 3rd ed. New York: Dover Publications.
Goldman, Emma. 1925. *My Disillusionment in Russia*. London: C. W. Daniel Company.
Gordon, David M. 1973. "Capitalism, Class and Crime in America." *Crime and Delinquency* 19:163–186.
Gordon, Lewis R. 1999. "A Short History of the 'Critical' in Critical Race Theory." *The APA Newsletter on Philosophy and the Black Experience* 98(2):23–26.
Greenberg, David F., ed. 1981. *Crime and Capitalism: Readings in Marxist Criminology*. Palo Alto, CA: Mayfield Publishing Company.
Hall, Walter P. 1948. "Review of *Enquiry Concerning Political Justice and Its Influence on Morals and Happiness*." *The Journal of Modern History* 20(4):345–346.
Hill, Michael R., and Susan Hoecker-Drysdale, eds. 2002. *Harriet Martineau: Theoretical and Methodological Perspectives*. New York: Routledge.
Jenkins, Philip. 1984. "Varieties of Enlightenment Criminology: Beccaria, Godwin, de Sade." *British Journal of Criminology* 24(2):112–130.
J. S. K. 1921. "Prince Kropotkin." *The Geographical Journal* 57(4):316–319.
Jurik, Nancy C. 1999. "Socialist Feminism, Criminology, and Social Justice." In *Social Justice/Criminal Justice: The Maturation of Critical Theory in Law, Crime, and Deviance*, edited by Bruce A. Arrigo, 31–50. Belmont, CA: West/Wadsworth.
Kramnick, Isaac. 1972. "On Anarchism and the Real World: William Godwin and Radical England." *The American Political Science Review* 66(1):114–128.
Kropotkin, Peter (Pierre Kropotkine). 1886. *Law and Authority: An Anarchist Essay*. London: International Publishing Company.
Kropotkin, Peter. [1905] 1975. "Anarchism." In *The Essential Kropotkin*, edited by Emile Capouya and Keitha Tompkins, 108–120. New York: Liveright.
Lengermann, Patricia Madoo, and Jill Niebrugge-Brantley. 2000. "Early Women Sociologists and Classical Sociological Theory: 1830–1930." In *Classical Sociological Theory*, 3rd ed., by George Ritzer, 289–321. Boston: McGraw-Hill.

Lipset, Seymour Martin. 1962. "Harriet Martineau's America." In Harriet Martineau's *Society in America,* edited by Seymour M. Lipset, 5–42. Garden City, NY: Anchor Books.

Lombroso, Cesare, and William Ferrero. [1893] 1903. *The Female Offender.* New York: D. Appleton and Company.

Lynch, Michael J. 2000. "The Power of Oppression: Understanding the History of Criminology as a Science of Oppression." *Critical Criminology* 9(1/2):144–152.

Lynch, Michael J., and W. Byron Groves. 1989. *A Primer in Radical Criminology.* 2nd ed. New York: Harrow and Heston.

Martineau, Harriet. [1855] 1877. *Harriet Martineau's Autobiography,* edited by Maria Weston Chapman. Two vols. Boston: James R. Osgood and Company.

Marx, Karl. [1844] 1964. "Economic and Philosophical Manuscripts." In *Karl Marx: Early Writings,* edited by T. B. Botomore, 61–219. New York: McGraw-Hill.

Marx, Karl. 1915. *Capital: A Critique of Political Economy. Volume I.* Translated by Samuel Moore and Edward Aveling. Chicago: Charles H. Kerr and Company.

Marx, Karl, and Frederick Engels. [1848] 1999. "The Communist Manifesto." Translated by Samuel Moore. In *The Communist Manifesto with Related Writings,* edited by John E. Toews, 62–96. Boston: Bedford/St. Martin's.

Miller, Jody. 2003. "Feminist Criminology." In *Controversies in Critical Criminology,* edited by Martin D. Schwartz and Suzanne E. Hatty, 15–28. Cincinnati, OH: Anderson Publishing Company.

Nielsen, Kai. 1995. "Engels, Friedrich." In *The Cambridge Dictionary of Philosophy,* edited by Robert Audi, 227. Cambridge: University of Cambridge Press.

Pashukanis, Evgeny B. [1924] 1978. *Law and Marxism: A General Theory.* Translated by B. Einhom. London: Ink Links.

Paul, C. Kegan. 1876. *William Godwin: His Friends and Contemporaries.* Boston: Roberts Brothers.

Pepinsky, Harold. 1978. "Communist Anarchism as an Alternative to the Rule of Criminal Law." *Contemporary Crisis* 2:315–327.

Quetelet, Adolphe. [1835] 1968. *A Treatise on Man and the Development of His Faculties.* Translated by R. Knox. New York: Burt Franklin.

Quinney, Richard. 1980. *Class, State, and Crime.* 2nd ed. New York: Longman.

Rusche, Georg, and Otto Kirchheimer. [1939] 2003. *Punishment and Social Structure.* New Brunswick, NJ: Transaction Publishers.

Russell, Katheryn K. 1999. "Critical Race Theory and Social Justice." In *Social Justice/Criminal Justice: The Maturation of Critical Theory in Law, Crime, and Deviance,* edited by Bruce A. Arrigo, 178–188. Belmont, CA: West/Wadsworth.

Saville, John. 1960. "Review of *Harriet Martineau: A Radical Victorian,* by R. K. Webb." *The Economic History Review* 13(2):293–294.

Schwartz, Martin D., and Suzanne E. Hatty. 2003. "Introduction." In *Controversies in Critical Criminology,* edited by Martin D. Schwartz and Suzanne E. Hatty, ix–xvii. Cincinnati, OH: Anderson Publishing.

Shub, David. 1953. "Kropotkin and Lenin." *The Russian Review* 12(4):227–234.

Tarnowsky, Pauline. 1889. *Étude anthropométrique sur les prostituées et les voleuses.* Paris: E. Lecrosnier et Babé.

Taylor, Edward. 1998. "A Primer on Critical Race Theory." *The Journal of Blacks in Higher Education* 19(Spring):122–124.

Tifft, Larry. 1979. "The Coming Redefinition of Crime: An Anarchist Alternative." *Social Problems* 26(4):392–402.

Tifft, Larry, and Dennis Sullivan. 1980. *The Struggle to be Human: Crime, Criminology, and Anarchism.* Orkney, UK: Cienfeugos.

Watkins, Frederick M. 1948. "Godwin's Enquiry Concerning Political Justice." *The Canadian Journal of Economics and Political Science* 14(1):107–112.

Webb, R. K. 1960. *Harriet Martineau: A Radical Victorian*. New York: Columbia University Press.

Wells-Barnett, Ida B. [1894] 1969. *On Lynchings*. New York: Arno.

Wheatley, Vera. 1957. *The Life and Work of Harriet Martineau*. London: Secker and Warburg.

Wilson, William Julius, Gerald Early, David Levering Lewis, Elijah Anderson, James E. Blackwell, Ronald Walters, and Chuck Stone. 1996. "Du Bois' *The Philadelphia Negro*: 100 Years Later." *The Journal of Blacks in Higher Education* 11(Spring):78–84.

Wonders, Nancy A. 1999. "Postmodern Feminist Criminology and Social Justice." In *Social Justice/Criminal Justice: The Maturation of Critical Theory in Law, Crime, and Deviance*, edited by Bruce A. Arrigo, 111–128. Belmont, CA: West/Wadsworth.

Zuckerman, Phil, ed. 2004. *The Social Theory of W.E.B. Du Bois*. Thousand Oaks, CA: Pine Forge Press.

CHAPTER 14

KARL MARX

The reading in this chapter is from Karl Marx's *Capital: A Critique of Political Economy, Volume I* (1915), pp. 788–797 and 805–814; translated by Samuel Moore and Edward Aveling; Chicago: Charles H. Kerr and Company. The first edition of *Capital* was published in German in 1867; a second German edition was published in 1873, a third in 1883, and a fourth in 1890. The selection presented here comes from a revision of Moore and Aveling's 1887 translation of the third German edition (edited by Frederick Engels); this translation was "revised and amplified according to the fourth German edition by Ernest Untermann." Chapter numbers have been removed and the footnotes have been renumbered. The full text of this version of *Capital* is available through the HathiTrust Digital Library (hathitrust.org).

Marx was writing during the mid-nineteenth century, just after the establishment of moral statistics and just before the emergence of the Italian and French schools. Although he did not write extensively on issues of law, crime, and punishment, he periodically provided an analysis that directly addressed an important issue of criminology. The reading in this chapter presents Marx's interpretation of the development and initial control of the proletariat. In this reading, he describes widespread class bias in the laws of England and other Western European societies on the threshold of capitalism. Marx begins by noting that the birth of modern capitalism depended on the existence of wage laborers; without a relatively large population of such laborers, it could not exist. From his viewpoint, starting around the late fifteenth century, large numbers of relatively self-sufficient peasants began to be forced from the lands they had farmed for generations. They were driven from feudal property, church property, common lands, and state lands. In other words, the creation of the proletariat occurred through the theft of land on a massive scale. Marx then argues that many of the victims of these crimes, many of the displaced peasants, could not find work immediately nor could they effectively adapt to their new circumstances. Thus "(t)hey were turned *en masse* into beggars, robbers, vagabonds. . . ." The response, Marx continues, was "a bloody legislation against vagabondage" that treated these victims as "'voluntary' criminals."

In short, the reading in this chapter represents a classic illustration of one of the principal concerns of critical criminologists—namely, that the laws do not protect everyone equally but instead serve the interests of a powerful minority often at the expense of the weaker segments of society. Although this inequity was more blatant in the past, critical theorists argue that it remains common in contemporary societies.

from CAPITAL: A CRITIQUE OF POLITICAL ECONOMY, VOLUME I
by Karl Marx

EXPROPRIATION OF THE AGRICULTURAL POPULATION FROM THE LAND

In England, serfdom had practically disappeared in the last part of the 14th century. The immense majority of the population[1] consisted then, and to a still larger extent, in the 15th century, of free peasant proprietors, whatever was the feudal title under which their right of property was hidden. In the larger seignorial domains, the old bailiff, himself a serf, was displaced by the free farmer. The wage-labourers of agriculture consisted partly of peasants, who utilised their leisure time by working on the large estates, partly of an independent special class of wage-labourers, relatively and absolutely few in numbers. The latter also were practically at the same time peasant farmers, since, besides their wages, they had alloted to them arable land to the extent of 4 or more acres, together with their cottages. Besides they, with the rest of the peasants, enjoyed the usufruct of the common land, which gave pasture to their cattle, furnished them with timber, fire-wood, turf, &c.[2] In all countries of Europe, feudal production is characterised by division of the soil amongst the greatest possible number of sub-feudatories. The might of the feudal lord, like that of the sovereign, depended not on the length of his rent roll, but on the number of his subjects, and the latter depended on the number of peasant proprietors.[3] Although, therefore, the English land, after the Norman conquest, was distributed in gigantic baronies, one of which often included some 900 of the old Anglo-Saxon lord-ships, it was bestrewn with small peasant properties, only here and there interspersed with great seignorial domains. Such conditions, together with the prosperity of the towns so characteristic of the 15th century, allowed of that wealth of the people which Chancellor Fortescue so eloquently paints in his "Laudes legum Angliæ;" but it excluded the possibility of capitalistic wealth.

The prelude of the revolution that laid the foundation of the capitalist mode of production, was played in the last third of the 15th, and the first decade of the 16th century. A mass of free proletarians was hurled on the labour-market by the breaking-up of the bands of feudal retainers, who, as Sir James Steuart well says, "everywhere uselessly filled house and castle." Although the royal power, itself a product of bourgeois development, in its strife after absolute sovereignty forcibly hastened on the dissolution of these bands of retainers, it was by no means the sole cause of it. In insolent conflict with king and parliament, the great feudal lords created an incomparably larger proletariat by the forcible driving of the peasantry from the land, to which the latter had the same feudal right as the lord himself, and by the usurpation of the common lands. The rapid rise of the Flemish wool manufactures, and the corresponding rise in the price of wool in England, gave the direct impulse to these evictions. The old nobility had been devoured by the great feudal wars. The new nobility was the child of its time, for which money was the power of all powers. Transformation of arable land into sheep-walks was, therefore, its cry. Harrison, in his "Description of England,

---

1. "The petty proprietors who cultivated their own fields with their own hands, and enjoyed a modest competence . . . then formed a much more important part of the nation than at present. If we may trust the best statistical writers of that age, not less than 160,000 proprietors who, with their families, must have made up more than a seventh of the whole population, derived their subsistence from little freehold estates. The average income of these small landlords . . . was estimated at between £60 and £70 a year. It was computed that the number of persons who tilled their own land was greater than the number of those who farmed the land of others." Macaulay: History of England, 10th ed., 1854, I. p. 333, 334. Even in the last third of the 17th century, 4/5 of the English people were agricultural. (1. c., p. 413.) I quote Macaulay, because as systematic falsifier of history he minimises as much as possible facts of this kind.

2. We must never forget that even the serf was not only the owner, if but a tribute-paying owner, of the piece of land attached to his house, but also a co-possessor of the common land. "Le paysan y (in Silesia, under Frederick II.) est serf." Nevertheless, these serfs possess common lands. "On n' a pas pu encore engager les Silésiens au partage des communes, tandis que dans la Nouvelle Marche, il n'y a guère de village où ce partage ne soit exécuté' avec le plus grand succès." (Mirabeau: De la Monarchie Prussienne. Londres, 1788, t. ii., pp. 125, 126.)

3. Japan, with its purely feudal organisation of landed property and its developed *petite culture,* gives a much truer picture of the European middle ages than all our history books, dictated as these are, for the most part, by bourgeois prejudices. It is very convenient to be "liberal" at the expense of the middle ages.

prefixed to Holinshed's Chronicle," describes how the expropriation of small peasants is ruining the country. "What care our great encroachers?" The dwellings of the peasants and the cottages of the labourers were razed to the ground or doomed to decay. "If," says Harrison, "the old records of euerie manour be sought . . . it will soon appear that in some manour seventeene, eighteene, or twentie houses are shrunk . . . that England was neuer less furnished with people than at the present. . . . Of cities and townes either utterly decaied or more than a quarter or half diminished, though some one be a little increased here or there; of townes pulled downe for sheepe-walks, and no more but the lordships now standing in them . . . I could saie some what." The complaints of these old chroniclers are always exaggerated, but they reflect faithfully the impression made on contemporaries by the revolution in the conditions of production. A comparison of the writings of Chancellor Fortescue and Thomas More reveals the gulf between the 15th and 16th century. As Thornton rightly has it, the English working-class was precipitated without any transition from its golden into its iron age.

Legislation was terrified at this revolution. It did not yet stand on that height of civilisation where the "wealth of the nation" (*i.e.*, the formation of capital, and the reckless exploitation and impoverishing of the mass of the people) figure as the *ultima Thule* of all state-craft. In his history of Henry VII., Bacon says: "Inclosures at that time (1489) began to be more frequent, whereby arable land (which could not be manured without people and families) was turned into pasture, which was easily rid by a few herdsmen; and tenancies for years, lives, and at will (whereupon much of the yeomanry lived) were turned into demesnes. This bred a decay of people, and (by consequence) a decay of towns, churches, tithes, and the like. . . . In remedying of this inconvenience the king's wisdom was admirable, and the parliament at that time . . . they took a course to take away depopulating inclosures, and depopulating pasturage." An Act of Henry VII., 1489, cap. 19, forbad the destruction of all "houses of husbandry" to which at least 20 acres of land belonged. By an Act, 25 Henry VIII., the same law was renewed. It recites, among other things, that many farms and large flocks of cattle, especially of sheep, are concentrated in the hands of a few men, whereby the rent of land has much risen and tillage has fallen off, churches and houses have been pulled down, and marvellous numbers of people have been deprived of the means wherewith to maintain themselves and their families. The Act, therefore, ordains the rebuilding of the decayed farmsteads, and fixes a proportion between corn land and pasture land, &c. An Act of 1533 recites that some owners possess 24,000 sheep, and limits the number to be owned to 2000.[4] The cry of the people and the legislation directed, for 150 years after Henry VII., against the appropriation of the small farmers and peasants, were alike fruitless. The secret of their inefficiency Bacon, without knowing it, reveals to us. "The device of King Henry VII.," says Bacon, in his "Essays, Civil and Moral," Essay 29, "was profound and admirable, in making farms and houses of husbandry of a standard; that is, maintained with such a proportion of land unto them as may breed a subject to live in convenient plenty, and no servile condition, and to keep the plough in the hands of the owners and not mere hirelings."[5] What the capital system demanded was, on the other hand, a degraded and almost servile condition of the mass of the people, the transformation of them into mercenaries, and of their means of labour into capital. During this transformation period, legislation also strove to retain the 4 acres of land by the cottage of the agricultural wage-labourer, and forbad him to take lodgers into his cottage. In the reign of James I. 1627, Roger Crocker of Front Mill, was condemned for having built a cottage on the manor of Front Mill without 4 acres of land attached to the same in perpetuity. As late as Charles I.'s

---

4. In his "Utopia," Thomas More says, that in England "your shepe that were wont to be so meke and tame, and so smal eaters, now, as I heare saye, be become so great devourers and so wylde that they eate up, and swallow downe, the very men themselfes." "Utopia," transl. by Robinson., ed. Arber, Lond., 1869, p. 41.

5. Bacon shows the connexion between a free, well-to-do peasantry and good infantry. "This did wonderfully concern the might and mannerhood of the kingdom to have farms as it were of a standard sufficient to maintain an able body out of penury, and did in effect amortize a great part of the lands of the kingdom unto the hold and occupation of the yeomanry or middle people, of a condition between gentlemen, and cottagers and peasants. . . . For it hath been held by the general opinion of men of best judgment in the wars . . . that the principal strength of an army consisteth in the infantry or foot. And to make good infantry it requireth men bred, not in a servile or indigent fashion, but in some free and plentiful manner. Therefore, if a state run most to noblemen and gentlemen, and that the husbandmen and ploughmen be but as their workfolk and labourers, or else mere cottages (which are but hous'd beggars), you may have a good cavalry, but never good stable bands of foot. . . . And this is to be seen in France, and Italy, and some other parts abroad, where in effect all is noblesse or peasantry . . . insomuch that they are inforced to employ mercenary bands of Switzers and the like, for their battalions of foot; whereby also it comes to pass that those nations have much people and few soldiers." ("The Reign of Henry VII." Verbatim reprint from Kennet's England. Ed. 1719. Lond., 1870, p. 808.)

reign, 1638, a royal commission was appointed to enforce the carrying out of the old laws, especially that referring to the 4 acres of land. Even in Cromwell's time, the building of a house within 4 miles of London was forbidden unless it was endowed with 4 acres of land. As late as the first half of the 18th century complaint is made if the cottage of the agricultural labourer has not an adjunct of one or two acres of land. Nowadays he is lucky if it is furnished with a little garden, or if he may rent, far away from his cottage, a few roods. "Landlords and farmers," says Dr. Hunter, "work here hand in hand. A few acres to the cottage would make the labourers too independent."[6]

The process of forcible expropriation of the people received in the 16th century a new and frightful impulse from the Reformation, and from the consequent colossal spoliation of the church property. The Catholic church was, at the time of the Reformation, feudal proprietor of a great part of the English land. The suppression of the monasteries, &c., hurled their inmates into the proletariat. The estates of the church were to a large extent given away to rapacious royal favourites, or sold at a nominal price to speculating farmers and citizens, who drove out, *en masse*, the hereditary sub-tenants and threw their holdings into one. The legally guaranteed property of the poorer folk in a part of the church's tithes was tacitly confiscated.[7] "Pauper ubique jacet," cried Queen Elizabeth, after a journey through England. In the 43rd year of her reign the nation was obliged to recognise pauperism officially by the introduction of a poor-rate. "The authors of this law seem to have been ashamed to state the grounds of it, for [contrary to traditional usage] it has no preamble whatever."[8] By the 16th of Charles I., ch. 4, it was declared perpetual, and in fact only in 1834 did it take a new and harsher form.[9]

These immediate results of the Reformation were not its most lasting ones. The property of the church formed the religious bulwark of the traditional conditions of landed property. With its fall these were no longer tenable.[10]

Even in the last decade of the 17th century, the yeomanry, the class of independent peasants, were more numerous than the class of farmers. They had formed the backbone of Cromwell's strength, and, even according to the confession of Macaulay, stood in favourable contrast to the drunken squires and to their servants, the country clergy, who had to marry their master's cast-off mistresses. About 1750,

---

6. Dr. Hunter, l. c., p. 134. "The quantity of land assigned (in the old laws) would now be judged too great for labourers, and rather as likely to convert them into small farmers." George Roberts: "The Social History of the People of the Southern Counties of England in past centuries." Lond., 1856, pp. 184–185.)

7. "The right of the poor to share in the tithe, is established by the tenour of ancient statutes." (Tuckett, l. c., Vol. II., pp. 804–805.)

8. William Cobbett: "A History of the Protestant Reformation," §471.

9. The "spirit" of Protestantism may be seen from the following, among other things. In the south of England certain landed proprietors and well-to-do farmers put their heads together and propounded ten questions as to the right interpretation of the poor-law of Elizabeth. These they laid before a celebrated jurist of that time, Sergeant Snigge (later a judge under James I.) for his opinion. "Question 9—Some of the more wealthy farmers in the parish have devised a skilful mode by which all the trouble of executing this Act (the 43rd of Elizabeth) might be avoided. They have proposed that we shall erect a prison in the parish, and then give notice to the neighbourhood, that if any persons are disposed to farm the poor of this parish, they do give in sealed proposals, on a certain day, of the lowest price at which they will take them off our hands; and that they will be authorised to refuse to any one unless he be shut up in the aforesaid prison. The proposers of this plan conceive that there will be found in the adjoining counties, persons, who, being unwilling to labour and not possessing substance or credit to take a farm or ship, so as to live without labour, may be induced to make a very advantageous offer to the parish. If any of the poor perish under the contractor's care, the sin will lie at his door, as the parish will have done its duty by them. We are, however, apprehensive that the present Act (43rd of Elizabeth) will not warrant a prudential measure of this kind; but you are to learn that the rest of the freeholders of the county, and of the adjoining county of B, will very readily join in instructing their members to propose an Act to enable the parish to contract with a person to lock up and work the poor; and to declare that if any person shall refuse to be so locked up and worked, he shall be entitled to no relief. This, it is hoped, will prevent persons in distress from wanting relief, and be the means of keeping down parishes." (R. Blakey: "The History of Political Literature from the earliest Times." Lond., 1855, Vol. II., pp. 84–85.) In Scotland, the abolition of serfdom took place some centuries later than in England. Even in 1698, Fletcher of Saltoun, declared in the Scotch parliament, "The number of beggars in Scotland is reckoned at not less than 200,000. The only remedy that I, a republican on principle can suggest, is to restore the old state of serfdom, to make slaves of all those who are unable to provide for their own subsistence." Eden, l. c., Book I., ch. 1, pp. 60–61, says, "The decrease of villenage seems necessarily to have been the era of the origin of the poor. Manufactures and commerce are the two parents of our national poor." Eden, like our Scotch republican on principle, errs only in this: not the abolition of villenage, but the abolition of the property of the agricultural labourer in the soil made him a proletarian, and eventually a pauper. In France, where the expropriation was effected in another way, the ordonnance of Moulins, 1571, and the Edict of 1656, correspond to the English poor-laws.

10. Professor Rogers, although formerly Professor of Political Economy in the University of Oxford, the hotbed of Protestant orthodoxy, in his preface to the "History of Agriculture" lays stress on the fact of the pauperisation of the mass of the people by the Reformation.

the yeomanry had disappeared,[11] and so had, in the last decade of the 18th century, the last trace of the common land of the agricultural labourer. We leave on one side here the purely economic causes of the agricultural revolution. We deal only with the forcible means employed.

After the restoration of the Stuarts, the landed proprietors carried, by legal means, an act of usurpation, effected everywhere on the Continent without any legal formality. They abolished the feudal tenure of land, *i.e.*, they got rid of all its obligations to the State, "indemnified" the State by taxes on the peasantry and the rest of the mass of the people, vindicated for themselves the rights of modern private property in estates to which they had only a feudal title, and, finally, passed those laws of settlement, which, *mutatis mutandis,* had the same effect on the English agricultural labourer, as the edict of the Tarter Boris Godunof on the Russian peasantry.

The "glorious Revolution" brought into power, along with William of Orange, the landlord and capitalist appropriators of surplus-value.[12] They inaugurated the new era by practising on a colossal scale thefts of state lands, thefts that had been hitherto managed more modestly. These estates were given away, sold at a ridiculous figure, or even annexed to private estates by direct seizure.[13] All this happened without the slightest observation of legal etiquette. The crown lands thus fraudulently appropriated, together with the robbery of the Church estates, as far as these had not been lost again during the republican revolution, form the basis of the to-day princely domains of the English oligarchy.[14] The bourgeois capitalists favoured the operation with the view, among others, to promoting free trade in land, to extending the domain of modern agriculture on the large farm-system, and to increasing their supply of the free agricultural proletarians ready to hand. Besides, the new landed aristocracy was the natural ally of the new bankocracy, of the newly-hatched *haute finance,* and of the large manufacturers, then depending on protective duties. The English bourgeoisie acted for its own interest quite as wisely as did the Swedish bourgeoisie who, reversing the process, hand in hand with their economic allies, the peasantry, helped the kings in the forcible resumption of the Crown lands from the oligarchy. This happened since 1604 under Charles X. and Charles XI.

Communal property—always distinct from the State property just dealt with—was an old Teutonic institution which lived on under cover of feudalism. We have seen how the forcible usurpation of this, generally accompanied by the turning of arable into pasture land, begins at the end of the 15th and extends into the 16th century. But, at that time, the process was carried on by means of individual acts of violence against which legislation, for a hundred and fifty years, fought in vain. The advance made by the 18th century shows itself in this, that the law itself becomes now the instrument of the theft of the people's land, although the large farmers make use of their little independent methods as well.[15] The parliamentary form of the robbery is that of Acts for enclosures of Commons, in other words, decrees by which the landlords grant themselves the people's land as private property, decrees of expropriation of the people. Sir F. M. Eden refutes his own crafty special pleading, in which he tries to represent communal property as the private property of the great landlords who have taken the place of the feudal lords, when he, himself, demands a "general "Act of Parliament for the enclosure of Commons," (admitting thereby that a parliamentary

---

11. A letter to Sir T. C. Banbury, Bart., on the High Price of Provisions. By a Suffolk Gentleman. Ipswich, 1795, p. 4. Even the fanatical advocate of the system of large farms, the author of the "Inquiry into the connection of large farms, etc., London, 1773," p. 133, says: "I most lament the loss of our yeomanry, that set of men who really kept up the independence of this nation; and sorry I am to see their lands now in the hands of monopolizing lords, tenanted out to small farmers, who hold their leases on such conditions as to be little better than vassals ready to attend a summons on every mischievous occasion."

12. On the private moral character of this bourgeois hero, among other things: "The large grant of lands in Ireland to Lady Orkney, in 1695, is a public instance of the king's affection, and the lady's influence. . . . Lady Orkney's endearing offices are supposed to have been—fœda labiorum ministeria." (In the Sloane Manuscript Collection, at the British Museum, No. 4224. The Manuscript is entitled: "The charakter and behaviour of King William, Sunderland, etc., as represented in Original Letters to the Duke of Shrewsbury, from Somors Halifax, Oxford, Secretary Vernon, etc." It is full of curiosa.)

13. "The illegal alienation of the Crown Estates, partly by sale and partly by gift, is a scandalous chapter in English history . . . a gigantic fraud on the nation." (F. W. Newman, Lectures on Political Economy. London, 1851, pp. 129, 130.) [For details as to how the present large landed proprietors of England came into their possessions see "Our Old Nobility. By Noblesse Oblige." London, 1879.—Ed.]

14. Read *e.g.,* E. Burke's Pamphlet on the ducal house of Bedford, whose offshoot was Lord John Russell, the "tomtit of Liberalism."

15. "The farmers forbid cottagers to keep any living creatures besides themselves and children, under the pretence that if they keep any beasts or poultry, they will steal from the farmers' barns for their support; they also say, keep the cottagers poor and you will keep them industrious, &c., but the real fact, I believe, is that the farmers may have the whole right of common to themselves." (A Political Inquiry into the consequences of enclosing Waste Lands. London, 1785, p. 75.)

coup d'état is necessary for its transformation into private property), and moreover calls on the legislature for the indemnification for the expropriated poor.[16]

Whilst the place of the independent yeoman was taken by tenants at will, small farmers on yearly leases, a servile rabble dependent on the pleasure of the landlords, the systematic robbery of the Communal lands helped especially, next to the theft of the State domains, to swell those large farms, that were called in the 18th century capital farms[17] or merchant farms,[18] and to "set free" the agricultural populations as proletarians for manufacturing industry. . . .

The spoliation of the church's property, the fraudulent alienation of the State domains, the robbery of the common lands, the usurpation of feudal and clan property, and its transformation into modern private property under circumstances of reckless terrorism, were just so many idyllic methods of primitive accumulation. They conquered the field for capitalistic agriculture, made the soil part and parcel of capital, and created for the town industries the necessary supply of a "free" and outlawed proletariat.

BLOODY LEGISLATION AGAINST THE EXPROPRIATED, FROM THE END OF THE 15TH CENTURY. FORCING DOWN OF WAGES BY ACTS OF PARLIAMENT

The proletariat created by the breaking up of the bands of feudal retainers and by the forcible expropriation of the people from the soil, this "free" proletariat could not possibly be absorbed by the nascent manufactures as fast as it was thrown upon the world. On the other hand, these men, suddenly dragged from their wanted mode of life, could not as suddenly adapt themselves to the discipline of their new condition. They were turned *en masse* into beggars, robbers, vagabonds, partly from inclination, in most cases from stress of circumstances. Hence at the end of the 15th and during the whole of the 16th century, throughout Western Europe a bloody legislation against vagabondage. The fathers of the present working-class were chastised for their enforced transformation into vagabonds and paupers. Legislation treated them as "voluntary" criminals, and assumed that it depended on their own goodwill to go on working under the old conditions that no longer existed.

In England this legislation began under Henry VII.

Henry VIII. 1530: Beggars old and unable to work receive a beggar's licence. On the other hand, whipping and imprisonment for sturdy vagabonds. They are to be tied to the carttail and whipped until the blood streams from their bodies, then to swear an oath to go back to their birthplace or to where they have lived the last three years and to "put themselves to labour." What grim irony! In 27 Henry VIII. the former statute is repeated, but strengthened with new clauses. For the second arrest for vagabondage the whipping is to be repeated and half the ear sliced off; but for the third relapse the offender is to be executed as a hardened criminal and enemy of the common weal.

Edward VI.: A statute of the first year of his reign, 1547, ordains that if anyone refuses to work, he shall be condemned as a slave to the person who has denounced him as an idler. The master shall feed his slave on bread and water, weak broth and such refuse meat as he thinks fit. He has the right to force him to do any work, no matter how disgusting, with whip and chains. If the slave is absent a fortnight, he is condemned to slavery for life and is to be branded on forehead or back with the letter S; if he runs away thrice, he is to be executed as a felon. The master can sell him, bequeath him, let him out on hire as a slave, just as any other personal chattel or cattle. If the slaves attempt anything against the masters, they are also to be executed. Justices of the peace, on information, are to hunt the rascals down. If it happens that a vagabond has been idling about for three days, he is to be taken to his birthplace, branded with a redhot iron with the letter V on the breast and be set to work, in chains, in the streets or at some other labour. If the vagabond gives a false birthplace, he is then to become the slave for life of this place, of its inhabitants, or its corporation, and to be branded with an S. All persons have the right to take away the children of the vagabonds and to keep them as apprentices, the young men until the 24th year, the girls until the 20th. If they run away, they are to become up to this age the slaves of their masters, who can put them in irons, whip them, &c., if they like. Every master may put an iron ring round the neck, arms or legs of his slave, by which to know

---

16. Eden, l. c. preface.
17. "Capital Farms." Two letters on the Flour Trade and the Dearness of Corn. By a person in business. London, 1767, pp. 19, 20.
18. "Merchant Farms." An inquiry into the present High Prices of Provisions. London, 1767, p. 11. Note.—This excellent work, which was published anonymously, is by the Rev. Nathaniel Forster.

him more easily and to be more certain of him.[19] The last part of the statute provides, that certain poor people may be employed by a place or by persons, who are willing to give them food and drink and to find them work. This kind of parish-slaves was kept up in England until far into the 19th century under the name of "roundsmen."

Elizabeth, 1572: Unlicensed beggars above 14 years of age are to be severely flogged and branded on the left ear unless some one will take them into service for two years; in case of a repetition of the offence, if they are over 18, they are to be executed, unless some one will take them into service for two years; but for the third offence they are to be executed without mercy as felons. Similar statutes: 18 Elizabeth, c. 13, and another of 1597.

James I: Any one wandering about and begging is declared a rogue and a vagabond. Justices of the peace in petty sessions are authorised to have them publicly whipped and for the first offence to imprison them for 6 months, for the second for 2 years. Whilst in prison they are to be whipped as much and as often as the justices of the peace think fit. . . . Incorrigible and dangerous rogues are to be branded with an R on the left shoulder and set to hard labour, and if they are caught begging again, to be executed without mercy. These statutes, legally binding until the beginning of the 18th century, were only repealed by 12 Ann, c. 23.[20]

Similar laws in France, where by the middle of the 17th century a kingdom of vagabonds (truands) was established in Paris. Even at the beginning of Louis XVI.'s reign (Ordinance of July 13th, 1777) every man in good health from 16 to 60 years of age, if without means of subsistence and not practising a trade, is to be sent to the galleys. Of the same nature are the statute of Charles V. for the Netherlands (October, 1537), the first edict of the States and Towns of Holland (March 10, 1614), the "Plakaat" of the United Provinces (June 26, 1649), &c.

Thus were the agricultural people, first forcibly expropriated from the soil, driven from their homes, turned into vagabonds, and then whipped, branded, tortured by laws grotesquely terrible, into the discipline necessary for the wage system.

It is not enough that the conditions of labour are concentrated in a mass, in the shape of capital, at the one pole of society, while at the other are grouped masses of men, who have nothing to sell but their labour-power. Neither is it enough that they are compelled to sell it voluntarily. The advance of capitalist production develops a working-class, which by education, tradition, habit, looks upon the conditions of that mode of production as self-evident laws of nature. The organization of the capitalist process of production, once fully developed, breaks down all resistance. The constant generation of a relative surplus-population keeps the law of supply and demand of labour, and therefore keeps wages, in a rut that corresponds with the wants of capital. The dull compulsion of economic relations completes the subjection of the labourer to the capitalist. Direct force, outside economic conditions, is of course still used, but only exceptionally. In the ordinary run of things, the labourer can be left to the "natural laws of production," *i.e.*, to his dependence on capital, a dependence springing from, and guaranteed in perpetuity by, the conditions of

---

19. The author of the Essay on Trade, etc., 1770, says, "In the reign of Edward VI. indeed the English seem to have set, in good earnest, about encouraging manufactures and employing the poor. This we learn from a remarkable statute which runs thus: 'That all vagrants shall be branded. &c.,'" l. c., p. 5.

20. In France, the régisseur, steward, collector of dues for the feudal lords during cormaraunte and very plage of his native contrey maye compasse aboute and inclose many thousand akers of grounde together within one pale or hedge, the husbandmen be thrust owte of their owne, or els either by coneyne and fraude, or by violent oppression they be put besydes it, or by wrongs and iniuries thei be so weried that they be compelled to sell all: by one meanes, therfore, or by other, either by hooke or crooke they muste needes departe awaye, poore, selye, wretched soules, men, women, husbands, wiues, fatherlesse children, widowes, wofull mothers with their yonge babes, and their whole household smal in substance, and muche in numbre, as husbandrye requireth many handes. Awaye thei trudge, I say, owte of their knowen accustomed houses, fyndynge no place to reste in. All their householde stuffe, which is very little woorthe, thoughe it might well abide the sale: yet beeynge sodainely thruste owte, they be constrayned to sell it for a thing of nought. And when they haue wandered abrode tyll that be spent, what can they then els doe but steale, and then iustly pardy be hanged, or els go about beggyng. And yet then also they be caste in prison as vagabondes, because theey go aboute and worke not; whom no man wyl set a worke though thei neuer so willyngly profre themselucs therto." Of these poor fugitives of whom Thomas More says that they were forced to thieve, "7200 great and petty thieves were put to death," in the reign of Henry VIII. (Hollinshed, "Description of England," Vol. 1., p. 186.) In Elizabeth's time, "rogues were trussed up apace, and that there was not one year commonly wherein three or four hundred were not devoured and eaten up by the gallowes." (Strype's Annals of the Reformation and Establishment of Religion, and other Various Occurrences in the Church of England during Queen Elizabeth's Happy Reign. Second ed., 1725, Vol. 2.) According to this same Strype, in Somersetshire, in one year, 40 persons were executed, 35 robbers burnt in the hand, 37 whipped, and 183 discharged as "incorrigible vagabonds." Nevertheless, he is of opinion that this large number of prisoners does not comprise even a fifth of the actual criminals, thanks to the negligence of the justices and the foolish compassion of the people; and the other counties of England were not better off in this respect than Somersetshire, while some were even worse.

production themselves. It is otherwise during the historic genesis of capitalist production. The bourgeoisie, at its rise, wants and uses the power of the state to "regulate" wages, *i.e.*, to force them within the limits suitable for surplus-value making, to lengthen the working-day and to keep the labourer himself in the normal degree of dependence. This is an essential element of the so-called primitive accumulation.

The class of wage-labourers, which arose in the latter half of the 14th century, formed then and in the following century only a very small part of the population, well protected in its position by the independent peasant proprietary in the country and the guild-organization in the town. In country and town master and workman stood close together socially. The subordination of labour to capital was only formal—*i.e.*, the mode of production itself had as yet no specific capitalistic character. Variable capital preponderated greatly over constant. The demand for wage-labour grew, therefore, rapidly with every accumulation of capital, whilst the supply of wage-labour followed but slowly. A large part of the national product, changed later into a fund of capitalist accumulation, then still entered into the consumption fund of the labourer.

Legislation on wage-labour, (from the first, aimed at the exploitation of the labourer and, as it advanced, always equally hostile to him),[21] is started in England by the Statute of Labourers, of Edward III., 1349. The ordinance of 1350 in France, issued in the name of King John, corresponds with it. English and French legislation run parallel and are identical in purport. . . .

The Statute of Labourers was passed at the urgent instance of the House of Commons. A Tory says naively: "Formerly the poor demanded such *high* wages as to threaten industry and wealth. Next, their wages are so *low* as to threaten industry and wealth equally and perhaps more, but in another way."[22] A tariff of wages was fixed by law for town and country, for piece-work and day-work. The agricultural labourers were to hire themselves out by the year, the town ones "in open market." It was forbidden, under pain of imprisonment, to pay higher wages than those fixed by the statute, but the taking of higher wages was more severely punished than the giving them. [So also in Sections 18 and 19 of the Staute of Apprentices of Elizabeth, ten days' imprisonment is decreed for him that pays the higher wages, but twenty-one days for him that receives them.] A statute of 1360 increased the penalties and authorised the masters to extort labour at the legal rate of wages by corporal punishment. All combinations, contracts, oaths, &c., by which masons and carpenters reciprocally bound themselves, were declared null and void. Coalition of the labourers is treated as a heinous crime from the 14th century to 1825, the year of the repeal of the laws against Trades' Unions. The spirit of the Statute of Labourers of 1349 and of its offshoots, comes out clearly in the fact, that indeed a maximum of wages is dictated by the State, but on no account a minimum.

In the 16th century, the condition of the labourers had, as we know, become much worse. The money wage rose, but not in proportion to the depreciation of money and the corresponding rise in the prices of commodities. Wages, therefore, in reality fell. Nevertheless, the laws for keeping them down remained in force, together with the ear-clipping and branding of those "whom no one was willing to take into service." By the Statute of Apprentices 5 Elizabeth, c. 3, the justices of the peace were empowered to fix certain wages and to modify them according to the time of the year and the price of commodities. James I. extended these regulations of labour also to weavers, spinners, and all possible categories of workers.[23] George II. extended the laws against coalitions of labourers to

---

21. "Whenever the legislature attempts to regulate the differences between masters and their workmen, its counsellors are always the masters," says A. Smith. "L'esprit des lois, c'est la propriété," says Linguet.

22. "Sophisms of Free Trade." By a Barrister. Lond., 1850, p. 53. He adds maliciously: "We were ready enough to interfere for the employer, can nothing now be done for the employed?"

23. From a clause of Statute 2 James I., c. 6, we see that certain cloth-makers took upon themselves to dictate, in their capacity of justices of the peace, the official tariff of wages in their own shops. In Germany, especially after the Thirty Years' War, statutes for keeping down wages were general. "The want of servants and labourers was very troublesome to the landed proprietors in the depopulated districts. All villagers were forbidden to let rooms to single men and women; all the latter were to be reported to the authorities and cast into prison if they were unwilling to become servants, even if they were employed at any other work, such as sowing seeds for the peasants at a daily wage, or even buying and selling corn. (Imperial privileges and sanctions for Silesia, I., 25.) For a whole century in the decrees of the small German potentates a bitter cry goes up again and again about the wicked and impertinent rabble that will not reconcile itself to its hard lot, will not be content with the legal wage; the individual landed proprietors are forbidden to pay more than the State had fixed by a tariff. And yet the conditions of service were at times better after the war than 100 years later: the farm servants of Silesia had, in 1652, meat twice a week, whilst even in our century, districts are known where they have it only three times a year. Further, wages after the war were higher than in the following century." (G. Freitag.)

manufactures. In the manufacturing period *par excellence,* the capitalist mode of production had become sufficiently strong to render legal regulation of wages as impracticable as it was unnecessary; but the ruling classes were unwilling in case of necessity to be without the weapons of the old arsenal. Still, 8 George II. forbade a higher day's wage than 2s. 7½d. for journeymen tailors in and around London, except in cases of general mourning; still 13 George III., c. 68, gave the regulation of the wages of silk-weavers to the justices of the peace; still, in 1706, it required two judgments of the higher courts to decide, whether the mandates of justices of the peace as to wages held good also for non-agricultural labourers; still, in 1799, an act of Parliament ordered that the wages of the Scotch miners should continue to be regulated by a statute of Elizabeth and two Scotch acts of 1661 and 1671. How completely in the meantime circumstances had changed, is proved by an occurrence unheard-of before in the English Lower House. In that place, where for more than 400 years laws had been made for the maximum, beyond which wages absolutely must not rise, Whitbread in 1796 proposed a legal minimum wage for agricultural labourers. Pitt opposed this, but confessed that the "condition of the poor was cruel." Finally, in 1813, the laws for the regulation of wages were repealed. They were an absurd anomaly, since the capitalist regulated his factory by his private legislation, and could by the poor-rates make up the wage of the agricultural labourer to the indispensable minimum. The provisions of the labour statutes as to contracts between master and workman, as to giving notice and the like, which only allows of a civil action against the contract-breaking master, but on the contrary permit a criminal action against the contract-breaking workman, are to this hour (1873) in full force. The barbarous laws against Trades' Unions fell in 1825 before the threatening bearing of the proletariat. Despite this, they fell only in part. Certain beautiful fragments of the old statute vanished only in 1859. Finally, the act of Parliament of June 29, 1871, made a pretence of removing the last traces of this class of legislation by legal recognition of Trades Unions. But an act of Parliament of the same date (an act to amend the criminal law relating to violence, threats, and molestation), re-established, in point of fact, the former state of things in a new shape. By this Parliamentary escamotage the means which the labourers could use in a strike or lock-out were withdrawn from the laws common to all citizens, and placed under exceptional penal legislation, the interpretation of which fell to the masters themselves in their capacity as justices of the peace. Two years earlier, the same House of Commons and the same Mr. Gladstone in the well-known straightforward fashion brought in a bill for the abolition of all exceptional penal legislation against the working-class. But this was never allowed to go beyond the second reading, and the matter was thus protracted until at last the "great Liberal party," by an alliance with the Tories, found courage to turn against the very proletariat that had carried it into power. Not content with this treachery, the "great Liberal party" allowed the English judges, ever complaisant in the service of the ruling classes, to dig up again the earlier laws against "conspiracy," and to apply them to coalitions of labourers. We see that only against its will and under the pressure of the masses did the English Parliament give up the laws against Strikes and Trades' Unions, after it had itself, for 500 years, held, with shameless egoism, the position of a permanent Trades' Union of the capitalists against the labourers.

During the very first storms of the revolution, the French bourgeoisie dared to take away from the workers the right of association but just acquired. By a decree of June 14, 1791, they declared all coalition of the workers as "an attempt against liberty and the declaration of the rights of man," punishable by a fine of 500 livres, together with deprivation of the rights of an active citizen for one year.[24] This law which, by means of State compulsion, confined the struggle between capital and labour within limits comfortable for capital, has outlived revolutions and changes of dynasties. Even the Reign of Terror left it untouched. It was but quite recently struck out of the Penal Code. Nothing is more characteristic than the pretext for this bourgeois coup d'état. "Granting," says Chapelier, the reporter of the Select Committee on this law, "that wages ought to be a little higher than they are, . . . that they ought to be high enough for him that receives them, to be

---

24. Article I. of this law runs: "L' anéantissement de toute espéce de corporations du méme état et profession étant l'une des bases fondamentales de la constitution française, il est défendu de les rétablir de fait sous quelque prétexte et sous quelque forme que ce soit." Article IV. declares, that if "des citoyens attachés aux mémes professions, arts et métiers prenaient des délibérations, faisaient entre eux des conventions tendantes à refuser de concert ou à n'accorder qu'à un prix déterminé le secours de leur industrie ou de leurs travaux, les dites délibérations et conventions . . . seront déclarées inconstitutionnelles, attentatoires à la liberté et à la declaration des droits de l'homme, &c.": felony, therefore, as in the old labour-statutes. ("Revolutions de Paris." Paris, 1791, t. III., p. 523.)

free from that state of absolute dependence due to the want of the necessaries of life, and which is almost that of slavery," yet the workers must not be allowed to come to any understanding about their own interests, nor to act in common and thereby lessen their "absolute dependence, which is almost that of slavery;" because, forsooth, in doing this they injure "the freedom of their cidevant masters, the present entrepreneurs," and because a coalition against the despotism of the quondam masters of the corporations is—guess what!—is a restoration of the corporations abolished by the French constitution.[25]

---

25. Buchez et Roux: "Histoire Parlementaire," t. x., p. 195.

CHAPTER 15

FREDERICK ENGELS

The reading in this chapter is from Frederick Engels's *The Condition of the Working Class in England in 1844* ([1845] 1887), pp. 63–68, 72–73, 76–78, 86–89, 188–189, and 190–195; translated by Florence Kelley Wischnewetzky; New York: John W. Lovell Company. The heading of the first section has been amended and the original footnote symbols have been changed.

The first edition of *The Condition of the Working Class* was published in 1845 in German when Engels was only in his mid-20s. It is a work of early sociology with a socialist orientation, and it devotes considerable attention to issues of law and crime. The reading in this chapter provides a historical complement to the analysis by Marx that was presented in Chapter 14. Although Marx's *Capital* (1867) was published well after *The Condition of the Working Class* (1845), the selection from *Capital* focused on an earlier stage in the evolution of capitalism; it was primarily concerned with the initial conditions that led to the emergence of capitalism. The excerpts from Engels's work, in contrast, focus on nineteenth-century industrial capitalism, a later stage in its development.

In the following reading, Engels addresses several issues that remain, in abstract, central concerns of contemporary Marxist criminology and, more generally, critical criminology. The reading begins with his conception of "social murder" and how it is committed on a massive scale by the bourgeoisie against the proletariat. For criminologists who question the idea of using the criminal law of a particular society as the basis for conceptualizing criminal behavior, for those who prefer to define crime as actions that violate basic human rights, Engels's discussion of social murder represents an important historical reference point. In this reading, Engels also presents his viewpoint on the demoralizing effects of early industrial capitalism, the conditions that drove many workers into a criminal lifestyle. Moreover, he provides an illustration of class bias in the law through his analysis of the poor laws of England, especially the New Poor Law; and, in connection with this topic, he describes the cruelty of workhouses—that is, "Poor Law Bastilles." Thus, in a somewhat fragmented and incomplete manner, Engels, like several other contributors to the early history of criminology (e.g., Garofalo and Durkheim), combined a theory of law and a theory of criminal behavior into a single conceptual framework.

from THE CONDITION OF THE WORKING CLASS IN ENGLAND IN 1844
by **Frederick Engels**

RESULTS [OF INDUSTRIAL CAPITALISM]

... When one individual inflicts bodily injury upon another, such injury that death results, we call the deed manslaughter; when the assailant knew in advance that the injury would be fatal, we call his deed murder. But when society[1] places hundreds of proletarians in such a position that they inevitably meet a too early and an unnatural death, one which is quite as much a death by violence as that by the sword or bullet; when it deprives thousands of the necessaries of life, places them under conditions in which they *cannot* live; forces them, through the strong arm of the law to remain in such conditions until that death ensues which is the inevitable consequence; knows that these thousands of victims must perish and yet permits these conditions to remain, its deed is murder just as surely as the deed of the single individual; disguised, malicious murder, murder against which none can defend himself which does not seem what it is, because no man sees the murderer, because the death of the victim seems a natural one, since the offence is more one of omission than of commission. But murder it remains. I have now to prove that society in England daily and hourly commits what the workingmens' organs, with perfect correctness, characterize as social murder, that it has placed the workers under conditions in which they can neither retain health nor live long; that it undermines the vital force of these workers gradually, little by little, and so hurries them to the grave before their time. I have further to prove, that society knows how injurious such conditions are to the health and the life of the workers, and yet does nothing to improve these conditions. That it *knows* the consequences of its deeds; that its act is, therefore, not mere manslaughter but murder, I shall have proved, when I cite official documents, reports of Parliament and of the Government, in substantiation of my charge.

That a class which lives under the conditions already sketched, and is so ill provided with the most necessary means of subsistence cannot be healthy and can reach no advanced age, is self-evident. Let us review the circumstances once more with especial reference to the health of the workers. The centralization of population in great cities exercises of itself an unfavorable influence; the atmosphere of London can never be so pure, so rich in oxygen, as the air of the country; two and a half million pairs of lungs, two hundred fifty thousand fires crowded upon an area three to four miles square, consume an enormous amount of oxygen which is replaced with difficulty, because the method of building cities in itself impedes ventilation. The carbonic acid gas, engendered by respiration and fire, remains in the streets by reason of its specific gravity, and the chief air current passes over the roofs of the city. The lungs of the inhabitants fail to receive the due supply of oxygen, and the consequence is mental and physical lassitude and low vitality. For this reason the dwellers in cities are far less exposed to acute, and especially to inflammatory affections, than rural populations, who live in a free normal atmosphere; but they suffer the more from chronic affections. And if life in large cities is, in itself, injurious to the health, how great must be the harmful influence of an abnormal atmosphere in the working peoples' quarters, where, as we have seen, everything combines to poison the air. In the country it may, perhaps, be comparatively innoxious to keep a dung heap adjoining one's dwelling, because the air has free ingress from all sides; but in the midst of a great city, among closely built lanes and courts that shut out all movement of the atmosphere, the case is different. All putrefying vegetable

---

1. When as here and elsewhere I speak of society as a responsible whole, having rights and duties, I mean, of course, the ruling power of society, the class which at present holds social and political control, and bears, therefore, the responsibility for the condition of those to whom it grants no share in such control. This ruling class in England, as in all other civilized countries, is the bourgeoisie. But that this society, and especially the bourgeoisie, is charged with the duty of protecting every member of society, at least in his life, to see to it, for example, that no one starves, I need not now prove to my *German* readers. If I were writing for the English bourgeoisie, the case would be different. (And so it is now in Germany. Our German capitalists are fully up to the English level, in this respect at least, in the year of grace, 1886.)

and animal substances give off gases decidedly injurious to the health, and if these gases have no free way of escape, they inevitably poison the atmosphere. The filth and stagnant pools of the working peoples' quarters in the great cities have therefore the worst effect upon the public health, because they produce precisely those gases which engender disease; so, too, the exhalations from contaminated streams. But this is by no means all. The manner in which the great multitude of the poor is treated by society to-day is revolting. They are drawn into the large cities where they breathe a poorer atmosphere than in the country; they are relegated to districts which, by reason of the method of construction, are worse ventilated than any others; they are deprived of all means of cleanliness, of water itself, since pipes are laid only when paid for, and the rivers so polluted that they are useless for such purposes; they are obliged to throw all offal and garbage, all dirty water, often all disgusting drainage and excrement into the streets, being without other means of disposing of them; they are thus compelled to infect the region of their own dwellings. Nor is this enough. All conceivable evils are heaped upon the heads of the poor. If the population of great cities is too dense in general, it is they in particular who are packed into the least space. As though the vitiated atmosphere of the streets were not enough, they are penned, in dozens, into single rooms, so that the air which they breathe at night is enough in itself to stifle them. They are given damp dwellings, cellar dens that are not water-proof from below, or garrets that leak from above. Their houses are so built that the clammy air cannot escape. They are supplied bad, tattered, or rotten clothing, adulterated and indigestible food. They are exposed to the most exciting changes of mental condition, the most violent vibrations between hope and fear; they are stirred up like game, and not permitted to attain peace of mind and quiet enjoyment of life. They are deprived of all enjoyments except that of sexual indulgence and drunkenness, are worked every day to the point of complete exhaustion of their mental and physical energies, and are thus constantly spurred on to the maddest excess in the only two enjoyments at their command. And if they surmount all this, they fall victims to want of work in a crisis when all the little is taken from them that had hitherto been vouchsafed them.

How is it possible, under such conditions, for the lower class to be healthy and long lived? What else can be expected than an excessive mortality, an unbroken series of epidemics, a progressive deterioration in the physique of the working population? Let us see how the facts stand.

That the dwellings of the workers in the worst portions of the cities, together with the other conditions of life of this class engender numerous diseases, is attested on all sides. The article already quoted from the *Artizan*,[2] asserts with perfect truth, that lung diseases must be the inevitable consequence of such conditions, and that indeed cases of this kind are disproportionately frequent in this class. That the bad air of London, and especially of the working peoples' districts, is in the highest degree favorable to the development of consumption, the hectic appearance of great numbers of persons sufficiently indicates. If one roams the streets a little, in the early morning when the multitudes are on their way to their work, one is amazed at the number of persons who look wholly or half consumptive. Even in Manchester the people have not the same appearance; these pale, lank, narrow-chested, hollow-eyed ghosts, whom one passes at every step, these languid, flabby faces, incapable of the slightest energetic expression, I have seen in such startling numbers only in London, though consumption carries off a horde of victims annually in the factory towns of the North. In competition with consumption stands typhus, to say nothing of scarlet fever, a disease which brings most frightful devastation into the ranks of the working class. Typhus, that universally diffused affliction, is attributed by the official report on the Sanitary Condition of the Working Class, directly to the bad state of the dwellings in the matters of ventilation, drainage and cleanliness. This report, compiled, it must not be forgotten, by the leading physicians of England from the testimony of other physicians, asserts that a single ill-ventilated court, a single blind alley without drainage, is enough to engender fever and usually does engender it, especially if the inhabitants are greatly crowded. This fever has the same character almost everywhere, and develops in nearly every case into specific typhus. It is to be found in the working people's quarters of all great towns and cities, and in single ill-built, ill-kept streets of smaller places, though it naturally seeks out single victims in better districts also. In London it has now prevailed for a considerable time; its extraordinary violence in the year 1837 gave rise to the Report already referred to. According to the annual report of Dr. Southwood Smith on the

---

2. The Artizan, October, 1842. [Editor's note: This reference is provided on page 25 of the original publication.]

London Fever Hospital, the number of patients in 1843 was 1,462, or 418 more than in any previous year. In the damp, dirty regions of the North, South and East districts of London, this disease raged with extraordinary violence. Many of the patients were working people from the country, who had endured the severest privation while migrating, and, after their arrival, had slept hungry and half naked in the streets, and so fallen victims to the fever. These people were brought into the hospital in such a state of weakness, that unusual quantities of wine, cognac, and preparations of ammonia and other stimulants were required for their treatment; 16½% of all patients died. This malignant fever is to be found in Manchester; in the worst quarters of the Old Town, Ancoats, Little Ireland, etc., it is rarely extinct; though here, as in the *English* towns generally, it prevails to a less extent than might be expected. In Scotland and Ireland, on the other hand, it rages with a violence that surpasses all conception. In Edinburgh and Glasgow it broke out in 1817, after the famine, and in 1826 and 1837, with especial violence, after the commercial crises subsiding somewhat each time after having raged about three years. In Edinburgh about 6,000 persons were attacked by the fever during the epidemic of 1817, and about 10,000 in that of 1837, and not only the number of persons attacked but the violence of the disease increased with each repetition.[3]

But the fury of the epidemic in all former periods seems to have been child's play in comparison with its ravages after the crisis of 1842. One-sixth of the whole indigent population of Scotland was seized by the fever, and the infection was carried by wandering beggars with fearful rapidity from one locality to another. It did not reach the middle and upper classes of the population, yet in two months there were more fever cases than in twelve years before. In Glasgow, twelve per cent. of the population were seized in the year 1843; 32,000 persons, of whom thirty-two per cent. perished, while the mortality of Manchester and Liverpool does not ordinarily exceed eight per cent. The illness reached a crisis on the seventh and fifteenth days; on the latter, the patient usually became yellow, which our authority[4] regards as an indication that the cause of the malady was to be sought in mental excitement and anxiety. In Ireland, too, these fever epidemics have become domesticated. During twenty-one months of the years 1817–1818, 39,000 fever patients passed through the Dublin hospital; and in a more recent year, according to Sheriff Alison,[5] 60,000. In Cork, the fever hospital received one-seventh of the population in 1817–1818, in Limerick in the same time one-fourth, and in the bad quarter of Waterford, nineteen-twentieths of the whole population were ill of the fever at one time.

When one remembers under what conditions the working people live, when one thinks how crowded their dwellings are, how every nook and corner swarms with human beings, how sick and well sleep in the same room, in the same bed, the only wonder is that a contagious disease like this fever does not spread yet further. And when one reflects how little medical assistance the sick have at command, how many are without any medical advice whatsoever, and ignorant of the most ordinary precautionary measures, the mortality seems actually small. Dr. Alison, who has made a careful study of this disease, attributes it directly to the want and the wretched condition of the poor, as in the report already quoted. He asserts that privations and the insufficient satisfaction of vital needs are what prepare the frame for contagion and make the epidemic widespread and terrible. He proves that a period of privation, a commercial crisis or a bad harvest, has each time produced the typhus epidemic in Ireland as in Scotland, and that the fury of the plague has fallen almost exclusively on the working class. It is a noteworthy fact, that according to his testimony, the majority of persons who perish by typhus are fathers of families, precisely the persons who can least be spared by those dependent upon them; and several Irish physicians whom he quotes, bear the same testimony.

Another category of diseases arises directly from the food rather than the dwellings of the workers. The food of the laborer, indigestible enough in itself, is utterly unfit for young children, and he has neither means nor time to get his children more suitable food. Moreover, the custom of giving children spirits, and even opium, is very general; and these two influences with the rest of the conditions of life prejudicial to bodily development, give rise to the most diverse affections of the digestive organs, leaving life-long traces behind them. Nearly all workers have stomachs more or less weak, and are yet forced to adhere to the diet which is the root of the evil. How should they know what is to blame for it? And if they knew, how could they obtain a more

---

3. Dr. Alison. Management of the Poor in Scotland.
4. Alison. Principles of Population, Vol. II.

5. Dr. Alison in an article read before the British Association for the Advancement of Science, October, 1844, in York.

suitable regimen so long as they cannot adopt a different way of living and are not better educated? But new disease arises during childhood from impaired digestion. Scrophula is almost universal among the working class, and scrophulous parents have scrophulous children, especially when the original influences continue in full force to operate upon the inherited tendency of the children. A second consequence of this insufficient bodily nourishment, during the years of growth and development, is rachitis, which is extremely common among the children of the working class. The hardening of the bones is delayed, the development of the skeleton in general is restricted, and deformities of the legs and spinal column are frequent, in addition to the usual rachitic affections. How greatly all these evils are increased by the changes to which the workers are subject in consequence of fluctuations in trade, want of work, and the scanty wages of times of crisis, it is not necessary to dwell upon. Temporary want of sufficient food, to which almost every workingman is exposed at least once in the course of his life, only contributes to intensify the effects of his usual sufficient but bad diet. Children who are half starved just when they most need ample and nutritious food—and how many such there are during every crisis and even when trade is at its best—must inevitably become weak, scrophulous, and rachitic in a high degree. And that they do become so, their appearance amply shows. The neglect to which the great mass of workingmen's children are condemned leaves ineradicable traces and brings the enfeeblement of the whole race of workers with it. Add to this, the unsuitable clothing of this class, the impossibility of precautions against colds, the necessity of toiling so long as health permits, want made more dire when sickness appears, and the only too common lack of all medical assistance; and we have a rough idea of the sanitary condition of the English working class. The injurious effects peculiar to single employments as now conducted, I shall not deal with here. . . .

Apart from the divers diseases which are the necessary consequence of the present neglect and oppression of the poorer classes, there are other influences which contribute to increase the mortality among small children. In many families the wife, like the husband, has to work away from home, and the consequence is the total neglect of the children who are either locked up or given out to be taken care of. It is therefore not to be wondered at if hundreds of them perish through all manner of accidents. Nowhere are so many children run over, nowhere are so many killed by falling, drowning or burning, as in the great cities and towns of England. Deaths from burns and scalds are especially frequent, such a case occurring nearly every week during the winter months in Manchester, and very frequently in London, though little mention is made of them in the papers. I have at hand a copy of the *Weekly Despatch* of December 15th, 1844, according to which, in the week from December 1st to December 7th inclusive, *six* such cases occurred. These unhappy children, perishing in this terrible way, are victims of our social disorder, and of the property holding classes interested in maintaining and prolonging this disorder. Yet one is left in doubt whether even this terrible torturing death is not a blessing for the children in rescuing them from a long life of toil and wretchedness, rich in suffering and poor in enjoyment. So far has it gone in England; and the bourgeoisie reads these things every day in the newspapers and takes no further trouble in the matter. But it cannot complain if, after the official and non-official testimony here cited which must be known to it, I broadly accuse it of social murder. Let the ruling class see to it that these frightful conditions are ameliorated, or let it surrender the administration of the common interests to the laboring class. To the latter course it is by no means inclined; for the former task, so long as it remains the bourgeoisie crippled by bourgeois prejudice, it has not the needed power. For if, at last, after hundreds of thousands of victims have perished, it manifests some little anxiety for the future, passing a "Metropolitan Buildings Act," under which the most unscrupulous overcrowding of dwellings is to be, at least in some slight degree, restricted; if it points with pride to measures which, far from attacking the root of the evil, do not by any means meet the demands of the commonest sanitary police, it cannot thus vindicate itself from the accusation. The English bourgeoisie has but one choice, either to continue its rule under the unanswerable charge of murder and in spite of this charge, or to abdicate in favor of the laboring class. Hitherto it has chosen the former course. . . .

Thus are the workers cast out and ignored by the class in power, morally as well as physically and mentally. The only provision made for them is the law, which fastens upon them when they become obnoxious to the bourgeoisie. Like the dullest of the brutes, they are treated to but one form of education, the whip, in the shape of force, not convincing but intimidating. There is therefore no cause for surprise if the workers, treated as brutes, actually become such; or if they can maintain their consciousness of manhood only by cherishing the most glowing hatred, the most unbroken inward rebellion against the bourgeoisie in power. They are men so long only as they burn with wrath against the reigning class. They become brutes the moment they bend in patience under the yoke, and merely strive to make life endurable while abandoning the effort to break the yoke.

This, then, is all that the bourgeoisie has done for the education of the proletariat—and when we take into consideration all the circumstances in which this class lives, we shall not think the worse of it for the resentment which it cherishes against the ruling class. The moral training which is not given to the worker in school is not supplied by the other conditions of his life; that moral training, at least, which alone has worth in the eyes of the bourgeoisie. His whole position and environment involves the strongest temptation to immorality. He is poor, life offers him no charm, almost every enjoyment is denied him, the penalties of the law have no further terrors for him; why should he restrain his desires, why leave to the rich the enjoyment of his birthright, why not seize a part of it for himself? What inducement has the proletarian not to steal? It is all very pretty and very agreeable to the ear of the bourgeois to hear the "sacredness of property" asserted; but for him who has none, the sacredness of property dies out of itself. Money is the God of this world; the bourgeois takes the proletarian's money from him and so makes a practical atheist of him. No wonder, then, if the proletarian retains his atheism and no longer respects the sacredness and power of the earthly God. And when the poverty of the proletarian is intensified to the point of actual lack of the barest necessities of life, to want and hunger, the temptation to the disregard of all social order does but gain power. This the bourgeoisie for the most part recognizes. Symonds[6] observes that poverty exercises the same ruinous influence upon the mind which drunkenness exercises upon the body; and Dr. Alison explains to property-holding readers, with the greatest exactness, what the consequences of social oppression must be for the working class.[7] Want leaves the workingman the choice between starving slowly, killing himself speedily, or taking what he needs where he finds it, in plain English, stealing. And there is no cause for surprise that most of them prefer stealing to starvation and suicide.

True, there are, within the working class, numbers too moral to steal even when reduced to the utmost extremity, and these starve or commit suicide. For suicide, formerly the enviable privilege of the upper classes, has become fashionable among the English workers, and numbers of the poor kill themselves to avoid the misery from which they see no other means of escape.

But far more demoralizing than his poverty in its influence upon the English workingman is the insecurity of his position, the necessity of living upon wages from hand to mouth, that in short which makes a proletarian of him. The smaller peasants in Germany are usually poor, and often suffer want, but they are less at the mercy of accident, they have at least something secure. The proletarian, who has nothing but his two hands, who consumes to-day what he earned yesterday, who is subject to every possible chance, and has not the slightest guarantee for being able to earn the barest necessities of life, whom every crisis, every whim of his employer may deprive of bread, this proletarian is placed in the most revolting, inhuman position conceivable for a human being. The slave is assured of a bare livelihood by the self-interest of his master, the serf has at least a scrap of land on which to live; each has at worst a guarantee for life itself. But the proletarian must depend upon himself alone, and is yet prevented from so applying his abilities as to be able to rely upon them. Everything that the proletarian can do to improve his position is but a drop in the ocean compared with the floods of varying chances to which he is exposed, over which he has not the slightest control. He is the passive object of all possible combinations of circumstances, and must count himself fortunate when he has saved his life even for a short time, and his character and way of living are naturally shaped by these conditions. Either he seeks to keep his head above water in this whirlpool, to rescue his manhood, and this he can do solely in rebellion[8] against the class which plunders him so mercilessly and then abandons him to his fate, which strives to hold him in this position so demoralizing to a human being; or he gives up the struggle against his fate as hopeless and strives to profit, so far as he can, by the most favorable moment. To save is unavailing, for at the utmost he cannot save more than suffices to sustain life for a short time, while if he falls out of work, it is

---

6. *Arts and Artizans*.
7. *Principles of Population*, Vol. II., p. 196, 197.

8. We shall see later how the rebellion of the working class against the bourgeoisie in England is legalized by the right of coalition.

for no brief period. To accumulate lasting property for himself is impossible; and if it were not, he would only cease to be a workingman and another would take his place. What better thing can he do, then, when he gets high wages than live well upon them? The English bourgeois is violently scandalized at the extravagant living of the workers when wages are high; yet it is not only very natural but very sensible of them to enjoy life when they can, instead of laying up treasures which are of no lasting use to them, and which in the end moth and rust (*i.e.* the bourgeoisie) get possession of. Yet such a life is demoralizing beyond all others. . . .

The contempt for the existing social order is most conspicuous in its extreme form, that of offences against the law. If the influences demoralizing to the workingman act more powerfully, more concentratedly than usual, he becomes an offender as certainly as water abandons the fluid for the vaporous state at 80 degrees, Réaumur. Under the brutal and brutalizing treatment of the bourgeoisie, the workingman becomes precisely as much a thing without volition as water, and is subject to the laws of nature with precisely the same necessity; at a certain point all freedom ceases. Hence with the extension of the proletariat, crime has increased in England, and the British nation has become the most criminal in the world. From the annual criminal tables of the Home Secretary, it is evident, that the increase of crime in England has proceeded with incomprehensible rapidity. The numbers of arrests for *criminal* offences reached in the years: 1805, 4,605; 1810, 5,146; 1815, 7,898; 1820, 13,710; 1825, 14,437; 1830, 18,107; 1835, 20,731; 1840, 27,187; 1841, 27,760; 1842, 31,309 in England and Wales alone. That is to say, they increased sevenfold in thirty-seven years. Of these arrests in 1842, 4,497 were made in Lancashire alone, or more than 14 per cent. of the whole; and 4,094 in Middlesex, including London, or more than 13 per cent. So that two districts which include great cities with large proletarian populations, produced one-fourth of the total amount of crime, though their population is far from forming one-fourth of the whole. Moreover, the criminal tables prove directly that nearly all crime arises within the proletariat; for, in 1842, taking the average, out of 100 criminals 32.35 could neither read nor write; 58.32 read and wrote imperfectly; 6.77 could read and write well; 0.22 had enjoyed a higher education, while the degree of education of 2.34 could not be ascertained. In Scotland crime has increased yet more rapidly. There were but 89 arrests for criminal offences in 1819, and as early as 1837 the number had risen to 3,176, and in 1842 to 4,189. In Lanarkshire, where Sheriff Alison himself made out the official report, population has doubled once in thirty years, and crime once in five and a half, or six times more rapidly than the population. The offences, as in all civilized countries, are, in the great majority of cases, against property, and have therefore arisen from want in some form; for what a man has, he does not steal. The proportion of offences against property to the population, which in the Netherlands is as 1:7,140, and in France, as 1:1,804, was in England when Gaskell wrote, as 1:799. The proportion of offences against persons to the population is, in the Netherlands, 1:28,904; in France, 1:17,573; in England, 1:23,395; that of crimes in general to the population in the agricultural districts, as 1:1,043; in the manufacturing districts as 1:840.[9] In the whole of England to-day the proportion is 1:660;[10] though it is scarcely ten years since Gaskell's book appeared!

These facts are certainly more than sufficient to bring any one, even a bourgeois, to pause and reflect upon the consequences of such a state of things. If demoralization and crime multiply twenty years longer in this proportion, (and if English manufacture in these twenty years should be less prosperous than heretofore, the progressive multiplication of crime can only continue the more rapidly), what will the result be? Society is already in a state of visible dissolution; it is impossible to pick up a newspaper without seeing the most striking evidence of the giving way of all social ties. I look at random into a heap of English journals lying before me; there is the Manchester *Guardian* for October 30, 1844, which reports for three days. It no longer takes the trouble to give exact details as to Manchester, and merely relates the most interesting cases: that the workers in a mill have struck for higher wages without giving notice and been condemned by a Justice of the Peace to resume work; that in Salford a couple of boys had been caught stealing, and a bankrupt tradesman tried to cheat his creditors. From the neighboring towns the reports are more detailed: In Ashton, two thefts, one burglary, one suicide; in Bury, one theft; in Bolton, two thefts, one revenue fraud; in Leigh, one theft; in Oldham, one strike for wages, one theft, one fight between Irish women, one non-

---

9. Manufacturing Population of England, chap. 10.
10. The total of population, about fifteen millions, divided by the number of convicted criminals, (22,733).

Union hatter assaulted by Union men, one mother beaten by her son, one attack upon the police, one robbery of a church; in Stockport, discontent of workingmen with wages, one theft, one fraud, one fight, one wife beaten by her husband; in Warrington, one theft, one fight; in Wigan, one theft, and one robbery of a church. The reports of the London papers are much worse; frauds, thefts, assaults, family quarrels crowd one another. A *Times* of September 12, 1844, falls into my hand, which gives a report of a single day, including a theft, an attack upon the police, a sentence upon a father requiring him to support his illegitimate son, the abandonment of a child by its parents, and the poisoning of a man by his wife. Similar reports are to be found in all the English papers. In this country social war is under full headway, every one stands for himself and fights for himself against all comers, and whether or not he shall injure all the others who are his declared foes, depends upon a cynical calculation as to what is most advantageous for himself. It no longer occurs to any one to come to a peaceful understanding with his fellow man; all differences are settled by threats, violence, or in a law court. In short, every one sees in his neighbor an enemy to be got out of the way or, at least, a tool to be used for his own advantage. And this war grows from year to year as the criminal tables show, more violent, passionate, irreconcilable. The enemies are dividing gradually into two great camps, the bourgeoisie on the one hand, the workers on the other. This war of each against all, of the bourgeoisie against the proletariat, need cause us no surprise, for it is only the logical sequel of the principle involved in free competition. But it may very well surprise us that the bourgeoisie remains so quiet and composed in the face of the rapidly gathering storm clouds, that it can read all these things daily in the papers without, we will not say indignation at such a social condition, but fear of its consequences, of a universal outburst of that which manifests itself symptomatically from day to day in the form of crime. But then it is the bourgeoisie, and from its standpoint cannot even see the facts, much less perceive their consequences. One thing only is astounding, that class prejudice and preconceived opinions can hold a whole class of human beings in such perfect, I might almost say such mad blindness. Meanwhile the development of the nation goes its way whether the bourgeoisie has eyes for it or not, and will surprise the property-holding class one day with things not dreamed of in its philosophy. . . .

THE ATTITUDE OF THE BOURGEOISIE TOWARDS THE PROLETARIAT

. . . Let us turn now to the manner in which the bourgeoisie as a party, as the power of the State, conducts itself towards the proletariat. Laws are necessary only because there are persons in existence who own nothing; and although this is directly expressed in but few laws, as for instance those against vagabonds, and tramps, in which the proletariat as such is outlawed, yet enmity to the proletariat is so emphatically the basis of the law that the judges, and especially the Justices of the Peace who are bourgeois themselves and with whom the proletariat comes most in contact, find this meaning in the laws without further consideration. If a rich man is brought up, or rather summoned to appear before the court, the judge regrets that he is obliged to impose so much trouble, treats the matter as favorably as possible and, if he is forced to condemn the accused, does so with extreme regret, etc., etc., and the end of it all is a miserable fine which the bourgeois throws upon the table with contempt and then departs. But if a poor devil gets into such a position as involves appearing before the Justice of the Peace, he has almost always spent the night in the station-house, with a crowd of his peers, is regarded from the beginning as guilty; his defense is set aside with a contemptuous "Oh! we know the excuses," and a fine imposed which he cannot pay and must work out with several months on the treadmill. And if nothing can be proved against him, he is sent to the treadmill, none the less, "as a rogue and a vagabond." The partisanship of the Justices of the Peace, especially in the country, surpasses all description, and it is so much the order of the day that all cases which are not too utterly flagrant are quietly reported by the newspapers, without comment. Nor is any thing else to be expected. For on the one hand, these Dogberries do merely construe the law according to the intent of the framers and, on the other, they are themselves bourgeois who see the foundation of all true order in the interests of their class. And the conduct of the police corresponds to that of the Justices of the Peace. The bourgeois may do what he will and the policeman remains ever polite, adhering strictly to the law, but the proletarian is roughly, brutally treated; his poverty both casts the suspicion of every sort of crime upon him and cuts him off from legal redress against any caprice of the administrators of the law; for him, therefore, the protecting forms of the law do not exist, the police force their way into his house without further ceremony, arrest and abuse him; and only when a workingmen's association, such as the miners, engages a Roberts, does it become evident how little the protective side of the law exists for the workingmen, how frequently he has to bear all the burdens of the law without enjoying its benefits. . . .

Meanwhile the most open declaration of war of the bourgeoisie upon the proletariat is Malthus' Law of Population and the New Poor Law framed in accordance with it. We have already alluded several times to the theory of Malthus. We may sum up its final result in these few words that the earth is perennially overpopulated, whence poverty, misery, distress and immorality must prevail; that it is the lot, the eternal destiny of mankind, to exist in too great numbers and therefore in diverse classes, of which some are rich, educated and moral, and others more or less poor, distressed, ignorant and immoral. Hence it follows in practice, and Malthus himself drew this conclusion, that charities and poor rates are, properly speaking, nonsense, since they serve only to maintain and stimulate the increase of the surplus population whose competition crushes down wages for the employed; that the employment of the poor by the Poor Law Guardians is equally unreasonable since only a fixed quantity of the products of labor can be consumed, and for every unemployed laborer thus furnished employment another hitherto employed, must be driven into enforced idleness whence private undertakings suffer at cost of Poor Law industry; that, in other words, the whole problem is not how to support the surplus population, but how to restrain it as far as possible. Malthus declares in plain English that the right to live, a right previously asserted in favor of every man in the world, is nonsense. He quotes the words of a poet, that the poor man comes to the feast of Nature and finds no cover laid for him, and adds that "she bids him begone," for he did not before his birth ask of society whether or not he is welcome. This is now the pet theory of all genuine English bourgeois, and very naturally, since it is the most specious excuse for them, and has moreover a good deal of truth in it under existing conditions. If then the problem is not to make the "surplus population" useful, to transform it into available population but merely to let it starve to death in the least objectionable way and to prevent its having too many children, this of course, is simple enough, provided the surplus population perceives its own superfluousness and takes kindly to starvation. There is, however, in spite of the violent exertions of the humane bourgeoisie, no immediate prospect of its succeeding in bringing about such a disposition among the workers. The workers have taken it into their heads that they, with their busy hands, are the necessary, and the rich capitalists, who do nothing, the surplus population.

Since, however, the rich hold all the power, the proletarians must submit, if they will not good-temperedly perceive it for themselves, to have the law actually declare them superfluous. This has been done by the New Poor Law. The Old Poor Law which rested upon the Act of 1601, (the 43d of Elizabeth), naively started from the notion that it is the duty of the parish to provide for the maintenance of the poor. Whoever had no work received relief, and the poor man regarded the parish as pledged to protect him from starvation. He demanded his weekly relief as his right, not as a favor, and this became, at last, too much for the bourgeoisie. In 1833, when the bourgeoisie had just come into power through the Reform Bill, and pauperism in the country districts had just reached its full development, the bourgeoisie began the reform of the Poor Law according to its own point of view. A commission was appointed, which investigated the administration of the Poor Laws, and revealed a multitude of abuses. It was discovered that the whole working class in the country was pauperized and more or less dependent upon the rates from which they receive relief when wages were low; it was found that this system by which the unemployed were maintained, the ill-paid and the parents of large families relieved, fathers of illegitimate children required to pay alimony and poverty, in general, recognized as needing protection—it was found that this system was ruining the nation, was:

> "A check upon industry, a reward for improvident marriage, a stimulus to increased population and a means of counterbalancing the effect of an increased population upon wages; a national provision for discouraging the honest and industrious, and protecting the lazy, vicious and improvident; calculated to destroy the bonds of family life, hinder systematically the accumulation of capital, scatter that which is already accumulated and ruin the taxpayers. Moreover, in the provision of aliment, it sets a premium upon illegitimate children."

(Words of the Report of the Poor Law Commissioner).[11] This description of the action of the Old

---
11. Extracts from Information received from the Poor Law Commissioners. Published by authority. London, 1833.

Poor Law is certainly correct; relief fosters laziness and increase of "surplus population." Under present social conditions it is perfectly clear that the poor man is compelled to be an egotist, and when he can choose, living equally well in either case, he prefers doing nothing to working. But what follows therefrom? That our present social conditions are good for nothing, and not as the Malthusian Commissioners conclude, that poverty is a crime and as such to be visited with heinous penalties which may serve as a warning to others.

But these wise Malthusians were so thoroughly convinced of the infallibility of their theory that they did not for one moment hesitate to cast the poor into the Procrustean bed of their economic notions and treat them with the most revolting cruelty. Convinced with Malthus and the rest of the adherents of free competition that it is best to let each one take care of himself, they would have preferred to abolish the Poor Laws altogether. Since, however, they had neither the courage nor the authority to do this, they proposed a Poor Law constructed as far as possible in harmony with the doctrine of Malthus, which is yet more barbarous than that of *laissez-faire,* because it interferes actively in cases in which the latter is passive. We have seen how Malthus characterizes poverty or rather the want of employment, as a crime under the title "superfluity," and recommends for it punishment by starvation. The commissioners were not quite so barbarous; death out-right by starvation was something too terrible even for a Poor Law Commissioner. "Good," said they, "we grant you poor a right to exist, but only to exist; the right to multiply you have not, nor the right to exist as befits human beings. You are a pest, and if we cannot get rid of you as we do of other pests, you shall feel, at least, that you are a pest, and you shall at least be held in check, kept from bringing into the world other "surplus" either directly or through inducing in others laziness and want of employment. Live you shall, but live as an awful warning to all those who might have inducements to become "superfluous."

They accordingly brought in the New Poor Law, which was passed by Parliament in 1834, and continues in force down to the present day. All relief in money and provisions was abolished; the only relief allowed was admission to the workhouses immediately built. The regulations for these workhouses, or as the people call them, Poor Law Bastilles, is such as to frighten away every one who has the slightest prospect of life without this form of public charity. To make sure that relief be applied for only in the most extreme cases and after every other effort had failed, the workhouse has been made the most repulsive residence which the refined ingenuity of a Malthusian can invent. The food is worse than that of the most ill-paid workingman while employed, and the work harder, or they might prefer the workhouse to their wretched existence outside. Meat, especially fresh meat, is rarely furnished, chiefly potatoes, the worst possible bread and oat-meal porridge, little or no beer. The food of criminal prisoners is better, as a rule, so that the paupers frequently commit some offense for the purpose of getting into jail. For the workhouse is a jail, too; he who does not finish his task gets nothing to eat; he who wishes to go out must ask permission, which is granted or not, according to his behavior or the inspector's whim; tobacco is forbidden, also the receipt of gifts from relatives or friends outside the house; the paupers wear a workhouse uniform, and are handed over helpless and without redress, to the caprice of the inspectors. To prevent their labor from competing with that of outside concerns, they are set to rather useless tasks; the men break stones "as much as a strong man can accomplish with effort in a day;" the women, children and aged men pick oakum, for I know not what insignificant use. To prevent the "superfluous" from multiplying and "demoralized" parents from influencing their children, families are broken up; the husband is placed in one wing, the wife in another, the children in a third, and they are permitted to see one another only at stated times after long intervals, and then only when they have, in the opinion of the officials, behaved well. And in order to shut off the external world from contamination by pauperism within these bastilles, the inmates are permitted to receive visits only with the consent of the officials, and in the reception rooms, to communicate in general with the world outside only by leave and under supervision.

Yet the food is supposed to be wholesome and the treatment humane with all this. But the intent of the law is too loudly outspoken for this requirement to be in any wise fulfilled. The Poor Law Commissioners and the whole English bourgeoisie deceive themselves if they believe the administration of the law possible without these results. The treatment, which the letter of the law prescribes, is in direct contradiction of its spirit. If the law in its essence proclaims the poor criminals, the workhouses prisons, their inmates beyond the pale of the law, beyond the pale of humanity, objects of disgust and repulsion, all commands to the contrary are unavailing. In practice, the spirit and not the letter of the law is followed in the treatment of the poor, as in the following few examples:

In the workhouse at Greenwich, in the summer of 1843, a boy five years old was punished by being shut into the dead-room, where he had to sleep upon the lids of the coffins. In the workhouse at Herne, the same punishment was inflicted upon a little girl for wetting the bed at night, and this method of punishment seems to be a favorite one. This workhouse, which stands in one of the most beautiful regions of Kent, is peculiar in so far as its windows open only upon the court, and but two, newly introduced, afford the inmates a glimpse of the outer world. The author who relates this in the *Illuminated Magazine,* closes his description with the words: "If God punished men for crimes as man punishes man for poverty, than woe to the sons of Adam!"

In November, 1843, a man died at Leicester, who had been dismissed two days before from the workhouse at Coventry. The details of the treatment of the poor in this institution are revolting. The man, George Robson, had a wound upon the shoulder, the treatment of which was wholly neglected; he was set to work at the pump, using the sound arm; was given only the usual workhouse fare, which he was utterly unable to digest by reason of the unhealed wound and his general debility; he naturally grew weaker, and the more he complained, the more brutally he was treated. When his wife tried to bring him her drop of beer, she was reprimanded and forced to drink it herself in the presence of the female warder. He became ill, but received no better treatment. Finally, at his own request, and under the most insulting epithets, he was discharged, accompanied by his wife. Two days later he died at Leicester, in consequence of the neglected wound and of the food given him, which was utterly indigestible for one in his condition, as the surgeon present at the inquest testified. When he was discharged, there were handed to him letters containing money, which had been kept back six weeks and opened, according to a rule of the establishment, by the inspector! In Birmingham such scandalous occurrences took place, that finally, in 1843, an official was sent to investigate the case. He found that four tramps had been shut up naked under a stair-case in a black hole, eight to ten days, often deprived of food until noon, and that at the severest season of the year. A little boy had been passed through all grades of punishment known to the institution, first locked up in a damp, vaulted, narrow, lumber-room; then in the dog-hole twice, the second time three days and three nights; then the same length of time in the old dog-hole, which was still worse; then the tramp-room, a stinking, disgustingly filthy hole, with wooden sleeping stalls, where the official, in the course of his inspection, found two other tattered boys, shrivelled with cold, who had been spending three days there. In the dog-hole there were often seven, and in the tramp-room twenty men huddled together. Women, also, were placed in the dog-hole because they refused to go to church, and one was shut four days into the tramp-room, with God knows what sort of company, and that while she was ill and receiving medicine! Another woman was placed in the insane department for punishment, though she was perfectly sane. In the workhouse at Bacton, in Suffolk, in January, 1844, a similar investigation revealed the fact that a feeble-minded woman was employed as nurse and took care of the patients accordingly, while sufferers who were often restless at night, or tried to get up, were tied fast with cords passed over the covering and under the bedstead to save the nurses the trouble of sitting up at night. One patient was found dead, bound in this way. In the St. Pancras workhouse in London (where the cheap shirts already mentioned are made), an epileptic died of suffocation during an attack in bed, no one coming to his relief; in the same house four to six, sometimes eight children, slept in one bed. In Shoreditch workhouse, a man was placed together with a fever patient violently ill, in a bed teeming with vermin. In Bethnal Green workhouse, London, a woman in the sixth month of pregnancy was shut up in the reception-room with her two-year-old child, from February 28th to March 20th, without being admitted into the workhouse itself, and without a trace of a bed or the means of satisfying the most natural wants. Her husband, who was brought into the workhouse, begged to have his wife released from this imprisonment, whereupon he received twenty-four hours imprisonment with bread and water as the penalty of his insolence. In the workhouse at Slough, near Windsor, a man lay dying in September, 1844. His wife journeyed to him, arriving at midnight, and hastening to the workhouse, was refused admission; she was not permitted to see her husband until the next morning, and then only in the presence of a female warder, who forced herself upon the wife at every succeeding visit, sending her away at the end of half an hour. In the workhouse at Middleton, in Lancashire, twelve and at times eighteen paupers, of both sexes, slept in one room. This institution is not embraced by the New Poor Law, but is administered under an old special act (Gilbert's Act.) The inspector had instituted a brewery in the house for his own benefit. In Stockport, July 31st, 1844, a man seventy-two years old, was brought before the Justice of the Peace for refusing to break stones, and insisting that by reason of his age and a stiff knee, he was unfit for this work. In vain did he offer to undertake any work adapted to his physical strength; he was sentenced to two weeks upon the treadmill. In the workhouse at Basford, an inspecting official found that the sheets had not been changed in thirteen weeks, shirts in four weeks, stockings in two to ten months, so that of forty-five boys but three had stockings, and all their shirts were in tatters. The beds swarmed with vermin, and the tableware was washed in the slop-pails. In the West of London workhouse, a porter who had infected four girls with syphilis was not discharged, and another who had concealed a deaf and dumb girl four days and nights in his bed was also retained.

As in life, so in death. The poor are dumped into the earth like infected cattle. The pauper burial ground of St. Brides, London, is a bare morass in use as a cemetery since the time of Charles II., and filled with heaps of bones; every Wednesday the paupers are thrown into a ditch fourteen feet deep, a curate rattles through the Litany at the top of his speed; the ditch is loosely covered in, to be reopened the next Wednesday, and filled with corpses as long as one more can be forced in. The putrefaction thus engendered contaminates the whole neighborhood. In Manchester, the pauper burial ground lies opposite to the Old Town, along the Irk; this, too, is a rough, desolate place. About two years ago, a railroad was carried through it. If it had been a respectable cemetery, how the bourgeoisie and the clergy would have shrieked over the desecration! But it was a pauper burial ground, the resting-place of the outcast and superfluous, so no one concerned himself about the matter. It was not even thought worth while to convey the partially decayed bodies to the other side of the cemetery; they were heaped up just as it happened, and piles were driven into newly-made graves, so that the water oozed out of the swampy ground, pregnant with putrefying matter, and filled the neighborhood with the most revolting and injurious gases. The disgusting brutality which accompanied this work I cannot describe in further detail.

Can any one wonder that the poor decline to accept public relief under these conditions? That they starve rather than enter these bastilles? I have the reports of five cases in which persons actually starving, when the guardians refused them outdoor relief, went back to their miserable homes and died of starvation rather than enter these hells. Thus far have the Poor Law Commissioners attained their object. At the same time, however, the workhouses have intensified more than any other measure of the party in power the hatred of the working class against the property holders, who very generally admire the New Poor Law. . . .

CHAPTER 16

PETER KROPOTKIN

This chapter presents Peter Kropotkin's *Law and Authority: An Anarchist Essay* (1886), which was first published as a pamphlet by the International Publishing Company (London). On the original publication, Kropotkin's name appears as "Pierre Kropotkine."

Shortly after Marx had passed away, Kropotkin wrote his major works of anarchist communism. Kropotkin's writings embodied the spirit of nineteenth-century natural science, socialism/communism, and anarchism. The integration of these three currents of thought provided the basis for his reality claims, his activism, and his theories of law, crime, and punishment. Kropotkin opposed economic systems that allow for great disparities of wealth and viewed law as a mechanism used by the elite to maintain their wealth and power. The fact that he adopted such a standpoint, that he developed an anarchist communist worldview, is remarkable given that his ascribed status was that of a prince within the Russian aristocracy.

In *Law and Authority*, Kropotkin provides a classic anarchist critique of law. He argues that people mistakenly view law as "a remedy for evil" when, in fact, it is more reasonable to view it as a source of evil. For instance, the law, for Kropotkin, is used to maintain the exploitation of workers and an uneven distribution of wealth, conditions that prompt a great deal of crime. He also maintains that the punishments imposed by the law are a cause of harmful conduct and concludes that offenders should receive "brotherly care" rather than punishment. Overall, Kropotkin's work anticipates several common contentions of contemporary critical criminology.

LAW AND AUTHORITY: AN ANARCHIST ESSAY
by **Peter Kropotkin**

I

"When ignorance reigns in society and disorder in the minds of men, laws are multiplied, legislation is expected to do everything, and each fresh law being a fresh miscalculation, men are continually led to demand from it what can proceed only from themselves, from their own education and their own morality." It is no revolutionist who says this, nor even a reformer. It is the jurist, Dalloy, author of the Collection of French law known as "Repertoire de la Legislation." And yet, though these lines were written by a man who was himself a maker and admirer of law, they perfectly represent the abnormal condition of our society.

In existing States a fresh law is looked upon as a remedy for evil. Instead of themselves altering what is bad, people begin by demanding a *law* to alter it. If the road between two villages is impassable, the peasant says:—"There should be a law about parish roads." If a park-keeper takes advantage of the want of spirit in those who follow him with servile observance and insults one of them, the insulted man says, "There should be a law to enjoin more politeness upon park keepers." If there is stagnation in agriculture or commerce, the husbandman, cattle-breeder, or corn speculator argues, "It is protective legislation that we require." Down to the old clothes-man there is not one who does not demand a law to protect his own little trade. If the employer lowers wages or increases the hours of labour, the politician in embryo exclaims, "We must have a law to put all that to rights," instead of telling the workers that there are other, and much more effectual means of settling these things straight; namely, recovering from the employer the wealth of which he has been despoiling the workmen for generations. In short, a law everywhere and for everything! A law about fashions, a law about mad dogs, a law about virtue, a law to put a stop to all the vices and all the evils which result from human indolence and cowardice.

We are so perverted by an education which from infancy seeks to kill in us the spirit of revolt, and to develop that of submission to authority; we are so perverted by this existence under the ferule of a law, which regulates every event in life—our birth, our education, our development, our love, our friendship—that, if this state of things continues, we shall lose all initiative, all habit of thinking for ourselves. Our society seems no longer able to understand that it is possible to exist otherwise than under the reign of Law, elaborated by a representative government and administered by a handful of rulers; and even when it has gone so far as to emancipate itself from the thraldom, its first care has been to reconstitute it immediately. "The Year I of Liberty" has never lasted more than a day, for after proclaiming it men put themselves the very next morning under the yoke of Law and Authority.

Indeed, for some thousands of years, those who govern us have done nothing but ring the changes upon "Respect for law, obedience to authority." This is the moral atmosphere in which parents bring up their children, and school only serves to confirm the impression. Cleverly assorted scraps of spurious science are inculcated upon the children to prove necessity of law; obedience to the law is made a religion; moral goodness and the law of the masters are fused into one and the same divinity. The historical hero of the schoolroom is the man who obeys the law, and defends it against rebels.

Later, when we enter upon public life, society and literature, impressing us day by day and hour by hour, as the water drop hollows the stone, continue to inculcate the same prejudice. Books of history, of political science, of social economy are stuffed with this respect for law; even the physical sciences have been pressed into the service by introducing artificial modes of expression, borrowed from theology and arbitrary power, into knowledge which is purely the result of observation. Thus our intelligence is successfully befogged, and always to maintain our respect for law. The same work is done by newspapers. They have not an article which does not preach respect for law, even where the third page proves every day to demonstrate the imbecility of that law, and shows how it is dragged through every variety of mud and filth by those charged with its administration. Servility before the law has become a virtue, and I doubt if there was ever even a revolutionist who did not begin in his youth as the defender of law against what are generally called "abuses," although these last are inevitable consequences of the law itself.

Art pipes in unison with would-be science. The hero of the sculptor, the painter, the musician shields Law beneath his buckler, and, with flashing eyes and distended nostrils stands ever ready to strike down the man who would lay hands upon her. Temples are raised to her; revolutionists themselves hesitate to touch the high priests consecrated to her service, and when revolution is about to sweep away some ancient institution, it is still by law that it endeavours to sanctify the deed.

The confused mass of rules of conduct called Law, which has been bequeathed to us by slavery, serfdom, feudalism, and royalty, has taken the place of those stone monsters before whom human victims used to be immolated, and whom slavish savages dared not even touch lest they should be slain by the thunder-bolts of heaven.

This new worship has been established with especial success since the rise to supreme power of the middle class—since the great French Revolution. Under the ancient *regime*, men spoke little of laws; unless, indeed, it were, with Montesquieu, Rousseau, and Voltaire, to oppose them to royal caprice; obedience to the good pleasure of the king and his lackeys was compulsory on pain of hanging or imprisonment. But during and after the Revolution, when the lawyers rose to power, they did their best to strengthen the principle upon which their ascendancy depended. The middle-class at once accepted it as a dike to dam up the popular torrent. The priestly crew hastened to sanctify it, to save their bark from foundering amid the breakers. Finally, the people received it as an improvement upon the arbitrary authority and violence of the past.

To understand this, we must transport ourselves in imagination into the eighteenth century. Our hearts must have ached at the story of the atrocities committed by the all-powerful nobles of that time upon the men and women of the people, before we can understand what must have been the magic influence upon the peasant's mind of the words, "Equality before the law, obedience to the law without distinction of birth or fortune." He, who until then, had been treated more cruelly than a beast, he who had never had any rights, he who had never obtained justice against the most revolting actions on the part of a noble, unless in revenge he killed him and was hanged—he saw himself recognised by this maxim, at least in theory, at least with regard to his personal rights, as the equal of his lord. Whatever this law might be, it promised to affect lord and peasant alike; it proclaimed the equality of rich and poor before the judge. The promise was a lie, and to-day we know it; but at that period it was an advance, a homage to justice, as hypocrisy is a homage rendered to truth. This is the reason that when the saviours of the menaced middle-class (the Robespierres and the Dantons) took their stand upon the writings of the Rousseaus and the Voltaires, and proclaimed "Respect for law, the same for every man," the people accepted the compromise; for their revolutionary impetus had already spent its force in the contest with a foe whose ranks drew closer day by day. They bowed the neck beneath the yoke of law to save themselves from the arbitrary power of their lords.

The middle class has ever since continued to make the most of this maxim, which, with another principle, that of representative government, sums up the whole philosophy of the bourgeois age, the XIX century. It has preached this doctrine in its schools, it has propagated it in its writings, it has moulded its art and science to the same purpose, it has thrust its beliefs into every hole and corner—like a pious Englishwoman, who slips tracts under the door—and it has done all this so successfully, that to-day we behold the issue in the detestable fact, that, at the very moment when the spirit of turbulent criticism is re-awakening, men who long for freedom begin the attempt to obtain it by entreating their masters to be kind enough to protect them by modifying the laws which these masters themselves have created!

But times and tempers are changed since a hundred years ago. Rebels are everywhere to be found, who no longer wish to obey the law without knowing whence it comes, what are its uses, and whither arises the obligation to submit to it, and the reverence with which it is encompassed. The rebels of our day are criticising the very foundations of Society, which have hitherto been held sacred, and first and foremost amongst them that fetish, law. Just for this reason, the upheaval which is at hand, is no mere insurrection, it is a *Revolution*.

The critics analyse the sources of law, and find there, either a god, product of the terrors of the savage, and stupid, paltry and malicious as the priests who vouch for its supernatural origin, or else, bloodshed, conquest by fire and sword. They study the characteristics of law, and instead of perpetual growth corresponding to that of the human race, they find its distinctive trait to be immobility, a tendency to crystalise what should be modified and developed day by day. They ask how law has been maintained, and in its service they see the atrocities of Byzantinism, the cruelties of the Inquisition, the tortures of the Middle Ages, living flesh torn by the lash of the executioner, chains, clubs, axes, the gloomy dungeons of prisons, agony, curses and tears. In our own days they see, as before, the axe, the cord, the rifle, the prison; on the one hand, the brutalised prisoner, reduced to the condition of a caged beast by the debasement of his whole moral being, and on the other, the judge, stripped of every feeling which does honor to human nature, living like a visionary in a world of legal fictions, revelling in the inflection of imprisonment and death, without even suspecting, in the cold malignity of his madness, the abyss of degradation into which he has himself fallen before the eyes of those whom he condemns.

They see a race of law-makers legislating without knowing what their laws are about; to-day voting a law on the sanitation of towns, without the faintest notion of hygiene, tomorrow making regulations for the armament of troops, without so much as understanding a gun; making laws about teaching and education without ever having given a lesson of any sort, or even an honest education to their own children; legislating at random in all directions, but never forgetting the penalties to be meted out to ragamuffins, the prison and the galleys, which are to be the portion of men a thousand times less immoral than these legislators themselves.

Finally, they see the gaoler on the way to lose all human feeling, the detective trained as a bloodhound, the police spy despising himself; "informing," metamorphosed into a virtue; corruption, erected into a system; all the vices, all the evil qualities of mankind countenanced and cultivated to insure the triumph of law.

All this we see, and, therefore, instead of inanely repeating the old formula, "Respect the law," we say, "Despise law and all its attributes!" In place of the cowardly phrase "Obey the law," our cry is "Revolt against all laws!"

Only compare the misdeeds accomplished in the name of each law, with the good it has been able to effect, and weigh carefully both good and evil, and you will see if we are right.

II

Relatively speaking, law is a product of modern times. For ages and ages mankind lived without any written law, even that graved in symbols upon the entrance stones of a temple. During that period, human relations were simply regulated by customs, habits and usages, made sacred by constant repetition, and acquired by each person in childhood, exactly as he learned how to obtain his food by hunting, cattle-rearing, or agriculture.

All human societies have passed through this primitive phase, and to this day a large proportion of mankind have no written law. Every tribe has its own manners and customs; customary law, as the jurists say. It has social habits, and that suffices to maintain cordial relations between the inhabitants of the village, the members of the tribe or community. Even amongst ourselves—the "civilized" nations—when we leave large towns, and go into the country, we see that there the mutual relations of the inhabitants are still regulated according to ancient and generally accepted customs, and not according to the written law of the legislators. The peasants of Russia, Italy, and Spain, and even of a large part of France and England, have no conception of written law. It only meddles with their lives to regulate their relations with the State. As to relations between themselves, though these are sometimes very complex, they are simply regulated according to ancient custom. Formerly, this was the case with mankind in general.

Two distinctly marked currents of custom are revealed by analysis of the usages of primitive people.

As man does not live in a solitary state, habits and feelings develop within him which are useful for the preservation of society and the propagation of the race. Without social feelings and usages, life in common would have been absolutely impossible. It is not law which has established them; they are anterior to all law. Neither is it religion which has ordained them; they are anterior to all religions. They are found amongst all animals living in society. They are spontaneously developed by the very nature of things, like those habits in animals which men call instinct. They spring from a process of evolution, which is useful, and, indeed, necessary, to keep society together in the struggle it is forced to maintain for existence. Savages end by no longer eating one another, because they find it in the long-run more advantageous to devote themselves to some sort of cultivation, than to enjoy the pleasure of feasting upon the flesh of an aged relative once a year. Many travelers have depicted the manners of absolutely independent tribes, where laws and chiefs are unknown, but where the members of the tribe have given up stabbing one another in every dispute, because the habit of living in society has ended by developing certain feelings of fraternity and oneness of interest, and they prefer appealing to a third person to settle their differences. The hospitality of primitive peoples, respect for human life, the sense of reciprocal obligation, compassion for the weak, courage, extending even to the sacrifice of self for others, which is first learnt for the sake of children and friends, and later, for that of members of the same community—all these qualities are developed in man anterior to all law, independently of all religion, as in the case of the social animals. Such feelings and practices are the inevitable results of social life. Without being, as say priests and metaphysicians, inherent in man, such qualities are the consequence of life in common.

But side by side with these customs, necessary to the life of societies and the preservation of the race, other desires, other passions, and therefore other habits and customs, are evolved in human associations. The desire to dominate others and impose one's own will upon them; the desire to seize upon the products of the labour of a neighbouring tribe; the desire to surround oneself with comforts, without producing anything, whilst slaves provide their master with the means of procuring every sort of pleasure and luxury—these selfish, personal desires give rise to another current of habits and customs. The priest and the warrior, the charlatan who makes a profit out of superstition, and after freeing himself from the fear of the devil, cultivates it in others; and the bully, who procures the invasion and pillage of his neighbours, that he may return laden with booty, and followed by slaves; these two, hand in hand, have succeeded in imposing upon primitive society customs advantageous to both of them, but tending to perpetuate their domination of the masses. Profiting by the indolence, the fears, the inertia of the crowd, and thanks to the continual repetition of the same acts, they have permanently established customs which have become a solid basis for their own domination.

For this purpose, they have made use, in the first place, of that tendency to run in a groove, so highly developed in mankind. In children and all savages it attains striking proportions, and it may also be observed in animals. Man, when he is at all superstitious, is always afraid to introduce any sort of change into existing conditions; he generally venerates what is ancient. "Our fathers did so and so; they got on pretty well; they brought you up; they were not unhappy; do the same!" the old say to the young, every time the latter wish to alter things. The unknown frightens them, they prefer to cling to the past, even when that past represents poverty, oppression, and slavery. It may even be said that the more miserable a man is, the more he dreads every sort of change, lest it may make him more wretched still. Some ray of hope, a few scraps of comfort, must penetrate his gloomy abode before he can begin to desire better things, to criticise the old ways of living, and prepare to imperil them for the sake of bringing about a change. So long as he is not imbued with hope, so long as he is not freed from the tutelage of those who utilise his superstition and his fears, he prefers remaining in his former position. If the young desire any change, the old raise a cry of alarm against the innovators. Some savages would rather die than transgress the customs of their country, because they have been told from childhood that the least infraction of established routine would bring ill-luck, and ruin the whole tribe. Even in the present day, what numbers of politicians, economists, and would-be revolutionists act under the same impression, and cling to a vanishing past. How many care only to seek for precedents. How many fiery innovators are mere copyists of bygone revolutions.

This spirit of routine, originating in superstition, indolence, and cowardice, has in all times been the mainstay of oppression. In primitive human societies, it was cleverly turned to account by priests and military chiefs. They perpetuated customs useful only to themselves, and succeeded in imposing them on the whole tribe. So long as this conservative spirit could be exploited so as to assure the chief in his encroachments upon individual liberty, so long as the only inequalities between men were the work of nature, and these were not increased a hundredfold by the concentration of power and wealth, there was no need for law, and the formidable paraphernalia of tribunals and ever-augmenting penalties to enforce it.

But as society became more and more divided into two hostile classes, one seeking to establish its domination, the other struggling to escape, the strife began. Now the conqueror was in a hurry to secure the results of his actions in a permanent form, he tried to place them beyond question, to make them holy and venerable by every means in his power. Law made its appearance under the sanction of the priest, and the warrior's club was placed at its service. Its office was to render immutable such customs as were to the advantage of the dominant minority. Military authority undertook to ensure obedience. This new function was a fresh guarantee to the power of the warrior; now he had not only mere brute force at his service; he was the defender of law.

If law, however, presented nothing but a collection of prescriptions serviceable to rulers, it would find some difficulty in insuring acceptance and obedience. Well, the legislators confounded in one code the two currents of custom, of which we have just been speaking, the maxims which represent principles of morality and social union wrought out as a result of life in common, and the mandates, which are meant to ensure eternal existence to inequality. Customs, absolutely essential to the very being of society, are, in the code, cleverly intermingled with usages imposed by the ruling caste, and both claim equal respect from the crowd. "Do not kill," says the code, and hastens to add, "And pay tithes to the priest." "Do not steal," says the code, and immediately after, "He who refuses to pay taxes, shall have his hand struck off."

Such was law; and it has maintained its twofold character to this day. Its origin is the desire of the ruling class to give permanence to customs imposed by themselves for their own advantage. Its character is the skilful co-mingling of customs useful to society, customs which have no need of law to ensure respect, with other customs useful only to rulers, injurious to the mass of the people, and maintained only by the fear of punishment.

Like individual capital, which was born of fraud and violence, and developed under the auspices of authority, law has no title to the respect of men. Born of violence and superstition, and established in the interests of consumer, priest and rich exploiter, it must be utterly destroyed on the day when the people desire to break their chains.

We shall be still better convinced of this when, in the next chapter, we have analysed the ulterior development of laws under the auspices of religion, authority and the existing parliamentary system.

III

We have seen in the previous chapter how law originated in established usage and custom, and how, from the beginning it has represented a skilful mixture of social habits, necessary to the preservation of the human race, with other customs, imposed by those who used popular superstition, as well as the right of the strongest, for their own advantage. This double character of law has determined its later development during the growth of political organization. Whilst in the course of ages the nucleus of social custom inscribed in law has been subjected to but slight and gradual modifications, the other portion has been largely developed in directions indicated by the interests of the dominant classes, and to the injury of the classes they oppress. From time to time these dominant classes have allowed a law to be extorted from them which presented, or appeared to present, some guarantee for the disinherited. But then such laws have but repealed a previous law, made for the advantage of the ruling caste. "The best laws," says Buckle, "were those which repealed the preceding ones." But what terrible efforts have been needed, what rivers of blood have been spilt, every time there has been a question of the repeal of one of these fundamental enactments serving to hold the people in fetters. Before she could abolish the last vestiges of serfdom and feudal rights, and break up the power of the royal court, France was forced to pass through four years of revolution and twenty years of war. Decades of conflict are needful to repeal the least of the iniquitous laws, bequeathed us by the past, and even then they scarcely disappear except in periods of revolution.

The history of the genesis of capital has already been told by Socialists many times. They have described how it was born of war and pillage, of slavery and serfdom, of modern fraud and exploitation. They have shown how it is nourished by the blood of the worker, and how little by little it has conquered the whole world. The same story, concerning the genesis and development of law has yet to be told. As usual, the popular intelligence has stolen a march upon the men of books. It has already put together the philosophy of this history, and is busy laying down its essential landmarks.

Law, in its quality of guarantee of the results of pillage, slavery and exploitation, has followed the same phases of development as capital; twin brother and sister, they have advanced hand in hand, sustaining one another with the suffering of mankind. In every country in Europe their history is approximately the same. It has differed only in detail; the main facts are alike; and to glance at the development of law in France or Germany is to know its essential traits, its phases of development, in most of the European nations.

In the first instance, law was a national part or contract. Such a contract was agreed upon between the legions and people at the Champs de Mars,[1] a relic of the same period is preserved even yet in the Field of May of the primitive Swiss cantons despite the alterations effected by the interference of centralising and middle-class civilization. It is true that this contract was not always freely accepted. Even in those early days the rich and strong were imposing their will upon the rest. But at all events they encountered an obstacle to their encroachments in the mass of the people, who often made them feel their power in return.

But as the Church on one side and the nobles on the other, succeeded in enthralling the people, the right of law-making escaped from the hands of the nation and passed into those of the privileged orders. Fortified by the wealth accumulating in her coffers, the Church extended her authority; she tampered more and more with private life, and under pretext of saving souls, she seized upon the labour of her serfs, she gathered taxes from every class, she increased her jurisdiction, she multiplied penalties, and enriched herself in proportion to the number of offences committed, for the produce of every fine poured into her coffers. Laws had no longer any connection with the interest of the nation. "They might

---

1. The annual assembly of the early Franks, originally held in March, there the first month of the year.

have been supposed to emanate rather from a council of religious fanatics than from legislators," observes an historian of French law.

At the same time, as the baron likewise extended his authority over labourers in the fields and artizans in the towns, he too, became legislator and judge. The few relics of national law dating from the tenth century are merely agreements regulating service, statute-labour, and tribute due from serf and vassals to their lord. The legislators of that period were a handful of brigands organized for the plunder of a people daily becoming more peaceful, as they applied themselves to agricultural pursuits. These robbers exploited the feeling for justice inherent in the people, they posed as the administrators of that justice, made a source of revenue for themselves out of its fundamental principles and concocted laws to maintain their own dominations.

Later on, these laws collected and classified by jurists, formed the foundation of our modern codes. And are we to talk about respecting these codes, the legacy of baron and priest?

The first revolution, the revolt of the townships, was successful in abolishing a portion only of these laws; the charters of enfranchised towns are, for the most part, a mere compromise between baronial and episcopal legislation, and the new relations created within the free borough itself. Yet what a difference between these laws and the laws we have now! The town did not take upon itself to imprison and execute citizens for reasons of State: it was content to expel anyone who plotted with the enemies of the city, and to raze his house to the ground. It confined itself to imposing fines for so-called "crimes and misdemeanours" and in the townships of the twelfth century may even be discerned the just principle to-day forgotten, which holds the whole community responsible for the misdoing of each of its members. The societies of that time looked upon crime as an accident or a misfortune; a conception common amongst the Russian peasantry at this moment. Therefore, they did not admit of the principle of personal vengeance, as preached by the Bible, but considered that the blame for each misdeed reverted to the whole society. It needed all the influence of the Byzantine Church, which imported into the West the refined cruelties of Eastern despotism, to introduce into the manners of Gauls and Germans the penalty of death, and the horrible tortures afterwards inflicted on those regarded as criminals. Just in the same way, it needed all the influence of the Roman code, the product of the corruption of Imperial Rome, to introduce the notions as to absolute property in land, which have overthrown the communistic customs of primitive people.

As we know, the free townships were not able to hold their own. Torn by internal dissensions between rich and poor, burgher and serf, they fell an easy prey to royalty. And as royalty acquired fresh strength, the right of legislation passed more and more into the hands of a clique of courtiers. Appeal to the nation was made only to sanction the taxes demanded by the King. Parliament summoned at intervals of two centuries, according to the good pleasure or caprice of the Court, "Councils Extraordinary," Assemblies of Notables, Ministers, scarce heeding the "grievances of the King's subjects"—these are the legislators of France. Later still, when all power is concentrated in a single man, who can say, "I am the State," edicts are concocted in the "secret counsels of the Prince," according to the whim of a minister, or of an imbecile King; and subjects must obey on pain of death. All judicial guarantees are abolished; the nation is the serf of royalty, and of a handful of courtiers. And at this period the most horrible penalties startle our gaze—the wheel, the stake, flaying alive, tortures of every description, invented by the sick fancy of monks and madmen, seeking delight in the sufferings of executed criminals.

The great Revolution began the demolition of this framework of law, bequeathed to us by feudalism and royalty. But after having demolished some portions of the ancient edifice, the Revolution delivered over the power of law-making to the bourgeoisie, who, in their turn, began to raise a fresh framework of laws intended to maintain and perpetuate middle-class domination amongst the masses. Their Parliament makes laws right and left, and mountains of law accumulate with frightful rapidity. But what *are* all these laws at bottom?

The major portion have but one object—to protect private property, *i.e.*, wealth acquired by the exploitation of man by man. Their aim is to open out to capital fresh fields for exploitation, and to sanction the new forms which that exploitation continually assumes, as capital swallows up another branch of human activity, railways, telegraphs, electric light, chemical industries, the expression of man's thought in literature and science, &c. The object of the rest of these laws is fundamentally the same. They exist to keep up the machinery of government, which serves to secure to capital the exploitation and monopoly of the wealth produced. Magistrature, police, army, public instruction, finance, all serve one God—capital; all have but one object—to facilitate the exploitation of the worker by the capitalist. Analyse all the laws passed for the last eighty years, and you will find nothing but this. The protection of the person, which is put forward as the true mission of law, occupies an imperceptible space amongst them, for, in existing society, assaults upon the person, directly dictated by hatred and brutality, tend to disappear. Now-a-days, if anyone is murdered, it is generally for the sake of robbing him; rarely from personal vengeance. But if this class of crimes and misdemeanours is continually diminishing, we certainly do not owe the change to legislation. It is due to the growth of humanitarianism in our societies, to our increasingly social habits rather than to the prescriptions of our laws. Repeal to-morrow every law dealing with the protection of the person, and to-morrow stop all proceedings for assault, and the number of attempts, dictated by personal vengeance and by brutality, would not be augmented by one single instance.

It will, perhaps, be objected that, during the last fifty years, a good many liberal laws have been enacted. But, if these laws are analysed, it will be discovered that this liberal legislation consists in the repeal of the laws bequeathed to us by the barbarism of preceding centuries. Every liberal law, every radical programme, may be summed up in these words, abolition of laws grown irksome to the middle-class itself, and return and extension to all citizens of liberties enjoyed by the townships of the twelfth century. The abolition of capital punishment, trial by jury for all "crimes" (there was a more liberal jury in the twelfth century), the election of magistrates, the right of bringing public officials to trial, the abolition of standing armies, free instruction, &c., everything that is pointed out as an invention of modern liberalism, is but a return to the freedom which existed before Church and King had laid hands upon every manifestation of human life.

Thus the protection of exploitation, directly by laws on property, and indirectly by the maintenance of the State, is both the spirit and the substance of our modern codes, and the one function of our costly legislative machinery. But it is time we gave up being satisfied with mere phrases, and learned to appreciate their real signification. The law, which on its first appearance presented itself as a compendium of customs useful for the preservation of society, is now perceived to be nothing but an instrument for the maintenance of exploitation, and the domination of the toiling masses by rich idlers. At the present day its civilising mission is *nil*; it has but one object, to bolster up exploitation.

This is what is told us by history as to the development of law. Is it in virtue of this history that we are called upon to respect it? Certainly not. It has no more title to respect than capital, the fruit of pillage; and the first duty of the revolutionists of the nineteenth century will be to make a bonfire of all existing laws, as they will of all titles to property.

IV

The millions of laws which exist for the regulation of humanity, appear upon investigation to be divided into three principal categories—protection of property, protection of persons, protection of government. And by analysing each of these three categories, we arrive at the same logical and necessary conclusion: *the uselessness and hurtfulness of law.*

Socialists know what is meant by protection of property. Laws on property are not made to guarantee either to the individual or to society the enjoyment of the produce of their own labor. On the contrary, they are made to rob the producer of a part of what he has created, and to secure to certain other people that portion of the produce which they have stolen either from the producer or from society as a whole. When, for example, the law establishes Mr. So-and-So's right to a house, it is not establishing his right to a cottage he has built for himself, or to a house he has erected with the help of some of his friends. In that case no one would have disputed his right. On the contrary, the law is establishing his right to a house which is *not* the product of his labor; first of all, because he has had it built for him by others, to whom he has not paid the full value of their work; and next, because that house represents a social value, which he could not have produced for himself. The law is establishing his right to what belongs to everybody in general and to nobody in particular. The same house built in the midst of Siberia would not have the value it possesses in a large town, and, as we know, that value arises from the labor of something like fifty generations of men who have built the town, beautified it, supplied it with water and gas, fine promenades, colleges, theatres, shops, railways, and roads leading in all directions. Thus, by recognising the right of Mr. So-and-So to a particular house in Paris, London, or Rouen, the law is unjustly appropriating to him a certain portion of the produce of the labour of mankind in general. And it is precisely because this appropriation and all other forms of property bearing the same character, are a crying injustice, that a whole arsenal of laws, and a whole army of soldiers, policemen, and judges are needed to maintain it against the good sense and just feeling inherent in humanity.

Well, half our laws, the civil code in each country, serves no other purpose than to maintain this appropriation, this monopoly for the benefit of certain individuals against the whole of mankind. Three-fourths of the causes decided by the tribunals are nothing but quarrels between monopolists—two robbers disputing over their booty. And a great many of our criminal laws have the same object in view, their end being to keep the workman in a subordinate position towards his employer, and thus afford security to exploitation.

As for guaranteeing the product of his labour to the producer, there are no laws which even attempt such a thing. It is so simple and natural, so much a part of the manners and customs of mankind, that law has not given it so much as a thought. Open brigandage, sword in hand, is no feature of our age. Neither does one workman ever come and dispute the produce of his labour with another. If they have a misunderstanding they settle it by calling in a third person, without having recourse to law. The only person who exacts from another what that other has produced, is the proprietor, who comes in and deducts the lion's share. As for humanity in general, it everywhere respects the right of each to what he has created, without the interposition of any special laws.

As all the laws about property, which make up thick volumes of codes, and are the delight of our lawyers, have no other object than to protect the unjust appropriation of human labour by certain monopolists, there is no reason for their existence, and, on the day of the Revolution, social revolutionists are thoroughly determined to put an end to them. Indeed, a bonfire might be made with perfect justice of all laws bearing upon the so-called "rights of property," all title-deeds, all registers, in a word, of all that is in any way connected with an institution which will soon be looked upon as a blot in the history of humanity, as humiliating as the slavery and serfdom of past ages.

The remarks just made upon laws concerning property are quite as applicable to the second category of laws; those for the maintenance of government, *i.e.*, Constitutional Law.

It again is a complete arsenal of laws, decrees, ordinances, orders in council, and what not, all serving to protect the diverse forms of representative government, delegated or usurped, beneath which humanity is writhing. We know very well—Anarchists have often enough pointed out in their perpetual criticism of the various forms of government—that the mission of all governments, monarchical, constitutional, or republican, is to protect and maintain by force the privileges of the classes in possession, the aristocracy, clergy, and traders. A good third of our laws—and each country possesses some tens of thousands of them—the fundamental laws on taxes, excise duties, the organization of ministerial departments and their offices, of the army, the police, the Church, &c., have no other end than to maintain, patch up, and develop the administrative machine. And this machine in its turn serves almost entirely to protect the privileges of the possessing classes. Analyse all these laws, observe them in action day by day, and you will discover that not one is worth preserving.

About such laws there can be no two opinions. Not only Anarchists, but more or less revolutionary radicals also, are agreed that the only use to be made of laws concerning the organization of government is to fling them into the fire.

The third category of law still remains to be considered, that relating to the protection of the person and the detection and prevention of "crime." This is the most important, because most prejudices attach to it; because, if law enjoys a certain amount of consideration, it is in consequence of the belief that this species of law is absolutely indispensable to the maintenance of security in our societies. These are laws developed from the nucleus of customs useful to human communities, which have been turned to account by rulers to sanctify their own domination. The authority of the chiefs of tribes, of rich families in towns, and of the king, depended upon their judicial functions, and even down to the present day, whenever the necessity of government is spoken of, its function as supreme judge is the thing implied. "Without a government men would tear one another to pieces," argues the village orator. "The ultimate end of all government is to secure twelve honest jurymen to every accused person," said Burke.

Well, in spite of all the prejudices existing on this subject, it is quite time that Anarchists should boldly declare this category of laws as useless and injurious as the preceding ones.

First of all, as to so-called "crimes"—assaults upon persons—it is well-known that two-thirds, and often as many as three-fourths, of such "crimes" are instigated by the desire to obtain possession of someone's wealth. This immense class of so-called "crimes and misdemeanours" will disappear on the day on which private property ceases to exist. "But," it will be said, "there will always be brutes who will attempt the lives of their fellow-citizens, who will lay their hands to a knife in every quarrel, and revenge the slightest offence by murder, if there are no laws to restrain and punishments to withhold them." This refrain is repeated every time the right of society *to punish* is called in question.

Yet there is one fact upon this head which at the present time is thoroughly established; the severity of punishment does not diminish the amount of crime. Hang, and, if you like, quarter murderers, and the number of murders will not decrease by one. On the other hand, abolish the penalty of death, and there will not be one murder more; there will be fewer. Statistics prove it. But if the harvest is good, and bread cheap, and the weather fine, the number of murders immediately decreases. This again is proved by statistics. The amount of crime always augments and diminishes in proportion to the price of provisions and the state of the weather. Not that all murderers are actuated by hunger. That is not the case. But when the harvest is good, and provisions are at an obtainable price, and when the sun shines, men, lighter hearted and less miserable than usual, do not give way to gloomy passions, do not from trivial motives, plunge a knife into the bosom of a fellow creature.

Moreover, it is also a well-known fact that the fear of punishment has never stopped a single murderer. He who kills his neighbour from revenge or misery does not reason much about consequences; and there have been few murderers who were not firmly convinced that they should escape prosecution.

Without speaking of a society in which a man will receive a better education, in which the development of all his faculties, and the possibility of exercising them, will procure him so many enjoyments, that he will not seek to poison them by remorse—without speaking of the society of the future—even in our society, even with those sad products of misery, whom we see to-day in the public-houses of great cities—on the day when no punishment is inflicted upon murderers, the number of murders will not augment by a single case; and it is extremely probable that it will be, on the contrary, diminished by all those cases which are due at present to habitual criminals, who have been brutalised in prisons.

We are continually being told of the benefits conferred by law, and the beneficial effect of penalties, but have the speakers ever attempted to strike a balance between the benefits attributed to laws and penalties, and the degrading effect of these penalties upon humanity? Only calculate all the evil passions awakened in mankind by the atrocious punishments formerly inflicted in our streets! Man is the cruellest animal upon earth; and who has pampered and developed the cruel instincts unknown, even amongst monkeys, if it is not the king, the judge, and the priest, armed with law, who caused flesh to be torn off in strips, boiling pitch to be poured into wounds, limbs to be dislocated, bones to be crushed, men to be sawn asunder to maintain their authority? Only estimate the torrent of depravity let loose in human society by the "informing," which is countenanced by judges, and paid in hard cash by governments, under pretext of assisting in the discovery of "crime." Only go into the gaols and study what man becomes when he is deprived of freedom and shut up with other depraved beings, steeped in the vice and corruption which oozes from the very walls of our existing prisons. Only remember that the more these prisons are reformed, the more detestable they become; our model modern penitentiaries are a hundred-fold more abominable than the dungeons of the middle ages. Finally, consider what corruption, what depravity of mind, is kept up amongst men by the idea of obedience, the very essence of law; of chastisement; of authority having the right to punish, to judge irrespective of our conscience and the esteem of our friends; of the necessity for executioners, gaolers, and informers—in a word, by all the attributes of law and authority. Consider all this, and you will assuredly agree with us in saying that a law inflicting penalties is an abomination which should cease to exist.

Peoples without political organization, and therefore less depraved than ourselves, have perfectly understood that the man who is called "criminal" is simply unfortunate; that the remedy is not to flog him, to chain him up, or to kill him on the scaffold or in prison, but to relieve him by the most brotherly care, by treatment based on equality, by the usages of life amongst honest men. In the next revolution we hope that this cry will go forth:

"Burn the guillotines; demolish the prisons; drive away the judges, policemen, and informers—the impurest race upon the face of the earth; treat as a brother the man who has been led by passion to do ill to his fellow; above all, take from the ignoble products of middle-class idleness the possibility of displaying their vices in attractive colours; and be sure that but few crimes will mar our society."

The main supports of crime are idleness, law and authority; laws about property, laws about government, laws about penalties and misdemeanours; and authority, which takes upon itself to manufacture these laws and to apply them.

No more laws! No more judges! Liberty, equality, and practical human sympathy are the only effectual barriers we can oppose to the anti-social instincts of certain amongst us.

CHAPTER 17

HARRIET MARTINEAU

The reading in this chapter comes from the second edition of Harriet Martineau's *Society in America*, Volume I (1839), pp. 162–181 and 199–207; London: Saunders and Otley. Both the first edition (1836–1837) and the second edition were published in three volumes. The full text of all three volumes is available through the HathiTrust Digital Library (hathitrust.org).

When *Society in America* was first published, the classical school was beginning to give way to the more empirical movements of phrenology, which was well established at this time, and moral statistics, which was just emerging. *Society in America* resembles the products of these latter movements in that it is an empirical work, but it is not based on the methods of the natural sciences, and it does not emphasize the collection and analysis of quantitative data. Rather, it is more ethnographic in its orientation, placing an emphasis on the collection and analysis of qualitative information. In this book, Martineau provides a sociological examination of several spheres of social life in the United States during the 1830s, including political, economic, and religious life. More importantly (for the field of criminology), *Society in America* contains an early feminist critique of justice in the United States. It is true that Martineau's work is rarely cited in the literature of criminology, but it is equally true that it offers a number of insights that are shared by contemporary feminist criminologists.

While Martineau's views clash with the Marxist standpoint on several issues concerning the interests of the working class and she certainly was not an anarchist, she nonetheless opposed several forms of oppression. Below two chapters from *Society in America* are presented—first "Allegiance to Law" and then "Political Non-Existence of Women." In these selections, Martineau opposes the institution of slavery and patriarchal social arrangements. In "Allegiance to Law," she describes the hardships faced by abolitionists and provides examples of how certain crimes committed by middle- and upper-class white males ("gentlemen") tend to be ignored or redescribed as noncriminal, at least when their victims occupy a lower social standing. In the "Political Non-Existence of Women," Martineau examines the exclusion of women from the political process and asks: Can a democracy apply a law in a just manner to a group when that group had little or no input regarding its content? This is a question criminologists need to keep in mind when examining laws of democratic societies and how they are applied. In short, these selections provide an early-nineteenth-century examination of the tendency of the criminal justice system to overlook harmful acts of powerful subpopulations and the undemocratic nature of some laws in a "democracy," two problems that continue to be analyzed by critical criminologists.

---

from SOCIETY IN AMERICA, VOLUME I
by Harriet Martineau

ALLEGIANCE TO LAW

It is notorious that there is a remarkable failure in this department of political morals among certain parties in the United States. The mobbing events of the last few years are celebrated; the abolition riots in New York and Boston; the burning of the Charleston Convent; the bank riots at Baltimore; the burning of the mails at Charleston; the hangings by Lynch-law at Vicksburg; the burning alive of a man of colour at St. Louis; the subsequent proceedings there towards the students of Marion College; and the abolition riots at Cincinnati. Here is a fearful list!

The first question that arises is, who has done these things? Whose hands have lighted green fagots round a living man? and strung up a dozen or twenty citizens on the same gallows? and fired and razed houses; and sent a company of trembling nuns flying for their lives at midnight? Here is evidence enough of ignorance,—of desperate, brutal ignorance. Whose ignorance?

In Europe, the instantaneous and natural persuasion of men who hear the tidings is, that the lowest classes in America have risen against the higher. In Europe, desperate, brutal ignorance is the deepest curse in the cursed life of the pauper and the serf. In Europe, mobbing is usually the outbreak of exasperated misery against laws which oppress, and an aristocracy which insults humanity. Europeans, therefore, naturally assume that the gentry of the United States are the sinned against, and the poor the sinners, in their social disturbances. They draw conclusions against popular government, and suppose it proved that universal suffrage dissolves society into chaos. They picture to themselves a rabble of ragged, desperate workmen, with torches in their hands; while the gentry look on in dismay, or tremble within their houses.

It is not so. I was informed, twenty times over, by gentlemen, that the Boston mob of last year was wholly composed of gentlemen. The only working man in it was the truck-man who saved the victim. They were the gentlemen of St. Louis who burned the black man, and banished the students of Marion College. They were the gentlemen of Cincinnati who denounced the abolitionists, and raised the persecution against them. They were the magistrates and gentry of Vicksburg who hanged way-farers, gamblers, and slaves in a long row. They were the gentlemen of Charleston who broke open the Post Office, and violated its sacred function, to the insult and injury of the whole country.

The case is plain. There are no paupers to rise against oppressive laws in a country, where the laws are made by all, and where pauperism is thereby excluded. There is no degraded class, subject to insults from the highest, which can be resented only by outrage. The assumption is a false one, that ignorance and poverty, knowledge and wealth, go together. Mobbing for European causes, and in European modes, is absolutely precluded where political rights are universal, and political power equally diffused through all classes.

The very few European causes which are in analogy with United States mobbing, are those riots for opinion, which bear only a subordinate relation to politics; such as the Birmingham riots, and the attempt of the Liverpool merchants to push Clarkson into the dock. The cases are very similar. The mobs of America are composed of high churchmen, (of whatever denomination,) merchants and planters, and lawyers.

One complete narrative of a riot, for the fidelity of which I can vouch, will expose the truth of the case better than a list of deeds of horror which happened beyond my sight. It is least revolting, too, to treat of a case whose terror lies in its existence, more than in its consequences. The actors in the riot, which it was my fortune to understand, were scarcely less guilty than if they had bathed their hands in blood; but it is easier to examine, undisturbed by passion, the case of those whose hands are, to the outward eye, clean.

A very few years ago, certain citizens in New England began to discover that the planters of the south were making white slaves in the north, nearly as successfully as they were propagating black slavery in the territories of the south and west. Charleston and Boston were affectionate friends in old times, and are so still, notwithstanding the hard words that passed between them in nullification days: that is, the merchants and professional men of Boston are fond of Charleston, on account of their commercial relations. This attachment has been carried to such an extreme as to be almost fatal to the liberties of some of the best citizens of the northern city. They found their brothers dismissed from their pastoral charges, their sons expelled from colleges, their friends excluded from professorships, and themselves debarred from literary and social privileges, if they happened to entertain and express opinions unfavourable to the peculiar domestic institution by which Charleston declares it to be her intention to abide. Such is the plea of those citizens of Boston who have formed associations for the purpose of opposing, by moral influence, an institution which they feel to be inconsistent with the first principles of morals and politics. For a considerable time before my visit to that part of the country, they had encountered petty persecutions of almost every conceivable kind. There is no law in Massachusetts by which the free expression of opinion on moral subjects is punishable. I heard many regret the absence of such law. Everything was done that could be done to make up for its absence. Books on any subject, written by persons who avow by association their bad opinion of slavery, are not purchased: clergymen are no longer invited to preach: the proprietors of public rooms will not let them to members of such associations; and the churches are shut against them. Their notices of public meetings are torn in the pulpits, while all notices of other public meetings are read. The newspapers pour contempt and wrath upon them in one continued stream. Bad practices are imputed to them, and their denial is drowned in clamour. As a single instance of this last; I was told so universally in the south and west that the abolitionists of Boston and New York were in the habit of sending incendiary tracts among the slaves, that it never occurred to me to doubt the fact; though I was struck with surprise at never being able to find any one who had seen any one who had actually seen one of these tracts. Nor did it occur to me that as slaves cannot read, verbal messages would be more to the purpose of all parties, as being more effectual and more prudent. Mr. Madison made the charge, so did Mr. Clay, so did Mr. Calhoun, so did every slave-holder and merchant with whom I conversed. I chose afterwards to hear the other side of the whole question; and I found, to my amazement, that this charge was wholly groundless. No Abolition Society of New York or Massachusetts has ever sent any anti-slavery paper south of Washington, except the circulars, addressed to public officers in the States, which were burnt at Charleston. The abolitionists of Boston have been denying this charge ever since it was first made, and offering evidence of its groundlessness; yet the calumny is persisted in, and, no doubt, honestly believed, to this hour, throughout the south, whither the voice of the condemned, stifled by their fellow-citizens, cannot reach.

Only mortal things, however, can be really suffocated; and there has never yet been an instance of a murder of opinion. There seemed, in 1835, so much danger of the abolitionists making themselves heard, that an emphatic contradiction was got up, it was hoped in good time.

The abolitionists had been, they believe illegally, denied by the city authority the use of Faneuil Hall; (called, in memory of revolutionary days, the "Cradle of Liberty.") Certain merchants and lawyers of Boston held a meeting there, in August, 1835, for the purpose of reprobating the meetings of the abolitionists, and denouncing their measures, while approving of their principles. The less that is said of this meeting,—the deepest of all the disgraces of Boston,—the better. It bears its character in its face. Its avowed object was to put down the expression of opinion by opprobrium, in the absence of gag laws. Of the fifteen hundred who signed the requisition for this meeting, there are many, especially among the younger and more thoughtless, who have long repented of the deed. Some signed in anger; some in fear; many in mistake; and of each of these there are some who would fain, if it were possible, efface their signatures with their blood.

It is an invariable fact, and recognized as such, that meetings held to supply the deficiency of gag laws are the prelude to the violence which supplies the deficiency of executioners under such laws. Every meeting held to denounce opinion is followed by a mob. This was so well understood in the present case that the abolitionists were warned that if they met again publicly, they would be answerable for the disorders that might ensue. The abolitionists pleaded that this was like making the rich man answerable for the crime of the thief who robbed him, on the ground that if the honest man had not been rich, the thief would not have been tempted to rob him. The abolitionists also perceived how liberty of opinion and of speech depended on their conduct in this crisis; and they resolved to yield to no threats of illegal violence; but to hold their legal meeting, pursuant to advertisement, for the despatch of their usual business. One remarkable feature of the case was that this heavy responsibility rested upon women. It was a ladies' meeting that was in question. Upon consultation, the ladies agreed that they should never have sought the perilous duty of defending liberty of opinion and speech at the last crisis; but, as such a service seemed manifestly appointed to them, the women were ready.

On the 21st of October, they met, pursuant to advertisement, at the office of their association, No. 46, Washington Street. Twenty-five reached their room, by going three-quarters of an hour before the appointed time. Five more made their way up with difficulty through the crowd. A hundred more were turned back by the mob.

They knew that a hand-bill had been circulated on the Exchange, and posted on the City Hall, and throughout the city, the day before, which declared that Thompson, the abolitionist, was to address them; and invited the citizens, under promise of pecuniary reward, to "snake Thompson out, and bring him to the tar-kettle before dark." The ladies had been warned that they would be killed, "as sure as fate," if they showed themselves on their own premises that day. They therefore informed the mayor that they expected to be attacked. The reply of the city marshal was, "You give us a great deal of trouble."

The committee-room was surrounded, and gazed into by a howling, shrieking mob of gentlemen, while the twenty-five ladies sat perfectly still, awaiting the striking of the clock. When it struck, they opened their meeting. They were questioned as to whether Thompson was there in disguise; to which they made no reply.

They began, as usual, with prayer; the mob shouting "Hurra! here comes Judge Lynch!" Before they had done, the partition gave way, and the gentlemen hurled missiles at the lady who was presiding. The secretary having risen, and begun to read her report, rendered inaudible by the uproar, the mayor entered, and insisted upon their going home, to save their lives. The purpose of their meeting was answered: they had asserted their principle; and they now passed out, two and two, amidst the execration of some thousands of gentlemen;—persons who had silver shrines to protect. The ladies, to the number of fifty, walked to the house of one of their members, and were presently struck to the heart by the news that Garrison was in the hands of the mob. Garrison is the chief apostle of abolition in the United States. He had escorted his wife to the meeting; and, after offering to address the ladies, and being refused, out of regard to his safety, had left the room, and, as they supposed, the premises. He was, however, in the house when the ladies left it. He was hunted for by the mob; dragged from behind some planks where he had taken refuge, and conveyed into the street. Here his hat was trampled under-foot, and brick-bats were aimed at his bare head; a rope was tied round him, and thus he was dragged through the streets. His young wife saw all this. Her exclamation was, "I think my husband will be true to his principles. I am sure my husband will not deny his principles." Her confidence was just. Garrison never denies his principles.

He was saved by a stout truckman, who, with his bludgeon, made his way into the crowd, as if to attack the victim. He protected the bare head, and pushed on towards a station house, whence the mayor's officers issued, and pulled in Garrison, who was afterwards put into a coach. The mob tried to upset the coach, and throw down the horses; but the driver laid about him with his whip, and the constables with their staves, and Garrison was safely lodged in jail for protection; for he had committed no offence.

Before the mayor ascended the stairs to dismiss the ladies, he had done a very remarkable deed;—he had given permission to two gentlemen to pull down and destroy the anti-slavery sign, bearing the inscription, "Anti-Slavery Office,"—which had hung for two years, as signs do hang before public offices in Boston. The plea of the mayor is, that he hoped the rage of the mob would thus be appeased: that is, he gave them leave to break the laws in one way, lest they should in another. The citizens followed up this deed of the mayor with one no less remarkable. They elected these two rioters members of the State legislature, by a large majority, within ten days.

I passed through the mob some time after it had begun to assemble. I asked my fellow-passengers in the stage what it meant. They supposed it was a busy foreign-post day, and that this occasioned an assemblage of gentlemen about the post-office. They pointed out to me that there were none but gentlemen. We were passing through from Salem, fifteen miles north of Boston, to Providence, Rhode Island; and were therefore uninformed of the events and expectations of the day. On the morrow, a visiter who arrived at Providence from Boston told us the story; and I had thenceforth an excellent opportunity of hearing all the remarks that could be made by persons of all ways of thinking and feeling, on this affair.

It excited much less attention than it deserved; less than would be believed possible by those at a distance who think more seriously of persecution for opinion, and less tenderly of slavery than a great many of the citizens of Boston. To many in the city of Boston the story I have told would be news; and to yet more in the country, who know that some trouble was caused by abolition meetings in the city, but who are not aware that their own will, embodied in the laws, was overborne to gratify the mercenary interests of a few, and the political fears of a few more.

The first person with whom I conversed about this riot was the president of a university. We were perfectly agreed as to the causes and character of the outrage. This gentleman went over to Boston for a day or two; and when he returned, I saw him again. He said he was happy to tell me that we had been needlessly making ourselves uneasy about the affair: that there had been no mob, the persons assembled having been all gentlemen.

An eminent lawyer at Boston was one of the next to speak upon it. "O, there was no mob," said he. "I was there myself, and saw they were all gentlemen. They were all in fine broad-cloth."

"Not the less a mob for that," said I.

"Why, they protected Garrison. He received no harm. They protected Garrison."

"From whom, or what?"

"O, they would not really hurt him. They only wanted to show that they would not have such a person live among them."

"Why should not he live among them? Is he guilty under any law?"

"He is an insufferable person to them."

"So may you be to-morrow. If you can catch Garrison breaking the laws, punish him under the laws. If you cannot, he has as much right to live where he pleases as you."

Two law pupils of this gentleman presently entered. One approved of all that had been done, and praised the spirit of the gentlemen of Boston. I asked whether they had not broken the law. Yes. I asked him if he knew what the law was. Yes; but it could not be always kept. If a man was caught in a house setting it on fire, the owner might shoot him; and Garrison was such an incendiary. I asked him for proof. He had nothing but hearsay to give. The case, as I told him, came to this. A. says Garrison is an incendiary. B. says he is not. A. proceeds on his own opinion to break the law, lest Garrison should do so.

The other pupil told me of the sorrow of heart with which he saw the law, the life of the republic, set at naught by those who should best understand its nature and value. He saw that the time was come for the true men of the republic to oppose a bold front to the insolence of the rich and the powerful, who were bearing down the liberties of the people for a matter of opinion. The young men, he saw, must brace themselves up against the tyranny of the monied mob, and defend the law; or the liberties of the country were gone. I afterwards found many such among the young men of the wealthier classes. If they keep their convictions, they and their city are safe.

No prosecutions followed. I asked a lawyer, an abolitionist, why. He said there would be difficulty in getting a verdict; and, if it was obtained, the punishment would be merely a fine, which would be paid on the spot, and the triumph would remain with the aggressors. This seemed to me no good reason.

I asked an eminent judge the same question; and whether there was not a public prosecutor who might prosecute for breach of the peace, if the abolitionists would not, for the assault on Garrison. He said it might be done; but he had given his advice against it. Why? The feeling was so strong against the abolitionists,—the rioters were so respectable in the city,—it was better to let the whole affair pass over without notice.

Of others, some knew nothing of it, because it was about such a low set of people; some could not take any interest in what they were tired of hearing about; some had not heard anything of the matter; some thought the abolitionists were served quite right; some were sure the gentlemen of Boston would not do anything improper; and some owned that there was such bad taste and meddlesomeness in the abolitionists, that people of taste kept out of the way of hearing anything about them.

Notwithstanding all this, the body of the people are sound. Many of the young lawyers are resolved to keep on the watch, to maintain the rights of the abolitionists in the legislature, and in the streets of the city. Many hundreds of the working men agreed to leave their work on the first rumour of riot, get sworn in as special constables, and keep the peace against the gentry; acting vigorously against the mob ringleaders, if such should be the magistrates of Boston themselves. I visited many of the villages in Massachusetts; and there everything seemed right. The country people are abolitionists, by nature and education, and they see the iniquity of mob-law. A sagacious gentleman told me that it did him good to hear, in New York, of this mob, because it proved the rest of Massachusetts to be in a sound state. It is always "Boston *versus* Massachusetts;" and when the city, or the aristocracy there, who think themselves the city, are very vehemently wrong, it is a plain proof that the country people are eminently right. This may, for the humour of the thing, be strongly put; but there is much truth in it.

The philosophy of the case is very easy to understand; and supremely important to be understood.

The law, in a republic, is the embodiment of the will of the people. As long as the republic is in a natural and healthy state, containing no anomaly, and exhibiting no gross vices, the function of the law works easily, and is understood and reverenced. Its punishments bear only upon individuals, who have the opposition of society to contend with for violating its will, and who are helpless against the righteous visitations of the law.

If there be any anomaly among the institutions of a republic, the function of the law is certain to be disturbed, sooner or later: and that disturbance is usually the symptom by the exhibition of which the anomaly is first detected, and then cured. It was so with free-masonry. It will be so with slavery; and with every institution inconsistent with the fundamental principles of democracy. The process is easily traceable. The worldly interests of the minority,—of perhaps a single class,—are bound up with the anomaly:—of the minority, because, if the majority had been interested in any anti-republican institution, the republic would not have existed. The minority may go on for a length of time in apparent harmony with the expressed will of the many,—the law. But the time comes when their anomaly clashes with the law. For instance, the merchants of the north trade in products which are, as they believe, created out of a denial that all men are born free and equal, and that the just powers of rulers are derived from the consent of the governed; while the contrary principles are the root which produces the law. Which is to be given up, when both cannot be held? If the pecuniary interest of merchants is incompatible with freedom of speech in fellow-citizens, which is to suffer?—The will of the majority, the lawmaker, is to decide. But it takes some time to awaken the will of the majority; and till it awakes, the interest of the faction is active, and overbears the law. The retribution is certain; the result is safe. But the evils meanwhile are so tremendous, that no exertion should be spared to open the eyes of the majority to the insults offered to its will. There is no fear that the majority will ultimately succumb to the minority,—the harmonious law to the discordant anomaly: but it is a fearful thing, meantime, that the brave should be oppressed by the mercenary, and oppressed in proportion to their bravery; that the masters of black slaves in the south should be allowed to make white slaves in the north; that power and wealth should be used to blind the people to the nature and dignity of the law, and to seduce them into a preference of brute force. These evils are so tremendous as to make it the duty of every citizen to bring every lawbreaker, high or low, to punishment; to strike out of the election list every man who tampers with the will of the majority; to teach every child what the law is, and why it must be maintained; to keep his eye on the rostrum, the bench, the bar, the pulpit, the press, the lyceum, the school, that no fallacy, no compromise with an anomaly, no surrender of principle be allowed to pass unexposed and unstigmatized.

One compound fallacy is allowed daily to pass unexposed and unstigmatized. "You make no allowance," said a friend who was strangely bewildered by it,—"you make no allowance for the great number of excellent people who view the anomaly and the law as you do, but who keep quiet, because they sincerely believe that by speaking and acting they should endanger the Union." This explains the conduct of a crowd of "excellent people," neither merchants, nor the friends of slave-holders, nor approving slavery, or mobbing, or persecution for opinion; but who revile or satirize the abolitionists, and, for the rest, hold their tongues. But is it possible that such do not see that if slavery be wrong, and if it be indeed bound up with the Union, the Union must fall? Is it possible that they do not see that if the question be really this,—that if the laws of God and the arrangements of man are incompatible, man's arrangements must give way?—I regard it as a false and mischievous assumption that slavery is bound up with the Union: but if I believed the dictum, I should not be for "putting off the evil day." Every day which passes over the unredressed wrongs of any class which a republic holds in her bosom; every day which brings persecution on those who act out the principles which all profess;

every day which adds a sanction to brute force, and impairs the sacredness of law; every day which prolongs impunity to the oppressor and discouragement to the oppressed, is a more evil day than that which should usher in the work of renovation.

But the dictum is not true. This bitter satire upon the constitution, and upon all who have complacently lived under it, is not true. The Union is not incompatible with freedom of speech. The Union does not forbid men to act according to their convictions. The Union has never depended for its existence on hypocrisy, insult, and injury; and it never will.

Let citizens but take heed individually to respect the law, and see that others do,—that no neighbour transgresses it, that no statesman despises it unrebuked, that no child grows up ignorant or careless of it; and the Union is as secure as the ground they tread upon. If this be not done, everything is in peril, for the season; not only the Union, but property, home, life and integrity. . . .

POLITICAL NON-EXISTENCE OF WOMEN

One of the fundamental principles announced in the Declaration of Independence is, that governments derive their just powers from the consent of the governed. How can the political condition of women be reconciled with this?

Governments in the United States have power to tax women who hold property; to divorce them from their husbands; to fine, imprison, and execute them for certain offences. Whence do these governments derive their powers? They are not "just," as they are not derived from the consent of the women thus governed.

Governments in the United States have power to enslave certain women; and also to punish other women for inhuman treatment of such slaves. Neither of these powers are "just;" not being derived from the consent of the governed.

Governments decree to women in some States half their husbands' property; in others one-third. In some, a woman, on her marriage, is made to yield all her property to her husband; in others, to retain a portion, or the whole, in her own hands. Whence do governments derive the unjust power of thus disposing of property without the consent of the governed?

The democratic principle condemns all this as wrong; and requires the equal political representation of all rational beings. Children, idiots, and criminals, during the season of sequestration, are the only fair exceptions.

The case is so plain that I might close it here; but it is interesting to inquire how so obvious a decision has been so evaded as to leave to women no political rights whatever. The question has been asked, from time to time, in more countries than one, how obedience to the laws can be required of women, when no woman has, either actually or virtually, given any assent to any law. No plausible answer has, as far as I can discover, been offered; for the good reason, that no plausible answer can be devised. The most principled democratic writers on government have on this subject sunk into fallacies, as disgraceful as any advocate of despotism has adduced. In fact, they have thus sunk from being, for the moment, advocates of despotism. Jefferson in America, and James Mill at home, subside, for the occasion, to the level of the author of the Emperor of Russia's Catechism for the young Poles.

Jefferson says,[1] "Were our State a pure democracy, in which all the inhabitants should meet together to transact all their business, there would yet be excluded from their deliberations,

"1. Infants, until arrived at years of discretion;

"2. Women, who, to prevent depravation of morals, and ambiguity of issue, could not mix promiscuously in the public meetings of men;

"3. Slaves, from whom the unfortunate state of things with us takes away the rights of will and of property."

If the slave disqualification, here assigned, were shifted up under the head of Women, their case would be nearer the truth than as it now stands. Woman's lack of will and of property, is more like the true cause of her exclusion from the representation, than that which is actually set down against her. As if there could be no means of conducting public affairs but by promiscuous meetings! As if there would be more danger in promiscuous meetings for political business than in such meetings for worship, for oratory, for music, for dramatic entertainments,—for any of the thousand transactions of civilized life! The plea is not worth another word.

Mill says, with regard to representation, in his Essay on Government, "One thing is pretty clear; that all those individuals, whose interests are involved in those of other individuals, may be struck off without inconvenience. . . . In this light, women may be regarded, the interest of almost all of whom is

---

1. Correspondence, vol. iv. p. 295.

involved, either in that of their fathers or in that of their husbands."

The true democratic principle is, that no person's interests can be, or can be ascertained to be, identical with those of any other person. This allows the exclusion of none but incapables.

The word "almost," in Mr. Mill's second sentence, rescues women from the exclusion he proposes. As long as there are women who have neither husbands nor fathers, his proposition remains an absurdity.

The interests of women who have fathers and husbands can never be identical with theirs, while there is a necessity for laws to protect women against their husbands and fathers. This statement is not worth another word.

Some who desire that there should be an equality of property between men and women, oppose representation, on the ground that political duties would be incompatible with the other duties which women have to discharge. The reply to this is, that women are the best judges here. God has given time and power for the discharge of all duties; and, if he had not, it would be for women to decide which they would take, and which they would leave. But their guardians follow the ancient fashion of deciding what is best for their wards. The Emperor of Russia discovers when a coat of arms and title do not agree with a subject prince. The King of France early perceives that the air of Paris does not agree with a free-thinking foreigner. The English Tories feel the hardship that it would be to impose the franchise on every artizan, busy as he is in getting his bread. The Georgian planter perceives the hardship that freedom would be to his slaves. And the best friends of half the human race peremptorily decide for them as to their rights, their duties, their feelings, their powers. In all these cases, the persons thus cared for feel that the abstract decision rests with themselves; that, though they may be compelled to submit, they need not acquiesce.

It is pleaded that half of the human race does acquiesce in the decision of the other half, as to their rights and duties. And some instances, not only of submission, but of acquiescence, there are. Forty years ago, the women of New Jersey went to the poll, and voted, at state elections. The general term, "inhabitants," stood unqualified;—as it will again, when the true democratic principle comes to be fully understood. A motion was made to correct the inadvertence; and it was done, as a matter of course; without any appeal, as far as I could learn, from the persons about to be injured. Such acquiescence proves nothing but the degradation of the injured party. It inspires the same emotions of pity as the supplication of the freed slave who kneels to his master to restore him to slavery, that he may have his animal wants supplied, without being troubled with human rights and duties. Acquiescence like this is an argument which cuts the wrong way for those who use it.

But this acquiescence is only partial; and, to give any semblance of strength to the plea, the acquiescence must be complete. I, for one, do not acquiesce. I declare that whatever obedience I yield to the laws of the society in which I live is a matter between, not the community and myself, but my judgment and my will. Any punishment inflicted on me for the breach of the laws, I should regard as so much gratuitous injury; for to those laws I have never, actually or virtually, assented. I know that there are women in England who agree with me in this—I know that there are women in America who agree with me in this. The plea of acquiescence is invalidated by us.

It is pleaded that, by enjoying the protection of some laws, women give their assent to all. This needs but a brief answer. Any protection thus conferred is, under woman's circumstances, a boon bestowed at the pleasure of those in whose power she is. A boon of any sort is no compensation for the privation of something else; nor can the enjoyment of it bind to the performance of anything to which it bears no relation. Because I, by favour, may procure the imprisonment of the thief who robs my house, am I, unrepresented, therefore bound not to smuggle French ribbons? The obligation not to smuggle has a widely different derivation.

I cannot enter upon the commonest order of pleas of all;—those which relate to the virtual influence of woman; her swaying the judgment and will of man through the heart; and so forth. One might as well try to dissect the morning mist. I knew a gentleman in America who told me how much rather he had be a woman than the man he is;—a professional man, a father, a citizen. He would give up all this for a woman's influence. I thought he was mated too soon. He should have married a lady, also of my acquaintance, who would not at all object to being a slave, if ever the blacks should have the upper hand; "it is so right that the one race should be subservient to the other!" Or rather,—I thought it a pity that the one could not be a woman, and the other a slave; so that an injured individual of each class might be exalted into their places, to fulfil and enjoy the duties and privileges which they despise, and, in despising, disgrace.

The truth is, that while there is much said about "the sphere of woman," two widely different notions are entertained of what is meant by the phrase. The narrow, and, to the ruling party, the more convenient notion is that sphere appointed by men, and bounded by their ideas of propriety;—a notion from which any and every woman may fairly dissent. The broad and true conception is of the sphere appointed by God, and bounded by the powers which he has bestowed. This commands the assent of man and woman; and only the question of powers remains to be proved.

That woman has power to represent her own interests, no one can deny till she has been tried. The modes need not be discussed here: they must vary with circumstances. The fearful and absurd images which are perpetually called up to perplex the question,—images of women on woolsacks in England, and under canopies in America, have nothing to do with the matter. The principle being once established, the methods will follow, easily, naturally, and under a remarkable transmutation of the ludicrous into the sublime. The kings of Europe would have laughed mightily, two centuries ago, at the idea of a commoner, without robes, crown, or sceptre, stepping into the throne of a strong nation. Yet who dared to laugh when Washington's super-royal voice greeted the New World from the presidential chair, and the old world stood still to catch the echo?

The principle of the equal rights of both halves of the human race is all we have to do with here. It is the true democratic principle which can never be seriously controverted, and only for a short time evaded. Governments can derive their just powers only from the consent of the governed.

CHAPTER 18

W. E. B. Du Bois

The reading in this chapter is from W. E. B. Du Bois's *The Philadelphia Negro: A Social Study* (1899), pp. 235–261, 264–265, and 267–268; Philadelphia: University of Pennsylvania Press. The selection includes nearly the entire chapter on "The Negro Criminal." The full text of this book is available through the HathiTrust Digital Library (hathitrust.org).

The Philadelphia Negro is based on research conducted by Du Bois about three decades after the Civil War and the abolition of slavery in the United States, a time when African Americans were still adjusting to their new, yet limited, freedom. In his "Preface," Du Bois describes this book as "part of a larger design of observation and research into the history and social condition of the transplanted Africans" (p. iii). His work was pioneering and represented a challenging area of inquiry. Not only was emancipation a relatively recent event, but this was a time when criminal anthropology, including its atavist theory, was at or near its peak of popularity. Nonetheless, in this context, Du Bois, a young African American scholar, proceeded to conduct an extensive study of the social factors that shaped the lives of African Americans. He joined the intellectual currents of the era that gave priority to social causation (e.g., the theorists of the French school and the Marxists) and, thus, contributed to the existing opposition to biological theories of crime.

The following reading from *The Philadelphia Negro* provides a groundbreaking analysis of African American crime. In this selection, Du Bois examines statistics from Eastern State Penitentiary and arrest figures from Philadelphia; he presents several descriptions of "typical" crimes by African Americans; and he integrates his analysis into a broader historical context, which adds significantly to the depth of the study. Du Bois's conclusions represent an important challenge to the biological reasoning on the race/crime relationship that was popular during this era. Viewing crime as an "open rebellion of an individual against his social environment" (p. 235), Du Bois suggested that many crimes by African Americans were the direct or indirect result of discrimination, a lack of opportunities, the disruptive effects of migration, and other social factors. He also noted that racial bias in the criminal justice system contributes to the overrepresentation of African Americans in prison. In short, Du Bois's study of race and crime presented in *The Philadelphia Negro* stands as an important precursor to contemporary critical race theory, a movement that has found a place in several fields and is gradually developing as a branch of critical criminology.

from THE PHILADELPHIA NEGRO: A SOCIAL STUDY
by W. E. B. Du Bois

THE NEGRO CRIMINAL

History of Negro Crime in the City.[1] —From his earliest advent the Negro, as was natural, has figured largely in the criminal annals of Philadelphia. Only such superficial study of the American Negro as dates his beginning with 1863 can neglect this past record of crime in studying the present. Crime is a phenomenon of organized social life, and is the open rebellion of an individual against his social environment. Naturally then, if men are suddenly transported from one environment to another, the result is lack of harmony with the new conditions; lack of harmony with the new physical surroundings leading to disease and death or modification of physique; lack of harmony with social surroundings leading to crime. Thus very early in the history of the colony characteristic complaints of the disorder of the Negro slaves is heard. In 1693, July 11, the Governor and Council approved an ordinance, "Upon the Request of some of the members of Council, that an order be made by the Court of Quarter Sessions for the Countie of philadelphia, the 4th July instant (proceeding upon a presentment of the Grand Jurie for the bodie of the sd countie), agt the tumultuous gatherings of the Negroes of the towne of philadelphia, on the first days of the weeke, ordering the Constables of philadelphia, or anie other person whatsoever, to have power to take up Negroes, male or female, whom they should find gadding abroad on the said first days of the weeke, without a ticket from their Mr. or Mris., or not in their Compa, or to carry them to gaole, there to remain that night, and that without meat or drink, and to Cause them to be publickly whipt next morning with 39 Lashes, well Laid on, on their bare backs, for which their sd. Mr. or Mris. should pay 15d. to the whipper," etc.[2]

Penn himself introduced a law for the special trial and punishment of Negroes very early in the history of the colony, as has been noted before.[3] The slave code finally adopted was mild compared with the legislation of the period, but it was severe enough to show the unruly character of many of the imported slaves.[4]

Especially in Philadelphia did the Negroes continue to give general trouble, not so much by serious crime as by disorder. In 1732, under Mayor Hasel, the City Council "taking under Consideration the frequent and tumultuous meetings of the Negro Slaves, especially on Sunday, Gaming, Cursing, Swearing, and committing many other Disorders, to the great Terror and Disquiet of the Inhabitants of this city," ordered an ordinance to be drawn up against such disturbances.[5] Again, six years later, we hear of the draft of another city ordinance for "the more Effectual suppressing Tumultuous meetings and other disorderly doings of the Negroes, Mulattos and Indian servts. and slaves."[6] And in 1741, August 17, "frequent complaints having been made to the Board that many disorderly persons meet every ev'g about the Court house of this city, and great numbers of Negroes and others sit there with milk pails and other things late at night, and many disorders are there committed against the peace and good government of this city," Council ordered the place to be cleared "in half an hour after sunset."[7]

Of the graver crimes by Negroes we have only reports here and there which do not make it clear how frequently such crimes occurred. In 1706 a slave is arrested for setting fire to a dwelling; in 1738 three Negroes are hanged in neighboring parts of New Jersey for poisoning people, while at Rocky Hill a slave is burned alive for killing a child and burning a barn. Whipping of Negroes at the public whipping post was frequent, and so severe was the punishment that in 1743 a slave brought up to be whipped committed suicide. In 1762 two

---

1. Throughout this chapter the basis of induction is the number of prisoners received at different institutions and *not* the prison population at particular times. This avoids the mistakes and distortions of the latter method. (Cf. Falkner: "Crime and the Census;" Publications of the American Academy of Political and Social Science, No. 190). Many writers on Crime among Negroes, as *e.g.*, F. L. Hoffman, and all who use the Eleventh Census uncritically, have fallen into numerous mistakes and exaggerations by carelessness on this point.
2. "Pennsylvania Colonial Records," I, 380–81.
3. See Chapter III, and Appendix B.
4. Cf. "Pennsylvania Statutes at Large," Ch. 56.
5. "Watson's Annals," I, 62.
6. *Ibid.*
7. *Ibid.*, pp. 62–63.

Philadelphia slaves were sentenced to death for felony and burglary; petitions were circulated in their behalf but Council was obdurate.[8]

Little special mention of Negro crime is again met with until the freedmen under the act of 1780 began to congregate in the city and other free immigrants joined them. In 1809 the leading colored churches united in a society to suppress crime and were cordially endorsed by the public for this action. After the war immigration to the city increased and the stress of hard times bore heavily on the lower classes. Complaints of petty thefts and murderous assaults on peaceable citizens now began to increase, and in numbers of cases they were traced to Negroes. The better class of colored citizens felt the accusation and held a meeting to denounce crime and take a firm stand against their own criminal class. A little later the Negro riots commenced, and they received their chief moral support from the increasing crime of Negroes; a Cuban slave brained his master with a hatchet, two other murders by Negroes followed, and gambling, drunkenness and debauchery were widespread wherever Negroes settled. The terribly vindictive insurrection of Nat Turner in a neighboring State frightened the citizens so thoroughly that when some black fugitives actually arrived at Chester from Southampton County, Virginia, the Legislature was hastily appealed to, and the whole matter came to a climax in the disfranchisement of the Negro in 1837, and the riots in the years 1830 to 1840.[9]

Some actual figures will give us an idea of this, the worst period of Negro crime ever experienced in the city. The Eastern Penitentiary was opened in 1829 near the close of the year. The total number of persons received here for the most serious crimes is given in the next table. This includes prisoners from the Eastern counties of the State, but a large proportion were from Philadelphia:[10]

Years.	Total Commitments.	Negroes.	Per Cent of Negroes.	Per Cent of Negroes of Total Population.
1829–34 ..	339	99	29.0	8.27 (1830)
1835–39 ..	878	356	40.5	7.39 (1840)
1840–44 ..	701	209	29.8	7.39 (1840)
1845–49 ..	633	151	23.8	4.83 (1850)
1850–54 ..	664	106	16.0	4.83 (1850)

8. "Pennsylvania Colonial Records," II, 275; IX, 6; "Watson's Annals," I, 309.
9. Cf. Chapter IV.
10. Reports Eastern Penitentiary.

Or to put it differently the problem of Negro crime in Philadelphia from 1830 to 1850 arose from the fact that less than one-fourteenth of the population was responsible for nearly a third of the serious crimes committed.

These figures however are apt to relate more especially to a criminal class. A better measure of the normal criminal tendencies of the group would perhaps be found in the statistics of Moyamensing, where ordinary cases of crime and misdemeanor are confined and which contains only county prisoners. The figures for Moyamensing prison are:

Years.	Total White Prisoners Received.	Total Negro Prisoners Received.	Per Cent of Negroes of Total Prisoners.	Per Cent of Negroes of Total Population.
1836–45 ..	1164	1087	48.29	7.39 (1840)
1846–55 ..	1478	696	32.01	4.83 (1850)
Total	2642	1783	...	.....

Here we have even a worse showing than before; in 1896 the Negroes forming 4 per cent of the population furnish 9 per cent of the arrests, but in 1850 being 5 per cent of the population they furnished 32 per cent of the prisoners received at the county prison. Of course there are some considerations which must not be overlooked in interpreting these figures for 1836–55. It must be remembered that the discrimination against the Negro was much greater then than now: he was arrested for less cause and given longer sentences than whites.[11] Great numbers of those arrested and committed for trial were never brought to trial so that their guilt could not be proven or disproven; of 737 Negroes committed for trial in six months of the year 1837, it is stated that only 123 were actually brought to trial; of the prisoners in the Eastern Penitentiary, 1829 to 1846, 14 per cent of the whites were pardoned and 2 per cent of the Negroes. All these considerations increase the statistics to the disfavor of the Negro.[12] Nevertheless making all reasonable allowances it is undoubtedly true that the crime of Negroes in this period reached its high tide for this city.

11. Average length of sentences for whites in Eastern Penitentiary during nineteen years, 2 years 8 months 2 days; for Negroes, 3 years 3 months 14 days. Cf. "Health of Convicts" (pam.), pp. 7, 8.
12. Ibid., "Condition of Negroes," 1838, pp. 15–18; "Condition," etc., 1848, pp. 26, 27.

The character of the crimes committed by Negroes compared with whites is shown by the following table, which covers the offences of 1359 whites and 718 Negroes committed to the Eastern Penitentiary, 1829–1846. If we take simply petty larceny we find that 48.8 per cent of the whites, and 55 per cent of the Negroes were committed for this offence.[13]

Kinds of Crime.	Whites.		Negroes.	
	Number.	Per Cent.	Number.	Per Cent.
Offences vs. the person	166	11.4	89	12.4
Offences vs. property with violence	191	13.1	165	22.9
Offences vs. property without violence	873	59.8	432	60.2
Malicious offences vs. property	22	1.5	14	2.0
Offences vs. Currency and forgery	167	11.5	7	1.0
Miscellaneous	40	27.0	11	1.5
All offences	1359	100	718	100

Negro Crime Since the War. —Throughout the land there has been since the war a large increase in crime, especially in cities. This phenomenon would seem to have sufficient cause in the increased complexity of life, in industrial competition, and the rush of great numbers to the large cities. It would therefore be natural to suppose that the Negro would also show this increase in criminality and, as in the case of all lower classes, that he would show it in greater degree. His evolution has, however, been marked by some peculiarities. For nearly two decades after emancipation he took little part in many of the great social movements about him for obvious reasons. His migration to city life, therefore, and his sharing in the competition of modern industrial life, came later than was the case with the mass of his fellow citizens. The Negro began to rush to the cities in large numbers after 1880, and consequently the phenomena attendant on that momentous change of life are tardier in his case. His rate of criminality has in the last two decades risen rapidly, and this is a parallel phenomenon to the rapid rise of the white criminal record two or three decades ago. Moreover, in the case of the Negro there were special causes for the prevalence of crime: he had lately been freed from serfdom, he was the object of stinging oppression and ridicule, and paths of advancement open to many were closed to him. Consequently the class of the shiftless, aimless, idle, discouraged and disappointed was proportionately larger.

In the city of Philadelphia the increasing number of bold and daring crimes committed by Negroes in the last ten years has focused the attention of the city on this subject. There is a widespread feeling that something is wrong with a race that is responsible for so much crime, and that strong remedies are called for. One has but to visit the corridors of the public buildings, when the courts are in session, to realize the part played in law-breaking by the Negro population. The various slum centres of the colored criminal population have lately been the objects of much philanthropic effort, and the work there has aroused discussion. Judges on the bench have discussed the matter. Indeed, to the minds of many, this is the real Negro problem.[14]

That it is a vast problem a glance at statistics will show;[15] and since 1880 it has been steadily growing. At the same time crime is a difficult subject to study, more difficult to analyze into its sociological elements, and most difficult to cure or suppress. It is a phenomenon that stands not alone, but rather as a symptom of countless wrong social conditions.

The simplest, but crudest, measure of crime is found in the total arrests for a period of years. The value of such figures is lessened by the varying efficiency and diligence of the police, by discrimination in the administration of law, and by unwarranted arrests. And yet the figures roughly measure crime. The total arrests and the number of Negroes is given in the next table for thirty-two years, with a few omissions:

---

13. "Condition of Negroes," 1849, pp. 28, 29. "Condition," etc., 1838, pp. 15–18.

14. "The large proportion of colored men who, in April, had been before the criminal court, led Judge Gordon to make a suggestion when he yesterday discharged the jurors for the term. 'It would certainly seem,' said the Court, 'that the philanthropic colored people of the community, of whom there are a great many excellent and intelligent citizens sincerely interested in the welfare of their race, ought to see what is radically wrong that produces this state of affairs and correct it, if possible. There is nothing in history that indicates that the colored race has a propensity to acts of violent crime; on the contrary, their tendencies are most gentle, and they submit with grace to subordination.'" Philadelphia *Record*, April 29, 1893; Cf. *Record*, May 10 and 12; *Ledger*, May 10, and *Times*, May 22, 1893.

15. Except as otherwise noted, the statistics of this section are from the official reports of the police department.

ARRESTS IN PHILADELPHIA, 1864–96.

Date.	Total Number Arrested.	Total Negroes Arrested.	Percentage of Negroes.
1864	34,221	3,114	9.1
1865	43,226	2,722	6.3
1869	38,749	2,907	7.5
1870	31,717	2,070	6.5
1873	30,400	1,380	4.5
1874	32,114	1,257	3.9
1875	34,553	1,539	4.5
1876	...	...	...
1877	44,220	2,524	5.7
1879	40,714	2,360	5.8
1880	44,097	2,204	4.98
1881	45,129	2,327	5.11
1882	46,130	2,183	4.73
1883	45,295	2,022	4.46
1884	49,468	2,134	4.31
1885	51,418	2,662	5.11
1886	...	...	...
1887	57,951	3,256	5.61
1888	46,899	2,910	6.20
1889	42,673	2,614	6.10
1890	49,148	3,167	6.44
1891	53,184	3,544	6.66
1892	52,944	3,431	6.48
1893	57,297	4,078	7.11
1894	61,478	4,805	7.81
1895	60,347	5,137	8.5
1896	58,072	5,302	9.1

We find that the total arrests in the city per annum have risen from 34,221 in 1864 to 61,478 in 1894, an increase of 80 per cent in crime, parallel to an increase of 85 per cent in population. The Negroes arrested have increased from 3114 in 1864 to 4805 in 1894, an increase of 54 per cent in crime, parallel to an increase of 77 per cent in the Negro population of the city. So, too, the percentage of Negroes in the total arrests is less in 1894 than in 1864. If, however, we follow the years between these two dates we see an important development: 1864 was the date bounding the antebellum period of crime; thereafter the proportion of Negro arrests fell steadily until, in 1874, the Negroes came as nearly as ever furnishing their normal quota of arrests, 3.9 per cent from 3.28 per cent (1870) of the population. Then slowly there came a change. With the Centennial Exposition in 1876 came a stream of immigrants, and once started the stream increased in speed by its own momentum. With this immigration the proportion of Negro arrests arose rapidly at first as a result of the exposition; falling off a little in the early eighties, but with 1885 rising again steadily and quickly to over 6 per cent in 1888, 6.4 per cent in 1890, 7 per cent in 1893, 8.5 per cent in 1895, 9 per cent in 1896. This is, as has been said before, but a rough indication of the amount of crime for which the Negro is responsible; it must not be relied on too closely, for the number of arrests cannot in any city accurately measure wrongdoing save in a very general way; probably increased efficiency in the police force since 1864 has had large effect; and yet we can draw the legitimate conclusion here that Negro crime in the city is far less, according to population, than before the war; that after the war it decreased until the middle of the seventies and then, coincident with the beginning of the new Negro immigration to cities,[16] it has risen pretty steadily.

These same phenomena can be partially verified by statistics of Moyamensing prison. If we take the tried and untried prisoners committed to this county prison from 1876 to 1895 we find the same gradual increase of crime:

MOYAMENSING PRISON: BOTH TRIED AND UNTRIED PRISONERS.

Date.	Total Receptions.	Negroes.	Per Cent of Negroes.
1876	21,736	1,530	7.8
1877	22,666	1,460	6.44
1878	22,147	1,356	6.12
1879	20,736	1,136	5.48
1880	22,487	1,030	4.58
1881	22,478	1,168	5.19
1882	24,176	1,274	5.27
1883	23,245	1,175	5.05
1884	25,081	1,218	4.86
1885	24,725	1,427	5.77
1886	27,286	1,708	6.26
1887	28,964	1,724	5.97
1888	21,399	1,399	6.54
1889	18,476	1,338	7.24
1890	20,582	1,611	7.83
1891	22,745	1,723	7.57
1892	22,460	1,900	8.46
1893	25,209	2,234	8.86
1894	25,777	2,452	9.51
1895	22,584	2,317	10.26
Total	464,959	31,180	6.70
1876–1885	229,477	12,774	5.57
1886–1895	235,482	18,406	7.81

---

16. Cf. Chapters IV and VII.

If we compare in this table the period 1876–85 with that of 1886–95 we find that the proportion of Negro criminals in the first period was 5.6 per cent, in the second 7.8 per cent.

The statistics of inmates of the House of Correction, where mild cases and juveniles are sent, for the last few years go to tell the same tale:

Year.	Total Receptions.	Negroes.	Percentage of Negroes.
1891	5907	274	4.6
1892	5297	254	4.8
1893	..	..	..
1894	6579	1055	16.0
1895	7548	672	8.9

Gathering up the statistics presented let us make a rough diagram of some of the results. First let us scan the record of the Negro in serious crime, such as entails incarceration in the Eastern Penitentiary. In these figures the Philadelphia convicts are not separated from those in the eastern counties of the state prior to 1885. A large proportion of the prisoners however are from Philadelphia; perhaps the net result of the error is somewhat to reduce the apparent proportion of Negroes in the earlier years. Taking then the proportion of Negro prisoners received to total receptions since the founding of the Penitentiary we have this diagram:

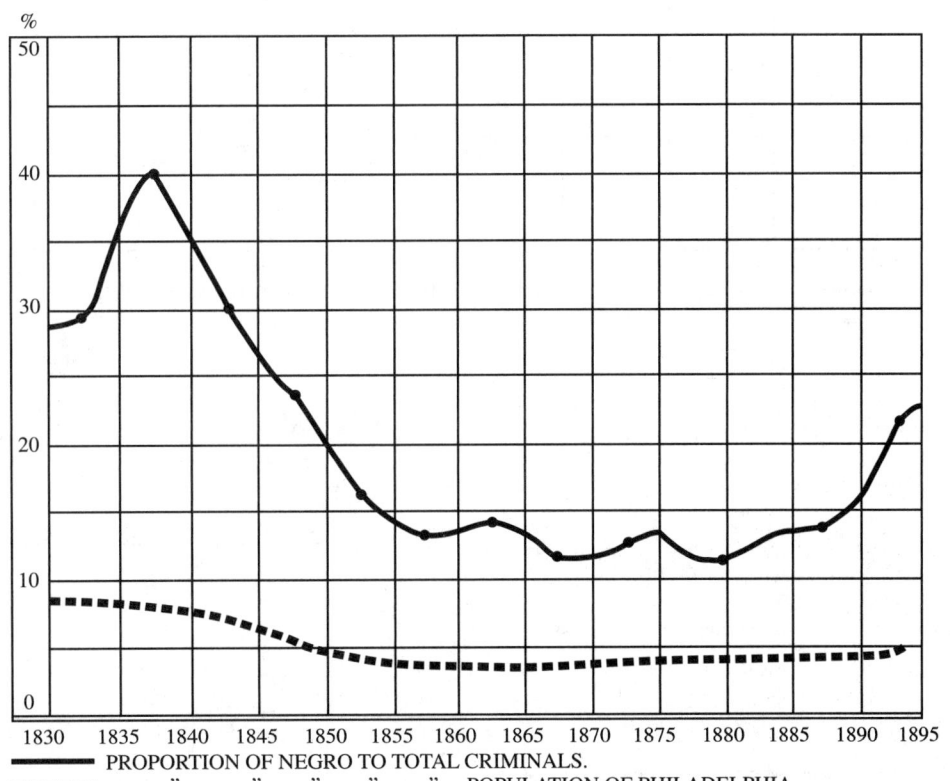

PROPORTION OF NEGROES TO TOTAL CONVICTS RECEIVED AT THE EASTERN PENITENTIARY, 1829–1895.

——— PROPORTION OF NEGRO TO TOTAL CRIMINALS.
∎∎∎∎∎   ”   ”   ”   ”   ”   POPULATION OF PHILADELPHIA.

The general rate of criminality may be graphically represented from the proportion of Negroes in the county prison, although changes in the policy of the courts make the validity of this somewhat uncertain:

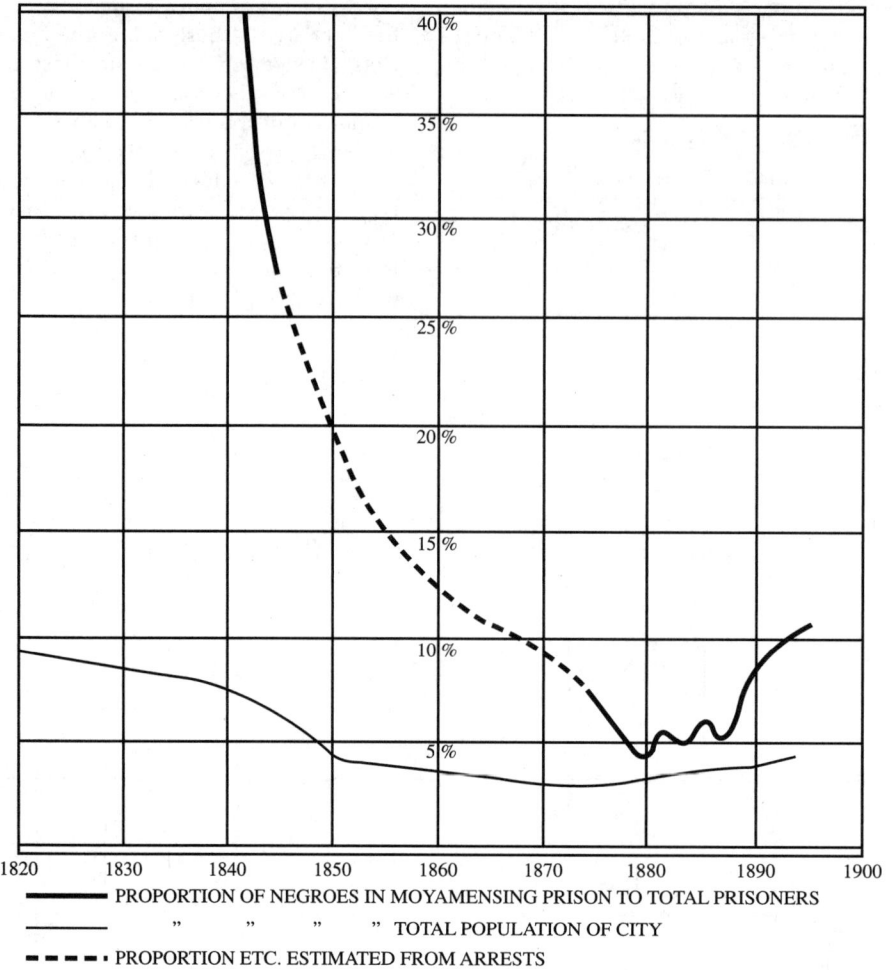

——— PROPORTION OF NEGROES IN MOYAMENSING PRISON TO TOTAL PRISONERS
———   "   "   "   "   TOTAL POPULATION OF CITY
- - - - PROPORTION ETC. ESTIMATED FROM ARRESTS

It thus seems certain[17] that general criminality as represented by commitments to the county prison has decreased markedly since 1840, and that its rapid increase since 1880 leaves it still far behind the decade 1830 to 1840. Serious crime as represented by commitments to the penitentiary shows a similar decrease but one not so marked indicating the presence of a pretty distinct criminal class.

---

17. The chief element of uncertainty lies in the varying policy of the courts, as for instance, in the proportion of prisoners sent to different places of detention, the severity of sentence, etc. Only the general conclusions are insisted on here.

CONVICTS COMMITTED TO THE EASTERN PENITENTIARY.

Years.	Total Commitments.	Negroes.	Percentage of Negroes.
1835–39	878	356	40.5
1855–59	941	126	13.4
1860–64	909	129	14.2
1865–69	1474	179	12.1
1870–74	1291	174	13.4
1875–79	2347	275	11.7
1880–84	2282	308	13.5
1885–89*	1583	223	14.09
1890–95*	1418	318	22.43

*Only convicts from Philadelphia; the statistics for the year 1891 are not available and are omitted.

The record of arrests per 1000 of Negro population 1864 to 1896 seems to confirm these conclusions for that period:

The increase in crime between 1890 and 1895 is not without pretty adequate explanation in the large Negro immigration cityward and especially in "the

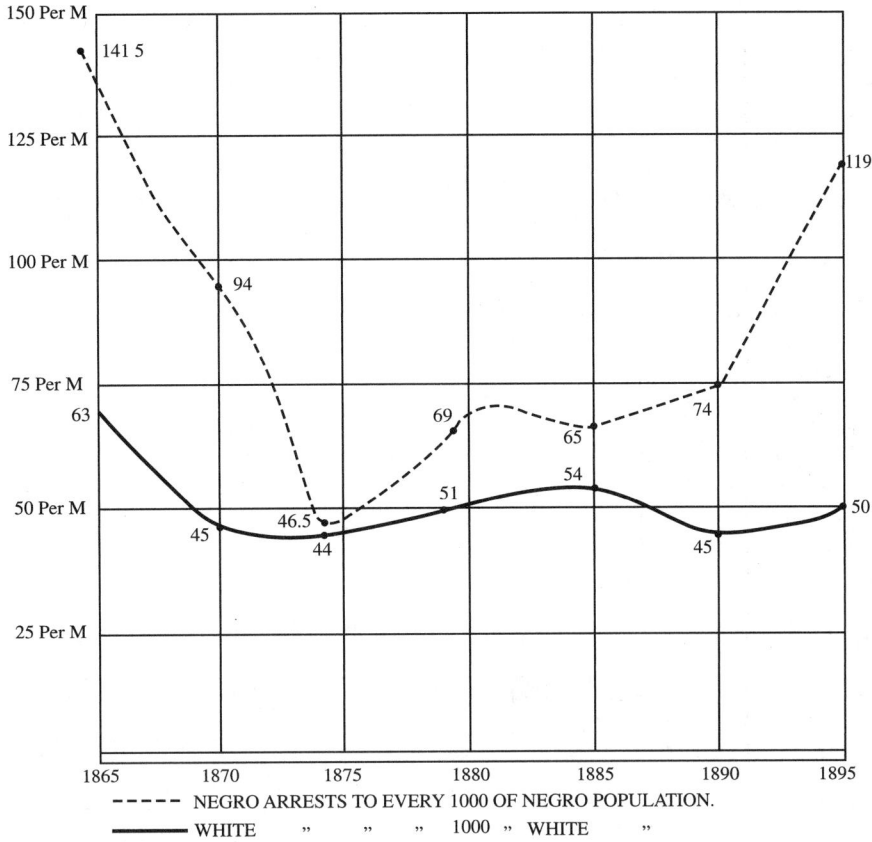

- - - - NEGRO ARRESTS TO EVERY 1000 OF NEGRO POPULATION.
———— WHITE "   "   " 1000 " WHITE "

terrible business depression of 1893" to which the police bureau attributes the increase of arrests. The effect of this would naturally be greater among the economic substrata.

This brings us to the question, Who are the Negro criminals and what crimes do they commit? To obtain an answer to this query let us make a special study of a typical group of criminals.

A Special Study in Crime.[18] —During ten years previous to and including 1895, there were committed to the Eastern Penitentiary, the following prisoners from the city of Philadelphia:

---

18. For the collection of the material here compiled, I am indebted to Mr. David N. Fell, Jr., a student of the Senior Class, Wharton School, University of Pennsylvania, in the year '96–'97. As before noted the figures in this Section refer to the number of prisoners received at the Eastern Penitentiary, and not to the total prison population at any particular time.

PHILADELPHIA WHITES AND NEGROES
COMMITTED TO THE EASTERN PENITENTIARY

Date.	Total Convictions.	Negroes.	Per Cent of Negroes.	
1885......	313	40	12.78	
1886......	347	45	12.97	
1887......	363	53	14.60	14.9
1888......	269	39	14.49	
1889......	291	46	15.81	
1890......	271	63	23.25	
1891*.....	..	..	..	
1892......	213	42	19.71	22.43
1893......	320	74	23.13	
1894......	329	69	20.97	
1895......	285	70	24.56	
Total......	3,001	541	18.2 average.	

*Statistics for this year were not available. Throughout this section, therefore, this year is omitted.

Let us now take the 541 Negroes who have been the perpetrators of the serious crimes charged to their race during the last ten years and see what we may learn. These are all criminals convicted after trial for periods varying from six months to forty years. It seems plain in the first place that the 4 per cent of the population of Philadelphia having Negro blood furnished from 1885 to 1889, 14 per cent of the serious crimes, and from 1890 to 1895, 22½ per cent. This of course assumes that the convicts in the penitentiary represent with a fair degree of accuracy the crime committed. The assumption is not wholly true; in convictions by human courts the rich always are favored somewhat at the expense of the poor, the upper classes at the expense of the unfortunate classes, and whites at the expense of Negroes. We know for instance that certain crimes are not punished in Philadelphia because the public opinion is lenient, as for instance embezzlement, forgery, and certain sorts of stealing; on the other hand a commercial community is apt to punish with severity petty thieving, breaches of the peace, and personal assault or burglary. It happens, too, that the prevailing weakness of ex-slaves brought up in the communal life of the slave plantation, without acquaintanceship with the institution of private property, is to commit the very crimes which a great centre of commerce like Philadelphia especially abhors. We must add to this the influences of social position and connections in procuring whites pardons or lighter sentences. It has been charged by some Negroes that color prejudice plays some part, but there is no tangible proof of this, save perhaps that there is apt to be a certain presumption of guilt when a Negro is accused, on the part of police, public and judge.[19] All these considerations modify somewhat our judgment of the moral status of the mass of Negroes. And yet, with all allowances, there remains a vast problem of crime.

The chief crimes for which these prisoners were convicted were:

Theft	243
Serious assaults on persons	139
Robbery and burglary	85
Rape	24
Other sexual crimes	23
Homicide	16
All other crimes	11
Total	541

Following these crimes from year to year we have:

Crime.	1885.	1886.	1887.	1888.	1889.	1890.	1892.	1893.	1894.	1895.	Total.
Theft, etc.	20	21	23	13	24	39	20	32	23	28	243
Robbery and burglary	2	8	8	5	5	9	7	14	19	8	85
Serious assaults	10	9	11	15	9	12	9	19	18	27	139
Homicide	.	.	3	2	5	.	2	1	1	2	16
Sexual crimes	6	7	7	4	4	4	4	5	3	3	47
All others	2	.	1	1	.	.	.	2	3	2	11
Total	40	45	53	40	47	64	42	73	67	70	541

The course of the total serious crime for this period may be illustrated by this diagram:

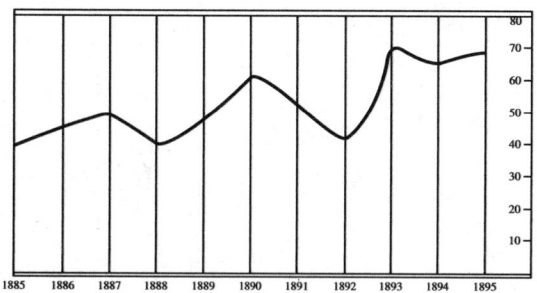

Drawing a similar diagram for the different sorts of crime we have:

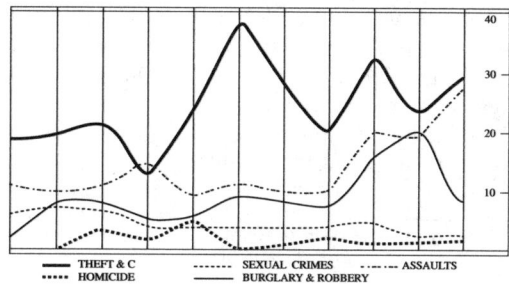

---

19. Witness the case of Marion Stuyvesant accused of the murder of the librarian, Wilson, in 1897.

In ten years convictions to the penitentiary for theft have somewhat increased, robbery, burglary and assault have considerably increased, homicide has remained about the same, and sexual crimes have decreased. Detailed statistics are given in the following table:

CRIMES OF 541 CONVICTS IN EASTERN PENITENTIARY, 1885–1895.

Crimes.	1885.	1886.	1887.	1888.	1889.	1890.	1892.	1893.	1894.	1895.
Assault and battery	3	.	1	2	.	1	.	.	.	.
Aggravated assault and battery	3	3	3	7	3	6	3	6	6	9
Assault to kill	4	6	7	6	6	5	4	13	11	17
Manslaughter	.	.	.	1	3	.	1	1	.	1
Murder	.	.	3	1	2	.	1	.	1	1
Assault to murder	.	.	1	.	.	.	.	.	.	.
Assault to steal	.	.	.	.	.	.	2	.	1	1
Larceny	20	21	23	13	24	39	17	27	22	28
Robbery	2	3	3	1	.	4	3	5	9	6
Burglary	.	5	5	4	5	5	4	9	10	2
Embezzlement	.	.	.	.	.	.	.	1	.	.
Sodomy	2	1	1	3	2	3	2	.	.	1
Abortion	1	.	.	.	.	1	.	.	.	.
Rape	1	.	.	.	.	.	.	2	1	.
Attempt to rape	1	6	1	1	1	1	1	3	2	1
Incest	1	.	.	.	.	.	.	.	.	.
Keeping bawdy house	.	.	4	.	.	.	.	.	.	1
Enticing female child	.	.	1	.	1	.	.	.	.	.
Carrying concealed weapons	1	.	.	.	.	.	.	1	.	.
Forgery	1	.	.	.	.	.	.	.	1	1
False pretence	.	.	.	1	.	.	1	.	1	.
Receiving stolen goods	.	.	.	.	.	.	2	4	1	.
Mayhem	.	.	.	.	.	.	.	1	.	.
Indecent exposure	.	.	.	.	.	.	.	.	.	1
Conspiracy	.	.	.	.	.	.	.	.	1	.
Total	40	45	53	40	47	64	42	73	67	70

The total crime can be classified also in this way:

Crimes against property	328	60.63 per cent.
Crimes against persons	157	29.02 per cent.
Crimes against persons and property	8	1.48 per cent.
Sexual crimes	48	8.87 per cent.
	541	100. per cent.

Age.	Number.	Percentage.	
15–19	58	10.73	
20–24	170	} 56.19	} 66.92
25–29	132		
30–39	132	24.03	
40–49	34	6.29	} 34.08
50–59	10	1.85	
60 and over	5	.91	
Total	541	100.	

Let us now turn from the crime to the criminals. 497 of them (91.87 per cent) were males and 44 (8.13 per cent) were females. 296 (54.71 per cent) were single, 208 (34.45 per cent) were married, and 37 (6.84 per cent) were widowed. In age they were divided as follows:

The mass of criminals are, it is easy to see, young single men under thirty. Detailed statistics of sex and age and conjugal condition are given in the next tables.

AGE AND SEX OF CONVICTS IN EASTERN PENITENTIARY. NEGROES, 1885–1895.

Ages.	Males.	Females.	Total.
15–19	53	5	58
20–24	153	17	170
25–29	119	13	132
30–34	80	5	85
35–39	45	2	47
40–44	21	1	22
45–49	11	1	12
50–59	3	.	3
60 and over	15	.	15
Total	497	44	541

CONJUGAL CONDITION OF CONVICTS IN EASTERN PENITENTIARY.

	Males.			Females.		
Age.	Single.	Married.	Widowed	Single.	Married.	Widowed.
15–19	48	5	0	4	1	0
20–24	117	35	0	7	9	1
25–29	59	54	8	3	10	0
30–34	30	38	6	0	4	1
35–39	11	30	4	0	0	2
40–49	8	16	8	0	2	0
50–59	3	3	4	0	0	0
60 and over	0	2	3	0	0	0

The convicts were born in the following States:

Philadelphia	114
Other parts of Pennsylvania	48
New Jersey	21
Maryland	99
Virginia	77
Delaware	37
District of Columbia	35
North Carolina	19
New York	11
South Carolina	9
Georgia	8
Other parts of the North	13
Other parts of the South	22
The West	13
Foreign Countries	15
	541

Altogether 21 per cent were natives of Philadelphia; 217 were born in the North, and 309, or 57 per cent, were born in the South. Two-thirds of the Negroes of the city, judging from the Seventh Ward, were born outside the city, and this part furnishes 79 per cent of the serious crime. 54 per cent were born in the South and this part furnishes 57 per cent of the crime, or more, since many giving their birthplace as in the North were really born in the South.

The total illiteracy of this group reaches 26 per cent or adding in those who can read and write imperfectly, 34 per cent compared with 18 per cent for the Negroes of the city in 1890. In other words the illiterate fifth of the Negro population furnished a third of the worst criminals.

ILLITERACY OF CONVICTS IN THE EASTERN STATE PENITENTIARY.

Year.	Read and Write.		Read and Write Imperfectly.		Totally Illiterate.	
	Number.	Per Cent.	Number.	Per Cent	Number.	Per Cent.
1885	20	50.0	6	15.0	14	35.0
1886	25	55.55	4	8.88	16	35.55
1887	27	50.94	13	24.53	13	24.53
1888	25	64.10	6	15.38	8	20.51
1889	26	56.52	10	21.74	10	21.74
1890	43	68.25	3	4.76	17	26.98
1892	33	78.57	0	0	9	21.43
1893	55	74.32	0	0	19	25.68
1894	49	71.01	0	0	20	28.99
1895	55	78.57	0	0	15	21.43
Total	358	66.17	42	7.76	141	26.06

Naturally as the general intelligence of a community increases the general intelligence of its criminals increases, though seldom in the same proportion, showing that some crime may justly be attributed to pure ignorance. The number of criminals able to read and write has increased from 50 per cent in 1885 to 79 per cent in 1895. The number of colored men from fifteen to thirty who can read and write was about 90 per cent in the Seventh Ward in 1896. This shows how little increased intelligence alone avails to stop crime in the face of other powerful forces. It would of course be illogical to connect these phenomena directly as cause and effect and make Negro crime the result of Negro education—in that case we should find it difficult to defend the public schools in most modern lands. Crime comes either in spite of intelligence or as a result of misdirected intelligence under severe economic and moral strain. Thus we find here, as is apparently true in France, Italy and Germany, increasing crime and decreasing illiteracy as concurrent phenomena rather than as cause and effect. However the rapid increase of intelligence in Negro convicts does point to some grave social changes: first, a large number of young Negroes are in such environment that they find it easier to be rogues than honest men; secondly, there is evidence of the rise of more intelligent and therefore more dangerous crime from a trained criminal class, quite different from the thoughtless, ignorant crime of the mass of Negroes.

A separation of criminals according to sex and age and the kind of crime is of interest. . . .

CRIMINALS IN EASTERN STATE PENITENTIARY.—FEMALES, BY AGE AND CRIME.

Ages.	Larceny.	Assault and Battery.	Aggravated Assault.	Assault to Kill.	Murder.	Bawdy and Disorderly Houses.	Accessory to Murder.	Abduction.
15–19	5	..	..	..	..	..	..	..
20–24	10	1	3	2	1	..	..	..
25–29	11	..	1	..	..	..	1	..
30–34	3	..	..	..	..	..	1	1
35–39	1	..	..	..	..	1	..	..
40–44	1	..	..	..	..	..	..	..
45–49	1	..	..	..	..	..	..	..

The women are nearly all committed for stealing and fighting. They are generally prostitutes from the worst slums. The boys of fifteen to nineteen are sentenced largely for petty thieving:

Whole number of male convicts, 15–19 years of age	53
Convicted for larceny	27
Convicted for assault and fighting	8
Convicted for sexual crimes	5
Convicted for burglary	5
Convicted for other crimes	8
	53

Making a similar table for two other age periods we have:

Men, 20–24 Years.		Men, 25–29 Years.	
Larceny	62	Larceny	45
Assault	41	Assault	33
Burglary and robbery	30	Burglary and robbery	22
Sexual crimes	6	Sexual crimes	13
Other crimes	14	Homicide	4
		Other crimes	3
	153		119

There is here revealed no especial peculiarity: stealing and fighting are ever the besetting sins of half-developed races.

It would be very instructive to know how many of the 541 criminals had been in the hands of the law before. This is however very difficult to ascertain correctly since in many, if not the majority of cases, the word of the prisoner must be taken. Even these methods however reveal the startling fact that only 315 or 58 per cent of these 541 convicts are reported as being incarcerated for the first time. 226 or 42 per cent can be classed as habitual criminals, who have been convicted as follows:

Twice	105	46.5 per cent.
Three times	60	26.5 per cent.
Four times	24	11.0 per cent.
Five times	19	8.0 per cent.
Six times	9	4.0 per cent.
Seven times	4	1.8 per cent.
Nine times	1	
Ten times	1	2.2 per cent.
Eleven times	2	
Twelve times	1	
	226	100 per cent.

When we realize that probably a large number of the other convicts are on their second or third term we begin to get an idea of the real Negro criminal class.[20]

---

20. The following Negroes were measured by the Bertillon system in Philadelphia during the last three years:

1893	64 (Whites 101).
1894	66 (Whites 248).
1895	56 (Whites 267).
1896	75 (Whites 347).

The arrests by detectives for five years are given on the following page. . . .

CRIMINALS IN EASTERN STATE PENITENTIARY.—MALES, BY AGE AND CRIME.

Ages	Larceny	Assault and Battery	Receiving Stolen Goods	Assault to Steal	Concealed Weapons	Aggravated Assault and Battery	Assault to Kill	Burglary	Robbery	Sodomy	Assault to Rape	Rape	Manslaughter	Forgery	Murder	Conspiracy	False Pretense	Embezzlement	Mayhem	Bawdy houses	Enticement to Rape	Indecent Exposure	Incest	Abortion
15–19	27	1	2	1	1	2	4	5	.	1	3	1	.	1	.	.	.	.	.	.	.	.	.	.
20–24	62	4	2	1	1	16	24	14	16	.	1	1	1	.	3	1	2	1	1	1	.	.	.	.
25–29	45	1	1	2	.	9	22	12	10	4	3	.	1	.	1	.	.	.	.	1	2	1	.	.
30–34	23	1	1	.	.	6	17	12	9	3	2	4	1	1	3	.	.	.	.	1	.	.	.	.
35–39	23	.	1	.	.	6	3	3	.	3	4	.	1	1	2	.	1	.	.	.	.	.	1	1
40–44	9	.	.	.	.	4	2	1	1	.	2	.	1	.	.	.	.	.	.	.	.	.	.	.
45–49	3	.	.	.	1	2	2	.	.	1	1	.	1	.	.	.	.	.	.	.	.	.	.	.
50–59	2	.	.	.	.	.	1	2	1	.	.	.	.	.	.	.	.	.	.	.	.	.	.	1
60 and over	3	.	.	.	.	.	1	.	.	3	.	.	1	.	.	.	.	.	.	.	.	.	.	.
Total	197	7	7	4	3	45	76	50	37	15	16	6	7	3	9	1	3	1	1	3	2	1	1	2

A few other facts are of interest: if we tabulate crime according to the illiteracy of its perpetrators, we have:

Larceny . . . . 31 per cent of illiteracy.
Assault, burglary and
 homicide . . . . 34 per cent of illiteracy.
Sexual crimes . . . . 55 per cent of illiteracy.

Or in other words, the more serious and revolting the crime the larger part does ignorance play as a cause. If we separate prisoners convicted for the above crimes according to length of sentence, we have:

Under five years 464   90.5 per cent.
Five and under ten years . 40   8.0 per cent.
Ten years and over   9   1.5 per cent.

                             513

Of the 49 sentenced for 5 years and over, 18 or 37 per cent were illiterate; of those sentenced for less than 5 years 160 or 35 per cent were illiterate.

CRIMES OF NEGROES ARRESTED BY DETECTIVES, 1887–1892.

Crimes.	1887.	1888.	1889.	1890.	1891.	1892.
Fugitives from justice	...	10	2	4	4	9
Larceny	10	19	17	19	18	29
Pickpocket	7	4	1	...	...	13
Burglary	1	...	2	...	2	4
Professional thief	1	4	2	1	2	3
Sodomy	...	...	...	...	...	1
Misdemeanor	...	1	...	1	...	1
Absconding	...	...	...	...	...	1
Assault to kill	5	6	1	1	4	4
Stabbing	...	...	...	...	...	1
False pretense	...	2	...	1	...	1
Forgery	...	...	...	...	...	1
Receiving stolen goods	1	4	8	...	3	...
Murder	3	2	1	3	2	...
Abortion	...	...	...	1	1	...
Breach of peace	...	...	...	2	...	...
Abandonment	...	...	1	1	...	...
Gambling house	...	4	...	5	...	...
Fornication and adultry	...	...	1	...	...	...
Infanticide	...	1	...	...	...	...
House robbery	...	1	...	...	...	...
Lottery	1	8	...	...	...	...
Embezzlement	...	1	...	...	...	...
Perjury	...	1	...	...	...	...
Seduction	1	...	...	...	...	...
Bawdy house	1	...	...	...	...	...

From this study we may conclude that young men are the perpetrators of the serious crime among Negroes; that this crime consists mainly of stealing and assault; that ignorance, and immigration to the temptations of city life, are responsible for much of this crime but not for all; that deep social causes underlie this prevalence of crime and they have so worked as to form among Negroes since 1864 a distinct class of habitual criminals; that to this criminal class and not to the great mass of Negroes the bulk of the serious crime perpetrated by this race should be charged.

Some Cases of Crime.—It is difficult while studying crime in the abstract to realize just what the actual crimes committed are, and under what circumstances they take place. A few typical cases of the crimes of Negroes may serve to give a more vivid idea than the abstract statistics give. Most of these cases are quoted from the daily newspapers.

First let us take a couple of cases of larceny:

Edward Ashbridge, a colored boy, pleaded guilty to the larceny of a quart of milk, the property of George Abbott. The boy's mother said he was incorrigible, and he was committed to the House of Refuge.

William Drumgoole, colored, aged thirty-one years, of Lawrenceville, Va., was shot in the back and probably fatally wounded late yesterday afternoon by William H. McCalley, a detective, employed in the store of John Wanamaker, Thirteenth and Chestnut streets. Drumgoole, it is alleged, stole a pair of shoes from the store, and was followed by McCalley to the corner of Thirteenth and Chestnut streets, where he placed him under arrest. Drumgoole broke away from the detective's grasp, and running down Thirteenth street turned into Drury street, a small thoroughfare above Sansom street. McCalley started in pursuit, calling upon him to stop, but the fugitive darted into an alleyway, and when his pursuer came up within a few yards of him, he threatened to "do him up" if he followed him any further. McCalley drew his revolver from his pocket, and as Drumgoole again broke into a run he pointed the weapon at his legs and fired. Drumgoole fell to the ground, and when McCalley came up to him he was unable to rise. McCalley saw at a glance that, instead of wounding him in the leg, as he had intended, the bullet had lodged in the man's back. He hurriedly sought assistance, and had the wounded man taken to the Jefferson Hospital. McCalley then surrendered himself to Reserve Policeman Powell, and was taken to the Central Station.

Fighting and quarreling among neighbors and associates is common in the slum districts:

> Etta Jones, colored, aged twenty-one years, residing on Hirst street, above Fifth, was stabbed near her home last night, it is alleged, by Lottie Lee, also colored, of Second and Race streets. The other woman was taken to the Pennsylvania Hospital, where her injuries were found to consist of several cuts on the left shoulder and side, none of which are dangerous. Her assailant was arrested later by Policeman Dean and locked up in the Third and Union streets station house. The assault is said by the police to have been the outcome of an old grudge.
>
> Joseph Cole, colored, aged twenty-four years, residing in Gillis' alley, was dangerously stabbed shortly before midnight on Saturday, as is alleged, by Abraham Wheeler, at the latter's house, on Hirst street. Cole was taken to the Pennsylvania Hospital, where it was found the knife had penetrated to within a short distance of the right lung. Wheeler fled from the house after the cutting and eluded arrest until yesterday afternoon, when he was captured by Policeman Mitchell, near Fifth and Lombard streets. When brought to the station house Wheeler denied having cut Cole, but acknowledged having struck him because he was insulting his wife. He was locked up, however, to await the result of Cole's injuries.

Sometimes servants are caught pilfering:

> Theodore Grant, colored, residing on Burton street, attempted to pledge a woman's silk dress for $15 at McFillen's, Seventeenth and Market streets, several days ago. The pawnbroker refused, under his rule, to take women's raiment from a man, and told Grant to bring the owner. Grant went away and returned with Ella Jones, a young colored woman, who consented to take $7 for the dress. Since that time C. F. Robertson, residing at Sixtieth and Spruce streets, made complaint to the police of the loss of the dress, and as the result of an investigation made by Special Policemen Gallagher and Ewing, Grant and Ella Jones were arrested yesterday charged with the larceny of the silk dress, which was recovered. Grant admitted to the special policemen that Ella had given him the dress to pawn, but asserted that he had nothing to do with the matter except to offer to pledge the article. At a hearing before Magistrate Jermon, at the City Hall, yesterday, Mr. Robertson stated that the girl had made a statement to him, saying that Grant had induced her to take the dress. He said the girl had been perfectly trustworthy up to the time of her acquaintance with Grant, and had been left in full charge of the house, and that nothing was ever missed. He said he also expected to show that Grant had been concerned in two or three robberies. Ella Jones, a neatly dressed girl, who said she came from Maryland, stated to the magistrate that Grant had been coming to see her for about a year past. She said he had been importuning her to take something and let him pawn it, so that he could raise some money, until she finally consented. After she started to go to her mistress' room to get the dress her heart failed and she turned back, but he persuaded her, telling her that Mrs. Robertson would not miss it, and then she took the dress. Mr. Robertson informed the magistrate, and Ella assented to the statement, that Grant had taken every cent of her earnings from her for weeks past and had also pawned all of her clothing, so that at the present time she was penniless and had not a single garment except what she wore. The magistrate said it was undoubtedly a hard case, but he would have to hold Grant and Ella on the charge of larceny, and Grant under additional bail for a further hearing next Thursday on the charges referred to by Mr. Robertson. The police say that Grant, who is a smooth-faced, cross-eyed mulatto, is a "crap fiend," and that whatever money he has managed to obtain by threats and cajolery from his victim, Ella Jones, has gone into the pockets of the small-fry gamblers.

... Cases of aggravated assaults, for various reasons, are frequent:

> Rube Warren, colored, thirty years, of Foulkrod and Cedar streets, was held in $1000 bonds, by Magistrate Eisenbrown, for an alleged aggravated assault and battery on Policeman Haug, of the Frankford station, during a dog fight about a month ago. The policeman attempted to stop the fight when Warren, it is charged, assisted by several companions, assaulted him, broke his club and took away his revolver. During the free fight that followed, in which other policemen took part, Warren escaped and went to Baltimore. There, it is said, he was sent to prison for thirty days. As soon as he was released he went back to Frankford, where he was arrested on Saturday night.
>
> William Braxton, colored, aged twenty-eight years, of Irving street, above Thirty-seventh, was yesterday held in $800 bail for a further hearing, charged with having committed an aggravated assault on William Keebler, of South Thirtieth street. The assault occurred about three o'clock yesterday morning on Irving street, near Thirty-seventh, where the colored folks of the neighborhood were having a party. Keebler and two friends, none of whom were colored, forced their company on the invited guests, it is said, and a fight ensued. Keebler was found a short time afterward lying in the snow with one eye almost gouged out. He was conveyed to the University Hospital and the police

of the Woodland avenue station, under Acting Sergeant Ward, upon being notified of the affair, hurried to the Irving street house and arrested twenty of the guests just in the height of their merrymaking. All of them, however, were discharged at the hearing, upon Braxton's being recognized as the man who struck Keebler. The physician at the hospital says that the injured man will very likely lose the sight of one eye.

... More and more frequently in the last few years, have crime, excess, and disappointment led to attempted suicide:

Policeman Wynne, of the Fifth and Race streets station, last evening found an unknown colored woman lying unconscious in an alleyway at Delaware avenue and Race street. Beside the woman was an empty bottle labeled benzine. Wynne immediately summoned the patrol wagon and had the woman removed to the Pennsylvania Hospital, where her condition was said to be critical. The physicians said there was no doubt the woman had drunk the contents of the bottle, and narcotics were at once administered to counteract the effect of the poison. At midnight the woman showed signs of returning consciousness and it was thought that she would recover. The police have no clue to her identity, as she could not tell her name, and the alleyway where she was found is surrounded by business houses, and no one could be found who knew her.

It is but fair to add that many unsustained charges of crime are made against Negroes, and possibly more in proportion than against other classes. Some typical cases of this sort are of interest:

W. M. Boley, colored, thirty years old, who said he resided in Mayesville, South Carolina, was a defendant before Magistrate Jermon, at the City Hall, yesterday, on the charge of assault with intent to steal. Detective Gallagher and Special Policeman Thomas testified that their attention was attracted to the prisoner by his actions in a crowd at the New York train gate at Broad street station on Saturday. He had with him several parcels which he laid on the floor near the gate, and they said they saw him make several attempts to pick women's pockets, and arrested him. The man however proved by documentary evidence that he was a clergyman, a graduate of Howard University, and financial agent of a Southern school. He was released.

Under instructions from Judge Finletter, a jury rendered a verdict of not guilty in the case of George Queen, a young colored man, charged with the murder of Joseph A. Sweeney and John G. O'Brien. Dr. Frederick G. Coxson, pastor of the Pitman Methodist Episcopal Church, at Twenty-third and Lombard streets, testified that on the night in question he was about to retire, when he heard a disturbance on the street. Upon going out he saw three young men, two of whom were leading the other and persuading him to come with them. At the same time the prisoner, Queen, came along in the middle of the street, walking leisurely. Immediately upon seeing him the three men attacked him, and were shortly afterward joined by three others, and the entire crowd, among whom were Sweeney and O'Brien, continued beating and striking the colored man. Suddenly the crowd scattered and Queen was placed under arrest; he had fatally stabbed two of his assailants. This testimony showed that the accused was not the aggressor, and without hearing the defence Judge Finletter ordered the jury to render a verdict of not guilty. The case, he said, was one of justifiable homicide, the defendant having a right to resist the attack by force. The judge further said he thought the case would have a tendency to repel the brutal attacks made on inoffensive persons in the community, and to make the streets safe for every man to walk on at any hour without fear.

. . .

APPENDIX: TIMELINE OF THE SELECTED READINGS

1734–1737 (1755) Francis Hutcheson's *A System of Moral Philosophy*

This book was reportedly written during the 1730s, but it was not published until 1755.

1748 Montesquieu's *The Spirit of Laws*

1764 Cesare Beccaria's *An Essay on Crimes and Punishments*

1775–1778 Johann Caspar Lavater's *Essays on Physiognomy*

1780 (1789) Jeremy Bentham's *An Introduction to the Principles of Morals and Legislation*

This book was printed in 1780 but was not published until 1789.

1825 Franz Joseph Gall's *Organology (On the Functions of the Brain and Each of Its Parts, Volume IV)*

Appendix: Timeline of the Selected Readings

1825

1833 André-Michel Guerry's *Essay on the Moral Statistics of France*

1835 Adolphe Quetelet's *A Treatise on Man and the Development of His Faculties*
This work includes much of Quetelet's *Research on the Propensity for Crime at Different Ages* (1831).

1837 Harriet Martineau's *Society of America*

1845 Frederick Engels's *The Condition of the Working Class in England in 1844*

1850

1867 Karl Marx's *Capital: A Critique of Political Economy*, Volume I

1875

1886 Peter Kropotkin's *Law and Authority: An Anarchist Essay*

1885 Raffaele Garofalo's *Criminology*

1893 & 1895 Cesare Lombroso's *The Female Offender*, with William Ferrero (1893) and *Criminal Anthropology: Its Origin and Application* (1895)

1890 Gabriel Tarde's *Penal Philosophy*

The first edition of Lombroso's best-known work, *Criminal Man*, was published in 1876.

1895 & 1900 Émile Durkheim's *The Rules of Sociological Method* (1895) *Two Laws of Penal Evolution* (1900)

1899 W. E. B. Du Bois's *The Philadelphia Negro: A Social Study*

1900

1901 (1906) Enrico Ferri's *The Positive School of Criminology: Three Lectures*

These lectures were given in 1901 and published in 1906. The first edition of Ferri's well-known work, *Criminal Sociology*, was published in 1881 under a different title.

AUTHOR INDEX

A

Akers, Ronald L., 6n6
Albee, Ernest, 13n2, 16n5, 16n6
Allen, Francis A., 77n17
Anderson, Elijah, 216n28, 217n29
Anon., 134
Atkinson, Charles Milner, 18n14

B

Baldwin, Roger N., 209n15, 210, 210n16, 211n17
Baradat, Leon P., 207n8, 207n9
Barale, Francesco, 79n23
Beccaria, Cesare, 14, 14n3, 17, 43, 280
Beck, Naomi, 9, 76n15, 77
Beck, Robert, 13
Becker, Gary S., 20
Becker, Howard, 140
Beeghley, Leonard, 16n8, 17n9
Beirne, Piers, 6, 9, 15, 16, 16n5, 16n8, 17, 17n10, 17n11, 69, 133n1, 134, 134n4, 135n6, 136n7, 136n9, 138, 138n12, 139, 139n13
Bentham, Jeremy, 9, 18, 18n4, 19, 55, 280
Berkman, Alexander, 207
Bernard, Thomas, 6n6, 75n12, 75n13, 76n15, 77n17
Bischoff, C.H.E., 90
Blackstone, William T., 15, 16n5, 16n7
Blackwell, James E., 216n28, 217n29
Bloom, Barbara, 212, 212n21
Bonger, Willem (William) Adrian, 138, 138n10, 138n11, 205n7, 206

C

Carpenter, Mary, 134, 213n23
Carrà, Giuseppe, 79n23
Chapman, Maria Weston, 213n24
Chesney-Lind, Meda, 212, 212n21
Clarke, Ronald V., 20
Cohen, Lawrence E., 20
Colvin, Mark, 206
Comte, Auguste, 2, 69, 214
Cornish, Derek B., 20
Coser, Lewis A., 134n5, 139
Cotterrell, Roger, 139n14
Critchley, MacDonald, 73n7, 73n9, 74
Cumberland, Richard, 13n2

D

Darwin, Charles, 75n12
Delgado, Richard, 215, 215n27

Desautels, Amy, 211n19, 212n21, 213n22
Dexter, Edwin Grant, 9
Dickman, Toby, 73n9, 74
DiCristina, Bruce, 70n2, 141n17, 211n18
Du Bois, W.E.B., 216, 264, 281
Dugdale, Richard L., 9, 80
Durkheim, Émile, 77n20, 139, 139n15, 140, 141, 141n17, 142, 186, 281

E

Early, Gerald, 216n28, 217n29
Ebenstein, William, 14, 16n8
Einstadter, Werner J., 6n6
Engels, Frederick, 202, 203, 204, 204n6, 206, 232, 281
Evans, Elizabeth C., 71, 73

F

Felson, Marcus, 20
Ferrell, Jeff, 207n8, 211
Ferrero, William, 100, 211, 281
Ferri, Enrico, 9, 15, 77, 114, 133, 206, 281
Feyerabend, Paul, 211n18
Flavin, Jeanne, 211n19, 212n21, 213n22
Fletcher, Joseph, 134
Foucault, Michel, 19, 201n2
Freud, Sigmund, 205
Friendly, Michael, 136, 136n7, 136n8

G

Gabbidon, Shaun L., 216, 216n28, 217n30
Gall, François (Franz) Joseph, 74, 89, 280
Galton, Francis, 80
Garland, David, 139n14, 140, 142, 202n3
Garofalo, Raffaele, 5, 9, 77, 77n18, 78, 78n19, 79, 125, 281
Geis, Gilbert, 18n14, 19
Gerould, Alexander L., 6n6
Giddens, Anthony, 3, 3n3, 139n14
Giddings, Franklin H., 138n12
Godwin, William, 209, 209n13
Goldman, Emma, 207, 207n9, 208
Gordon, David M., 206
Gordon, Lewis R., 215n27, 216
Goring, Charles, 80
Graham, John, 71, 71n3, 72, 72n4
Greenberg, David F., 202n3, 206
Greene, Helen Taylor, 217n30
Groves, W. Byron, 202n3, 206
Guerry, André-Michel, 9, 134, 134n3, 136, 136n7, 136n9, 137, 138n11, 139n15, 157n12, 281

H

Halfpenny, Peter, 69, 139n15
Hall, Walter P., 209
Hankins, Frank H., 134n4
Hatty, Suzanne E., 205, 206
Henry, Stuart, 6n6
Hill, Michael R, 213n24
Hirschi, Travis, 140
Hobbes, Thomas, 14
Hoecker-Drysdale, Susan, 213n24
Hooton, Earnest, 7, 79
Horton, David M., 5
Howard, John, 9
Hufeland, C.W., 90
Hutcheson, Francis, 16, 16n5, 22, 280

J

Jenkins, Philip, 17n10, 20n15, 137, 208n12, 209
J.S.K., 209n15, 210
Jurik, Nancy C., 211n19, 212n21

K

Kant, Immanuel, 20, 20n16
Kirchheimer, Otto, 206
Kramnick, Isaac, 208n12, 209, 209n14
Kretschmer, Ernst, 79
Kropotkin, Peter Alexeivich, 207, 208, 208n10, 209, 210–211, 244, 281

L

LaCapra, Dominick, 139n14
Lavater, Johann (John) Caspar, 70, 71, 72, 83, 280
Lengermann, Patricia Madoo, 213, 213n23, 213n24, 214n26
Levin, Yale, 1, 76n15, 134, 136, 136n7, 137
Lewis, David Levering, 216n28, 217n29
Lindesmith, Alfred, 1, 76n15, 134, 136, 136n7, 137
Lindsey, Edward, 138n12
Lipset, Seymour Martin, 213n24, 214, 214n25
Lombroso, Cesare, 9, 75, 75n12, 76, 100, 211, 281
Lombroso-Ferrero, Gina, 9, 79
Lukes, Steven, 139n14
Lurguin, Constant, 134n4
Lynch, Michael J., 201n2, 202n3, 206

M

Marongiu, Pietro, 6, 15, 17n10, 18, 43n, 137
Martineau, Harriet, 213, 213n24, 214, 255, 281
Marx, Karl, 19, 202, 203, 203n5, 204, 205, 222, 232, 281
McKay, Henry D., 134n3
Merton, Robert, 140

Miller, Jody, 211n19, 212n21
Monachesi, Elio, 15, 17n10, 18n13
Montagu, Ashley, 140
Montesquieu, 9, 16, 16n8, 17, 31, 280

N

Neibrugge-Brantley, Jill, 213, 213n23, 213n24, 214n26
Newman, Graeme R., 6, 15, 17n10, 18, 43n, 137
Nielsen, Kai, 203

P

Paolucci, Henry, 15, 17n10, 18
Parsons, Talcott, 139n14
Pashukanis, Evgeny B., 206
Paul, C. Kegan, 208n12
Pauly, John, 206
Pepinsky, Harold, 211
Percival, Melissa, 71n3, 72
Pinel, Philippe, 79, 137
Powers, Charles H., 16n8, 17n9
Prichard, James Cowles, 79

Q

Quetelet, Lambert Adolphe Jacques, 9, 134, 134n3, 134n4, 135, 135n6, 137, 138n11, 145, 211, 281
Quinney, Richard, 206

R

Radcliffe, Elizabeth S., 16n5
Rafter, Nicole, 5, 73n7, 73n8, 74, 77n21, 79, 138
Rawson, Rawson W., 134
Ray, Isaac, 79
Riegel, Robert E., 73, 73n7, 74
Rusche, Georg, 206
Rush, Benjamin, 9, 79
Russell, Katherine K., 215, 215n27

S

Saville, John, 214n25
Savitz, Leonard, 73n9, 74
Scarre, Geoffrey, 13, 13n1
Schwartz, Martin D., 205, 206
Sellers, Christine S., 6n6
Sellin, Thorsten, 76n15
Shaw, Clifford R., 134n3
Sheldon, William H., 7, 79
Shichor, David, 138, 138n10
Shklar, Judith N., 16, 16n8, 17
Shub, David, 209n15, 210
Simpson, Donald, 73n7, 73n9, 74
Snipes, Jeffrey B., 6n6
Sorel, Albert, 16n8
Stafford, Mark C., 20

Staum, Martin, 71*n*3, 72, 72*n*5, 72*n*6, 73*n*7, 73*n*8, 73*n*9, 74
Stefancic, Jean, 215, 215*n*27
Stone, Chuck, 216*n*28, 217*n*29
Sullivan, Dennis, 211
Sutherland, Edwin, 5
Sylvester, Sawyer F., 134*n*4

T

Tarde, Gabriel, 138, 138*n*11, 139, 141, 170, 281
Tarnowsky, Pauline, 213*n*23
Taylor, Edward, 215, 215*n*27
Tifft, Larry, 211
Tilly, Charles, 3*n*3
Tosti, Gustavo, 138*n*12
Tsouna, Voula, 71, 73
Turner, Jonathan H., 16*n*8, 17*n*9
Turner, Stanley H., 73*n*9, 74

V

van Wyhe, John, 73*n*7, 73*n*9, 73*n*10, 74*n*11
Vine, Margaret S., 138*n*12, 139
Vold, George B., 75*n*12, 75*n*13, 76*n*15, 77*n*17

W

Wallas, Graham, 18, 18*n*14, 19
Walters, Ronald, 216*n*28, 217*n*29
Warr, Mark, 20
Watkins, Frederick M., 209
Webb, R.K., 213*n*24, 214*n*25
Wells-Barnett, Ida B., 213*n*23
Wheatley, Vera, 213*n*24
Whitt, Hugh P., 134*n*2, 136, 136*n*7, 136*n*9, 139*n*15
Wilson, William Julius, 216*n*28, 217*n*29
Wolfgang, Marvin E., 75, 75*n*12, 75*n*13, 76, 79
Wonders, Nancy A., 212*n*21, 213

Y

Young, Robert M., 73*n*7, 73*n*9, 74
Young, Vernetta D., 217*n*30

Z

Zimmern, Helen, 8, 138
Zuckerman, Phil, 216, 216*n*28

SUBJECT INDEX

A

Abolitionists, 256–261
Abortion, 105–106, 276, 277
Absolute government, punishment and, 190–191
Adams, John, 18
Adultery, 128, 150, 178
African Americans and crime, 216–217, 264–279
   history of in Philadelphia, 265–267
   since Civil War, 267–271
   unsustained charges, 279
Age
   of African American offenders, 273–274, 275, 276
   criminal behavior and, 135, 151–157, 212
   punishment and young, 61
Akers, Ronald, 170
Alcibiades, 84, 85
"Allegiance to Law" (Martineau), 255, 256–261
Altruistic criminals, 114, 121
Altruistic sentiments, natural crime and, 130
American Revolution, law and, 2
Anarchism
   altruistic view of human nature, 208
   governmental authority and, 206–207
   individualist, 208n10
   Marxists and, 206
   philosophical, 209
Anarchist communism, 210, 244
Anarchist criminology, 206–211
Anarcho-syndicalism, 207
Anomic suicide, 140
Anomie, 187
Anthropological causes of crime, 77, 114, 117–119, 124
Anthropométrie (Quetelet), 135n6
Arcadius, 40, 42
Aristippus, 207
Aristotle, 71, 85, 181n28
Arrests, of African Americans in Philadelphia, 267–268, 271
Arson, 177
Assassination, 128, 149, 150, 177, 184
Assassins, 111
Atavistic criminal, 102–104, 121
   female, 109–113
Atavist theory, 7, 75, 76, 100
Athens, punishment in ancient, 193–194
Augustus, 42
Aurelian, 94, 98

B

Bacon, Francis, 224n5
Bakunin, Mikhail, 207
Balbi, Adriano, 136
Balestrini, Roberto, 105
Balzac, Honoré de, 128
Beccaria, Cesare, 5, 6, 15, 138n11. *See also An Essay on Crimes and Punishments* (Beccaria)
   career of, 17–18
   criticism of works of, 201
   on punishment, 14
   as reformer, 195
   science and, 133
Becker, Howard, 140
Belgium
   age and crime in, 155, 156
   sex and propensity to crime in, 151
Bell, Derrick, 215
Bentham, Jeremy, 5, 6, 13, 15
   career of, 18–19
   on cases unmeet for punishment, 60–63
   criticism of works of, 201
   on four sanctions/sources of pleasure and pain, 58–60
   free will and, 55–56
   An Introduction to the Principles of Morals and Legislation, 55, 56–67, 280
   panopticon and, 9, 18, 19
   on principle of utility, 56–58
   on punishment, 63–67, 116
   science and, 133
   utilitarianism and, 55, 56–58
Bentham, Samuel, 19
Bertillon system, 275
Bigamy, 128
Biological causes of human behavior, 100
The Black North in 1901 (Du Bois), 216
Blanc, Jean J.C. Louis, 204
Bonger, Willem (William) Adrian, 206
Born criminals, 105, 106, 107, 123
Bourgeoisie, 203–204
   attitude toward proletariat, 239–243
   social murder and, 232, 233–239
Brain
   characteristics of criminal, 102–103
   phrenology and, 73–75
Brain organs
   carnivorous, 95–99
   Gall's 27, 89–90
Branding, 195

Brigandage, 194
   of nobility, 177–178
   rural *vs.* urban, 173
Brigands, 176n15, 178n20
Burglary, 272, 273, 275, 276, 277

C

Caesar, 35
Caligula, 93, 99
Candolle, Alphonse de, 146, 146n1
Capital, law and, 249, 250–251
Capital crimes, regional differences and, 163
Capitalism
   Bentham and, 19
   emergence of criminology and, 3–4
   Marxist criminology and, 203–205
   social murder and, 233–239
Capitalist societies, crime and, 204–205
Capital (Marx), 202, 202n4, 205–206, 222, 223–231, 232, 281
Capital punishment
   under absolute monarchy, 195
   Beccaria on, 51–53
   city-states and use of, 194
   Hutcheson on, 27
   Montesquieu on, 38
   Quetelet on, 147n3
   Socrates on, 14
   worsened by additional corporal punishment, 192–193
Capitolinus, 36
Carnivorous instinct to kill, 89, 91–95
Carnivorous organ in brain, 95–99
Carpenter, Mary, 134, 213n23
Carrara, Francesco, 117, 124
Cartographic method, 136, 137, 158, 159–169
Cassius, 42
Catherine de Medicis, 94, 98
Catherine the Great, 18
Champneuf, Jacques Guerry de, 136
Charles I, 224–225
Charles II, 36
Charles V, 178n20
Charles X, 226
Charles XI, 226
Chastity, acts wounding, 127
Chicago School, 158
Children, assault upon, 179
China
   high treason in, 40
   Montesquieu on punishment in, 36
Chivalrous romance, 178n20
Cities, attraction for criminals, 179–180
City-state, punishment under, 191–192, 193–194
Civil law, Hutcheson and, 25–30

Civil War, African American crime since, 267–271
Class bias, in law, 222, 232, 240–243
Classical penitentiary school, 9
Classical school of criminology, 6, 13–20. *See also* Beccaria, Cesare; Bentham, Jeremy; Hutcheson, Francis; Montesquieu
   criticism of, 6
   Ferri critique of, 114, 115–116, 122, 123, 124
   limitation and contemporary relevance of, 20
   theoretical framework, 13–15
Clemency, 53–54
Clement IV, 194
Clergy, crime and distribution of, 167–169
Climate. *See also* Telluric causes of crime
   crime and, 120
   law and, 9
Colajanni, 138n11
Collective crime, 106
Colonialism, emergence of criminology and, 2, 3, 3n4
Colvin, Mark, 206
Combe, George, 73
Communal property, 226–227
Communism, 204, 205
   anarchist, 210, 244
   Kropotkin and, 210
The Communist Manifesto (Marx & Engels), 203
Community, principle of utility and, 57
"Comparative Statistics of the Educational Situation and the Number of Crimes . . . Districts of France" (Guerry & Balbi), 136
Compensation for crime
   Bentham on, 60–61
   Hutcheson on, 22, 23, 24, 26, 28
Compte général de l'administration de la justice criminelle (Champneuf), 136
Comte, Auguste, 2, 69, 134n5, 214
Condillac, Étienne Bonnot de, 15
The Condition of the Working Class in England in 1844 (Engels), 203, 206, 232, 233–243, 281
Conjugal condition of African American prisoners, 274
The Conquest of Bread (Kropotkin), 210
Conservatives, physiognomy and phrenology and, 72n5
"The Consideration on the Rise and Declension of the Roman Grandeur," 36

Considerations sur la Statistique des Delits (Candolle), 146*n*1
Constantine, 36
Constantine Ducas, 36
Constitutional law, 252–253
Control theories, 140
Corporal punishment
    Beccaria on, 49–50
    Hutcheson on, 22, 27
    Montesquieu on, 37
Corporations, punishment of, 28
Corruption, 111
Counterfeiting, 177
Cremutius Cordus, 42
Crenshaw, Kimberlé W., 215
Crime
    African Americans and, 216–217, 264–279
    age and, 135, 151–157, 212, 273–274, 275, 276
    anthropological causes of, 114, 117–119, 124
    capitalist societies and, 204–205
    climate and, 120
    against collective things, 196–197
    committed by females, 76, 107, 109–113, 110
    cultural relativism of, 140
    development of propensity to, 146–147
    different remedies for different criminals, 123
    distribution of clergy and, 167–169
    disturbing public tranquillity, 38
    economic conditions and, 120–121, 135, 209
    evolution of, 190–199
    Ferri and causes of, 114, 116–117
    geographical distribution of, 135, 160–169
    heredity and, 9, 79–80, 104
    high treason, 40–42
    human nature and, 15
    imitation and, 139, 170, 171–185
    against individuals (*See* Crimes against persons)
    industrial development and, 165–166
    lack of sociological definition of, 126
    lottery and, 161–162
    moral, 38
    natural, 78, 125–131
    offenses excluded as, 130–131
    political, 128–129
    poverty and, 165
    punishment in proportion to, 31, 36, 37–38, 45–46, 50, 63–67
    religious, 37–38
    seasons and, 120, 147, 156–157
    secular conception of, 2
    separation from idea of sin, 2
    sex and (*See* Sex)
    social causes of, 114, 117, 120–121, 124, 171–185
    social evolution and, 141–142
    as social fact, 140–141, 186, 187–190
    social mobility and, 180
    sorts of, 37–38
    telluric causes of, 114, 117, 119–120, 124
    wealth and, 120, 163–165, 167–169
    working class and, 237–239
Crime against nature, 31, 39–40
"Crime as a Normal Social Fact" (Durkheim), 186, 187–190
Crimes against persons, 196–197
    African Americans and, 267, 273
    age and propensity to, 152
    geographical distribution in France, 160–163, 166
    seasons and, 147
    sex and propensity to, 148–151
Crimes against property, 152
    African Americans and, 267, 273
    geographical distribution in France, 163–169
    seasons and, 147
    sex and propensity to, 148–151
Crime statistics. *See also* African Americans and crime; Moral statistics
    Quetelet and, 145–157
Criminal anthropology, 75–76, 75*n*14, 100, 101–109, 264
"Criminal Anthropology" (Lombroso), 76, 100, 101–109, 281
Criminal behavior
    biological causes of, 100
    imitation patterns of, 170, 171–185
    Italian school view of control of, 70
    as learned, 139
Criminal code
    Ferri on, 122–123
    Lombroso on reform of, 107–109
La Criminalité compareé (Tarde), 139
Criminality
    delimitation of, 129–131
    human, 196, 197–198
    religious, 196–197, 198
Criminal justice, criminology *vs.*, 5*n*5
Criminal justice system
    Beccaria and secular, 17
    classical school definition of, 14
Criminal Man (Lombroso), 76, 281
Criminaloid, 105

Criminal psychology, 9, 78, 78n20, 79
Criminals
    atavism of, 102–104, 121
    attraction to cities, 179–180
    born criminals, 105, 106, 107, 123
    characteristics of brain of, 102–103.
        See also Phrenology
    egoistic vs. altruistic, 114, 121
    epilepsy of, 104–105
    evolutionary, 121
    female, 76, 107, 109–113
    habitual, 123–124
    insane, 9, 102, 105, 106, 123
    occasional, 124
    passionate, 105, 124
    types of, 105
Criminal saturation, 124
Criminal sociology, 76–77, 78
Criminal Sociology (Ferri), 8, 77, 114, 281
Criminal therapeutics, 108–109
"The Criminal Type in Women and Its Atavistic Origin" (Lombroso), 109–113
"Criminels avec Atlas" (Ferri), 106–107
Criminology
    criminal justice vs., 5n5
    critical (See Critical criminology)
    defining, 5
    divisions of, 5
    establishment of, 1–21
    historical context of emergence of, 1–4
    historical trajectories in, 5–9
    positive, 69
Criminology (Garofalo), 5, 77–78, 125, 126–131, 281
Critical criminology, 201–217
    anarchist criminology, 206–211
    critical race theory, 214–217
    feminist criminology, 211–214
    Marxist criminology, 202–206, 205
Critical race theory (CRT), 8, 213n23, 214–217. See also Du Bois, W.E.B.
Crucifixion, 194
Cumberland, Richard, 13, 13n2
Custom, fashion passing to, 181–185
Customary law, 247–249

D
d'Alembert, Jean Le Rond, 15, 18
Damages, compensation for, 28
Darwin, Charles, 72, 75n12, 76, 77, 182, 182n31
De Aramburu, Felix, 130
Death penalty. See Capital punishment

Decemvirs, 35
Defamation, 106
Defence, right to, 23–24
The Defence of Usury (Bentham), 18
Dei delitti e delle pene (Beccaria), 195
De legibus naturae (Cumberland), 13n2
Delgado, Richard, 215
The Descent of Man (Darwin), 75n12
Desertion, 26, 33, 167–169
Despotic governments, punishment under, 32, 33–34
Determinism, 7–8
    classical school and, 15
    Italian school and, 69
    Tarde and, 139
Deterrence, 6, 20
    Beccaria and, 17, 43–44, 46, 50
    Bentham and, 60n9
    classical school and, 15
    death penalty and, 51–52
    Hutcheson and, 16, 22, 24, 26
    Kropotkin and, 253
Dialectics of Nature (Engels), 203
Diderot, Denis, 15
Dionysius, 41
Dismemberment, 179
The Division of Labor in Society (Durkheim), 140
Domitian, 94
Dostoiewski, Fyodor, 105
Douglas, Frederick, 215
Du Bois, W.E.B., 8, 202, 215–217, 264
    The Philadelphia Negro, 264–279, 281
Duchatelet, Parent, 113
Duel, 175n11, 184n33
Dugdale, Richard L., 80
Durkheim, Émile, 5, 8, 186–187
    career of, 139–142
    crime as social fact, 187–190
    criticism of social arrangements, 201
    criticism of work, 142
    French school and, 137, 138
    on natural crime, 78n20
    punishment and law of quantitative variations, 190–199
    The Rules of Sociological Method, 140–141, 186, 187–190, 281
    social evolution and crime, 141–142
    Two Laws of Penal Evolution, 141, 186, 190–199, 281

E
Eastern State Penitentiary, statistics on African American prisoners in, 264, 266, 269, 270, 271–277

Ecological research, 134*n*3, 158
"Economic and Philosophical Manuscripts" (Marx), 203, 203*n*5
Economic approach to crime, 20
Economic conditions, crime and, 120–121, 135, 209
Economic determinism, 118–119
Economic inequality, crime and, 209
Eden, M., 226
Educational level
  of African American prisoners, 274–275
  crime and criminal's, 151, 157
Edward III, 229
Edward VI, 227–228, 228*n*19
Egoistic criminals, 114, 121
Egoistic suicide, 140
Egypt, punishment in ancient, 192, 193
The Elementary Forms of Religious Life (Durkheim), 140
Elizabeth I, 225, 228, 229
Ellis, Havelock, 107, 138*n*11
Elmira Reformatory, 108
Emperor Alexander, 40–41
Emperor Basil, 36
Empirical inquiry
  emergence of criminology and emphasis on, 2
  Italian school and, 69, 70
Engels, Frederick, 5, 8, 138*n*11
  career of, 202, 203–204, 206, 232
  The Condition of the Working Class in England in 1844, 232, 233–243, 281
  on New Poor Law, 232, 240–243
  social murder, 232, 233–239
Enlightenment, 2
  Scottish, 16, 17*n*11
Enquiry Concerning Political Justice and Its Influence on Modern Morals and Happiness (Godwin), 209
Environmental factors in crime, 78*n*19
Epicurus, 13, 13*n*1
Epilepsy, of criminals, 104–105
An Essay on Crimes and Punishments (Beccaria), 15*n*4, 17–18, 43, 44–54, 72, 280
  acts of violence, 49–50
  advantage of immediate punishment, 49
  death penalty, 51–53
  estimating degree of crimes, 46
  intent of punishment, 46
  mildness of punishments, 50
  origin of punishment, 44
  pardons, 53–54
  proportion between crimes and punishments, 45–46
  right to punish, 44–45
  torture, 46–49
Essay on the Moral Statistics of France (Guerry), 136–137, 145, 157*n*12, 158, 159–169, 281
Essays on Physiognomy (Lavater), 71–72, 83, 84–88, 280
Establishments of St. Louis, 194
Ethnicity. *See* Critical race theory (CRT)
Eugenics movement, 79
Evolutionary criminal, 121
Evolutionary theory, Lombroso and, 76
Executions, 22

F
Facial features, examination of. *See* Physiognomy
Family, acts against, 127–128
Fashion passing to custom, 181–185
Fathers
  parricide, 149, 195
  punishment of for children's crimes, 37
Faustinian, 41
Female African American prisoners, 275
Female criminals, 76, 107, 109–113, 275. *See also* Sex; Women
The Female Offender (Lombroso), 76, 100, 281
Feminism, branches of, 212
Feminist criminology, 211–214. *See also* Martineau, Harriet
Feminist criticism, 8
Feminist epistemologies, 213*n*22
Ferrell, Jeff, 211
Ferrero, William, 75, 76, 281
  "The Criminal Type in Women and Its Atavistic Origin," 100, 109–113
Ferri, Enrico (Henry), 7, 8, 9, 75, 105, 106, 138*n*11, 211*n*17
  career of, 76–77, 100, 114
  Criminal Sociology, 77, 114, 281
  criticism of classical school, 6
  in France, 137
  Marx and Engels and, 206
  The Positive School of Criminology, 114, 115–124, 281
  on Quetelet and Guerry, 133
  science and, 133
Feudalism, 179, 194, 223–226
Fields, Factories, and Workshops (Kropotkin), 210
Fines, as punishment, 27. *See also* Compensation
  Montesquieu on, 37

Fletcher, Joseph, 134
Foucault, Michel, 137
Fourier, Charles, 201n1
Fragment on Government (Bentham), 18, 57n4
France
    ancient laws of, 32
    laws against unions, 230–231
    laws on wages, 228
Francis II, 74, 201
Freeman, Alan, 215
Free will
    Bentham and, 55–56
    classical school and, 15, 116
    Ferri and, 105
    positive school and, 116
    positivism and, 70
    Tarde and, 139
French Revolution, 2, 145
French school of criminology, 8, 137–142.
    See also Durkheim, Émile; Tarde, Gabriel
    existing social arrangements and, 201, 201n1
    moral statistics and, 142
Freud, Sigmund, 205
Friedrich II, 18
On the Functions of the Brain and of Each of Its Parts (Gall), 74, 89, 91–99
    carnivorous instinct in man, 91–95
    carnivorous organ in brain, 95–99
    disposition to murder, 94–95

G

Gall, Franz Joseph, 7, 79
    career of, 73–74, 89–90
    in France, 137
    Francis II and, 201
    Organology, 73n10, 74, 89, 91–99, 280
    On the Functions of the Brain and of Each of Its Parts, 74, 89, 91–99
Galleys, 195
Galton, Francis, 80
Gambling, 120–121
Garofalo, Raffaele, 7, 9, 75, 100, 138n11
    career of, 77–78, 125–126
    criminal psychology and, 78, 79
    Criminology, 77–78, 125, 126–131, 281
    defining criminology, 5
    natural crime, 125–131
    science and, 133
Garrison, William Lloyd, 258, 259
Gender-ratio problem, 135, 145, 211, 212
Genetics, crime and, 9, 79–80, 104
Geographical distribution of crime, 118, 119, 135, 160–169
George II, 229–230

George III, 230
The German Ideology (Marx & Engels), 203
Germany, laws on wages, 229n23
Glaser, Daniel, 170
God, punishment from, 46
Godwin, William, 138n11, 207, 208–209, 210n16, 211n19
Goldman, Emma, 207, 207n9, 211n19
Goncourt, Edmond de, 105
Gordon, David M., 206
Goring, Charles, 80
Government
    anarchists and authority of, 206–207
    derivation of power of, 261
    law and, 249–251, 252–253
    obligations of subjects to, 28–30
    principle of utility and, 57
    right to punish and, 14
    severity of punishment and power of, 190–199
    severity of punishment and type of, 32, 33–34
Greatest happiness/greatest felicity principle, 56n1, 58n4
Greenberg, David F., 206
Groves, W. Byron, 206
Guerry, André-Michel, 8
    career of, 133–134, 135–137, 158
    Essay on the Moral Statistics of France, 136–137, 157n12, 158, 159–169, 281
    seasons and crime, 120

H

Habitual criminals, 123–124
Halfpenny, Peter, on positivism, 69–70
Happiness, utilitarianism and, 16
Hebrew people, punishment among, 193
Hedonism, 55
Helvétius, Claude Adrien, 15, 18, 93
Henry III, 177
Henry IV, 179n22
Henry VII, 224, 227
Henry VIII, 41, 94, 224, 227
Heredity, crime and, 9, 79–80, 104
Heresy, 31, 38–39, 194
High treason, 36n34, 40–42
Highway robbery, 149
Hippocrates, 73
Hirschi, Travis, 140
Historical materialism, 118–119
H.M.S. Beagle, 72
Hobbes, Thomas, 14, 15
Homicide. *See* Murder
Honorius, 42
Hooton, Earnest, 79

House of Corrections, African American inmates at, 269
How to Observe Morals and Manners (Martineau), 214
Human criminality, 186, 196, 197–198, 199
Human nature, crime and, 15
Humboldt, Alexander von, 159
Hume, David, 13, 15, 16, 18
Hutcheson, Francis, 6, 15
  career of, 16, 22–23
  on civil laws, 25–30
  on compensation for victims, 22, 23, 24, 26, 28
  deterrence and, 22, 24, 26
  on punishment, 22, 24–30
  on rights arising from injuries and damages done by others, 23–25
  A System of Moral Philosophy, 22, 23–30, 31, 280

I
Illustrations of Political Economy (Martineau), 213–214
Imitation, criminal behavior and, 139, 170, 171–185
Imitation-customs, 181
Imitation-fashions, 181
Impunity, 50
Index Librorum Prohibitorum, 6, 17, 201
Individual, principle of utility and, 57
Individualist anarchism, 208n10
Industrial development, crime and, 165–166, 167–169
Industrial Revolution, 3, 145
Infanticide, 105–106, 111, 149, 167–169, 277
Insane criminals, 9, 102, 105, 106, 123
Insanity
  crime and, 79
  as defense, 107
  punishment and, 61
International Working Men's Association, 206
Intoxication, punishment and, 61
An Introduction to the Principles of Morals and Legislation (Bentham), 18, 19, 55, 56–67, 280
  cases unmeet for punishment, 60–63
  four sanctions or sources of pain and pleasure, 58–60
  on principle of utility, 56–58
  proportion between punishments and offenses, 63–67
Italian school of positive criminology, 7, 75–80. *See also* Ferri, Enrico; Garofalo, Raffaele; Lombroso, Cesare
  criticism of classical school, 20

J
Jack the Ripper, 102, 180
James I, 176, 228, 229, 229n23
Japan
  insufficiency of laws of, 33–34
  punishment of women in, 42
Jefferson, Thomas, 18, 261
John (King), 229
Justice, 44–45
Juvenile Delinquency and Urban Areas (Shaw & McKay), 134n3

K
Kant, Immanuel, 197
  criticism of classical school, 6, 20
Killing. *See also* Murder
  carnivorous instinct and, 91–95
  disposition to, 94–95
Kirchheimer, Otto, 206
Knife blows, 184
Kretschmer, Ernst, 79
Kropotkin, Peter, 5, 8, 202, 207, 208
  career of, 209–211, 244
  Law and Authority, 244–254, 281

L
Lacassagne, Alexandre, 107, 138, 138n11
Land, creation of proletariat and theft of, 222, 223–227
Lavater, Johann Caspar, 7, 23, 70
  career of, 71–72, 83–84
  Essays on Physiognomy, 83, 84–88, 280
  science and, 133
Law and Authority (Kropotkin), 210, 211, 244–254, 281
Lawrence, Charles R., III, 215
Law(s) anarchist critique of, 244–254
  ancient French, 32
  capital and, 249, 250–251
  class bias in, 232, 240–243
  customary, 247–249
  function of, 260
  of imitation, 173–175
  of insertion, 181–185
  Japanese, 33–34
  of Manu, 192, 193
  Marxist critique of, 239–243
  New Poor Law, 240–243
  origin of punishments and, 44
  proportion of punishment to offense and, 67
  protection of government and, 251, 252
  protection of people and, 251, 252–253
  protection of property and, 251–252
  of quantitative variations, 186, 190–199

response to unjust, 29–30
Roman, 35–36
serving interests of powerful in society, 222
on wages, 227–231
The Laws of Imitation (Tarde), 139
Learning theory, 170
Left-handedness, criminal behavior and, 103, 104
Lenin, Vladimir, 210
Leviathan (Hobbes), 14
Liberals, physiognomy and phrenology and, 72n5
Life-course criminology, 135, 145
Literacy
 of convicts in Eastern State Penitentiary, 274, 277
 propensity to crime and, 151, 157
Livy, 32n4, 35, 194
Locke, John, 14, 15
Logic, positivism and, 70n2
Lombroso, Cesare, 7, 8, 9, 79, 138n11
 atavist theory and, 75–76
 career of, 100–101
 "Criminal Anthropology," 101–109
 Criminal Man, 76, 281
 "The Criminal Type in Women and Its Atavistic Origin," 109–113
 criticism of classical school, 6
 The Female Offender, 76, 281
 French school and, 137, 138
 on insanity and crime, 79
 physiognomy and, 102–104, 117
 science and, 133
Lottery, crime and, 161–162, 167–169
Louis XI, 93, 98
Louis XIII, 179n22
Louis XIV, 191
Lyall, Alfred, 173n8
Lynch, Michael J., 206

M
Malthus, Thomas Robert, 182n31
Malthus' Law of Population, 240–241
Manouvrier, Léonce, 138n11
Manslaughter, 115, 276
Manuel Comnenus, 39
Maps, Guerry's use of, 136, 158, 159–169
Maria Theresa of Austria, 18
Martineau, Harriet, 8, 202
 career of, 213–214, 255–256
 Society in America, 255–263, 281
Marx, Karl, 8, 139
 on Bentham, 19
 Capital, 222, 223–231, 232, 281
 career of, 202–204, 205–206, 222
 Kropotkin and, 210

Marxist criminology, 202–206. See also Engels, Frederick; Marx, Karl
 criticism of, 205
Marxist criticism
 of classical school, 20
 of social arrangements, 8
Marxist scientific socialism, Ferri and, 77, 79
Materialism, Lombroso and, 76
Matsuda, Mari J., 215
Mattoid, 105, 106
Maximinus, 36
McKay, Henry D., 134n3, 158
Memoirs of a Revolutionist (Kropotkin), 210
Men, propensity to crime and, 148–151, 156. See also Sex
Merton, Robert, 140
Middle class, law and, 246
Military desertion, 167–169
Mill, James, 13, 261–262
Mill, John Stuart, 13
Miscarriage, 149
Misoneism, 106
Missupposal, punishment and, 61
Mobs, 171–173, 256, 258–259
Modesty, acts wounding, 127
Monarchy, punishment under, 195
Montaigne, 99, 177
Montesquieu, 6, 8n8, 9, 15, 66n38, 137, 245. See also *The Spirit of Laws* (Montesquieu)
 career of, 16–17, 31–32
 criticism of works of, 201
 on punishment, 44
Moral crimes, 38
Moral education, 140
Moral/popular sanction, 58, 59, 62n18
Moral power, 135
Morals and Manners Among Negro Americans (Du Bois), 216
Moral sense
 development of, 125
 Hutcheson and, 16
Moral statistics, 133–137. See also Guerry, André-Michel; Quetelet, Adolphe
 examination of, 7–8
 French school and, 142
 influence on Durkheim, 139n15
More, Thomas, 224, 224n4
Mortifications, 194
Mosaic law, 193
Moyamensing prison, statistics on African American prisoners in, 266, 268, 269

Murder
    by bravos, 176–177
    carnivorous instinct and, 91–95
    carnivorous organ in brain and, 95–99
    conviction of African Americans for, 272, 273, 276, 277
    Ferri on, 106–107
    propensity to, 94–95, 154
    sex and propensity to, 111, 149, 150
    social, 206, 232, 233–239
Mussolini, Benito, 77
Mutilation, 180, 193, 194, 195
Mutual Aid (Kropotkin), 210
Mutualism, 207

N
Nation-states, emergence of criminology and, 2–3
Natural crime, 78, 78n20, 125–131
    rationale of, 126–129
"The Negro and Crime" (Du Bois), 216
Nero, 93, 99
New Poor Law, Engels on, 232, 240–243
Nobility, crimes propagated to people from, 174–179

O
Obesity, of prostitutes/criminals, 113
Occasional criminal, 124
Offender, proportion of punishment to offense and, 67
Old Poor Law, 240–241
On the Functions of the Brain and of Each of Its Parts (Gall), 280
Organology (Gall), 73n10, 74, 89, 91–99, 280
The Origin of the Family, Private Property, and the State (Engels), 203

P
Panopticon prison design, 9, 18, 19
Pardons, 53–54
Parents, attacks against, 160, 161, 162, 167–169
Parricide, 149, 195
Pashukanis, Evgeny B., 206
Passionate criminal, 124
Paulinus, 40
Pauly, John, 206
Pecuniary fines, as punishment, 27
Penal law
    evolution of, 194
    reform of, 195
Penal Philosophy (Tarde), 139, 170, 171–185, 281
Penal systems, evolution of, 192

Penances, 194
Penn, William, 265
Pepinsky, Harold, 211
The Persian Letters (Montesquieu), 17
Persons, laws and protection of, 251, 252–253. *See also* Crimes against persons
Philadelphia
    African American crime in, 265–279
    age and crime in, 156
The Philadelphia Negro (Du Bois), 216, 217, 264–279, 281
Philip II, 174
Philip the Long, 39
Philosophical anarchism, 209
"Philosophy of Fashion" (Zimmern), 111
Phrenology, 7, 73–75, 73n7, 73n8, 73n10, 79. *See also* Gall, Franz Joseph; *On the Functions of the Brain and of Each of Its Parts* (Gall)
    Guerry and, 136n9
Physical appearance theories, 6–7, 71
    See also Physiognomy
Physical sanction, 58, 59
Physiognomy, 7, 71–73. *See also* Lavater, Johann Caspar
    Essays on Physiognomy (Lavater), 83, 84–88
    Guerry and, 162
    Lombroso and, 102–104
    physiognomic examination of Socrates, 83–88
Pilfering, 278
Pinel, Philippe, 79, 137
Pity, natural crime and, 125–127, 129
Plato, 14, 37n41
Pleasure/pain
    Bentham and, 55, 56, 58–60
    classical school and, 15
    sources of, 58–60
Plunder, 178
Plutarch, 33
Poaching, 176
Poisonings, 149, 150, 156, 161, 176
Political crimes, 128–129
Political criminals, 105
"Political Non-Existence of Women" (Martineau), 255, 261–263
Political sanction, 58
Popularity/unpopularity, 172n7
Popular sanction, 58
Population concentration, effect on crime, 160, 163, 179–180
Population growth, emergence of criminology and, 4
Porta, Giambattista della, 71
Positive criminology, 7, 69

Positive Philosophy (Comte), 214
Positive school of criminology, Ferri on, 114, 116
The Positive School of Criminology (Ferri), 77, 114, 115–124, 281
Positivism, 2, 69–70, 76
    Quetelet and, 145
    sociological, 186
Poverty, crime and, 165
Prichard, James Cowles, 79
Principle of utility, 13n2, 14
    Bentham on, 56–58
    punishment and, 55
Principles of Criminology (Sutherland), 5
Prisons, overrepresentation of African Americans in, 264–279
"Prisons and Their Moral Influence on Prisoners" (Kropotkin), 210–211, 211n17
Private property, law and, 250–252
Probity, natural crime and, 125–127, 129
Procopius, 39
Professional Ethics and Civic Morals (Durkheim), 141n17
Professional thieves, 166
Progress, historical trajectory of criminology and, 8–9, 217
Proletariat
    attitude of bourgeoisie toward, 239–243
    crime and, 203–204
    development and control of, 222, 223–227
    social murder and, 233–239
Propensity to crime, 146–147
    age and, 151–157
    sex and, 148–151, 156
Prostitutes, 180
    obesity of, 113
    studies of, 107, 109–110, 111
Proudhon, Pierre-Joseph, 201n1, 207
Psychological tradition of criminology, 9
Public, proportion of punishment to offense and, 67
Public peace, nonpolitical crime and, 129
Punishment. *See also* Capital punishment; Corporal punishment; *An Essay on Crimes and Punishments* (Beccaria)
    Bentham on, 60–63, 60n9
    breach of modesty in, 42
    classical school on, 14
    consideration of circumstances of, 107
    Durkheim on, 140
    evolution of, 190–199
    of father for child's crimes, 37
    Ferri on, 116, 122
    fines as, 27, 37
    fitting to individual criminal, 122–123
    four sanctions, 58–60
    Hutcheson on appropriate, 22, 24–30
    Kropotkin on, 253–254
    Montesquieu on (See *The Spirit of Laws* (Montesquieu))
    power of, 33
    principle of utility and, 55, 56–58
    in proportion to crime, 31, 36, 37–38, 45–46, 50, 63–67
    social development and severity of, 186, 190–199
    state of nation and severity of, 54
    type of government and severity of, 32, 33–34
Pythagoras, 71, 99

Q

Qualitative studies, in feminist criminology, 212–213, 255
Quetelet, Adolphe, 8, 9, 124
    career of, 133–135, 145
    in France, 137
    seasons and crime and, 120
    Tarde on, 138n11
    A Treatise on Man and the Development of His Faculties, 145, 146–157, 281
Quinney, Richard, 206

R

Race. *See also* Critical race theory (CRT)
    criminality and, 118–119
Rack, 36–37
Rape, 149, 178
Rational choice theory, 6, 20
Rawson, Rawson W., 134
Ray, Isaac, 79
Recidivists, 107
Reformation, punishment and, 60n9
Reformation (religious), effect on private property, 225
Regicides, 177
Regions, criminality and, 118, 119, 135, 160–169
Religion, Hutcheson and, 22–23
Religious crimes, 37–38, 186, 196–197, 198–199
Religious sanctions, 58–59, 62n18
Research on the Propensity for Crime at Different Ages (Quetelet), 135, 145, 281
Retaliation, 37
Revenge, 124
Revolver, 180

Rewards, 25, 63n22
Rights, arising from injuries and damages done by others, 23–25
Riots, 256
Robbery, 33
    conviction of African Americans for, 272, 273, 275, 276
Roleswinck, Werner, 177
Roman Catholic Church
    criticism of Beccaria, 17
    criticism of classical school, 6, 20
    criticism of Montesquieu, 17
    punishment under, 194–195
Roman law, 35–36
Rome
    punishment in ancient, 191–192, 193, 194
    punishment of women in ancient, 42
Rousseau, Jean-Jacques, 14, 245, 246
Routine activities theory, 20
The Rules of Sociological Method (Durkheim), 140–141, 186, 187–190, 281
Rural brigandage, urban bridgandage *vs.*, 173
Rusche, Georg, 206
Rush, Benjamin, 23, 79
In Russian and French Prisons (Kropotkin), 210

S
Sacrilege, 40, 195
Sade, Marquis de, 137
Saint Louis, 37n42, 182, 194
Sanction, defined, 58n5
Satirical writing, 42
Science, criminology and, 7, 133
Science of man, Beccaria and, 17, 17n11
Scientific socialism, 77, 79
Scientific thought, Hutcheson and, 22–23
Scottish Enlightenment, 16, 17n11
Seasons, crime and, 120, 147, 156–157
Secularism, emergence of criminology and, 2
Seduction, 149
Self-report data, 70n2
Septemberists, 171n5
Septimus Severus, 94, 99
Sex. *See also* Men; Women
    of African American offenders, 273–274, 275, 276
    age and first offense, 153
    propensity to crime and, 145, 148–151, 156
Sexual selection, female offenders and, 112
Sfregio, 184
Shakespeare, William, 105
Shaw, Clifford R., 134n3, 158
Sheldon, William, 79
Sidgwick, Henry, 13
Sighele, 106
Sin, crime *vs.*, 2
Slavery
    death penalty *vs.* perpetual, 52
    Martineau on, 256–261
Smith, Adam, 16
Smoking habit, imitation of, 176
Social bond theory, 140
Social causes of crime
    Ferri on, 76–77, 114, 117, 120–121, 124
    French school and, 8
    Tarde on, 171–185
    women offenders and, 111–112
Social class, violent crime and, 121–122
Social contract theory, classical school and, 6, 13, 14
Social control, 4
    classical school and, 13
Social evolution, crime and, 141–142
Social evolution theory, 78
Socialism (Engels), 203
The Socialist Superstition (Garofalo), 77n18
Social Laws: An Outline of Sociology (Tarde), 139
Social mechanics, 134
Social mobility, crime and, 180
Social murder, 206, 232, 233–239
Social physics, 134, 134n5
Social superiors, imitation of, 174–175
Society in America (Martineau), 213, 214, 255–263
    slavery, 256–261
    women's political non-existence, 261–263
Society of America (Martineau), 281
Socioeconomic system, Marxist criminology and, 204–205
Sociological positivism, 139n15, 186
Sociology, 134n5
Socrates
    as criminal, 189
    death penalty and, 14
    physiognomic examination of, 71, 72, 83–88
Solitary confinement, 122
Some Notes on Negro Crime, Particularly in Georgia (Du Bois), 216
"The Spawn of Slavery" (Du Bois), 216
Speech, punishment for indiscreet, 41–42
Spencer, Herbert, 77, 78, 125, 182n30, 191, 192n2
The Spirit of Laws (Montesquieu), 17, 31, 32–42, 280
    accusations requiring moderation and prudence, 38–39

breach of modesty in punishing crimes, 42
crime against nature, 39–40
French laws, 32
high treason, 40–41
indiscreet speech, 41–42
just proportion between punishments and crime, 36
laws of Japan, 33–34
liberty and punishments, 37–38
pecuniary and corporal punishments, 37
power of punishments, 33
punishment of fathers for crimes of children, 37
the rack, 36–37
retaliation, 37
Roman laws, 35–36
severity of punishments in different governments, 32
thoughts, 41
Valerian law, 32–33
writings, 42
Spurzheim, Johann Gaspar, 73, 73n8, 74, 94, 98
Stake, 194
Stateville Penitentiary, 19
Statute of Labourers, 229
Steuart, James, 223
Stirner, Max, 208n10
Suicide, 140, 158, 171, 237, 279
Suicide (Durkheim), 139n15, 140
Sullivan, Dennis, 211
Süssmilch, Johann Peter, 133n1
Sutherland, Edwin, 5, 170
Sylla, 35, 35n20, 94, 99
Systematic observation, Italian school's emphasis on, 79
A System of Moral Philosophy (Hutcheson), 16, 16n7, 22, 23–30, 31, 280

T
Tachianthropometer, 108
Tarde, Gabriel, 8
  career of, 138–139, 170
  on Durkheim, 139
  French school and, 137, 138
  Penal Philosophy, 139, 170, 171–185, 281
Tarnowsky, Pauline, 107, 109, 111, 213n23
Tattooing, 103
Telluric causes of crime, 7, 7n7, 9, 77, 114, 117, 119–120, 124
Theft
  conviction of African Americans for, 272
  propensity to, 154
  sex and propensity to, 111, 149–150
  Tarde on, 177, 180
Theodorus Lascarus, 39

Theodosius, 40, 42
The Theory of Reward (Dumont), 60n9
Thoreau, Henry David, 207, 207n9
Thoughts, punishment for, 41
Tiberius, 42, 94
Tifft, Larry, 211
Tolstoy, Leo, 121, 207, 208n11, 209, 210n16
Torture, 27, 31, 194, 195
  Beccaria on, 46–49
A Treatise on Man and the Development of His Faculties (Quetelet), 135, 145, 146–157, 281
Two Laws of Penal Evolution (Durkheim), 141, 186, 190–191, 281
Tyrannicide, 177

U
Unconsciousness, punishment and, 61
Unintentionality, punishment and, 61
Unions, laws against, 229–231
United States, criminal therapeutics in, 108–109
Urban brigandage, rural brigandage vs., 173
Urbanization, emergence of criminology and, 4
Utilitarianism. *See also* Principle of utility
  Bentham and, 55, 56–58
  classical school and, 6, 13–14
  Hutcheson and, 16
Utilitarians, 197

V
Valentinian, 40
Valerian law, 32–33
Valerius Publicola, 32n4
Verri, Pietro and Alessandro, 15, 18
Violence, social class and, 121–122
Violent crimes, 49–50
Vitriol, 179–180
Voltaire, 8n8, 15, 18, 43, 137, 245, 246

W
Wages, legislation on, 227–231
War madness, 172
Wealth, crime and, 120, 163–165, 167–169
Weather conditions, crime and, 9. *See also* Telluric causes of crime
Weber, Max, 139
Wedderburn, Alexander, 57–58n4
Wells-Barnett, Ida B., 213n23, 215
Western State Penitentiary (Pittsburgh), 19
Williams, Patricia J., 215
Witchcraft, 31, 38–39
Wollstonecraft, Mary, 208–209, 211n19
Women. *See also* Sex
  criminals, 76, 107 109–113, 275
  mutilation of, 180

propensity to crime and, 148–151, 156
  punishment of, 42
Workhouses, 206, 232, 241–243
Working class, crime and, 237–239
Writings, punishment for, 42

Z
Zeno, 207
Zimmern, Helen, 111
Zola, Émile, 105
Zopyrus, 72, 84, 85, 86